Acronyms, Initialisms & Abbreviations Dictionary

Supplement

ISSN 0270-4404

Acronyms, Initialisms & Abbreviations Dictionary

Supplement

Volume 2 of
Acronyms, Initialisms & Abbreviations Dictionary
Twenty-Seventh Edition

*A Guide to Acronyms, Abbreviations,
Contractions, Alphabetic Symbols, and Similar Condensed Appellations*

Covering: Aerospace, Associations, Banking, Biochemistry, Business, Data Processing,
Domestic and International Affairs, Economics, Education, Electronics, Genetics,
Government, Information Technology, Internet, Investment, Labor, Law, Language, Medicine, Military
Affairs, Periodicals, Pharmacy, Physiology, Politics, Religion, Science, Societies, Sports, Technical
Drawings and Specifications, Telecommunications, Trade, Transportation, and Other Fields

Mary Rose Bonk,
Editor

Pamela Dear,
Associate Editor

Phyllis Spinelli
Assistant Editor

GALE GROUP

Detroit
New York
San Francisco
London
Boston
Woodbridge, CT

Editor: Mary Rose Bonk

Associate Editor: Pamela Dear
Assistant Editor: Phyllis Spinelli

Data Capture Manager: Ron Montgomery
Data Entry Coordinator: Beverly Jendrowski

Manufacturing Manager: Dorothy Maki
Buyer: Nekita McKee

Graphic Services Manager: Barbara J. Yarrow
Graphic Artist: Gary Leach

Manager, Technical Support Services: Theresa A. Rocklin
Programmer: Charles Beaumont

Library of Congress Catalog Number 84-643188
ISBN 0-7876-2861-1
ISSN 0270-4404

Printed in the United States of America

Contents

A Word about *Acronyms, Initialisms & Abbreviations Dictionary Supplement*.............................vii

User's Guide ix

List of Selected Sources xi

Acronyms, Initialisms and Abbreviations

    By Acronym...1

    By Meaning...87

Gale's publications in the acronyms and abbreviations field include:

Acronyms, Initialisms & Abbreviations Dictionary series:

Acronyms, Initialisms & Abbreviations Dictionary (Volume 1). A guide to acronyms, initialisms, abbreviations, and similar contractions, arranged alphabetically by abbreviation.

Acronyms, Initialisms & Abbreviations Supplement (Volume 2). An interedition supplement in which terms are arranged alphabetically both by abbreviation and by meaning.

Reverse Acronyms, Initialisms & Abbreviations Dictionary (Volume 3). A companion to Volume 1 in which terms are arranged alphabetically by meaning of the acronym, initialism, or abbreviation.

Acronyms, Initialisms & Abbreviations Dictionary Subject Guide series:

Computer & Telecommunications Acronyms (Volume 1). A guide to acronyms, initialisms, abbreviations, and similar contractions used in the field of computers and telecommunications in which terms are arranged alphabetically both by abbreviation and by meaning.

Business Acronyms (Volume 2). A guide to business-oriented acronyms, initialisms, abbreviations, and similar contractions in which terms are arranged alphabetically both by abbreviation and by meaning.

International Acronyms, Initialisms & Abbreviations Dictionary series:

International Acronyms, Initialisms & Abbreviations Dictionary (Volume 1). A guide to foreign and international acronyms, initialisms, abbreviations, and similar contractions, arranged alphabetically by abbreviation.

Reverse International Acronyms, Initialisms & Abbreviations Dictionary (Volume 2). A companion to Volume 1, in which terms are arranged alphabetically by meaning of the acronym, initialism, or abbreviation.

Periodical Title Abbreviations series:

Periodical Title Abbreviations: By Abbreviation (Volume 1). A guide to abbreviations commonly used for periodical titles, arranged alphabetically by abbreviation.

Periodical Title Abbreviations: By Title (Volume 2). A guide to abbreviations commonly used for periodical titles, arranged alphabetically by title.

New Periodical Title Abbreviations (Volume 3). An interedition supplement in which terms are arranged alphabetically both by abbreviation and by title.

A Word about
Acronyms, Initialisms & Abbreviations
Dictionary Supplement

> Contains over 10,000 newly coined or newly found terms

As acronyms continue to simplify and accelerate modern communication, the need for timely access remains essential. Publication of this supplement to the twenty-seventh edition of *Acronyms, Initialisms & Abbreviations Dictionary (AIAD)* makes terms available while their currency is at a peak, keeping you informed and up to date in a constantly expanding field.

Timely Coverage

The more dynamic fields of endeavor tend to generate the largest number of acronyms. *Acronyms, Initialisms & Abbreviations Dictionary Supplement (AIAD-S)* reflects this trend by providing increased coverage in:

- Environment

- Genealogy

- Library Science

- Medicine

- Weather

Current events and new technology often produce abbreviated designations intended as time and space savers. Colorful examples in this supplement include:

- MOODS................................Music Object-Oriented Distributed System

- PEAK....................................Pricing Electronic Access to Knowledge

- SMURFS..............................Southern Michigan Unorganized Regional Festival of Stargazers

- TIGER..................................Trans-Iron Galactic Element Recorder

Major Sources Cited

AIAD-S, like *AIAD*, contains entries from a wide variety of sources. Although many terms are from published sources, the majority of entries are sent by outside contributors, are uncovered through independent research by the editorial staff, or are located in miscellaneous broadcast or print media references. Therefore, it is impossible to cite a source on every entry in *AIAD-S*. It was felt, however, that the citation of selected sources would assist the user in his or her research.

A code for the source of the entry (represented in small capital letters within parentheses) is given only for those print sources that provided at least 50 items. Complete bibliographical information about the publications cited can be found in the List of Selected Sources following the User's Guide. The editor will provide further information upon request.

Acknowledgments

In addition to the in-house staff, other people have contributed significantly to the compilation of this supplement. The editor wishes to thank Monica Langley, James U. Rose, Janet I. Rose, Stuart E. Rose, and Tracey Head Turbett for their contributions.

Available in Electronic Format

AIAD and *AIAD-S* are available for licensing on magnetic tape or diskette in a fielded format. The database is available for internal data processing and nonpublishing purposes only. For more information, call 800-877-GALE.

Comments and Suggestions Are Welcome

Users can make unique and important contributions to future supplements and new editions by notifying the editor of subject fields that are not adequately covered, by suggesting sources for covering such fields, and even by sending individual terms they feel should be included.

User's Guide

Acronyms, Initialisms & Abbreviations Dictionary Supplement comprises two sections, providing numeric and alphabetic access to entries either by acronym or by meaning.

By Acronym Section

Acronyms are arranged alphabetically in letter-by-letter sequence, regardless of spacing, punctuation, or capitalization. If the same abbreviation has more than one meaning, the various meanings are then subarranged alphabetically in word-by-word sequence. Entries may contain some of the elements noted in the example below:

Abbreviation or acronym

Location

English Translation

Sponsoring Organization

AP................Absolute Pardon	Meaning or Phrase
A/P................Account-Purchase Phrase	
A & P............Agricultural and Pastoral	
ap..................Antiperiplanar [*Chemistry*]	Subject area
AP..................Appendectomy	
APA ....Automobile Protection Association [*Canada*]	
APB ....All Points Bulletin	
APC ....Anno post Christum Natum [*Latin*]	Language
APC ....Archives Publiques du Canada [*Public Archives of Canada*]	
APC ....Area Planning Council [*Department of Education*]	
APCA............Aft Power Controller Assembly (MCD)	Source code (Decoded in the List of Selected Sources)

By Meaning Section

Terms are arranged in word-by-word sequence according to the explanation of the acronym. Minor parts of speech (articles, conjunctions, prepositions) are generally not considered in the alphabetizing. If a particular explanation of the acronym has more than one initialism representing it, the various choices are then subarranged alphabetically, letter-by-letter, as they are in the *By Acronym* section.

Meaning or Phrase

Second Audio Program... SAP	Abbreviation or Acronym
Second Audio Program... SAPRO	
Second Audio Program... SECAP	
Second Base [*Baseball*] 2B	
Secondary School Admission Test Board [*Princeton, NJ*]... SSATB	
Secretariat for Catholic-Jewish Relations .... CJR	
Secretariat Europeen des Fabricants d'Emballages Metalliques Legers [*European Secretariat of Manufacturers of Light Metal Packages*] .... SEFEL	
Secretariat for Hispanic Affairs [*National Conference of Catholic Bishops*] .... SHA	
Secundum [*Latin*] .... SEC	
Secure Acoustic Data Relay.................................. SADR	

List of Selected Sources

Each of the print sources included in the following list contributed at least 50 terms. It would be impossible to cite a source for every entry because the majority of terms are sent by outside contributors, are uncovered through independent research by the editorial staff, or are located in miscellaneous broadcast or print media references.

Unless further described in an annotation, the publications listed here contain no additional information about the acronym, initialism, or abbreviation. The editor will provide further information about these sources upon request.

(BEE)   *"The Beeline."* <http://www.bton.com/tb17/abbr/a.html> (17 November 1999)

(BROA)   *Broadcasting and Cable Yearbook 1999.* New Providence, NJ: Reed Elsevier, Inc., 1999.

(EOSA)   *"Earth Observing System (EOS) Acronyms and Abbreviations."* <http://eospso.gsfc.nasa.gov/eos_homepage/misc> (5 October 1999)

(EPAT)   *"Terms of Environment."* <http://www.epa.gov/OCEPAterms/aaad.html> (3 November 1999)

(GEAB)   *"Genealogy Abbreviations."* <http://www.genweb.net/~samcasey/abbr.html> (17 November 1999)

(GEOI)   *"Dictionary of Abbreviations and Acronyms in Geographic Information Systems, Cartography, and Remote Sensing."* By Philip Hoehn and Mary Lynette Larsgaard. <http://www.lib.berkeley.edu/EART/abbrev.html> (June 1999)

(GVA)   *"Glossary of Veterinary Acronyms."* <http://www/spvs.org.uk/glossary.htm> (October 1999)

(IUSS)   *"IUSS Acronyms."* <http://206.239.241.41/Acronym/a.html> (12 October 1999)

(MELL)   *Melloni's Illustrated Dictionary of Medical Abbreviations.* By John Melloni and Ida G. Dox. Pearl River, NY: Parthenon Publishing Group, Inc., 1998.

(MILB)   *The Military Balance 1998/99.* London, England: Oxford University Press for the International Institute for Strategic Studies, 1998.

(NFLA)   *"National Football League Abbreviations and Team Histories."* <http://maxwell.uhh.hawaii.edu/football/archive/nflAbbreviations.html> (1998)

(PROS)   *Prospector's Choice. User's Guide.* Detroit, MI: The Taft Group, 1997.

(QUAC)   *"Dictionary of Quaternary Acronyms."* <http://www.ualberta.ca/~abeaudoi/cap/diction/atoc.html> (12 October 1999)

(SG)   *Standard & Poor's Stock Guide.* New York, NY: Standard & Poor's, 2000.

(WEAT)   *"Weather Abbreviations."* <http://www.ukweather.freeserve.co.uk/abbrev.html> (16 November 1999)

(WORL)   *World Guide to Libraries.* Edited by Willemina van der Meer. 14th ed. Munich, Germany: Saur, 1999.

Numerics
By Acronym

1/d .... One Time a Day [*Medicine*] (MELL)
2/d .... Two Times a Day [*Medicine*] (MELL)
2-DR .... Two-Door [*Automobile*]
3-A.............. Dairy & Food Industries Supply Association, Inc.
3/d .... Three Times a Day [*Medicine*] (MELL)
3-D CAE....... Three-Dimensional Computer-Aided Engineering
3-DR .... Three-Door [*Automobile*]

4A's .... Associated Actors and Artistes of America (EA)
4CYL............ Four-Cylinder [*Engine*]
4/d .... Four Times a Day [*Medicine*] (MELL)
4-DR .... Four-Door [*Automobile*]
4ID.............. 4th Infantry Division [*Army*]
5-SPD .... Five-Speed [*Manual transmission*]
6-SPD .... Six-speed [*Manual transmission*]

A
By Acronym

A .... Auto House (GEOI)
AA .... Accountable Area [*Environmental science*] (EPAT)
AA .... Active Area
AA .... Alcoa, Inc. [*NASDAQ symbol*] (SG)
AA .... Auto-Alerting (IUSS)
AAA .... Alaska Anthropological Association (QUAC)
AAACC .... U.S. Pan-Asian Chamber of Commerce (EA)
AABM .... Association of American Battery Manufacturers, Inc.
AAC .... Affirmative Action Clause
AAC .... Arcadia Financial Ltd. [*NYSE symbol*] (SG)
AAC .... Autoclaved Aerated Concrete
AACA .... Airborne Anti-Submarine Warfare Coordination Aircraft (IUSS)
AACB .... Alliance Atlantis Communic'B' [*NASDAQ symbol*] (SG)
AACCCM ...... Anglo-American Cataloguing Committee for Cartographic Materials (GEOI)
AACCH .... American Association of Cereal Chemists
AACE .... American Association of Cat Enthusiasts (EA)
AAD .... Advanced Acoustic Decoy [*Military*] (IUSS)
AADA .... American Autoduel Association (EA)
AADI .... Adjusted Acceptable Daily Intake
AAFHV .... American Association of Food Hygiene Veterinarians (GVA)
AAFS .... Advanced Aerial Fire Support System [*Military*] (IUSS)
AAHC .... American Accreditation Health Care Commission
AAHC .... Australian Animal Health Council (GVA)
AAHL .... Australian Animal Health Laboratory
AAI .... American Society for Personnel Administration Accreditation Institute
AAI .... Aqua Alliance'A' [*AMEX symbol*] (SG)
AAII .... Applied Analytical Industries [*NASDAQ symbol*] (SG)
AAIR .... AirTran Hldgs [*NASDAQ symbol*] (SG)
AAM .... All About Marilyn [*An association*] (EA)
AAMOF .... As a Matter of Fact [*Online dialog*]
AAM/R .... Air-to-Air Missile/Refuelling (MILB)
AAN .... ABN AMRO Holding ADS [*NYSE symbol*] (SG)
A&G .... Aiming and Guidance [*Military*] (IUSS)
AANWR .... Alaskan Arctic National Wildlife Refuge (EPAT)
AAO .... Affirmative Action Officer
AAORS .... Amphibious Assault Oceanographic Reconnaissance System [*Military*] (IUSS)
AAPA .... American Association of Professional Apiculturalists (QUAC)
AAPG .... American Association of Petroleum Geologists (QUAC)
AAPHV .... American Association of Public Health Veterinarians (GVA)
AARLS .... Arkansas Association of Registered Land Surveyors (GEOI)
AARS .... Asian Association on Remote Sensing (GEOI)
AAS .... Advanced Array Sensor [*Military*] (IUSS)
AASLBM .... Airborne Anti-Submarine-Launched Ballistic Missile [*Military*] (IUSS)
AASP .... American Antiquarian Society Proceedings (GEAB)
AATA .... American Athletic Trainers Association and Certification Board (EA)
AATC .... Airborne Anti-Submarine Warfare Tactical Coordinator (IUSS)
AATC/DAIR... Amphibious Air Traffic Control/Direct Altitude and Identity Readout [*Military*] (IUSS)
AATK .... Amer Acess Technologies [*NASDAQ symbol*] (SG)
AATSR .... Advanced Along-Track Scanning Radiometer (EOSA)
AAV .... Amphibious Armoured Vehicle (MILB)
AAVCB .... Australian Association of Veterinary Conservation Biologists (GVA)
AAVDM .... American Academy of Veterinary Disaster Medicine (GVA)
AAVI .... American Academy of Veterinary Informatics (GVA)
AAVI .... American Association of Veterinary Immunologists (GVA)
AAW .... Amry's Acquisition Workforce
AAW .... Army Acquisition Workforce
AAWCS .... Anti-Air Weapon Control System [*Military*] (IUSS)
ab .... Abbey (GEAB)
ab .... About (BEE)
ab .... Abridgment
AB .... Antigua and Barbuda (MILB)
AB .... Arts, Bachelor of (PROS)
AB .... Cannon Express [*AMEX symbol*] (SG)
ABAG .... Association of Bay Area Governments [*California*] (GEOI)
ABB .... Associacao Brasileira de Buiatria [*Brazilian Veterinary Cattle Association*] (GVA)
ABC .... Airborne Corps (IUSS)
ABCR .... ABC-Naco Inc. [*NASDAQ symbol*] (SG)
abd .... Abdicated (GEAB)
ABD .... AutoBond Acceptance [*AMEX symbol*] (SG)
ABDH .... Association of British Dogs' Homes (GVA)
ABDR .... Abacus Direct [*NASDAQ symbol*] (SG)
ABF .... Automatic Beam Forming [*Military*] (IUSS)

ABG .... Alpha Beta Gamma International (EA)
ABG .... Aluminum, Brick, and Glass Workers International Union
ABH .... Amer Bank Note Holographics [*NYSE symbol*] (SG)
ABI .... Amer Bankers Insur Grp [*NYSE symbol*] (SG)
ABI .... Automatic Bearing Instrumentation (IUSS)
ABIT .... Airborne Imagery Transmission [*Military*] (IUSS)
ABL .... Australian Bat Lyssavirus
ABM .... ABM Industries, Inc. [*NYSE symbol*] (SG)
ABMC .... American Belgian Malinois Club (EA)
Abp .... Archbishop (GEAB)
ABR .... Airborne Relay [*Military*] (IUSS)
ABR .... Atlantic Premium Brands [*AMEX symbol*] (SG)
ABRAVAS..... Associacao Brasileira de Veterinarios de Animais Selvagens [*Brazilian Small Animal Veterinary Association*] (GVA)
abs .... Abstract (GEAB)
ABS .... Australian Bureau of Statistics (GEOI)
ABSM .... Alberta Bureau of Surveying and Mapping [*Canada*] (GEOI)
ABSURD .... Airborne/Shipboard Universal Recovery Device (IUSS)
ABTL .... autobytel.com, Inc. [*NASDAQ symbol*] (SG)
ABY .... Abitibi-Consolidated [*NYSE symbol*] (SG)
AC .... Acquisition Command [*Army*]
AC .... Actual Commitment (EPAT)
A/C .... Air Conditioning
AC .... American Cartographer [*A publication*] (GEOI)
A/C .... Analyzer/Classifier (IUSS)
AC .... Ancestor Chart [*Genealogy*] (GEAB)
AC .... Antonio Castro (GFOI)
AC .... Attach Center [*Military*] (IUSS)
ACA .... Acrodermatitis Chronica Atrophicans [*Dermatology*]
ACA .... Aerial Cartographics of America (GEOI)
ACA .... Automovil Club Argentino (GEOI)
ACACIA .... Arid Climate, Adaptation, and Cultural Innovation in Africa (QUAC)
ACAF .... Advisory Committee on Animal Feedingstuffs (GVA)
ACAHF .... Australian Companion Animal Health Foundation (GVA)
ACAI .... Atlantic Coast Airlines Hldgs [*NASDAQ symbol*] (SG)
AC&C .... Office of Aeronautical Charting and Cartography (GEOI)
AC&E .... Advanced Concepts and Engineering [*Military*] (IUSS)
ACAP .... Air Command Acoustic Processing (IUSS)
ACAPHS .... Advisory Committee on Agricultural Product Health and Safety [*European Union*] (GVA)
ACAPS .... Automated Chart Production System (GEOI)
ACAS .... Amer Capital Strategies [*NASDAQ symbol*] (SG)
ACC .... Academia de Ciencias de Cuba (GEOI)
Acc .... Accessories
ACC .... Acoustic (IUSS)
ACC .... Amphibious Control Center [*Military*] (IUSS)
ACC .... Amplifier Control Cabinet [*Military*] (IUSS)
ACC .... Application Control Center
ACC .... Atlantic Climate Change
AcCast .... Altocumulus Castellanas Cloud (WEAT)
ACCC .... Afloat Contingency Command Center [*Military*] (IUSS)
ACCF .... American Chamber of Commerce in France (EA)
ACCM .... Asynchronous Communication Channel Multiplexer (IUSS)
ACCMPS ...... Automated Command and Control Message Processing System [*Military*] (IUSS)
acco .... Account (GEAB)
ACCS .... Afloat Cryptologic Support System [*Military*] (IUSS)
acct .... Accountant (PROS)
accu .... Accurate (GEAB)
ACE .... Advanced Cartographic Environment (GEOI)
ACE .... Advanced Cartographic Equipment (GEOI)
ACE .... Advanced Concept Excursion [*Army*]
ACE .... Alternating Conditional Expectation
ACE .... Any Credible Evidence [*Environmental science*] (EPAT)
ACES .... Active Control Equivalence Studies
ACES .... Arts Create Excellent Schools [*Program*]
ACFA .... American Cat Fanciers Association (EA)
ACG .... Acquisition Coordinating Group (IUSS)
ACI .... Aerosol-Cloud Interactions (QUAC)
ACI .... Arch Coal [*NYSE symbol*] (SG)
ACIC .... Automated Cartographic Information Center [*University of Minnesota Library*] (GEOI)
ACID .... Active Change Initiating Document (IUSS)
ackd .... Acknowledged (GEAB)
ACL .... Allowance Components List (IUSS)
ACLAD .... American Committee on Laboratory Animal Diseases (GVA)

AcLent	Altocumulus Lenticularis Cloud (WEAT)
ACLS	Association of Canadian Land Surveyors (GEOI)
ACM	Asynchronous Channel Multiplexer (IUSS)
ACMCA	Advertising Cup and Mug Collectors of America (EA)
ACME	Association of Coffee Mill Enthusiasts (EA)
ACMGIS	Association of Computing Machinery Geographic Information Systems (GEOI)
ACML	Association of Canadian Map Libraries (GEOI)
ACMS	Automated Census Mapping System (GEOI)
ACM-SIGGRAPH	Association of Computing Machinery Special Interest Group on Graphics (GEOI)
ACMSV	Advisory Committee on the Microbiological Safety of Food (GVA)
ACP	Agriculture Control Program [*Environmental Protection Agency*] (EPAT)
ACP	Arms Control Proposal [*Military*] (IUSS)
ACP	Association Canadienne des Palynologues (QUAC)
ACPAT	Association of Chartered Physiotherapists in Animal Therapy (GVA)
ACPT	Air Campaign Planning Tool [*Military*] (IUSS)
ACQ	Ammoniacal Copper Quaternary
ACR	Absolute Cryogenic Radiometer
ACR	Amer Retirement [*NYSE symbol*] (SG)
ACRB	Acquisition Civilian Record Brief [*Army*]
ACR-F	Allowance Change Request-Fixed (IUSS)
ACRS	Asian Conference on Remote Sensing (GEOI)
ACS	Active Control Station (IUSS)
ACS	Advanced Cartographic Systems (GEOI)
ACS	Affiliated Computer Services 'A' [*NYSE symbol*] (SG)
ACS	Air Control Supervisor [*Military*] (IUSS)
ACS	American Community Survey (GEOI)
ACS	Automated Cartographic Systems (GEOI)
ACSC	Automobile Club of Southern California (GEOI)
ACSI	Altocumulus Standing Lenticular Cloud (WEAT)
ACSTTO	Association of Certified Survey Technicians and Technologists of Ontario [*Canada*] (GEOI)
ACT	Abbott Consortium for Technology
actg	Acting (GEAB)
ACVT	Advisory Committee on Veterinary Training [*European Union*] (GVA)
ACWM	Asbestos-Containing Waste Material (EPAT)
ACY	Aerocentury Corp. [*AMEX symbol*] (SG)
A-D	Arm-Disarm [*Military*] (IUSS)
AD	Attachment Disorder [*Medicine*]
ADA	Allen Osborne Associates, Inc. (GEOI)
ADAAC	Affiliated Distributed Active Archive Center (EOSA)
ADALT	Advanced Radar Altimeter (EOSA)
ADAP	Adaptive Broadband [*NASDAQ symbol*] (SG)
ADAS	Air-Deployable Array Sonobuoy [*Military*] (IUSS)
ADATP	Allied Data Publication (IUSS)
ADB	Acoustic Database (IUSS)
ADBMS	Acoustic Data Base Management System (IUSS)
ADBSS	Acoustic Data Base System (IUSS)
ADC	Acoustic Display Console (IUSS)
ADC	Aeronautical Charting Division (GEOI)
ADC	Affiliated Data Center (EOSA)
ADC	After-Death Communication
ADC	Alexandria Drafting Company (GEOI)
ADC	Astronomical Data Center
ADC	Atlantic Data Coverage
AD/CAC	Automated Detection/Computer-Aided Classification (IUSS)
ADD	Authorized Development Deviation
ADDA	National Attention Deficit Disorder Association
ADDS-DP	Automated Data System-Development Plan (IUSS)
ADE	AutoCAD Data Extension (GEOI)
ADEC	Accumulated Deductible Employee Contributions
ADEC	Adaptive Detection, Estimation, and Correlation (IUSS)
ADEO	Advanced Earth Observing Satellite (GEOI)
ADFC	AdForce, Inc. [*NASDAQ symbol*] (SG)
ADFG	Alaska Department of Fish and Game (GEOI)
ADFM	Association Democratique des Femmes du Maroc [*Morocco*]
ADG	Advanced Communications Grp. [*NYSE symbol*] (SG)
ADGO	Adams Golf [*NASDAQ symbol*] (SG)
ADHS	Appalachian Development Highway System
ADIC	Abu Dhabi Investment Company
adj	Adjusted (MILB)
adj	Adjutant (GEAB)
ADL	Alexandria Digital Library (GEOI)
Adm	Admiralty (GEOI)
adm	Admission (GEAB)
ADM	Archer-Daniels-Midland [*NYSE symbol*] (SG)
ADMG	Advanced Matis Group [*NQS*] (SG)
admin	Administrator (GEAB)
ADMIT	Analytical Detection Methods for the Irradiation Treatment of Foods
ADNR	Alaska Department of Natural Resources (GEOI)
ADOT	Arizona Department of Transportation (GEOI)
ADOTPF	Alaska Department of Transportation and Public Facilities (GEOI)
ADP	Advanced Development Phase (IUSS)
ADP	Advanced Development Program (IUSS)
ADPDP	Alaska Division of Policy Development and Planning (GEOI)
ADPSWG	Automated Data Processing Standardization Working Group (IUSS)
ADQ	Audits of Data Quality [*Environmental science*] (EPAT)
ADR	Acoustic Data Relay (IUSS)
ADR	Aerial Data Reduction Associates, Inc. (GEOI)
ADRES	Advanced Reconnaissance Sensor [*Military*] (IUSS)
ADRG	Arc Digitized Raster Graphics (GEOI)
ADRS	American Depositary Receipts
ADS	Asteroid Detection System

AdSt	Adolf Stieler (GEOI)
ADSX	Applied Digital Solutions [*NASDAQ symbol*] (SG)
ADT	Advanced Data Technologies, Inc. (GEOI)
ADTC	Army Development Test Command
ADTN	Adtran, Inc. [*NASDAQ symbol*] (SG)
ADVBA	American Deaf Volleyball Association (EA)
ADVICE	Annual to Decadal Variability in Climate in Europe (QUAC)
ADW	Agricultural Drainage Well (GEOI)
ADWR	Arizona Department of Water Resources (GEOI)
AE	Acquisition Engineer [*Military*] (IUSS)
AEA	Association for Environmental Archaeology (QUAC)
AEC	Aerial Experimental Component [*Military*] (IUSS)
AECCM	Active Electronic Countermeasures (IUSS)
AECT	Association for Educational Communications & Technology
AEE	Ameren Corp. [*NYSE symbol*] (SG)
AEELS	Automatic Electronic Intelligence Emitter Location System (IUSS)
AEF	Active Emitter File (IUSS)
AEF	Alliance for Environmental Education (GEOI)
AEG	AEGON N.V. Ord [*NYSE symbol*] (SG)
AEM	Atmospheric Explorer Mission (GEOI)
AEM	Automatic Experimental Monitoring (IUSS)
AER	Aegis Realty [*AMEX symbol*] (SG)
AER	Atmospheric and Environmental Research (EOSA)
AERHO	National Broadcasting Society-Alpha Epsilon Rho [*Formerly, Alpha Epsilon Rho*] (EA)
AERI	Atmospheric Emitted Radiance Interferometer
AERL	Aerial Communications [*NASDAQ symbol*] (SG)
Aeron	Aeronautics (BEE)
AERS	Advanced Earth Resources Satellite (GEOI)
AESE	Association of Earth Science Editors (GEOI)
AESP	Advanced Elect Support Pds [*NASDAQ symbol*] (SG)
AETE	Acquisition Education, Training, and Experience [*Army*]
AETTA	Antique Engine, Tractor, and Toy Association (EA)
AEWCC	Airborne Early Warning Control Center [*Military*] (IUSS)
AEWS	Advanced Early Warning System [*Military*] (IUSS)
af	Affidavit (GEAB)
AFA	American Ferret Association (GVA)
AFB	Aluminum Four-Barrel [*Automotive term*]
AFB/S	Air Force Base/Station (MILB)
AFC	Advanced Force Commander (IUSS)
AFC	Air Force Center (IUSS)
AFCI	Advanced Fibre Communication [*NASDAQ symbol*] (SG)
AFCS	Adaptive Fire Control System [*Military*] (IUSS)
AFCS	Automatic Facilities Control Subsystem (IUSS)
Aff	Affairs (PROS)
affil	Affiliation (PROS)
Afg	Afghanistan (MILB)
AFIS	Air Force Intelligent System (IUSS)
AFM	AMFM, Inc. [*NYSE symbol*] (SG)
AFPL	Air Force Phillips Laboratory
Afro-Amer	African-American (BEE)
AFS	Active Fleet Ships (IUSS)
AF/SA	Air Force Studies and Analysis (IUSS)
AFSAT	Air Force Satellite (IUSS)
AFT	Ambiguity Function Technique (GEOI)
AFT	Ash Fusion Temperature [*Coal industry*]
AG	About Good [*Numismatic term*]
Ag	Algeria (MILB)
AG	Array Gain (IUSS)
AG	Attack Group [*Military*] (IUSS)
AGC	Arkansas Geological Commission (GEOI)
AGC	Attack Group Commander [*Military*] (IUSS)
AgDB	Agriculture Network Information Center [*Internet resource*]
AGDS	Automated Graphics Digitizing System (GEOI)
AGE	Edwards(AG), Inc. [*NYSE symbol*] (SG)
AGH	Atlantis Plastics [*AMEX symbol*] (SG)
AGI	Alpine Group [*NYSE symbol*] (SG)
AGI	Association for Geographic Information [*London, England*] (GEOI)
AGIC	Arizona Geographic Information Council (GEOI)
AGII	Argonaut Group [*NASDAQ symbol*] (SG)
AGIS	Automated Geographic Information System (GEOI)
AGMA	Federal Agricultural Mtge'A' [*NYSE symbol*] (SG)
AGN	Active Galactic Nuclei
AGNPS	Agricultural Non-Point Source [*Environmental science*]
AGR	Argentaria Banco Hipotecario ADS [*NYSE symbol*] (SG)
Agric	Agriculture (BEE)
AGS	Alberta Geological Survey [*Canada*] (GEOI)
AGT	AimGlobal Technologies [*AMEX symbol*] (SG)
AGTO	Agritope, Inc. [*NASDAQ symbol*] (SG)
AGTX	Applied Graphics Tech [*NASDAQ symbol*] (SG)
AGX	Agribrands Intl. [*NYSE symbol*] (SG)
AGY	Argosy Gaming [*NYSE symbol*] (SG)
A/H	Amplitudes/Hour
AH	Armor Holdings [*NYSE symbol*] (SG)
AHAA	Alpha Indus [*NASDAQ symbol*] (SG)
AHAP	Alaska High-Altitude Aerial Photography (GEOI)
AHBA	American Hardboard Association
AHC	Alternating Hemiplegia of Childhood [*Medicine*]
AHC	Amerada Hess [*NYSE symbol*] (SG)
AHCC	American-Hellenic Chamber of Commerce (EA)
AHDAS	Adaptable Hydrologic Data Acquisition System (GEOI)
AHE	Amer Health Pro [*NYSE symbol*] (SG)
AHEAD	Animal Health/Emerging Animal Diseases (GVA)
AHES	Archive for History of Exact Sciences [*A publication*]
AHG	Apria Healthcare Grp [*NYSE symbol*] (SG)

AHI............. Allied Holdings [*NYSE symbol*] (SG)
AHL............. Amer Heritage Life [*NYSE symbol*] (SG)
AHO............. Ahold Ltd. ADR [*NYSE symbol*] (SG)
AHP............. Advanced Humionics Platform [*Military*]
AHP............. Amer Home Products [*NYSE symbol*] (SG)
AHPI............ Allied Healthcare Prod [*NASDAQ symbol*] (SG)
AHR............. Anthracite Capital [*NYSE symbol*] (SG)
AHTC.......... AHT Corp. [*NASDAQ symbol*] (SG)
AHVG.......... Animal Health and Veterinary Group [*British*] (GVA)
AI................. Associative Ionization
AIA.............. Amer Ins Mtge Inv L.P. [*AMEX symbol*] (SG)
AI/ANA........ American Indian/Alaska Native Area (GEOI)
AIC.............. Active to Inert Conversion [*Environmental science*] (EPAT)
AIC.............. Australian Institute of Cartographers (GEOI)
AIC.............. Auxiliary Interface Cabinet (IUSS)
AICHE .... American Institute of Chemical Engineers
AIF.............. Applications Interface (IUSS)
AIG.............. Amer Intl. Group [*NYSE symbol*] (SG)
AIG.............. Amplifier Interface Group (IUSS)
AIGER .... American Industry Government Emissions Research Consortium
AII............... Amer Ins Mtge Inv Ser 85 [*AMEX symbol*] (SG)
AIJ............... Amer Ins Mtge Inv Ser 86 [*AMEX symbol*] (SG)
AIK.............. Amer Ins Mtge Inv Ser 88 [*AMEX symbol*] (SG)
AIL.............. Automated Integrated Language (IUSS)
AILESP........ American Indian Lands Environmental Support Project (GEOI)
AILSIN .... Automated Integrated Language System Identification Number (IUSS)
AIM.............. American Institute for Management
AIM.............. Americans in Milan [*An association*]
AIMS........... Airborne Integrated Mapping System (GEOI)
A IN B.......... Auto in Basement (GEAB)
AIO.............. Attitudes, Interests, and Opinions
AIP.............. Accuracy Improvement Program (IUSS)
AIPA........... Association Internationale de Palynologie Africaine [*International Association of African Palynology*] (QUAC)
AIPRC .... American Indian Policy Review Commission
Air............... Air Conditioner
AIR.............. Alternation Installation Requirements (IUSS)
AIR.............. American Indian Reservation (GEOI)
Aireps......... Aircraft Reports (WEAT)
AIRS .... Amer Aircarriers Support [*NASDAQ symbol*] (SG)
AIS.............. Acoustic Intercept System (IUSS)
AIS.............. Ampal-Amer Israel'A' [*AMEX symbol*] (SG)
AJR.............. Asociation de Juventud Rebelde [*Association of Rebel Youth*]
AK............... Ackerley Group [*NYSE symbol*] (SG)
AKDC .... Automatic Key Distribution Center (IUSS)
AKK.............. Armstrong World Ind 7.45% 'QUIBS' [*NYSE symbol*] (SG)
AL................ Ambassador at Large
Ala.............. Alabama (BEE)
ALAE........... Atmospheric Lyman Alpha Emissions (GEOI)
ALARS .... Alaska Land and Resources System (GEOI)
ALC.............. Alltrista Corp. [*NYSE symbol*] (SG)
ALCN .... Alternate Logistic Control Number (IUSS)
ald............... Alderman (GEAB)
ALF.............. Alien Life-Form
ALFA........... Assessment of Long-Range Fleet Architecture [*Military*] (IUSS)
Alg.............. Algebra (BEE)
ALGO .... Algos Pharmaceutical [*NASDAQ symbol*] (SG)
Algon.......... Algonquian (BEE)
ALGX .... Allegiance Telecom [*NASDAQ symbol*] (SG)
ALI.............. Alterra Healthcare [*AMEX symbol*] (SG)
ALI.............. Amplitude Line Integration (IUSS)
ALIAS......... Arctic Logistics Information Access Service (QUAC)
ALIS............ Automated Land Information System (GEOI)
ALLC........... Allied Capital [*NASDAQ symbol*] (SG)
alleg........... Allegiance (GEAB)
ALLR........... Allaire Corp. [*NASDAQ symbol*] (SG)
ALLS........... Allstar Systems [*NASDAQ symbol*] (SG)
ALN.............. Allen Telecom [*NYSE symbol*] (SG)
ALOHA........ Aerial Locations of Hazardous Atmospheres (GEOI)
ALP.............. Automated Lands Project (GEOI)
ALR.............. Action Leakage Rate [*Environmental science*] (EPAT)
ALRE........... Annuity & Life Re [*NASDAQ symbol*] (SG)
ALRS........... Alaris Medical [*NASDAQ symbol*] (SG)
ALS.............. Airborne Link Segment [*Military*] (IUSS)
als............... Alias (GEAB)
ALS.............. ALSTOM ADS [*NYSE symbol*] (SG)
Alsk............. Alaska (BEE)
ALT.............. Allegheny Teledyne [*NYSE symbol*] (SG)
alt............... Alternative (BEE)
ALTA........... Active Long-Term Archive (EOSA)
alter........... Alteration (BEE)
Alum........... Aluminum
ALV.............. Autoliv, Inc. [*NYSE symbol*] (SG)
AM............... Alternating Magnetic (IUSS)
AM............... Amer Greetings Cl'A' [*NYSE symbol*] (SG)
AM............... Autoallergic Myositis [*Dermatology*]
AMA............. Asociacion Mexicana Automovilistica (GEOI)
AMAD .... Airborne Missions and Applications Division [*Ames Research Center*] (GEOI)
AMAP........... Arctic Monitoring and Assessment Program (GEOI)
AMASS .... Advanced Marine Airborne Signal Intelligence System (IUSS)
AMB............. Acquisition Management Branch [*Army*]
AMB............. AMB Property [*NYSE symbol*] (SG)
AMC............. American Muslim Council
AMC............. Atmospheric Mesoscale Campaigns (QUAC)

AMCC.......... Applied Micro Circuits [*NASDAQ symbol*] (SG)
AMCHAM .... American Chamber of Commerce in Belgium (EA)
AmCham..... American Chamber of Commerce in Italy [*An association*]
AMCHAM .... American Chamber of Commerce in New Zealand (EA)
AMCHAM .... American Chamber of Commerce in Okinawa (EA)
AMCHAM .... American Chamber of Commerce in the Netherlands (EA)
AmCham..... Costa Rican-American Chamber of Commerce (EA)
AmCham-Argentina... American Chamber of Commerce in Argentina (EA)
AMCHAM Egypt... American Chamber of Commerce-Egypt (EA)
AMCHAM EL SALVADOR... American Chamber of Commerce of El Salvador (EA)
AMCHAM IRELAND... U.S. Chamber of Commerce in Ireland (EA)
AMCHAM KOREA... American Chamber of Commerce in Korea (EA)
AMCHAM Paraguay... Paraguayan-American Chamber of Commerce (EA)
AMCHAM PERU... American Chamber of Commerce of Peru (EA)
AMCHAM-Sao Paulo... American Chamber of Commerce for Brazil-Sao Paulo (EA)
AMCPC .... AMC Pacer Club (EA)
AMCT.......... AMRESCO Capital Tr [*NASDAQ symbol*] (SG)
AME............. Aero-Metric Engineering, Inc. (GEOI)
AmerInd...... American Indian (BEE)
AmerSp....... American Spanish (BEE)
Amex.......... American Stock Exchange
AMG............. Affiliated Managers Grp [*NYSE symbol*] (SG)
AMG............. Australian Map Grid (GEOI)
AMH............. AmerUs Life Holdings'A' [*NYSE symbol*] (SG)
AMI............. Analytical Methods/Inorganic
AMI............. Applied Mapping, Inc. (GEOI)
AMICA .... Automatic Musical Instrument Collectors Association International (EA)
AMIF........... Airglow Measurements of Infrared Measurements Emissions (GEOI)
AMIS........... Aviation Management Information System (GEOI)
AMISAR ...... Active Microwave Imager Synthetic Aperture Radar (GEOI)
AMKR.......... Amkor Technology [*NASDAQ symbol*] (SG)
AML............. Asymmetric Maximum Likelihood [*Statistics*]
AML............. Asymmetric Maximum Liklihood
AMM............ Advantage Marketing System [*AMEX symbol*] (SG)
AMM............ American Mathematical Monthly [*A publication*]
AMMVEPE... Asociacion Mexicana de Medicos Veterinarios Especialistas en Pequenas Especies [*Mexican Small Animal Veterinary Association*] (GVA)
AMNH .... American Museum of Natural History
AMO............. Analytical Methods/Organic
AMO............. Atomic, Molecular, and Optical
AMOS .... Air Management Oversight System [*Environmental science*] (EPAT)
AMP............. Americans for Medical Progress (GVA)
AMP............. Analysis of Mobility Platform [*Military*] (IUSS)
AMP............. Analytical Methods/Partial
AMPE.......... Automated Message Processing Equipment (IUSS)
AMRAD .... Advanced Research Project Agency Measurement Radar (IUSS)
AMRC.......... Antarctic Meteorology Research Center
AMRIR......... Advanced Medium Resolution Infrared Radiometer
AMS............. Attitude Measurement Sensor (GEOI)
AMS............. Australian Mammal Society (GVA)
AMS............. Automated Mapping System (GEOI)
AMSAA .... Army Materiel Systems Analysis Activity
AMSD .... Adjusted Mapping Support Data (GEOI)
AMSO .... Army Modeling and Simulation Office
AMSU-A ...... Advanced Microwave Sounding Unit-A (EOSA)
AMSY.......... Amer Mgmt Systems [*NASDAQ symbol*] (SG)
AMT............. Amer Tower'A' [*NYSE symbol*] (SG)
AMT............. Avionics Maintenance Trainer [*Military*] (IUSS)
AMTD.......... AmeriTrade Holding'A' [*NASDAQ symbol*] (SG)
AMTRA .... Animal Medicines Training and Regulatory Authority (GVA)
AMTS.......... Advanced Moisture and Temperature Sounder (EOSA)
AMVC.......... Advanced Mach Vision Ci'A' [*NASDAQ symbol*] (SG)
AMVQ.......... Academie de Medecine Veterinaire du Quebec (GVA)
AMZ............. Amer Medical Security Grp [*NYSE symbol*] (SG)
AMZN.......... Amazon.com [*NASDAQ symbol*] (SG)
AN............... AutoNation, Inc. [*NYSE symbol*] (SG)
ANA .... All Nippon Airways
ANAD........... ANADIGICS, Inc. [*NASDAQ symbol*] (SG)
ANAPROP... Anomalous Propagation [*Meteorology*] (WEAT)
ANARE........ Australian National Antarctic Research Expeditions (GEOI)
ANB .... Anterior Neural Boundary Organizer
anc............. Ancestry (GEAB)
ANC............. Ashore Navigation Center [*Military*] (IUSS)
ANDR........... Andrew [*Stock market symbol*]
AnF/SW....... Angel Flight/Silverwings [*An association*] (EA)
ANGCEL....... Angle Cell [*Military*] (IUSS)
ANH............. Anworth Mortgage Asset [*AMEX symbol*] (SG)
ANK .... Atlantic Tele-Network [*AMEX symbol*] (SG)
ANMCCSD... Alternate National Military Command Center Software Directorate (IUSS)
annot .... Annotated (GEAB)
ano............. Another (GEAB)
Anon........... Anonymous (BEE)
ANRC........... Alaska Native Regional Corp. (GEOI)
ANS............. AirNet Systems [*NYSE symbol*] (SG)
ANS............. Applications Network Software (IUSS)
ANS............. Asteroid Negation System
ANSS .... ANSYS, Inc. [*NASDAQ symbol*] (SG)
ant............. Antiquary (GEAB)
antiq........... Antiquities (GEAB)
ANU Pr .... ANZ Exch Pfd Tr [*NYSE symbol*] (SG)
ANV .... Alaska Native Village (GEOI)
ANVSA........ Alaska Native Village Statistical Area (GEOI)

ANZCCART... Australian and New Zealand Council for the Care of Animals in Research and Teaching (GVA)
ANZLIC .... Australia New Zealand Land Information Council (GEOI)
AO .... Amphibious Operations [*Military*] (IUSS)
AO .... Ars Orientalis: The Arts of Islam and the East [*A publication*]
AO/ASIF ...... Arbeitsgemeinschaft fuer Osteosynthesefragen-Association for the Study of Internal Fixation (GVA)
AOB .... Average on Board (IUSS)
AOC .... Allied Operational Center [*Military*] (IUSS)
AOCC .... Air Operations Control Center (IUSS)
AOFC .... Apple Octopus Now [*An association*] (EA)
AOI .... Apple Orthodontix'A' [*AMEX symbol*] (SG)
AOIPS .... Atmospheric and Oceanographic Image Processing System (GEOI)
AO LLC .... American Ordnance Limited Liability Corporation
AOLS .... Association of Ontario Land Surveyors [*Canada*] (GEOI)
AONA .... Arbeitsgemeinschaft fuer Osteosynthesefragen North America (GVA)
AOO .... Air Operations Officer [*Military*] (IUSS)
AOO .... American Oceanographic Organization (GEOI)
AOP .... American Order of Pioneers (GEAB)
AOR .... Aurora Foods [*NYSE symbol*] (SG)
AOSS .... Ashtech Office Suite for Survey (GEOI)
AOTC .... Army Operational Test Command
AOU .... Approved for Operational Use (IUSS)
A/P .... Alert Pending [*Military*] (IUSS)
AP .... Analytical Plotter (GEOI)
AP .... Arboreal Pollen (QUAC)
AP .... Armed for Anti-Personnel Attack (MILB)
APA .... Adaptive Phased Array [*Military*] (IUSS)
APA .... Alternate Proficiency Assessments
APA .... Anti-Phopholipid Antibody [*Medicine*]
APAC .... APAC Customer Services [*NASDAQ symbol*] (SG)
APAFO .... Advanced Particles and Fields Observer (EOSA)
APAS .... Advanced Passive Sensors [*Military*] (IUSS)
APAS .... Astrophysical, Planetary, and Atmospheric Sciences
APBC .... Association of Pet Behavior Counsellors (GVA)
APC .... Acquisition Planning Conference (IUSS)
APC .... Animal Procedures Committee (GVA)
APC .... Average Percent Complete (IUSS)
APCC .... Amer Power Conversion [*NASDAQ symbol*] (SG)
APCM .... Aerial Photography Contract Management System (GEOI)
APD .... Alpha Phi Delta (EA)
APDF .... Automated Product Development Framework
APDIC .... Arizona Poison and Drug Information Center
APDIP .... Asia Pacific Development Information Programme
APEX .... Apex, Inc. [*NASDAQ symbol*] (SG)
APG .... Association of Polish Geomorphologists (QUAC)
APIS .... Aerial Photography Information System (GEOI)
APJI .... Association for Protection of Jewish Immigrants (GEAB)
APL .... Anti-Personnel Land-Mine (MILB)
APM .... Array Position Message (IUSS)
APM .... Assistant Program Manager (IUSS)
APMC .... Advanced Program Management Course [*Army*]
APMI .... Aerial Photography Micrographic Index (GEOI)
APO .... Acquisition Project Officer (IUSS)
APO .... Amer Community Properties Tr [*AMEX symbol*] (SG)
Apo .... Apogee (GEOI)
APP .... Amyloid Precursor Protein
app .... Appreciation
appar .... Apparently (BEE)
APPEAL .... Academic Press Print and Electronic Access License
APPP .... Acoustic Performance Prediction Program (IUSS)
apprd .... Appeared (GEAB)
approx .... Approximately (GEAB)
APPS .... Acoustic Performance Prediction System (IUSS)
APPSR .... Aerial Photography Progress Summary Report (GEOI)
APQF .... Aerial Photography Quad File (GEOI)
APR .... Amer Precision Indus [*NYSE symbol*] (SG)
Apr .... April (BEE)
APRB .... Acquisition Program Review Board (IUSS)
APS .... Acquisition Planning System (IUSS)
APS .... Acquisition Program Sponsor (IUSS)
APS .... Adaptive Planning System
APSA .... Asiatic Parrot Society of America (EA)
APSR .... Aerial Photography Summary Record (GEOI)
APSRS .... Aerial Photography Summary Record System (GEOI)
APT .... Admissions per Thousand [*Hospitalization*]
APT .... All Purpose Tracker [*Military*] (IUSS)
APT .... Annular Proton Telescope
APTS .... Aerial Profiling of Terrain System (GEOI)
APTS .... Automated Package Test System (IUSS)
APVMA .... American Pre-Veterinary Medical Association (GVA)
APWG .... Acquisition Policy Working Group (IUSS)
APWWA ...... American Public Water Works Association (GEOI)
APZ .... Applied Indus Technologies [*NYSE symbol*] (SG)
AQ .... Allowance Quantity (IUSS)
AQCP .... Air Quality Control Program [*Environmental Protection Agency*] (EPAT)
AQMP .... Air-Quality Management Plan [*Environmental Protection Agency*] (EPAT)
AQR .... Applied Quaternary Studies (QUAC)
AQUA .... Autralasian Quaternary Association (QUAC)
AR .... Acquisition Request (IUSS)
Ar .... Arabic (BEE)
AR .... As Received

ARAC .... Acid Rain Advisory Committee [*Environmental Protection Agency*] (EPAT)
ARAV .... Association of Reptilian & Amphibian Veterinarians (GVA)
ARAZPA ...... Australasian Regional Association of Zoological Parks and Aquaria (GVA)
ARB .... Anti-Roll Bar
arb .... Arbitrageur [*Business term*]
ARBA .... Ariba, Inc. [*NASDAQ symbol*] (SG)
ARC .... Acquisition Review Council (IUSS)
ARC .... Alberta Research Council [*Canada*] (QUAC)
ARC .... Ames Research Center [*NASA*] (GEOI)
ARC .... Atlantic Richfield [*NYSE symbol*] (SG)
ArcFM .... Arc Facilities Manager (GEOI)
Archeol .... Archeology (BEE)
ARE .... Alexandria R.E. Equities [*NYSE symbol*] (SG)
AREC .... Air Resources Element Coordinator (IUSS)
ARFA .... American Running & Fitness Association
ARG .... Annual Real Growth (IUSS)
ARGOS .... Argos Data Collection and Location System [*France*] (EOSA)
ARI .... Arden Realty [*NYSE symbol*] (SG)
Ari .... Arizona Cardinals [*National Football League*] [*1994-present*] (NFLA)
ARIADNE ..... Anti-Submarine Warfare Surveillance System [*Military*] (IUSS)
ARIS .... Arizona Resources Information System (GEOI)
ARISE .... Associates for Research into the Science of Enjoyment
ARISTOTELES... Applications and Research Involving Space Technologies Observing the Earth's Field from a Low Earth Orbiting Satellite (EOSA)
Ariz .... Arizona (BEE)
ARJ .... Arch Chemicals [*NYSE symbol*] (SG)
ARK .... Ambac Financial Group [*NYSE symbol*] (SG)
Ark .... Arkansas (BEE)
ARL .... American Roque and Croquet Association [*Formerly, American Roque League*] (EA)
ARL/UT .... Applied Research Laboratory/University of Texas (IUSS)
ARM .... Airborne Remote Mapping (GEOI)
ARM .... ARM Financial Grp'A' [*NYSE symbol*] (SG)
ARM .... Artillery, Mortars, Cruise Missiles, Antiradiation Missiles [*Military*]
ARM .... Asphalt Roofing Manufacturers Association
armd .... Armored (MILB)
Armd Cav Regt... Armored Cavalry Regiment
ARMHY .... ARM Holdings ADS [*NASDAQ symbol*] (SG)
ARMIS .... Arkansas Resource Management Information System (GEOI)
AR-Net .... Amateur Radio Network (EA)
ARNEWS ..... Acid Rain National Early Warning Systems (EPAT)
ARP .... Annual Review of Progress
ARPL .... Authorized Replacement Parts List (IUSS)
ARRSTC ...... Asian Regional Remote Sensing Training Centre (GEOI)
ARS .... Automatic Reporting System (IUSS)
ARSA .... Auguste Reymond, SA
ARSC .... Australian Remote Sensing Conference (GEOI)
ARSF .... U.S. Amateur Confederation of Roller Skating (EA)
ART .... Alternative Risk Transfer [*Finance*]
ART .... Assisted Reproductive Technology [*Medicine*]
ARTS .... Annual Records of Tropical Systems (QUAC)
ARTT .... Advanced Radio Telecom [*NASDAQ symbol*] (SG)
arty .... Artillery (MILB)
ARX .... Experimental Repair Ship [*Military*] (IUSS)
AS .... Adolf Schild
As .... Altostratus Cloud (WEAT)
AS .... Anti-Spoofing (GEOI)
AS .... Asperger's Syndrome [*Medicine*]
AS .... Automatic Sprinklers (GEOI)
ASA .... Anti-Sperm Antibody [*Medicine*]
ASA .... Archaeological Survey of Alberta [*Canada*] (QUAC)
ASAALT .... Assistant Secretary of the Army for Acquistion, Logistics, and Technology
ASA(ILE) ...... Assistant Secretary of the Army for Installations, Logistics and Environment
ASAM .... Advanced Surface/Air Missile (IUSS)
ASAM .... ASAHI/America [*NASDAQ symbol*] (SG)
ASAP .... Advanced Scientific Array Processors (GEOI)
ASAP .... Agricultural Sciences Advisory Panel (GEOI)
ASAP .... Antarctic Space Analog Program [*NASA*]
A-SAR .... Advanced Synthetic Aperture Radar (EOSA)
ASAVA .... Australian Small Animal Veterinary Association (GVA)
ASBCI .... Asbestos-Covered Frame Building (GEOI)
ASBR .... American/Saudi Business Roundtable (EA)
ASC .... Allowance Support Code (IUSS)
ASC .... Antique Souvenir Collectors (EA)
ASC .... Archaeological Survey of Canada (QUAC)
A-SCAT .... Advanced Scatterometer (EOSA)
ascert .... Ascertain (GEAB)
ASCF .... Ames Satellite Communications Facility (GEOI)
ASCI .... Advanced Strategic Computing Initiative [*Department of Energy*]
ASCM .... Advanced Spaceborne Computer Module (IUSS)
ASCS .... Advanced Submarine Combat System [*Military*] (IUSS)
ASCS .... Airborne Strategic Communication System (IUSS)
ASE .... Advanced Sensor Exploration [*Military*] (IUSS)
ASE .... Amer Science & Engr [*AMEX symbol*] (SG)
ASEM .... Asia-Europe Meeting
ASF .... Administaff, Inc. [*NYSE symbol*] (SG)
ASF .... American Sailing Association Foundation (EA)
asgd .... Assigned (GEAB)
ASHTD .... American Association of State Highway and Transportation Officials (GEOI)

ASI	Acquisition Streamlining Initiative (IUSS)
ASI	Agenzia Spaziale Italiana [*Italy*] (EOSA)
ASI	Amer Safety Ins Grp [*NYSE symbol*] (SG)
ASI	Analytical Surveys, Inc. (GEOI)
ASIC	All-Source Information Center (IUSS)
ASIP	All-Source Imagery Processing System [*Marine Corps*] (IUSS)
ASKJ	ASK Jeeves [*NASDAQ symbol*] (SG)
asl	Above Sea Level (QUAC)
ASLA	Australia School Library Association
ASLE	Association for the Study of Literature and the Environment (QUAC)
aslt	Assault (MILB)
ASM	Audio Switching Matrix (IUSS)
ASMI	ASM Intl. N.V. [*NASDAQ symbol*] (SG)
ASML	ASM Lithography Hldg NV [*NASDAQ symbol*] (SG)
ASN	Autonomous System Number
ASO	Associated Service Organization
ASO	Australian Survey Office (GEOI)
ASP	Arabic Sciences and Philosophy [*A publication*]
ASPG	Automated Data Processing Standards Policy Group (IUSS)
ASPLS	Alaska Society of Professional Land Surveyors (GEOI)
ASPS	Arkansas Society of Professional Surveyors (GEOI)
asr	Assessor (GEAB)
Ass	Association (GEOI)
ASSA	Adolph Schild, S.A.
ASSA	Application for State School Aid
ASSI	Airglow Solar Spectrometer Instrument
Assn	Association (PROS)
assocs	Associates (BEE)
AST	Advanced Secondary Treatment [*Environmental science*] (EPAT)
ASTAC	Anti-Submarine Warfare Tactical Support Center [*Military*] (IUSS)
ASTE	At Sea Tactical Exercises [*Military*] (IUSS)
ASTEC	Australian Science and Technology Council
ASTER	Advanced Spaceborne Thermal Emission and Reflection Radiometer (EOSA)
ASTER	Advance Spaceborne Thermal Emission and Reflectance Radiometer
ASTF	Atchinson, Topeka, & Santa Fe Railway Co.
ASTM	American Society for Testing Materials (GEOI)
ASTSF	ASE Test Ltd. [*NASDAQ symbol*] (SG)
ASU-USA	Amateur Speedskating Union of the United States (EA)
ASVO	Association of State Veterinary Officers (GVA)
ASWCCS	Anti-Submarine Warfare Command, Control, and Communications Systems [*Military*] (IUSS)
ASWM	Anti-Submarine Warfare Module [*Military*] (IUSS)
ASWS	Advanced Surveillance Workstation [*Military*] (IUSS)
ASWS	Anti-Submarine Warfare School [*Military*] (IUSS)
ASW/SAR	Anti-Submarine Warfare/Search and Rescue [*Military*] (IUSS)
ASWSP	Anti-Submarine Warfare Systems Project [*Military*] (IUSS)
ASY	Airport Systems Intl. [*AMEX symbol*] (SG)
AT	Acquisition Team (IUSS)
AT	Aero-Triangulation (GEOI)
ATAC	Aftermarket Technology [*NASDAQ symbol*] (SG)
AT&T	Atlantic Telephone & Telegraph
ATARF	Abbreviated Tracking and Reporting Form (IUSS)
ATC	Aberdeen Test Center
ATC	Advanced Technology Classroom (IUSS)
ATC	AmTec, Inc. [*AMEX symbol*] (SG)
ATC	Animal Test Certificate (GVA)
ATC	Animal Treatment Center (GVA)
ATC	Approved Training Center (GVA)
ATC	Army Tank Contractor
ATC	Army Transportation Command (IUSS)
ATCS	Air Traffic Control System (IUSS)
ATD	Above-Threshold Dissociation
ATEN	At Entertainment, Inc. [*NASDAQ symbol*] (SG)
ATHM	At Home Corp.'A' [*NASDAQ symbol*] (SG)
ATHY	AppliedTheory Corp. [*NASDAQ symbol*] (SG)
ATI	Allied Telesyn International Corp.
ATIDS	Automated Tactical Information Display System (IUSS)
ATIS	Advanced Tissue Sciences [*NASDAQ symbol*] (SG)
ATIS	Automated Tactical Information System (IUSS)
ATL	Atalanta/Sosnoff Capital [*NYSE symbol*] (SG)
Atl	Atlanta Falcons [*National Football League*] [*1966-present*] (NFLA)
ATLAS	Argonne Tandem Linear Accelerator System
ATM	Adaptive Triangular Mesh (GEOI)
ATM	Automated Technical Manual (IUSS)
ATMHS	Automated Text Message Handling System (IUSS)
ATMI	ATMI, Inc. [*NASDAQ symbol*] (SG)
ATMP	Air Tour Management Plan
ATOD	Alcohol, Tobacco, and Other Drugs
ATOS	Anti-Submarine Warfare Operations Center-Tape Operation Systems [*Military*] (IUSS)
ATP	Acceptance Test Procedure (IUSS)
ATP	Advance Tracker Prototype (IUSS)
ATP	Automatic Telecommunications Program (IUSS)
ATPX	Advanced Technical Products [*NASDAQ symbol*] (SG)
ATRS	Advanced Tactical Radar System (IUSS)
ATS	Allowance Tracking System [*Environmental science*] (EPAT)
ATS	APT Satellite Hldg Ltd ADS [*NYSE symbol*] (SG)
ATS	Automated Technical Systems (GEOI)
ATSIC	Aboriginal and Torres Strait Islander Commission [*Australia*]
ATSN	Artesyn Technologies [*NASDAQ symbol*] (SG)

ATT	Advanced Testing Technology (IUSS)
ATTC	AT&T Canada'B' [*NASDAQ symbol*] (SG)
ATW	Advanced Technical Workstation (IUSS)
ATW	Atwood Oceanics [*NYSE symbol*] (SG)
ATX	Automatic Transmission
ATX	Cross CI'A' [*AMEX symbol*] (SG)
AU	About Uncirculated [*Numismatic term*]
AU	Alopecia Universalis [*Dermatology*]
AU	Anglogold Ltd. ADS [*NYSE symbol*] (SG)
aud	Auditor (GEAB)
aug	Augmentative (BEE)
Aug	August (BEE)
AUR	Air Unit Risk [*Environmental Science*]
AURIO	Auroral Imaging Observatory (EOSA)
AURISA	Australasian Urban and Regional Information Systems Association (GEOI)
Aus	Australia (MILB)
AUSDEC	Australasian Data Exchange Centre (GEOI)
AUSLIG	Australian Surveying and Land Information Group (GEOI)
Aust	Australian (BEE)
Auto	Automatic Transmission
AUTO	Automatic Transmission
AUTOSEVCOMII	Automatic Secure Voice Communications Network, Phase II (IUSS)
AUWS	Advanced Underwater Weapons System [*Military*] (IUSS)
Av	Avenue (GEOI)
AVA	Anti-Ovarian Antibody [*Medicine*]
AVA	Australian Veterinary Association (GVA)
AVA	Avista, Corp. [*NYSE symbol*] (SG)
AVAR	Association of Veterinarians for Animal Rights (GVA)
AVC	Association of Veterinary Consultants (GVA)
AVCA	American Veterinary Chiropractic Association (GVA)
AVCA	Audio-Visual and Cartographic Archives Division [*National Archives of Canada*] (GEOI)
AVCPT	Association for Veterinary Clinical Pharmacology and Therapeutics (GVA)
AVD	Amer Vanguard [*AMEX symbol*] (SG)
AVDC	American Veterinary Dental College (GVA)
AVDO	Avado Brands [*NASDAQ symbol*] (SG)
AVE	Anterior Visceral Endodermal
AVECCT	Academy of Veterinary Emergency & Critical Care Technicians (GVA)
AVG	Average Circulated [*Numismatic term*]
AVH	Academy of Veterinary Homeopathy (GVA)
AVI	Association for Veterinary Informatics (GVA)
AVI	Association of Veterinarians in Industry (GVA)
AVI	Avis Rent A Car [*NYSE symbol*] (SG)
AVIRIS	Advanced Visible/InfraRed Imaging Spectrometer (GEOI)
AVL	Alabama Virtual Library
AVMF	American Veterinary Medical Foundation (GVA)
avn	Aviation (MILB)
AVO	Audio/Visual Object (GEOI)
AVRI	Arizona Vegetation Resource Inventory (GEOI)
AVS	Aviation Sales [*NYSE symbol*] (SG)
AVSPNI	Association of Veterinary Surgeons Practicing in Northern Ireland (GVA)
AVSS	Automated Voice Switching System (IUSS)
AVT&RW	Association of Veterinary Teachers and Research Workers (GVA)
AVZ	AMVESCAP PLC ADS [*NYSE symbol*] (SG)
AW	Allied Waste Ind [*NYSE symbol*] (SG)
AWA	America West Holdings'B' [*NYSE symbol*] (SG)
AWAR	American Women's Association of Rome [*Italy*]
AWC	Advanced Web Creations
AWC	Asia Pacific Wire & Cable [*NYSE symbol*] (SG)
AWC	Aviation Weather Center
AWE	Army Warfighting Experiments
AWEB	Autoweb.com, Inc. [*NASDAQ symbol*] (SG)
AWF	Animal Welfare Foundation (GVA)
AWFC	Another World Fan Club (EA)
AWI	American Watchmakers-Clockmakers Institute
AWMSAS	Arc View Marine Spill Analysis System (GEOI)
AWP	American Wire Producers Association
AWP	Any Willing Provider [*Insurance*]
AWR	Amer States Water [*NYSE symbol*] (SG)
AWSELVA	Animal Welfare, Science, Ethics, and Law Veterinary Association (GVA)
AWSIM	Air Warfare Simulation Model [*Military*] (IUSS)
AWSS	Acquisition Workforce Support Specialist [*Army*]
AWX	Avalon Holdings'A' [*AMEX symbol*] (SG)
AX	Alpha Chi (EA)
AXAF-I	Advanced X-Ray Astrophysics Facility-Imaging [*NASA*]
AXL	Amer Axle & Manufacturing [*NYSE symbol*] (SG)
AXL	Anderson Exploration [*Toronto Stock Exchange symbol*] (SG)
AXM	Apex Mortgage Capital [*NYSE symbol*] (SG)
AXPH	AxyS Pharmaceuticals [*NASDAQ symbol*] (SG)
AYES	Automotive Youth Employment Services
AYVS	Army Year of Values Scales
AZ	Alexander Zakreski (GEOI)
Az	Azerbaijan (MILB)
AzMAP	Arizona Mapping Advisory Council (GEOI)
AZN	AstraZeneca ADR [*NYSE symbol*] (SG)
AZX	Azurix Corp. [*NYSE symbol*] (SG)
AZZ	Aztec Mfg Co. [*NYSE symbol*] (SG)

B
By Acronym

B .... Bel
ba .... Bachelor (GEAB)
BAAMA .... Bay Area Automated Mapping Association (GEOI)
BAC .... Bank of America [*NYSE symbol*] (SG)
BAC .... Bioremediation Action Committee [*Environmental science*] (EPAT)
BACE .... Beta-Site Amyloid Precursor Protein-Cleaving Enzyme
bach .... Bachelor (BEE)
Bacteriol ...... Bacteriology (BEE)
BADGER .... Bay Area Digital GeoResource (GEOI)
BAE .... British Aerospace
BAFSAM ...... British Association of Feed Supplement and Additives Manufacturers (GVA)
BAK .... Back at Keyboard [*Online dialog*]
BAL .... Balanced Care [*AMEX symbol*] (SG)
Bal .... Baltimore Colts [*National Football League*] [*1950, 1953-83*] (NFLA)
BALTEX .... Baltic Sea Experiment (QUAC)
BAMS .... Bulletin of the Australian Mathematical Society [*A publication*]
B&G .... Blue and Gold Macaw [*Bird*]
B&L .... Boggs and Lewis (GEOI)
B&S .... Bore and Stroke
B&W .... Birds and Wildlife
Banobras ..... Banco Nacional de Obras y Servicios Publicos [*Mexico*] (GEOI)
BAO .... Beijing Astronomical Observatory [*China*]
bap .... Baptism (GEAB)
BAP .... Credicorp Ltd. [*NYSE symbol*] (SG)
BAPMON ...... Background Air Pollution Monitoring (QUAC)
BAR .... British Antarctic Survey (QUAC)
BARCIS .... Bar Code Information System (GEOI)
Bas .... Basket
BASE .... Beaufort and Arctic Storms Experiment (QUAC)
BASE .... United States Base Association (EA)
BASINS .... Better Assessment Science Integrating Point and Nonpoint Systems (GEOI)
BATERISTA... Biosphere-Atmosphere Transfers and Ecological Research in Situ Studies in Amazonia (QUAC)
BATGE .... Biosphere-Atmosphere Trace Gas Exchange in the Tropics (QUAC)
BB .... Banco BHIF ADS [*NYSE symbol*] (SG)
BB .... Baseball
BBC .... Bahamas Billfish Championship
BBFC .... Beach Boys Fan Club (EA)
BBFC .... Boston Bruins Hockey Fan Club (EA)
BBFCI .... Billy Blanton Fan Club International (EA)
BBFN .... Bye Bye for Now [*Online dialog*]
Bbl .... Barrel [*Automotive term*]
bbr .... Bomber (MILB)
BBr .... Boston Braves [*National Football League*] [*1932*] (NFLA)
BBT .... BB&T Corp. [*NYSE symbol*] (SG)
BBX .... BankAtlantic Bancorp 'A' [*NYSE symbol*] (SG)
BBY .... Best Buy [*NYSE symbol*] (SG)
BC .... Blue Crown Conure [*Bird*]
BCA .... Bird Clubs of America (EA)
BCAA .... Branched-Chain Amino Acid
BCC .... Airdance, Inc. [*Formerly, Bellanca-Champion Club*] (EA)
BCC .... Biological Chemicals of Concern [*Environmental science*]
BCCA .... British Columbia Agency
BCCF .... British Columbia Cancer Foundation
BCCI .... British Chamber of Commerce for Italy
BCCRC .... British Columbia Cancer Research Centre
BCDC .... Bay Conservation and Development Commission (GEOI)
bcer .... Birth Certificate (GEAB)
BCGS .... Board of Coast and Geodetic Survey [*Philippines*] (GEOI)
BCHE .... BioChem Pharma [*NASDAQ symbol*] (SG)
BCICF .... Bell Canada Intl. [*NASDAQ symbol*] (SG)
BCL .... BLC Financial Svcs [*AMEX symbol*] (SG)
BCM .... Business Card Museum [*An association*] (EA)
BCM .... Canadian Imperial Blk Commerce [*NYSE symbol*] (SG)
BCMFC .... Bob Crane Memorial Fan Club (EA)
BCMS .... British Cattle Movement Service (GVA)
BCPCT .... Best Conventional Pollutant Control Technology (EPAT)
BCS .... Belleek Collectors' International Society (EA)
BCS .... Bragg Crystal Spectrometer
BCS .... Broadband Cable System
BCTGM .... Bakery, Confectionary, Tobacco Workers, and Grain Millers International Union
BCVA .... Belgian Veterinary Computer Association (GVA)
BCX .... BCE Mobile Communic [*NYSE symbol*] (SG)

bd .... Below Datum (QUAC)
BD .... Budget Group 'A' [*NYSE symbol*] (SG)
bd .... Buried (GEAB)
BDAT .... Best Demonstrated Achievable Technology [*Environmental science*] (EPAT)
BDBC .... British Dog Breeders' Council (GVA)
BDCT .... Best Demonstrated Control Technology [*Environmental science*] (EPAT)
bde .... Brigade (MILB)
BDE .... Brilliant Digital Entertain't [*AMEX symbol*] (SG)
BDET .... Bengston, DeBell, Elkin & Titus Ltd. (GEOI)
bdgt .... Budget (MILB)
BDLNR .... Bedliner
BDN .... Bob Dylan Newsletter [*An association*] (EA)
Bds .... Barbados (MILB)
BDS .... Bridgestreet Accomodations [*AMEX symbol*] (SG)
bdt .... Birth Date (GEAB)
Be .... Belgium (MILB)
BE .... Benguet Corp.CI'B' [*NYSE symbol*] (SG)
BE .... Brick Enclosed Elevator (GEOI)
BE2 .... Bare Eyed Cockatoo [*Bird*]
BEA .... Bernhard, Eisenbraun and Associates (GEOI)
BEAS .... BEA Systems [*NASDAQ symbol*] (SG)
bec .... Became (GEAB)
BEC .... Beckman Coulter [*New York City*] (SG)
BEEM .... Ballistic Electron Emission Spectroscopy
BEG .... Big Evil Grin [*Online dialog*]
BEG .... Bureau of Economic Geology [*Texas*] (GEOI)
BEIQ .... BEI Technologies [*NASDAQ symbol*] (SG)
Bel .... Belarus (MILB)
BELFA .... Bel Fuse, Inc.'A' [*NASDAQ symbol*] (SG)
BEOFC .... Barbara Eden's Official Fan Club (EA)
BESI .... BE Semiconductor Indus [*NASDAQ symbol*] (SG)
BETS .... Brunson Electronic Triangulation System (GEOI)
BEV .... Blacksburg Electronic Village
Bf .... Beaufort Force (WEAT)
BFA .... Blue Fronted Amazon [*Bird*]
BFCGDS .... Beatles Fan Club: Good Day Sunshine (EA)
Bfly .... Butterfly
BFO .... Bestfoods [*NYSE symbol*] (SG)
BFT .... Bally Total Fitness Holding [*NYSE symbol*] (SG)
BFX .... BFX Hospitality Group [*AMEX symbol*] (SG)
Bg .... Bulgaria (MILB)
BG .... Green Bay Packers [*National Football League*] [*1921-present*] (NFLA)
BGALY .... Banc Galicia-Buenos AiresADR [*NASDAQ symbol*] (SG)
BGC .... Business Geographics Conference (GEOI)
BGF .... Big Flower Holdings [*NYSE symbol*] (SG)
BH .... Bristol Hotel & Resorts [*NYSE symbol*] (SG)
BHA .... Bilateral Hilar Adenopathy [*Dermatology*]
BHAG .... BHA Group [*NASDAQ symbol*] (SG)
BHB .... Bar Harbor Bankshares [*AMEX symbol*] (SG)
BHB .... British Horseracing Board (GVA)
BHE .... Benchmark Electronics [*NYSE symbol*] (SG)
BHFC .... Bret Hart Fan Club (EA)
BHG .... Blown Head Gasket [*Automotive term*]
BHIC .... British Horse Industry Confederation (GVA)
BHP .... Biodegradation, Hydrolysis and Photolysis
BHRA .... British House Rabbit Association (GVA)
BHS .... Boston Harbor Software, Inc. (GEOI)
BHVMA .... British Holistic Veterinary Medicine Association (GVA)
BI .... Bullous Ichthyosis [*Dermatology*]
BIB .... Blocked Impurity Band
BICI .... Book Item Contribution Identifer (GEOI)
Bicuc .... Bicuculline
BiH .... Bosnia-Herzegovina (MILB)
BILL .... Billing Concepts [*NASDAQ symbol*] (SG)
BIMA .... Berkeley-Illinois-Maryland Array
BIMA .... Bulletin of the Institute of Mathematics and Its Applications [*A publication*]
BIND .... Berkeley Internet Name Domain [*California*]
BIOC .... Bricklin International Owners Club (EA)
BIOMAPS ...... Biodiversity Mapping for Protection and Sustainable Use of Natural Resources (GEOI)
BIP .... Band Interleaved by Pixel (GEOI)
BIRMD .... Balanced Incomplete Repeated Measures Design

bish .... Bishop (GEAB)
BJ .... BJ's Wholesale Club [*NYSE symbol*] (SG)
BJHS .... British Journal for the History of Science [*A publication*]
BJS .... BJ Services [*NYSE symbol*] (SG)
BKB .... BankBoston Corp. [*NYSE symbol*] (SG)
BKC/L .... Berlin Kommandatura Commandents' Letter
BkD .... Brooklyn Dodgers [*National Football League*] [*1930-43*] (NFLA)
BKE .... Buckle, Inc. [*NYSE symbol*] (SG)
bkf .... Bankfull (QUAC)
BKLY .... Berkley, W.R. [*NASDAQ symbol*] (SG)
BKN .... Broken Cloud (WEAT)
BKR .... Baker, Michael [*AMEX symbol*] (SG)
BkT .... Brooklyn Tigers [*National Football League*] [*1944*] (NFLA)
BKW .... Bent Knee Walker [*Doll collecting*]
BKX .... Beta Kappa Chi (EA)
bl .... Bibliography (GEAB)
BL .... Blood Lead
Bl .... Boulevard (GEOI)
BLAST .... Bell Labs Layered Space-Time
BLBIFC .... Bonnie Lou Bishop International Fan Club (EA)
BLC .... B-Lymphocyte Chemoattractant
BLDP .... Ballard Power Systems [*NASDAQ symbol*] (SG)
BLG .... Binary Line Generalization (GEOI)
BLM .... Blimpie Int'l. [*AMEX symbol*] (SG)
Blmfld .... Bloomfield (BEE)
BLPG .... Boron LePore & Assoc [*NASDAQ symbol*] (SG)
BLPU .... Basic Land and Property Unit (GEOI)
BLR .... Business & Legal Reports, Inc.
BLS .... Bahamas Lands and Surveys Department (GEOI)
BM .... Baume & Mercier
BMA .... Botswana Ministry Agriculture (GEOI)
BMG .... Bureau of Mines and Geosciences [*Philippines*] (GEOI)
BMM .... Bulletin of the Metals Museum [*A publication*] [*Sendai, Japan*]
BMR .... Bureau Mineral Resources [*Austalia*] (GEOI)
BMS .... British Micropalaeontological Society (QUAC)
BMW CCA ... BMW Car Club of America (EA)
BMW RA ...... BMW Riders Association (EA)
BN .... Banta Corp. [*NYSE symbol*] (SG)
bn .... Battalion (MILB)
Bn .... Benin (MILB)
BNBN .... barnesandnoble.com, Inc.'A' [*NASDAQ symbol*] (SG)
BND .... Boundless Corp. [*AMEX symbol*] (SG)
BNDES .... Brazilian National Development Bank
bndsmn .... Bondsman (GEAB)
BNE .... Bowne & Co. [*NYSE symbol*] (SG)
BNFL .... British Nuclear Fuels
Bng .... Bangladesh (MILB)
BNKU .... Bank United 'A' [*NYSE symbol*] (SG)
BNL .... Bunzl PLC ADS [*NYSE symbol*] (SG)
BNO .... Benton Oil & Gas [*NYSE symbol*] (SG)
BNPC .... Bathymetric Navigation Planning Chart (GEOI)
BNPD .... Bivariate Normal Probability Density (GEOI)
BNV .... Bencklser N.V.'B' [*NYSE symbol*] (SG)
BOA .... Basic Order Agreement
BOA .... Building Omission Area (GEOI)
BOBJ .... Business Objects ADS [*NASDAQ symbol*] (SG)
BOC .... Bureau of the Census (GEOI)
BOFI .... Bofors Optronic Fire Control Instrument (MILB)
BOFRS .... Books and Open-File Report Section (GEOI)
Bon .... Bonsai
BONY .... Bank of New York
BOP .... Bureau of Printing (GEOI)
BOR .... Burns Intl. Services [*NYSE symbol*] (SG)
Boro .... Borough (BEE)
BORPELS ..... Board of Registration for Professional Engineers and Land Surveyors [*California*]
BOS .... Airboss of America [*Toronto Stock Exchange symbol*] (SG)
Bos .... Boston Patriots [*National Football League*] [*1960-70*] (NFLA)
Bot .... Botany (BEE)
BOUT .... About.com, Inc. [*NASDAQ symbol*] (SG)
BOX .... BOC Group ADS [*NYSE symbol*] (SG)
BOY .... Boykin Lodging [*NYSE symbol*] (SG)
bp .... Birthplace (GEAB)
BPA .... BP Amoco ADS [*NYSE symbol*] (SG)
BPA .... British Pig Association (GVA)
BPAA .... Battle Point Astronomical Association
BPEG .... Bureau of Planning and Entitlement Grants
BPF .... Brazilian Purpuric Fever [*Medicine*]
BPI .... Business Periodicals Index
bpl .... Birthplace (GEAB)
BPO .... Brookfield Properties [*NYSE symbol*] (SG)
BPPT .... Badan Pembinaan dan Penerapan Teknologi [*Indonesia*] (GEOI)
bpt .... Baptized (GEAB)
BQ .... Best Qualified
BQD .... Berlin Quadripartite Document
Br. .... Brazil (MILB)
Br. .... British (GEAB)
br. .... Brother (GEAB)
BrAVO .... British Association for Veterinary Ophthalmology (GVA)

BRB .... Babe Ruth Baseball/Softball [*An association*] (EA)
BRC .... Brady Corp.'A' [*NYSE symbol*] (SG)
BRCD .... Brocade Communic Sys [*NASDAQ symbol*] (SG)
BRCM .... Broadcom Corp.'A' [*NASDAQ symbol*] (SG)
BRC/TCU ..... Brotherhood Railway Carmen Division/Transportation Communications Union (EA)
BRd .... Boston Redskins [*National Football League*] [*1933-36*] (NFLA)
BRET .... Biomedical Research Education Trust (GVA)
BRG .... BG plc ADS [*NYSE symbol*] (SG)
BRH .... Comp Cervelaria Brahma Pfd ADS [*NYSE symbol*] (SG)
BRICMICS .... British and Irish Committee for Map Information and Cataglogue Systems (GEOI)
Brig Hq .... Brigade Headquarters
Brit. .... British (BEE)
BRKL .... Brookline Bancorp [*NASDAQ symbol*] (SG)
BRKT .... Brooktrout, Inc. [*NASDAQ symbol*] (SG)
BRL .... Barr Laboratories [*NYSE symbol*] (SG)
Brn .... Bahrain (MILB)
BrO .... Bromine Monoxide (EOSA)
BRO .... Brown & Brown [*NYSE symbol*] (SG)
BRS .... Banco Rio De La Plata ADS [*NYSE symbol*] (SG)
Bru .... Brunei (MILB)
BRv .... Baltimore Ravens [*National Football League*] [*1996-present*] (NFLA)
bs .... Below Surface (QUAC)
BS .... Bureau of Statistics [*Japan*] (GEOI)
BSAP .... South Carolina Basic Skills Assessment Program
BSAS .... British Society of Animal Science (GVA)
BSC .... Boston Survey Consultants (GEOI)
BSCH .... Banco Santander Central Hispano [*Spain*]
BSE .... BEC Energy [*NYSE symbol*] (SG)
BSF .... International Brotherhood of Boilermakers, Iron Ship Builders, Blacksmiths, Forgers and Helpers (EA)
BSI .... Blackhawk Standbys [*An association*] (EA)
BSI .... Blue Square-Israel ADS [*NYSE symbol*] (SG)
BSI .... Bromeliad Society (EA)
bskb .... Basketball
BSQ .... Band Sequential (GEOI)
BSRG .... British Sedimentological Research Group (QUAC)
BSU .... Base Spatial Unit (GEOI)
BT .... Base Topo (GEOI)
BTAS .... Batman the Animated Series [*Television program*]
BTC .... Big Ten Conference (EA)
BTF .... Berlin Task Force
BTHS .... Benthos, Inc. [*NASDAQ symbol*] (SG)
BTJ .... Bolt Technology [*AMEX symbol*] (SG)
Bton .... Bloomington (BEE)
BTS .... BCT.TELUS Communications [*Toronto Stock Exchange symbol*] (SG)
BTTFTFC ..... Back to the Future, the Fan Club (EA)
Btwa .... Botswana (MILB)
BTWC .... Biological and Toxin Weapons Convention
bty .... Battery (MILB)
Bu .... Burundi (MILB)
BUDC .... Before Upper Dead Center
Buf .... Buffalo Bills [*National Football League*] [*1960-present*] (NFLA)
BULL .... Bull Run [*NASDAQ symbol*] (SG)
BUPNIS .... Beijing Underground-Network Information System [*China*] (GEOI)
bur .... Buried (GEAB)
BV .... Benvenuto Club [*Milan, Italy*]
BV .... Biological Values
BVC .... Bay View Capital [*NYSE symbol*] (SG)
BVCA .... British Veterinary Camelid Association (GVA)
BVDA .... British Veterinary Dental Association (GVA)
BVU .... Brightness Value Unit (GEOI)
B/W .... Black and White
BW .... Blackwall [*Automotive term*]
BWC .... Bandwidth Compression (GEOI)
BWC .... Bowhunters of America (EA)
BWC .... Buttes Watch Co.
BWE .... BancWest Corp. [*NYSE symbol*] (SG)
BWE .... Bandwith Expansion (GEOI)
BWEB .... BackWeb Technologies [*NASDAQ symbol*] (SG)
BWG .... Bouygues Offshore ADS [*NYSE symbol*] (SG)
BWLA .... Bowl America CI'A' [*AMEX symbol*] (SG)
BWN .... Bowlin Outdoor Adv/Travel [*AMEX symbol*] (SG)
BWS .... Brown Shoe [*NYSE symbol*] (SG)
BWY WS ...... Broadway Stores Wrrt [*NYSE symbol*] (SG)
BXH .... Box Hill Systems [*NYSE symbol*] (SG)
BXM .... Biomatrix, Inc. [*NYSE symbol*] (SG)
BXP .... Boston Properties [*NYSE symbol*] (SG)
BXS .... BancorpSouth [*NYSE symbol*] (SG)
BYH .... Beijing Yanhua Petrochem'H' ADS [*NYSE symbol*] (SG)
BYk .... Boston Yanks [*National Football League*] [*1944-48*] (NFLA)
BYKT .... But You Knew That [*Online dialog*]
BYND .... Beyond.com Corp. [*NASDAQ symbol*] (SG)
byp .... Bypass (BEE)
BYS .... Bay State Bancorp [*AMEX symbol*] (SG)
byte .... Binary Digit Eight
Bze .... Belize (MILB)

C

By Acronym

C .... Cartography (GEOI)
C .... Citigroup, Inc. [NYSE symbol] (SG)
c .... Cousin (GEAB)
C4I .... Command, Control, Communications, Computers, and Intelligence
C4IEWS .... Command, Control, Communications, Computers, Intelligence, Electronic Warfare, and Sensors [Army]
CA .... Antonio Castro (GEOI)
Ca .... Canada (MILB)
CA .... Cloud to Air Lightning (WEAT)
CAA .... Capital Alliance Income Tr [AMEX symbol] (SG)
CAAD .... Center for Advanced Computation [University of Illinois] (GEOI)
CAAD .... Compressed Aeronautical Chart (GEOI)
CAC .... Camden National [AMEX symbol] (SG)
CAC .... Contract Addenda Committee
CACS .... Canadian Active Control System (GEOI)
CAD .... Carbohydrate Addict's Diet
CADMAP ...... Computer-Aided Drafting, Mapping, and Photogrammetry (GEOI)
CAE .... CAE, Inc. [Toronto Stock Exchange symbol] (SG)
CAEN .... Chemically Assembled Electronic Nanocomputers
CAFF .... Conservation of Arctic Flora and Fauna (GEOI)
CAG .... Congo African Grey [Bird]
CaGIS .... Cartography and Geographic Information Science [A publication] (GEOI)
CAGIS .... Cartography and Geographic Information Society (GEOI)
CaGIS .... Cartography and Geographic Information Systems [A publication] (GEOI)
CAIS .... CAIS Internet [NASDAQ symbol] (SG)
cal .... Calibration (MILB)
CAL .... Contl Airlines'B' [NYSE symbol] (SG)
CALCM .... Conventional Air-Launched Cruise Missile (MILB)
CALMIT .... Center for Advanced Land Management Information Technologies [University of Nebraska-Lincoln] (GEOI)
CALS .... Computer Assisted Land Survey System (GEOI)
Caltech .... California Institute of Technology
Cal/Val .... Calibration/Validation (EOSA)
Cam .... Cambodia (MILB)
CAM .... Computer-Aided Machining
CAM .... Computer Aided Mapping (GEOI)
CAM .... Cooper Cameron [NYSE symbol] (SG)
CAM .... Cost Account Managers
CAMFER ...... Center for the Assessment and Monitoring of Forest and Environmental Resources [University of California, Berkeley] (GEOI)
CAN .... Amer Natl Can Group [NYSE symbol] (SG)
CAN .... Canadian Air Mail Collectors Club (EA)
can .... Cannon (MILB)
CANDE .... Candies, Inc. [NASDAQ symbol] (SG)
C & E .... Cough and Expectoration (MELL)
C & F .... Chills and Fever (MELL)
C&MT .... Communications & Measurement Technologies Ltd. (GEOI)
C & P .... Chloroquine and Primaquine [Medicine] (MELL)
C & T .... Color and Temperature [Medicine] (MELL)
CANNY .... Canon, Inc. ADR [NASDAQ symbol] (SG)
CAO .... CSK Auto [NYSE symbol] (SG)
CAOF .... Coalition Against On-Line Forms
CAP .... California Civil Addict Program
Cap .... Capitation
CaP .... Card-Pitt [National Football League] [1944] (NFLA)
CAP .... College of American Pathology
CAP .... Cooperative Agreements Program (GEOI)
CAPD .... Central Auditory Processing Disorder [Medicine]
CAPDU .... Canadian Association of Public Data Users (GEOI)
CAPE .... Circumpolar Arctic Paleo Environments (QUAC)
CAPMoN ...... Canadian Air and Precipitation Monitoring Network (EPAT)
capt .... Captured (GEAB)
CAPTA .... Canadian Association of Provincial and Territorial Archaeologists (QUAC)
Car .... Carolina (BEE)
Car .... Carolina Panthers [National Football League] [1995-present] (NFLA)
CAR .... Curriculum, Accreditation and Registration Committee (GEOI)
CARBICE ...... Carbon Dioxide Intercalibration Experiment (QUAC)
CARD .... Canadian Archaeological Radiocarbon Database (QUAC)
CARES .... Center for Agricultural, Resource, and Environmental Systems [University of Missouri] (GEOI)
CARL .... CarelInsite, Inc. [NASDAQ symbol] (SG)
CARP .... Cache Array Routing Protocol [Computer science]

CAR=PGa ..... Committee for the Advancement of Role-Playing Games (EA)
CARS .... Capital Automotive REIT [NASDAQ symbol] (SG)
CART .... Classification and Regression Tree Technique [Statistics]
CASA .... Centre for Advanced Spatial Analysis [University College, London] (GEOI)
CASE .... Centre for Analysis of Social Exclusion [Great Britain]
casevac ...... Casualty Evacuation (MILB)
CASM .... Conventionally Armed Stand-Off Missiles (MILB)
CASP .... Critical Assessment of Methods of Protein Structure Prediction
CASS .... Cassette Player
Cat .... Category (MILB)
CAT .... Cold Air Induction
CAT .... Computer Assisted Thermography (GEOI)
catal .... Catalogue (GEAB)
CATIA .... Computer-Aided Three-Dimensional Interactive Application
CATS .... Consequences Assessment Tool Set (GEOI)
CATTS .... Center for Advanced Telecommunications Systems and Services
CAUP .... College of Architecture and Urban Planning
CAUZ .... Consortium of Aquariums, Universities, and Zoos (GVA)
CAVE .... Core Automated Virtual Environment
CAVO .... Canadian Association of Veterinary Ophthalmology (GVA)
CAWC .... Companion Animal Welfare Council (GVA)
CB .... Cement Block [Construction] (GEOI)
CB .... Column Builder (GEOI)
cba .... Cabana
CBBA .... Carolina Brahman Breeders Association (GVA)
CBCN .... Canadian Botanical Conservation Network (QUAC)
CBD .... Companhia Brasileira ADS [NYSE symbol] (SG)
CBDQ-FM .... Labrador City, NF [FM radio station call letters] (BROA)
CBEP .... Community Based Environmental Project (EPAT)
CBEP .... Community-Based Environmental Protection (GEOI)
CBET .... Concrete Block Enclosed Elevator (GEOI)
CBH .... Commerce Bancorp [NYSE symbol] (SG)
CBI .... Chicago Bridge & Iron N.V. [NYSE symbol] (SG)
CBID .... Certified Degree of Indian Blood (GEAB)
CBIN .... Canadian Biodiversity Information Network (QUAC)
CBIZ .... Century Business Svcs [NASDAQ symbol] (SG)
CBL .... Calibration Base Line (GEOI)
CBLA-FM .... Toronto, ON [FM radio station call letters] (BROA)
CbMam .... Cumulonimbus Mamatus Cloud (WEAT)
CBME-FM .... Montreal, PQ [FM radio station call letters] (BROA)
CBN .... Cooperative Base Network (GEOI)
CBN .... Cornerstone Bancorp [AMEX symbol] (SG)
CBPI .... Canadian Business Periodicals Index
CBR .... CIBER, Inc. [NYSE symbol] (SG)
CBR .... Concrete, Lime, Cinder or Cement Brick (GEOI)
CBS .... Community Base Station (GEOI)
CBSG .... Conservation Breeding Specialist Group (GVA)
CBSI .... Complete Business Solutions [NASDAQ symbol] (SG)
cbt .... Combat (MILB)
CBU .... Community Bank System [NYSE symbol] (SG)
CBVX-FM .... Quebec, PQ [FM radio station call letters] (BROA)
CBWCA .... Classic Bicycle and Whizzer Club (EA)
CBWE .... Corn Blight Watch Experiment (GEOI)
CBZ .... Cort Business Services [NYSE symbol] (SG)
CC .... Cartographic Catalog (GEOI)
CC .... Circuit City Strs-CrctCty Grp [NYSE symbol] (SG)
Cc .... Cirrocumulus Cloud (WEAT)
CC .... Closed Cup
CC .... Cloud to Cloud Lightning (WEAT)
CC .... Cruise Control [Automotive term]
CCA .... Canonical Correspondence Analysis (QUAC)
CCAC .... Clear Cell Adenocarcinoma [Medicine] (MELL)
CCAL .... Consumer Consortium on Assisted Living
CCAP .... Climate Change Action Plan [Environmental Protection Agency] (EPAT)
CCAP .... Coastal Change Analysis Project (QUAC)
CCAP .... Competative Cooperative Agreements Program (GEOI)
CCB .... Carbon-Carbon Bond (MELL)
CCB .... Cold Cup Biopsy [Medicine] (MELL)
CCBCCM ...... Canadian Committee for the Bibliographic Control of Cartographic Materials (GEOI)
CCBG .... Capital City Bank Grp [NASDAQ symbol] (SG)
CCBL .... C-COR.net Corp [NASDAQ symbol] (SG)
CCC .... Chronic Catarrhal Colitis [Medicine] (MELL)
CCC .... Chronic Cigarette Cough (MELL)

CCC............ Clear Cell Carcinoma [*Medicine*] (MELL)
CCC............ Comprehensive Care Clinic (MELL)
CCCELS........ California Council of Civil Engineers and Land Surveyors (GEOI)
CCCG .... Cavum Conchal Cartilage Graft [*Medicine*] (MELL)
CCCS .... Core Curriculum Content Standards
CCD .... Calcium Compensation Depth (QUAC)
CCD .... Central Core Disease (MELL)
CCD .... Cerebellar Cortical Degeneration [*Medicine*] (MELL)
CCD .... Cerebral Cortical Degeneration [*Medicine*] (MELL)
CCD .... Colony Count for Diarrhea [*Medicine*] (MELL)
CCEB .... Culture Collection of Entomogenous Bacteria (MELL)
CCFC .... Creepy Crawlers Fan Club (EA)
CCGE .... Canadian Council on Geographic Education (GEOI)
CCI............. Classic Chevy Club International (EA)
CCIRN .... Coordinating Committee for Intercontinental Research
CCISA .... Congress of Cartographic Information Specialist Associations (GEOI)
CCM........... Calcium Citrate Malate (MELL)
CCM........... Canada Centre for Mapping (GEOI)
CCM........... Closed Chest Massage [*Medicine*] (MELL)
CCM........... Costoclavicular Maneuver [*Medicine*] (MELL)
CCMS.......... Cerebro-Costo-Mandibular Syndrome [*Medicine*] (MELL)
CCN .... Condylocephalic Nail (MELL)
CCN .... Critical Care Nursing (MELL)
CCN .... Curved Calapinto Needle [*Medicine*] (MELL)
CCOA .... Cougar Club of America (EA)
CCP............ Canadian Climate Program (QUAC)
CCP............ Chronic Constrictive Pericarditis [*Medicine*] (MELL)
CCP............ Complete Cleft Palate (MELL)
CCP............ Cryptococcal Pneumonitis [*Medicine*] (MELL)
CCPA .... Council of Canadian Personnel Associations
CCR .... Carotid Chemoreflex [*Medicine*] (MELL)
CCR .... Central Contractor Register
CCRD .... Concord Communications [*NASDAQ symbol*] (SG)
CCRN .... Canadian Climate Research Network (QUAC)
CCRT .... CompuCredit Corp. [*NASDAQ symbol*] (SG)
CCSA .... Core Curriculum Content Standards Aid
CCSL .... Cirrocumulus Standing Lenticular Cloud (WEAT)
CCT............ Cancer Chemotherapy [*Medicine*] (MELL)
CCT............ Central Conduction Time (MELL)
CCT............ Certified Cardiographic Technician (MELL)
CCT............ Chronic Catarrhal Tonsillitis [*Medicine*] (MELL)
CCT............ Closed Cerebral Trauma (MELL)
CCT............ Combat-Capable Trainer (MILB)
CCT............ Communication, Culture, and Technology Program
CCUA .... Clean Catch Urinalysis [*Medicine*] (MELL)
CCV .... Critical Care Ventilator (MELL)
CCVM.......... Congenital Cardiovascular Malformation [*Medicine*] (MELL)
CCW........... Countryside Council for Wales (GVA)
CCWR .... Cross-Content Workplace Readiness
CCX .... Con-way Central Express
CD.............. Capillary Drainage [*Medicine*] (MELL)
CD.............. Cardiac Dysrhythmia [*Medicine*] (MELL)
CD.............. Cerebellar Degeneration [*Medicine*] (MELL)
CD.............. Cervical Dysplasia [*Medicine*] (MELL)
CD.............. Chemical Dependency (MELL)
CD.............. Chronic Dialysis [*Medicine*] (MELL)
CD.............. Chronic Diarrhea [*Medicine*] (MELL)
CD.............. Climatological Data (EPAT)
CD.............. Clinical Death (MELL)
CD.............. Cognition Disorder (MELL)
CD.............. Conductive Deafness (MELL)
CD.............. Congenital Deafness (MELL)
CD.............. Congenital Defect (MELL)
CD.............. Culminating Demonstration
CD.............. Cumulative Dose [*Medicine*] (MELL)
CD.............. Cystine Deficiency [*Medicine*] (MELL)
CDA .... Colorado Department of Agriculture (GEOI)
CDA .... Cordiant Communic Grp ADS [*NYSE symbol*] (SG)
CDAPCA....... Comprehensive Drug Abuse Prevention and Control Act (MELL)
CDC .... California Department of Conservation (GEOI)
CDC .... Carey Diversified LLC [*NYSE symbol*] (SG)
CDC .... Certified Drug Counselor (MELL)
CDC .... Chronic Disseminated Candidiasis [*Medicine*] (MELL)
CDC .... Congenital Dacryocystocele [*Medicine*] (MELL)
CDC .... Coronary Dilatation Catheter [*Medicine*] (MELL)
CDCR .... Conceptual Design and Cost Review (EOSA)
CDD .... Cervical Disk Disease [*Medicine*] (MELL)
CDD .... Clot Dissolving Drug [*Medicine*] (MELL)
CDD .... Cordant Technologies [*NYSE symbol*] (SG)
CDDD.......... Cervical Degenerative Disk Disease [*Medicine*] (MELL)
CDED .... Canadian Digital Elevation Data (GEOI)
CDF............ Cadillac Fairview [*NYSE symbol*] (SG)
CDF............ California Department of Forestry (GEOI)
CDFG .... California Department of Fish and Game (GEOI)
CDGS .... Carbohydrate Deficient Glycoprotein Syndrome [*Medicine*]
CDH .... Communications and Data Handling (GEOI)
CDH .... Congenital Dysplastic Hip (MELL)
CDHRUI ...... Coalition for the Defense of Human Rights Under Islam
CDK .... Congenital Dislocation of Knee (MELL)
CDK .... Cyclin-Dependent Kinases
CDL............ California Digital Library
CDLT .... Carbon Dioxide LASER Therapy [*Medicine*] (MELL)
CDM........... Chondrodystrophic Myotonia [*Medicine*] (MELL)
CDM........... Clean Development Mechanism
CDMG .... California Division of Mines and Geology (GEOI)

CDML.......... Carbon Dioxide Membrane Lung [*Medicine*] (MELL)
CDN .... Coordinates, Definitions, and Notations (GEOI)
cdo .... Commando (MILB)
CDOW .... Colorado Division of Wildlife (GEOI)
CDP .... Cartographer Development Program (GEOI)
CDP .... Census Designated Place (GEOI)
CDP .... Chemical Dependence Profile [*Medicine*] (MELL)
CDP .... Chondrodysplasia Punctata [*Medicine*] (MELL)
CDP .... Chronic Destructive Periodontitis [*Medicine*] (MELL)
CDP .... Colorado Division of Planning (GEOI)
CDR .... Continuing Disability Review (MELL)
CDS .... Caudal Dysplasia Syndrome [*Medicine*] (MELL)
CDS .... Cervical Disk Syndrome [*Medicine*] (MELL)
CDS .... Chronic Dislocating Shoulder [*Medicine*] (MELL)
CDS .... Closed Drainage System [*Medicine*] (MELL)
CDS .... Coronal Diagnostic Spectrometer
CDSS .... Cystic Duct Stump Syndrome [*Medicine*] (MELL)
CDT .... Cable Design Technologies [*NYSE symbol*] (SG)
CDT .... Combination Drug Therapy (MELL)
CDT .... Computer Display Terminal (GEOI)
CDT .... Constrained Delaunay Triangulation (GEOI)
CDTED .... Compressed Digital Terrain Elevation Data (GEOI)
CDUS .... Carotid Doppler Ultrasonography [*Medicine*] (MELL)
CDV .... Cartographic Data Visualizer (GEOI)
CDV .... Chrysler Data Visualizer
CDV .... Consol Delivery & Logistics [*AMEX symbol*] (SG)
CDWR .... California Department of Water Resources (GEOI)
CDX .... Canadex Resources [*Toronto Stock Exchange symbol*] (SG)
CDX .... Chloriazepoxide [*Medicine*] (MELL)
CE.............. Cardiac Embolism [*Medicine*] (MELL)
CE.............. Categorical Exclusion (EPAT)
CE.............. Cerebral Embolism [*Medicine*] (MELL)
CE.............. Collaborative Environment
CEA .... China Eastern Airlines ADS [*NYSE symbol*] (SG)
CEA .... Cost and Economic Assessment (EPAT)
CEC .... Cartier Ebel Christalor
CEC .... Commission for Environmental Cooperation [*Environmental Protection Agency*] (EPAT)
CECS........... Chronic Exertional Compartment Syndrome [*Medicine*]
CECW.......... Consulting Engineers Council of Washington (GEOI)
CED............ Civil Engineering Data
CED............ Cosmic Exposure Dating (QUAC)
CEDAC .... Comprehensive Economic Data Atlas of China (GEOI)
CEDD .... Committee on the Exchange of Digital Data (GEOI)
CEE .... Childhood Epileptic Encephalopathy [*Medicine*] (MELL)
CEF .... Cuban Expeditionary Force
CEG .... Constellation Energy Group [*NYSE symbol*] (SG)
CEI .... Clinical Ecological Illness (MELL)
CEI .... Coexisting Illness (MELL)
CEIFA.......... Comprehensive Educational Improvement and Financing Act
CEL .... Check Engine Light [*Automotive term*]
CELSOC ...... Consulting Engineers and Land Surveyors of California (GEOI)
Cem .... Cemetery (GEOI)
cem .... Cemetery (GEAB)
CEM........... ChemFirst, Inc. [*NYSE symbol*] (SG)
CEMA.......... Colorado Educational Media Association
cen .... Census (GEAB)
cen.............. Central (BEE)
CEN .... Ceridian Corp. [*NYSE symbol*] (SG)
CENREN ...... Centro de Recursos Naturales [*El Salvador*] (GEOI)
cent .... Century (GEAB)
CENTA .... Centro Nacional de Tecnologia Agropecuaria [*El Salvador*] (GEOI)
ceo .... Chief Executive Officer (PROS)
CEO .... European Centre for Earth Observation (GEOI)
CEP .... Celestial Ephemeris Pole (GEOI)
CEP .... Chronic Eosinophilic Pneumonia [*Medicine*] (MELL)
cer .... Certificate (GEAB)
CER .... Cholesterol Ester Ratio [*Medicine*] (MELL)
CER............ Cortical Evoked Response [*Medicine*] (MELL)
CERCG .... Centre d'Etudes et de Realisations Cartographiques Geographiques [*France*] (GEOI)
CERD .... Catalog of Environmental Resource Data (GEOI)
CERES .... California Environmental Resource Evaluation System (GEOI)
CERES plot... Combining Conditional Expectations and Residuals Plot
CERG .... Ceres Group [*NASDAQ symbol*] (SG)
CERN .... Chinese Ecological Research Network (QUAC)
CERR .... Centre d'Ecologie des Ressources Renouvelables [*France*] (GEOI)
CES............. Cauda Equina Syndrome [*Medicine*] (MELL)
CES............. Cerebral Edema Syndrome [*Medicine*] (MELL)
CES............. Coalition of Essential Schools
CES............. Conditioned Escape Response [*Medicine*] (MELL)
CES............. Conjugated Estrogen Substance [*Medicine*] (MELL)
CES............. Cranial Electrical Stimulation [*Medicine*] (MELL)
CESC........... Chorda Equina of Spinal Cord [*Medicine*] (MELL)
CET .... Commission on Education and Training
CETENAL...... Comision de Estudios del Territorio Nacional [*Mexico*] (GEOI)
CETS........... Chromosome Eighteen Trisomy Syndrome [*Medicine*] (MELL)
CETS........... Chromosome Eight Trisomy Syndrome [*Medicine*] (MELL)
CEUS .... Cerebral Embolism of Unknown Source [*Medicine*] (MELL)
CEV .... California Encephalitis Virus [*Medicine*] (MELL)
CEW............ Center for the Education of Women
CF .... Calcaneus Fracture (MELL)
CF .... Calcarine Fissure (MELL)
CF .... Cavus Foot (MELL)
CF .... Cerebral Fissure [*Medicine*] (MELL)

CF	Chip Fracture (MELL)
CF	Clotting Factor [*Medicine*] (MELL)
CF	Compact-Flash [*Computer science*]
CF	Condylar Fracture (MELL)
CF	Coronary Force (MELL)
CF	Cotton Fracture (MELL)
CF	Cough Frequency (MELL)
CF	Crush Syndrome [*Medicine*] (MELL)
CF	Cubital Fossa [*Medicine*] (MELL)
CFA	Cervicofacial Actinomycosis [*Medicine*] (MELL)
CFA	Chemfab Corp. [*NYSE symbol*] (SG)
CFA	Colony-Forming Assay [*Medicine*] (MELL)
CFA	Confirmatory Factor Analysis
CFA	Coronado 15 Association (EA)
CFA	Cystic Fibrosis Association (MELL)
CFB	Center for Bioethics (MELL)
CFC	Common Fund for Commodities
CFCC	Census Feature Class Code (GEOI)
CFCP	Cystic Fibrosis Chest Pain [*Medicine*] (MELL)
CFD	Central Fracture Dislocation [*Medicine*] (MELL)
CFD	Chronic Foot Dermatitis [*Medicine*] (MELL)
CFD	Congenital Facial Diplegia [*Medicine*] (MELL)
CFD	Craniofacial Dysostosis [*Medicine*] (MELL)
CFERR	Commission on Food, Environment, and Renewable Resources [*National Association of State Universities and Land-Grant Colleges*] (GVA)
CFF	Cartographic Feature File (GEOI)
CFFN	Capital Federal Financial [*NASDAQ symbol*] (SG)
CFG	Chronic Follicular Gastritis [*Medicine*] (MELL)
CFI	Canada Foundation for Innovation
CFI	Culp, Inc. [*NYSE symbol*] (SG)
CFIA	Canadian Food Inspection Agency (GVA)
CFIC	Clever Fellows Innovation Consortium
CFIT	Controlled Flights into Terrain [*Aviation*]
CFMV	Conselho Federal de Medicina Veterinaria [*Brazil*] (GVA)
cfo	Chief Financial Officer (PROS)
CFON	C-Phone Corp. [*NASDAQ symbol*] (SG)
CFR	Cullen/Frost Bankers [*NYSE symbol*] (SG)
CFT	Capillary Filling Time [*Medicine*] (MELL)
CFT	Capillary Fragility Test [*Medicine*] (MELL)
CFT	Chronic Fibrous Thyroiditis [*Medicine*] (MELL)
CFT	Conjoint Family Therapy (MELL)
CFW	Computron Software [*AMEX symbol*] (SG)
CG	Cerebral Gigantism [*Medicine*] (MELL)
CG	Columbia Energy Group [*NYSE symbol*] (SG)
CG	Congenital Glaucoma (MELL)
CG	Control Group [*Medicine*] (MELL)
CG	Corneal Grafting (MELL)
CGA	Cayman Golf Association (EA)
CGA	Collegiate Gymnastics Association (EA)
CGC	Climate and Global Change
CGC	Commission Geologique du Canada (GEOI)
CGCP	Canadian Global Change Program (EOSA)
CGDB	Central Geographic Data Base (GEOI)
CGDI	Canadian Geospatial Data Infrastructure (GEOI)
CGE	Centris Group [*NYSE symbol*] (SG)
CGIC	Canadian Geoscience Information Centre (GEOI)
CGLA	Cagle's Inc.'A' [*AMEX symbol*] (SG)
CGNHS	Connecticut Geological and Natural History Survey (GEOI)
CGO	Atlas Air [*NYSE symbol*] (SG)
CGS	Caregiver Stress (MELL)
CGS	Cryogenic Surgery [*Medicine*] (MELL)
CGUSARLANT	Comanding General, United States, Army, Atlantic
CGW	Computer Graphics World [*A publication*] (GEOI)
CGX	Consolidated Graphics [*NYSE symbol*] (SG)
CH	Capillary Hemorrhage [*Medicine*] (MELL)
CH	Cardiac Hypertrophy [*Medicine*] (MELL)
CH	Case History [*Medicine*] (MELL)
CH	Cerebral Hemisphere [*Medicine*] (MELL)
CH	Charley-Horse [*Spasm*] (MELL)
CH	Chemical Sampling Information
CH	Chief Hydrologist (GEOI)
ch	Children (GEAB)
CH	Chronic Hepatitis (MELL)
CH	Chronic Hypertension (MELL)
CH	Completely Healed (MELL)
Cha	Chad (MILB)
chan	Chancery (GEAB)
Chap	Chapter (PROS)
CHB	Carbon-Hydrogen Bond (MELL)
CHC	Charter Muni Mtg Acceptance [*AMEX symbol*] (SG)
ChC	Chicago Cardinals [*National Football League*] [*1920-59*] (NFLA)
CHC	Comprehensive Health Care (MELL)
CHC	Consumer Health Care (MELL)
CHCC	Comprehensive Healthcare Clinic (MELL)
CHCl	Cocaine Hydrochloride [*Medicine*] (MELL)
CHD	Cartilage Hair Dysplasia (MELL)
CHD	Claw Hand Deformity (MELL)
CHE	Chronic Hepatic Encephalopathy [*Medicine*] (MELL)
CHE	Chronic Hypertrophic Emphysema [*Medicine*] (MELL)
CHEEC	Center for Health Effects of Environmental Contamination [*University of Iowa*] (GEOI)
CHES	Certified Health Education Specialist
CHG	China Energy Resources [*AMEX symbol*] (SG)
CHGS	Center for Human Genome Studies [*Internet resource*]
CHH	Choice Hotels Intl. [*NYSE symbol*] (SG)
Chi	Chicago Bears [*National Football League*] [*1922-present*] (NFLA)
CHI	Chlorine Institute, Inc.
CHIA	Cumulative Hydrologic Impact Assessment (GEOI)
ChiCom	Chinese Communist
CHINA	China.com Corp. [*NASDAQ symbol*] (SG)
CHIP	Catastrophic Health (MELL)
CHIPS	Cosmic Hot Interstellar Plasma Spectrometer [*NASA*]
CHK	Chesapeake Energy [*NYSE symbol*] (SG)
CHKF-FM	Calgary, AB [*FM radio station call letters*] (BROA)
CHKP	Check Point Software Tech [*NASDAQ symbol*] (SG)
Chl	Chile (MILB)
CHL	China Telecom Hong Kong ADS [*NYSE symbol*] (SG)
CHL	Conductive Hearing Loss (MELL)
CHL	Coracohumeral Ligament (MELL)
chldn	Children (GEAB)
CHM	Charleston Museum [*South Carolina*]
CHM	Congestive Hepatomegaly [*Medicine*] (MELL)
CHNL	Channell Commercial [*NASDAQ symbol*] (SG)
CHNM	Marine Channel (GEOI)
CHOICES	Community Health Onsite Information Centers [*New York Public Library*]
chp	Chairperson (PROS)
CHR	Cerebrohepatorenal [*Medicine*] (MELL)
chr	Christened (GEAB)
chr	Church (BEE)
CHRW	C.H. Robinson Worldwide [*NASDAQ symbol*] (SG)
ChS	Chicago Staleys [*National Football League*] [*1921*] (NFLA)
CHS	Composite Healthcare System (MELL)
CHS	Congenital Hip Subluxation [*Medicine*] (MELL)
CHS	Congenital Hypoventilation Syndrome [*Medicine*] (MELL)
CHSMG	Canine Health Schemes Management Group [*British*] (GVA)
CHSU-FM	Kelowna, BC [*FM radio station call letters*] (BROA)
CHT	Chemohormonal Therapy [*Medicine*] (MELL)
CHT	Combined Hormonal Therapy [*Medicine*] (MELL)
chwn	Chairwoman (PROS)
CHZ	Chittenden Corp. [*NYSE symbol*] (SG)
Ci	Cirrus Cloud (WEAT)
CI	Compass and Inclinometer (GEOI)
CIA	Common Iliac Artery [*Medicine*] (MELL)
CIA	Congenital Intestional Aganglionosis [*Medicine*] (MELL)
CIACER	Centro de Investigacion y Aplicacion de Sensores Remotos [*Bolivia*] (GEOI)
CIAQ	Council on Indoor Air Quality [*Environmental Protection Agency*] (EPAT)
CIB	Controlled Image Base (GEOI)
CIC	Calcium Ion Concentration (MELL)
CIC	Chronic Inflammatory Cell [*Medicine*] (MELL)
CIC	Common Iliac Catheter [*Medicine*] (MELL)
CIC	Crisis Intervention Center (MELL)
CICA	Centro Informatico Cientifico de Andalucia [*Group of eight universities in Spain*]
CICAEDAS	Committee Investigating Cartographic Entity, Definitions, and Standards (GEOI)
CICD	Chronic Irritant Contact Dermatitis (MELL)
CICD	Circulating Immune-Complex Disease [*Medicine*] (MELL)
CICS	Canadian Institute for Climate Studies (QUAC)
CIE	Classified Image Editor (GEOI)
CIE	Congenital Ichtyosisform Erythroderma [*Dermatology*]
CIE	International Lighting Commission
CIEN	Cervical Intraepithelial Neoplasia [*Medicine*] (MELL)
CIEN	CIENA Corp. [*NASDAQ symbol*] (SG)
CIEN	Conjunctival Intraepithelial Neoplasia [*Medicine*] (MELL)
CIF	Clipping Injury Fracture (MELL)
CIG	Climate Interest Group (GEOI)
CIG	Cloud Ceiling Height (WEAT)
CIGP	Council of Ivy Group Presidents (EA)
CIHD	Chronic Ischemic Heart Disease [*Medicine*] (MELL)
CII	Catheter-Induced Infection [*Medicine*] (MELL)
CII	Chronic Intestinal Ischemia [*Medicine*] (MELL)
CII	Continuous Insulin Infusion [*Medicine*] (MELL)
CIKM	Conference on Information Knowledge Management (GEOI)
CILN	Common Iliac Lymph Node [*Medicine*] (MELL)
CILT-FM	Steinbach, MB [*FM radio station call letters*] (BROA)
CIM	Chronic Idiopathic Megacolon [*Medicine*] (MELL)
CIM	Collection Insertion Map (GEOI)
CIMP	Closed Intramedullary Pinning [*Medicine*] (MELL)
CIN	Central Inhibition [*Medicine*] (MELL)
Cin	Cincinnati Bengals [*National Football League*] [*1968-present*] (NFLA)
CINDI	Center for Integration of Natural Disaster Information (GEOI)
CIN I	Cervical Intraepithelial Neoplasia [*Mild*] [*Medicine*] (MELL)
CIN II	Cervical Intraepithelial Neoplasia [*Moderate*] [*Medicine*] (MELL)
CINN-FM	Hearst, ON [*FM radio station call letters*] (BROA)
CINS	Composites Institute
CINT	Saskatoon, SK [*AM radio station call letters*] (BROA)
CIO	Chlorine Dioxide (MELL)
CIOI-FM	Hamilton, ON [*FM radio station call letters*] (BROA)
CIP	Chronic Intestinal Pseudoobstruction [*Medicine*] (MELL)
CIP	Contour Interpolation Program (GEOI)
CIPD	Chronic Intermittent Peritoneal Dialysis [*Medicine*] (MELL)
CiR	Cincinnati Reds [*National Football League*] [*1933-34*] (NFLA)
cir	Circa (GEAB)
Circ	Circumcision (MELL)
CIRF	Cocaine-Induced Respiratory Failure [*Medicine*] (MELL)
CIRSS	California Integrated Remote Sensing System (GEOI)

CIS.............. Carcinoma in Situ [*Medicine*] (MELL)
CIS.............. Color Imaging Systems (GEOI)
CIS.............. Con-way Intergrated Services
CIs.............. Counterirritants (MELL)
CISAB .... Center for the Integrative Study of Animal Behavior (GVA)
CISC.......... Carcinoma in Situ of Cervix [*Medicine*] (MELL)
CISC.......... Contl Information Sys [*NASDAQ symbol*] (SG)
CISD .... Cook Islands Department of Survey (GEOI)
CISIG .... Geographic Information Systems Interest Group (GEOI)
CISP .... Cast Iron Soil Pipe Institute
CISP .... Chronic Intractable Shoulder Pain (MELL)
CIST .... Centre d'Information Sur les Sciences de la Terre [*Canada*] (GEOI)
CISV .... Carcinoma in Situ of Vagina [*Medicine*] (MELL)
CIT .... Casoni Intradermal Test [*Medicine*] (MELL)
CIT .... CIT Group 'A' [*NYSE symbol*] (SG)
CIT .... Conventional Insulin Therapy (MELL)
CITC.......... Citadel Communications [*NASDAQ symbol*] (SG)
CITH.......... Cytomegalovirus-Induced Thrombocytopenia and Hemolysis [*Medicine*] (MELL)
CITYG .... City Graphic (GEOI)
CITZ .... CFS Bancorp [*NASDAQ symbol*] (SG)
civ............ Civil (GEAB)
CIV............ Conectiv, Inc. [*NYSE symbol*] (SG)
CIVII.......... Continuous Intravenous Insulin Infusion [*Medicine*] (MELL)
civ pol ..... Civilian Police (MILB)
CIX............ CompX Intl.'A' [*NYSE symbol*] (SG)
CIZN-FM ..... Cambridge, ON [*FM radio station call letters*] (BROA)
CJ............. Charcot Joint (MELL)
CJ............. Chopart Joint (MELL)
CJ............. County Judge (GEAB)
CJA........... Columbus SoPwr 7.92% Sub Db [*NYSE symbol*] (SG)
CJCJ .... Centre on Juvenile and Criminal Justice
CJES.......... Canadian Journal of Earth Sciences [*A publication*] (QUAC)
CJFP-FM..... Riviere du Loup, PQ [*FM radio station call letters*] (BROA)
CJIL-TV ...... Lethbridge, AB [*Television station call letters*] (BROA)
CJLM-FM.... Joliette, PQ [*FM radio station call letters*] (BROA)
CJMC-FM.... Ste. Anne des Monts, PQ [*FM radio station call letters*] (BROA)
CJMT-FM.... Canmore, AB [*FM radio station call letters*] (BROA)
CJPX-FM..... Montreal, PQ [*FM radio station call letters*] (BROA)
CJRRU .... Casey Jones Railroad Unit [*An association*] (EA)
CJSI-FM...... Calgary, AB [*FM radio station call letters*] (BROA)
CJTT-FM..... New Liskeard, ON [*FM radio station call letters*] (BROA)
CJUM-FM .... Winnipeg, MB [*FM radio station call letters*] (BROA)
CK............ Congenital-Kyphosis [*Medicine*] (MELL)
CK............ Crush Kidney [*Medicine*] (MELL)
CKAJ-FM..... Jonquiere, PQ [*FM radio station call letters*] (BROA)
CKC.......... Continental Kennel Club (GVA)
CKCB-FM .... Collingwood, ON [*FM radio station call letters*] (BROA)
CKD .... Cement Kiln Dust (EPAT)
CKDX-FM..... Newmarket, ON [*FM radio station call letters*] (BROA)
CKEM-TV ..... Edmonton, AB [*Television station call letters*] (BROA)
CKER-FM..... Edmonton, AB [*FM radio station call letters*] (BROA)
CKLS-FM..... La Sarre, PQ [*FM radio station call letters*] (BROA)
CKLU-FM..... Sudbury, ON [*FM radio station call letters*] (BROA)
CKLY-FM ..... Lindsay, ON [*FM radio station call letters*] (BROA)
CKMG-FM.... Maniwaki, PQ [*FM radio station call letters*] (BROA)
CKNR-FM..... Elliot Lake, ON [*FM radio station call letters*] (BROA)
CKNU-FM.... Donnacona, PQ [*FM radio station call letters*] (BROA)
CKOM-FM.... Saskatoon, SK [*FM radio station call letters*] (BROA)
CKP........... Compartmental Knee Prosthesis (MELL)
CK-PL .... Check Plotter (GEOI)
CKQR-FM..... Castlegar, BC [*FM radio station call letters*] (BROA)
CKRB-FM..... St. Georges-de-Beauce, PQ [*FM radio station call letters*] (BROA)
CKRC .... Cement Kiln Recycling Coalition (EPAT)
CKRX-FM..... Fort Nelson, BC [*FM radio station call letters*] (BROA)
CKUA-FM..... Edmonton, AB [*FM radio station call letters*] (BROA)
CKUW-FM.... Winnipeg, AB [*FM radio station call letters*] (BROA)
CKX-FM ..... Brandon, MB [*FM radio station call letters*] (BROA)
CKXX-FM..... Corner Brook, NF [*FM radio station call letters*] (BROA)
CKYX-FM..... Fort McMurray, AB [*FM radio station call letters*] (BROA)
CL.............. Capillary Lumen [*Medicine*] (MELL)
CL.............. Cardiac Lipomas [*Medicine*] (MELL)
CL.............. Cholelithiasis (MELL)
CL.............. Cirrhosis of Liver [*Medicine*] (MELL)
CL.............. Cleft Lip (MELL)
CL.............. Coin Lesion (MELL)
CL.............. Contact Lens (MELL)
CI.............. Cote d'Ivoire (MILB)
CL.............. Crab Lice (MELL)
CL.............. Cruciate Ligament [*Medicine*] (MELL)
CL.............. Cruciform Ligament [*Medicine*] (MELL)
CL.............. Cutis Laxa [*Loose skin*] (MELL)
CLA........... Cutaneous Lichen Amyloidosis [*Medicine*] (MELL)
CIB............ Cleveland Browns [*National Football League*] [*1999-present*] (NFLA)
CLB........... Core Labortories N.V. [*NYSE symbol*] (SG)
CLC........... Corpus Luteum Cyst [*Medicine*] (MELL)
CLCP......... Certified Literate Community Program
cld .... Called
CLD........... Center Line Data (GEOI)
CLD........... Childhood Language Disorder (MELL)
CLD........... Congenital Lactase Deficiency [*Medicine*] (MELL)
CLDB......... Common Land Data Base (GEOI)
Cle............ Cleveland Browns [*National Football League*] [*1950-95*] (NFLA)
CLE........... Congenital Lobar Emphysema [*Medicine*] (MELL)
CLE........... Continuous Lumbar Epidural [*Medicine*] (MELL)

CLF............ Cerebral Longitudinal Fissure [*Medicine*] (MELL)
CLF............ Chinese Liver Fluke [*Medicine*] (MELL)
CLF............ Cross Leg Flap (MELL)
CLG............ Colonial Gas [*NYSE symbol*] (SG)
CLH............ Corpus Luteum Hormone [*Medicine*] (MELL)
CLID........... Class Identifier (GEOI)
CLIRSEN ..... Remote Sensing Center [*Ecuador*] (GEOI)
CLIVAR .... Climate Variability
CLJ............ Crestline Capital [*NYSE symbol*] (SG)
Clk............ Clerk (GEOI)
clk............ Clerk (GEAB)
CLL............ Corrected Line Length (GEOI)
CLM........... Cutaneous Larva Migrans [*Medicine*] (MELL)
CLN........... Caseouslike Necrosis Cervical Lymph Node [*Medicine*] (MELL)
CLN........... Cloquet's Lymph Node [*Medicine*] (MELL)
CLO........... Caldwell-Luc Operation [*Medicine*] (MELL)
CIO............ Chlorine Monoxide (EOSA)
CLOB......... Central Limit Order Book [*Singapore*]
CLOMA .... Confidential Letters of Map Amendment (GEOI)
CLR............ Clarion Commercial Hldgs'A' [*NYSE symbol*] (SG)
CIR............ Cleveland Rams [*National Football League*] [*1937-45*] (NFLA)
CLRN.......... Clarent Corp. [*NASDAQ symbol*] (SG)
CLS............ Capillary-Like Space [*Medicine*] (MELL)
CLS............ Carcinoid-Like Syndrome [*Medicine*] (MELL)
CLS............ Celestica, Inc. [*NYSE symbol*] (SG)
CLS............ Cerebral Lateral Sulcus [*Medicine*] (MELL)
CLSA.......... California Land Surveyors Association (GEOI)
CLT............ Cholesterol-Lowering Therapy [*Medicine*] (MELL)
CLT............ Clotting Time [*Medicine*] (MELL)
CLTR.......... Coulter Pharmaceutical [*NASDAQ symbol*] (SG)
CLUMP .... Canada Land Use Monitoring Program (GEOI)
CLV............ Cutaneous Leukocytoclastic Vasculitis [*Medicine*] (MELL)
CM............ Cardiac Muscle [*Medicine*] (MELL)
CM............ Chromosome Mapping [*Medicine*] (MELL)
CM............ Chylomicrons (MELL)
CM............ Congestive Mastitis [*Medicine*] (MELL)
CM............ Consanguineous Marriage (MELL)
CM............ Conus Medullaris (MELL)
CM............ Crescendo Murmur [*Medicine*] (MELL)
CM............ Cushieri Maneuver [*Medicine*] (MELL)
CMA.......... California Medical Association (MELL)
CMA.......... Carpometacarpal Articulation [*Medicine*] (MELL)
CMA.......... Central Mapping Agency [*New South Wales*] (GEOI)
CMA.......... China Meteorological Administration
CMA.......... Cingulate Motor Area [*Part of brain's cortex*]
CMA.......... Compound Myopic Astigmatism [*Medicine*] (MELL)
CMADL .... Controlled Medical Assistance Drug List (MELL)
CMAJ.......... Canadian Medical Association Journal [*A publication*] (MELL)
CMB.......... Certified Mortgage Banker
CMC.......... Canadian Museum of Civilization (QUAC)
CMC.......... Cell-Mediated Cytotoxicity [*Medicine*] (MELL)
CMCL......... Carpometacarpal Ligament [*Medicine*] (MELL)
CMD.......... Current Meter Digitizer (GEOI)
CMDC......... CareMatrix Corp. [*NASDAQ symbol*] (SG)
CMDRH........ Center for Medical Devices and Radiologic Health (MELL)
CMDS......... Command Ship (MILB)
CMDX......... Chemdex Corp. [*NASDAQ symbol*] (SG)
CME.......... Core Materials [*AMEX symbol*] (SG)
CMF.......... Carbonaceous Mass Fraction (QUAC)
CMG.......... Congenital Myasthenia Gravis [*Medicine*] (MELL)
CMGI .... CMGI, Inc. [*NASDAQ symbol*] (SG)
CMI........... CMI Corp. CI'A' [*NYSE symbol*] (SG)
CMI........... Corvallis Microtechnology, Inc. (GEOI)
CMIB.......... Controlled Multispectral Image Base (GEOI)
CMJ............ College Mathematics Journal [*A publication*]
CMJD......... Carpometacarpal Joint Dislocation [*Medicine*] (MELL)
CML........... Chronic Myelogenous Leukemia [*Medicine*]
CMLS......... Cumulus Media 'A' [*NASDAQ symbol*] (SG)
CMM.......... Cross-Modality Matching (MELL)
CMN.......... Canadian Museum of Nature (QUAC)
CMNH .... Carnegie Museum of Natural History
CMO.......... Calculated Mean Organism (MELL)
CMO.......... Canada Map Office (GEOI)
CMO.......... Competitive Medical Organization (MELL)
CMOL......... Chronic Monocytic Leukemia [*Medicine*] (MELL)
CMOTS .... Cartographic Material Order and Tracking System (GEOI)
CMP.......... Carbon Monoxide Poisoning (MELL)
CMP.......... Coastal Mapping Program (GEOI)
CMP.......... Cow's Milk Protein (MELL)
CMPB......... Chronic Mucopurulent Bronchitis [*Medicine*] (MELL)
CMPF......... Cow's Milk, Protein-Free (MELL)
CMRC......... Commerce One [*NASDAQ symbol*] (SG)
CMS.......... California Map Society (GEOI)
CMS.......... Chronic Maxillary Sinusitis [*Medicine*] (MELL)
CMS.......... Chronic Myelodysplastic Syndrome [*Medicine*] (MELL)
CMSDU....... Commission on Map Use and Spatial Data Use (GEOI)
CMSM........ Committee on Marine Surveying and Mapping (GEOI)
CMSU........ Clean Midstream Urine [*Specimen*] [*Medicine*] (MELL)
CMT.......... Cell-Mediated Toxicity [*Medicine*] (MELL)
CMT.......... Corvallis Microtechnology, Inc. (GEOI)
CMTL......... Comtech Telecommns [*NASDAQ symbol*] (SG)
CMTN......... Cooper Mtn Networks [*NASDAQ symbol*] (SG)
CMTO......... Com21, Inc. [*NASDAQ symbol*] (SG)
CMV........... Continuous Mandatory Ventilation (MELL)
CMVO .... Continuous Mixed Venous Oximetry (MELL)

CNAG..........	Chronic Narrow Angle Glaucoma (MELL)
CNB...........	Connected Network Backup [CMP]
CNCX..........	Concentric Network [NASDAQ symbol] (SG)
CNDC..........	Chronic Nonspecific Diarrhea of Childhood [Medicine] (MELL)
CNDR..........	Condor Tech Solutions [NASDAQ symbol] (SG)
CNET..........	CNET, Inc. [NASDAQ symbol] (SG)
CNEXO........	Centre National pour l'Exploitation des Oceans [France] (GEOI)
CNF...........	CNF Transportation [NYSE symbol] (SG)
CNFL.........	Confluence (GEOI)
CNHA..........	Congenital Nonspherocytic Hemolytic Anemia [Medicine] (MELL)
CNI...........	Canadian Natl Railway [NYSE symbol] (SG)
CNITV........	Centre National d'Informations Toxicologiques Veterinaires (GVA)
CNJ...........	Cuneonavicular Joint (MELL)
CNL...........	Chronic Neutrophilic Leukemia [Medicine] (MELL)
CNL...........	Cleco Corp. [NYSE symbol] (SG)
CNM..........	Carcinomatous Neuromyopathy [Medicine] (MELL)
CNMS.........	Compaq Networking Management Software [Computer science]
CNP..........	Cranial Nerve Palsy [Medicine] (MELL)
CNQ..........	Canadian Natural Resources [Toronto Stock Exchange symbol] (SG)
CNRA.........	Commission on National and Regional Atlases (GEOI)
CNRG..........	Centre National de Recherches Geomorphologiques [Belgium] (GEOI)
CNROA........	Centro Nacional de Reconhecimento e Ordenamento Agrario [Portugal] (GEOI)
CNRST........	Centre National de la Recherche Scientifique et Technologique [Burkina Faso] (GEOI)
CNS...........	Congenital Nephrotic Syndrome [Medicine] (MELL)
CNS...........	Cranial Nerve Syndrome [Medicine] (MELL)
CNSD.........	Central Nervous System Dysfunction [Medicine] (MELL)
CNSRT........	Computer Network Security Response Team
CNT...........	CenterPoint Prop TrSBI [NYSE symbol] (SG)
cntr..........	Center (BEE)
CNU..........	Continucare Corp. [AMEX symbol] (SG)
CNV..........	CVF Technologies [AMEX symbol] (SG)
CNVSPA......	Conference Nationale des Veterinaires Specialises en Petits Animaux [France] (GVA)
CNW..........	Chicago and Northwestern Railway Co.
CNX..........	CONSOL Energy [NYSE symbol] (SG)
CNXT.........	Conexant Systems [NASDAQ symbol] (SG)
CO............	Calcium Oxalate (MELL)
CO............	Cartometric Operations (GEOI)
CO............	Central Obesity (MELL)
CO............	Chiari Osteotomy [Medicine] (MELL)
CO............	Cochlear Occlusion [Medicine] (MELL)
CO............	Cochlear Ossification [Medicine] (MELL)
Co............	Colombia (MILB)
CO............	Corrective Osteotomy [Medicine] (MELL)
COA..........	Conchologists of America (EA)
CoA..........	Council of the Americas (EA)
COAA.........	Centro de Observacao Astronomica no Algarve
COAS.........	Cervico-Oculo-Acoustic Syndrome [Medicine] (MELL)
COBRIG.......	Council of British Geography (GEOI)
COC..........	Calcifying Odontogenic Cyst [Medicine] (MELL)
COC..........	Certificate of Coverage [Insurance]
COCCID.......	Coccidioidomycosis [Medicine] (MELL)
COCM.........	Congestive Cardiomyopathy [Medicine] (MELL)
CODA.........	Child of a Deaf Adult
CODMAC......	Committee on Data Management, Archiving, and Computation (EOSA)
CODUC.......	Calcium Oxalate Dihydrate Urinary Calculi [Medicine] (MELL)
COE..........	Cardiac Output Estimation [Medicine] (MELL)
CoE..........	College of Engineering
COE..........	Court-Ordered Examination [Medicine] (MELL)
COFPAES.....	Committee on the Federal Procurement of Architect and Engineer Services (GEOI)
COFSS.......	Cerebro-Oculo-Facio-Skeletal Syndrome [Medicine] (MELL)
COGGER......	Canadian Options for Greenhouse Gas Emissions Reduction (QUAC)
COI..........	Chilhood-Onset Insomnia [Medicine] (MELL)
COI..........	Cutaneous Occupational Infection [Medicine] (MELL)
COL..........	Agricultural Colony (GEOI)
col..........	Colonel (GEAB)
col..........	Colony (BEE)
COLM.........	Columbia Sportswear [NASDAQ symbol] (SG)
Colmbs.......	Columbus (BEE)
COLT.........	COLT Telecom Group ADS [NASDAQ symbol] (SG)
COM..........	Chronic Opioid Medication [Medicine] (MELL)
COM..........	Chronic Osteomyelitis [Medicine] (MELL)
com..........	Commander (GEAB)
Com..........	Commission (GEOI)
com..........	Common (BEE)
COM..........	Corpuscle of Meissner [Medicine] (MELL)
COMAFTASKOR...	Commander, Air Force Task Force
COMAP.......	Continuous Area Pattern Mapping (GEOI)
comd.........	Command (MILB)
Comdg.......	Commanding (GEOI)
COMETS......	Communications and Broadcasting Engineering Test Satellite
COMIS.......	Cartographic Operations Management Information System (GEOI)
COMISA......	World Federation of the Animal Health Industry (GVA)
comm........	Commissioners (GEAB)
comm........	Committee (PROS)
comm........	Communication (BEE)
commn.......	Commission (PROS)
commnr......	Commissioner (PROS)
comms........	Communications (MILB)
comp........	Company (GEAB)
compar......	Comparative (BEE)
COMPAS......	Coastal Ocean Management, Planning, and Assessment System (GEOI)
COMPASS....	Computerized Optimization Model for Predicting and Analyzing Support Structures [Army]
comptr......	Comptroller (PROS)
con...........	Concert (BEE)
CONCERT....	Communications for North Carolina Education, Research, and Technology Network
confed.......	Confederation (PROS)
confer.......	Conferred (GEAB)
CONICET....	Council for Science and Technology [Buenos Aires, Argentina]
conject......	Conjecture (GEAB)
CONPS.......	Carbon, Oxygen, Nitrogen, Phosphorus, and Sulphur (QUAC)
CONRIM.....	Committee on Natural Resource Information Management [Alaska] (GEOI)
CONS.........	Constant (WEAT)
Consult.......	Consultant (PROS)
contr.........	Contract (GEAB)
contr.........	Controller (PROS)
CONV.........	Convergent Communications [NASDAQ symbol] (SG)
CONVINCE...	Consortium of North American Veterinary Interactive New Concept Education (GVA)
coo...........	Chief Operating Officer (PROS)
COO..........	Cooper Cos. [NYSE symbol] (SG)
Cop...........	Copernican (BEE)
COP/BOP......	City of Portland Bureau of Planning [Oregon] (GEOI)
COR..........	Closed Observation Room (MELL)
cor...........	Coroner (BEE)
COR..........	Corrected Report (WEAT)
COR..........	Crystal Gas Storage [AMEX symbol] (SG)
CORL.........	Corel Corp. [NASDAQ symbol] (SG)
corp.........	Corporal (GEAB)
CORS.........	Continuously Operated Reference Station (GEOI)
CORSE.......	Conference on Remote Sensing Education (GEOI)
COS.........	Calcium Oxalate Stone [Medicine] (MELL)
COS.........	Central Office of Statistics [Malta] (GEOI)
COS.........	Clinically Observed Seizures (MELL)
COS.........	Cooperation for Open Systems
COSA.........	Child of a Substance Abuser
COS-B.......	Cosmic Ray Satellite-B [European Space Agency]
COSEWIC.....	Committee on the Status of Endangered Wildlife in Canada (QUAC)
COSMI......	Committee on Southern Map Libraries (GEOI)
COST........	Costco Cos. [NASDAQ symbol] (SG)
COTE........	Complete Occupational Therapy Evaluation (MELL)
COU.........	Chronic Obstructive Uropathy [Medicine] (MELL)
Counc........	Council (PROS)
couns........	Counsel (PROS)
couns........	Counsellor (GEAB)
cous.........	Cousin (GEAB)
COVD........	Covad Communications Grp [NASDAQ symbol] (SG)
coven........	Covenant (BEE)
COVIS........	Commonwealth of Virginia Information Systems (GEOI)
COW.........	Circle of Willis [Medicine] (MELL)
coy..........	Company (MILB)
CP...........	Cancer Procoagulant [Medicine] (MELL)
CP...........	Carotid Pulse [Medicine] (MELL)
CP...........	Cartographic Perspectives [A publication] (GEOI)
CP...........	Celiac Plexus [Medicine] (MELL)
CP...........	Cellulitic Phlegmasia [Medicine] (MELL)
CP...........	Cervical Plexus [Medicine] (MELL)
CP...........	Chemoprophylaxis [Medicine] (MELL)
CP...........	Chronic Pharyngitis [Medicine] (MELL)
CP...........	Chronic Pleurisy (MELL)
CP...........	Chronic Polyarthritis [Medicine] (MELL)
CP...........	Colonic Polyposis [Medicine] (MELL)
CP...........	Cooperative Polygyny
CPA.........	Center for Patient Advocacy (MELL)
CPA.........	Chlorpropamide [Medicine] (MELL)
CPAM.......	Continental Polluted Air Mass (QUAC)
CPBP.........	Cardiopulmonary Bypass [Medicine] (MELL)
CPC.........	Central Parking [NYSE symbol] (SG)
CPC.........	Chronic Pain Center (MELL)
CPC.........	Comanche Portable Cockpit [Army]
CPC.........	Constrictive Pericarditis [Medicine] (MELL)
CPD.........	Calcium Pyrophosphate Deposition [Medicine] (MELL)
CPD.........	Cardiopulmonary Disease (MELL)
CPD.........	Chronic Pain Disorder (MELL)
CPD.........	Chronic Peritoneal Dialysis [Medicine] (MELL)
CPD.........	Chronic Protein Deprivation [Medicine] (MELL)
CPD.........	Congenital Polycystic Disease [Medicine] (MELL)
CPD.........	Critical Point Drying (MELL)
CPE.........	Callon Petroleum [NYSE symbol] (SG)
Cpe..........	Coupe
CPEA........	Comparative Performance Exploratory Analysis
CPF.........	Cancer-Prone Family (MELL)
CPF.........	Cardiac Pump Function [Medicine] (MELL)
CPF.........	Cardiac Purkinje Fiber [Medicine] (MELL)
CPFS........	Colorado Plateau Field Station (GEOI)
CPH.........	Cartographic Publishing House [China] (GEOI)
CPH.........	Chronic Paroxysmal Hemicrania [Medicine] (MELL)
CPH.........	Corticotropin-Releasing Hormone [Medicine] (MELL)
CPHA........	Campaign for the Protection of Hunted Animals (GVA)
CPI..........	Capital Properties [AMEX symbol] (SG)
CPI..........	Christian Periodical Index [A publication]

CPI	Corruption-Perception Index
CPIA	Cultural Property Implementation Act
CPJ	Chateau Communities [*NYSE symbol*] (SG)
CPLAR	Community Perspectives on Land and Agrarian Reform [*South Africa*] (GEOI)
CPM	Cardiac Pacemaker (MELL)
CPM	Chronic Progressive Myelopathy [*Medicine*] (MELL)
CPM	Condylar Process of Mandible [*Medicine*] (MELL)
CPM	Coronoid Process of Mandible [*Medicine*] (MELL)
CPO	Corn Products Intl. [*NYSE symbol*] (SG)
CPOSSU	Chemistry and Physics on Stamps Study Unit [*An association*] (EA)
CPP	Chronic Pelvic Pain (MELL)
CPP	Chronic Pigmented Purpura [*Medicine*] (MELL)
CPP	Cornerstone Properties [*NYSE symbol*] (SG)
CPS	Cardiopulmonary Support [*Medicine*] (MELL)
CPS	Cervical Pain Syndrome [*Medicine*] (MELL)
CPS	Chest Pain Syndrome [*Medicine*] (MELL)
CPS	Child Personality Scale [*Medicine*] (MELL)
CPS	ChoicePoint, Inc. [*NYSE symbol*] (SG)
CPS	Chronic Prostatitis Syndrome [*Medicine*] (MELL)
CPS	Consumer Product Safety Commission (MELL)
CPT	Cancer Pain Treatment (MELL)
CPTA	Cerebral Percutaneous Transluminal Angioplasty [*Medicine*] (MELL)
CPTH	Critical Path [*NASDAQ symbol*] (SG)
CPTL	CTC Communications [*NASDAQ symbol*] (SG)
CPUE	Chest Pain of Undetermined Etiology [*Medicine*] (MELL)
CPV	Correctional Properties Tr [*NYSE symbol*] (SG)
CPW	Central Pocket Whorl [*Fingerprint*] (MELL)
CQM	Close-Quarter Marksmanship
CR	Carrier Replacement [*Insurance*]
CR	Central Region (GEOI)
CR	Chemoreceptor [*Medicine*] (MELL)
CR	Chief Resident [*Medicine*] (MELL)
CR	Chronic Rejection [*Medicine*] (MELL)
CR	Circadian Rhythm (MELL)
CR	Code Red (MELL)
CR	Congenital Rubella [*Medicine*] (MELL)
CR	Conjugal Rights (MELL)
CR	Continuous Radon (EPAT)
CR	Corn Refiners Association, Inc.
CR	Corona Radiata [*Medicine*] (MELL)
CR	Cremaster Reflex [*Medicine*] (MELL)
Cr	Croatia (MILB)
CR	Customer Representative
CRA	Chronic Respiratory Alkalosis [*Medicine*] (MELL)
CRA	Chronic Rheumatoid Arthritis (MELL)
CRA	Church Records Archives (GEAB)
CRAF	Conscript Ratio in the Air Forces
CRAG	Columbia Region Association of Governments (GEOI)
CRAIGES	Cartographic Reproduction and Interactive Graphic Editing System (GEOI)
cranial I	Cranial Nerve I [*Olfactory nerve*] [*Medicine*] (MELL)
cranial II	Cranial Nerve II [*Optic nerve*] [*Medicine*] (MELL)
cranial III	Cranial Nerve III [*Oculomotor nerve*] [*Medicine*] (MELL)
cranial IV	Cranial Nerve IV [*Trochlear nerve*] [*Medicine*] (MELL)
cranial IX	Cranial Nerve IX [*Glossopharyngeal nerve*] [*Medicine*] (MELL)
cranial V	Cranial Nerve V [*Trigeminal nerve*] [*Medicine*] (MELL)
cranial VI	Cranial Nerve VI [*Abducent nerve*] [*Medicine*] (MELL)
cranial VII	Cranial Nerve VII [*Facial nerve*] [*Medicine*] (MELL)
cranial VIII	Cranial Nerve VIII [*Vestibulocochlear nerve*] [*Medicine*] (MELL)
cranial X	Cranial Nerve X [*Vagus nerve*] [*Medicine*] (MELL)
CRASH	Community Resources Against Street Hoodlums [*An association*]
CRB	Certified Real Estate Brokerage Manager
CRBSI	Catheter-Related Bloodstream Infection [*Medicine*] (MELL)
CRBT	Centre de Recherches Biologiques Tropicales [*Algeria*] (GEOI)
CRC	Consejo Revolucionario Cubano [*Cuban Revolutionary Council*]
CRCA	Congenital Red Cell Anemia [*Medicine*] (MELL)
CRCL	Circle International Group [*NASDAQ symbol*] (SG)
CrCl	Creatinine Clearance (MELL)
CRD	Capsaicin-Related Drug (MELL)
CRD	Child Resistant Device (MELL)
CRD	Chronic Radiodermatitis [*Medicine*] (MELL)
CRD	Circadian Rhythm Disorder [*Medicine*] (MELL)
CRD	Congenital Rubella Deafness [*Medicine*] (MELL)
CRDA	Casino Reinvestment Development Authority
CRDB	Coal Reserves Data Base
CRDIP	Chronic Relapsing Demyelinating Inflammatory Polyneuropathy [*Medicine*] (MELL)
CRE	Corn Residue Equivalents [*Environmental science*]
CRE	Counselor of Real Estate
CRES	Center for the Reproduction of Endangered Species
CRESP	Consortium for Risk Evaluation with Stakeholder Participation (GEOI)
CRF	Cardiorenal Failure [*Medicine*] (MELL)
CRF	Cardiorespiratory Failure [*Medicine*] (MELL)
CRG	Chest Roentgenogram [*Medicine*] (MELL)
CRI	Cambridge Research Instrumentation
CRI	Cardiac Risk Index [*Medicine*] (MELL)
CRI	Cartographic Research Laboratory (GEOI)
CRI	Chronic Respiratory Insufficiency [*Medicine*] (MELL)
CRIM	Centre de Recherche Informatique de Montreal [*Canada*]
CRMV-RJ	Conselho Regional de Medicina Veterinaria do Rio de Janeiro (GVA)
CRMV-SP	Conselho Regional de Medicina Veterinaria de Sao Paulo (GVA)
Crn	Cameroon (MILB)
CRN	Canadian Road Network (GEOI)
CRN	Cornell Corrections [*NYSE symbol*] (SG)
CRNS	Cronos Group [*NASDAQ symbol*] (SG)
CRP	Child-Resistant Packaging (EPAT)
CRPD	City Real Property Database (GEOI)
CRPRC	California Regional Primate Research Center (GVA)
CRRR	Captec Net Lease Realty [*NASDAQ symbol*] (SG)
CRS	Catheter-Related Sepsis [*Medicine*] (MELL)
CRS	Cell Recovery System [*Medicine*] (MELL)
CRS	Cervical Rib Syndrome [*Medicine*] (MELL)
CRS	Cherry-Red Spot [*Tay's sign*] [*Medicine*] (MELL)
CRS	Cholinergic Receptor Site [*Medicine*] (MELL)
CRS	Colorectal Surgery [*Medicine*] (MELL)
CRS	Comparative Respiratory Society (GVA)
crs	Crease
CRS	Crestar Energy [*Toronto Stock Exchange symbol*] (SG)
CRSC	California Remote Sensing Council (GEOI)
crspd	Correspond (GEAB)
CRT	Capillary Refill Test [*Medicine*] (MELL)
CRT	Collagen Replacement Therapy [*Medicine*] (MELL)
CRT	Computerized Renal Tomography [*Medicine*] (MELL)
CRT	Congenital Retinal Telangiectasia [*Medicine*] (MELL)
CRT	Controlled-Release Tablet Corrected [*Medicine*] (MELL)
CR/TE	Cost Reduction/Technical Excellence
CRTR	Crater (GEOI)
CrUnc	Crisp Uncirculated [*Numismatic term*]
CRW	Common Ragweed (MELL)
CRXA	Corixa Corp. [*NASDAQ symbol*] (SG)
CRY	CryoLife, Inc. [*NYSE symbol*] (SG)
CRYSYS	Cryospheric System (EOSA)
CS	Calcaneal Spur (MELL)
CS	Cardarelli's Sign [*Medicine*] (MELL)
CS	Caries Susceptible [*Medicine*] (MELL)
CS	Cayuga Syndrome [*Reproductive disturbance in fish*]
CS	Celiac Syndrome [*Medicine*] (MELL)
CS	Cervical Collar (MELL)
CS	Cervical Smear (MELL)
CS	Cervical Sponge (MELL)
CS	Chanarin Syndrome [*Medicine*]
Cs	Cirrostratus Cloud (WEAT)
CS	Color Scanner (GEOI)
CSA	Careside, Inc. [*AMEX symbol*] (SG)
CSA	Central Sleep Apnea [*Medicine*] (MELL)
CSA	Chief School Administrator
CSA	Childhood Sexual Abuse (MELL)
CSA	Child Sexual Abuse (MELL)
CSAC	Census Statistical Area Committee (GEOI)
CSAC	Company Services Advisory Committee [*British*] (GVA)
CSAP	Colorado Student Assessment Program
CSAV	Czechoslovak Academy of Sciences (GEOI)
CSB	Cat-Scratch Bacillus [*Medicine*] (MELL)
CSB	Cheyne-Stokes Breathing [*Medicine*] (MELL)
CSB	Coil Spring Brace [*Medicine*] (MELL)
CSBA	Canadian Swine Breeders Association (GVA)
CSC	Chimney Sweeps Cancer [*Medicine*] (MELL)
CSC	Commercial Space Centers
CSC	Computer Sciences Corporation (GEOI)
CSCAR	Center for Statistical Consultation and Research
CSD	Calcium Store Disease [*Medicine*] (MELL)
CSD	Conduction System Disease [*Medicine*] (MELL)
CSD	Craniospinal Defect [*Medicine*] (MELL)
CSDB	Click2Send Safe Deposit Box [*Digital storage*]
CSDGM	Content Standard for Digital Geospatial Metadata (GEOI)
CSDH	Chronic Subdural Hematoma [*Medicine*] (MELL)
CSE	Con-way Southern Express
CSF	Clay Shoveler's Fracture [*Medicine*] (MELL)
CSFS	Colorado State Forest Service (GEOI)
CSG	Cartography Special Group [*Association of American Geographers*] (GEOI)
CSHFI	Cervical Spine Hyperextension-Flexion Injury [*Medicine*] (MELL)
CSI	Cavernous Sinus Infiltration [*Medicine*] (MELL)
CSI	Cervical Spine Injury [*Medicine*] (MELL)
CSI	Chase Industries [*NYSE symbol*] (SG)
CSI	Chronic Smoke Inhalation (MELL)
CSI	Common Sense Initiative [*Environmental science*] (EPAT)
CSI	Continuous Subcutaneous Infusion [*Medicine*] (MELL)
CSI	Cranial Spinal Irradiation [*Medicine*] (MELL)
CSIC	Consejo Superior de Investigaciones Cientificas [*Spain*] (GEOI)
CSIN	Computer Systems Information Network (GEOI)
CSIP	Continental Scale International Project (GEOI)
CSK	Convertible Slip Knot (MELL)
CSL	Central Science Laboratory (GVA)
CSL	Community Service Learning
CSLA	California School Library Association
CSM	Crop Simulation Model
CSME	Cotton-Spot Macular Edema [*Medicine*] (MELL)
CSML	Committee on Southern Map Libraries (GEOI)
CSN	Congenital Sensory Neuropathy [*Medicine*] (MELL)
CSN	Crucible Swell Number
CSP	Carotid Sympathetic Plexus [*Medicine*] (MELL)
CSP	Chondroitin Sulfate Protein (MELL)
CSP	Conformal Space Projection (GEOI)
CSQ	Cognitive Strategies Questionnaire (MELL)
CSR	Central Serous Retinopathy [*Medicine*] (MELL)
CSR	Class Size Reduction
CSR	Continued Stay Review [*Medicine*] (MELL)
CSRC	Computer Security Resource and Response Center

CSRD.......... Comprehensive School Reform Demonstration
CSRS.......... Canadian Spatial Reference System (GEOI)
CSS............. Carotid Sinus Syndrome [*Medicine*] (MELL)
CSS............. Cavernous Sinus Syndrome [*Medicine*] (MELL)
CST............. Chi-Square Test (MELL)
CST............. Computer Scatter Tomography (MELL)
CST............. Corticoid Suppression Test (MELL)
CSTF........... Clinical Studies Trust Fund (GVA)
CSU .... Capital Senior Living [*NYSE symbol*] (SG)
CT .... Capital Trust 'A' [*NYSE symbol*] (SG)
CT .... Cardiac Tamponade (MELL)
CT .... Cell Therapy [*Medicine*] (MELL)
CT .... Census Tract (GEOI)
CT .... Chronotherapeutics (MELL)
CT .... Closed Thoracotomy [*Medicine*] (MELL)
CT .... Conjoined Twins (MELL)
CT .... Cryotherapy [*Medicine*] (MELL)
CTA .... Center Trust [*NYSE symbol*] (SG)
CTA .... Chemotactic Activity [*Medicine*] (MELL)
CTA .... Chemotactic Agent [*Medicine*] (MELL)
CTAP.......... Computed Tomography Angiographic Portography [*Medicine*] (MELL)
CTAP.......... Connective Tissue Activating Peptide [*Medicine*] (MELL)
CTC .... Confederacion de Trabajadores Cubanos [*Confederation of Cuban Workers*]
CTCO .... Commonwealth Tel Enterp [*NASDAQ symbol*] (SG)
CTCP.......... Carbon Tetrachloride Poisoning [*Medicine*] (MELL)
CTCP.......... Clinical Toxicology and Commercial Products (MELL)
CTCQ .... Check Technology [*NASDAQ symbol*] (SG)
CTD .... Chief, Topographic Division (GEOI)
CTE .... Cardiotech Intl. [*AMEX symbol*] (SG)
CTEST......... Consortium for Equity in Standards and Testing
CTFS........... Complete Testicular Feminization Syndrome (MELL)
CTFV.......... Colorado Tick Fever Virus (MELL)
CTG............. CTG Resources [*NYSE symbol*] (SG)
CTH............. Chronic Tension Headache (MELL)
CTH............. Corticotropic Hormone [*Medicine*] (MELL)
CTI .... Carbon Tetrachloride Intoxication (MELL)
CTI .... Continues to Improve (MELL)
CTIA........... Cerebral Transient Ischemic Attack [*Medicine*] (MELL)
CTIX........... Cheap Tickets [*NASDAQ symbol*] (SG)
CTL .... Cartographic Technology Laboratory (GEOI)
CTL .... Century Tel, Inc. [*NYSE symbol*] (SG)
CTLN........... Cricothyroid Lymph Node [*Medicine*] (MELL)
CTN............. Classroom Teacher Network
CTO............. Cable Twister Orthosis [*Medicine*] (MELL)
CTO............. Caribbean Tourism Organization, American Branch (EA)
CTO............. Carpal-Tarsal Osteolysis [*Medicine*] (MELL)
CTOG .... Contour to Grid (GEOI)
CTPVO .... Chronic Thrombotic Pulmonary Vascular Obstruction [*Medicine*] (MELL)
CTR............. Cabot Industrial Tr [*NYSE symbol*] (SG)
CTR............. Calcaneal Tendon Reflex [*Medicine*] (MELL)
CTRA .... Cardiac T Rapid Assay [*Medicine*] (MELL)
CTS............. Cattle Tracing System (GVA)
CTS............. Chaddock's Toe Sign [*Medicine*] (MELL)
CTV............. Commscope, Inc. [*NYSE symbol*] (SG)
CTZ............. Chicago Title [*NYSE symbol*] (SG)
CU............... Cause Undetermined [*Medicine*] (MELL)
CU............... Circuity Upgrade
CU............... Cleft Uvula [*Medicine*] (MELL)
CU............... Compania Cervecerias Unidas ADS [*NYSE symbol*] (SG)
Cu............... Cumulus Cloud (WEAT)
CUC............. Cystourethrocele [*Medicine*] (MELL)
CuCon......... Cumulus Congestus Cloud (WEAT)
CUD .... Chancroid Ulcer Disease [*Medicine*] (MELL)
CUDS.......... Closed Urinary Drainage System [*Medicine*] (MELL)
Cu Ft.......... Cubic Feet
CUGiK.......... Centralny Urzad Geodezji i Kartografil [*Poland*] (GEOI)
CuHu........... Cumulus Humilis Cloud (WEAT)
CUI.............. Coach USA [*NYSE symbol*] (SG)
Cu In.......... Cubic Inch
CuMed........ Cumulus Medicoris Cloud (WEAT)
CUPS .... Cancer of Unknown Primary Site [*Medicine*] (MELL)
CURE .... Connecticut United for Research Excellence (GVA)
curr............ Current (PROS)
CUS .... Chronic Ulcerative Stomatitis [*Medicine*]
CUSEC .... Central United States Earthquake Consortium (GEOI)

cust............ Customer (PROS)
CUST .... CustomTracks Corp. [*NASDAQ symbol*] (SG)
CUT............. Carbohydrate Utilization Test [*Medicine*] (MELL)
CUTS .... Consumer Unity & Trust Society
CUTW .... Connecticut Union of Telephone Workers
CV.............. Cardiac Volume [*Medicine*] (MELL)
CV.............. Cavernous Sinus [*Medicine*] (MELL)
CV.............. Central VT Pub Svc [*NYSE symbol*] (SG)
CV.............. Cerebrovascular [*Medicine*] (MELL)
CV.............. Chemical Vocabulary (EPAT)
CV.............. Chorionic Villi [*Medicine*] (MELL)
c/v.............. City View
CV.............. Contrast Ventriculography [*Medicine*] (MELL)
CV.............. Corporate Venturing [*Business term*]
CV.............. Coxa Vera [*Medicine*] (MELL)
CVAE.......... Cardiovascular Adverse Effects [*Medicine*] (MELL)
CVD .... Chemical-Vapour-Deposited
CVD .... Covance, Inc. [*NYSE symbol*] (SG)
CVF............. Cardiovascular Failure [*Medicine*] (MELL)
CVF............. Cervicovaginal Fistula [*Medicine*] (MELL)
CVF............. Cervicovaginal Fluid [*Medicine*] (MELL)
CVG............. Convergys Corp. [*NYSE symbol*] (SG)
CVHD .... Chronic Valvular Heart Disease [*Medicine*] (MELL)
CVI............. Central Venous Infusions [*Medicine*] (MELL)
CVI............. Cerebrovascular Incident [*Medicine*] (MELL)
CVIR........... Cost Avoidance to Total Investment Ratio
CVJ............. Costovertebral Joint (MELL)
CVM............ Christian Veterinary Mission (GVA)
CVMC.......... Christian Veterinary Missions of Canada (GVA)
CVOD .... Corporal Veno-Occlusive Dysfunction [*Medicine*] (MELL)
CVP............. Circumvallate Papilla [*Medicine*] (MELL)
CVPM.......... Certificate in Veterinary Practice Management (GVA)
CVS............. Conrad Veidt Society (EA)
CVT............. Congenital Vertical Talus [*Medicine*] (MELL)
CVTY........... Coventry Health Care [*NASDAQ symbol*] (SG)
CW............. Cerclage Wire (MELL)
CW............. Civil War (GEAB)
CW............. Common Wart (MELL)
CW............. Continuous Wave [*Radar*]
cw.............. Continuous Wave
CWC............ Cortebert Watch Company
CWF............ Cartwheel Fracture (MELL)
CWF............ Compassion in World Farming (GVA)
CWG .... CanWest Global Commun [*NYSE symbol*] (SG)
CWIHP .... Cold War International History Project [*Woodrow Wilson International Center for Scholars*] [*Internet resource*]
CWL........... Chartwell Re [*NYSE symbol*] (SG)
CWL........... Coffee Worker's Lung (MELL)
CWM........... Can We Meet [*Online dialog*]
CWP............ Cable & Wireless ADS [*NYSE symbol*] (SG)
CWP............ Chest Wall Pain (MELL)
CWRA .... Canadian Water Resources Program (GEOI)
CWRA .... Clean Water Restoration Act (MELL)
CWS............ Cartographic Workstation (GEOI)
CWT............ Calif Water Svc Grp [*NYSE symbol*] (SG)
CWT............ Con-way Truckload Services
CWTR .... Coldwater Creek [*NASDAQ symbol*] (SG)
CWX............ Con-way Western Express
CWZ............ Cable & Wireless Communic ADS [*NYSE symbol*] (SG)
Cx.............. Convex (MELL)
CxBx .... Cervical Biopsy [*Medicine*] (MELL)
CXR .... Cox Radio 'A' [*NYSE symbol*] (SG)
CxTx.......... Cervical Traction [*Medicine*] (MELL)
c/y.............. Courtyard
Cy.............. Cyprus (MILB)
CYBS .... CyberSource [*Stock market symbol*]
CYL............. Community Capital [*AMEX symbol*] (SG)
Cyl.............. Cylinder
CYMI........... Cymer, Inc. [*NASDAQ symbol*] (SG)
CYP............. Cape York Peninsula (GEOI)
CYP............. Cypros Pharmaceutical [*AMEX symbol*] (SG)
CYPLUS ...... Cape York Peninsula Land Use Strategy (GEOI)
CYSP .... Cybershop Intl. [*NASDAQ symbol*] (SG)
CZ.............. Club Zoologico [*Universiti Putra Malaysia*] [*University student group*] (GVA)
Cz .... Czech Republic (MILB)
CZS............. Cefazolin Sodium (MELL)

D
By Acronym

D	Dalton (MELL)	db	Date of Birth (MELL)
D	Decamethonium (MELL)	DB	Direct Bronchoscopy [Medicine] (MELL)
d	Decrease (MELL)	DB&C	Dwelling, Building, and Contents
D	Diastolic (MELL)	DBD	Definite Brain Damage (MELL)
D	Dilated (MELL)	dbd	Depth Below Datum (QUAC)
D	Dilution (MELL)	DBD	Diffuse Brain Damage (MELL)
D	Dwelling (GEOI)	DBD	Disruptive Behavior Disorder (MELL)
D1	Day One [First day seen for treatment] [Medicine] (MELL)	DBDB	Digital Bathymetry Data Base (GEOI)
D3	Cholecalciferol [Medicine] (MELL)	DBF	Dashboard Fracture [Medicine] (MELL)
D/3	Distal Third [Medicine] (MELL)	DBIFC	David Birney International Fan Club (EA)
DA	Dacryoadenitis [Medicine] (MELL)	Dbl	Double
Da	Denmark (MILB)	DBPPWG	Data Base Population Planning Working Group (GEOI)
DA	Deoxyadenosine (MELL)	DBPWG	Data Base Population Working Group (GEOI)
DA	Diabetic Acidosis [Medicine] (MELL)	DBS	Data Base Specifications (GEOI)
DA	Dissecting Aneurysm [Medicine] (MELL)	dbs	Depth Below Surface (QUAC)
DA	Distended Abdomen (MELL)	DBS	Diamond-Blackfan Syndrome [Medicine] (MELL)
DA	Dopamine Agonist [Medicine] (MELL)	DBS	Doctor at Bedside (MELL)
DA	Drug Abuse (MELL)	DBS	Duck-Billed Speculum [Medicine] (MELL)
DA	Duodenal Atresia [Medicine] (MELL)	DBT	DBT Online [NYSE symbol] (SG)
DAA	Dementia Associated with Alcoholism (MELL)	DBT	Dialectical Behavior Therapy [Medicine] (MELL)
DAA	Dream Anxiety Attack (MELL)	DBT	Double-Blind Test [Medicine] (MELL)
DA&SM	Data Acquisitions and Systems Maintenance (GEOI)	DBT	Double-Blind Trial [Medicine] (MELL)
DAASC	Defense Automated Addressing System Center (GEOI)	DBT	Dumbbell Tumor [Medicine] (MELL)
DAB	Dave & Buster's [NYSE symbol] (SG)	DC	Dental Caries (MELL)
DAB	Days after Birth (MELL)	DC	Deputy Clerk (GEAB)
DAB	Dictionary of American Biography [A publication] (GEAB)	DC	Dermoid Cyst [Medicine] (MELL)
DABR	David's Bridal [NASDAQ symbol] (SG)	DC	Dietary Chaos (MELL)
DAC	Differentiated Adenomatous Carcinoma [Medicine] (MELL)	DC	Digital Clubbing (MELL)
DAC	Diffuse Alveolar Consolidation [Medicine] (MELL)	DC	Dilatation Catheter [Medicine] (MELL)
DAC	Direct-Acting Carcinogen [Medicine] (MELL)	DC	Direct Coombs [Test] [Medicine] (MELL)
DACH	Deputy Assistant Chief Hydrologist (GEOI)	DC	Dislocated Civilian
DADS	Data Archive and Distribution System (EOSA)	DC	District Chief (GEOI)
DADS	Digital Assisted Data Base System (GEOI)	DC	District of Columbia (GEOI)
DAFZ	Dubai Airport Free Zone	DC	Dressing Change [Medicine] (MELL)
DAH	Diffuse Alveolar Hemorrhage [Medicine] (MELL)	DC	Drug Combination [Medicine] (MELL)
DAH	Disarticulation of Hip (MELL)	DC	Dual Choice [Insurance]
DAI	Diarthrodial Joint (MELL)	DCA	Department of Civil Aviation
DAJ	Daimler-Benz 5.75% Sub Notes [NYSE symbol] (SG)	DCA	Department of Community Affairs [Montana] (GEOI)
DAK	Disarticulation of Knee (MELL)	DC&A	Data Collection and Analysis (GEOI)
Dal	Dallas Cowboys [National Football League] [1960-present] (NFLA)	DCASS	Digital Cartographic Software System (GEOI)
DAMA	Discharged against Medical Advice (MELL)	DCC	Daimler-Chrysler Corporation
DAMES	Defense Automated Message Exchange Service (GEOI)	DCC	Dorsal Cell Column (MELL)
DANASAT	Direct Ascent Nuclear Antisatellite	DCC	Double-Current Catheter [Medicine] (MELL)
D & A	Discharge and Advise [Medicine] (MELL)	DCC	Dystrophic Cardiac Calcinosis [Medicine] (MELL)
D & C	Direct and Consensual (MELL)	DCCC	Disabled Collectors' Correspondence Club (EA)
D & D	Death and Dignity (MELL)	DCCO	Diffusing Capacity of Carbon Monoxide (MELL)
D & D	Dysphagia and Dysphonia [Medicine] (MELL)	DCDSTF	Digital Cartographic Data Standards Task Force (GEOI)
D & G	Deafness and Goiter (MELL)	DCES	Direct Current Electrical Stimulation (MELL)
D & R	Desquamation and Regeneration [Medicine] (MELL)	DCF	Digital Cartographic File (GEOI)
D & T	Dependence and Tolerance (MELL)	DCG	Descendants of Colonial Governors (GEAB)
DANE	Departamento Administrativo Nacional de Estadstica [Colombia] (GEOI)	DCH	Day-Care Home (MELL)
DANNASAT	Direct Ascent Nonnuclear Antisatellite	DCHUM	Digital Chart Update Manual (GEOI)
DAP	Delayed-Action Preparation [Medicine] (MELL)	DCI	Differential Corrections, Inc. (GEOI)
DAP	Delayed after Depolarization [Medicine] (MELL)	DCI	Duplicate Coverage Inquiry [Insurance]
DAP	Dextroamphetamine Phosphate [Medicine] (MELL)	DCIFC	David Copperfield International Fan Club (EA)
DAP	Diastolic Arterial Pressure [Medicine] (MELL)	DCLCO	Diffusing Capacity of Lung for Carbon Monoxide (MELL)
DAP	Dorsal Artery of Penis [Medicine] (MELL)	DCLK	DoubleClick, Inc. [NASDAQ symbol] (SG)
DAR	Darling International [AMEX symbol] (SG)	DCN	Depressed, Cognitively Normal [Medicine] (MELL)
DAR	Death after Resuscitation (MELL)	DCO	Ducommun, Inc. [NYSE symbol] (SG)
DAR	Drug-Abuse Reporting (MELL)	DCP	Digital Cartographic Production (GEOI)
DARA	Deutsche Agentur fur Raumfahrtangelegenheiten [Germany] (EOSA)	DCP	Diphencyprone [Medicine]
DARF	Direct Aerosol Radiative Forcing (QUAC)	DCPN	Direction Changing Positional Nystagmus [Medicine] (MELL)
DAS	Dead-Arm Syndrome [Medicine] (MELL)	DCPS	Digital Cartographic Production Segment (GEOI)
DAS	Delaware Assocation of Surveyors (GEOI)	DCR	Debt Coverage Ratio [Business term]
DAS	Doctor-Assisted Suicide (MELL)	DCR	Design Concept Review (GEOI)
DASA	Daimler Chrysler Aerospace	DCS	Del Castillo Syndrome [Medicine] (MELL)
DASE	Dutch Association of Safety Experts	DCS	Delerium/Confusional State [Medicine] (MELL)
DAST	Drug Abuse Screening Test (MELL)	DCS	Diffuse Cutaneous Scleroderma [Medicine] (MELL)
DASTY	Dassault Systems ADS [NASDAQ symbol] (SG)	DCS	Digital Cartography Section (GEOI)
DaT	Dallas Texans [National Football League] [1952] (NFLA)	DCS	Displaced Child Syndrome (MELL)
DATIS	Digital Airborne Topographic Imaging System (GEOI)	DCS	DONCASTERS plc ADS [NYSE symbol] (SG)
DATPE	Direction de l'Amernagement du Territoire et de la Protection de l'Environnement [Haiti] (GEOI)	DCS	Double-Contrast Study (MELL)
		DCSF	Diba Consulting Software Engineers (GEOI)
dau	Daughter (GEAB)	DCS/RSE	Data Collection System Receiving Site Equipment (GEOI)
		DCST	Data Collection System Tape (GEOI)
DAV	Domestic Abuse and Violence (MELL)	DCT	Direction Topographique et du Cadastre [Congo] (GEOI)

DCVMA	District of Columbia Veterinary Medical Association (GVA)
DCX	DaimlerChryler AG [*NYSE symbol*] (SG)
DD	Dandruff (MELL)
DD	Day of Delivery [*Medicine*] (MELL)
DD	Deferent Duct [*Medicine*] (MELL)
DD	Degenerated Disk [*Medicine*] (MELL)
DD	Delivery Date [*Medicine*] (MELL)
DD	Delusional Disorder [*Medicine*] (MELL)
DD	Dental Decay (MELL)
DD	Designer Drug [*Medicine*] (MELL)
DD	Developmental Dyslexia [*Medicine*] (MELL)
DD	Dewey Decimal (GEOI)
DD	Digestive Disorder (MELL)
DD	Dignified Dying (MELL)
DD	Direct Diagnosis [*Medicine*] (MELL)
DD	Discharge Diagnosis [*Medicine*] (MELL)
DD	Drug Dependence (MELL)
DD	Dual Diagnosis [*Medicine*] (MELL)
DD	Dual Disorder [*Medicine*] (MELL)
DDA	Data Descriptive Area (GEOI)
DDA	Dementia Associated with Alcoholism [*Medicine*] (MELL)
DDACM	Deputy Director for Acquisition Career Management [*Army*]
DDB	Defined Dollar Benefit
DDD	Chequemate Intl. [*AMEX symbol*] (SG)
DDD	Den Danske Dyrlaegeforening [*Danish Veterinary Association*] (GVA)
DDE	Distributive Data Environment
DDES	Digital Data Editing System (GEOI)
DDF	Data Descriptive File (GEOI)
DDF	Dideoxy Finger-Printing (MELL)
DDFC	Dave Durham Fan Club (EA)
DDG	Deoxy-D-Glucose (MELL)
DDG	Development and Discretionary Grants Bureau
DDH	Development Dysplasia of Hip [*Medicine*] (MELL)
DDI	Design Data, Inc. (GEOI)
DDIS	Depository Distribution Information System (GEOI)
DDLE	Disseminated Discoid Lupus Erythematosus [*Medicine*]
DDM	Documents Data Miner (GEOI)
DDN	Dynamex, Inc. [*AMEX symbol*] (SG)
DDN SCC	Defense Data Network Security Coordination Center
ddpm	Dial Divisions per Minute
DDPN	Deafness, Diabetes, Photomyoclonus and Nephropathy [*Medicine*] (MELL)
DDPO	Defense Dissemination Program Office (GEOI)
DDPS	Desktop Digital Photogrammetry System (GEOI)
DDR	Data Descriptive Record (GEOI)
DDRC	Drug Dose-Response Curve [*Medicine*] (MELL)
DDS	Descriptor Differential Scale [*Medicine*] (MELL)
DDS	Dillard's Inc.'A' [*NYSE symbol*] (SG)
DDS	Disease-Disability Scale [*Medicine*] (MELL)
DDS	Domestic Data Service
DDS	Dry Dock Shelter (MILB)
DDT	Deferent Duct Tumor [*Medicine*] (MELL)
DDT	Dillard's Cap Tr 7.50% Cap Sec [*NYSE symbol*] (SG)
DDT	Double Diffusion Test [*Medicine*] (MELL)
DDTC	Drug Dependence Treatment Center (MELL)
DDTP	Drug Dependence Treatment Program (MELL)
DE	Data Extraction (GEOI)
DE	Dependent Edema [*Medicine*] (MELL)
DE	Diagnostic Error [*Medicine*] (MELL)
DE	Donor Eggs [*Medicine*]
DE	Doppler Effect (MELL)
dea	Deacon (GEAB)
Dec	Decatur Staleys [*National Football League*] [*1920*] (NFLA)
dec	Declination (GEOI)
decis	Decision (GEAB)
DED	Debrancher Enzyme Deficiency [*Medicine*] (MELL)
def	Defense (MILB)
defn	Definition (MILB)
degr	Degree (GEAB)
del	Delegate (PROS)
del	Delineation (GEOI)
DEL	Deltic Timber [*NYSE symbol*] (SG)
delt	Delineator (GEOI)
DEM	Digital Elevation Matrix (GEOI)
DEM	Dysplasia Epiphysalis Multiplex [*Medicine*] (MELL)
DEM-G	Digital Elevation Model-Graphic (GEOI)
DEM-P	Digital Elevation Model-Planar (GEOI)
DEMVFY	Digital Elevation Model Verify (GEOI)
Den	Denver Broncos [*National Football League*] [*1960-present*] (NFLA)
DEP	Department of Environmental Protection (GEOI)
dep	Depot (GEAB)
DEP	Diabetic Encephalopathy [*Medicine*] (MELL)
DEP	Diesel Exhaust Particulates [*Medicine*] (MELL)
DEPA	Demonstrably Effective Program Aid
DEPA	Dual Energy Photon Absorptiometry (MELL)
DepFonMin	Deputy Foreign Minister
depr	Depreciation
Deptel	Department of State Telegram
DERV	Duck Embryo Rabies Vaccine (MELL)
DE/S	Data Extraction Segment (GEOI)
DES	Delta Epsilon Sigma (EA)
DES	Digital Editing Station (GEOI)
desc	Descendant (GEAB)
DESG	Defence Engineering and Science Group
DESI	Diversified Energy Services, Inc. (GEOI)

DET	DECS Trust 8.50% 2000 [*NYSE symbol*] (SG)
det	Detachment (MILB)
Det	Detroit Lions [*National Football League*] [*1934-present*] (NFLA)
DETR	Department of Environment, Transport, and the Regions
DETR	Department of the Environment, Transport, and the Regions
devis	Devised (GEAB)
DF	Dengue Fever [*Medicine*] (MELL)
DF	Depressed Fracture [*Medicine*] (MELL)
DF	Dermatofibroma [*Medicine*] (MELL)
DF	Drug Free (MELL)
DF	Duodenal Flexure [*Medicine*] (MELL)
DFA	Difficulty Falling Asleep (MELL)
DFC	Delta Financial [*NYSE symbol*] (SG)
DFC	Devils Fan Club (EA)
DFD	Degenerative Facet Disease [*Medicine*] (MELL)
DFG	Delphi Fin'l Group 'A' [*NYSE symbol*] (SG)
DFG	Department of Fish and Game (GEOI)
DFIIP	Digital Flight Information Publication (GEOI)
DFS	Dead Fetus Syndrome (MELL)
DFS	Drop Foot Splint (MELL)
DFU	Diabetic Foot Ulcer [*Medicine*] (MELL)
DFW	Department of Fish and Wildlife (GEOI)
DFW	Drug-Free Workplace (MELL)
DFZ	Drug-Free Zone (MELL)
DGC	Direct Geodetic Constraint (GEOI)
DGCM	Direct Geodetic Constraint Method (GEOI)
DGCM	Division of Grants and Contracts Management (MELL)
DGCR	Defective Glucose Counterregulation [*Medicine*] (MELL)
DGDF	Digital Geospatial Data Files (GEOI)
DGEC	Direccion General de Estadistica y Censos [*Costa Rica*] (GEOI)
DGF	Department of Game and Fish (GEOI)
DGGM	Direccion General de Geologia y Minas [*Colombia*] (GEOI)
DGI	Direktorat Geologi [*Indonesia*] (GEOI)
DGIAI	Direccion General de Integracion y Analisis de la Informacion [*Mexico*] (GEOI)
DGII	Digi International [*NASDAQ symbol*] (SG)
DGIWG	Ditigal Geographic Information Working Group (GEOI)
DGMG	Direccion General de Minas y Geologia [*Venezuela*] (GEOI)
DGMP	Direccion de Geologia, Minas y Petrolio [*Costa Rica*] (GEOI)
DGN	Domestic Geographic Name (GEOI)
DGNR	Domestic Geographic Names Report (GEOI)
DGO	Direccion General de Oceanografia [*Mexico*] (GEOI)
DGP	Digital Graphic Product (GEOI)
DGPA	Direccion General de la Produccion Agraria [*Spain*] (GEOI)
DGPS	Differential Global Positioning Satellite (GEOI)
DGRM	Direccion General de Recursos Minerales [*Panama*] (GEOI)
DGS	Delaware Geological Survey (GEOI)
DGS	Dollar Gen'l 8.50%'STRYPES' [*NYSE symbol*] (SG)
DGSF	Department of Geological Survey and Exploration [*Burma*] (GEOI)
DGU	Danmarks Geologiske Undersogelse (GEOI)
DGV	Digital Lava [*AMEX symbol*] (SG)
DH	Definitive Host (MELL)
DH	Dissociative Hysteria [*Medicine*] (MELL)
DH	Dowager's Hump [*Medicine*] (MELL)
DH	Drill Hole (GEOI)
DH	Dry Heaves [*Medicine*] (MELL)
DHD	Doghouse Disease (MELL)
DHF	Diastolic Heart Failure [*Medicine*] (MELL)
DHI	Deafness, Hyperprolinuria, and Ichthyosis [*Medicine*] (MELL)
DHI	Defense Hydrographic Initiative (GEOI)
DHS	Delayed Hypersensitivity [*Medicine*] (MELL)
DHS	Diabetic Hyperosmolar State [*Medicine*] (MELL)
DI	Desert Inn
DI	Digital Image (GEOI)
DI	Digitalis Intoxication [*Medicine*] (MELL)
DI	Drug-Induced (MELL)
DI	Drug Intoxication (MELL)
DI	Dry Ice (MELL)
DIA	Department of Indian Affairs (GEOI)
DIA	Department of International Affairs (GEOI)
DIA	Design Institute of America
DIA	DIAMONDS Trust, Series 1 [*AMEX symbol*] (SG)
DIAA	Drug-Induced Aplastic Anemia [*Medicine*] (MELL)
DIAL	Dialog Corp. ADS [*NASDAQ symbol*] (SG)
DIAPPERS	Delirium, Infection, Atrophic Urethritis, Pharmaceuticals, Psychologic Depressi on, Excessive Urination, Restricted Mobility, and Stool Impaction [*Causes of transient urinary incontinence*] [*Medicine*] (MELL)
DIC	Direct Illumination Component (MELL)
DIC	Drip Infusion Cholangiography [*Medicine*] (MELL)
DIC	Drug-Induced Constipation [*Medicine*] (MELL)
DID	Data Information Delivery
DID	Data Information Description (GEOI)
DID	Digital Image Data (GEOI)
DIED	Died in Emergency Department (MELL)
DIER	Died in Emergency Room (MELL)
DIES	Digital Image Enhancement System (GEOI)
DIF	Dairy Industry Federation (GVA)
DIFP	Diffuse Interstitial Fibrosing Pneumonitis [*Medicine*] (MELL)
DiG	DiGeorge Syndrome [*Medicine*]
DIGCAT	Digital Catalog (GEOI)
DIGL	Digital Lightwave [*NASDAQ symbol*] (SG)
DIGX	Digex Inc.'A' [*NASDAQ symbol*] (SG)
DIH	Died in Hospital (MELL)
DIH	Drug-Induced Headache [*Medicine*] (MELL)

DIHE	Drug-Induced Hepatic Encephalopathy [*Medicine*] (MELL)
DIIBF	Dorel Industries'B' [*NASDAQ symbol*] (SG)
DILD	Diffuse Interstitial Lung Disease [*Medicine*] (MELL)
DIM	Digital Image Matching (GEOI)
DIMD	Drug-Induced Movement Disorder [*Medicine*] (MELL)
dio	Diocese (GEAB)
DIP	Data Integration Program (GEOI)
DIPB	Deep Infrapatellar Bursa [*Medicine*] (MELL)
DIPD	Diagnostic Interview for Personality Disorders (MELL)
DIPF	Diffuse Interstitial Pulmonary Fibrosis [*Medicine*] (MELL)
DIPI	Direct Intra-Peritoneal Insemination [*Medicine*]
DIR	Deep Inguinal Ring [*Medicine*] (MELL)
DIR	Diurnal Insulin Resistance [*Medicine*] (MELL)
DIR	Donald, Luf & Jen-DLJdirect [*NYSE symbol*] (SG)
DIS	Data and Information System (EOSA)
dis	Disability (MELL)
dis	Discharge (GEAB)
dis	Disease (MELL)
DISA	Digital Intravenous Subtraction Angiography [*Medicine*] (MELL)
discip	Discipline (GEAB)
DISHIDROS	Dinas Hidro Oceanografi [*Indonesia*] (GEOI)
DISI	Directory Information Services Infrastructure
DISTDAHS	Distributed Satellite Telemetry Data Handling System (GEOI)
Distr	Distributor (PROS)
DIT	Deferoxamine Infusion Test [*Medicine*] (MELL)
DIT	Drug-Induced Thrombocytopenia [*Medicine*] (MELL)
div	Divorced (GEAB)
Dj	Djibouti (MILB)
DJOA	Dominant Juvenile Optic Atrophy [*Medicine*] (MELL)
DK	Diabetic Ketoacidosis [*Medicine*] (MELL)
DK	Donna Karan Intl. [*NYSE symbol*] (SG)
dkfz	Deutsches Krebsforschungszentrum [*Germany*]
DKS	Disseminated Kaposi Sarcoma [*Medicine*]
DL	Data Logging (GEOI)
DLA	Dole Food $2.7475'TRACES' [*AMEX symbol*] (SG)
DLCW	Department of Land and Water Conservation (GEOI)
DLD	Date of Last Drink [*Medicine*] (MELL)
DLG2DEM	Digital Line Graph to Digital Elevation Model (GEOI)
DLG-E	Digital Line Graph-Enhanced (GEOI)
DLGF	Digital Line Graph-Framework (GEOI)
DLG-O	Digital Line Graph-Optional (GEOI)
DLI	Data Liberation Initiative [*Canada*] (GEOI)
DLIA	dELiAs, Inc. [*NASDAQ symbol*] (SG)
DLM	Del Monte Foods [*NYSE symbol*] (SG)
DLNR	Department of Land and Natural Resources (GEOI)
DLO-NL	Netherlands Organization for Agricultural Research (GVA)
DLP	Dislocation of Patella [*Medicine*] (MELL)
DLP	Dorsal Lithotomy Position [*Medicine*] (MELL)
DLR	Deutsches Zentrum Fuer Luft- und Raumfahrt
DLS	Department of Lands and Survey [*Guyana*] (GEOI)
DLS	Digitalis-Like Substance [*Medicine*] (MELL)
DLS	Dynamic Limb Sounder (EOSA)
DLT	Double Lumen Tube [*Medicine*] (MELL)
DLT	Double-Lung Transplantation [*Medicine*] (MELL)
DLTR	Dollar Tree Stores [*NASDAQ symbol*] (SG)
DLVD	Diastolic Left Ventricular Dysfunction [*Medicine*] (MELL)
DLW	Double Loop Whorl [*Fingerprint*] (MELL)
DLWC	Department of Land and Water Conservation [*Australia*] (GEOI)
DM	Danbury Mint
DM	Defensive Medicine (MELL)
DM	Descemet's Membrane [*Medicine*] (MELL)
DM	Diffuse Myalgia [*Medicine*] (MELL)
DM	Distal Metastases [*Medicine*] (MELL)
DM	Distolic Murmur [*Medicine*] (MELL)
DMA	Denervated Muscle Atrophy [*Medicine*] (MELL)
DMA	Digital Model Assembly
DMAFF	Defense Mapping Agency Feature File (GEOI)
DMAIAGS	Defense Mapping Agency Inter-American Geodetic Survey (GEOI)
DMASPOEM	Defense Mapping Agency Special Program Office for Exploitation Modernization (GEOI)
DMAT	Disaster Medical Assistance Team (MELL)
DMCB	Dairy Mart Conven Str'B' [*AMEX symbol*] (SG)
DMD	Distal Muscular Dystrophy [*Medicine*] (MELL)
DMD	Doppler Method of Diagnosis [*Medicine*] (MELL)
DME	Department of Mines and Energy [*Nova Scotia*] (GEOI)
DMFC	Dennis Miller Fan Club (EA)
DMH	Ducati Motor Hldg ADS [*NYSE symbol*] (SG)
DMI	Depomed, Inc. [*AMEX symbol*] (SG)
DMMG	Direccion Nacional de Mineria y Geologia [*Uruguay*] (GEOI)
DMMR	Deputy Ministry for Mineral Resources [*Saudi Arabia*] (GEOI)
DMN	Dysplastic Melanocytic Nevi [*Medicine*]
DMP	Dimercaprol [*Medicine*] (MELL)
DMRT	Department of Mineral Resources of Thailand (GEOI)
DMS	Defense Mobilization Ship (MILB)
DMS	Distribution Management System (GEOI)
DMSI	Data Management Segment Interface [*Control Document*] (GEOI)
DMSO	Defense Mapping School Operations Office (GEOI)
DMTI	Desktop Mapping Technologies, Inc. (GEOI)
DMU	Defense Mapping Unit [*Singapore*] (GEOI)
DMVA	Direct Mechanical Ventricular Actuator [*Medicine*] (MELL)
DMW	Daft, McCune, Walker (GEOI)
DN	Delphian Node [*Medicine*] (MELL)
DN	Diabetic Nephropathy [*Medicine*] (MELL)
DN	Digital Number (GEOI)
DNA	Deoxyribose Nucleic Acid

DNA	Diabetes Nutritional Assessment (MELL)
DNA	Directional Neighbourhoods Approach
DNB	Destructive Nerve Block [*Medicine*] (MELL)
DNC	Digital Nautical Chart (GEOI)
DNCC	Dunn Computer [*NASDAQ symbol*] (SG)
DNG	Diffuse Nontoxic Goiter [*Medicine*] (MELL)
DNH	Directory of Nursing Homes [*A publication*] (MELL)
DNHL	Diffuse Non-Hodgkin's Lymphoma [*Medicine*] (MELL)
DNIG	De Novo Inflammatory Growth [*Medicine*] (MELL)
DNLL	Dorsal Nucleus of Lateral Lemniscus [*Medicine*] (MELL)
DNM	Dilator Naris Muscle [*Medicine*] (MELL)
DNPCT	Direction National de Production Cartographique et Topographique [*Mali*] (GEOI)
DNR	Denbury Resources [*NYSE symbol*] (SG)
DNR	Dorsal Nerve Root [*Medicine*] (MELL)
DNRC	Department of Natural Resources and Conservation [*Montana*] (GEOI)
DNREP	Department of Natural Resources and Environmental Protection [*Kentucky*] (GEOI)
DNRP	Department of Natural Resource Protection
DNS	Dextrose in Normal Solution [*Medicine*] (MELL)
DNT	Delta Air Lines 8.125% Nts [*NYSE symbol*] (SG)
DNT	Direccion Nacional de Topografia [*Uruguay*] (GEOI)
DO	Digital Ortho (GEOI)
DO	Drug Overdose (MELL)
DO	Drug Oxidation (MELL)
DOA-DRA	Dead on Arrival Despite Resuscitation Attempt (MELL)
DOC	Date of Conception (MELL)
DOC	Drug of Choice (MELL)
DOD	Date of Discharge [*Medicine*] (MELL)
DOD	Dentino-Osseous Dysplasia [*Medicine*] (MELL)
DOD	Drug Overdose (MELL)
DODS	Distributed Ocean Data System
DOELAP	Department of Energy Laboratory Accreditation Program
DOI	Date of Illness (MELL)
DOI	Date of Implant (MELL)
DOI	Date of Investigation (MELL)
DOI	Document Object Identifier (GEOI)
DOIN	Donny Osmond International Network (EA)
DOMS	Delayed-Onset Muscle Soreness
DON	Determination of Need (MELL)
DON	Donnelly Corp.Cl'A' [*NYSE symbol*] (SG)
don	Donor (PROS)
DOPC	Determined Osteogenic Precursor Cell [*Medicine*] (MELL)
DOPLID	Doppler Lidar (EOSA)
DOQ	Digital Orthophoto Quadrangle (GEOI)
DOQQ	Digital Orthophoto Quarter Quadrangle (GEOI)
DOR	Endorex Corp. [*AMEX symbol*] (SG)
DORIS	Decision-Oriented Resource Information System [*Ventura County, CA*] (GEOI)
DORIS	Determination d'Orbite et Radiopositionement Integre par Satellite (EOSA)
DOS	Dialysis Osteomalacia Syndrome [*Medicine*] (MELL)
DOS	Digital Orthophoto System (GEOI)
DOS	Dysosteosclerosis [*Medicine*] (MELL)
DOSLI	Department of Survey and Land Information [*New Zealand*] (GEOI)
DOW	Doppler on Wheels
DOX	Amdocs Ltd. [*NYSE symbol*] (SG)
DP	Demand Pacemaker (MELL)
DP	Dental Plaque (MELL)
DP	Digital Photogrammetry (GEOI)
DP	Distal Phalanx [*Medicine*] (MELL)
DP	Double Pneumonia (MELL)
DP	Dying Patient (MELL)
DPA	Directorate of Presidential Affairs
DP & AD	Depressive Personality and Allied Disorders (MELL)
DPC	Days Post Coitum [*Medicine*] (MELL)
DPC	Direct Platelet Count [*Medicine*] (MELL)
DPCS	Dedham Pottery Collectors Society (EA)
DPE	Data Processing Environment (GEOI)
DPED	Department of Planning and Economic Development (GEOI)
DPH	Delphi Automotive Systems [*NYSE symbol*] (SG)
DPI	Daily Permissible Intake [*Medicine*] (MELL)
DPI	Doppler Perfusion Index [*Medicine*] (MELL)
DPIE	Department of Primary Industries and Energy [*Australia*] (GEOI)
DPL	Data Programming Language (GEOI)
dpl	Death Place (GEAB)
DPL	Diagnostic Peritoneal Lavage [*Medicine*] (MELL)
DPM	Dopamine [*Medicine*] (MELL)
DPMI	DuPont Photomasks [*NASDAQ symbol*] (SG)
DPN	Diabetic Proximal Neuropathy [*Medicine*] (MELL)
DPPDB	Digital Point Positioning Data Base (GEOI)
DPRL	Digital Property Rights Language
DPS	Department of Public Safety [*Arizona*]
DPS	Descending Perineum Syndrome [*Medicine*] (MELL)
DPS	Digital Production System (GEOI)
DPS	Dysesthetic Pain Syndrome [*Medicine*] (MELL)
DPSC	Detainees Parents' Support Committee
DPSL	Database Publishing Systems Limited
Dpt	Department (GEOI)
DPUD	Duodenal Peptic Ulcer Disease [*Medicine*] (MELL)
DPUS	Directory of Physicians in the United States [*A publication*] (MELL)
DPV	Dorsal Penis Vein [*Medicine*] (MELL)
DPW	Digital Power [*AMEX symbol*] (SG)

DPZ.............. Deutsches Primatenzentrum GmbH Goettingen [*German Primate Center*] (GVA)
DQZ............. Duquesne Light 7.375% Bonds [*NYSE symbol*] (SG)
DR.............. Date Rape (MELL)
DR.............. Deoxyribose (MELL)
DR.............. Detached Retina (MELL)
DR.............. Diaper Rash (MELL)
DR.............. Diocesan Registry (GEAB)
DR.............. Directives
DR.............. Dominican Republic (MILB)
Dr .... Door
DR.............. Drifting (WEAT)
DR.............. Drug Receptor (MELL)
DR.............. Drug Residue (MELL)
DR.............. Drug Resistance (MELL)
DR.............. Ductus Reuniens (MELL)
DRA............ Democratic Republic of Afghanistan
DRA............ Drug-Related Admission (MELL)
DRB............ Demonstrated Reserve Base
DRC............ Dain Rauscher [*NYSE symbol*] (SG)
DRD............ Dorsal Root Damage (MELL)
DRD............ Drug-Related Dementia (MELL)
DRD............ Duane Reade [*NYSE symbol*] (SG)
DRE............ Duke-Weeks Realty [*NYSE symbol*] (SG)
DRES .... Dietary Risk Evaluation System [*Environmental Protection Agency*] (EPAT)
DRF .... Dan River 'A' [*NYSE symbol*] (SG)
drg.............. Drainage (MELL)
DRGE.......... Drainage (MELL)
DRM .... Digital Rights Management
DRM .... Donor-Recipient Matching [*Medicine*] (MELL)
DROC.......... Democratic Republic of Congo (MILB)
DRP .... Drug-Related Problem (MELL)
DRQ............ Diagnostic Radiographic Quality (MELL)
DRQ............ Dril-Quip, Inc. [*NYSE symbol*] (SG)
DRR............ Data Review Record [*Environmental Protection Agency*] (EPAT)
DRRA.......... Dura Automotive Sys'A' [*NASDAQ symbol*] (SG)
DRS .... Disability Rating Scale (MELL)
DRS .... Duane's Retraction Syndrome [*Medicine*] (MELL)
DRT .... Dermal Regeneration Template [*Medicine*] (MELL)
DRT .... Distal Renal Tubular Acidosis [*Medicine*] (MELL)
DRTRS......... District Report of Transported Resident Students
DS.............. Decompression Sickness (MELL)
DS.............. Deep Sedative (MELL)
DS.............. Deep Sleep (MELL)
DS.............. Diffuse Scleroderma [*Medicine*] (MELL)
DS.............. Discharge Summary [*Medicine*] (MELL)
DS.............. Disorganized Schizophrenia [*Medicine*] (MELL)
DS.............. Dressler's Syndrome [*Medicine*] (MELL)
DS.............. Drug Screening (MELL)
DS.............. Dry Socket [*Medicine*] (MELL)
DSAC .... Defense Systems Affordability Council
DSB .... Direct Sounding Broadcast (EOSA)
DSCM .... drugstore.com, Inc. [*NASDAQ symbol*] (SG)
dsct............. Descendant (GEAB)
DSD .... Dayton Superior'A' [*NYSE symbol*] (SG)
DSE............. Deep Sky Exploration
DSE............. Diffuse Spasm of Esophagus [*Medicine*] (MELL)
DSE............. Dry Skin Eczema (MELL)
DSF .... Diffuse Sound Field (MELL)
DSG .... Dry Sterile Gauze (MELL)
DSHS .... Deliberate Self-Harm Syndrome [*Medicine*] (MELL)
DSL.............. Downey Financial [*NYSE symbol*] (SG)
DSM............. Diamond-Shaped Murmur [*Medicine*] (MELL)
DSM............. Disposable Surgical Mask (MELL)
DSMIV .... Diagnostic and Statistical Manual, 4th Edition [*A publication*]
DSNT .... Distant (WEAT)
DSOFC......... Dark Shadows Official Fan Club (EA)

DSP .... Decreased Sensory Perception (MELL)
DSP .... Delayed Sleep Phase (MELL)
DSP .... Digital Subtraction Phlebography (MELL)
DSP .... DSP Communications [*NYSE symbol*] (SG)
DSPD........... Delayed Sleep-Phase Disorder (MELL)
DSR .... Dry Sterile Dressing [*Medicine*] (MELL)
DSRCT......... Desmoplastic Small Round-Cell Tumor [*Medicine*] (MELL)
DS-RP.......... Deafness Sensorineural, Recessive Profound [*Medicine*] (MELL)
DSS .... Direct State Services
dSSc .... Diffuse Systemic Sclerosis
DSTP .... Delaware State Testing Program
DSU .... Day Surgery Unit (MELL)
DSWS .... Disorders of Sleep-Wake Schedule (MELL)
dsx............. Doublesex
DT.............. Desmoid Tumor [*Medicine*] (MELL)
DT.............. Deutsche Telekom ADS [*NYSE symbol*] (SG)
DT.............. Diet Therapy (MELL)
DT.............. Diuretic Therapy [*Medicine*] (MELL)
DT.............. Dog Tick (MELL)
DT.............. Dominant Trait (MELL)
DT.............. Drug Therapy (MELL)
DT.............. Drug Toxicity (MELL)
DTaP........... Diptheria and Tetanus Toxoids Combined with Acellular Pertussis Vaccine [*Medicine*] (MELL)
DTB............ Detroit Edison 7.54% 'QUIDS' [*NYSE symbol*] (SG)
DTC............ Distal Transverse Crease (MELL)
DTG .... Date-Time-Group
DTG .... Diffuse Toxic Goiter [*Medicine*] (MELL)
DTG .... Dollar Thrifty Auto Grp [*NYSE symbol*] (SG)
DTH .... Detroit Edison 7.375% 'QUIDS' [*NYSE symbol*] (SG)
DTICH .... Delayed Traumatic Intracerebral Hematoma [*Medicine*] (MELL)
DTL .... Dal-Tile Intl. [*NYSE symbol*] (SG)
DTP .... Distal Tingling on Pressure [*Medicine*] (MELL)
dtr.............. Daughter (GEAB)
DTS .... Detector Test System
DTW .... Duty to Warn (MELL)
DTx............ Dallas Texans [*National Football League*] [*1960-62*] (NFLA)
DU .... Device Upgrade
DU .... Dual-Use
DU .... Dust in Suspension in the Air (WEAT)
DUA .... Dorsal Uterine Artery [*Medicine*] (MELL)
DUAP.......... Dual-Use Applications Program
DUD .... Duodenal Ulcer Diet [*Medicine*] (MELL)
DUF .... Drug Use Forecast (MELL)
DUID........... Driving Under the Influence of Drugs (MELL)
DUO .... Disk Unseen Object
DUT .... Duke Energy 6.60% Sr Notes'C' [*NYSE symbol*] (SG)
d/v .... Danube View
DVC .... Direct Visualization of Vocal Cords (MELL)
DVD .... Dover Downs Entertainment [*NYSE symbol*] (SG)
DVG .... Deutsche Veterinaermedizinische Gesellschaft [*German Veterinary Association*] (GVA)
DVI............. DVI, Inc. [*NYSE symbol*] (SG)
DVM........... Divisional Veterinary Manager (GVA)
DVNT .... Diversinet Corp. [*NASDAQ symbol*] (SG)
DW............. Deworming (MELL)
DW............. Doing Well (MELL)
DWCC .... Differential White Cell Count [*Medicine*] (MELL)
DWF............ Dollywood Foundation (EA)
DWL............ Detergent Worker's Lung [*Medicine*] (MELL)
DWS .... Dandy-Walker Syndrome [*Medicine*] (MELL)
DWS .... Doppler Wind Sensor (EOSA)
DWS .... Double Whammy Syndrome [*Medicine*] (MELL)
DWT .... Duck Waddle Test (MELL)
DX............. Dynex Capital [*NYSE symbol*] (SG)
dy .... Died Young (GEAB)
DYH .... Double Yellow Headed Amazon [*Bird*]
DYS .... Distribucion y Servico ADS [*NYSE symbol*] (SG)
DZT............. Dizygotic (MELL)

E

By Acronym

E	Endogenous (MELL)
E	Ephelis (MELL)
E	Expected Value
E	Kinetic Energy (MELL)
EA	Early Amniocentesis [*Medicine*] (MELL)
EA	Edetic Acid (MELL)
EA	Elder Abuse (MELL)
EA	Embryonic Antibody [*Medicine*] (MELL)
EA	Endometrial Ablation [*Medicine*] (MELL)
EA	Epidural Abscess [*Medicine*] (MELL)
EA	Erythrocyte Antiserum [*Medicine*] (MELL)
Ea	Estonia (MILB)
EAA	Electro-Acupuncture Analgesia [*Medicine*] (MELL)
EAA	Everglades Agricultural Area
EAA	Extrinsic Allergic Alveolitis [*Medicine*] (MELL)
EAC	Evaluation Analysis Center [*Army*]
EACOA	Endometrioid Endocarcinoma of Ovary [*Medicine*] (MELL)
EAD	Early After-Depolarization [*Medicine*] (MELL)
EAD	Exogenous Antigen Disease [*Medicine*] (MELL)
EAE	Edetic Acid Eugenics [*Medicine*] (MELL)
EAEVE	European Association of Establishments for Veterinary Education (GVA)
EAF	Extra-Articular Fracture [*Medicine*] (MELL)
EAG	Electroarteriography [*Medicine*] (MELL)
E & A	Evaluate and Advise [*Medicine*] (MELL)
E & E	Eye and Ear (MELL)
E & H	Euchromatin and Heterochromatin [*Medicine*] (MELL)
E & U	Erosion and Ulcer [*Medicine*] (MELL)
EAP	Ectopic Abdominal Pregnancy (MELL)
EAPA	Employee Assistance Program Association
EAPG	European Association of Petroleum Geologists (QUAC)
EASVO	European Association of State Veterinary Officers (GVA)
EAWS	Enlisted Aviation Warfare Specialist
EAZWVS	European Association of Zoo and Wildlife Veterinary Surgeons (GVA)
EB	Endometrial Biopsy [*Medicine*]
EB	Escape Beat [*Medicine*] (MELL)
EB	Excisional Biopsy [*Medicine*] (MELL)
EBA	Euro Banking Association
EBAA	Electric Boat Association of the Americas (EA)
EBAY	eBay, Inc. [*NASDAQ symbol*] (SG)
EBC	EdperBrascan Corp.'A' [*AMEX symbol*] (SG)
EBCT	Electron Beam Computed Tomography
EBFP	Enhanced Blue Fluorescent Protein
EBH	Epidermolysis Bullosa Hereditaria [*Dermatology*]
EBI	Electron Beam Instrumentation (MELL)
EBI	Equality Bancorp [*AMEX symbol*] (SG)
EBL	Endoscopic Band Ligation (MELL)
EBM	Evidence-Based Medicine
E-box	Electronic Box
EBRA	European Biomedical Research Association (GVA)
EBS	Elastic Back Strap (MELL)
EBS	Emergency Bypass Surgery (MELL)
EBS	Equal Breath Sounds (MELL)
EBv	Epstein-Barr Virus (MELL)
EBV-1	Epstein-Barr Virus Type 1 (MELL)
EBV-2	Epstein-Barr Virus Type 2 (MELL)
EBVS	European Board of Veterinary Specialisation (GVA)
EC	Early China
EC	Ectopia Cordis [*Medicine*] (MELL)
Ec	Ecuador (MILB)
EC	Electrocautery [*Medicine*] (MELL)
EC	Electrode Catheter [*Medicine*] (MELL)
EC	Endotracheal Catheter [*Medicine*] (MELL)
EC	Esophageal Chalasia [*Medicine*] (MELL)
EC	Excitation-Contraction [*Medicine*] (MELL)
ECA	Echinococcus Antibody [*Medicine*] (MELL)
ECA	Economic Community for Africa (EPAT)
ECA	Electrode Catheter Ablation [*Medicine*] (MELL)
ECA	Encal Energy [*NYSE symbol*] (SG)
ECA	Endocervical Aspiration [*Medicine*] (MELL)
ECA	Endocervical Aspirator [*Medicine*] (MELL)
ECA	Enteric Coated Aspirin (MELL)
ECA	External Carotid Artery [*Medicine*] (MELL)
ECAC	Enhanced Counter Air Capability [*Military*]
ECACC	European Council of American Chambers of Commerce (EA)
ECAR	European College for Animal Reproduction (GVA)
ECD	Epithelial Corneal Dystrophy [*Medicine*] (MELL)
ECF	Extracapsular Fracture [*Medicine*] (MELL)
ECG	Electrocardiography [*Medicine*] (MELL)
ECG	Endocrine Gland [*Medicine*] (MELL)
ECGM	Electrocardiagraphic Monitoring [*Medicine*] (MELL)
ECGO	Amer Eco [*NASDAQ symbol*] (SG)
ECH	Endocardial Hemorrhage [*Medicine*] (MELL)
ECH	Epicardial Hemorrhage [*Medicine*] (MELL)
ECH	Episodic Cluster Headache (MELL)
ECHA	Executive Committee for Humanitarian Affairs [*United Nations*]
ECIS	Environmental Concern Interaction Score
ECM	Enchondromatosis [*Medicine*] (MELL)
ECM	Esophagocardiomyotomy [*Medicine*] (MELL)
ECM	Extracellular Mass [*Medicine*] (MELL)
ECML	Electronic Commerce Modeling Language
ECMO	Extracorporeal Membrane Oxidation [*Medicine*] (MELL)
ECNS	Electronic Trading Systems [*Finance*]
ECO157	Escherichia Coli 0157 [*Virulent strain of the bacterium E. coli*] [*Medicine*] (MELL)
ecol	Ecology (BEE)
econ	Economics (BEE)
EconMin	Economics Minister
ECOS	Environmental Council of the States (EPAT)
ECOS	Extracardiac Obstructive Shock [*Medicine*] (MELL)
ECP	Effective Core Potential
ECP	Emitter Current Programmer (MELL)
ECPA	Early Childhood Program Aid
ECPAT	End Child Prostitution and Trafficking [*An association*]
ECPD	External Counterpressure Device [*Medicine*] (MELL)
ECPR	External Cardiopulmonary Resuscitation [*Medicine*] (MELL)
ECR	Enforcement Case Review [*Environmental science*] (EPAT)
ECSGY	ECsoft Group ADR [*NASDAQ symbol*] (SG)
ECTR	Endoscopic Carpal Tunnel Release [*Medicine*] (MELL)
ECU	Electrocautery Unit [*Medicine*] (MELL)
ECV	Epithelial Cell Vacuolization [*Medicine*] (MELL)
ECVA	European College of Veterinary Anaesthesia (GVA)
ECVCN	European College of Veterinary and Comparative Nutrition (GVA)
ECVIM-CA	European College of Veterinary Internal Medicine-Companion Animals (GVA)
ECVO	European College of Veterinary Ophthalmologists (GVA)
ECVP	European College of Veterinary Pathologists (GVA)
ECVPH-PM-FS	European College for Veterinary Public Health, Population Medicine, and Food Scince (GVA)
ECVS	European College of Veterinary Surgeons (GVA)
ED	Eating Disorder (MELL)
Ed	Edible
ed	Education (BEE)
ED	Ejaculatory Dysfunction [*Medicine*] (MELL)
ED	Elbow Dislocation (MELL)
ED	Entering Diagnosis [*Medicine*] (MELL)
ED	Equivalent Dose (QUAC)
ED	Erb Disease [*Medicine*] (MELL)
ED	Erectile Dysfunction [*Medicine*] (MELL)
ED	Esophageal Diverticulum [*Medicine*] (MELL)
ED50	Median Effective Dose
EDA	Engineering Design Agreement
EDA	Epidermal Abscess [*Medicine*] (MELL)
EDA	Epidural Anesthesia [*Medicine*] (MELL)
EDAC	Early Defibrillation/Advanced Care [*Medicine*] (MELL)
EDI	Endosseous Dental Implant
EDI/EDA	Electronic Data Interchange and Electronic Data Access
EDL	End-Diastolic Load [*Medicine*] (MELL)
EDMC	Education Management [*NASDAQ symbol*] (SG)
EDP	EDP-Electricidade Portugal ADS [*NYSE symbol*] (SG)
EDP	Emergency Department Physician
EDR	Early Diastolic Relaxation [*Medicine*] (MELL)
EDR	Edrophonium [*Medicine*] (MELL)
EDR	Enzyme-Dependent Reaction [*Medicine*] (MELL)
EDS	Electronic Data Systems [*NYSE symbol*] (SG)
EDS	Engineering Design Simulator
EDT	End-Diastolic Thickness [*Medicine*] (MELL)
edu	Education (BEE)
EDUT	EduTrek Intl.'A' [*NASDAQ symbol*] (SG)
EDX	Electronic Data Exchange (EPAT)
EE	Esterified Estrogen [*Medicine*] (MELL)
EE	External Ear (MELL)

EEAP	Environmental Effects Assessment Panel
EEE	Canadian 88 Energy [*AMEX symbol*] (SG)
EEE	Edema, Erythema, and Exudate [*Medicine*] (MELL)
EEG	Echo-Encephalography [*Medicine*] (MELL)
EELN	E-Loan, Inc. [*NASDAQ symbol*] (SG)
EELV	End-Expiratory Lung Volume [*Medicine*] (MELL)
EEM	Ebauches Electronic Marin
EERP	Extended Endocardial Resection Procedure [*Medicine*] (MELL)
EEUA	End-to-End Ureteral Anastomosis [*Medicine*] (MELL)
EEV	Eastern Equine Virus (MELL)
EF	Enteric Fistula [*Medicine*] (MELL)
EF	Epicondylar Fracture [*Medicine*] (MELL)
EF	Extended Field (MELL)
EFA	Enhancing Factor of Allergy [*Medicine*] (MELL)
EFA	Everglades Forever Act
EFAB	Electrochemical Fabrication
EFAS	Embryo-Fetal Alcohol Syndrome (MELL)
EFAX	eFax.com, Inc. [*AMEX symbol*] (SG)
EFB	Evening School for Foreign Born
EFC	EFC Bancorp [*AMEX symbol*] (SG)
EFD	Episode Free Day [*Medicine*] (MELL)
EFD	Erlenmeyer Flask Deformity [*Medicine*] (MELL)
EFDEX	Electronic Food and Beverage Exchange
EFNT	Efficient Networks [*NASDAQ symbol*] (SG)
EFO	Equivalent Field Office [*Environmental Protection Agency*] (EPAT)
EFT	Erythrocyte Fragility Test [*Medicine*] (MELL)
EFT	Essential-Familial Tremor [*Medicine*] (MELL)
EFU	Evaluation and Follow-Up [*Medicine*] (MELL)
EG	Equatorial Guinea (MILB)
EG	Estrogen Gel [*Medicine*] (MELL)
EG	Exfoliation Glaucoma [*Medicine*] (MELL)
EGA	Efferent Glomerular Arteriole [*Medicine*] (MELL)
EGAS	Energy Search [*NASDAQ symbol*] (SG)
EGC	Early Gastric Carcinoma [*Medicine*] (MELL)
EGC	Early Glottic Carcinoma [*Medicine*] (MELL)
EGC	Epiglottic Cartilage [*Medicine*] (MELL)
EGG	Electrogastrography [*Medicine*] (MELL)
EGGS	Egghead.com, Inc. [*NASDAQ symbol*] (SG)
EGLO	eGlobe, Inc. [*NASDAQ symbol*] (SG)
EGNB	Enteric Gram Negative Bacteria [*Medicine*] (MELL)
EGRET	Epidemiological, Graphics, Estimation, and Testing [*Program*]
EGRP	E Trade Group [*NASDAQ symbol*] (SG)
Egypt	Egyptian (BEE)
EH	Endometrial Hyperplasia [*Medicine*] (MELL)
EH	Epidermolytic Hyperkeratosis [*Dermatology*]
EH	Epidural Hematoma [*Medicine*] (MELL)
EHBP	Essential High Blood Pressure (MELL)
EHD	Environmental Hypersensitivity Disease [*Medicine*] (MELL)
EHS	Ectopic-Hypercalcemia Syndrome [*Medicine*] (MELL)
EHS	Employee Health Service (MELL)
EHT	Essential Hypertension (MELL)
EI	Ectopic Implantation [*Medicine*] (MELL)
EI	Emotional Intelligence (MELL)
EI	Erythema Infectiosum [*Medicine*] (MELL)
EIA	Early Infantile Autism [*Medicine*] (MELL)
EIA	Energy Information Agency
EIB	Electrophoretic Immunoblotting [*Medicine*] (MELL)
EID	Espace d'Interpellation Democratique [*Forum for Democratic Consultation*] [*Mali*]
EIDC	Extreme Intervertebral Disk Collapse [*Medicine*] (MELL)
EIDD	Epileptic Intentional Deficit Disorder (MELL)
EIDSY	Eidos PLC ADR [*NASDAQ symbol*] (SG)
EIEC	Enteroinvasive E. coli [*Medicine*] (MELL)
EIEE	Early Infantile Epileptic Encephalopathy [*Medicine*] (MELL)
EIEN	Endometrial Intraepithelial Neoplasia [*Medicine*] (MELL)
EIFL Direct	Electronic Information for Libraries Direct
EIL	Electrochemical Ind (1952) [*AMEX symbol*] (SG)
EIM	E-Sim Ltd. [*AMEX symbol*] (SG)
EIMI	Exercise-Induced Myocardial Ischemia [*Medicine*] (MELL)
EIN	Echelon International [*NYSE symbol*] (SG)
EIN	Endometrial Intraepithelial Neoplasia [*Medicine*] (MELL)
EIP	Enterprise Information Portals
EIPSL	Entry Age Normal with Frozen Initial Past Service Liability [*Business term*]
EIV	External Iliac Vein (MELL)
EJN	External Jugular Vein (MELL)
EJP	European Journal of Physics [*A publication*]
EKG	Electrocardiography [*Medicine*] (MELL)
EKO	Ekco Group [*AMEX symbol*] (SG)
EKS	Epidemic Kaposi's Sarcoma [*Medicine*] (MELL)
EL	Ectopia Lentis [*Medicine*] (MELL)
EL	Emergency Laparotomy [*Medicine*] (MELL)
EL	Epidemic Listeriosis [*Medicine*] (MELL)
EL	Excimer Laser [*Medicine*] (MELL)
EL	Exploratory Laparotomy [*Medicine*] (MELL)
ELB	Early-Labeled Bilirubin [*Medicine*] (MELL)
ELB	Florida P&L 7.05% CABCO Tr Debs [*NYSE symbol*] (SG)
ELBO	Electronics Boutique Hldgs [*NASDAQ symbol*] (SG)
ELC	Expression-Linked Copy (MELL)
ELCP	European Lake Coring Project (QUAC)
ELCRA	Elliott-Larsen Civil Rights Act [*Michigan*]
ELD	Emergency Laparotomy Drain [*Medicine*] (MELL)
ELD	Endolymphatic Duct [*Medicine*] (MELL)
ELDP	European Lake Drilling Program (QUAC)
elect	Electrical (BEE)

electr	Electricity (BEE)
ELIA	Enzyme-Linked Immunoassay (MELL)
E-LIDAR	Experimental Lidar (EOSA)
ELIX	Electric Lightwave 'A' [*NASDAQ symbol*] (SG)
elm	Element (MILB)
ELMG	EMS Technologies [*NASDAQ symbol*] (SG)
ELN	Encapsulated Lymph Node [*Medicine*] (MELL)
ELNK	Earthlink Network [*NASDAQ symbol*] (SG)
ELOT	Executone Info Sys [*NASDAQ symbol*] (SG)
ELP	Comp Paranaense Energia 'B' ADS [*NYSE symbol*] (SG)
EIS	El Salvador (MILB)
ELS	Endolymphatic Sac [*Medicine*] (MELL)
ELSI	Electrosource, Inc. [*NASDAQ symbol*] (SG)
ELT	Euglobulin Lysis Test [*Medicine*] (MELL)
ELV	Efferent Lymphatic Vessel [*Medicine*] (MELL)
ElvisNet EPFC	Elvisnet Elvis Presley Fan Club (EA)
EM	Early Melanoma [*Medicine*] (MELL)
EM	Electron Microscopy [*Medicine*] (MELL)
em	Emirates (BEE)
EM	Erythema Migrans [*Medicine*] (MELL)
EM	Extracellular Matrix [*Medicine*] (MELL)
EMA	Elephant Managers Association (GVA)
EMAN	Ecological Monitoring and Assessment Network [*Canada*] (QUAC)
EMANJ	Educational Media Association of New Jersey
Emb	Embassy
emb	Embryo (MELL)
EMBD	Embedded (WEAT)
EMBM	Environment-Mapped Bump Mapping [*Computer science*]
EmbOff	Embasy Office
EMC	Endometrial Cancer [*Medicine*] (MELL)
EMC	Endometrial Carcinoma [*Medicine*] (MELL)
EMC	Endometrial Curettage [*Medicine*] (MELL)
EMC	Essential Mixed Cryoglobulinemia [*Medicine*] (MELL)
EMCB	Endomyocardial Biopsy [*Medicine*] (MELL)
EMD	Electromyocardial Dissociation [*Medicine*] (MELL)
EMD	Erythema Multiforme [*Medicine*] (MELL)
EMD	Esophageal Myotonia Dystrophica [*Medicine*] (MELL)
EMF	Elastomyofibrosis [*Medicine*] (MELL)
EMF	Electronic Fetal Monitoring [*Medicine*] (MELL)
EMFF	Edward Mulhare's Foundations (EA)
EMG	Electromyelogram [*Medicine*] (MELL)
EMG	Essential Monoclonal Gammopathy [*Medicine*] (MELL)
EMI	Egg Marketing Inspectorate (GVA)
EMI	Elderly and Mentally Infirmed (MELL)
EMI	Emergency Medical Identification (MELL)
EMIS	Emergency Medical Indentification Symbol (MELL)
EMLNG	External Mammary Lymph Node Group [*Medicine*] (MELL)
EMP	Extraocular Muscle Palsy [*Medicine*] (MELL)
empl	Employment (PROS)
EMPS	Exertional Muscle Pain Syndrome [*Medicine*] (MELL)
EMR	Endoscopic Mucosal Resection [*Medicine*] (MELL)
EMR	Extra-Mural Rotations (GVA)
EMS	Early Morning Stiffness (MELL)
EMS	Early Mortality Syndrome [*Reproductive disturbance in fish*]
EMS	Elvis Presley Memorial Society (EA)
EMS	Endoscopic Mucosectomy (MELL)
EMS	Extra-Mural Studies (GVA)
EMSA	Eugene Meylan, SA
EMSU	Early Morning Specimen of Urine (MELL)
EMT	Embratel Participacoes ADS [*NYSE symbol*] (SG)
EMT	Emergency Medical Team (MELL)
EMT	Ergonovine Maleate Test [*Medicine*] (MELL)
EMTM	Executive Master's in Technology Management
EMTS	Environmental Monitoring Testing Site (EPAT)
EMU	Early Morning Urine (MELL)
EMU	Epilepsy Monitoring Unit [*Medicine*] (MELL)
EMUS	Early Morning Urine Specimen (MELL)
EN	Efferent Nerve [*Medicine*] (MELL)
EN	Endoscopy [*Medicine*] (MELL)
EN	Enteritis Necroticans [*Medicine*] (MELL)
EN	Entrapment Neuropathy [*Medicine*] (MELL)
EN	Essentially Negative (MELL)
EN	Euro-Nevada Mining [*Toronto Stock Exchange symbol*] (SG)
ENAM	European North Atlantic Margin (QUAC)
ENBS	Early Neurobehavioral Score (MELL)
ENBX	Einstein/Noah Bagel [*NASDAQ symbol*] (SG)
ENC	Enesco Group [*NYSE symbol*] (SG)
END	Early Neonatal Death (MELL)
ENDL	Evaluated Nuclear Data Library
Eng	English (BEE)
ENGA	Engage Technologies [*NASDAQ symbol*] (SG)
Engin	Engineering (BEE)
engr	Engineer (PROS)
ENGSY	Energis PLC ADS [*NASDAQ symbol*] (SG)
ENN	Equity Inns [*NYSE symbol*] (SG)
eno	Enough (GEAB)
ENP	Everglades National Park
EnPA	Environmental Performance Agreement (EPAT)
ens	Ensign (GEAB)
ENS	Epidermal Nevus Syndrome [*Medicine*]
ensu	Ensuing (GEAB)
ENT	EQUANT N.V. ADS [*NYSE symbol*] (SG)
Entomol	Entomology (BEE)
ENTRI	Environmental Treaties and Resource Indicators [*Internet resource*]
ENTU	Entrust Technologies [*NASDAQ symbol*] (SG)

EOA............	External Oblique Aponeurosis [*Medicine*]	(MELL)
EOA............	External Ostomy Appliance [*Medicine*]	(MELL)
EOB............	Exstrophy of Bladder [*Medicine*]	(MELL)
EOBC	Early-Onset Breast Cancer	(MELL)
EOC............	Early Ovarian Cancer	(MELL)
EOC............	Empresa Nac'l De El Chile, ADS [*NYSE symbol*]	(SG)
EOC............	Enema of Choice [*Medicine*]	(MELL)
EOC............	Epiphyseal Ossification Center [*Medicine*]	(MELL)
EOC............	Epithelial Ovarian Cancer	(MELL)
EOD............	End-Organ Dysfunction [*Medicine*]	(MELL)
eod	Every Other Day	(MELL)
EOD............	Extent of Disease	(MELL)
EOEC..........	Early-Onset Endocarditis [*Medicine*]	(MELL)
EO-ICWG.....	Earth Observations International Coordination Working Group	(EOSA)
EOJ............	Extrahepatic Obstructive Jaundice [*Medicine*]	(MELL)
EOL............	End of Lecture [*Online dialog*]	
EOLC..........	End-of-Life Care	(MELL)
EOM............	Extraocular Movement [*Medicine*]	(MELL)
EOP............	End of Pipe	(EPAT)
EOP............	External Occipital Protuberance [*Medicine*]	(MELL)
EOPM..........	Electro-Optic Phase Modulation	(EOSA)
EOSP	Earth Observing Scanner Polarimeter	
EOSP	Earth Observing Scanning Polarimeter	(EOSA)
EP............	Ectopic Pacemaker	(MELL)
EP............	Edematous Pancreatitis [*Medicine*]	(MELL)
EP............	Emergency Physician	(MELL)
EP............	Erb Paralysis [*Medicine*]	(MELL)
EP............	Ergot Poisoning	(MELL)
EP............	Estrogen Patch	(MELL)
EP............	Experimental Product	(EPAT)
EPC............	Elevated Plasma Cholesterol	(MELL)
EPC............	Endoscopic Pancreatocholangiography [*Medicine*]	(MELL)
EPD............	Emergency Planning District [*Environmental science*]	(EPAT)
EPD............	Enterprise Products Partners [*NYSE symbol*]	(SG)
EPD............	European Pollen Database	(QUAC)
EPH............	Edema, Proteinuria, and Hypertension [*Medicine*]	(MELL)
EPH............	Episodic Paroxysmal Hemicrania [*Medicine*]	(MELL)
EPH............	Extensor Proprius Hallucis [*Medicine*]	(MELL)
EPH............	Extrapyramidal Hypertonia [*Medicine*]	(MELL)
EPHSOC.......	Ephemera Society of America	(EA)
EPI............	Consolidated Ed 7.35%'PINES' [*NYSE symbol*]	(SG)
EPI............	Environmental Preference Inventory	
EPIC............	Electronic Publishing Initiative at Columbia	
EPIC............	Epicor Software [*NASDAQ symbol*]	(SG)
EPLI............	Employment Practices Liability Insurance	
EPOP	European Polar-Orbiting Platform	(EOSA)
EPP............	Epiphyseal Plate [*Medicine*]	(MELL)
EPPB	End Positive-Pressure Breathing	(MELL)
EPR............	Entertainment Properties Tr [*NYSE symbol*]	(SG)
EPRS	Electron Pulse Radiolysis System [*Medicine*]	(MELL)
EPS............	Enzyme Pancreatic Secretion [*Medicine*]	(MELL)
EPS............	European Polar Satellite	
EPSA..........	Elevated Prostate-Specific Antigen [*Medicine*]	(MELL)
EPSAL..........	Elevated Prostate-Specific Antigen Level [*Medicine*]	(MELL)
EPV............	External Pudendal Vein [*Medicine*]	(MELL)
eqpt	Equipment	(MILB)
EQT............	Environmental Quality Technology	
EQY............	Equity One [*NYSE symbol*]	(SG)
ER............	Ecosystem Restoration [*Environmental Protection Agency*]	(EPAT)
ER............	Electroresection [*Medicine*]	(MELL)
ER............	Ergonomics	
Er............	Eritrea	(MILB)
ER............	Erythrocyte Receptor [*Medicine*]	(MELL)
ER............	Escape Rhythm [*Medicine*]	(MELL)
ER............	Esophageal Reflux [*Medicine*]	(MELL)
ER............	Extrarespiratory	
ERA............	Estradiol Receptor Assay [*Medicine*]	(MELL)
ERA............	Exercise-Related Anaphylaxis [*Medicine*]	(MELL)
ERAS	Endogenous Reninangiotensin System [*Medicine*]	(MELL)
ERC............	Energy Research [*AMEX symbol*]	(SG)
ERD............	Early Retirement for Disability	(MELL)
ERGATT	European Research Group for Alternatives in Toxicity Testing	(GVA)
ERHD..........	Exposure-Related Hypothermic Death	(MELL)
ERICY	Ericsson, L.M., Tel'B'ADS [*NASDAQ symbol*]	(SG)
ERM............	Exposure Radical Mastectomy	(MELL)
ERMS..........	Exacerbating-Remitting Multiple Sclerosis	(MELL)
EROS	Electric Resonance Optothermal Spectrometer	
ERP............	Enzyme-Releasing Peptide	(MELL)
ERPF..........	Estimated Renal Plasma Flow [*Medicine*]	(MELL)
ERS............	Emergency Response System	(MELL)
ERT............	Emergency Room Triage	(MELL)
ERT............	Enzyme Replacement Therapy [*Medicine*]	(MELL)
ERT............	Extended-Release Tablets [*Medicine*]	(MELL)
ERTH	EarthShell Corp. [*NASDAQ symbol*]	(SG)
ERTS-1	Earth Resources Technology Satellite-1	(EOSA)
ES............	Egypt Suez [*Crude oil*]	
ES............	Elastic Stockings	(MELL)
ES............	Embryonic Stem [*Medicine*]	(MELL)
ES............	Embryonic System [*Medicine*]	
ES............	Emotional Stress	(MELL)
ES............	Entotic Sound [*Medicine*]	(MELL)
ES............	Esophageal Spasm [*Medicine*]	(MELL)
ESA............	Extended Stay Amer. [*NYSE symbol*]	(SG)
ESAD	Earth Science and Applications Division [*NASA*]	(EOSA)
ESAT..........	Esat Telecom Group ADS [*NASDAQ symbol*]	(SG)

ESAT..........	Extrasystolic Atrial Tachycardia [*Medicine*]	(MELL)
ESCC..........	Epidural Spinal Cord Compression [*Medicine*]	(MELL)
ESD............	Electrical Overstress/Electrostatic Discharge Association, Inc.	
ESEP..........	Extreme Somatosensory Evoked Potential [*Medicine*]	(MELL)
ESES..........	Electrical Status Epilepticus during Sleep [*Medicine*]	(MELL)
ESFM..........	European Society of Feline Medicine	(GVA)
ESH............	Earth System History	(QUAC)
ESI............	Epidural Steroid Injection [*Medicine*]	(MELL)
ESKD..........	End-Stage Kidney Disease	(MELL)
ESLF..........	End-Stage Liver Failure	(MELL)
ESLP..........	Electric Shocklike Pain	(MELL)
ESM............	Endometrial Stromal Meiosis [*Medicine*]	(MELL)
ESM............	Erector Spinae Muscle [*Medicine*]	(MELL)
ESMSA........	18 Square Meter Sailing Association	(EA)
ESOA..........	Employee Stock Ownership Association	
ESP............	Electric Shock Protector	(MELL)
ESP............	Endometritis, Salpingitis, and Peritonitis [*Medicine*]	(MELL)
ESP............	Extended Service Program	
ESPA..........	Elementary School Proficiency Assessment	
ESPA..........	Elementary School Proficiency Test	
ESPI...........	e.spire Communications [*NASDAQ symbol*]	(SG)
ESPRIT	Espatriate Turin [*Italy*] [*An association*]	
esq............	Esquire	(BEE)
ESR............	Experimental Storage Ring	
ESREF..........	ESG Re Ltd [*NASDAQ symbol*]	(SG)
ESSL..........	Eco Soil Systems [*NASDAQ symbol*]	(SG)
est	Estate	(GEAB)
establ	Establishment	(GEAB)
estd	Estimated	(GEAB)
ESTEC..........	European Space Research and Space Technology Centre	(EOSA)
ESTH..........	Economic Swiss Time Holding	
ESTIV..........	European Society of Toxicology in Vitro	(GVA)
ESU............	Electrosurgical Unit	(MELL)
ESVOT	European Society of Veterinary Orthopaedics and Traumatology	(GVA)
ESWL..........	Electroshock Wave Lithotripsy [*Medicine*]	(MELL)
Et	Egypt	(MILB)
ET	Electrophoretic Type [*Medicine*]	(MELL)
ET	Endocrine Therapy [*Medicine*]	(MELL)
ET	Enterotoxin	(MELL)
ET	Epidemic Threshold	(MELL)
ET	Expiratory Time	(MELL)
ET	Extrathoracic	
ETA............	Embryo Toxicity Assay [*Medicine*]	
ETA............	Endotracheal Airway [*Medicine*]	(MELL)
ETA............	Endotracheal Anesthesia [*Medicine*]	(MELL)
ETD............	Eustachian Tube Dysfunction [*Medicine*]	(MELL)
ETF............	Embryo Toxic Factor [*Medicine*]	
ETI............	Ejection Time Index	(MELL)
ETI............	Endotracheal Intubation [*Medicine*]	(MELL)
ETIG............	Equine Tetanus Immune Globulin	(MELL)
ETIPT..........	Environmental Technology Integrated Process Team	
ETIYRA	El Toro International Yacht Racing Association	(EA)
ETM............	Entercom Communications'A' [*NYSE symbol*]	(SG)
ETN............	Erythrityl Tetranitrate [*Medicine*]	(MELL)
ETOA..........	Estimated Time of Arrival	(MELL)
ETP............	Ephedrine, Theophylline and Phenobarbital [*Medicine*]	(MELL)
ETR............	Emergency Treatment Record	(MELL)
ETS............	Emissions Tracking System [*Environmental Protection Agency*]	(EPAT)
ETS............	Environmental Tobacco Smoke	(MELL)
ETT	ElderTrust SBI [*NYSE symbol*]	(SG)
ETT	Epinephrine Tolerance Test [*Medicine*]	(MELL)
ETTC	Environmental Technology Technical Council	
ETV............	E4L, Inc. [*NYSE symbol*]	(SG)
ETV............	Environmental Technology Verification Program	(EPAT)
ETYS..........	eToys, Inc. [*NASDAQ symbol*]	(SG)
EU	Emotionally Unstable	(MELL)
EU	Etiology Unknown [*Medicine*]	(MELL)
EUG............	Excretory Urography [*Medicine*]	(MELL)
EUnet..........	Europe Network	
EUP............	End-Use Product	(EPAT)
EUP............	Extrauterine Pregnancy	(MELL)
EURADOS	European Radiation Dosimetry Group	
EV	Eaton Vance [*NYSE symbol*]	(SG)
EV	Ebola Virus [*Medicine*]	(MELL)
EV	Echovirus [*Medicine*]	(MELL)
EV	Emissary Vein [*Medicine*]	(MELL)
EV	Enteroviruses [*Medicine*]	(MELL)
EVA............	Echo Virus Antibody [*Medicine*]	(MELL)
EVANE	Evans, Inc. [*NASDAQ symbol*]	(SG)
EVB............	Esophageal Variceal Bleeding [*Medicine*]	(MELL)
EVCI............	Educational Video Conferencing [*NASDAQ symbol*]	(SG)
EVD............	Ebola Virus Disease [*Medicine*]	(MELL)
EVDC..........	European Veterinary Dental College	(GVA)
EVF............	Enterovaginal Fistula [*Medicine*]	(MELL)
EVL............	Enveloping Layer	
EVLG..........	European Veterinary Libraries Group	(GVA)
EVMC..........	Enteroviral Meningitis in Childhood [*Medicine*]	(MELL)
EVMS..........	Earned Value Management System	
EVP............	Enteric Viral Pathogens [*Medicine*]	(MELL)
EVP............	Episcleral Venous Pressure [*Medicine*]	(MELL)
EVP............	Evoked Visual Response [*Medicine*]	(MELL)
EVP............	Extroverted Personality	(MELL)
EVR............	EVEREN Capital [*NYSE symbol*]	(SG)

EVRS .... Early Ventricular Repolarization Syndrome [*Medicine*] (MELL)
EVSSAR .... European Veterinary Society for the Study of Small Animal Reproduction (GVA)
EVT .... External Vacuum Therapy (MELL)
EVV .... Environmental Safeguards [*AMEX symbol*] (SG)
EVZS .... Edinburgh Veterinary Zoological Society (GVA)
EW .... Earwax (MELL)
EWA .... WEBS, Australia Index Series [*AMEX symbol*] (SG)
EWBX .... EarthWeb, Inc. [*NASDAQ symbol*] (SG)
EWC .... WEBS, Canada Index Series [*AMEX symbol*] (SG)
EWD .... WEBS, Sweden Index Series [*AMEX symbol*] (SG)
EWG .... WEBS, Germany Index Series [*AMEX symbol*] (SG)
EWH .... WEBS, Hong Kong Index Series [*AMEX symbol*] (SG)
EWI .... WEBS, Italy Index Series [*AMEX symbol*] (SG)
EWJ .... WEBS, Japan Index Series [*AMEX symbol*] (SG)
EWK .... WEBS, Belgium Index Series [*AMEX symbol*] (SG)
EWL .... Estimated Weight Loss (MELL)
EWL .... WEBS, Switzerland Index Series [*AMEX symbol*] (SG)
EWM .... WEBS, Malaysia(Free)Index Series [*AMEX symbol*] (SG)
EWN .... WEBS, Netherlands Index Series [*AMEX symbol*] (SG)
EWO .... WEBS, Austria Index Series [*AMEX symbol*] (SG)
EWP .... WEBS, Spain Index Series [*AMEX symbol*] (SG)
EWQ .... WEBS, France Index Series [*AMEX symbol*] (SG)
EWS .... WEBS, Singapore(Free)Index Series [*AMEX symbol*] (SG)
EWT .... Erupted Wisdom Teeth (MELL)

EWU .... WEBS, U.K. Index Series [*AMEX symbol*] (SG)
EWW .... WEBS, Mexico(Free)Index Series [*AMEX symbol*] (SG)
EXAFS .... Edge X-Ray Absorption Fine Structure
EXBD .... Corporate Executive Board [*NASDAQ symbol*] (SG)
EXBT .... Exabyte Corp. [*NASDAQ symbol*] (SG)
exc .... Escision (MELL)
Exc .... Excellent
excl .... Excludes (MILB)
EXDS .... Exodus Communications [*NASDAQ symbol*] (SG)
EXEA .... Extendicare, Inc. [*NASDAQ symbol*] (SG)
EXM .... Excel Maritime Carriers [*AMEX symbol*] (SG)
EXO .... Exophoria [*Medicine*] (MELL)
exox .... Executrix (GEAB)
exp .... Expenditure (MILB)
EXP .... Exploloratory [*Medicine*] (MELL)
ExS .... Ex-Smoker (MELL)
ExS .... Extra-Strength (MELL)
Ext .... Exterior
EXTR .... Extreme Networks [*NASDAQ symbol*] (SG)
EXTUB .... Extubation [*Medicine*] (MELL)
exx .... Executrix (GEAB)
EXXA .... EXX, Inc.'A' [*AMEX symbol*] (SG)
EYFP .... Enhanced Yellow Fluorescent Protein
EZ .... Erogenous Zone (MELL)
EZMA .... E-Z EM, Inc.'A' [*AMEX symbol*] (SG)
EZR .... Easyriders, Inc. [*AMEX symbol*] (SG)

By Acronym

F	Fascia	(MELL)
f	Father	(GEAB)
F	Femur	(MELL)
F	Fever	(MELL)
F	Fibroblast	(MELL)
F	Fibula	(MELL)
F	Flexion	(MELL)
F	Floaters	(MELL)
F	Folacin	(MELL)
F	Fontanel	(MELL)
F	Fossa	(MELL)
F	Fundus	(MELL)
fa	Father	(GEAB)
FA	Fludaradine [*Medicine*]	(MELL)
FA	Food Allergy	(MELL)
FAA	Febrile Antigen Agglutination [*Medicine*]	(MELL)
FAA	Formaldehyde, Acetic Acid, and Alcohol	(MELL)
FAAT	Fluorscent Antinuclear Antibody Test	(MELL)
FAB	Antigen Binding Fragments	(MELL)
FAB	Fibroadenoma of Breast [*Medicine*]	(MELL)
FAB	FirstFed Amer Bancorp [*AMEX symbol*]	(SG)
FACE	Free-Air Carbon Dioxide Enrichment	(QUAC)
FACO	First Alliance 'A' [*NASDAQ symbol*]	(SG)
FACS	Facility for Access Control and Security [*RadWare*]	
FACT	Functional Assessment of Cancer Therapy	(MELL)
FAD	Familial Alzheimer's Dementia	(MELL)
FAD	First Appearance of Date	(QUAC)
FAI	Folic Acid Injection	(MELL)
FAI	Food Allergy Insomnia	(MELL)
FAIR	Fund for Appalachian Industrial Restraining	
FairTest	National Center for Fair & Open Testing	
FAJ	Fused Apophyseal Joint [*Medicine*]	(MELL)
FAK	Floating Arm Keyboard	(MELL)
FAL	Fall River Gas [*AMEX symbol*]	(SG)
FALP	Fluoro-Assisted Lumbar Puncture [*Medicine*]	(MELL)
fam	Family	(GEAB)
F & C	Fever and Chills	(MELL)
F & N	Fetus and Neonate	(MELL)
F & S	Fatigue and Sleep	(MELL)
FAP	Family Auto Plan	
FAP	First Appearance	(QUAC)
FAP	Fixed Action Potential	(MELL)
FAPC	Food Animal Practitioners Club [*Ohio State University*]	(GVA)
FARC	Revolutionary Armed Forces of Colombia	
FAS	Functional Acquisition Specialist [*Army*]	
FASC	Fasciculation [*Medicine*]	(MELL)
FASG	Fellow American Society of Genealogists	(GEAB)
FAWC	Farm Animal Welfare Council	(GVA)
FB	Fever Blister	(MELL)
FB	Football	
FB	Footling Breech [*Medicine*]	(MELL)
FB	Frostbite	(MELL)
FBB	Frank Breech Presentation [*Medicine*]	(MELL)
FBC	Flexion Body Cast	(MELL)
FBCP	Familial Benign Chronic Pemphigus [*Medicine*]	(MELL)
FBD	Foreign Born Doctor	(MELL)
FBF	Football Finger	(MELL)
FBHH	Familial Benign Hypocalciuric Hypercalcemia [*Medicine*]	(MELL)
FBI	Foodborne Illness	(MELL)
f/b/o	For the Benefit Of	(PROS)
FBP	First Bancorp [*NYSE symbol*]	(SG)
FBP	Footling Breech Presentation [*Medicine*]	(MELL)
fbr	Fire-Broken Rock [*Archaeology*]	(QUAC)
FBR	Foreign Body Reaction	(MELL)
FBR	Friedman Billings Ramsey Gp'A' [*NYSE symbol*]	(SG)
FBS	Failed Back Syndrome	(MELL)
FBS	Fibrocystic Breast Syndrome [*Medicine*]	(MELL)
FBS	Flabby Back Syndrome [*Medicine*]	(MELL)
FBS	Foreign-Body Sarcoma [*Medicine*]	(MELL)
FBS	Functional Bladder Syndrome [*Medicine*]	(MELL)
FBSS	Failed Back Surgery Syndrome [*Medicine*]	(MELL)
FC	Facial Canal	(MELL)
fc	Fall Color	
FC	Fat Cell	(MELL)
FC	Flail Chest	(MELL)
FC	Flow Cytometry [*Medicine*]	(MELL)

FC	Foster Care	(MELL)
FC	Fovea Centralis	(MELL)
Fc	Fractocumulus Cloud	(WEAT)
FC	Funnel Chest	(MELL)
FCA	Fluorescent Cytoprint Assay	(MELL)
FCAT	Florida Comprehensive Achievement Test	
FCBD	Fibrocystic Breast Disease [*Medicine*]	(MELL)
FCCL	Follicular Center Cell Lymphoma [*Medicine*]	(MELL)
FCCSET	Federal Coordinating Committee on Science	
FCD	Fatal Childhood Diarrhea [*Medicine*]	(MELL)
FCDB	Fibrocystic Disorder of Breast [*Medicine*]	(MELL)
FCF	Fasciocutaneous Flap [*Medicine*]	(MELL)
FCI	Flow Cytometric Immunophenotyping [*Medicine*]	(MELL)
FCI	Food Chemical Intolerance	(MELL)
FCIN	Flour City Intl. [*NASDAQ symbol*]	(SG)
FCIS	Flint Colon Injury Scale [*Medicine*]	(MELL)
FCM	Franklin Telecommunications [*AMEX symbol*]	(SG)
FCMVS	Fetal Cytomegalovirus Syndrome [*Medicine*]	(MELL)
FCN	FTI Consulting [*AMEX symbol*]	(SG)
FCNA	Foxhound Club of North America	(EA)
FCO	Fibrocytoma of Ovary [*Medicine*]	(MELL)
FCOM	Focal Communications [*NASDAQ symbol*]	(SG)
FCRV	Family Campers and Rivers [*An association*]	(EA)
FCS	Fetal Cocaine Syndrome [*Medicine*]	(MELL)
FCS	Fever, Chills, and Sweating	(MELL)
FCS	Foot Compartment Syndrome	(MELL)
FCSIL	Flight Control System Integration Laboratory [*Army*]	
FCST	Flycast Communications [*NASDAQ symbol*]	(SG)
FCT	Ferric Chloride Test [*Medicine*]	(MELL)
FCT	Foramen Cecum of Tongue [*Medicine*]	(MELL)
FD	Fabry's Disease [*Medicine*]	(MELL)
FD	Facial Dyskinesias [*Medicine*]	(MELL)
FD	Fairbanks Dysostosis [*Medicine*]	(MELL)
FD	Fetal Death	(MELL)
FD	Fetal Distress	(MELL)
FD	Fibrous Dysplasia	(MELL)
fd	Field	(MILB)
FD	Folate Deficiency	(MELL)
FD	Footdrop	(MELL)
FDB	First-Degree Burn	(MELL)
FDBLP	Familial Dysbetalipoproteinemia [*Medicine*]	(MELL)
FDC	First-Dollar Coverage [*Insurance*]	(MELL)
FDD	First Digitized Division [*Army*]	
FDM	Fused Deposition Modeling	
fdn	Foundation	(BEE)
FDP	Fresh Del Monte Produce [*NYSE symbol*]	(SG)
fdr	Founder	(PROS)
FDS	FactSet Research Systems [*NYSE symbol*]	(SG)
FDT	Forced Duction Test	(MELL)
FDX	FDX Corp. [*NYSE symbol*]	(SG)
FDY	Atchison Casting [*NYSE symbol*]	(SG)
FDZ	Fetal Danger Zone	(MELL)
FE	Fat Embolism	(MELL)
FE	Fertilled Egg	(MELL)
FE	Forced Expiration	(MELL)
FEA	Field-Emitter Arrays	
FEB	Free Erythrocyte Protoporphyrin [*Medicine*]	(MELL)
FEBP	Fetal Estrogen-Binding Protein	(MELL)
FECAVA	Federation of European Companion Animal Veterinary Associations (GVA)	
Fed	Federal Reserve Board	
FedRep	Federal Republic of Germany	
FEDRT	Federal Tax Rate	
FEDS	Field-Emitter Displays	
FEEVA	Federation of European Equine Veterinary Associations	(GVA)
FEFANA	European Feed Additives Manufacturers Association	(GVA)
FELE	Franklin Electric [*NASDAQ symbol*]	(SG)
FEN	Forest Ecology Network	
FEP	Fibroepithelial Polyp [*Medicine*]	(MELL)
FESCO	Faisalabad Electric Supply Company [*Pakistan*]	
FET	Frozen Embryo Transfer [*Medicine*]	
FEVR	Familial Exudative Vitreoretinopathy [*Medicine*]	(MELL)
FF	Fatal Facts	
FF	Fatigue Factor	(MELL)
FF	Fatigue Fracture	(MELL)
FF	Fibula Fracture	(MELL)

FF .... Fog Fever (MELL)
FF .... Follicular Fluid (MELL)
ff .... Ford Foundation
FF .... Freeze-Fracturing (MELL)
FFCP .... Forme Fruste of Chickenpox (MELL)
FFD .... Fat-Free Diet (MELL)
FFG .... FBL Financial Group'A' [*NYSE symbol*] (SG)
FFH .... Farm Family Holdings [*NYSE symbol*] (SG)
FFI .... Fauna and Flora International
FFIH .... Familial Fat-Induced Hyperlipemia [*Medicine*] (MELL)
FFL .... Floral Variant of Follicular Lymphoma [*Medicine*] (MELL)
FFN .... Fetal Fibronectin [*Medicine*] (MELL)
FFP .... Filiform Papilla [*Medicine*] (MELL)
FFP .... Fungiform Papilla [*Medicine*] (MELL)
FFR .... Freedom from Relapse (MELL)
FFROM .... Free and Full Range of Motion (MELL)
FFRP .... Fans and Friends of Ray Price [*An association*] (EA)
FFS .... Flexible Fiberoptic Sigmoidoscopy [*Medicine*] (MELL)
FFS .... Frost-Free Season (QUAC)
FFT .... Finger-to-Finger Test [*Medicine*] (MELL)
FG .... Free Gingiva (MELL)
FGAH .... First-Generation Antihistamine [*Medicine*] (MELL)
FGFRI .... Finnish Game and Fisheries Research Institute
FGI .... Friede Goldman Intl. [*NYSE symbol*] (SG)
FGL .... Fasting Gastrin Level [*Medicine*] (MELL)
FGRA .... Family Group Record Archives [*Genealogy*] (GEAB)
FGV .... Fasting Glucose Value [*Medicine*] (MELL)
FH .... Fasting Hemoglobin [*Medicine*] (MELL)
FH .... Femoral Hernia [*Medicine*] (MELL)
FH .... Fetal Hemoglobin [*Medicine*] (MELL)
FHC .... Family History Center [*Genealogy*] (GEAB)
FHC .... Friends' Health Connection (EA)
FHCC .... First Health Group [*NASDAQ symbol*] (SG)
FHE .... Fatal Hyponatremic Encephalopathy [*Medicine*] (MELL)
FHL .... Family History Library [*Genealogy*] (GEAB)
FHRA .... Fetal Heart Rate Acceleration (MELL)
FHS .... Foundation Health Systems'A' [*NYSE symbol*] (SG)
FHWA .... Federal Highway Administration Office of Highway Safety
FI .... Fibula (MELL)
FI .... Firearm Injury (MELL)
FI .... Food Intolerance (MELL)
FI .... Fructose Intolerance (MELL)
FI .... Fulminating Infection [*Medicine*] (MELL)
FI .... Fungal Infection (MELL)
FIAS .... Forging Industry Association
FICUS .... Florida Internet Center for Understanding Sustainability
FID .... Fungal Immunodiffusion [*Medicine*] (MELL)
fidel .... Fidelity (GEAB)
FIF .... Financial Federal [*NYSE symbol*] (SG)
FII .... Federated Investors 'B' [*NYSE symbol*] (SG)
FILM .... Children's Broadcasting [*NASDAQ symbol*] (SG)
FIN .... Fishmeal Information Network (GVA)
FinLAS .... Finnish Laboratory Animal Scientists (GVA)
FIP .... Familial Intestinal Polyposis [*Medicine*] (MELL)
FIS .... Floppy Infant Syndrome [*Medicine*] (MELL)
FIS .... Forced Inspiratory Spirogram [*Medicine*] (MELL)
FISU .... Westinghouse Federation of Independent Salaried Unions
FITB .... Fill in the Blank [*Online dialog*]
FIV .... Forced Inspiratory Volume (MELL)
FIVC .... Forced Inspiratory Vital Capacity (MELL)
FIX .... Comfort Systems USA [*NYSE symbol*] (SG)
Fji .... Fiji (MILB)
FJP .... Familial Juvenile Polyposis [*Medicine*] (MELL)
FJS .... Facet Joint Syndrome (MELL)
FJS .... Finger Joint Size (MELL)
FJUS .... FJ United States [*An association*] (EA)
FKE .... Full Knee Extension (MELL)
FL .... Face Lift (MELL)
FL .... Farmer's Lung (MELL)
Fl .... Floor (PROS)
FL .... Foodborne Listeriosis [*Medicine*] (MELL)
FLA .... Fluorescent-Labeled Antibody [*Medicine*] (MELL)
FLAS .... FlashNet Communications [*NASDAQ symbol*] (SG)
FLC .... Fatty Liver Cell (MELL)
FLC .... Frontal Lobe of Cerebrum [*Medicine*] (MELL)
FLD .... Fibrotic Lung Disease (MELL)
FLD .... Full Lower Denture (MELL)
FLEX .... Flextronics Intl. [*NASDAQ symbol*] (SG)
FLGS .... Flagstar Bancorp [*NASDAQ symbol*] (SG)
FLKS .... Fatty Liver and Kidney Syndrome (MELL)
FLLD .... Familial Lipoprotein Lipase Deficiency [*Medicine*] (MELL)
FLP .... Frog-Leg Position [*Medicine*] (MELL)
FLS .... Flowserve Corp. [*NYSE symbol*] (SG)
flt .... Flight (MILB)
flw .... Flower
FLYR .... Navigant International [*Stock market symbol*]
FLZ .... Flurazepam Hydrochloride [*Medicine*] (MELL)
FM .... Familial Melanoma [*Medicine*] (MELL)
FM .... Fetal Medicine (MELL)
FM .... Fetal Membranes (MELL)
FM .... Fetal Monitor (MELL)
FM .... Fibromyalgia
FM .... Flint's Murmur [*Medicine*] (MELL)
FM .... Franklin Mint
FM .... Friends of Mineralogy

FM .... Furuncular Myiasis [*Medicine*] (MELL)
FMA .... Fibromyalgia Syndrome [*Medicine*]
FMA/F/S ...... Foreign Military Assistance/Financing/Sales (MILB)
FMAP .... Financial Management Assistance Project [*Environmental Protection Agency*] (EPAT)
FMAX .... Franchise Mtge Acceptance [*NASDAQ symbol*] (SG)
FMC .... Fetal Movement Count (MELL)
FMC .... Focal Macular Choroidopathy [*Medicine*] (MELL)
FMC .... Fulminating Meningococcemia [*Medicine*] (MELL)
FMD .... Familial Metaphyseal Dysplasia [*Medicine*] (MELL)
FME .... Fetal-Maternal Exchange [*Medicine*] (MELL)
FMERC .... Factory Mutual Engineering & Research Corp.
FMK .... FiberMark, Inc. [*NYSE symbol*] (SG)
FMM .... FFP Marketing [*AMEX symbol*] (SG)
FMM .... Front Motor Mount [*Automotive term*]
FMO .... Flavin Monooxygenases
FMRR .... Financial Management Rate of Return [*Business term*]
FMS .... Fibromyalgia Syndrome [*Medicine*]
FMS .... Fresenius Medical AG ADS [*NYSE symbol*] (SG)
FMT .... Fremont Genl [*NYSE symbol*] (SG)
FMU .... First-Morning Urine (MELL)
FMX .... Fomento Economico ADS [*NYSE symbol*] (SG)
FNC .... First National Corp. [*AMEX symbol*] (SG)
FNCM .... Finet.com, Inc. [*NASDAQ symbol*] (SG)
FNF .... Fidelity Natl Finl [*NYSE symbol*] (SG)
FNH .... Familial Neonatal Hypoglycemia [*Medicine*] (MELL)
FNHR .... Febrile Nonhemolytic Reaction [*Medicine*] (MELL)
FNT .... Finger-to-Nose Test (MELL)
FNTT .... Femoral Nerve Traction Test [*Medicine*] (MELL)
FOCFC .... Friends of the Cassidys [*An association*] (EA)
FOD .... Familial Osseous Dystrophy [*Medicine*] (MELL)
FOD .... First Occurence of Date (QUAC)
FOH .... Familial Orthostatic Hypotension [*Medicine*] (MELL)
FOHBC .... Federation of Historical Bottle Collectors (EA)
FOISD .... Fiber Optic Isolated Spherical Dipole Antenna (EPAT)
FOJI .... Friends of Julio International (EA)
Fomoco .... Ford Motor Company
FonMin .... Foreign Minister
FonOff .... Foreign Office
FONX .... Fonix Corp. [*NASDAQ symbol*] (SG)
FOR .... Boyds Collection [*NYSE symbol*] (SG)
FORD .... Ford Motor Company
FORR .... Forrester Research [*NASDAQ symbol*] (SG)
FOS .... Fiber Optic Sigmoidoscope [*Medicine*] (MELL)
FOS .... Fiberoptic Sigmoidoscopy [*Medicine*] (MELL)
FOS .... Frank Orthogonal System [*Medicine*] (MELL)
FOS .... Fructooligosaccharides [*Type of carbohydrate*]
FOX .... Fox Entertainment Grp 'A' [*NYSE symbol*] (SG)
FP .... Facial Pain (MELL)
FP .... Familial Polyposis [*Medicine*] (MELL)
FP .... Family Physician (MELL)
FP .... Fat Pad (MELL)
FP .... Feeding Pump (MELL)
FP .... Fetal Presentation [*Medicine*] (MELL)
FP .... Foot Pad (MELL)
FP .... Fungiform Papilla [*Medicine*] (MELL)
FPAS .... Foreign Purchase Acknowledgement Statements (EPAT)
FPBG .... Fingerprick Blood Glucose [*Medicine*] (MELL)
FPCA .... Federal Pay Comparability Act of 1970
FPE .... False-Positive Error [*Medicine*] (MELL)
FPE .... Fatal Pulmonary Embolism [*Medicine*] (MELL)
FPIC .... FPIC Insurance Grp [*NASDAQ symbol*] (SG)
FPL .... Fasting Plasma Lipids [*Medicine*] (MELL)
FPPA .... Federal Pollution Prevention Act (EPAT)
FPR .... False Positive Rate (MELL)
FPR .... Familial Polyposis Registry (MELL)
FPS .... Fleet Patrol Ship (MILB)
FPUSA .... Federation of Petanque U.S.A. (EA)
FPWR .... Fountain Powerboat Ind [*NASDAQ symbol*] (SG)
FPX .... Fortune Natural Res [*AMEX symbol*] (SG)
Fr .... Fair [*Numismatic term*]
f/r .... Fair Rate
FR .... Family Registry (GEAB)
FR .... Flow Regime
FR .... Fluid Restriction (MELL)
FR .... Fluid Retention (MELL)
Fr .... French (BEE)
Fra .... Fragrant
FRC .... Functional Residual Capacity (MELL)
FRCA .... Farming and Rural Conservation Agency (GVA)
FRD .... Fat-Restricted Diet (MELL)
FRD .... Fiber-Rich Diet (MELL)
FRDT .... Flexion-Rotation Drawer Test (MELL)
FREE .... Freeserve plc ADS [*NASDAQ symbol*] (SG)
freem .... Freeman (GEAB)
freq .... Frequentative (BEE)
FRG .... Filtration-Resistant Glaucoma (MELL)
FRI .... Firearm-Related Injury (MELL)
FRIET .... Finite Real Estate Investment Trust
FRK .... Florida Rock Indus [*NYSE symbol*] (SG)
FROM .... Full Range of Movements (MELL)
FRS .... Fecal Reducing Substance [*Medicine*] (MELL)
FRS .... Female Reproductive System (MELL)
FRS .... Fetal Radiation Syndrome [*Medicine*] (MELL)
FRS .... Fetal Rubella Syndrome [*Medicine*] (MELL)

frs .... Fruits
FRW .... First Wash Realty Trust [*NYSE symbol*] (SG)
FRY .... Federal Republic of Yugoslavia (MILB)
FS .... Four Seasons Hotels [*NYSE symbol*] (SG)
Fs .... Fractostratus Cloud (WEAT)
FS .... Fracture Site (MELL)
FS .... Frozen Shoulder (MELL)
FSA .... Financial Supervisory Agency [*Japan*]
FSA .... Food Standards Agency (GVA)
FSA/CM .... Foundation for the Study of the Arts and Crafts Movement at Roycroft (EA)
FSBG .... Fingerstick Blood Glucose [*Medicine*] (MELL)
FSCS .... Future Scout and Cavalry System [*Army*]
FSE .... Fini Sec Assurance 6.95%Sr'QUIDS' [*NYSE symbol*] (SG)
FSI .... Foreign Substance Inhalation [*Medicine*] (MELL)
FSI .... Freedom Securities [*NYSE symbol*] (SG)
FSM .... Factory Service Manual
FSNE .... Flower-Spray Nerve Ending (MELL)
FSPB .... Food Safety Promotion Board [*Ireland*] (GVA)
FSPT .... FirstSpartan Financial [*NASDAQ symbol*] (SG)
FSS .... Fetal Scalp Sampling [*Medicine*] (MELL)
FSS .... Fetal Solvent Syndrome [*Medicine*] (MELL)
FSS .... Fetal Syphilis Syndrome [*Medicine*] (MELL)
FSS .... Focal Segmental Sclerosis [*Medicine*] (MELL)
FSS .... Frequency-Selective Saturation [*Medicine*] (MELL)
FST .... Field Support Terminal (EOSA)
FST .... Forest Oil [*NYSE symbol*] (SG)
fsu .... Former Soviet Union
FSV .... Fat-Soluble Vitamins (MELL)
FSW .... flightserv.com [*AMEX symbol*] (SG)
FT .... Fecal Trypsin [*Medicine*] (MELL)
FT .... Filum Terminale [*Medicine*] (MELL)
FT .... Finger Tip (MELL)
FT .... Fissured Tongue (MELL)
FT .... Fluoride Treatment (MELL)
Ft .... Fort (PROS)
FT .... Free Testosterone (MELL)
FTAAT .... Fluorescent Treponemal Antibody Absorption Test [*Medicine*] (MELL)
FTB .... Full-Thickness Burn (MELL)
FTC .... Fallopian Tube Carcinoma [*Medicine*] (MELL)
FTE .... France Telecom ADS [*NYSE symbol*] (SG)
FTG............. Free Tendon Graft [*Medicine*] (MELL)
FTIR .... Fourier Transform Infrared
FT-IRAS .... Fourier Transform-Infrared Reflection Absorption Spectroscopy
FTKA .... Failed to Keep Appointment (MELL)
FTLR .... Fallopian Tube Ligation Ring [*Medicine*] (MELL)
FTM .... Fourier Transform Microwave

FTMS .... Fourier Transform Microwave Spectroscopy
FTMTF .... Fantom Technologies [*NASDAQ symbol*] (SG)
FTN .... First Tenn Natl [*NYSE symbol*] (SG)
FTO .... Frontier Oil [*NYSE symbol*] (SG)
FTOP .... First Trimester of Pregnancy (MELL)
FTOS .... Full-Time Outservice (MELL)
FTP .... Fallopian Tube Papilloma [*Medicine*] (MELL)
FTP .... Finger-Trap Phenomenon [*Medicine*] (MELL)
FTP .... Full-Term Pregnancy (MELL)
ftr .... Fighter (MILB)
FTR .... Fractional Tubular Reabsorption [*Medicine*] (MELL)
FTRS .... Full-Text Retrieval System (MELL)
FTS .... Fallopian Tube Sarcoma [*Medicine*] (MELL)
FTS .... Fetal Tobacco Syndrome [*Medicine*] (MELL)
FTS .... Fissured Tongue Syndrome [*Medicine*] (MELL)
FTSD .... Full-Term Spontaneous Delivery [*Medicine*] (MELL)
FTSS .... Flight Test Simulation Station
FTT .... Fat Tolerance Test [*Medicine*] (MELL)
FTT .... Finning Intl. [*Toronto Stock Exchange symbol*] (SG)
FTT .... Free Tissue Transfer [*Medicine*] (MELL)
FTTS .... Failure to Thrive Syndrome [*Medicine*] (MELL)
FTUS .... Factory 2-U Stores [*NYSE symbol*] (SG)
FU .... Fudan University [*China*]
FUD .... Full Upper Denture (MELL)
furn .... Furnishing (BEE)
FV .... Facial Vein (MELL)
FVA .... Finnish Veterinary Association (GVA)
FVBG .... Free Vascularized Bone Graft [*Medicine*] (MELL)
FVCX .... FVC.com, Inc. [*NASDAQ symbol*] (SG)
FVH .... Fahnestock Viner Hldgs'A' [*NYSE symbol*] (SG)
FVL .... Flexible Video Laparoscope [*Medicine*] (MELL)
FVN .... Familial Visceral Neuropathy [*Medicine*] (MELL)
FVO .... Femoral Valgus Osteotomy [*Medicine*] (MELL)
FVS .... Floppy Valve Syndrome [*Medicine*] (MELL)
FVV .... Fossa of Vestibule of Vagina [*Medicine*] (MELL)
fw .... Fresh Water (MELL)
FWDP .... Fourth World Documentation Project [*Center for World Indigenous Studies*] [*Internet resource*]
FWG............ FREDDIE MAC 6.688%'98 Debs [*NYSE symbol*] (SG)
FWI .... Fire Weather Index (QUAC)
FWLS .... Fever Without Localizing Signs (MELL)
Fx .... Fracture (MELL)
FXF .... Fragile X Foundation (MELL)
FXXILW .... Force XXI Land Warrior [*Military*]
FY .... Fiscal Year (MELL)
FYS .... Five-Year Survival (MELL)
FZS .... Frontozygomatic Suture [*Medicine*] (MELL)

G

By Acronym

G	Gastrulation	(MELL)
g	Gender	(MELL)
G	Gland	(MELL)
G	Granulocyte	(MELL)
g	Gravitational Constant	(MELL)
g	Great	(GEAB)
g	Group	(MELL)
GA	Galea Aponeurotica	(MELL)
GA	Gamma Alpha	(EA)
GA	Gastric Acid	(MELL)
GA	Genome Analysis	(MELL)
GA	Geriatric Assessment	(MELL)
GA	Gouty Arthritis	(MELL)
GA	Group Army	(MILB)
GAAT	Glacial Acetic Acid Test	(MELL)
GAC	Geological Association of Canada	(QUAC)
GAC	Gulfstream Aeorspace [NYSE symbol]	(SG)
GACE	Gamma-Site Amyloid Precursor Protein-Cleaving Enzyme	
GACT	Granular Activated Carbon Treatment	(EPAT)
GAD	Gross Air Dried	
Gael	Gaelic	(BEE)
GAI	Global-Tech Appliances [NYSE symbol]	(SG)
Gal	Gallon	
GALEX	Galaxy Evolution Explorer	
GALT	Galileo Technology [NASDAQ symbol]	(SG)
GALVA	Gay and Lesbian Veterinary Association [Australia]	(GVA)
Gam	Gambia	(MILB)
GAM	Geographical Analysis Machine	
GAM	Great Adductor Muscle [Medicine]	(MELL)
GAMS	Guide to Available Mathematical Software [Internet resource]	
GANA	Gem Artists of North America	
GAR	Garaged [Automobile]	
gar	Garden	(BEE)
GAR	Gross as Received	
GARCH	Generalized Autoregressive Conditional Heteroskedasticy Process	
GARD	General Aviation Recovery Devices	
GATC	Gay Airline and Travel Club	(EA)
GBC	Glassblower's Cataract	(MELL)
GBF	Gesellschaft fuer Biotechnologische Forschung mbH [Germany]	
GBL	Gabelli Asset Management'A' [NYSE symbol]	(SG)
GBL	Glucose-Blood Level [Medicine]	(MELL)
GBLX	Global Crossing Ltd. [NASDAQ symbol]	(SG)
GBM	Geosphere-Biosphere Models	(QUAC)
Gbn	Gabon	(MILB)
GBO	Geosphere-Biosphere Observatories	(QUAC)
GBS	Gas-Bloat Syndrome [Medicine]	(MELL)
GBS	Gastric Bypass Surgery	(MELL)
GBT	Global Light Telecommun. [AMEX symbol]	(SG)
GBT	Gordon's Biological Test	(MELL)
GBW	General Body Weakness	(MELL)
GC	Genetic Code	(MELL)
GC	Genetic Counseling	(MELL)
GC	Glandular Cancer	(MELL)
GC	Glycocalyx [Medicine]	(MELL)
GC	Goblet Cells [Medicine]	(MELL)
GC	Green Cheeked Conure [Bird]	
GC	Guide Catheter [Medicine]	(MELL)
GCADA	Governor's Council on Alcoholism and Drug Abuse [New Jersey]	
GCC	Germ Cell Cancer	(MELL)
GCC	Glassy Cell Carcinoma	(MELL)
GCC	Global Change Category	(EOSA)
gch	Grandchildren	(GEAB)
GCI	Gestational Carbohydrate Intolerance [Medicine]	(MELL)
GCL	Gastrocolic Ligament [Medicine]	(MFII)
GCM	Global Computer Model	(WEAT)
GCP	Giant Cell Pneumonia [Medicine]	(MELL)
GCP	Granulocytopenia [Medicine]	(MELL)
GCR	Galactic Cosmic Ray [Astronomy]	
GCRIO	Global Change Research Information Office	(QUAC)
GCS	Gas Chemical Sterlization	(MELL)
GCS	Giant-Cell Sarcoma	(MELL)
GCS	Gluteus Compartment Syndrome	(MELL)
GCSI	Government Computer Sales, Inc.	
GCTI	Genesys Telecommunications [NASDAQ symbol]	(SG)
GCV	Granulose Cell Tumor	(MELL)
GCV	Great Cephalic Vein [Medicine]	(MELL)
GCVTC	Grand Canyon Visibility Transport Commission	(EPAT)
GCW	Gerber Childrenswear [NYSE symbol]	(SG)
GD	Gaucher's Disease	(MELL)
GD	Gauze Dressing	(MELL)
GD	Genetic Disorder	(MELL)
GD	Gestational Diabetes	(MELL)
gd	Guard	(MILB)
GDA	Gastroduodenal Artery [Medicine]	(MELL)
GDE	Generic Data Exemption	(EPAT)
GDF	Gel Diffusion Precipitin [Medicine]	(MELL)
GDF	Guidaut Defibrillator [Medicine]	(MELL)
GDI	Gardner Denver [NYSE symbol]	(SG)
GDI	Global Defense Initiative	
GDID	Genetically Determined Immunodeficiency Disease	(MELL)
GDL	Graduate Driver Licensing	
GDLS	Generals Dynamics Land Systems	
gdn	Guardian	(GEAB)
GDOS	General Dynamics Ordnance Systems	
Ge	Germany	(MILB)
GEAG	Gastroepiploic Artery Graft [Medicine]	(MELL)
GEB	Genetronics Biomedical [Toronto Stock Exchange symbol]	(SG)
GECC	Golf Entertainment [NASDAQ symbol]	(SG)
GED	Genetically Engineered Drug	(MELL)
GEDEX	Greenhouse Effect Detection Experiment	(EOSA)
GENI	Global Employer's Network, Inc.	
GENXY	Genset ADR [NASDAQ symbol]	(SG)
Geol	Geology	(BEE)
Geom	Geometry	(BEE)
GEPA	Grade Eight Proficiency Assessment	
GEPH	Gestational Edema with Proteinuria and Hypertension [Medicine] (MELL)	
GER	Gene Expression Regulation [Medicine]	(MELL)
GER	Global Environmental Research	(QUAC)
GES	Guess, Inc. [NYSE symbol]	(SG)
GESO	Gurkha Ex-Servicemen's Organisation	
GF	Gingival Fibromatosis [Medicine]	(MELL)
GF	Glandular Fever [Medicine]	(MELL)
GF	Glenoid Fossa [Medicine]	(MELL)
gf	Gold Filled [Watch]	
GF	Greenstick Fracture [Medicine]	(MELL)
GF	Ground Frost	(WEAT)
GF	Growth Failure	(MELL)
GFAC	Glucose-Fatty Acid Cycle	(MELL)
gFARAD	Global Food Animal Residue Avoidance Databank	(GVA)
GFB	Gas-Forming Bacteria	(MELL)
GFCL	Giant Follicular Cell Lymphoma [Medicine]	(MELL)
GFD	Galeazzi Fracture-Dislocation [Medicine]	(MELL)
GFL	Germ-Free Life	(MELL)
GFN	Ganglion of Facial Nerve [Medicine]	(MELL)
GFN	Genitofemoral Nerve [Medicine]	(MELL)
GFO	Grant Funding Order	(EPAT)
GFR	Growth Factor Receptors	(MELL)
GG	Gamma Globulinemia [Medicine]	(MELL)
GG	Gas Gangrene	(MELL)
GG	Gestational Glaucoma	(MELL)
GGA	Global Gecko Association	(GVA)
GGB	Gerdau S.A. ADS [NYSE symbol]	(SG)
GGY	Compagnie Genl Geophy ADS [NYSE symbol]	(SG)
GH	Gestational Hypotension [Medicine]	(MELL)
GH	Gingival Hyperplasia [Medicine]	(MELL)
GHA	Gay and Homosexually Active	
Gha	Ghana	(MILB)
GHG	Greenhouse Gases	
GHIH	Growth Hormone Inhibiting Hormone	(MELL)
GHM	Geniohyoid Muscle	(MELL)
GHz	Gigahertz	
GI	Gas Insufflation	(MELL)
GI	Genomic Imprinting	(MELL)
GI	Gingival Index	(MELL)
GI	Glucose Intolerance	(MELL)
GI	Gold Inlay	(MELL)
GI	Granuloma Inguinale [Medicine]	(MELL)
GI	Gym Itch	(MELL)
GIA	Gastrointestinal Anthrax [Medicine]	(MELL)
GIB	CGI Group [NYSE symbol]	(SG)
GIBA	Gastrointestinal Bleeding from Aspirin	(MELL)

GID	Gastrointestinal Disease (MELL)
GID	Gastrointestinal Disorder (MELL)
GIF	Gastrointestinal Fistula [*Medicine*] (MELL)
GIF	Giant Intestinal Fluke [*Medicine*] (MELL)
GIF	Glycosylation Inhibition Factor [*Medicine*] (MELL)
GIL	Gildan Activewear'A' [*AMEX symbol*] (SG)
GIM	Gastrointestinal Myiasis [*Medicine*] (MELL)
GIM	Gross Income Multiplier [*Business term*]
GIMPS	Great Internet Mersenne Prime Search
GINA	Girls in National Alliance [*An association*]
GIO	Gastrointestinal Obstruction [*Medicine*] (MELL)
GIS	Gas Imaging Spectrometer
GISP	Government Information Sharing Project [*Internet resource*]
GK	GenTek, Inc. [*NYSE symbol*] (SG)
Gk	Greek (BEE)
GKAP	Georgia Kindergarten Assessment Program
GL	Gastric Lavage [*Medicine*] (MELL)
GL	Genomic Library (MELL)
GL	Germ Line [*Medicine*] (MELL)
GL	Gland (MELL)
GL	Gold Line [*Automotive tires*]
GL	Great Lakes REIT [*NYSE symbol*] (SG)
GLAS	Geoscience Laser Altimeter System (EOSA)
GLAST	Gamma-Ray Large Area Space Telescope
GLC	Galileo Intl. [*NYSE symbol*] (SG)
GLC	Genealogical Library Catalog (GEAB)
GLC	Granulosa Lutein Cell [*Medicine*] (MELL)
GLD	Granulomatous Lung Disease (MELL)
GLFA	Gays and Lesbians in Foreign Affairs [*An association*] (EA)
GLH	Gallaher Group ADS [*NYSE symbol*] (SG)
GLH	Generalized Lymphoid Hyperplasia [*Medicine*] (MELL)
GLHSC	Gay and Lesbian History Stamp Club (EA)
GLI	Global Imager (EOSA)
GLM	Genetic Linkage Map [*Medicine*] (MELL)
GLN	Gastric Lymph Node [*Medicine*] (MELL)
GLRS-A	Geoscience Laser Ranging System-Altimeter (EOSA)
GLRS-R	Geoscience Laser Ranging System-Ranger (EOSA)
GLSLB	Great Lakes-St. Lawrence Basin (QUAC)
GLSO	Group Legal Services Organization
GLTS	Gun-Launch to Space
GLTT	Glucose-Lactase Tolerance Test [*Medicine*] (MELL)
GLXW	GalaxiWorld.com [*NASDAQ symbol*] (SG)
GM	Geriatric Medicine (MELL)
GM	German Measles (MELL)
gm	Grandmother (GEAB)
Gmc	Germanic (BEE)
GMCD	Grand Mal Convulsive Disorder [*Medicine*] (MELL)
GMD	Glutamate Dehydrogenase [*Medicine*] (MELL)
GMD	Gower's Muscular Dystrophy [*Medicine*] (MELL)
GMK	Gruma S.A. ADS [*NYSE symbol*] (SG)
GMM	Generalized Mixed Models
GMM	Gluteus Maximus Muscle (MELL)
GMP	Glucose Monophosphate [*Medicine*] (MELL)
GMST	Gemstar Intl. Group [*NASDAQ symbol*] (SG)
GMTC	Geometric Mean Titer of Controls (MELL)
GMWL	Global Mean Water Line (QUAC)
GN	Gouty Nephropathy [*Medicine*] (MELL)
GN	Gouty Node [*Medicine*] (MELL)
GNC	Gram Negative Cocci [*Medicine*] (MELL)
GNDC	Gram-Negative Diplococci [*Medicine*] (MELL)
GNE	Generalized Nash-Equilibrium [*Game*]
GNET	g02net, Inc. [*NASDAQ symbol*] (SG)
GNI	Gram-Negative Infection [*Medicine*] (MELL)
GNS	Gram-Negative Sepsis [*Medicine*] (MELL)
GNSS	Genesis Microchip [*NASDAQ symbol*] (SG)
GOA	Gardeners of America (EA)
GOA	Government of Argentina
GOB	Government of Brazil
GOC	General Occupational Classification
GOC	Government of Cuba
godf	Godfather (GEAB)
godm	Godmother (GEAB)
GOF	Government of France
GOG	Gynecologic Oncology Group (MELL)
GOS	Geomagnetic Observing System (EOSA)
GOSL	Government of Sri Lanka
GOT	Goal of Treatment [*Medicine*] (MELL)
GOTO	GoTo.com, Inc. [*NASDAQ symbol*] (SG)
GOV	Gouverneur Bancorp [*AMEX symbol*] (SG)
GP	Gangliocytic Paraganglioma [*Medicine*] (MELL)
GP	Gastric Polyp [*Medicine*] (MELL)
GP	General Physician (MELL)
GP	Girard-Perregaux
GP	Glycophorins (MELL)
GP	Growth Plate (MELL)
GPAI	Genealogical Periodical Annual Index (GEAB)
GPB	Gram-Positive Bacilli (MELL)
GPB	Gram-Positive Bacteria (MELL)
GPC	Giant Pyramidal Cell (MELL)
GPCI	General Purpose Channel Interface
GPF	Gram Parsons Foundation (EA)
GPF	Greater Palatine Foramen (MELL)
GPI	Group 1 Automotive [*NYSE symbol*] (SG)
GPI	Growth Plate Injury (MELL)
GPIFC	Gene Pitney International Fan Club (EA)
GPL	Gastrophrenic Ligament (MELL)
Gpm	Gallons per Minute
GPM	Getty Petroleum Mktg. [*NYSE symbol*] (SG)
GPM	Greater Pectoral Muscle (MELL)
GPRS	General Packet Radio Service
GPSDR	Global Positioning System Demonstration Receiver (EOSA)
GPSI	Great Plains Software [*NYSE symbol*] (SG)
GPVEC	Great Plains Veterinary Educational Center [*University of Nebraska*] (GVA)
GPX	GP Strategies [*NYSE symbol*] (SG)
GR	Genetic Recombination [*Medicine*] (MELL)
gr	Graduate (GEAB)
Gr	Greece (MILB)
GRE	Guardian Royal Exchange [*Great Britain*]
GREENTIE	Global Remedy for the Environment and Energy Use--Technology Information Exchange
GRF	Gastrin-Releasing Factor [*Medicine*] (MELL)
grf	Grandfather (GEAB)
GRI	Graduate Realtors Institute
GRL	Gulf Indonesia Resources [*NYSE symbol*] (SG)
grmo	Grandmother (GEAB)
grs	Grandson (GEAB)
GRU	Geomorphic Response Unit (QUAC)
GS	Genetic Screening (MELL)
GS	Ghost Surgery (MELL)
GS	Glucagonoma Syndrome [*Medicine*] (MELL)
GS	Glycogen Synthesis [*Medicine*] (MELL)
GS	Goldman Sachs Group [*NYSE symbol*] (SG)
GS	Gram Stain [*Medicine*] (MELL)
GS	Granulocytic Sarcoma [*Medicine*] (MELL)
GS	Grebe Syndrome [*Medicine*] (MELL)
GS	Ground Substance [*Medicine*] (MELL)
GSB	Golden State Bancorp [*NYSE symbol*] (SG)
GSC	Genome Sequence Centre
GSC	Greater Sulphur Crested Cockatoo [*Bird*]
GSD	Gamma Sigma Delta (EA)
GSD	Glycogen Synthetase Deficiency [*Medicine*] (MELL)
GSD	Gunstock Deformity [*Medicine*] (MELL)
GSE	Gundle/SLT Environmental [*NYSE symbol*] (SG)
GSF	Greater Sciatic Foramen [*Medicine*] (MELL)
GSF	Greenstick Fracture [*Medicine*] (MELL)
GSF	Gunshot Fracture [*Medicine*] (MELL)
GSI	Gestational Stress Incontinence [*Medicine*] (MELL)
GSI	Graduate Student Instructor
GSMP	Global Services Management Platform [*Newbridge Network*]
GSN	Greater Sciatic Notch [*Medicine*] (MELL)
GSR	Glutathione Reductase [*Medicine*] (MELL)
GSRA	Graduate Student Research Assistant
GSSA	Graduate Student Staff Assistant
GST	Genetic Screening Test (MELL)
GST	Gold Steel Titanium
GST	Gravity Stress Test (MELL)
GSTH	Ground Surface Temperature Histories (QUAC)
GSTX	GST Telecommunications [*NASDAQ symbol*] (SG)
GSY	Guest Supply [*NYSE symbol*] (SG)
GT	Gamekeeper Thumb (MELL)
GT	Gastric Tonometry [*Medicine*] (MELL)
GT	Gene Therapy (MELL)
GT	Genetic Transduction (MELL)
GT	Geographic Tongue [*Medicine*] (MELL)
GT	Glyceryl Trinitrate [*Medicine*] (MELL)
GTA	Golf Trust of America [*AMEX symbol*] (SG)
GTAC	Gene Therapy Advisory Committee (GVA)
GTC	Gestational Trophoblastic Carcinoma [*Medicine*] (MELL)
GTCE	Global Tropospheric Chemistry Experiment (EOSA)
GTCS	Generalized Tonic-Clonic Seizure [*Medicine*] (MELL)
GTG	Glycerol Tolerant Gel (MELL)
GTHR	Generalized Thyroid Hormone Resistance [*Medicine*] (MELL)
GTLL	Golden Triangle Ind. [*NASDAQ symbol*] (SG)
GTOAA	GTO Association of America (EA)
GTRC	Guitar Center [*NASDAQ symbol*] (SG)
GTSG	Global TeleSystems Grp. [*NASDAQ symbol*] (SG)
GTT	Gestational Trophoblastic Tumor [*Medicine*] (MELL)
GTW	Gateway, Inc. [*NYSE symbol*] (SG)
GTY	Getty Realty [*NYSE symbol*] (SG)
GU	Giant Urticaria [*Medicine*] (MELL)
GU	Glucose Uptake [*Medicine*] (MELL)
Gua	Guatemala (MILB)
GuB	Guinea-Bissau (MILB)
Gui	Guinea (MILB)
GUT	Genitourinary Tract [*Medicine*] (MELL)
GUVMA	Glasgow University Veterinary Medical Association (GVA)
GUVZS	Glasgow University Veterinary Zoological Society (GVA)
Guy	Guyana (MILB)
GV	Genu Valgum (MELL)
GV	Genu Varum (MELL)
GV	Gingivectomy [*Medicine*] (MELL)
GV	Gonorrheal Vaginitis [*Medicine*] (MELL)
GVA	Granite Construction [*NYSE symbol*] (SG)
GVC	Gold-Veneer Crown (MELL)
GVE	Grove Property Trust [*NYSE symbol*] (SG)
GVG	Global Vacation Grp. [*NYSE symbol*] (SG)
GVG	Greater-Vestibular Gland (MELL)
GVHD	Graft-Versus Host Disease [*Medicine*]
GVP	GSE Systems [*AMEX symbol*] (SG)

GVS .... Gastric Vertical Stapling [*Medicine*] (MELL)
GVS .... Goat Veterinary Society (GVA)
GW .... Genital Warts (MELL)
GW .... Global Warming (QUAC)
GW .... Gymnast's Wrist (MELL)

GWC .... General Watch Co.
GWDS .... Generalized Work Distress Scale (MELL)
GWPS .... Groundwater Protection Strategy [*Environmental science*] (EPAT)
GWT .... Gardner-Wells Tongs (MELL)
GWWR .... Gateway Western Railway Co.

H
By Acronym

H	Hair	(MELL)
H	Hallucis	(MELL)
H	Handage	(MELL)
h	Heiress	(GEAB)
H	Hemorrhoid	(MELL)
H	Heparin [*Medicine*]	(MELL)
H	Histidinemethemoglobin [*Medicine*]	(MELL)
H	Hospice	(MELL)
H	Humalog	(MELL)
H	Hypertension	(MELL)
HA	Halothane Anesthia [*Medicine*]	(MELL)
HA	Hemadsorbent	(MELL)
HA	Hepatic Agenesis	(MELL)
HA	Hippuric Acid	(MELL)
HA	Human Albumin	(MELL)
HAC	Hanging Arm Cast	(MELL)
HAC	Hyperactive Child	(MELL)
HAC	Hyperadrenocorticism [*Medicine*]	(MELL)
HACA	Hammered Aluminum Collectors Association	(EA)
HACV	Heavy Armored Combat Vehicle	(MILB)
HAD	Heterologous Antibody Disease [*Medicine*]	(MELL)
HAE	Hereditary Angioedema [*Medicine*]	(MELL)
HAIN	Hain Food Group [*Toronto Stock Exchange symbol*]	(SG)
HAL	Hypoplastic Acute Leukemia [*Medicine*]	(MELL)
HAM	Home Apnea Monitoring [*Medicine*]	(MELL)
HAM	Hospital-Acquired Meningitis	(MELL)
H & C	Hepatitis and Cirrhosis	(MELL)
H & C	Hypoventilation and Cyanosis [*Medicine*]	(MELL)
H & R	Hysteria and Repression	(MELL)
H & S	Hearing and Speech	(MELL)
H & S	Hemorrhage and Shock	(MELL)
H & S	Hypocalcemia and Seizures	(MELL)
HAO	Hip Osteoarthritis [*Medicine*]	(MELL)
HAP	Hazardous Air Pollutant	(QUAC)
HAP	Hospital-Acquired Pneumonia	(MELL)
HAPD	Home-Automated Peritoneal Dialysis [*Medicine*]	(MELL)
HAR	High-Altitude Retinopathy [*Medicine*]	(MELL)
HARI	Hospital-Acquired Respiratory Infection	(MELL)
HARM	Hypertension, Anemia, Renal, Malabsorption [*Medicine*]	(MELL)
HAS	Hepatic Angiosarcoma [*Medicine*]	(MELL)
HAS	High Altitude Syncope [*Medicine*]	(MELL)
HAS	High Apgar Score [*Medicine*]	(MELL)
HAS	Holmes-Adie Syndrome [*Medicine*]	(MELL)
HAS	Hygiene Assessment System [*British*]	(GVA)
HASHD	Hypertensive Arteriosclerotic Heart Disease	(MELL)
HAT	Hospital Arrival Time	(MELL)
Haw	Hawaii	(BEE)
HB	Heartburn	(MELL)
HB	Hunchback	(MELL)
HB	Hyoid Bone	(MELL)
HBC	HSBC Holdings ADS [*NYSE symbol*]	(SG)
HBCA	Hudson's Bay Company Archives [*Canada*]	(QUAC)
HbCO	Carbon Monoxide Hemoglobin [*Medicine*]	(MELL)
HbCO	Carboxyhemoglobin [*Medicine*]	(MELL)
HBI	HomeBase, Inc. [*NYSE symbol*]	(SG)
HBIX	Hagler Bailly [*NASDAQ symbol*]	(SG)
HBK	Hatchback	
HBL	Habib Bank Limited [*Pakistan*]	
HBMT	Haploidentical Bone Marrow Transplantation [*Medicine*]	(MELL)
HBOC	Hereditary Breast Ovarian Cancer	(MELL)
HBP	Handlebar Palsy [*Medicine*]	(MELL)
HBP	Helicobacter Pylori [*Medicine*]	(MELL)
HBT	Homologous Blood Transfusion	(MELL)
HBT	Hydrogen Breath Test	(MELL)
HC	Hanging Cast	(MELL)
HC	Hanover Compressor [*NYSE symbol*]	(SG)
HC	Hard Cancer	(MELL)
HC	Heart Catheterization	(MELL)
HC	Heparin Cofactor [*Medicine*]	(MELL)
HC	Hepatic Candidiasis [*Medicine*]	(MELL)
HC	Histamine Challenge [*Medicine*]	(MELL)
HC	Hot Compress	(MELL)
HC	Hydatid Cyst	(MELL)
HC	Hysterical Convulsions	(MELL)
HCA	Hoverclub of America	(EA)
HCBS	Hot Cross Bun Skull	(MELL)

HCC	Himalayan Climate Centre	(QUAC)
HCC	Hurthle Cell Cancer	(MELL)
HCC	Husband-Coached Childbirth	(MELL)
HCCD	Historical Canadian Climate Dataset	(QUAC)
HCD	Heavy Chain Deposition [*Medicine*]	(MELL)
HCD	Herniated Cervical Disk [*Medicine*]	(MELL)
HCD	High-Calorie Diet	(MELL)
HCDJ	Hyperostosis Corticalis Deformans Invenilis [*Medicine*]	(MELL)
HCGR	Heavy Chain Gene Rearrangement [*Medicine*]	(MELL)
HCHS	Hydrocortisone Hemisuccinate [*Medicine*]	(MELL)
HCl	Hydrochloric Acid	(MELL)
HCIN	Hydrocarbon-Induced Neoplasm [*Medicine*]	(MFLL)
HCL	Hilar Cell Tumor [*Medicine*]	(MELL)
HCM	Hanover Capital Mtg. [*AMEX symbol*]	(SG)
HCM	Hostile Cervical Mucus [*Medicine*]	(MELL)
HCMM/AEM-1	Heat Capacity Mapping Mission/Applications Explorer Mission-1	(EOSA)
HCN	Hereditary Chronic Nephritis [*Medicine*]	(MELL)
HCN	Hypercalcemic Nephropathy [*Medicine*]	(MELL)
HCPA	Health-Care Power of Attorney [*Medicine*]	(MELL)
HCR	HCR Manor Care [*NYSE symbol*]	(SG)
HCR	Host Cell Reactivation [*Medicine*]	(MELL)
HCRF	Hypercarbic Respiratory Failure	(MELL)
HCRI	Healthcare Recoveries [*NASDAQ symbol*]	(SG)
HCSS	Hypersensitive Carotid Sinus Syndrome	(MELL)
HCT	Heat Coagulation Test	(MELL)
HCT	Hector Communications [*AMEX symbol*]	(SG)
HCT	Hematopoietic Cell Transplantation [*Medicine*]	(MELL)
HCW	Health Care Worker	(MELL)
HD	Haglund Deformity [*Medicine*]	(MELL)
HD	Hank's Dilator [*Medicine*]	(MELL)
HD	Hartnup Disease [*Medicine*]	(MELL)
HD	Hematologic Disorder [*Medicine*]	(MELL)
HD	Hemolytic Disease [*Medicine*]	(MELL)
HD	Hepatic Disease [*Medicine*]	(MELL)
HD	Hip Dislocation	(MELL)
HDC	Hemoglobin Dissociation Curve [*Medicine*]	(MELL)
HDC	High-Dose Chemotherapy [*Medicine*]	(MELL)
HDDT	Heavy-Duty Diesel Truck	(EPAT)
HDGT	Heavy-Duty Gasoline Truck	(EPAT)
HDM	Host Defense Mechanism [*Medicine*]	(MELL)
HDT	Half Disappearance Time	(MELL)
HDTP	Hardtop	
hdwr	Hardware	(BEE)
HE	Heat Exhaustion	(MELL)
HE	Heterologous	(MELL)
HEAB	High Energy Astrophysics Branch [*NASA*]	
HEB	Hemispherx BioPharma [*AMEX symbol*]	(SG)
HEFCW	Higher Education Funding Council for Wales	(GVA)
hel	Helicopter	(MILB)
HELCOM	Helsinki Commission	
HEPA	Hamster Egg Penetration Assay	
HERBA	Herbalife Intl'A' [*NASDAQ symbol*]	(SG)
HERCULES	Heavy Equipment Recovery Combat Utility Lift and Evacuation System [*Military*]	
HERF	High-Energy Radio Frequency	
HESSI	High Energy Solar Spectroscopic Imager	
HETE	Hydroxyarachidonic Acid	(MELL)
HEV	Hepatitis E Virus	(MELL)
HEVRA	Heads of European Veterinary Regulatory Agencies	(GVA)
HF	Hair Follicle	(MELL)
HF	Hangman's Fracture [*Medicine*]	(MELL)
HF	Head of Fetus	(MELL)
HF	Heller Financial 'A' [*NYSE symbol*]	(SG)
HF	Hemofiltration	(MELL)
HF	Hepatic Fibrosis [*Medicine*]	(MELL)
HF	Hip Fracture	(MELL)
HF	Hot Flashes	(MELL)
HFC	Hydrofluorocarbon	
HFEA	Human Fertilization Embryo Authority [*Great Britain*]	
HFI	Hyperostosis Frontalis Interna	(MELL)
HFRS	Hemorrhagic Fever with Renal Stones [*Medicine*]	(MELL)
HG	Human Genome [*Medicine*]	(MELL)
HGD	Hypersensitivity Glomerular Disease [*Medicine*]	(MELL)
HGD	Hysterical Gait Disorder [*Medicine*]	(MELL)
HGI	Hardgrove Grindability Index	

HGL	Hemoglobin Gene Loci [*Medicine*] (MELL)
HGM	Hepatogastric Ligament [*Medicine*] (MELL)
HGM	Human Glucose Monitoring [*Medicine*] (MELL)
HGM	Hyoglossus Muscle [*Medicine*] (MELL)
HGMIS	Human Genome Management Information System
HGN	Hypoglossal Nerve [*Medicine*] (MELL)
HGSIL	High-Grade Squamous Intraepithelial Lesion [*Medicine*] (MELL)
HGSIL	High-Grade Squamous Intraepithelial Lesions [*Medicine*]
HGT	Hugoton Royalty Trust [*NYSE symbol*] (SG)
HH	Hepatic Hydatidosis [*Medicine*] (MELL)
HH	High Heels [*Doll collecting*]
HHAB	Hig-Hinge Abduction Brace [*Medicine*] (MELL)
HHC	Hepatic Hydatid Cyst [*Medicine*] (MELL)
HHCS	High Altitude Hypertrophic Cardiomyopathy Syndrome [*Medicine*] (MELL)
HHI	Herfindahl-Hirschmann Index [*Economics*]
HHS	Hereditary Hemolytic Syndrome [*Medicine*] (MELL)
HHS	Home Health Services (MELL)
HHT	Head Balter Traction (MELL)
HHT	Hypothalamo-Hypophyseal Tract [*Medicine*] (MELL)
HIC	Hydrogen Ion Concentration [*Medicine*] (MELL)
HICH	Hypertensive Intracranial Hemorrhage [*Medicine*] (MELL)
HIG	Hartford Finl Svcs Gp. [*NYSE symbol*] (SG)
HIH-WFJD	Hearts in Harmony - World Family of John Denver [*An association*] (EA)
HIMSS	High-Resolution Microwave Spectrometer Sounder (EOSA)
Hind	Hindustani (BEE)
HIP	Health Insurance Plan (MELL)
HIPAA	Health Insurance Portability & Accountability Act
HIPAA	Health Insurance Portability and Accountability Act of 1996
HiPerf	High Performance
HIPP	Himalayan Interdisciplinary Paleoclimate Project (QUAC)
HIR	Diversified Corp. Resources [*AMEX symbol*] (SG)
HIRDLS	High-Resolution Dynamics Limb Sounder (EOSA)
HIS	High Resolution Interferometer Sounder (EOSA)
HIS	Home Incapacity Scale (MELL)
hist	Historian (GEAB)
HIT	Home Infusion Therapy (MELL)
HIT	Home Intravenous Therapy (MELL)
HIU	Head Injury Unit (MELL)
HIVAT	Home Intravenous Antibiotic Therapy (MELL)
HIVSS	Highlands and Islands Veterinary Services Scheme (GVA)
HJC	Henderson-Jones Chondromatosis [*Medicine*] (MELL)
HK	Hyperkeratosis [*Medicine*] (MELL)
HK	Hypokalemia [*Medicine*] (MELL)
HKA	Hypokalemic Alkalosis [*Medicine*] (MELL)
HKI	Hong Kong Influenza (MELL)
HKRP	Hinged Knee Replacement Prosthesis (MELL)
HKT	Cable & Wireless HKT ADR [*NYSE symbol*] (SG)
HKT	Heterotopic Kidney Transplant (MELL)
HKTDC	Hong Kong Trade Development Council (EA)
HL	Hairy Leukemia (MELL)
HL	Hyperlipemia [*Medicine*] (MELL)
HLE	Heat-Labile Enterotoxin [*Medicine*] (MELL)
HLI	Hartford Life 'A' [*NYSE symbol*] (SG)
HLYW	Hollywood Entertainment [*NASDAQ symbol*] (SG)
HM	Hahns Macaw [*Bird*]
HM	Heimlich Maneuver [*Medicine*] (MELL)
HM	Heloma Molle [*Medicine*] (MELL)
HM	Hemifacial Microsomia [*Medicine*] (MELL)
HM	Hispanic Male (MELL)
HM	Historia Mathematica [*A publication*]
HM	Holosystolic Murmur [*Medicine*] (MELL)
HM	Humidity Mask (MELL)
HMK	HA-LO Industries [*NYSE symbol*] (SG)
HMK	Housemaid's Knee (MELL)
HMM	Horizon Mission Methodology [*NASA*]
HMP	Health Maintenance Program (MELL)
HMP	Heavy Metal Poisoning (MELL)
HMP	Heineke-Mikulicz Pyloroplasty [*Medicine*] (MELL)
HMS	Harvard Medical School
HMSN	Hereditary Motor and Sensory Neuropathy [*Medicine*] (MELL)
HMWC	High Molecular Weight Component (MELL)
HN	Haygarth's Node [*Medicine*] (MELL)
HN	Hensen's Node [*Medicine*] (MELL)
HN	Hydronephrosis [*Medicine*] (MELL)
HNAD	Hyperosmolar Nonacidotic Diabetes [*Medicine*] (MELL)
HNI	Hospitalization not Indicated (MELL)
HNKC	Hyperosmolar Nonketotic Coma [*Medicine*] (MELL)
HNL	Histiocytic Necrotizing Lymphadenitis [*Medicine*] (MELL)
HNM	High Neonatal Morality (MELL)
HNP	Human Neurophysin [*Medicine*] (MELL)
HNPCC	Hereditary Non-Polyposis Colorectal Cancer (MELL)
HNS	Hypernasal Speech (MELL)
HO	Hippocratic Oath (MELL)
HO	Homologous (MELL)
HO	Hyperostosis [*Medicine*] (MELL)
HOA	High Oxygen Affinity (MELL)
HOC	Hydroxycorticoid (MELL)
HOC	Hyperosmolar Coma (MELL)
HOE	Head of Epididymis [*Medicine*] (MELL)
HOF	High Output Failure [*Medicine*] (MELL)
HOK	Hilum of Kidney (MELL)
Hon	Honeybees
hon	Honorable (GEAB)

honor	Honorably (GEAB)
honor	Honorary (GEAB)
HOOV	Hoover's Inc. [*NASDAQ symbol*] (SG)
HOPA	Hospital-Based Organ Procurement Agency (MELL)
HORF	High Output Renal Failure [*Medicine*] (MELL)
HORT	Hines Horticulture [*NASDAQ symbol*] (SG)
Hot	Hypotropia [*Medicine*] (MELL)
Hou	Houston Oilers [*National Football League*] [*1960-96*] (NFLA)
how	Howitzer (MILB)
HP	Hannah's Prayer [*Christian infertility/pregnancy loss group*]
HP	Hard Palate [*Medicine*] (MELL)
HP	Harvard Pump [*Medicine*] (MELL)
HP	Hip Prosthesis (MELL)
HP	Horizontal Plane (MELL)
HP	Humeroscapular Periarthritis [*Medicine*] (MELL)
HP	Hydrogen Peroxide (MELL)
HP	Hyperperistalsis [*Medicine*] (MELL)
HP	Hyperplasia [*Medicine*] (MELL)
hPa	Hectopascals (WEAT)
HPCHA	High Red Cell Phosphatidylcholine Anemia [*Medicine*] (MELL)
HPD	Histrionic Personality Disorder [*Medicine*] (MELL)
HPD	Hypothalamic-Pituitary Dsyfunction [*Medicine*] (MELL)
HPE	Hydrostatic Permeability Edema [*Medicine*] (MELL)
HPK	Hollywood Park [*NYSE symbol*] (SG)
HPLC	High Pressure Liquid Chromatographic
HPM	High-Pitched Murmur [*Medicine*] (MELL)
HPNA	Home Phoneline Networking Alliance
HPP	Hinged Penile Prosthesis [*Medicine*] (MELL)
HPP	Hyperplastic Polyps [*Medicine*] (MELL)
HPP	Hypokalemic Periodic Paralysis [*Medicine*] (MELL)
HPR	Hypophosphatemic Rickets [*Medicine*] (MELL)
HPS	Heel Pain Syndrome (MELL)
HPS	Hepatoportal Sclerosis [*Medicine*] (MELL)
HPS	Human Platelet Suspension [*Medicine*] (MELL)
HPTM	Home Prothrombin Time Monitoring [*Medicine*] (MELL)
HPVC	Hypoxic Pulmonary Vasoconstriction [*Medicine*] (MELL)
HPVI	Human Papillomavirus [*Medicine*] (MELL)
Hpx	Hemopexin [*Medicine*] (MELL)
HQ	Hambrecht & Quist Group [*NYSE symbol*] (SG)
HR	Heat Rash (MELL)
Hr	Honduras (MILB)
HR	Hormone Receptor (MELL)
HRBT	Hudson River Bancorp [*NASDAQ symbol*] (SG)
HRCT	High-Resolution Computed Tomography (MELL)
HRE	Hepatic Reticuloendothelial [*Medicine*] (MELL)
HRF	Homologous Restriction Factor [*Medicine*] (MELL)
HRF	Hypothalamic Releasing Factor [*Medicine*] (MELL)
HRMA	High Resolution Mirror Assembly
HROI	High Resolution Optical Instrument (EOSA)
HRP	High-Risk Pregnancy (MELL)
HRPI	High-Risk Premature Infant (MELL)
HRS	Hamman-Rich Syndrome [*Medicine*] (MELL)
HRTS	Hyper-Real-Time Simulation
HRV	High Resolution Video (EOSA)
HRZ	Hertz Corp'A' [*NYSE symbol*] (SG)
HS	Hamstring (MELL)
HS	Hazardous Substance (MELL)
HS	Home Service [*British*] (MILB)
HSA	Health Scientist Administrator (MELL)
HSA	Health Security Act (MELL)
HSA	Horseshoe Abscess [*Medicine*] (MELL)
HSAC	High Speed Access [*NASDAQ symbol*] (SG)
HSAN	Hereditary, Sensory, and Autonomic Neuopathy [*Medicine*] (MELL)
HSB	HSB Group [*NYSE symbol*] (SG)
HSCD	Hand-Schueller-Christian Disease (MELL)
HSH	Hydrogenated Starch Hydrolysates [*Medicine*] (MELL)
HSI	Home Security Intl. [*AMEX symbol*] (SG)
HSK	Horseshoe Kidney [*Medicine*] (MELL)
HSL	Health and Safety Laboratory
HSM	Heterosexual Male (MELL)
HSM	Hussmann Intl. [*NYSE symbol*] (SG)
HSN	Heart Sounds Normal [*Medicine*] (MELL)
HSOR	Hydroxysteroid Oxidoreductase [*Medicine*] (MELL)
HSP	High Speed Photometer
HSPA	High School Proficiency Assessment
HSPH	Harvard School of Public Health (MELL)
HSPN	Henoch-Schonlein Purpura Nephritis [*Medicine*] (MELL)
HSPT	High School Proficiency Test
HSR	Heated Serum Reagin [*Medicine*] (MELL)
HSV1	Herpes Simplex, Type 1 [*Medicine*]
HSV2	Herpes Simplex, Type 2 [*Medicine*]
HSV2	Herpes Simplex Virus Type 2
HT	Halo Test [*Medicine*] (MELL)
HT	Heat Therapy (MELL)
HT	Hematologic Toxin [*Medicine*] (MELL)
HT	Hemothorax [*Medicine*] (MELL)
HT	Hersha Hospitality Trust [*AMEX symbol*] (SG)
HT	High Tracheostomy [*Medicine*] (MELL)
HTBK	Hatchback
HTC	Hypertrophic Cicatrix [*Medicine*] (MELL)
HTCVD	Hypertensive Cardiovascular Disease (MELL)
HTD	Heat Transfer Division
HTDS	Host Terminal Data Server
HTE	Hypothenar Eminence [*Medicine*] (MELL)
HTF	Hard to Find [*Collectibles*]

HTL..............	Hot Tub Lung (MELL)
HTL..............	Human T-cell Leukemia (MELL)
HTT..............	High Touch Therapy (MELL)
HTX..............	Hemothorax [*Medicine*] (MELL)
HU	Hudson United Bancorp [*NYSE symbol*] (SG)
Hu	Hungary (MILB)
HU	Hydroureter [*Medicine*] (MELL)
HUC	Human Use Committee
HUD	Hypertonic Uterine Dysfunction [*Medicine*] (MELL)
HUD	Hypotonic Uterine Dysfunction [*Medicine*] (MELL)
HUGH..........	Human Growth Hormone (MELL)
Hum.............	Hummingbird
HUMC	Hummingbird Communications [*NASDAQ symbol*] (SG)
HUN	Hyperuricemic Nephropathy [*Medicine*] (MELL)
hund	Hundred (GEAB)
hus..............	Husband (GEAB)
h/v	Harbour View
HVA	Hypervitamintosis A [*Medicine*] (MELL)
HVO	Hallux Valgus Orthosis [*Medicine*] (MELL)
HVS	Herpes Virus Sensitivity [*Medicine*] (MELL)

HVS	Hirsutism-Virilizing Syndromes [*Medicine*] (MELL)
HVS	Hypovolemic Shock [*Medicine*] (MELL)
HW..............	Herpetic Whitlow [*Medicine*] (MELL)
HW..............	Hookworm (MELL)
HW..............	Hot Wheels [*Mattel*]
HWD	Hollywood Casino'A' [*AMEX symbol*] (SG)
HWM	Howmet International [*NYSE symbol*] (SG)
HWP	Hot Wet Pack (MELL)
HWS	Hospitality Worldwide Svcs. [*AMEX symbol*] (SG)
HWY MI.......	Highway Miles
HXT..............	Houston Industries 7 Percent,'ACES' [*NYSE symbol*] (SG)
hy	Heavy (MILB)
HYC	Hypercom Corp. [*NYSE symbol*] (SG)
HYD	Hydration (MELL)
HYPT	Hyperion Telecommunications'A' [*NASDAQ symbol*] (SG)
HZAN	Herpes Zoster Acute Neuralgia [*Medicine*] (MELL)
HZI..............	Hemizona Assay Index [*Medicine*] (MELL)
HZI..............	Herpes Zoster Infection [*Medicine*] (MELL)
HZL..............	Herpes Zoster Lesion [*Medicine*] (MELL)
HZP..............	Horizon Pharmacies [*!AMX*] (SG)

I

By Acronym

I.................. I-Band (MELL)
I.................. Implantation (MELL)
I.................. Incision (MELL)
I.................. Inspiration (MELL)
I.................. Insulin (MELL)
I.................. Iris (MELL)
I.................. Ischium (MELL)
IA................ Immunoadsorbent [*Medicine*] (MELL)
IA................ Indolic Acid (MELL)
IA................ Infantile Apnea [*Medicine*] (MELL)
IA................ Infectious Arthritis (MELL)
IA................ Inhalation Anesthesia (MELL)
Ia................ Iowa (BEE)
IAA.............. Iliac Artery Aneurysm [*Medicine*] (MELL)
IAA.............. Infra-Abdominal Abscess [*Medicine*] (MELL)
IAA.............. International Association for Aerobiology (QUAC)
IAAI............ Intra-Articular Anesthetic Injection [*Medicine*] (MELL)
IAAP........... International Association of African Palynology (QUAC)
IAB.............. Induced Abortion (MELL)
IABD........... Ischemic-Anoxic Brain Damage [*Medicine*] (MELL)
IABM........... Idiopathic Aplastic Bone Marrow [*Medicine*] (MELL)
IAC.............. Image Analysis Computer (MELL)
IAC.............. Inpatient Acute Care (MELL)
IAC.............. Intra-Arterial Catheter [*Medicine*] (MELL)
IACD........... Implantable Automatic Cardioverter-Defibrillator [*Medicine*] (MELL)
IACG........... Intermittent Angle-Closure Glaucoma (MELL)
IACP........... International Academy of Compounding Pharmacists (GVA)
IADCCT....... International Association of Duncan Certified Ceramic Teachers (EA)
IADN........... Integrated Atmospheric Deposition Network [*Environmental Protection Agency*] (EPAT)
IAEP........... International Association of Equine Practitioners (GVA)
IAF.............. Inhibiting Activity Factor [*Medicine*] (MELL)
IAG.............. Internal Audit Group [*British*] (GVA)
IAGT........... Indirect Antiglobulin Test [*Medicine*] (MELL)
IAH.............. Isonicotinic Acid Hydrazide [*Medicine*] (MELL)
IAHS........... Infection-Associated Hemophagocytic Syndrome [*Medicine*] (MELL)
IAI.............. Idiopathic Autonomic Insufficiency [*Medicine*] (MELL)
IAJ.............. Immoblization of Ankle Joint (MELL)
IAM............. Altos Hornos de Mexico ADS [*NYSE symbol*] (SG)
IAMA........... International Association of Machinists and Aerospace Workers, Woodworkers District Lodge 1 (EA)
I & E.......... Inspiratory and Expiratory [*Medicine*] (MELL)
IAP.............. Islamic Association for Palestine
IAR.............. Immediate Asthma Reaction (MELL)
IAS.............. Idiopathic Ankylosing Spondylitis [*Medicine*] (MELL)
IAS.............. Infant Appnea Syndrome [*Medicine*] (MELL)
IAS.............. Infantile Arteriosclerosis [*Medicine*] (MELL)
IAS.............. Insulin Autoimmune Syndrome [*Medicine*] (MELL)
IASC........... International Association of Skateboard Companies (EA)
IASI............ Improved Atmospheric Sounding Interferometer (EOSA)
IASI............ Infrared Atmospheric Sounding Interferometer
IAVA........... International AIDS Vaccine Initiative
IAVI............ Italian Academy of Veterinary Informatics (GVA)
IB................ Infant Botulism [*Medicine*] (MELL)
IBBT........... International Brotherhood of Bikers' Teardrops (EA)
IBDA........... International Bird Dog Association (EA)
IBED........... Inborn Error of Development (MELL)
IBG.............. Iliac Bone Graft [*Medicine*] (MELL)
IBHFM........ International Boxing Hall of Fame Museum (EA)
IBOW.......... Intact Bag of Waters [*Medicine*] (MELL)
IBQ.............. Illness Behavior Questionnaire (MELL)
IBRFC......... International Buddy Rich Fan Club (EA)
IBU.............. Inland Boatmen's Union of the Pacific
IC................ Iliac Crest [*Medicine*] (MELL)
IC................ Immediate Care [*Medicine*] (MELL)
IC................ Immunocompromised [*Medicine*] (MELL)
IC................ Immunoconjugate [*Medicine*] (MELL)
IC................ Impetigo Contagiosa [*Medicine*] (MELL)
IC................ Incompetent Cervix [*Medicine*] (MELL)
ICA.............. Integrated Color Analysis (QUAC)
ICAA........... Internal Carotid Artery Aneurysm [*Medicine*] (MELL)
ICAAE......... International Center for Aquaculture and Aquatic Environments (GVA)
ICAHM........ International Committee on Archaeological Heritage Management (QUAC)
ICANN........ Internet Corporation for Assigned Names and Numbers
ICANN........ Internet Corporation of Assigned Names and Numbers

ICAR........... International Congress on Animal Reproduction (GVA)
ICAR........... Italian Car Registry (EA)
ICB.............. Intercostal Block [*Medicine*] (MELL)
ICCB........... Institute of Chemistry and Cell Biology [*Harvard Medical School*]
ICCC........... International Christian Cycling Club USA (EA)
ICCI............ Insight Communications [*NASDAQ symbol*] (SG)
ICCK........... Immunoreactive Cholecystokinin [*Medicine*] (MELL)
ICCP........... International Climate Change Partnership (EPAT)
ICCT........... Intracavitary Chemotherapy [*Medicine*] (MELL)
ICD.............. Impulse Control Disorder (MELL)
ICD.............. Internal Cardioverter Defibrillator [*Medicine*] (MELL)
ICDC........... Implantable Cardioverter Defibrillator Catheter [*Medicine*] (MELL)
ICE.............. Intracochlear Electrodes [*Medicine*] (MELL)
ICEDA......... Intracranial Epidural Abscess [*Medicine*] (MELL)
ICEI............ Internal Combustion Engine Institute, Inc.
ICES........... Information, Communication, Entertainment, Safety, and Security
ICF.............. Instrument Control Facility (EOSA)
ICGX........... ICG Communications [*NASDAQ symbol*] (SG)
ICH.............. Infantile Cortical Hyperostosis [*Medicine*] (MELL)
ICH.............. Intracortical Hemorrhage [*Medicine*] (MELL)
ICH.............. Intracranial Hypertension [*Medicine*] (MELL)
ICI.............. Intracavitary Irradiation [*Medicine*] (MELL)
Icl.............. Iceland (MILB)
ICL.............. Industrial Code and Logic
ICLAS......... International Council for Laboratory Animal Science (GVA)
ICM............. Intercostal Muscle [*Medicine*] (MELL)
ICM............. International Connections Manager
ICMA........... Intracranial Microaneurysm [*Medicine*] (MELL)
ICMI........... Imperial Credit Comm'l Mtg. [*NASDAQ symbol*] (SG)
ICN.............. Immune Complex Nephritis [*Medicine*] (MELL)
ICNSH........ Idiopathic Central Nervous System Hypersommia [*Medicine*] (MELL)
ICO.............. InaCom Corp. [*NYSE symbol*] (SG)
ICO.............. Intracartilaginous Ossification [*Medicine*] (MELL)
ICP.............. Immunocompromised Patient [*Medicine*] (MELL)
ICP.............. Intermittent Catheterization Protocol [*Medicine*] (MELL)
ICP.............. Intraperitoneal Cisplatinum [*Medicine*] (MELL)
ICPT........... InterCept Group [*NASDAQ symbol*] (SG)
ICR.............. Intracavitary Radium [*Medicine*] (MELL)
ICS.............. Internet Caching Service [*Computer science*]
ICSL........... Innovative Clinical Solutions [*NASDAQ symbol*] (SG)
ICT.............. Impaired Glucose Tolerance [*Medicine*] (MELL)
ICT.............. Interstitial Cell Tumor [*Medicine*] (MELL)
ICT.............. Intracranial Tumor [*Medicine*] (MELL)
ICTC........... Inferior Cornu of Thyroid Cartilage [*Medicine*] (MELL)
ICV.............. Ileocecal Valve [*Medicine*] (MELL)
ICV.............. Intracellular Volume [*Medicine*] (MELL)
ICZN........... International Code of Zoological Nomenclature (QUAC)
ID................ Idiotype (MELL)
ID................ Inappropriate Disability (MELL)
IDA.............. Idacorp, Inc. [*NYSE symbol*] (SG)
Ida.............. Idaho (BEE)
IDA.............. Initial Data Analysis [*Statistics*]
IDA.............. International Dark-Sky Association
IDAL........... Illinois Digital Academic Library
IDAM........... Infant of Drug-Abusing Mother (MELL)
IDAM........... Infant of Drug-Addicted Mother (MELL)
IDBC........... Infiltrating Ductal Breast Cancer (MELL)
IDBT........... Immune Dot-Blot Test [*Medicine*] (MELL)
IDC.............. Industrial Democracy Commission
IDCT........... Inverse Discrete Cosine Transform [*Electronics*]
IDD.............. Iodotyrosine Deiodinase Deficiency [*Medicine*] (MELL)
IDEAL......... International Decade of East African Lakes (QUAC)
IDF.............. Idiopathic Diffuse Fibrosis [*Medicine*] (MELL)
IDG.............. Industrial Distribution Grp. [*NYSE symbol*] (SG)
IDG.............. Interdisciplinary Group (MELL)
IDI.............. Implantable Defibrillator Insertion [*Medicine*] (MELL)
IDI.............. Intradiskal Injection [*Medicine*] (MELL)
IDP.............. Idiopathic Pulmonary Hemosiderosis [*Medicine*] (MELL)
IDP.............. Intraductal Papilloma [*Medicine*] (MELL)
IDR.............. Intrawest Corp. [*NYSE symbol*] (SG)
IDS.............. Industrial Data Systems [*AMEX symbol*] (SG)
IDS.............. Interdisciplinary Science (EOSA)
IDT.............. Indicator Dilution Technique [*Medicine*] (MELL)
IE................ Impacted Embolism [*Medicine*] (MELL)
IE................ Inflammatory Exudate [*Medicine*] (MELL)
IE................ Inner Ear (MELL)

IEC.............	Infectious Endocarditis [*Medicine*] (MELL)
IEC.............	Infective Endocarditis [*Medicine*] (MELL)
IED.............	Intraepithelial Dysplasia [*Medicine*] (MELL)
IEE.............	Integrated Electrical Svcs. [*NYSE symbol*] (SG)
IEN.............	Internet Experimental Note
IEOAM	Inborn Errors of Organic Acid Metabolism [*Medicine*] (MELL)
IEOS............	International Earth Observing System (EOSA)
IEPT............	Intermediate End Point of Therapy (MELL)
IES.............	Ineffective Erythropoiesis Syndrome [*Medicine*] (MELL)
IES.............	Inferior Esophageal Sphincter [*Medicine*] (MELL)
IES.............	Institute of Environmental Sciences
IEST............	Implanted Electrode Stimulation Therapy [*Medicine*] (MELL)
IET.............	International Embryo Transfer Society (GVA)
IEWG...........	International Elbow Working Group (GVA)
IEXAS...........	Institute of Experimental Animal Sciences [*Osaka University*] (GVA)
IF...............	Ictal Fear [*Medicine*] (MELL)
IF...............	Immunofixation [*Medicine*] (MELL)
IF...............	Implant Failure [*Medicine*] (MELL)
IF...............	Inferior Facet [*Medicine*] (MELL)
IF...............	Infrapatellar Fat [*Medicine*] (MELL)
IFA.............	Indirect Immunofluorescence Assay [*Medicine*] (MELL)
IFAR...........	International Fund for Avian Research (GVA)
IFCS...........	International Forum on Chemical Safety (EPAT)
IFMA..........	Information Resources Management Association
IFPA...........	International Flipper Pinball Association (EA)
Ifs.............	Independent Front Suspension
IFSE...........	Internal Fetal Scalp Electrode [*Medicine*] (MELL)
IG..............	Infantile Glaucoma (MELL)
IG..............	Inflammatory Glaucoma (MELL)
IG..............	Intestinal Gas (MELL)
IGAP	Illinois Goal Assessment Program
IGAP	International Global Aerosol Program (EOSA)
IGB............	Ischiogluteal Bursa [*Medicine*] (MELL)
IGB............	Ischiogluteal Bursitis [*Medicine*] (MELL)
IGFA...........	International Group of Funding Agencies for Global Change Research (QUAC)
IGM............	Internet Grateful Med [*Program for assisted searching of MEDLINE*] (MELL)
IGS.............	International Glaciospeleological Society (QUAC)
IGTN	Ingrown Toenail (MELL)
IGU	Iminoglycinuria [*Medicine*] (MELL)
IH..............	ICH Corp. [*AMEX symbol*] (SG)
IH..............	Idiopathic Hirsutism [*Medicine*] (MELL)
IH..............	Imperforate Hymen [*Medicine*] (MELL)
IH..............	Incisional Hernia [*Medicine*] (MELL)
IH..............	Incompletely Healed [*Medicine*] (MELL)
IH..............	Intracranial Hematome [*Medicine*] (MELL)
IHB............	Intermittent Heartburn (MELL)
IHDP	International Human Dimensions Program on Global Environmental Change (QUAC)
IHDT	Integrated Helicopter Design Tool
IHEP...........	Institute for Higher Education Policy
IHF............	International Home Foods [*NYSE symbol*] (SG)
IHI.............	Information Holdings [*NYSE symbol*] (SG)
IHIC...........	International Hydrocarbon Intercomparison Committee (QUAC)
IHK............	Imperial Sugar [*AMEX symbol*] (SG)
IHMF..........	International Herpes Management Forum
IHN............	Iliohypogastric Nerve [*Medicine*] (MELL)
IHP............	Indicated Horsepower
IHU............	Impaired Hepatic Uptake [*Medicine*] (MELL)
II..............	Impaired Intellect (MELL)
II..............	Incapacitating Illness (MELL)
II..............	Incapacitating Injury (MELL)
II..............	Inhalation Injury (MELL)
II..............	Intellectual Impairment (MELL)
II..............	Intentional Injury (MELL)
II..............	Interdisciplinary Investigator (EOSA)
II..............	Intestional Ischemia [*Medicine*] (MELL)
IICA...........	Intracranial Internal Carotid Artery [*Medicine*] (MELL)
IICAB	Institute for International Cooperation in Animal Biologics (GVA)
IIDM..........	Insulin-Independent Diabetes Mellitus [*Medicine*] (MELL)
IIH............	Institute of International Health (GVA)
IIJ.............	Internet Initiative Japan, Inc.
IIP............	Idiopathic Interstitial Pneumonitis [*Medicine*] (MELL)
IIP............	Integrated Image Processing (MELL)
IIR............	IRI International [*NYSE symbol*] (SG)
IISD	International Institute for Sustainable Development (QUAC)
IIVTG	Industrial in Vitro Toxicology Group (GVA)
IIXC...........	IXC Communications [*NASDAQ symbol*] (SG)
IIXL...........	iXL Enterprises [*NASDAQ symbol*] (SG)
IJBFC.........	International Jack Benny Fan Club (EA)
IJO............	Idiopathic Juvenille Osteoporosis [*Medicine*] (MELL)
IKE............	Imperial Klingon Embassy/Star Trek [*An association*] (EA)
IKN............	Ikon Office Solutions [*NYSE symbol*] (SG)
II..............	Israel (MILB)
ILAN...........	Israel Network
ILC............	Intermediate Longitudinal Crease [*Medicine*] (MELL)
ILD............	Inflammatory Lung Disease (MELL)
ILE............	Infantile Lobar Emphysema [*Medicine*] (MELL)
ILECS.........	Incumbent Local Exchange Carriers
ILF............	Indicated Low Forceps [*Medicine*] (MELL)
ILL............	Iliolumbar Ligament [*Medicine*] (MELL)
Ill.............	Illinois (BEE)
Illit...........	Illiterate (BEE)
ILN............	Inguinal Lymph Node [*Medicine*] (MELL)

ILS.............	Infared Liver Scan [*Medicine*] (MELL)
ILX.............	ILX Resorts [*AMEX symbol*] (SG)
IM.............	Indonesia Minas [*Crude oil*]
IM.............	Inferior Mediastinum [*Medicine*] (MELL)
IM.............	Inherent Moisture [*Coal industry*]
IM.............	Innocent Murmur [*Medicine*] (MELL)
IM.............	Internal Monitor [*Medicine*] (MELL)
IMAC..........	International Mobile Air Conditioning Association, Inc.
IMAL..........	i-Mall, Inc. [*NASDAQ symbol*] (SG)
IMAX..........	Imax Corp. [*NASDAQ symbol*] (SG)
IMB............	Investigator of Micro-Biosphere (EOSA)
IMB............	Irish Medicines Board (GVA)
IMC............	Intermittent Catheterization [*Medicine*] (MELL)
IMC............	Interstitial Myocarditis [*Medicine*] (MELL)
IMCA..........	International Mistral Class Association (EA)
IMCI...........	Induced Myocardial Ischemia [*Medicine*] (MELL)
IMG............	Interferometric Monitor of Greenhouse Gases (EOSA)
IMI............	Impending Myocardial Infarction [*Medicine*] (MELL)
IMI............	Isolated Meconium Ileus [*Medicine*] (MELL)
IMI............	Istituto Bancario Ital ADS [*NYSE symbol*] (SG)
imit...........	Imitative (BEE)
IMLN..........	Internal Mammary Lymph Node [*Medicine*] (MELL)
IMN............	Imation Corp. [*NYSE symbol*] (SG)
IMN............	Infectious Mononucleosis [*Medicine*] (MELL)
IMN............	Initial Malignant Neoplasm [*Medicine*] (MELL)
IMN............	Inmet Mining Toronto Stock Exchange symbol (SG)
IMON..........	ImaginOn, Inc. [*NASDAQ symbol*] (SG)
IMP............	Imperial Bancorp [*NYSE symbol*] (SG)
imp...........	Importation (GEAB)
imp...........	Improved (MILB)
IMP............	Intermenstrual Pain (MELL)
IMP............	Ischemic Muscle Pain (MELL)
IMPACC	Intestinal Multiple Polyposis and Colorectal Cancer (MELL)
IMPS..........	International Mensan Philatelists Society (EA)
IMR............	Internet Monthly Report
IMRS..........	IMRglobal Corp. [*NASDAQ symbol*] (SG)
IMRSA	International Medical Regulatory and Shipping Association (GVA)
IMS............	Infertile Male Syndrome (MELL)
IMSG..........	International Medical School Graduate (MELL)
IN.............	Industrial Nurse (MELL)
IN.............	Insulin Neuritis [*Medicine*] (MELL)
IN.............	Internist (MELL)
INA............	International Nannoplankton Association (QUAC)
INAD..........	In No Apparent Distress [*Medicine*] (MELL)
IN-ADDR	Inverse Addressing
INB............	Community Independent Bank [*AMEX symbol*] (SG)
INC............	National Institute of Culture
INCIID.........	International Council on Infertility Information Dissemination
INCX..........	INFOCURE Corp. [*NASDAQ symbol*] (SG)
Ind	India (MILB)
Ind	Indiana (BEE)
Ind	Indianapolis Colts [*National Football League*] [*1984-present*] (NFLA)
Ind	Indians (GEAB)
INDA..........	Investigational New Drug Application (MELL)
indep..........	Independent (MILB)
INDG..........	Indigo N.V. [*NASDAQ symbol*] (SG)
Indo	Indonesia (MILB)
INDOEX.......	Indian Ocean Experiment [*National Science Foundation project*]
Indpls.........	Indianapolis (BEE)
IndyCar.......	Championship Auto Racing Teams [*An association*] (EA)
INet...........	Indiana Network
inf	Infant (BEE)
inf	Infantry (MILB)
INF............	Infarction [*Medicine*] (MELL)
INF............	Interferon [*Medicine*] (MELL)
INF............	Intravenous Nutritional Feeding (MELL)
Inf Bde........	Infantry Brigade
infl............	Influenced (BEE)
INFN...........	Italian National Institute for Nuclear Physics
INFY...........	Infosys Technologies ADS [*NASDAQ symbol*] (SG)
inh	Inherited (GEAB)
inhab	Inhabitant (GEAB)
INIT...........	Interliant, Inc. [*NASDAQ symbol*] (SG)
INKT...........	Inktomi Corp. [*NASDAQ symbol*] (SG)
INPA..........	Instituto Nacional de Pesquisas de Amazonia [*Brazil*] (EOSA)
INPE..........	Instituto Nacional de Pesquisas Espaciais [*Brazil*] (EOSA)
INS............	Idiopathic Neurologic Syndrome [*Medicine*] (MELL)
INS............	Illuminated Nasal Speculum [*Medicine*] (MELL)
INSA..........	Institut National des Sciences Appliques [*France*] (EOSA)
INSITE	International Network of Somewhere in Time Enthusiasts (EA)
inst	Institute (BEE)
INST...........	Instrumental (MELL)
INSW	InsWeb Corp. [*NASDAQ symbol*] (SG)
Int.............	Interior
int.............	Interred (GEAB)
intens	Intensive (BEE)
INTI...........	Inet Technologies [*NASDAQ symbol*] (SG)
INV............	Amer Residential Inv Trust [*NYSE symbol*] (SG)
INVI...........	Integral Vision [*NASDAQ symbol*] (SG)
IOAL..........	Intraoperative Abdominal Lavage [*Medicine*] (MELL)
IOB............	Implantation of Blastocyst [*Medicine*] (MELL)
IOB............	Institute of Biology (GVA)
IOC............	Industrial Operations Command [*Army*]
IOC............	Intergovernmental Oceanographic Commission (EOSA)
IOCG..........	Intraoperative Cholecystogram [*Medicine*] (MELL)

IODAM	Infant of Drug-Addicted Mother (MELL)
IOF	Infraorbital Foramen [*Medicine*] (MELL)
IOF	Intraorbital Foramen [*Medicine*] (MELL)
IOH	Infundibulum of Hypophysis [*Medicine*] (MELL)
IOI	Integrated Orthopaedics [*AMEX symbol*] (SG)
IOI	Intraocular Implant [*Medicine*] (MELL)
IOL	Iron Overload [*Medicine*] (MELL)
IOL	Islet of Langerhans [*Medicine*] (MELL)
IOLC	Inoperable Lung Cancer (MELL)
IOLI	Intraocular Lens Implantation [*Medicine*] (MELL)
IOM	Iomega Corp. [*NYSE symbol*] (SG)
IOMM&P	International Organization of Masters, Mates, and Pilots
ION	Infraorbital Nerve [*Medicine*] (MELL)
IONA	IONA Technologies ADR [*NASDAQ symbol*] (SG)
IOPA	Independent Organ Procurement Agency [*Medicine*] (MELL)
IOR	Immature Oocyte Retrieval [*Medicine*]
IOT	Intraocular Tumor [*Medicine*] (MELL)
IOW	Infected Open Wound (MELL)
IOX	Iomed, Inc. [*AMEX symbol*] (SG)
IP	Idiopathic Parkinsonism [*Medicine*] (MELL)
IP	Inactivated Pepsin [*Medicine*] (MELL)
IP	Incompetent Patient (MELL)
IPA	Independent Pilots Association
IPA	Industries Perforators Association, Inc.
IPA	International Permafrost Association (QUAC)
IPA	Invasion Plasmid Antigens [*Medicine*] (MELL)
IPAP	Investment Promotion Action Plan [*Bangkok*]
IPAR	Inter Parfums [*NASDAQ symbol*] (SG)
IPAS	International Projects Assistance Services
IPC	Indirect Platelet Count [*Medicine*] (MELL)
IPC	International Palynological Congress (QUAC)
IPC	Intraperitoneal Chemotherapy [*Medicine*] (MELL)
IPC	Ion Pair Chromatography [*Medicine*] (MELL)
IPC	Ischemic Preconditioning [*Medicine*] (MELL)
IPCT	Intraperitoneal Chemotherapy [*Medicine*] (MELL)
IPD	Imaging Photon Detector (QUAC)
IPD	Incurable Problem Drinker (MELL)
IPD	Infantile Polycystic Disease [*Medicine*] (MELL)
IPD	Interplanetary Dust [*Science*]
IPDAS	Intestinal Protective Drug Absorption System [*Medicine*] (MELL)
IPF	International Pen Friends (EA)
IPG	Inter-Professional Group (GVA)
IPHP	Intraperitoneal Hyperthermic Perfusion [*Medicine*] (MELL)
IPIE	Intrapulmonary Interstitial Emphysema [*Medicine*] (MELL)
IPIS	Incomplete Pulmonary Infarction [*Medicine*] (MELL)
IPKD	Infantile Polycystic Kidney Disease [*Medicine*] (MELL)
IPL	Internet Public Library [*Established by the University of Michigan in 1995*]
IPL	Isolated Perfused Lung [*Medicine*] (MELL)
IPM	Immediate Pigment Darkening [*Medicine*] (MELL)
IPM	Infectious Polymyositis [*Medicine*] (MELL)
IPOC	International Partner Operations Center (EOSA)
IPP	Intractable Pelvic Pain [*Medicine*] (MELL)
IPV	Infectious Peritonitis Virus [*Medicine*] (MELL)
IR	Internet Registry
Ir	Iran (MILB)
Ir	Irish (BEE)
IRA	Immunoradioassay [*Medicine*] (MELL)
IRA	Implant Resection Arthroplasty [*Medicine*] (MELL)
IRAF	Image Reduction and Analysis Facility
Iran	Iranian (BEE)
IRAS	Infared Astronomical Satellite [*Launched in January 1983*]
IRD	Infantile Refsum's Syndrome [*Medicine*] (MELL)
IRE	Bank of Ireland Governor & Co ADS [*NYSE symbol*] (SG)
IRID	Iridium World Communications'A' [*NASDAQ symbol*] (SG)
IRIS	Infrared Radiation Interferometer Spectrometer
Irl	Ireland (MILB)
IRLS	Iteratively Reweighted Least Squares
IRM	Immune Response Modifier [*Medicine*] (MELL)
IRM	Iron Mountain [*NYSE symbol*] (SG)
IRMC	Inter-Regulatory Risk Management Council [*Environmental science*] (EPAT)
IRPGN	Idiopathic Rapidly Progressive Glomerulonephritis [*Medicine*] (MELL)
Irq	Iraq (MILB)
Irs	Independent Rear Suspension
IRTR	Impaired Renal Tubular Reabsorption [*Medicine*] (MELL)
IS	Ichthyosis Simplex [*Medicine*] (MELL)
IS	Infectious Spondylitis [*Medicine*] (MELL)
IS	Inguinal Syndrome [*Medicine*] (MELL)
IS	Intestinal Stenosis [*Medicine*] (MELL)
IS	Isometric Strength [*Medicine*] (MELL)
IS	Isotonic Strength [*Medicine*] (MELL)
ISAS	Institute for Space and Astronautical Science
ISAZ	International Society for Anthrozoology (GVA)
ISBFA	International Sphynx Breeders and Fanciers' Association (EA)
ISCA	International Specialty Car Association (EA)
ISCR	Intrastromal Corneal Ring [*Medicine*] (MELL)
ISD	Immune-Suppression Drug (MELL)
ISD	Interventricular Septal Defect [*Medicine*] (MELL)
ISD	Intractable Seizure Disorder [*Medicine*] (MELL)
ISD	Intrinsic Sleep Disorder [*Medicine*] (MELL)
ISD	Iron-Storage Disease [*Medicine*] (MELL)
ISGA	International Sprout Growers Association
ISIS	Integrated Shape Imaging System (MELL)

ISLD	Digital Island [*NASDAQ symbol*] (SG)
ISM	Illinois State Museum (QUAC)
ISO	Independent System Operator
ISO	Isolette (MELL)
ISPI	International Society for Performance Improvement
ISPV	In Situ Plasma Vitrification
ISS	Inferior Sagittal Sinus [*Medicine*] (MELL)
ISS	International Staging System [*Medicine*] (MELL)
ISS	Irritable Stomach Syndrome [*Medicine*] (MELL)
ISSRA	Individual Social Security Retirement Account
ISSX	ISS Group [*NASDAQ symbol*] (SG)
IST	Immunosuppressive Therapy [*Medicine*] (MELL)
IST	Instrument Support Terminal (EOSA)
IST	Inversion Stress Test [*Medicine*] (MELL)
IST	ISPAT Intl'A' [*NYSE symbol*] (SG)
ISTEP	Indiana Statewide Testing for Educational Progress
ISV	InSite Vision [*AMEX symbol*] (SG)
ISVMA	Illinois State Veterinary Medical Association (GVA)
ISVP	International Society of Veterinary Perinatology (GVA)
ISY	International Space Year [*1992*] (EOSA)
IT	Impacted Tooth [*Medicine*] (MELL)
IT	Infective Thrombosis [*Medicine*] (MELL)
IT	Infective Thrombus [*Medicine*] (MELL)
IT	Insulin Therapy [*Medicine*] (MELL)
IT	Intermittent Traction [*Medicine*] (MELL)
It	Italy (MILB)
ITA	Influenza Type A [*Medicine*] (MELL)
ITA	Internal Thoracic Artery [*Medicine*] (MELL)
ITASE	International Trans-Antarctic Scientific Expedition (QUAC)
ITC	Innovative Technology Council (EPAT)
ITC	International Thunderbird Club (EA)
ITCD	ITC DeltaCom [*NASDAQ symbol*] (SG)
ITEX	International Tundra Experiment (QUAC)
ITG	Investment Tech Group [*NYSE symbol*] (SG)
ITIR	Infrared Thermal Imaging Radiometer (EOSA)
ITLA	ITLA Capital [*NASDAQ symbol*] (SG)
ITN	Independent Transportation Network
ITO	Intertrochanteric [*Medicine*] (MELL)
ITOY	International Tropospheric Ozone Year (QUAC)
ITP	Islet-Cell Tumor of Pancreas [*Medicine*] (MELL)
ITR	Integrated Trans Ntwk Grp. [*AMEX symbol*] (SG)
ITS	Inflatable Tubular Structure
ITS	Inhaled Tobacco Smoke (MELL)
ITS	Internet Technology Series
ITTR	Inflatable Tubular Torso Restraint
ITVU	InterVU, Inc. [*NASDAQ symbol*] (SG)
ITX	IT Group [*NYSE symbol*] (SG)
ITY	Imperial Tobacco Grp ADS [*NYSE symbol*] (SG)
IUBS	International Union of Biological Sciences (QUAC)
IUD	Incoordinate Uterine Dsyfunction [*Medicine*] (MELL)
IUF	International Underwater Foundation (EA)
IUJH	International Union of Journeyman Horseshoers
IUP	Intended Use Plan [*Environmental science*] (EPAT)
IV	Influenza Vaccination [*Medicine*] (MELL)
IV	Initial Visit [*Medicine*] (MELL)
IV	Interview [*Medicine*] (MELL)
IVA	Irish Veterinary Association (GVA)
IVBT	Intravascular Brachytherapy [*Medicine*]
IVC	Intravascular Catheter [*Medicine*] (MELL)
IVC	Invacare Corp. [*NYSE symbol*] (SG)
IVCOD	IVC Industries (New) [*NASDAQ symbol*] (SG)
IVD	Induced Vestibular Dysfunction [*Medicine*] (MELL)
IVD	Intraventricular Delay [*Medicine*] (MELL)
IVD	Ischemic Vascular Disease [*Medicine*] (MELL)
IVDD	Intervertebral Disk Disease [*Medicine*] (MELL)
IVF	Intervertebral Foramen [*Medicine*] (MELL)
IVF	Intravenous Feeding [*Medicine*] (MELL)
IVFA	Intravenous Fluorescein Angiogram [*Medicine*] (MELL)
IVFT	Intravenous Fluid Therapy [*Medicine*] (MELL)
IVGG	Intravenous Gamma Globulin [*Medicine*] (MELL)
IVIL	iVillage, Inc. [*NASDAQ symbol*] (SG)
IVM	Intervertebral Muscle [*Medicine*] (MELL)
IVM	Involuntary Muscle [*Medicine*] (MELL)
IVN	Inferior Vertebral Notch [*Medicine*] (MELL)
IVNTA	International Veterinary Nurses and Technicians Association (GVA)
IVU	Irish Veterinary Union (GVA)
IVUS	Interventional Ultrasonography [*Medicine*] (MELL)
IVV	Influenza Virus Vaccine [*Medicine*] (MELL)
IVWL	Intracapsular Volar Wrist Ligament [*Medicine*] (MELL)
IWA	International Wheelchair Aviators (EA)
IWC	International Watch Co.
IWC	International Welcome Club
IWEC	International Wildlife Education & Conservation (GVA)
IWF	Iliac Wing Fracture [*Medicine*] (MELL)
IWGDMGC	Interagency Working Group on Data Management for Global Change (EOSA)
IWI	Inferior Wall Infarct [*Medicine*] (MELL)
IWJG	International Watch and Jewelry Guild
IWMI	International Water Management Institute
IWNFC	International Willie Nelson Fan Club (EA)
IWT	Impacted Wisdom Tooth (MELL)
IXX	Ivex Packaging [*NYSE symbol*] (SG)
IYO	International Year of the Ocean [*1998*] (QUAC)
IZ	Infarction Zone [*Medicine*] (MELL)

J
By Acronym

Ja .... Jamaica (MILB)
JA .... Juvenile Arthritis (MELL)
Jac.............. Jacksonville Jaguars [*National Football League*] [*1995-present*]
                  (NFLA)
JADF........... Jordan Airports Duty Free
JAIN........... Japan Academic Inter-University Network
JALAM........ Japanese Association for Laboratory Animal Medicine (GVA)
JAPCA........ Journal of Air Pollution Control Association [*A publication*] (EPAT)
JAVMA........ Journal of American Veterinary Medical Association [*A publication*]
                  (GVA)
JAX .... J. Alexander's Corp. [*NYSE symbol*] (SG)
JAZ .... JCC Holding 'A' [*AMEX symbol*] (SG)
JBL .... Jabil Circuit [*NYSE symbol*] (SG)
JC .... Jacket Crown (MELL)
JC .... Joint Contracture [*Medicine*] (MELL)
JC .... Juvenile Cataract (MELL)
JCCINY .... Japanese Chamber of Commerce and Industry of New York (EA)
JD.............. Jaundice [*Medicine*] (MELL)
JDC............ Jackson Development Corporation
JDC............ Juvenile Detention Center
JDEC........... J D Edwards [*NYSE symbol*] (SG)
JDSU .... JDS Uniphase Corp. [*NASDAQ symbol*] (SG)
JE .... Jacksonian Epilepsy [*Medicine*] (MELL)
JEA .... Japan Environmental Agency (QUAC)
JEB .... Junctional Escape Beat [*Medicine*] (MELL)
JEOS........... Japanese Earth Observing Satellite (EOSA)
JERS .... Japanese Earth Resources Satellite
JERS-1........ Japanese Earth Remote-Sensing Satellite-1 (EOSA)
JFAX .... JFAX.COM, Inc. [*NASDAQ symbol*] (SG)
JFSSG........ Joint Food Safety and Standards Group [*British*] (GVA)
JH............. Jogger's Heel (MELL)
JHPC.......... JLM Couture [*NYSE symbol*] (SG)
JHUP .... Johns Hopkins University Press
JI .... Joint Implementation
JIMS .... Job Information Matrix System
JK .... Jumper's Knee (MELL)
JK .... Just Kidding [*Online dialog*]

JL .... Johnny Lightnings [*Topper Toys*]
JLC .... Jaeger LeCoultre
JLK .... JLK Direct Distribution'A' [*NYSE symbol*] (SG)
JLL .... Jones Lang LaSalle [*NYSE symbol*] (SG)
JLS .... Jet Lag Syndrome (MELL)
JMPR......... Joint Meeting on Pesticide Residues [*Environmental Protection
                  Agency*] (EPAT)
JN .... Junctional Nevus [*Medicine*] (MELL)
JNH............ Journal of Negro History [*A publication*] (GEAB)
JNPR .... Juniper Networks [*NASDAQ symbol*] (SG)
JOC............ Job Ordering Contract
JOS............ Journal of Quaternary Science [*A publication*] (QUAC)
JPA .... Juvenile Psoriatic Arthritis [*Medicine*] (MELL)
JPC............ Joint Partnering Contracting
JPL .... Japan Planetarium Laboratory
JPOP.......... Japanese Polar Orbiting Platform (EOSA)
JRC............ Journal Register [*NYSE symbol*] (SG)
JRJ .... Jamaica Association of Villas and Apartments (EA)
JRRI........... Juvenile Risk Reduction Initiative
JSAP.......... Journal of Small Animal Practice [*A publication*] (GVA)
JSB .... JSB Financial [*NYSE symbol*] (SG)
JSI .... JumboSports, Inc. [*NYSE symbol*] (SG)
JSLAE .... Japanese Society for Laboratory Animal and Environment (GVA)
JSS .... Joshua Slocum Society (EA)
JST .... Jinpan Intl. [*AMEX symbol*] (SG)
JSTARS....... Joint Strategic Airborne Reconnaissance System (MILB)
JSVS........... Japanese Society of Veterinary Science (GVA)
JT .... Japan Tobacco, Inc.
JTE .... Javelin Thrower's Elbow (MELL)
JTF............. Junior Tennis Foundation (EA)
JTUAV........ Joint Tactical Unmanned Aerial Vehicle
judic .... Judicial (GEAB)
junr............ Junior (GEAB)
JVD............ Jugular Venous Distention [*Medicine*] (MELL)
JvNCnet...... John von Neumann Center Network
JVS .... Jamaican Vomiting Sickness (MELL)
JWEB .... Juno Online Svcs. [*NASDAQ symbol*] (SG)
JWGFC........ John Wilson Gill Fan Club (EA)

K
By Acronym

K .... Keloid (MELL)
K .... Keratometry (MELL)
K .... Kilocalorie (MELL)
K .... Kilodalton (MELL)
k .... King (GEAB)
KA .... Ketoaciduria (MELL)
KABC-DT .... Los Angeles, CA [*Television station call letters*] (BROA)
KABO .... Lewiston, MT [*Television station call letters*] (BROA)
KAECT .... Kansas Association for Educational Communications & Technology
KAF .... Conglutinogen Activating Factor [*Medicine*] (MELL)
KAFC-FM .... Anchorage, AK [*FM radio station call letters*] (BROA)
KALZ-FM ...... Fresno, CA [*FM radio station call letters*] (BROA)
KANG-FM .... lake Havasu City, AZ [*FM radio station call letters*] (BROA)
KANM .... Modesto, CA [*FM radio station call letters*] (BROA)
KATH-FM .... El Paso, TX [*FM radio station call letters*] (BROA)
KATU-DT ...... Portland, OR [*Television station call letters*] (BROA)
KATZ-FM ...... Alton, IL [*FM radio station call letters*] (BROA)
KAUJ-FM ...... Walhalla, ND [*FM radio station call letters*] (BROA)
KAVA .... Pueblo, CO [*AM radio station call letters*] (BROA)
KAVW-FM .... Amarillo, TX [*FM radio station call letters*] (BROA)
KAVX-FM .... Lufkin, TX [*FM radio station call letters*] (BROA)
KAWV-FM .... Lihue-Kauai, HI [*FM radio station call letters*] (BROA)
KAXV-FM .... Bastrop, LA [*FM radio station call letters*] (BROA)
KAYM-FM .... Weatherford, OK [*FM radio station call letters*] (BROA)
KAYT-FM ...... Jena, LA [*FM radio station call letters*] (BROA)
Kaz .... Kazakstan (MILB)
KAZJ .... Seattle, WA [*AM radio station call letters*] (BROA)
KAZX-FM .... Kirtland, NM [*FM radio station call letters*] (BROA)
KBAJ-FM .... Deer River, MN [*FM radio station call letters*] (BROA)
KBAP-FM .... King City, CA [*FM radio station call letters*] (BROA)
KBCM .... Fort Worth, TX [*AM radio station call letters*] (BROA)
KBCV-FM .... Paris, TX [*FM radio station call letters*] (BROA)
KBCW-FM .... McAlester, OK [*FM radio station call letters*] (BROA)
KBCX-FM .... Big Spring, TX [*FM radio station call letters*] (BROA)
KBCZ .... Holbrook, AZ [*Television station call letters*] (BROA)
KBDA-FM .... Great Bend, KS [*FM radio station call letters*] (BROA)
KBDC-FM .... Mason City, IA (BROA)
KBDD-FM .... Winfield, KS [*FM radio station call letters*] (BROA)
KBDE-FM .... Gatesville, TX [*FM radio station call letters*] (BROA)
KBDH-FM .... San Ardo, CA [*FM radio station call letters*] (BROA)
KBDJ-FM .... Ruston, LA [*FM radio station call letters*] (BROA)
KBDK .... Hoisington, KS [*Television station call letters*] (BROA)
KBDO-FM .... Des Arc, AR [*FM radio station call letters*] (BROA)
KBDQ-FM .... Owensville, MO [*FM radio station call letters*] (BROA)
KBDS-FM .... Arvin, CA [*FM radio station call letters*] (BROA)
KBDT-FM .... Oraibi, AZ [*FM radio station call letters*] (BROA)
KBDU-FM .... Hayden, CO [*FM radio station call letters*] (BROA)
KBEB-FM .... Hamilton, MT [*FM radio station call letters*] (BROA)
KBED-FM .... Shreveport, LA [*FM radio station call letters*] (BROA)
KBEF-FM ...... Gibsland, LA [*FM radio station call letters*] (BROA)
KBEG .... Clovis, CA [*AM radio station call letters*] (BROA)
KBEI .... Durango, CO [*Television station call letters*] (BROA)
KBEJ .... Fredericksburg, TX [*Television station call letters*] (BROA)
KBEO .... Jackson, WY [*Television station call letters*] (BROA)
KBEV-FM .... Dillon, MT [*FM radio station call letters*] (BROA)
KBEX-FM .... Billings, MT [*FM radio station call letters*] (BROA)
KBFA .... Wolfforth, TX [*Television station call letters*] (BROA)
KBFE-FM .... Grand Junction, CO [*FM radio station call letters*] (BROA)
KBFF-FM ...... Gallup, NM [*FM radio station call letters*] (BROA)
KBFH-FM .... Moose Lake, MN [*FM radio station call letters*] (BROA)
KBFJ-FM ...... Mountain Home, AR [*FM radio station call letters*] (BROA)
KBFO-FM .... Aberdeen, SD [*FM radio station call letters*] (BROA)
KBFQ .... Enid, OK [*AM radio station call letters*] (BROA)
KBFR-FM .... Bridgeport, TX [*FM radio station call letters*] (BROA)
KBFV-FM .... Carlsbad, NM [*FM radio station call letters*] (BROA)
KBFZ-FM .... Kimball, NE [*FM radio station call letters*] (BROA)
KBGC .... Pullman, WA [*Television station call letters*] (BROA)
KBGD .... Farwell, TX [*Television station call letters*] (BROA)
KBGF .... Douglas, AZ [*Television station call letters*] (BROA)
KBGG .... Des Moines, IA [*AM radio station call letters*] (BROA)
KBGJ-FM .... Marble Hill, MO [*FM radio station call letters*] (BROA)
KBGL .... Larned, KS [*FM radio station call letters*] (BROA)
KBGM-FM .... Park Hills, MO [*FM radio station call letters*] (BROA)
KBGP-FM .... Bellview, MN [*FM radio station call letters*] (BROA)
KBGQ-FM .... Harrisburg, AR [*FM radio station call letters*] (BROA)
KBGT-FM ...... Hastings, NE [*FM radio station call letters*] (BROA)

KBGU-FM .... Ingalls, KS [*FM radio station call letters*] (BROA)
KBGV-FM .... Clear Lake, SD [*FM radio station call letters*] (BROA)
KBGX-FM .... Newport, OR [*FM radio station call letters*] (BROA)
KBGY-FM .... Fairbault, MN [*FM radio station call letters*] (BROA)
KBGZ-FM .... Galena, KS [*FM radio station call letters*] (BROA)
KBHA-FM .... Wake Village, TX [*FM radio station call letters*] (BROA)
KBHD-FM .... Gregory, TX [*FM radio station call letters*] (BROA)
KBHH-FM .... Kerman, CA [*FM radio station call letters*] (BROA)
KBHI-FM ...... Miner, MO [*FM radio station call letters*] (BROA)
KBHJ-FM ...... Jackson, WY [*FM radio station call letters*] (BROA)
KBHM-FM .... Johannesburg, CA [*FM radio station call letters*] (BROA)
KBHN-FM .... Hydesville, CA [*FM radio station call letters*] (BROA)
KBHO-FM .... Boonville, MO [*FM radio station call letters*] (BROA)
KBHQ-FM .... Moapa Valley, NV [*FM radio station call letters*] (BROA)
KBHV-FM .... Wellton, AZ [*FM radio station call letters*] (BROA)
KBHX-FM .... Shingletown, CA [*FM radio station call letters*] (BROA)
KBHY-FM .... Atkins, AR [*FM radio station call letters*] (BROA)
KBIE-FM ...... Ingalls, KS [*FM radio station call letters*] (BROA)
KBIH-FM ...... Coeur d'Alene, ID [*FM radio station call letters*] (BROA)
KBII-FM ...... Hatfield, AR [*FM radio station call letters*] (BROA)
KBIJ-FM ...... Mena, AR [*FM radio station call letters*] (BROA)
KBIL-FM ...... Grand Isle, LA [*FM radio station call letters*] (BROA)
KBIO-FM ...... Natchitoches, LA [*FM radio station call letters*] (BROA)
KBIV .... El Paso, TX [*AM radio station call letters*] (BROA)
KBIY-FM ...... Van Buren, MO [*FM radio station call letters*] (BROA)
KBJA .... Sandy, UT [*AM radio station call letters*] (BROA)
KBJC .... Kansas City, KS [*AM radio station call letters*] (BROA)
KBJD .... Denver, CO [*AM radio station call letters*] (BROA)
KBJE .... Monroe, LA [*AM radio station call letters*] (BROA)
KBJF-FM ...... Shelby, MT [*FM radio station call letters*] (BROA)
KBJG-FM .... Mesquite, NV [*FM radio station call letters*] (BROA)
KBJL .... Sheridan, WY [*Television station call letters*] (BROA)
KBJN .... Ely, NV [*Television station call letters*] (BROA)
KBJO .... Avalon, CA [*Television station call letters*] (BROA)
KBJQ-FM .... Bronson, KS [*FM radio station call letters*] (BROA)
KBJU-FM .... Bagdad, AZ [*FM radio station call letters*] (BROA)
KBKC-FM .... Moberly, MO [*FM radio station call letters*] (BROA)
KBKF-FM .... Snyder, OK [*FM radio station call letters*] (BROA)
KBKH-FM .... Ilwaco, WA [*FM radio station call letters*] (BROA)
KBKK-FM .... Pillager, MN [*FM radio station call letters*] (BROA)
KBL .... Keebler Foods [*NYSE symbol*] (SG)
KBLD-FM .... Kennewick, WA [*FM radio station call letters*] (BROA)
KBLI .... Blackfoot, ID [*AM radio station call letters*] (BROA)
KBLT-FM ...... Leakey, TX [*FM radio station call letters*] (BROA)
KBME .... Houston, TX [*AM radio station call letters*] (BROA)
KBME-DT .... Bismarck, ND [*Television station call letters*] (BROA)
KBNF-FM .... Chester, CA [*FM radio station call letters*] (BROA)
KBOP-FM .... Jourdanton, TX [*FM radio station call letters*] (BROA)
KBSX-FM .... Boise, ID [*FM radio station call letters*] (BROA)
KBSZ .... Wickenburg, AZ [*AM radio station call letters*] (BROA)
KBTA-FM .... Batesville, AR [*FM radio station call letters*] (BROA)
KBTE-FM .... Rockport, TX [*FM radio station call letters*] (BROA)
KBTL-FM ...... El Dorado, KS [*FM radio station call letters*] (BROA)
KBUL .... Billings, MT [*AM radio station call letters*] (BROA)
KBUL-FM .... Carson City, NV [*FM radio station call letters*] (BROA)
KBUW-FM .... Buffalo, WY [*FM radio station call letters*] (BROA)
KBWB .... San Francisco, CA [*Television station call letters*] (BROA)
KBZG-FM .... Payson, AZ [*FM radio station call letters*] (BROA)
KC .... Kangaroo Care [*Medicine*] (MELL)
KC .... Kansas City Chiefs [*National Football League*] [*1963-present*] (NFLA)
KCAS-FM .... McCook, TX [*FM radio station call letters*] (BROA)
KCBS-DT .... Los Angeles, CA [*Television station call letters*] (BROA)
KCCF .... Ferndale, WA [*FM radio station call letters*] (BROA)
KCET-DT .... Los Angeles, CA [*Television station call letters*] (BROA)
KCHC .... Conroe, TX [*AM radio station call letters*] (BROA)
KCHT .... Astoria, OR [*FM radio station call letters*] (BROA)
KCI .... Potassium Chloride (MELL)
KCJK .... Iowa City, IA [*AM radio station call letters*] (BROA)
KCKK-FM .... Longmont, CO [*FM radio station call letters*] (BROA)
KCLH-FM .... Yankton, SD [*FM radio station call letters*] (BROA)
KCLR-FM .... Boonville, MO [*FM radio station call letters*] (BROA)
KCLS-FM .... Ely, NV [*FM radio station call letters*] (BROA)
KCMG-FM .... Los Angeles, CA [*FM radio station call letters*] (BROA)
KCML-FM .... St. Joseph, MN [*FM radio station call letters*] (BROA)
KCMT-FM .... Billings, MT [*FM radio station call letters*] (BROA)
KCOP-DT .... Los Angeles, CA [*Television station call letters*] (BROA)

KCP .... Knee-Chest Position (MELL)
KCPT-DT ...... Kansas City, MO [*Television station call letters*] (BROA)
KCRL-FM ..... Sunrise Beach, MO [*FM radio station call letters*] (BROA)
KCRZ-FM ..... Tipton, CA [*FM radio station call letters*] (BROA)
KCSG .... Cedar City, UT [*Television station call letters*] (BROA)
KCSH-FM ..... Ellensburg, WA [*FM radio station call letters*] (BROA)
KCSX-FM ..... Moberly, MO [*FM radio station call letters*] (BROA)
KCWC-TV ..... Lander, WY [*Television station call letters*] (BROA)
KCWE .... Kansas City, MO [*Television station call letters*] (BROA)
KCWU-FM .... Ellensburg, WA [*FM radio station call letters*] (BROA)
KCWY .... Casper, WY [*Television station call letters*] (BROA)
KCYO-FM ..... Ozark, MO [*FM radio station call letters*] (BROA)
KCYT-FM ..... Lead, SD [*FM radio station call letters*] (BROA)
KCZN-FM ..... Santa Paula, CA [*FM radio station call letters*] (BROA)
KD .... Kappa Delta (EA)
KD .... Kohler Disease (MELL)
KDAV .... Lubbock, TX [*AM radio station call letters*] (BROA)
KDDJ-FM ..... Globe, AZ [*FM radio station call letters*] (BROA)
KDFM-FM ..... Falfurrias, TX [*FM radio station call letters*] (BROA)
KDFW-DT ..... Dallas, TX [*Television station call letters*] (BROA)
KDKA-DT ..... Pittsburgh, PA [*Television station call letters*] (BROA)
KDLT-TV ..... Sioux Falls, SD [*Television station call letters*] (BROA)
KDLV-TV ..... Mitchell, SD [*Television station call letters*] (BROA)
KDNZ .... Cedar Falls, IA [*AM radio station call letters*] (BROA)
KDOS-FM ..... Gainesville, TX [*FM radio station call letters*] (BROA)
KDOX .... Henderson, NV [*AM radio station call letters*] (BROA)
KDU .... Kidney Dialysis Unit (MELL)
KDXX .... Dallas, TX [*AM radio station call letters*] (BROA)
KDXX-FM ..... Corsicana, TX [*FM radio station call letters*] (BROA)
KDYA .... Vallejo, CA [*AM radio station call letters*] (BROA)
KDZY-FM ..... McCall, ID [*FM radio station call letters*] (BROA)
KE .... Kagel Exercise (MELL)
KEDD-FM ..... Johannesburg, CA [*FM radio station call letters*] (BROA)
KEDG-FM ..... Alexandria, LA [*FM radio station call letters*] (BROA)
Keet .... Parakeet [*Bird*]
KEKO-FM ..... Hebronville, TX [*FM radio station call letters*] (BROA)
KEOT-FM ..... St. George, UT [*FM radio station call letters*] (BROA)
KEPCO .... Korea Electric Power Corp.
KESO-FM ..... South Padre Island, TX [*FM radio station call letters*] (BROA)
KESQ .... Indio, CA [*AM radio station call letters*] (BROA)
KEUG-FM ..... Cottage Grove, OR [*FM radio station call letters*] (BROA)
KEUL-FM ..... Girdwood, AK [*FM radio station call letters*] (BROA)
KEZQ-FM ..... Island Park, ID [*FM radio station call letters*] (BROA)
KEZZ .... Estes Park, CO [*AM radio station call letters*] (BROA)
KFAT-FM ..... Anchorage, AK [*FM radio station call letters*] (BROA)
KFBN-FM ..... Fargo, ND [*FM radio station call letters*] (BROA)
KFEB-FM ..... Campbell, MO [*FM radio station call letters*] (BROA)
KFI .... Krause's Furniture [*AMEX symbol*] (SG)
KFJO-FM ..... Walnut Creek, CA [*FM radio station call letters*] (BROA)
KFLV-FM ..... Wilber, NE [*FM radio station call letters*] (BROA)
KFLX-FM ..... Kachina Village, AZ [*FM radio station call letters*] (BROA)
KFMB-DT ..... Sand Diego, CA [*Television station call letters*] (BROA)
KFMK-FM .... Round Rock, TX [*FM radio station call letters*] (BROA)
KFNX .... Cave Creek, AZ [*AM radio station call letters*] (BROA)
KFPX .... Newton, IA [*Television station call letters*] (BROA)
KFRZ-FM ..... Green River, WY [*FM radio station call letters*] (BROA)
KFT .... Kidney Function Test [*Medicine*] (MELL)
KFXE-FM ..... Cuba, MO [*FM radio station call letters*] (BROA)
KFXJ-FM ..... Nampa, ID [*FM radio station call letters*] (BROA)
KFXP .... Pocatello, ID [*Television station call letters*] (BROA)
KFXX .... Vancouver, WA [*AM radio station call letters*] (BROA)
KFY .... Korn/Ferry Intl. [*NYSE symbol*] (SG)
KG .... Keratoglobus [*Medicine*] (MELL)
KGA .... Ketoglutaric Acid (MELL)
KGAR-FM ..... Garden City, MO [*FM radio station call letters*] (BROA)
KGDP-FM ..... Orcutt, CA [*FM radio station call letters*] (BROA)
KGER-FM ..... Quincy, WA [*FM radio station call letters*] (BROA)
KGGF-FM ..... Fredonia, KS [*FM radio station call letters*] (BROA)
KGIM-FM ..... Redfield, SD [*FM radio station call letters*] (BROA)
KGKS-FM ..... Scott City, MO [*FM radio station call letters*] (BROA)
KGMM .... Abilene, TX [*AM radio station call letters*] (BROA)
KGNT-FM ..... Smithfield, UT [*FM radio station call letters*] (BROA)
KGO-DT ..... San Francisco, CA [*Television station call letters*] (BROA)
KGPX .... Spokane, WA [*Television station call letters*] (BROA)
KGTV-DT ..... San Diego, CA [*Television station call letters*] (BROA)
KGUL-FM ..... Edna, TX [*FM radio station call letters*] (BROA)
KGUM-FM .... Dededo, GU [*FM radio station call letters*] (BROA)
KGW-DT ..... Portland, OR [*Television station call letters*] (BROA)
Kgz .... Kyrgyzstan (MILB)
KHBX-FM ..... El Dorado, AR [*FM radio station call letters*] (BROA)
KHCH .... Huntsville, TX [*AM radio station call letters*] (BROA)
KHFX-FM ..... Ball, LA [*FM radio station call letters*] (BROA)
KHIM-FM ..... Mangum, OK [*FM radio station call letters*] (BROA)
KHIX-FM ..... Ely, NV [*FM radio station call letters*] (BROA)
KHJP-FM ..... Leone, AS [*FM radio station call letters*] (BROA)
KHJQ-FM ..... Susanville, CA [*FM radio station call letters*] (BROA)
KHJS-FM ..... Pago Pago, AS (BROA)
KHOC-FM ..... Casper, WY [*FM radio station call letters*] (BROA)
KHOU-DT ..... Houston, TX [*Television station call letters*] (BROA)
KHPN .... Loveland, CO [*AM radio station call letters*] (BROA)
KHTE-FM ..... Lonoke, AR [*FM radio station call letters*] (BROA)
KHTZ .... Albuquerque, NM [*AM radio station call letters*] (BROA)
KHVO-DT ..... Hilo, HI [*Television station call letters*] (BROA)
KHXR-FM ..... Sun Valley, NV [*FM radio station call letters*] (BROA)
KIBR-FM ..... Sandpoint, ID [*FM radio station call letters*] (BROA)
KIDS .... Kids in Integrated Day Care Settings (MELL)
KIKN .... Port Angeles, WA [*AM radio station call letters*] (BROA)
KILE .... Bellaire, TX [*AM radio station call letters*] (BROA)
KING-DT ..... Seattle, WA [*Television station call letters*] (BROA)
KINZ-FM ..... Humboldt, KS [*FM radio station call letters*] (BROA)
KIOD-FM ..... McCook, NE [*FM radio station call letters*] (BROA)
KIQN .... Tooele, UT [*AM radio station call letters*] (BROA)
KIRIS .... Kentucky Instructional Results Information System
KIRO-DT ..... Seattle, WA [*Television station call letters*] (BROA)
KISF-FM ..... Las Vegas, NV [*FM radio station call letters*] (BROA)
KISK-FM ..... Shasta Lake City, CA [*FM radio station call letters*] (BROA)
KIST-FM ..... Santa Barbara, CA [*FM radio station call letters*] (BROA)
KISU-FM ..... Pocatello, ID [*FM radio station call letters*] (BROA)
KITV-DT ..... Honolulu, HI [*Television station call letters*] (BROA)
KIXD-FM ..... Oracle, AZ [*FM radio station call letters*] (BROA)
KIXK-FM ..... Linden, TX [*FM radio station call letters*] (BROA)
KIXO-FM ..... Sulphur, OK [*FM radio station call letters*] (BROA)
kJ .... Kilojoule (EOSA)
KJFK-FM ..... Lampasas, TX [*FM radio station call letters*] (BROA)
KJHA-FM ..... Houston, AK [*FM radio station call letters*] (BROA)
KJJM-FM ..... Baker, MT [*FM radio station call letters*] (BROA)
KJJZ-FM ..... Indio, CA [*FM radio station call letters*] (BROA)
KJLA .... Ventura, CA [*Television station call letters*] (BROA)
KJUN-FM ..... Tillamook, OR [*FM radio station call letters*] (BROA)
KKAP .... Little Rock, AR [*Television station call letters*] (BROA)
KKAW-FM ..... Albin, WY [*FM radio station call letters*] (BROA)
KKCN-FM ..... Sterling City, TX [*FM radio station call letters*] (BROA)
KKDD .... San Bernardino, CA [*AM radio station call letters*] (BROA)
KKED-FM ..... Fairbanks, AK [*FM radio station call letters*] (BROA)
KKEN .... Duncan, OK [*AM radio station call letters*] (BROA)
KKEN-FM ..... Duncan, OK [*FM radio station call letters*] (BROA)
KKER-FM ..... Kerrville, TX [*FM radio station call letters*] (BROA)
KKGJ .... Grand Junction, CO [*AM radio station call letters*] (BROA)
KKGT .... Portland, OR [*AM radio station call letters*] (BROA)
KKHN-FM ..... Naipahu, HI [*FM radio station call letters*] (BROA)
KKI .... Kenpo Karate International (EA)
KKIK-FM ..... La Junta, CO [*FM radio station call letters*] (BROA)
KKLF .... Denison-Sherman, TX [*AM radio station call letters*] (BROA)
KKLQ-FM ..... Vancouver, WA [*FM radio station call letters*] (BROA)
KKRS-FM ..... Davenport, WA [*FM radio station call letters*] (BROA)
KKSB-FM ..... Goleta, CA [*FM radio station call letters*] (BROA)
KKSC .... Brawley, CA [*AM radio station call letters*] (BROA)
KKSD-FM ..... Milbank, SD [*FM radio station call letters*] (BROA)
KKSN .... Oregon City, OR [*AM radio station call letters*] (BROA)
KKTL-FM ..... Cleveland, TX [*FM radio station call letters*] (BROA)
KKTT-FM ..... Eugene, OR [*FM radio station call letters*] (BROA)
KKUU-FM ..... Indio, CA [*FM radio station call letters*] (BROA)
KKWB .... El Paso, TX [*Television station call letters*] (BROA)
KKWY .... Fox Farm, WY [*AM radio station call letters*] (BROA)
KKYC-FM ..... Clovis, NM [*FM radio station call letters*] (BROA)
KKYK-TV ..... El Dorado, AR [*Television station call letters*] (BROA)
KKZQ-FM ..... Tehachapi, CA [*FM radio station call letters*] (BROA)
KKZY-FM ..... Bemidji, MN [*FM radio station call letters*] (BROA)
KLA .... Kansas Library Association
KLAC .... KLA-Tencor Corp. [*NASDAQ symbol*] (SG)
KLB .... Audio Book Club (SG)
KLCA-FM ..... Tahoe City, CA [*FM radio station call letters*] (BROA)
KLCI-FM ..... Princeton, MN [*FM radio station call letters*] (BROA)
KLCX-FM ..... St. Charles, MN [*FM radio station call letters*] (BROA)
KLDZ-FM ..... Fremont, CA [*FM radio station call letters*] (BROA)
KLEY-FM ..... Floresville, TX [*FM radio station call letters*] (BROA)
KLFO .... Florence, OR [*FM radio station call letters*] (BROA)
KLJT-FM ..... Jacksonville, TX [*FM radio station call letters*] (BROA)
KLJZ-FM ..... Yuma, AZ [*FM radio station call letters*] (BROA)
KLNC-FM ..... Killeen, TX [*FM radio station call letters*] (BROA)
KLNQ-FM ..... Des Moines, IA [*FM radio station call letters*] (BROA)
KLNT .... Laredo, TX [*AM radio station call letters*] (BROA)
KLNV-FM ..... San Diego, CA [*FM radio station call letters*] (BROA)
KLOV-FM ..... Winchester, OR [*FM radio station call letters*] (BROA)
KLPC .... Krypton Laser Photocoagulation [*Medicine*] (MELL)
KLPL-FM ..... Lake Providence, LA [*FM radio station call letters*] (BROA)
KLPQ-FM ..... Arkansas City, KS [*FM radio station call letters*] (BROA)
KLQV-FM ..... San Diego, CA [*FM radio station call letters*] (BROA)
KLRU-DT ..... Austin, TX [*Television station call letters*] (BROA)
KLS .... Kleine-Levin Syndrome [*Medicine*] (MELL)
KLSI-FM ..... Hutchinson, KS [*FM radio station call letters*] (BROA)
KLSN-FM ..... Santa Cruz, CA [*FM radio station call letters*] (BROA)
KLTI-FM ..... Ames, IA [*FM radio station call letters*] (BROA)
KLTW-FM ..... Rayne, LA [*FM radio station call letters*] (BROA)
KLTX .... Long Beach, CA [*AM radio station call letters*] (BROA)
KLUV .... Dallas, TX [*AM radio station call letters*] (BROA)
KLVJ-FM ..... Julian, CA [*FM radio station call letters*] (BROA)
KLVK-FM ..... Kingsburg, CA [*FM radio station call letters*] (BROA)
KLVP .... Tigard, OR [*AM radio station call letters*] (BROA)
KLVP-FM ..... Cherryville, OR [*FM radio station call letters*] (BROA)
KLVU-FM ..... Sweet Home, OR [*FM radio station call letters*] (BROA)
KLVW-FM ..... Odessa, TX [*FM radio station call letters*] (BROA)
KLWT .... Kirsch Laser Welding Technique [*Medicine*] (MELL)
KLXK-FM ..... Breckenridge, TX [*FM radio station call letters*] (BROA)
KLXQ-FM ..... Hot Springs, AR [*FM radio station call letters*] (BROA)
KLYF .... Thousand Oaks, CA [*AM radio station call letters*] (BROA)
KM .... Kneading Massage (MELL)
KMAP-FM ..... Castana, IA [*FM radio station call letters*] (BROA)
KMAU-DT ..... Wailuku, HI [*Television station call letters*] (BROA)
KMAX-TV ..... Sacramento, CA [*Television station call letters*] (BROA)

KMCG .... Casper, WY [*AM radio station call letters*] (BROA)
KMCM-FM ... Odessa, TX [*FM radio station call letters*] (BROA)
KMDX-FM .... San Angelo, TX [*FM radio station call letters*] (BROA)
KMDY-FM .... Keokuk, IA [*FM radio station call letters*] (BROA)
KMJM-FM .... Columbia, IL [*FM radio station call letters*] (BROA)
KMKP-FM .... Honolulu, HI [*FM radio station call letters*] (BROA)
KMKX-FM .... Rock Springs, WY [*FM radio station call letters*] (BROA)
KMKY .... Oakland, CA [*AM radio station call letters*] (BROA)
KMLT-FM ..... Thousand Oaks, CA [*FM radio station call letters*] (BROA)
KMMG-FM ... Santa Fe, NM [*FM radio station call letters*] (BROA)
KMOV-DT ..... St. Louis, MO [*Television station call letters*] (BROA)
KMPC .... Abilene, TX [*AM radio station call letters*] (BROA)
KMSE-FM .... Rochester, MN [*FM radio station call letters*] (BROA)
KMSL .... Ontario, CA [*AM radio station call letters*] (BROA)
KMSX-FM .... Carlsbad, CA [*FM radio station call letters*] (BROA)
KMTF .... Helena, MT [*Television station call letters*] (BROA)
KMX .... Circuit City Strs-CarMx Grp [*NYSE symbol*] (SG)
KMXB-FM .... Henderson, NV [*FM radio station call letters*] (BROA)
KMXF-FM .... Lowell, AR [*FM radio station call letters*] (BROA)
KMXP-FM .... Phoenix, AZ [*FM radio station call letters*] (BROA)
KMYR .... Wichita, KS [*AM radio station call letters*] (BROA)
KMZL-FM ..... Missoula, MT [*FM radio station call letters*] (BROA)
kn .... Knot
KNBC-DT ...... Los Angeles, CA [*Television station call letters*] (BROA)
KNCW-FM .... Omak, WA [*FM radio station call letters*] (BROA)
KNDL-FM ..... Angwin, CA [*FM radio station call letters*] (BROA)
KNDN-FM .... Sacramento, CA [*FM radio station call letters*] (BROA)
KNDX .... Bismarck, ND [*Television station call letters*] (BROA)
KNEC-FM ..... Yuma, CO [*FM radio station call letters*] (BROA)
KNHK-FM ..... Reno, NV [*FM radio station call letters*] (BROA)
KNLG-FM ..... New Bloomfield, MO [*FM radio station call letters*] (BROA)
KNMvD .... Royal Netherlands Veterinary Association (GVA)
KNNS .... Larned, KS [*AM radio station call letters*] (BROA)
KNNT .... Farmington, NM [*AM radio station call letters*] (BROA)
KNOM .... Nome, AK [*AM radio station call letters*] (BROA)
KNRS .... Salt Lake City, UT [*AM radio station call letters*] (BROA)
KNSD-DT ..... San Diego, CA [*Television station call letters*] (BROA)
KNSY-FM ..... Amarillo, TX [*FM radio station call letters*] (BROA)
knt .... Knight (GEAB)
KNTB .... Lakewood, WA [*AM radio station call letters*] (BROA)
KNVN .... Chico, CA [*Television station call letters*] (BROA)
KNWP-FM .... Port Angeles, WA [*FM radio station call letters*] (BROA)
KNXV-DT ...... Phoenix, AZ [*Television station call letters*] (BROA)
KNYN-FM ..... Fort Bridger, WY [*FM radio station call letters*] (BROA)
KOCL-FM ..... Arthur, ND [*FM radio station call letters*] (BROA)
KOES-FM ..... Stamford, TX [*FM radio station call letters*] (BROA)
KOFR-FM ..... Post, TX [*FM radio station call letters*] (BROA)
KOFT .... Farmington, NM [*Television station call letters*] (BROA)
KOGCC .... Kelley Oil & Gas [*NASDAQ symbol*] (SG)
KOIN-DT ...... Portland, OR [*Television station call letters*] (BROA)
KOKE .... Pflugerville, TX [*AM radio station call letters*] (BROA)
KOKP .... Perry, OK [*AM radio station call letters*] (BROA)
KOLI-FM ...... Electra, TX [*FM radio station call letters*] (BROA)
KOLT-FM ..... Gering, NE [*FM radio station call letters*] (BROA)
KOMC-FM .... Kimberking City, MO [*FM radio station call letters*] (BROA)
KOMO-DT .... Seattle, WA [*Television station call letters*] (BROA)
KOOK-FM ..... Junction, TX [*FM radio station call letters*] (BROA)
KOOP .... drkoop.com, Inc. [*NASDAQ symbol*] (SG)
KOOR .... Clovis, CA [*AM radio station call letters*] (BROA)
KOSB-FM ..... Perry, OK [*FM radio station call letters*] (BROA)
KOSS-FM ..... Rosamond, CA [*FM radio station call letters*] (BROA)
KOUU .... Pocatello, ID [*AM radio station call letters*] (BROA)
KOVA-FM ..... Rosenberg, TX [*FM radio station call letters*] (BROA)
KOVE-FM ..... Port Arthur, TX [*FM radio station call letters*] (BROA)
KOWS .... Texarkana, TX [*AM radio station call letters*] (BROA)
KOXZ-FM ..... Comanche, TX [*FM radio station call letters*] (BROA)
KOZL-FM ..... New Boston, TX [*FM radio station call letters*] (BROA)
KPAM .... Troutdale, OR [*AM radio station call letters*] (BROA)
KPBE-FM ..... Brownwood, TX [*FM radio station call letters*] (BROA)
KPBM-FM .... McCamey, TX [*FM radio station call letters*] (BROA)
KPFC-FM ..... Callisburg, TX [*FM radio station call letters*] (BROA)
KPFN-FM ..... Seward, AK [*FM radio station call letters*] (BROA)
KPG .... King Power Intl. [*AMEX symbol*] (SG)
KPHN .... Kansas City, MO [*AM radio station call letters*] (BROA)
KPHO-DT ..... Phoenix, AZ [*Television station call letters*] (BROA)
KPHR-FM ..... Ortonville, MN [*FM radio station call letters*] (BROA)
KPIX-DT ...... San Francisco, CA [*Television station call letters*] (BROA)
KPLN-FM ..... San Diego, CA [*FM radio station call letters*] (BROA)
KPMR .... Santa Barbara, CA [*Television station call letters*] (BROA)
KPNX-DT ..... Mesa, AZ [*Television station call letters*] (BROA)
KPOW-FM .... La Monte, MO [*FM radio station call letters*] (BROA)
KPPX .... Tolleson, AZ [*Television station call letters*] (BROA)
KPQZ-FM ..... Amarillo, TX [*FM radio station call letters*] (BROA)
KPRB-FM ..... Brush, CO [*FM radio station call letters*] (BROA)
KPRC-DT ..... Houston, TX [*Television station call letters*] (BROA)
KPRH-FM ..... Montrose, CO [*FM radio station call letters*] (BROA)
KPRU-FM ..... Delta, CO [*FM radio station call letters*] (BROA)
KPRV-FM ..... Heavener, OK [*FM radio station call letters*] (BROA)
KPSG .... Oklahoma City, OK [*Television station call letters*] (BROA)
KPTE-FM ..... Durango, CO [*FM radio station call letters*] (BROA)
KPTT .... Reno, NV [*AM radio station call letters*] (BROA)
KPUB-FM ..... Prescott, AZ [*FM radio station call letters*] (BROA)
KPWB-TV ..... Ames, IA [*Television station call letters*] (BROA)
KPWW-FM ... Hooks, TX [*FM radio station call letters*] (BROA)
KPXC-TV ...... Denver, CO [*Television station call letters*] (BROA)
KPXD .... Arlington, TX [*Television station call letters*] (BROA)
KPXE .... Kansas City, MO [*Television station call letters*] (BROA)
KPXF .... Porterville, CA [*Television station call letters*] (BROA)
KPXG .... Salem, OR [*Television station call letters*] (BROA)
KPXK .... Odessa, TX [*Television station call letters*] (BROA)
KPXL .... Uvalde, TX [*Television station call letters*] (BROA)
KPXO .... Kaneohe, HI [*Television station call letters*] (BROA)
KPXR .... Cedar Rapids, IA [*Television station call letters*] (BROA)
KQBT-FM ..... Taylor, TX [*FM radio station call letters*] (BROA)
KQDI .... Great Falls, MT [*AM radio station call letters*] (BROA)
KQED-DT ..... San Francisco, CA [*Television station call letters*] (BROA)
KQIB-FM ...... Idabel, OK [*FM radio station call letters*] (BROA)
KQIS-FM ...... Basile, LA [*FM radio station call letters*] (BROA)
KQJD .... West Fargo, ND [*AM radio station call letters*] (BROA)
KQJZ-FM ..... Grover City, CA [*FM radio station call letters*] (BROA)
KQKK-FM ..... Walker, MN [*FM radio station call letters*] (BROA)
KQLI-FM ...... Geneseo, IL [*FM radio station call letters*] (BROA)
KQLV-FM ..... Grants, NM [*FM radio station call letters*] (BROA)
KQQA .... Creedmoor, TX [*AM radio station call letters*] (BROA)
KQQQ-FM .... Hutto, TX [*FM radio station call letters*] (BROA)
KQRV-FM ..... Deer Lodge, MT [*FM radio station call letters*] (BROA)
KQWB .... Fargo, ND [*AM radio station call letters*] (BROA)
KR .... Kennedy Round
KRAM .... West Klamath, OR [*AM radio station call letters*] (BROA)
KRAR-FM ..... Brigham City, UT [*FM radio station call letters*] (BROA)
KRBT .... Eveleth, MN [*AM radio station call letters*] (BROA)
KRC .... Kilroy Realty [*NYSE symbol*] (SG)
KRCM .... Beaumont, TX [*AM radio station call letters*] (BROA)
KRDG-FM ..... Shingletown, CA [*FM radio station call letters*] (BROA)
KRDR-FM ..... Red River, NM [*FM radio station call letters*] (BROA)
KREO-FM ..... Superior, MT [*FM radio station call letters*] (BROA)
KRIV-DT ...... Houston, TX [*Television station call letters*] (BROA)
KRKH-FM ..... Harwood, ND [*FM radio station call letters*] (BROA)
KRKR-FM ..... Lincoln, NE [*FM radio station call letters*] (BROA)
KRMJ .... Grand Junction, CO [*Television station call letters*] (BROA)
KRMP-FM .... Portland, TX [*FM radio station call letters*] (BROA)
KRNM-FM .... Saipan, MP [*FM radio station call letters*] (BROA)
KRON-DT ..... San Francisco, CA [*Television station call letters*] (BROA)
KROO .... Breckenridge, TX [*AM radio station call letters*] (BROA)
KROR-FM .... Hastings, NE [*FM radio station call letters*] (BROA)
KROW-FM .... Huntsville, MO [*FM radio station call letters*] (BROA)
KRRE-FM ..... Shingle Springs, CA [*FM radio station call letters*] (BROA)
KRRK-FM ..... Lake Havasu City, AZ [*FM radio station call letters*] (BROA)
KRRNY .... King's Royal Regiment of New York (GEAB)
KRRW-FM .... St. James, MN [*FM radio station call letters*] (BROA)
KRRX-FM ..... Burney, CA [*FM radio station call letters*] (BROA)
KRSK-FM ..... Salem, OR [*FM radio station call letters*] (BROA)
KRSR-FM ..... Santa Rosa, NM [*FM radio station call letters*] (BROA)
KRTK .... Chubbuck, ID [*AM radio station call letters*] (BROA)
KRVK-FM ..... Midwest, WY [*FM radio station call letters*] (BROA)
KRVQ-FM ..... Blanchard, LA [*FM radio station call letters*] (BROA)
KRXY .... Shelton, WA [*FM radio station call letters*] (BROA)
KRXZ-FM ..... Erath, LA [*FM radio station call letters*] (BROA)
KRY .... Crystallex Intl. [*AMEX symbol*] (SG)
KS .... Kallmann's Syndrome [*Medicine*] (MELL)
KS .... Kehr's Sign [*Medicine*] (MELL)
KS .... Kernig's Sign [*Medicine*] (MELL)
KS .... Ketosteroid [*Medicine*] (MELL)
KS .... Koplik's Spots [*Medicine*] (MELL)
KS .... Krackow Suture [*Medicine*] (MELL)
KSCC .... Hutchinson, KS [*Television station call letters*] (BROA)
KSCI .... Long Beach, CA [*Television station call letters*] (BROA)
KSFF-FM ...... Caledonia, MN [*FM radio station call letters*] (BROA)
KSFS .... Sioux Falls, SD [*AM radio station call letters*] (BROA)
KSIB-FM ...... Creston, IA [*FM radio station call letters*] (BROA)
KSIL-FM ...... Wallace, ID [*FM radio station call letters*] (BROA)
KSIZ-FM ...... Maumelle, AR [*FM radio station call letters*] (BROA)
KSKD-FM ..... Chowchilla, CA [*FM radio station call letters*] (BROA)
KSMH .... Auburn, CA [*AM radio station call letters*] (BROA)
KSMM .... Shakopee, MN [*AM radio station call letters*] (BROA)
KSNN-FM ..... St. George, UT [*FM radio station call letters*] (BROA)
KSNX-FM ..... Show Low, AZ [*FM radio station call letters*] (BROA)
KSOB-FM ..... Dell Rapids, SD [*FM radio station call letters*] (BROA)
KSOF-FM ..... Dinuba, CA [*FM radio station call letters*] (BROA)
KSQB-FM ..... Flandreau, SD [*FM radio station call letters*] (BROA)
KSRZ-FM ..... Omaha, NE [*FM radio station call letters*] (BROA)
KSSE-FM ..... Riverside, CA [*FM radio station call letters*] (BROA)
KSTJ-FM ...... Boulder City, NV [*FM radio station call letters*] (BROA)
KSTV-FM ..... Dublin, TX [*FM radio station call letters*] (BROA)
KSUH .... Puyallup, WA [*AM radio station call letters*] (BROA)
KSWN-FM .... McCook, NE [*FM radio station call letters*] (BROA)
KSYR-FM ..... Minden, LA [*FM radio station call letters*] (BROA)
K-T .... Cretaceous-Tertiary
KT .... Kelling's Test [*Medicine*] (MELL)
KT .... Kerner's Test [*Medicine*] (MELL)
KT .... Killian's Test [*Medicine*] (MELL)
KT .... Kiloton (MILB)
KT .... Kinberg's Test [*Medicine*] (MELL)
KT .... Klimow's Test [*Medicine*] (MELL)
KT .... Knapp's Test [*Medicine*] (MELL)
KT .... Kober Test [*Medicine*] (MELL)
KTAS .... San Luis Obispo, CA [*Television station call letters*] (BROA)
KTBK .... Denison-Sherman, TX [*AM radio station call letters*] (BROA)
KTBR-FM ..... Myrtle Point, OR [*FM radio station call letters*] (BROA)
KTBU .... Conroe, TX [*Television station call letters*] (BROA)

KTC.............. Korea Telecom ADS [*NYSE symbol*] (SG)
KTCI-DT........ St. Paul, MN [*Television station call letters*] (BROA)
KTGS-FM..... Ada, OK [*FM radio station call letters*] (BROA)
KTHK-FM..... Milton-Freewater, OR [*FM radio station call letters*] (BROA)
KTHU-FM..... Los Molinos, CA [*FM radio station call letters*] (BROA)
KTKY-FM..... Refugio, TX [*FM radio station call letters*] (BROA)
KTKZ.......... Sacramento, CA [*AM radio station call letters*] (BROA)
KTLA-DT...... Los Angeles, CA [*Television station call letters*] (BROA)
KTLC-FM...... Canon City, CO [*FM radio station call letters*] (BROA)
KTLM.......... Rio Grande City, TX [*Television station call letters*] (BROA)
KTMW.......... Salt Lake City, UT [*Television station call letters*] (BROA)
KTOF............ Cedar Rapids, IA [*AM radio station call letters*] (BROA)
KTRK-DT...... Houston, TX [*Television station call letters*] (BROA)
KTRN-FM..... White Hall, AR [*FM radio station call letters*] (BROA)
KTRQ-FM..... Brinkley, AR [*FM radio station call letters*] (BROA)
KTRS.......... St. Louis, MO [*AM radio station call letters*] (BROA)
KTSP.......... St. George, UT [*AM radio station call letters*] (BROA)
KTTA-FM...... Esparto, CA [*FM radio station call letters*] (BROA)
KTTV-DT...... Los Angeles, CA [*Television station call letters*] (BROA)
KTUB.......... Farmersville, TX [*AM radio station call letters*] (BROA)
KTUZ-FM..... Chickasha, OK [*FM radio station call letters*] (BROA)
KTVF-DT...... Fairbanks, AK [*Television station call letters*] (BROA)
KTVI-DT...... St. Louis, MO [*Television station call letters*] (BROA)
KTVT-DT...... Fort Worth, TX [*Television station call letters*] (BROA)
KTVU-DT...... Oakland, CA [*Television station call letters*] (BROA)
KTXI-FM...... Ingram, TX [*FM radio station call letters*] (BROA)
KTXM-FM..... Hallettsville, TX [*FM radio station call letters*] (BROA)
KTXX.......... Salinas, CA [*AM radio station call letters*] (BROA)
KTZN.......... Anchorage, AK [*AM radio station call letters*] (BROA)
KUB........... Kidney Ultrasound Biopsy [*Medicine*] (MELL)
KUBD.......... Ketchikan, AK [*Television station call letters*] (BROA)
KUHB.......... St. Paul, AK [*AM radio station call letters*] (BROA)
KUJ-FM........ Walla Walla, WA [*FM radio station call letters*] (BROA)
KULH-FM..... Wheeling, MO [*FM radio station call letters*] (BROA)
KULL-FM..... Abilene, TX [*FM radio station call letters*] (BROA)
KULU-FM..... Seaside, OR [*FM radio station call letters*] (BROA)
KUMX-FM..... Houma, LA [*FM radio station call letters*] (BROA)
KUPB.......... Midland, TX [*Television station call letters*] (BROA)
KUPL.......... Portland, OR [*AM radio station call letters*] (BROA)
KUPN.......... Mission, KS [*AM radio station call letters*] (BROA)
KUPX.......... Provo, UT [*Television station call letters*] (BROA)
KUST-FM..... Huntsville, TX [*FM radio station call letters*] (BROA)
KUUL-FM..... East Moline, IL [*FM radio station call letters*] (BROA)
KUUY-FM..... Glendo, WY [*FM radio station call letters*] (BROA)
KUWB.......... Ogden, UT [*Television station call letters*] (BROA)
KUYI-FM..... Holevilla, AZ [*FM radio station call letters*] (BROA)
KV.............. Kraurosis Vulvae [*Medicine*] (MELL)
KVAK-FM..... Valdez, AK [*FM radio station call letters*] (BROA)
KVCU.......... Boulder, CO [*AM radio station call letters*] (BROA)
KVFX-FM..... Logan, UT [*FM radio station call letters*] (BROA)
KVJM-FM..... Hearme, TX [*FM radio station call letters*] (BROA)
KVMA.......... Kansas Veterinary Medical Association (GVA)
KVMA.......... Kentucky Veterinary Medical Association (GVA)
KVNR.......... Santa Ana, CA [*AM radio station call letters*] (BROA)
KVOP-FM..... Plainview, TX [*FM radio station call letters*] (BROA)
KVPC-FM..... San Joaquin, CA [*FM radio station call letters*] (BROA)
KVRN-FM..... Marvell, AR [*FM radio station call letters*] (BROA)
KVRO-FM..... Stillwater, OK [*FM radio station call letters*] (BROA)
KVTY-FM..... Lewiston, ID [*FM radio station call letters*] (BROA)
KVVN.......... Santa Clara, CA [*AM radio station call letters*] (BROA)
KVWB.......... Las Vegas, NV [*Television station call letters*] (BROA)
KWB........... Koch-Weeks Bacillus [*Medicine*] (MELL)
KWBM.......... Harrison, AR [*Television station call letters*] (BROA)
KWBQ.......... Santa Fe, NM [*Television station call letters*] (BROA)
KWBT.......... Muskogee, OK [*Television station call letters*] (BROA)
KWCY-FM..... Glendale, AZ [*FM radio station call letters*] (BROA)
KWEG-FM..... Warm Springs, OR [*FM radio station call letters*] (BROA)
KWF............ Kirschner Wire Fixation (MELL)

KWFS.......... Wichita Falls, TX [*AM radio station call letters*] (BROA)
KWGB-FM.... Colby, KS [*FM radio station call letters*] (BROA)
KWHY-DT.... Los Angeles, CA [*Television station call letters*] (BROA)
KWJG-FM.... Kasilof, AK [*FM radio station call letters*] (BROA)
KWLW......... North Salt Lake City, UT [*AM radio station call letters*] (BROA)
KWMM-FM.... Osage, IA [*FM radio station call letters*] (BROA)
KWMO........ Washington, MO [*AM radio station call letters*] (BROA)
KWMR-FM.... Point Reyes Station, CA [*FM radio station call letters*] (BROA)
KWMX-FM.... Williams, AZ [*FM radio station call letters*] (BROA)
KWPX......... Bellevue, WA [*Television station call letters*] (BROA)
KWRD-FM.... Arlington, TX [*FM radio station call letters*] (BROA)
KWSH-FM.... Wewoka, OK [*FM radio station call letters*] (BROA)
Kwt............ Kuwait (MILB)
KWTR-FM.... Big Lake, TX [*FM radio station call letters*] (BROA)
KWYY-FM.... Casper, WY [*FM radio station call letters*] (BROA)
KXAS-DT.... Fort Worth, TX [*Television station call letters*] (BROA)
KXBA-FM..... Nikiski, AK [*FM radio station call letters*] (BROA)
KXBK......... Bryan, TX [*FM radio station call letters*] (BROA)
KXCA......... Lawton, OK [*AM radio station call letters*] (BROA)
KXEZ-FM..... Farmersville, TX [*FM radio station call letters*] (BROA)
KXFS......... Ventura, CA [*AM radio station call letters*] (BROA)
KXKK-FM.... Park Rapids, MN [*FM radio station call letters*] (BROA)
KXL-FM....... Portland, OR [*FM radio station call letters*] (BROA)
KXLY-DT..... Spokane, WA [*Television station call letters*] (BROA)
KXME-FM.... Kaneohe, HI [*FM radio station call letters*] (BROA)
KXND......... Minot, ND [*Television station call letters*] (BROA)
KXNT......... North Las Vegas, NV [*AM radio station call letters*] (BROA)
KXOL......... Brigham City, UT [*AM radio station call letters*] (BROA)
KXPS......... Thousand Palms, CA [*AM radio station call letters*] (BROA)
KXTA......... Los Angeles, CA [*AM radio station call letters*] (BROA)
KXTZ-FM..... Pismo Beach, CA [*FM radio station call letters*] (BROA)
KXXL-FM.... Sun Valley, NV [*FM radio station call letters*] (BROA)
KXXM-FM.... San Antonio, TX [*FM radio station call letters*] (BROA)
KXXT......... Santa Barbara, CA [*AM radio station call letters*] (BROA)
KXZN-FM.... Sanger, TX [*FM radio station call letters*] (BROA)
Kya........... Kenya (MILB)
KYBB-FM.... Canton, SD [*FM radio station call letters*] (BROA)
KYCM-FM.... Bastrop, TX [*FM radio station call letters*] (BROA)
KYIZ......... Renton, WA [*AM radio station call letters*] (BROA)
KYLA-FM.... Homer, LA [*FM radio station call letters*] (BROA)
KYLV-FM.... Oklahoma City, OK [*FM radio station call letters*] (BROA)
KYOR-FM.... Yucca Valley, CA [*FM radio station call letters*] (BROA)
KYPX......... Little Rock, AR [*Television station call letters*] (BROA)
KYSY-FM.... Ankeny, IA [*FM radio station call letters*] (BROA)
KYUL-FM.... Harker Heights, TX [*FM radio station call letters*] (BROA)
KYW-DT...... Philadelphia, PA [*Television station call letters*] (BROA)
KZAT-FM..... Belle Plaine, IA [*FM radio station call letters*] (BROA)
KZBE-FM..... Omak, WA [*FM radio station call letters*] (BROA)
KZBN......... Santa Barbara, CA [*AM radio station call letters*] (BROA)
KZCY-FM.... Cheyenne, WY [*FM radio station call letters*] (BROA)
KZDF-FM..... McKinney, TX [*FM radio station call letters*] (BROA)
KZDL-FM..... Terrell, TX [*FM radio station call letters*] (BROA)
KZDY-FM..... Cawker City, KS [*FM radio station call letters*] (BROA)
KZEG-FM..... Clinton, IA [*FM radio station call letters*] (BROA)
KZEW-FM.... Wheatland, WY [*FM radio station call letters*] (BROA)
KZFX-FM..... Lincoln, NE [*FM radio station call letters*] (BROA)
KZIA-FM..... Cedar Rapids, IA [*FM radio station call letters*] (BROA)
KZIO-FM..... Two Harbors, MN [*FM radio station call letters*] (BROA)
KZJZ......... St. Louis, MO [*AM radio station call letters*] (BROA)
KZLO-FM.... Bozeman, MT [*FM radio station call letters*] (BROA)
KZMP......... Fort Worth, TX [*AM radio station call letters*] (BROA)
KZNR-FM.... Lakeville, MN [*FM radio station call letters*] (BROA)
KZNZ-FM.... Eden Prairie, MN [*FM radio station call letters*] (BROA)
KZSF......... San Jose, CA [*AM radio station call letters*] (BROA)
KZTR-FM..... Franklin, TX [*FM radio station call letters*] (BROA)
KZYQ-FM.... Lake Village, AR [*FM radio station call letters*] (BROA)
KZZD-FM..... Wichita, KS [*FM radio station call letters*] (BROA)
KZZM-FM.... Dayton, WA [*FM radio station call letters*] (BROA)
KZZP-FM..... Mesa, AZ [*FM radio station call letters*] (BROA)

L

By Acronym

L .... Law (GEAB)
L .... Leptin (MELL)
L .... Leukocyte (MELL)
L .... Lithuania (MILB)
LA .... Lactic Acidosis [*Medicine*] (MELL)
La .... Lanthanum (MELL)
LA .... Laryngeal Atresia [*Medicine*] (MELL)
LA .... Latex Allergy (MELL)
LA .... Lenticular Astigmatism (MELL)
LA .... Leucinamide (MELL)
LA .... Linea Aspera (MELL)
LA .... Linolenic Acid (MELL)
LA .... Locomotor Ataxia [*Medicine*] (MELL)
La .... Louisiana (BEE)
LA .... Lunula (MELL)
LA .... Lupus Anticoagulant [*Medicine*] (MELL)
LA .... Lyme Arthritis (MELL)
LAA .... Lead Agency Attorney (EPAT)
LABC .... Lymphadenosis Benigna Cutis [*Medicine*]
LABH .... Lab Holdings [*NASDAQ symbol*] (SG)
labr .... Laborer (GEAB)
LAC .... Los Angeles Chargers [*National Football League*] [*1960*] (NFLA)
LACM .... Los Angeles County Museum of Natural History [*California*]
LACO .... Erich Lacher Co.
LAD .... Lithia Motors'A' [*NYSE symbol*] (SG)
LADD .... Lowest Acceptable Daily Dose (EPAT)
LAFM .... Limited-Area Fine Mesh
LAI .... Laboratory Audit Inspection [*Environmental Protection Agency*] (EPAT)
LAKBC .... Los Angeles Kings Booster Club (EA)
LAM .... Levator Ani Muscle (MELL)
LAMA .... Laser-Assisted Microanastomosis [*Medicine*] (MELL)
LAMI .... Laminectomy [*Medicine*] (MELL)
LAMR .... Lamar Advertising 'A' [*NASDAQ symbol*] (SG)
LanChile ..... Linea Aerea Nacional de Chile
L & C .... Laxatives and Cathartics (MELL)
Landsat....... Land Remote Sensing Satellite (EOSA)
LANIC .... Latin American Network Information Center [*Internet resource*]
LANSA .... Latin American Paper Money Society (EA)
Lao .... Laos (MILB)
LAOF .... Longitudinal Arch of Foot (MELL)
LAP .... Leukocyte Adhesion Stimulator [*Medicine*] (MELL)
LAPD .... Latin American Pollen Database (QUAC)
LAR .... Los Angeles Raiders [*National Football League*] [*1982-94*] (NFLA)
LaRC .... Langley Research Center (EOSA)
LAS .... Lateral Amyotrophic Sclerosis [*Medicine*] (MELL)
LAS .... Low Apgar Score [*Medicine*] (MELL)
LAS .... Lupus Anticoagulant Syndrome [*Medicine*] (MELL)
Lat .... Latin (BEE)
Lat .... Latvia (MILB)
LAUN .... Launch Media [*NASDAQ symbol*] (SG)
LAVV .... Left Atrioventricular Valve [*Medicine*] (MELL)
LAWTE....... Laboratory Animal Welfare Training Exchange (GVA)
Lb .... Liberia (MILB)
LB .... Liver Biopsy [*Medicine*] (MELL)
LB .... Lung Biopsy [*Medicine*] (MELL)
LBA .... Left Brachial Artery [*Medicine*] (MELL)
LBAT .... Leukocyte Bactericidal Assay Test [*Medicine*] (MELL)
LBC .... Letter Book Copy (GEAB)
LBCV .... Left Brachiocephalic Vein [*Medicine*] (MELL)
LBD .... Lamellar Body Density [*Medicine*] (MELL)
LBFC .... Long Beach Finl'. [*NASDAQ symbol*] (SG)
LBIR .... Low Background Infrared Radiometry
LBR .... Labor Room (MELL)
LBRS .... Low Background Reference System
LBRT .... Liberate Technologies [*NASDAQ symbol*] (SG)
LBT .... Lupus Band Test [*Medicine*]
LBV .... Lateral Boundary Value (QUAC)
LCA .... Left Coronary Artery [*Medicine'*] (MELL)
LCA .... Leukocyte Common Antigen [*Medicine*] (MELL)
LCD .... Left Crus of Diaphragm [*Medicine*] (MELL)
LCD .... Light-Chain Deposition (MELL)
LCD .... Lobster-Claw Deformity (MELL)
LCD .... Low Calorie Diet (MELL)
LCFC .... Lou Christie Official Fan Club (EA)
LCGU .... Lesser Curve Gastric Ulcer (MELL)

LCH/M/T/U/VP... Landing Craft, Heavy/Merchanised/Tank/Utility/Vehicles and Personnel (MILB)
LCI .... Local Cerebral Ischemia [*Medicine*] (MELL)
LCL .... Lateral Capsular Ligament [*Medicine*] (MELL)
LCL .... Lumbocostal Ligament [*Medicine*] (MELL)
LCOC .... Lincoln and Continental Owners Club (EA)
LCP .... Loews Cineplex Entertain't. [*NYSE symbol*] (SG)
LCSFP......... Low Cerebrospinal Fluid Pressure [*Medicine*] (MELL)
L/D .... Labor and Delivery (MELL)
LD .... Labyrinthine Dysfunction [*Medicine*] (MELL)
LD .... Lactase Deficiency [*Medicine*] (MELL)
LD .... Land Disposal (EPAT)
LD .... Large Date [*Numismatic term*]
LD .... Last Dose (MELL)
LD .... Leigh's Disease [*Medicine*] (MELL)
LD .... Leukodystrophy [*Medicine*] (MELL)
L/D .... Lift-Drag Ratio [*Aerodynamics*]
LD .... Lipodystrophy [*Medicine*] (MELL)
LD .... Lisfranc Dislocation [*Medicine*] (MELL)
LD50 .... Lethal Dose 50
LDA............ Local Data Acquisition
LD & B .... Lyme Disease and Babesiosis [*Medicine*] (MELL)
LDEQ .... Louisana Department of Environmental Quality
LDGT .... Light-Duty Gasoline Truck (EPAT)
LDIR .... Low-Dose Ionizing Radiation (MELL)
LDL .... Lambda Delta Lambda (EA)
ldr .... Leader (GEAB)
LDS............ Lucey-Driscoll Syndrome [*Medicine*] (MELL)
LDSH .... Ladish Co. [*NASDAQ symbol*] (SG)
LDT............ Lowest Dose Tested [*Environmental science*] (EPAT)
LDV .... Laser Doppler Velocimetry [*Medicine*] (MELL)
LE .... Lazy Eye (MELL)
LE .... Leukocyte Esterase (MELL)
LE .... Life Expectancy (MELL)
LE .... Low Exposure (MELL)
LEAP .... Louisiana Educational Assessment Program
LEC .... Lower East Coast
LECCE .... Left Extracapsular Cataract Extraction (MELL)
LEEP .... Left End-Expiratory Pressure [*Medicine*] (MELL)
LEFI .... Local Electrical Field Instrument (EOSA)
LEH .... Linear Enamel Hypoplasias (QUAC)
LEM .... Light Emission Microscopy (MELL)
LERC.......... Local Emergency Response Committee (EPAT)
LERTS......... Laboratoire d'Etudes et de Recherches en Teledetection Spatiale [*France*] (EOSA)
LF .... Lassa Fever [*Medicine*] (MELL)
LF .... Lethal Factor (MELL)
LF .... Leukotactic Factor [*Medicine*] (MELL)
LF .... Ligamenta Flava [*Medicine*] (MELL)
LF .... Liver Fluke [*Medicine*] (MELL)
LF .... Lung Fluke [*Medicine*] (MELL)
LFA .... Lavage Fluid Analysis [*Medicine*] (MELL)
LFD .... Lateral Facial Dysplasia [*Medicine*] (MELL)
LFD .... Low Fiber Diet (MELL)
LFG .... Landamerica Financial Grp. [*NYSE symbol*] (SG)
LFIN .... Local Financial [*NASDAQ symbol*] (SG)
LFJ .... Lumbar Facet Joints [*Medicine*] (MELL)
LFT .... Lexford Residential TR SBI [*NYSE symbol*] (SG)
lg .... Large (BEE)
LG .... Lateral Geniculate [*Medicine*] (MELL)
LGA .... Left Gastric Artery [*Medicine*] (MELL)
LGA .... Local Government Association (GVA)
LGD .... Lou Gehrig Disease [*Medicine*] (MELL)
LGF .... Lions Gate Entertainment [*AMEX symbol*] (SG)
LGI .... Lower Gastrointestinal [*Medicine*] (MELL)
LGM............ Lymphogranuloma [*Medicine*] (MELL)
LGS............ Last Glacial Stage (QUAC)
LGVMA .... Lesbian & Gay Veterinary Medical Association (GVA)
LH .... Lanugo Hair (MELL)
LH .... Laparoscopic Herniorrhaphy [*Medicine*] (MELL)
LH .... Lidocaine Hydrochloride [*Medicine*] (MELL)
LHDDV .... Light Heavy-Duty Diesel Vehicle (EPAT)
LHE .... Lateral Humeral Epicondylalgia [*Medicine*] (MELL)
LHE .... Lateral Humeral Epicondylitis [*Medicine*] (MELL)
LHO .... LaSalle Hotel Properties [*NYSE symbol*] (SG)
LHPT........... Loculated Hydropneumothorax [*Medicine*] (MELL)

LHSC	Lateral Horn of Spinal Cord [*Medicine*] (MELL)
LI	Lactose Intolerance [*Medicine*] (MELL)
LI	Laser Iridotomy [*Medicine*] (MELL)
LI	Liver Infarct [*Medicine*] (MELL)
lib	Library (GEAB)
lic	License (BEE)
lieut	Lieutenant (GEAB)
LIF	Left Index Finger (MELL)
LIFE	League of Independent Ferret Enthusiasts (EA)
LIH	Leucine-Induced Hypoglycemia [*Medicine*] (MELL)
LIH	Leukocyte Inhibiting Factor [*Medicine*] (MELL)
LII	Lennox Intl. [*NYSE symbol*] (SG)
Limo	Limousine
LIN	Linens'n Things [*NYSE symbol*] (SG)
Ling	Linguistics (BEE)
LINUS	Local Independently Nucleated Units of Structure (MELL)
LIO	Laser Indirect Ophthalmoscope [*Medicine*] (MELL)
LION	Literature Online [*Chadwyck-Healey*]
LIS	Lightning Imaging Sensor
LIS	Locked-in Syndrome [*Medicine*] (MELL)
LISFAN	Lost in Space Fannish Alliance (EA)
LIT	Leukocyte Immunization Therapy [*Medicine*]
LITE	Lidar In-Space Technology Experiment (EOSA)
LJ	Lockjaw (MELL)
LJBF	Let's Just Be Friends [*Online dialog*]
LK	Lamellar Keratoplasty [*Medicine*] (MELL)
Lkc	Leukocyte (MELL)
LKS	Landau-Kleffer Syndrome [*Medicine*]
LLC	Laparoscopic Laser Cholecystectomy [*Medicine*] (MELL)
LLCC	Long-Leg Cylinder Cast [*Medicine*] (MELL)
LLD	Late-Life Depression (MELL)
LLD	Lipid-Lowering Drug (MELL)
LLF	Lower Limb Fracture (MELL)
LLL	L-3 Communications Hldgs. [*NYSE symbol*] (SG)
LLL	Left Liver Lobe (MELL)
LLL	Left Lower Leg (MELL)
LLL	Left Lower Lid (MELL)
LLLE	Low-Level Lead Exposure (MELL)
LLMS	Longitudinal Layer of Muscles of Stomach (MELL)
LLN	Lower Limit of Normal [*Medicine*] (MELL)
LLS	Later-Life Sexuality (MELL)
LLS	Little League Shoulder (MELL)
lm	Light-Minute
LM	Long March [*Launch vehicle*]
LMM	Laser Mortgage Mgmt. [*NYSE symbol*] (SG)
lmmd	Low Molecular Weight Dextran [*Medicine*] (MELL)
LMOP	Landfill Methane Outreach Program [*Environmental Protection Agency*] (EPAT)
LMP	Left Mentoposterior [*Medicine*] (MELL)
LMP	Low Malignant Potential [*Medicine*] (MELL)
LMS	Lateral Medullary Syndrome [*Medicine*] (MELL)
LMS	Levator Muscle of Scapula [*Medicine*] (MELL)
LMS	Levator Muscle Syndrome [*Medicine*] (MELL)
LMV	Larva Migrans Visceralis [*Medicine*] (MELL)
Ln	Lane (PROS)
LNB	Lumbar Nerve Block [*Medicine*] (MELL)
LNB	Lymph Node Biopsy [*Medicine*] (MELL)
LNC	Leonard Nimoy Club (EA)
LNIB	Like New in Box [*Watch collecting*]
LNK	Clublink Corp. [*Toronto Stock Exchange symbol*] (SG)
LNN	Lindsay Mfg. [*NYSE symbol*] (SG)
LNN	Lower Nephron Nephrosis [*Medicine*] (MELL)
LNR	LNR Property [*NYSE symbol*] (SG)
LNT	Alliant Energy [*NYSE symbol*] (SG)
LOA	Lateral Osseous Ampulla [*Medicine*] (MELL)
LOA	Leber's Optic Atrophy [*Medicine*] (MELL)
LOA	Left Anterior Oblique [*Medicine*] (MELL)
LOA	Loners of America [*An association*] (EA)
LOAN	Local Officials' Administration Network (EA)
LOAX	Log On America
LOCE	Last Observation Carried Forward
LOD	Last Occurrence of Date (QUAC)
LOD	Lodgian, Inc. [*NYSE symbol*] (SG)
log	Logistic (MILB)
LOHF	Late-Onset Hepatic Failure [*Medicine*] (MELL)
LOIS	Lesbians Organising in Solidarity [*An association*]
LOP	Lactosuria of Pregnancy (MELL)
LOP	Level of Pain (MELL)
Los.	Los Angeles Rams [*National Football League*] [*1946-94*] (NFLA)
LOS	Lost in Space [*Television Program*]
LOU	Limited Official Use
LP	Labor Pain (MELL)
LP	Lactic Peroxidase [*Medicine*] (MELL)
LP	Lead Poisoning (MELL)
LP	Lichen Planus (MELL)
LP	Lipid Pneumonia (MELL)
LPA	Lightning Position Analyser (QUAC)
LPD	Legg-Perthes Disease [*Medicine*] (MELL)
LPD	Lymphoproliferative Disorder [*Medicine*] (MELL)
LPD/H	Landing Platform, Dock/Helicopter (MILB)
LPF	Lead Pipe Fracture (MELL)
LPHL	Leisureplanet Holdings [*NASDAQ symbol*] (SG)
LPI	Laser Peripheral Iridectomy [*Medicine*] (MELL)
LPI	Long Process of Incus [*Medicine*] (MELL)
LPR	Low Power Radio
LQ	Lower Quadrant [*Medicine*] (MELL)
LQER	Lesser Quantity Emission Rates (EPAT)
LQID	Liquid Audio [*NASDAQ symbol*] (SG)
LR	Lacrimation Reflex [*Medicine*] (MELL)
LR	Laser Retroreflector (EOSA)
LR	Low Renin [*Medicine*] (MELL)
LR	Low Resolution (QUAC)
LRA	Laser Retroreflector Array (EOSA)
LRD	Low-Residue Diet (MELL)
LRIFC	Lauren Robbins International Fan Club (EA)
LRPT	Low-Resolution Picture Transmission (EOSA)
LRRC	Lionel Railroaders Club (EA)
LRSB	Low Right Sternal Border [*Medicine*] (MELL)
LRT	Lymphoreticular Tissue [*Medicine*] (MELL)
LRTD	Living Relative Transplant Donor (MELL)
LRU	Landscape Response Unit (QUAC)
LRU	Line Replaceable Unit
LRW	Labor Ready [*NYSE symbol*] (SG)
LS	Larcher's Sign [*Medicine*] (MELL)
LS	Laser Surgery (MELL)
LS	Latent Syphilis (MELL)
LS	Lecithin Supplement (MELL)
LS	Leichtenstern's Sign [*Medicine*] (MELL)
Ls	Lesotho (MILB)
LS	Lichen Sclerosis [*Medicine*] (MELL)
LS	Lichen Simplex [*Medicine*] (MELL)
ls	Light-Second
LS	Liver Scan [*Medicine*] (MELL)
LS	Lladro Society (EA)
LS2	Lesser Sulphur-Crested Cockatoo [*Bird*]
LSA	Lumbosacral Agenesis [*Medicine*] (MELL)
LSD	Life-Sustaining Device (MELL)
LSD	Lipid Storage Disease (MELL)
LSD	Low Salt Diet (MELL)
LSD/H/M/T	Landing Ship, Dock/Heavy/Medium/Tank (MILB)
LSE	Low-Set Ear (MELL)
LSF	Last Spring Frost (QUAC)
LSF	Lesser Sciatic Foramen [*Medicine*] (MELL)
LSH	LaSalle Re Holdings [*NYSE symbol*] (SG)
LSL	Left Short Leg (MELL)
LSL	Lymphosarcoma Leukemia [*Medicine*] (MELL)
LSN	Leasing Solutions [*NYSE symbol*] (SG)
LSN	Lesser Sciatic Notch [*Medicine*] (MELL)
LSON	Lason, Inc. [*NASDAQ symbol*] (SG)
LSP	Left Sacroposterior [*Medicine*] (MELL)
LSP	Lumbosacral Plexus [*Medicine*] (MELL)
LSRI	Lumbosacral Root Injury (MELL)
LSS	Laparoscopic Surgery (MELL)
LSS	Lateral Spinal Stenosis [*Medicine*] (MELL)
LSS	Limb-Salvage Surgery (MELL)
LSS	Lumbar Spinal Stenosis [*Medicine*] (MELL)
LST	Large Simple Trial [*Statistics*]
LSV	Lateral Sacral Vein [*Medicine*] (MELL)
LSV	Left Sinus of Valsalva [*Medicine*] (MELL)
LT	Lamaze Technique [*Medicine*] (MELL)
LTB	Lead-Time Bias (MELL)
LTB	Length-Time Bias (MELL)
LTBG	Lightbridge, Inc. [*NASDAQ symbol*] (SG)
LTC	Long-Term Complication (MELL)
LTC	Long-Term Consequence (MELL)
LTC	Low Transverse Cervical [*Medicine*] (MELL)
LTPA	Leisure-Time Physical Activity (MELL)
LTR	Long-Term Residential
LTT	Lactose Tolerance Test [*Medicine*] (MELL)
LTTPBA	Late Third Trimester Partial Birth Abortion (MELL)
LTUI	Low Transverse Uterine Incision [*Medicine*] (MELL)
LTVC	Long-Term Venous Catheter [*Medicine*] (MELL)
LTWO	Learn2.com, Inc. [*NYSE symbol*] (SG)
Lu	Luxembourg (MILB)
LUCE	Low Urinary Calcium Excretion [*Medicine*] (MELL)
LUIS	Label Use Information System [*Environmental Protection Agency*] (EPAT)
LUMD	Lowest Usual Maintenance Dose [*Medicine*] (MELL)
LUT	Limited User Testing
l/v	Lake View
LV	Laryngeal Vestibule [*Medicine*] (MELL)
LV	Lateral Ventricle [*Medicine*] (MELL)
LV	Latino Virus [*Medicine*] (MELL)
L/V	Loan-to-Value Ratio [*Business term*]
LVIS	Low Velocity Intense Source
LVLT	Level 3 Communications [*NASDAQ symbol*] (SG)
LVM	Lateral Vastus Muscle [*Medicine*] (MELL)
LVOTO	Left Ventricular Outflow Tract Obstruction [*Medicine*] (MELL)
LVSO	Left Ventricular Systolic Output [*Medicine*] (MELL)
LWOT	Left Without Therapy (MELL)
LWS	Lavage with Saline [*Medicine*] (MELL)
lx	Larynx (MELL)
ly	Light-Year

M
By Acronym

M .... Macrophage (MELL)
M .... Malta (MILB)
M .... Mandible (MELL)
M .... Marijuana (MELL)
M .... Married (MELL)
M .... Maternal (MELL)
M .... Maxilla (MELL)
M .... Measles (MELL)
M .... Meatus (MELL)
M .... Medicare (MELL)
M .... Meningeal (MELL)
M .... Modiolus (MELL)
m .... Molality (MELL)
M .... Molarity (MELL)
M .... Mucus (MELL)
M2 .... Moluccan Cockatoo [Bird]
MA .... Malignant Astrocytoma [Medicine] (MELL)
MA .... Masseter [Medicine] (MELL)
MA .... Mechanical Atherectomy [Medicine] (MELL)
MA .... Megaloblastic Anemia [Medicine] (MELL)
MA .... Metabolic Acidosis [Medicine] (MELL)
MA .... Microadenoma [Medicine] (MELL)
MA .... Monkeein' Around [An association] (EA)
MA .... Monomorphic Adenoma [Medicine] (MELL)
MAC .... Macrophage (MELL)
MAC .... Macula (MELL)
MAC .... Maintained Anesthesia Care (MELL)
MAC .... Mastoid Air Cell [Medicine] (MELL)
MAC .... Mobil Air Conditioner (EPAT)
MACOM .... Major Commands [Military]
MACSU .... Maximum Card Study Unit [An association] (EA)
MACT .... Multiple-Agent Chemotherapy [Medicine] (MELL)
MAD .... Milk-Alkali Disease [Medicine] (MELL)
MADA .... Muscle Adenylate Deaminase [Medicine] (MELL)
MADAM .... Mean and Dispersion Additive Model [Statistics]
MADS .... Mixed Anxiety/Depression Syndrome [Medicine] (MELL)
MAEQW .... Moves All Extremities Quite Well [Medicine] (MELL)
MAFA .... Movement-Associated Fetal Acceleration [Medicine] (MELL)
MAGI .... Microscope Assisted Guided Intervention [Medical technique]
Magsat .... Magnetic Field Satellite (EOSA)
MAHLOVS..... Middle and High Latitudes Oceanic Variability Study (EOSA)
maint........... Maintenance (MILB)
maj .... Major (GEAB)
MAJC .... Microprocessor Architecture for Lava Computing
Mal .... Malaysia (MILB)
MALS.......... Median Arcuate Ligament Syndrome [Medicine] (MELL)
MALTL .... Mucosa-Associated Lymphoid Tissue Lymphoma [Medicine] (MELL)
MAME .... Michigan Association for Media in Education
MAME .... Michigan Association of Media Educators
MAMS......... Multispectral Atmospheric Mapping Sensor
M&N .... Mydriacyl and Neosynephrine [Medicine] (MELL)
M&P .... Melphenal and Prednisone [Medicine] (MELL)
M&T........... Muscles and Tendons (MELL)
MAP........... Maxilla Alveolar Process [Medicine] (MELL)
MAP........... Methyl Alcohol Poisoning [Medicine] (MELL)
MAP........... Microwave Anisotropy Probe
MAP........... Missouri Assessment Program
MAP........... Multiple Antigen Peptide [Medicine] (MELL)
MAP estimate... Maximum a Posteriori Estimate
MAPS......... Measurement of Atmospheric Pollution from Satellites (EOSA)
Mar............ March (BEE)
MarCorps..... Marine Corps
MARPS .... Marine Petrol Tr. [NASDAQ symbol] (SG)
MARS .... Multiple-Angle Reference System
MARS .... Multivariate Adaptive Regression Splines
MaRV .... Maneuvering Reentry Vehicle
MAS .... Malabsorption Syndrome (MELL)
MASD .... Menstrual-Associatied Sleep Disorder [Medicine] (MELL)
MASL .... Missouri Association of School Librarian
MASL .... Missouri Association of School Librarians
Mass........... Massachusetts (BEE)
MAST .... Medical Antishock Trausers (MELL)
MASU .... Mid-Atlantic State University
mat .... Maternal (GEAB)
MAT .... Mean Absorption Time [Medicine] (MELL)
MAT .... Microagglutination Test [Medicine] (MELL)

MATVY......... Matav-Cable Sys ADS [NASDAQ symbol] (SG)
MAU........... Microalbuminuria [Medicine] (MELL)
MAVMA....... Massachusetts Veterinary Medical Association (GVA)
MAX SOCIETY... Maximilian Numismatic and Historical Society (EA)
MAYA .... Muslim Arab Youth Association
MB .... Matchbox [Mattel]
MB .... Milwaukee Brace [Medicine] (MELL)
MB .... Mucosal Barrier [Medicine] (MELL)
MB .... Mucosal Bleeding [Medicine] (MELL)
MBCC .... Matchbox Challenge Cars [Toy collection]
MBD........... Maple Bark Disease [Medicine] (MELL)
MBD........... Marble Bone Disease [Medicine] (MELL)
MBD........... Marchiafava-Bignami Disease [Medicine] (MELL)
MBD........... Marie-Bamberger Disease [Medicine] (MELL)
MBD........... Metabolic Bone Disease [Medicine] (MELL)
MBD........... Meyer-Betz Disease [Medicine] (MELL)
MBD........... Moeller-Barlow Disease [Medicine] (MELL)
MBE........... Malibu Entmt Intl. [AMEX symbol] (SG)
MBE........... Molecular Beam Epitaxy
MBFC.......... Magic of Bewitched Fan Club (EA)
MBI........... Maximal Blink Index [Medicine] (MELL)
MBI........... Methylene Bisphenyl Isocyanate [Medicine] (MELL)
MBI........... Mycobacterial Infection [Medicine] (MELL)
MBP........... Malignant Bone Pain (MELL)
MBP........... Mid Penn Bancorp [AMEX symbol] (SG)
MBP........... Modified Bagshawe Protocol [Medicine] (MELL)
MBPS......... Munchausen-by-Proxy Syndrome [Medicine] (MELL)
MBRW .... Matchbox Regular Wheels [Toy collection]
MBS........... Managed Bandwidth Service
MBSF......... Matchbox Superfast [Toy collection]
MBT........... Massive Blood Transfusion [Medicine] (MELL)
MBT........... Motion Base Technologies
MBX........... Matchbox [Toy collection]
MBYY......... Matchbox Models of Yesteryear [Toy collection]
MC .... Macula Coloboma [Medicine] (MELL)
MC .... Malignant Carcinoid [Medicine] (MELL)
MC .... Mature Cataract (MELL)
MC .... Mazda Club (EA)
MC .... Medial Canthus (MELL)
MC .... Medullary Cavity [Medicine] (MELL)
MC .... Megalocornea (MELL)
MCA............ Maserati Club of America (EA)
MCA............ Monetary Control Act
MCAR .... Missing Completely at Random
MCAT .... Monoclonal Antibody Therapy (MELL)
MCB........... Motor Company of Botswana
MCBs.......... Metacarpal Bone [Medicine] (MELL)
MCC........... Mesenchymal Cell Concentration [Medicine] (MELL)
MCC........... Metacentric Chromosome [Medicine] (MELL)
MCC........... Microfilm Card Catalog (GEAB)
MCC........... Multichannel Cochlear Implant [Medicine] (MELL)
MCCI........... Mucocutaneous Candidiasis [Medicine] (MELL)
MCD........... Mad Cow Disease [Medicine] (MELL)
MCD........... Municipal Civil District (GEAB)
MCDV......... Maritime Coastal Defense Vessel (MILB)
MCE........... Myocardial Embolism [Medicine] (MELL)
MCEA......... Maryland Classified Employees Association
MCF........... Middle Cranial Fossa [Medicine] (MELL)
MCF........... Myocardial Fascicles [Medicine] (MELL)
MCFS......... Median Cleft Face Syndrome [Medicine] (MELL)
MCFS......... Middle Cranial Fossa Syndrome [Medicine] (MELL)
MCHB......... Maternal and Child Health Bureau (MELL)
MCL........... Mature Corpus Luteum [Medicine] (MELL)
MCM........... Controladora Comer'l Mex GDS [NYSE symbol] (SG)
MCM........... Meningococcal Meningitis [Medicine] (MELL)
MCM........... Metastatic Carcinomatous Meningitis [Medicine] (MELL)
MCMC......... Markov Chain Monte Carlo Method
MCMCC....... Mid-Century Mercury Car Club (EA)
MCM/CS ..... Mine Countermeasures/Command and Support Ship (MILB)
MCMP......... Middle Constrictor Muscle of Pharynx [Medicine] (MELL)
MCN........... Malignant Cystic Neoplasm [Medicine] (MELL)
MCN........... Musculocutaneous Nerve [Medicine] (MELL)
MCO........... Multicystic Ovary [Medicine] (MELL)
MCP........... Managed Care Program (MELL)
MCP........... Meteorological Communications Package (EOSA)
MCP........... Midclavicular Plane [Medicine] (MELL)

MCP............ Minimum Convex Polygon
MCP............ Mucin Clot Prevention [*Medicine*] (MELL)
MCP............ Mullet-Channel Plate [*Spectrometry*]
MCR............ Mutual Climatic Range (QUAC)
MCRD.......... Medullary Cystic Renal Disease [*Medicine*] (MELL)
MCRE.......... MetaCreations Corp. [*NASDAQ symbol*] (SG)
MCS............ Malignant Carcinoid Syndrome [*Medicine*] (MELL)
MCS............ Metachronous Seeding [*Medicine*] (MELL)
MCS............ Multi-Chemical Sensitivity [*Medicine*] (MELL)
MCT............ Manual Cervical Traction [*Medicine*] (MELL)
MCT............ Mature Cystic Teratoma [*Medicine*] (MELL)
MCU............ Mobile Calibration Unit
MCV............ Meningococcus Vaccine [*Medicine*] (MELL)
MCV............ Middle Cardiac Vein [*Medicine*] (MELL)
Md.............. Maryland (BEE)
MDA............ Media Arts Group [*NYSE symbol*] (SG)
MD-BD........ Major Depression and Bipolar Disorder [*Medicine*] (MELL)
MDC............ Max-Delbrueck-Center [*Berlin, Germany*]
MDC............ Milk Development Council (GVA)
MDC............ Mullerian Duct Cyst [*Medicine*] (MELL)
MDCA.......... MDC Corp. Cl'A' [*NASDAQ symbol*] (SG)
MDCLC........ Medical Control, Inc. [*NASDAQ symbol*] (SG)
MDCR.......... Michigan Department of Civil Rights
MDD............ Male Development Disorder (MELL)
MDD............ Manic Depressive Disorder (MELL)
Mdg............ Madagascar (MILB)
MDI............ Multiple Daily Injection [*Medicine*] (MELL)
MDP............ Minimum Distance Probability
MDRF.......... Materials Dosimetry Reference Facility
MDRI.......... Multidrug-Resistant Infection (MELL)
MDRT.......... Multidrug-Resistant Tuberculosis (MELL)
MDRX.......... Allscripts, Inc. [*NASDAQ symbol*] (SG)
MDS............ Midas, Inc. [*NYSE symbol*] (SG)
MDS............ Myocardial-Dysplasia Syndrome [*Medicine*] (MELL)
MDT............ Maintainability Development Test [*Army*]
MDu............ Middle Dutch (BEE)
MDVMA........ Maryland Veterinary Medical Association (GVA)
ME.............. Male Escutcheon [*Medicine*] (MELL)
ME.............. Manic Episode [*Medicine*] (MELL)
ME.............. Maximal Efficacy [*Medicine*] (MELL)
ME.............. Medication Error [*Medicine*] (MELL)
ME.............. Microemboli [*Medicine*] (MELL)
ME.............. Multiple Embolisms [*Medicine*] (MELL)
ME.............. Multiple Exostoses [*Medicine*] (MELL)
MEBA.......... Michigan Elk Breeders Association (GVA)
MEBA/NMU... Marine Engineers' Beneficial Association/National Maritime Union (EA)
MEC............ Model Energy Code [*Environmental Protection Agency*] (EPAT)
Mech .... Mechanics (BEE)
mech .... Mechanized (MILB)
MECH........ MECH Financial [*NASDAQ symbol*] (SG)
MECHRIC.... Middle East Christian Committee
med .... Medieval (BEE)
MED............ Multiple Endocrin Deficiency [*Medicine*] (MELL)
MEF/B/U... Marine Expeditionary Force/Brigade/Unit (MILB)
MEI.............. Metastatic Efficiency Index [*Medicine*] (MELL)
MEI.............. Middle-Ear Infection (MELL)
MEL 1.......... Military Education Level One [*Army*]
MELAS........ Mitochrondrial Encephalomyopathy with Acidosis and Stroke [*Medicine*] (MELL)
MELISSA...... Micro Ecological Life Support Alternative [*European Space Agency*]
Meml.......... Memorial (PROS)
MEN............ Meningitis [*Medicine*] (MELL)
MENIC........ Middle East Network Information Center [*Internet resource*]
MENS.......... Microamperage Electrical Nerve Stimulation [*Medicine*] (MELL)
Mep .... Mean Effective Pressure
MEP............ Migrant Education Projects
MER............ Medical Error Reduction (MELL)
MERK.......... Merkert American [*NASDAQ symbol*] (SG)
MERLIN........ Medical Emergency Relief International (MELL)
MESS.......... Mangled Extremity Severity Score [*Medicine*] (MELL)
MET............ Medium Energy Telescope
META.......... Megachannel Extra-Terrestrial Assay
Metall.......... Metallurgy (BEE)
METAR........ Meteorological Actual Report (WEAT)
Meteorol...... Meteorology (BEE)
METEOSAT... Geosynchronous Meteorology Satellite (EOSA)
MEV............ Maximal Exercise Ventilation (MELL)
MEV............ Middle Ear Ventilation (MELL)
MEVMA........ Maine Veterinary Medical Association (GVA)
MEXnet........ Mexico Network
MF.............. Maisonneuve Fracture [*Medicine*] (MELL)
M/F............ Male or Female
MF.............. Mallet Finger (MELL)
MF.............. Mallet Fracture [*Medicine*] (MELL)
MF.............. Mandibular Foramen [*Medicine*] (MELL)
MF.............. March Fracture [*Medicine*] (MELL)
MF.............. Microfilament (MELL)
MFA............ America First Mtg Investments [*NYSE symbol*] (SG)
MFA............ Macrofollicular Adenoma [*Medicine*] (MELL)
MFBE.......... Minority/Female Business Enterprise
MFCS.......... Mason Fracture Classification System [*Medicine*] (MELL)
MFD............ Monteggia Fracture-Dislocation [*Medicine*] (MELL)
MFEnet........ Magnetic Fusion Energy Network
MFG............ Magnetic Field Gradient (MELL)

Mfg .... Manufacturing (PROS)
M/F/H........ Minorities, Females, Handicapped
MFI............ MicroFinancial, Inc. [*NYSE symbol*] (SG)
MFM............ Maternal-Fetal Medicine (MELL)
MFNX.......... Metromedia Fiber Network'A' [*NASDAQ symbol*] (SG)
mfpm .... Made from Purchased Materials [*Manufacturing*]
Mfr............. Manufacturer (PROS)
MFS............ Medicated Feeding Stuff (GVA)
MFW............ M&F Worldwide [*NYSE symbol*] (SG)
MG............ Media Guide
MG............ Minister of the Gospel (GEAB)
MGA............ Mammary Gland Adenoma [*Medicine*] (MELL)
MGCAX........ Managers Capital Appreciation Fund
MGCE.......... Multifocal Giant Cell Encephalitis [*Medicine*] (MELL)
MGCT.......... Mixed Germ Cell Tumor [*Medicine*] (MELL)
MGD............ Maternal Genetic Disease (MELL)
MGD............ Mixed Gonadal Dysgenesis (MELL)
MGE............ Megaloblastic Erythropoiesis [*Medicine*] (MELL)
MGF............ Multipotent Growth Factor [*Medicine*] (MELL)
MGH............ Mammogenic Hormone [*Medicine*] (MELL)
MGH............ Monosodium Glutamate Headache [*Medicine*] (MELL)
Mgl............ Mongolia (MILB)
MGR............ Marrow Graft Rejection [*Medicine*] (MELL)
MGT............ Multiple Glomus Tumor [*Medicine*] (MELL)
MGT............ Multiplex Genetic Testing [*Medicine*] (MELL)
MH............ Migraine Headache (MELL)
MH............ Morgagni Hernia [*Medicine*] (MELL)
MH............ Myocardial Hypertrophy [*Medicine*] (MELL)
MHC............ Mason & Hanger Corp.
MHCA.......... Tumor Histocompatibility Antigen [*Medicine*] (MELL)
MH/CD........ Mental Health/Chemical Dependency
MHC/I/O........ Minehunter, Coastal/Inshore/Offshore (MILB)
MHDA.......... Multiplex Heteroduplex Analysis [*Medicine*] (MELL)
MHDDV........ Medium Heavy-Duty Diesel Vehicle (EPAT)
MHG............ Middle High German (GEAB)
MHI............ Meat Hygiene Inspector (GVA)
MHI............ Minor Head Injury (MELL)
MHI............ Morrison Management Specialists [*NYSE symbol*] (SG)
MHK............ Mohawk Industries [*NYSE symbol*] (SG)
MHN............ Morbus Hemolyticus Neonatorum [*Medicine*] (MELL)
MHN............ Musical Heritage Network [*Internet resource*]
MHN............ Mylohyoid Nerve [*Medicine*] (MELL)
MHO............ Medical House Officer (MELL)
MHR............ Magnum Hunter Resources [*AMEX symbol*] (SG)
MHR............ Maternal Heart Rate (MELL)
MHS............ Meat Hygiene Service (GVA)
MHS............ Microwave Humidity Sounder (EOSA)
MH/SA........ Mental Health/Substance Abuse
MHU............ MIIX Group [*NYSE symbol*] (SG)
MHWL........ Mean High Water Level (QUAC)
MI............ Mechanical Incontinence [*Medicine*] (MELL)
MI............ Mexican Isthmus [*Crude oil*]
MI............ Mitosis Index [*Medicine*] (MELL)
Mia............ Miami Dolphins [*National Football League*] [*1966-present*] (NFLA)
MIAAHC........ Michigan Alliance Against Hate Crimes
MICA............ Midwest Insulation Contractors Association
MICI............ Metadata Information Clearinghouse Interactive
MID............ Median Incisal Diastema [*Medicine*] (MELL)
MID............ Minimal Infecting Dose [*Medicine*] (MELL)
MID............ Minimal Irradiation Dose [*Medicine*] (MELL)
MIDAS........ Munich Image Data Analysis System
MIDCAB........ Minimally Invasive Direct Coronary Artery Bypass [*Medicine*] (MELL)
MIE............ Medical Improvement Expectation
MIF............ Maximum Inspiratory Force [*Medicine*] (MELL)
MIFR.......... Maximal Inspiratory Flow Rate [*Medicine*] (MELL)
MIFR.......... Mullerian Inhibiting Factor [*Medicine*] (MELL)
MIH............ Migraine with Interval Headache (MELL)
MIHL.......... MIH Limited'A' [*NASDAQ symbol*] (SG)
MIIF............ Maintenance of Inactive Industrial Facilities
mil.............. Military (BEE)
MIL STD ..... Military Standard
MIMB.......... Mint in a Mint Box [*Collectibles*]
MIME.......... Multimedia Internet Mail Extension
MIMIC model... Multiple Indicator Multiple Cause Model
MIMP.......... Mint in Manufacturer's Packaging [*Collectibles*]
MIMP.......... Mint in Mint Package [*Collectibles*]
MIMR.......... Multi-Frequency Imaging Microwave Radiometer (EOSA)
MIMS.......... MIM Corp. [*NASDAQ symbol*] (SG)
Min.............. Minnesota Vikings [*National Football League*] [*1961-present*] (NFLA)
MIN............ Motor Interneuron (MELL)
Mineral........ Mineralogy (BEE)
MINMB........ Mint in a Near Mint Box [*Collectibles*]
MINMP........ Mint in Near Mint Package [*Collectibles*]
MinPres........ Minister President
MIP............ Mean Incubation Perios (MELL)
MIPAS .... Michelson Interferometric Passive Atmosphere Sounder (EOSA)
MIRLYN........ Michigan Research Library Network
MISG.......... Modified Immune Serum Globulin [*Medicine*] (MELL)
MISI............ Metro Information Svcs. [*NASDAQ symbol*] (SG)
MISMR .... Michigan Society for Medical Research (GVA)
MISR.......... Multi-Angle Imaging Spectroradiometer (EOSA)
MIT............ Myocardial Infarction Triage [*Medicine*] (MELL)
mitse .... Made in the Same Establihment [*Manufacturing*]
MJ.............. Minerva Jacket [*Medicine*] (MELL)
MKA............ Metrika Systems [*AMEX symbol*] (SG)

MKC	McCormick & Co. [*NYSE symbol*] (SG)
MKC	Megakaryocyte [*Medicine*] (MELL)
MKL	Markel Corp. [*NYSE symbol*] (SG)
MKSI	MKS Instruments [*NASDAQ symbol*] (SG)
MKTW	MarketWatch.com [*NYSE symbol*] (SG)
ML	Macula Lutea (MELL)
ML	Mail Label
ML	Marine Limit (QUAC)
ML	Maurice Lacroix
ML	Memory Loss (MELL)
ML	Milk Letdown (MELL)
MLA	Monophosphoryl Lipid A [*Medicine*] (MELL)
MLAN	Midland Co. [*NASDAQ symbol*] (SG)
MLBP	Mechanical Low Back Pain (MELL)
MLBW	Moderately Low Birth Weight (MELL)
MLC	Multilumen Catheter [*Medicine*] (MELL)
MLL	Middle Lobe of Lung (MELL)
MLN	Mediastinal Lymph Node [*Medicine*] (MELL)
MLN	Membranous Lupus Nephropathy [*Medicine*] (MELL)
MLO	Mesio-Linguo-Occlusal [*Dentistry*] (MELL)
MLP	Maui Land & Pineapple [*AMEX symbol*] (SG)
MLRS	Multiple Launch Rocket System
MLSE	Malformed Low-Set Ears (MELL)
ML Society	Magic Latern Society of the United States and Canada (EA)
Mlw	Malawi (MILB)
MLW	Military Land Warrant (GEAB)
MLWL	Mean Low Water Level (QUAC)
MM	Military Macaw [*Bird*]
MM	Mitral Murmur [*Medicine*] (MELL)
MMA	Main Mission Antennas
MMA	Minor Motor Aphasia [*Medicine*] (MELL)
MMA	Monosil Manufacturers Association
MMB	Mouth-to-Mouth Breathing (MELL)
MMC	Meningomyelocele [*Medicine*] (MELL)
MMC	Microcar and Minicar Club (EA)
MMC	Microsoft Management Console
MMCN	MMC Networks [*NASDAQ symbol*] (SG)
MMD	Milkmaid's Dislocation [*Medicine*] (MELL)
MME	Milkmaid's Elbow [*Medicine*] (MELL)
MMH	Meristar Hotels & Resorts [*NYSE symbol*] (SG)
MMMT	Malignant Mixed Mesodermal Tumor [*Medicine*] (MELL)
MMMT	Metastatic Mixed Mullerian Tumor [*Medicine*] (MELL)
MMPT	Modem Media.Poppe Tyson'A' [*NASDAQ symbol*] (SG)
MMR	McMoRan Exploration [*NYSE symbol*] (SG)
MMR	Mild Mental Retardation (MELL)
MMR	Mouth-to-Mouth Resuscitation (MELL)
MMS	MAXIMUS, Inc. [*NYSE symbol*] (SG)
MMS	Megacystis-Megaureter Syndrome [*Medicine*] (MELL)
MMS	Milkman's Syndrome [*Medicine*] (MELL)
MMS	Minimum Methadone Service [*Medicine*] (MELL)
MMT	Malignant Mixed Tumor [*Medicine*] (MELL)
MMT	Medial Meniscus Tear [*Medicine*] (MELL)
MMT	Methadone Mainetnance Treatment [*Medicine*] (MELL)
MMWW	Metamor Worldwide [*NASDAQ symbol*] (SG)
MMXI	Media Metrix [*NASDAQ symbol*] (SG)
MN	Melanocytic Nevus [*Medicine*] (MELL)
MN	Membranous Nephropathy [*Medicine*] (MELL)
MNB	Mandibular Nerve Block [*Medicine*] (MELL)
MNBCCS	Multi-Nevoid Basal-Cell Carcinoma Syndrome [*Medicine*] (MELL)
MNC	Monaco Coach [*NYSE symbol*] (SG)
MNC	Multinucleated Cell [*Medicine*] (MELL)
MNES	Median Nerve Entrapment Syndrome [*Medicine*] (MELL)
MNF	Myelinated Nerve Fiber [*Medicine*] (MELL)
MNI	Media Networks, Inc.
MNM	Motile with Normal Morphology [*Medicine*] (MELL)
MNN	Median Nerve Neuropathy [*Medicine*] (MELL)
MNP	Median Nerve Palsy [*Medicine*] (MELL)
MNS	MSC.Software Corp. [*NYSE symbol*] (SG)
MNT	Morton's Neuroma of Toe [*Medicine*] (MELL)
MNT	Mouse Infection Neutralization Test [*Medicine*] (MELL)
MNY	MONY Group [*NYSE symbol*] (SG)
MO	Mechanical Obstruction (MELL)
MO	Medulla Oblongata [*Medicine*] (MELL)
Mo	Missouri (BEE)
mo	Mother (GEAB)
MO	Mumps Orchitis [*Medicine*] (MELL)
MOA	Monoamine Oxidase (MELL)
MOC	Mint on Card [*Collectibles*]
MOCO	MOCON, Inc. [*NASDAQ symbol*] (SG)
MODIS	Moderate Resolution Imaging Spectroradiometer (EOSA)
MODIS-N	Moderate Resolution Imaging Spectrometer-Nadir (EOSA)
MODIS-T	Moderate Resolution Imaging Spectrometer-Tilt (EOSA)
MOF	Mal-Union of Fracture [*Medicine*] (MELL)
MOF	Mature Ovarian Follicle [*Medicine*] (MELL)
Mol	Moldova (MILB)
MOLA	Mars Orbiter Laser Altimeter
MOM	Main Outcome Measure [*Medicine*] (MELL)
MOM	Mission Operations Manager (EOSA)
MOMC	Mint on a Mint Card [*Collectibles*]
MOMC	Mint on Mint Card [*Toy collection*]
MOMS	Mothers Offering Maternal Support [*An association*] (MELL)
MONMC	Mint on Near Mint Card [*Collectibles*]
MONT-PEA	Montana Public Employees Association
MOODS	Music Object-Oriented Distributed System
MOP	Multiple Oocytes per Disk [*Medicine*] (MELL)

MOP	Myositis Ossificans Progressiva [*Medicine*] (MELL)
MOR	Main Operating Room (MELL)
MOR	Morphology (MELL)
MOS	Macula of Saccule [*Medicine*] (MELL)
MOS	Myocardial Oxygen Supply [*Medicine*] (MELL)
MOSF	Multiple Organ System Failure [*Medicine*] (MELL)
MOU	Macula of Utricle [*Medicine*] (MELL)
MOUT	Military Operations in Urban Terrain
mov	Moved (GEAB)
MOX	Mixed Uranium Plutonium Oxide
MOY	Matchbox Models of Yesteryear [*Toy collection*]
MP	Macrophage (MELL)
MP	Malpractice (MELL)
MP	Manganese Poisoning [*Medicine*] (MELL)
MP	Mastoid Process [*Medicine*] (MELL)
MP	Mercury Poisoning [*Medicine*] (MELL)
MPAN	Macrosopic Polyarteritis Nodosa [*Medicine*] (MELL)
MPAQ	McGill Pain Assessment Questionnaire (MELL)
MPB	Mucopurulent Bronchitis [*Medicine*] (MELL)
MPC	Mean Plasma Concentration [*Medicine*] (MELL)
Mpc	Megaparseo
MPC	Meningococcal Protein Conjugate [*Medicine*] (MELL)
MPC	Midpalmar Crease [*Medicine*] (MELL)
MPC	Mucopurulent Cervicitis [*Medicine*] (MELL)
MPC	Multipolar Cell [*Medicine*] (MELL)
MPCA	Microbial Pest Control Agent (EPAT)
MPD	Myeloprofiferative Disorder [*Medicine*] (MELL)
MPE	Malignant Pericardial Effusion [*Medicine*] (MELL)
MPEC	Minor Planet Electronic Circular [*A publication*]
MPEC	Molt Periosteal Elevator [*Medicine*] (MELL)
MPEC	Multipolar Electrocoagulation [*Medicine*] (MELL)
MPED	Minimal Phototoxic Erythema Dose [*Medicine*] (MELL)
Mpg	Miles per Gallon
MPGT	Mediastinal Paraganglionic Tumor [*Medicine*] (MELL)
MPH	Championship Auto Racing [*NYSE symbol*] (SG)
MPH	Mesh Plug Hernioplasty [*Medicine*] (MELL)
Mph	Miles per Hour
MPHD	Multiple Pituitary Hormone Deficiency [*Medicine*] (MELL)
MPHP	Maximal Predicted Heart Rate [*Medicine*] (MELL)
MPN	Maximum Possible Number (EPAT)
MPO	Minimal Perceptible Odor (MELL)
MPO	MotivePower Indus. [*NYSE symbol*] (SG)
MPOA	Medical Power of Attorney (MELL)
MPP	Malleable Penile Prosthesis [*Medicine*] (MELL)
MPP	Master's Degree in Public Policy
MPP	Medial Pterygoid Plate [*Medicine*] (MELL)
MPPP	MP3.com, Inc. [*NASDAQ symbol*] (SG)
MPPS	Mammary Gland Physiology and Pathology Society (GVA)
MPR	Maximal Pulse Rate [*Medicine*] (MELL)
MPR	Myeloproliferative Reaction [*Medicine*] (MELL)
MPRMAC	Military Participation Ratio of the Military Age Cohorts
MPS	Mean Prognostic Score [*Medicine*] (MELL)
MPS	Modis Professional Svcs. [*NYSE symbol*] (SG)
MPTH	Mpath Interactive [*NASDAQ symbol*] (SG)
MPU	Malposition of Uterus [*Medicine*] (MELL)
MPUA	Military and Police Uniform Association (EA)
MPWC	Multiprocess Wet Cleaning (EPAT)
MPWG	MPW Industrial Svcs. [*NASDAQ symbol*] (SG)
MQ	Mayflower Quarterly [*A publication*] (GEAB)
MQA	Measurement Quality Assurance
MQSA	Mammography Quality Standards Act
MQST	MapQuest.com, Inc. [*NASDAQ symbol*] (SG)
MR	Moro's Reflex [*Medicine*] (MELL)
MRBA	Marimba, Inc. [*NASDAQ symbol*] (SG)
MRC	Major Renal Calix [*Medicine*] (MELL)
MRC	Minor Renal Calix [*Medicine*] (MELL)
MRD	MacDermid, Inc. [*NYSE symbol*] (SG)
MRD	Metabolic Renal Disease [*Medicine*] (MELL)
MRD	Minimal Renal Disease [*Medicine*] (MELL)
mRF	Monoclonal Rheumatoid Factor [*Medicine*] (MELL)
MRID	Master Record Identification Number (EPAT)
MRKHS	Mayer-Rokitansky-Kuester-Hauser Syndrome [*Medicine*] (MELL)
MRM	Modified Radical Mastectomy [*Medicine*] (MELL)
MRM	Multiple Residue Method [*Medicine*] (MELL)
MRN	Malignant Renal Neoplasm [*Medicine*] (MELL)
M-ROVER	Michigan's Remote Operated Vehicle for Education and Research
MRPS	Midline Retroperitoneal Syndrome [*Medicine*] (MELL)
MRS	Meritor Automotive [*NYSE symbol*] (SG)
MRSh	Modern Red Schoolhouse
MRT	Median Reaction Time (MELL)
MRT	Median Relapse Time (MELL)
MRT	Minimal Resolvable Temperature
Ms	Mauritius (MILB)
MS	Maxillary Sinus [*Medicine*] (MELL)
MS	Megalosperm [*Medicine*] (MELL)
MS	Menkes' Syndrome [*Medicine*] (MELL)
MS	Milestone Scientific [*AMEX symbol*] (SG)
MS	Milk Sugar (MELL)
MS	Morel Syndrome [*Medicine*] (MELL)
MS	Munchausen's Syndrome [*Medicine*] (MELL)
MS	Myelosclerosis [*Medicine*] (MELL)
MSA	Major Serologic Antigen [*Medicine*] (MELL)
MSA	Middle Sacral Artery [*Medicine*] (MELL)
MSA	Millennium Star Atlas [*A publication*]
MSAS	Military Sponsored Air Service

MSC/I/O/R.... Minesweeper, Coastal/Inshore/Offshore/Riverine (MILB)
MSD............. Maple-Syrup Disease [*Medicine*] (MELL)
MSD............. Microsurgical Discectomy [*Medicine*] (MELL)
MSDI .... Martin Suicide Depression Inventory (MELL)
MSE............. Muscle Strengthening Exercise (MELL)
MSI.............. Multiple Subcutaneous Injections [*Medicine*] (MELL)
msl .... Missile (MILB)
MSLA.......... Manitoba School Library Association
MSLP........... Mean Sea Level Pressure (WEAT)
MSM............ Mid-Systolic Murmur [*Medicine*] (MELL)
MSM............ Muscat Securities Market
MSMR .... Massachusetts Society for Medical Research (GVA)
MSO............ Mentally Stable and Oriented (MELL)
MSPAP .... Maryland School Performance Assessment Program
MSRM .... Mars Sample Return Mission [*NASA*]
MST............. Movement of Landless Rural Workers [*Brazil*]
MSTR........... MicroStrategy Inc'A' [*NASDAQ symbol*] (SG)
MSU-PVMA... Michigan State University Pre-Veterinary Medical Association (GVA)
MSWG .... Military Spending Working Group
MT .... Marathoner's Toe (MELL)
MT .... Mathematics Teacher [*A publication*]
MT .... Melatonin (MELL)
MT .... Morton Toe (MELL)
MT .... Multiple Tics (MELL)
MT .... Muscle Testing (MELL)
MT .... Muscle Trauma (MELL)
MTA............ Magyar TavKozlesi ADS [*NYSE symbol*] (SG)
MTA............ Manufacturing Technical Assistance
MTBCA........ M.T. Bottle Collectors Association (EA)
MTD............ Mettler-Toledo Intl. [*NYSE symbol*] (SG)
MTE .... Multiple Trace Elements [*Medicine*] (MELL)
MTEC........... Meridian Medical Tech. [*NASDAQ symbol*] (SG)
MTF............. Mild Thyroid Failure [*Medicine*] (MELL)
MtF............. Monitoring the Future [*University of Michigan project*]
MTF............. Murine Typhus Fever [*Medicine*] (MELL)
mtg.............. Meeting (BEE)
mtg.............. Mortgage (GEAB)
MTHL........... Medial Thyrohyoid Ligament [*Medicine*] (MELL)
MTHS.......... Middle Turbinate Headache Syndrome [*Medicine*] (MELL)
MTI.............. Multigraphics, Inc. [*AMEX symbol*] (SG)
MTIC........... MTI Technology
MTIX........... Micro Therapeutics
MTMM .... Multitrait-Multimethod Model
mtn .... Mountain (MILB)
MTP............. Maximum Tolerated Pressure (MELL)
MTP............. Medical Termination of Pregnancy (MELL)
MTPB........... Malaysia Tourism Promotion Board (EA)

MTS............. Microwave Temperature Sounder (EOSA)
MTSS.......... Medial Tibial Stress Syndrome [*Medicine*] (MELL)
MTW............ Mountain Waves (WEAT)
MTX............. Manual Transmission
MTZ............. MasTec, Inc. [*NYSE symbol*] (SG)
MUD .... Matched Unrelated Donor [*Medicine*] (MELL)
MUE............ Medication Use Evaluated (MELL)
MUI............. Metals USA [*NYSE symbol*] (SG)
MUP............ Maximal Urethral Pressure [*Medicine*] (MELL)
MUPS .... Metastases with Unknown Primary Site [*Medicine*] (MELL)
MUS............ Midstream Urine Specimen [*Medicine*] (MELL)
MUSE........... Micromuse, Inc. [*NASDAQ symbol*] (SG)
musm.......... Museum (BEE)
MVa............ Minute Ventilatory Volume for Experimental Animal Species
MVC............ Mitral Valve Cusps [*Medicine*] (MELL)
MVD............ Microvascular Decompression [*Medicine*] (MELL)
mvd .... Moved (GEAB)
MVh............ Minute Ventilatory Volume for Human
MVho........... Minute Ventilatory Volume for Human in an Occupational Environment
MVL............ Marvel Enterprises [*NYSE symbol*] (SG)
MVRT........... Multivoltage Radiation Therapy (MELL)
MVS............ Mature Vesicular Follicle [*Medicine*] (MELL)
MVS............ Mesenteric Venous System [*Medicine*] (MELL)
MVS............ Midvoid Stream [*Medicine*] (MELL)
MW............. Midwife (MELL)
MW............. Mosaic Wart [*Medicine*] (MELL)
MW............. Multiple Warts [*Medicine*] (MELL)
MWBMT....... Mint with Both Mint Tags [*Collectibles*]
MWG .... Maternal Weight Gain (MELL)
MWH .... Baycorp Holdings [*AMEX symbol*] (SG)
MWL............ Mail-Well, Inc. [*NYSE symbol*] (SG)
MWMT......... Mint with Mint Tag [*Collectibles*]
MWR........... Microwave Radiation (MELL)
MWS........... Mallory-Weiss Syndrome [*Medicine*] (MELL)
MWS........... Muckle-Wells Syndrome [*Medicine*] (MELL)
MWT........... Maintenance of Wakefulness Test (MELL)
MXD............ Maximum-Latewood-Density
MXT............ Metris Cos. [*NYSE symbol*] (SG)
M/Y............. Model Year
My .... Myanmar (Burma) (MILB)
MYFC.......... Mike Yager Fan Club (EA)
MyG............ Myasthenia Gravis [*Medicine*] (MELL)
Myr.............. Million Years
Myth .... Mythology (BEE)
MZ............... Milacron, Inc. [*NYSE symbol*] (SG)
MZM............ Movado Zenith Mondia

N
By Acronym

N	Nasion (MELL)	NBAE	National Basketball Association Entertainment
N	Nepal (MILB)	NBBP	National Board of Boiler & Pressure Vessel Inspectors
n	Nephew (GEAB)	NBC	Nasobiliary Catheter [*Medicine*] (MELL)
N	Nevus (MELL)	NBC	No Back Cover
NA	Nasal Allergy (MELL)	NBC	Nursing Bottle Caries [*Medicine*] (MELL)
na	Naturalized (GEAB)	NBD	No Brain Damage (MELL)
NA	Nuclear Antigen (MELL)	NBF	Not Breast Fed (MELL)
NAA	N-Acetyl Aspartate (MELL)	NBICU	Newborn Intensive Care Unit (MELL)
NAA	National Aeronca Association (EA)	NBIOME	Northern Biosphere Observation and Modelling Experiment (EOSA)
NAA	Neutrophil Aggregation Activity (MELL)	NBIS	Northern Biosphere Information System (EOSA)
NAAC	No Apparent Anesthesia Complication [*Medicine*] (MELL)	NBP	Needle Biopsy of Prostate [*Medicine*] (MELL)
NAAEC	North American Agreement on Environmental Cooperation (EPAT)	NBS	National Bird-Feeding Society (EA)
Nab	Neutralizing Antibodies [*Medicine*] (MELL)	NBT	Natl Bancshares Texas [*AMEX symbol*] (SG)
NAB	Nitric Acid Burns [*Medicine*] (MELL)	NC	Nasal Catheter [*Medicine*] (MELL)
NAB	North American Blastomycosis [*Medicine*] (MELL)	NC	Nose Clip (MELL)
NAB	Not at Bedside [*Medicine*] (MELL)	NCA	National Camp Association (EA)
NABADA	Association of Container Reconditioners	NCA	National Catfishing Association (EA)
NABX	Needle Aspiration Biopsy [*Medicine*] (MELL)	NCA	National Climate Archive (QUAC)
NAC	National Ability Center (EA)	NCA	Netherlands Centre Alternatives to Animal Use (GVA)
NACE	Nace International	NCA	No Congenital Abnormalities [*Medicine*] (MELL)
NACFT	National Association of Cattle Foot Trimmers (GVA)	NCA	Norwegian Council for Africa
NACGS	North American Cottage Garden Society	NCAH	National Child Abuse Hotline (MELL)
NADTCA	North American Diecast Toy Collectors Association (EA)	NC&C	Normal Coitus and Climax (MELL)
NAERIC	North American Equine Ranching Information Council (GVA)	NCAP	Nasal Continuous Airway Pressure [*Medicine*] (MELL)
NAFM	National Association of Farmers' Markets (GVA)	NCBA	National Cattlemen's Beef Association (GVA)
NAGB	National Assessment Governing Board	NCD	AT&T Capital 8.25% 'PINES' [*NYSE symbol*] (SG)
NAGO	National Association of Greyhound Owners (GVA)	NCE	Naughton Cardiac Exercise (MELL)
NAIC	Network Applications and Information Center	NCE	Neurologic Clinical Examination [*Medicine*] (MELL)
NAIVPP	National Association of Independent Veterinary Practices and Practitioners (GVA)	NCE	New Century Energies [*NYSE symbol*] (SG)
NAM	National Arbitration & Mediation	NCEN	New Century Financial
NAM	Normal Adult Male (MELL)	NCEP	National Cholesterol Education Program
NAME	National Association of Medical Examiners (MELL)	NCES	National Center for Education Standards
NAME	National Association of Name Plate Manufacturers, Inc.	NCF	AT&T Capital 8.125% 'PINES' [*NYSE symbol*] (SG)
NAME	Nevi, Atrial Myxoma, Myxoid Neurofibroma, and Ephilides [*Syndrome*] [*Medicine*] (MELL)	NCFB	National Collection of Food Bacteria (MELL)
N&A	Nipple and Areola [*Medicine*] (MELL)	NCI	Navigant Consulting [*NYSE symbol*] (SG)
N&D	Nodular and Diffuse [*Medicine*] (MELL)	NCIM	National Commission on Infant Mortality (MELL)
N&T	Nicotine and Tobacco (MELL)	NCMRWF	National Centre for Medium Range Weather Forecasting [*New Delhi, India*]
NANs	Negative Axillary Node [*Medicine*] (MELL)	NCN	Nasociliary Nerve [*Medicine*] (MELL)
NAP	Nerve Action Potential [*Medicine*] (MELL)	NCPPA	National Coalition for Promoting Physical Activity (MELL)
NAP	Non-Arboreal Pollen [*Palynology*] (QUAC)	NCPR	National Center for Patient's Rights (MELL)
NAPD	North American Pollen Database (QUAC)	NCR	NCR Corp. [*NYSE symbol*] (SG)
NAPS	National Air Pollution Surveillance (EPAT)	NCRA	National Coal Resource Assessment
NAR	No Adverse Reaction [*Medicine*] (MELL)	NCRC	National Climate Research Committee (QUAC)
NAR	Not at Risk (MELL)	NCRC	Non-Child-Resistant Container (MELL)
NARA	N3N Restorers Association (EA)	NCS	National Cockatiel Society (EA)
NARA	National Agrichemical Retailers Association (EPAT)	NCS	National Conference of States on Building Codes and Standards, Inc.
NarAnon	Narcotics Anonymous (MELL)	NCS	NCI Building Systems [*NYSE symbol*] (SG)
Narcs	Narcotics (MILB)	NCSC	Neighborhood Community Service Centers
NARD	Nonarticular Rheumatic Disorder [*Medicine*] (MELL)	NCSE	Nonconvulsive Status Epilepticus [*Medicine*] (MELL)
NARGS	North American Rock Garden Society (EA)	NCSTRL	Networked Computer Science Technical Reference Library
NARSTO	North American Research Strategy for Tropospheric Ozone (EPAT)	NCT	Newcourt Credit Group [*NYSE symbol*] (SG)
NAS	No Abnormality Seen [*Medicine*] (MELL)	NCT	Noncontact Tonometry (MELL)
NASC	Network Access Solutions [*NASDAQ symbol*] (SG)	NCT	Nursing Care Technician (MELL)
Nashvl	Nashville (BEE)	NCTOG	North Central Texas Council of Governments
NASP	North Atlantic Seaboard Program (QUAC)	NCVMA	North Carolina Veterinary Medical Association (GVA)
NASSA	North American State Securities Administrators	NCX	NOVA Chemicals [*NYSE symbol*] (SG)
NASWSC	North American Society for Water and Soil Conservation	ND	Neutron Density
NATAC	North Atlantic Chemistry Experiment (QUAC)	ND	Nutritionally Deprived (MELL)
NATE	National Association of Trade Exchanges	ND	Nutrition Disorder (MELL)
NATT	Northern Australian Tropical Transect (QUAC)	NDA	New Drug Approval (MELL)
NavAide	Naval Aide	NDAA	Non-Developmental Airlift Aircraft [*Military*]
NAVCA	North American Veterinary College Administrators (GVA)	NDDA	National Demolition Derby Association (EA)
NAVTA	North American Veterinary Technician Association (GVA)	NDHIA	National Dairy Herd Improvement Association (GVA)
NAWW, Inc.	National Association of Wheat Weavers (EA)	NDLTD	Networked Digital Library of Theses and Dissertations
NAY	Not Available Yet [*Numismatic term*]	NDMC	National Drought Mitigation Center
NB	Nephroblastoma [*Medicine*] (MELL)	NE	Necrotic Enteritis [*Medicine*] (MELL)
NB	Nerve Block [*Medicine*] (MELL)	NE	Nervous Exhaustion (MELL)
NB	Nigerian Bonny [*Crude oil*]	NE	New England Patriots [*National Football League*] [*1971-present*] (NFLA)
NB	Night Blindness (MELL)		
NB	Nosebleed (MELL)	NE	Noble Drilling Corp. [*NYSE symbol*] (SG)
NB	Nutrient Broth (MELL)	NEAT	Nonexercise activity thermogenesis
Nba	Nambia (MILB)	NEG	Energy East [*NYSE symbol*] (SG)
NBA	National Beef Association (GVA)	NEJM	New England Journal of Medicine [*A publication*]
NBAC	National Bioethics Advisory Commission	NELM	Northeastern Lumber Manufacturers Association
		NEM	No Evidence of Malignancy [*Medicine*] (MELL)

NEMO	Navy EarthMap Explorer
NEO	Neonatology [*Medicine*] (MELL)
NEOM	No Evidence of Malignancy [*Medicine*] (MELL)
NEON	New Era of Networks [*NASDAQ symbol*] (SG)
NEP	Northeast Pennsylvania Finl. [*AMEX symbol*] (SG)
neph	Nephew (GEAB)
NEPIRC	Northeastern Pennsylvania Industrial Resource Center
NEPPS	National Environmental Performance Partnership System
NERL	Northeast Research Libraries
NET	Neuroendocrine Transducer [*Medicine*] (MELL)
NETG	NetGravity, Inc. [*NASDAQ symbol*] (SG)
NETN	Networks North [*NASDAQ symbol*] (SG)
NETO	NetObjects, Inc. [*NASDAQ symbol*] (SG)
NETP	Net Perceptions [*NASDAQ symbol*] (SG)
NEUIC	National Employee Union Information Center (EA)
neut	Neuter (BEE)
NEVA	North of England Veterinary Association (GVA)
NEWRAD	New Radiometry
NF	New Face [*Collectibles*]
NFC	Newsline II Fan Club (EA)
NFC	No Front Cover
NFD	No Family Doctor (MELL)
NFD	Non-Familial Disease (MELL)
NFF	Neff Corp'A' [*NYSE symbol*] (SG)
NFI	NovaStar Financial [*NYSE symbol*] (SG)
NFL Alumni	National Football League Alumni [*An association*] (EA)
NFO	NFO Worldwide [*NYSE symbol*] (SG)
NFOR	National Forest Products Association
NFS	Nationwide Finl Svcs'A' [*NYSE symbol*] (SG)
NFSH	National Federation of State High School Associations
NFT	No Further Treatment [*Medicine*] (MELL)
NG	Nodular Goiter [*Medicine*] (MELL)
NG	Normoglycemia [*Medicine*] (MELL)
Nga	Nigeria (MILB)
NGB	Neurogenic Bladder [*Medicine*] (MELL)
NGH	Nabisco Group Holdings [*NYSE symbol*] (SG)
NGI	Nasogastric Intubation [*Medicine*] (MELL)
NGISC	National Gambling Impact Study Commission
NGPE	Neurogenic Pulmonary Edema [*Medicine*] (MELL)
Ngr	Niger (MILB)
NH	Neurohormone [*Medicine*] (MELL)
NH	New Holland N.V. [*NYSE symbol*] (SG)
NHC	Nursing Home Care (MELL)
NHEIAP	New Hampshire Educational Improvement and Assessment Program
NHGRI	National Human Genome Research Institute
NHL	Noise Interference Level (MELL)
NHL	Normal Hearing Level (MELL)
NHL	Normal Hormone Level (MELL)
NHMC	National Hotline for Missing Children (MELL)
NHP	Nodular Hyperplasia of Prostate [*Medicine*] (MELL)
NHP	Nonhemoglobin Protein [*Medicine*] (MELL)
NHR	Natl Health Realty [*AMEX symbol*] (SG)
NI	New Initiatives
NI	NiSource, Inc. [*NYSE symbol*] (SG)
nia	Niacin (MELL)
NIAGRC	National Institute on Aging's Gerontology Research Center (MELL)
NIB	New in Box [*Watch collecting*]
NIC	Neonatal Inclusion Conjunctivitis [*Medicine*] (MELL)
NIC	Nursing Interim Care (MELL)
NICE	National Institute for Clinical Excellence
NICE	NICE-Systems ADR [*NASDAQ symbol*] (SG)
NICT	National Incident Coordination Team [*Environmental science*] (EPAT)
NID	Non-Immunologic Disease [*Medicine*] (MELL)
NID	Not in Distress [*Medicine*] (MELL)
NIDS	National Institutional Delivery System
NIL	Nothing in Light Microscopy (MELL)
NIM	Normal-Incidence Monochromator
NIMC	National Institute of Materials and Chemical Research [*Japan*]
NIS	No Inflammatory signs [*Medicine*] (MELL)
NISS	Nosocomial Infection Surveillance System [*Medicine*] (MELL)
NIT	New Investment Technology
NITD	Noninsulin-Treated Disease [*Medicine*] (MELL)
NITR	Nonimmune Transfusion Reaction [*Medicine*] (MELL)
NIVA	North of Ireland Veterinary Association (GVA)
NJHMFA	New Jersey Housing & Mortgage Finance Agency
NKB	No Known Basis (MELL)
NKS	Needle-Knife Sphincterotomy [*Medicine*] (MELL)
Nl	Netherlands (MILB)
NLC	Natural Language Command [*Computer science*]
NLC	Nocturnal Leg Cramps [*Medicine*] (MELL)
NLC&C	Normal Libido, Coitus and Climax [*Medicine*] (MELL)
NLD	Nasolabial Distance [*Medicine*] (MELL)
NLDI	Nasolacrimal Duct Impatency [*Medicine*] (MELL)
NLDO	Nasolacrimal Duct Obstruction [*Medicine*] (MELL)
NLE	Neonatal Lupus Erythematosus [*Medicine*] (MELL)
NLEA	National Lupus Erythematosus Association (MELL)
NLF	National Laser Facility
NLMC	Nocturnal Leg Muscle Cramp [*Medicine*] (MELL)
NLY	Annaly Mortgage Mgmt [*NYSE symbol*] (SG)
nm	Nautical Mile (MILB)
NM	Neomycin [*Medicine*] (MELL)
NM	Neonatal Meningitis [*Medicine*] (MELL)
NM	Nocturnal Myoclonus [*Medicine*] (MELL)
NM	None Minted [*Numismatic term*]
NM	Nonmalignant [*Medicine*] (MELL)

NMD	Neosynephrine/Mydriacil Dilation [*Medicine*] (MELL)
NMD	Neuromuscular Disease [*Medicine*] (MELL)
NMD	Neuromyodysplasia [*Medicine*] (MELL)
NMDA	N-Methyl-D-Aspartate [*Medicine*] (MELL)
NMGC	NeoMagic Corp. [*NASDAQ symbol*] (SG)
NMI	No Meaningful Improvement (MELL)
NML	No Mail Label
NML	Nonocclusive Mesenteric Infarction [*Medicine*] (MELL)
NML	Normal Male Infant (MELL)
NMP	National Military Park
NMR	National Museum of Racing and Hall of Fame (EA)
NMS	Natural Matrix Standard
NMT	Nuclear Medicine Technologist (MELL)
NMTI	NMT Medical [*NASDAQ symbol*] (SG)
NMVMA	New Mexico Veterinary Medical Association (GVA)
NN	Nevocellular Nevus (MELL)
NN	Normal Nutrition (MELL)
NNA	Nonnarcotic Analgesics [*Medicine*] (MELL)
NNBC	Node-Negative Breast Cancer (MELL)
NNL	No New Laboratory (MELL)
NNPBD	National Network to Prevent Birth Defects (MELL)
NO	New Orleans Saints [*National Football League*] [*1967-present*] (NFLA)
No	Norway (MILB)
NOA	Notice of Arrival [*Environmental Protection Agency*] (EPAT)
NOAC	Nature of Action Code [*Environmental science*] (EPAT)
NOBL	Noble International [*NASDAQ symbol*] (SG)
NOBLE	North of Boston Library Exchange
NOBT	Nonoperative Biopsy Technique [*Medicine*] (MELL)
No-CPR	No Cardiopulmonary Resuscitation [*Medicine*] (MELL)
NOD	New-Onset Diabetes [*Medicine*] (MELL)
NODS	NASA Ocean Data System (EOSA)
NOFAS	National Organization on Fetal Alcohol Syndrome (MELL)
NOG	Nuclear Oncogenes [*Medicine*] (MELL)
NOGAPS	National Oceanographic Global Atmospheric Prediction System (WEAT)
NOIC	Notice of Intent to Cancel [*Environmental Protection Agency*] (EPAT)
NOIS	Notice of Intent to Suspend [*Environmental Protection Agency*] (EPAT)
NOISE	Netscape, Oracle, IBM, Sun-and Everybody Else
Nonpr	Nonprofit (PROS)
nonstand	Nonstandard (BEE)
NOR	NorthWestern Corp. [*NYSE symbol*] (SG)
NORDUNet	Nordic Countries Network
NORS	National Organization for Rivers (EA)
NORTEL	Northern Telecom
Norw	Norwegian (BEE)
NOS	Nonobese Subject (MELL)
NOS	No Organisms Seen (MELL)
NOSI	Nitric Oxide Synthase Inhibitor [*Medicine*] (MELL)
NOY	Not Online Yet (BEE)
NPAC	Nonconducted Premature Atrial Contractions [*Medicine*] (MELL)
NPBFC	National Pat Boone Fan Club (EA)
NPC	Nasal Point of Conversion [*Medicine*] (MELL)
NPC	Nasopancreatic Catheter [*Medicine*] (MELL)
NPC	Nonproductive Cough (MELL)
NPD	Nocturnal Paroxysmal Dystonia [*Medicine*] (MELL)
NPD	Nonprescription Drug (MELL)
NPESA	National Printing Equipment & Supply Association, Inc.
NPG	Nonpregnant (MELL)
NPHAP	National Pesticide Hazard Assessment Program (EPAT)
NPI	Nasopharyngeal Intubation [*Medicine*] (MELL)
NPIA	National Pet Insurance Association (GVA)
NPIN	National Parent Education Network
NPIN	National Prevention Information Network [*Internet resource*]
NPK	Natl Presto Indus. [*NYSE symbol*] (SG)
NPLS	Network Plus [*NASDAQ symbol*] (SG)
NPNT	NorthPoint Communic Grp. [*NASDAQ symbol*] (SG)
NPOP	NASA Polar Orbiting Platform (EOSA)
NPP	Net Primary Production
NPP	Neuropathic Pain [*Medicine*] (MELL)
NPP	Neuroperfusion Pump [*Medicine*] (MELL)
NPP	Normal Postpartum [*Medicine*] (MELL)
NPPU	Net Postprandial Protein Utilization
NPQ	Not Physically Qualified (MELL)
NPres	National Preserve
NPRI	Nasopharyngeal Radium Irradiation [*Medicine*] (MELL)
NPT	Neuroectodermal Pigmented Tumor [*Medicine*] (MELL)
NPTRE	Nuclear-Powered Turbo-Reciprocating Engine
NPTT	Nocturnal Penile Tumescence Test [*Medicine*] (MELL)
NPV	Negative Pressure Ventilation [*Medicine*] (MELL)
NR	Negligible Risk
NR	Nerve Root (MELL)
nr	Non Recorded [*Genealogy*] (GEAB)
NR	No Radiation (MELL)
NR	No Respiration (MELL)
NRAF	Nonrheumatic Atrial Fibrillation [*Medicine*] (MELL)
NRB	Nerve Root Block (MELL)
NRC	National Rehabilitation Center (MELL)
NRC	Nerve Root Canal (MELL)
NRC	Nerve Root Compression (MELL)
NRCS	Natural Resources Conservation Service
NRD	Nerve Root Damage (MELL)
NRDS	Neonatal Respiratory Distress Syndrome [*Medicine*] (MELL)
NRF	Never Removed from Box [*Doll collecting*]

NRI	Nationsrent, Inc. [*NYSE symbol*] (SG)
NRM	Normal Range of Motion (MELL)
NRMCI	Northeast Rat and Mouse Club (EA)
NRSP	Nonrestorative Sleep Pattern (MELL)
NRTC	National Rotorcraft Technology Center
NRW	NCL Holdings ADS [*NYSE symbol*] (SG)
NS	Name Server
NS	Neoplasm Staging [*Medicine*] (MELL)
Ns	Nimbostratus Cloud (WEAT)
NSA	National Steeplechase Association (EA)
NSAD	No Sign of Acute Disease (MELL)
NSAS	Nonsystemic Antacid Suspension [*Medicine*] (MELL)
NSC	National Stinson Club - 108 Series (EA)
NSC	Norwegian Space Center (EOSA)
NSE	Normal Saline Enema [*Medicine*] (MELL)
NSEC	National System for Emergency Coordination (EPAT)
NSEP	National System for Emergency Preparedness (EPAT)
NSF	National Sleep Foundation (MELL)
NSF	Nightstick Fracture [*Medicine*] (MELL)
NSI	Nonspecific Infection [*Medicine*] (MELL)
NSI	Nonstreptococcal Infection [*Medicine*] (MELL)
NSM	National Student Marketing
NSO	nSTOR Technologies [*AMEX symbol*] (SG)
NSOL	Network Solutions [*NASDAQ symbol*] (SG)
NSPA	National Stolen Property Act
NSPK	NetSpeak Corp. [*NASDAQ symbol*] (SG)
NSPR	INSpire Insurance Solutions [*NASDAQ symbol*] (SG)
NSR	National Scenic Riverway
NSS	Non-Seasalt Sulphate (QUAC)
NSSC	Normal Size, Shape, and Consistency [*Medicine*] (MELL)
NSSO	National Second Surgical Opinion Program (MELL)
NST	National Scenic Trail
NSV	Natl Equipment Svcs. [*NYSE symbol*] (SG)
NSX	Neurosurgical Examination (MELL)
NT	Nortel Networks [*NYSE symbol*] (SG)
NTA	New Testament Abstracts [*A publication*]
NTA	New Transatlantic Agenda
NTBK	Net.Bank [*NASDAQ symbol*] (SG)
NTC	Norwegian Trade Council (EA)
NTCC	National Type Culture Collection (MELL)
NTCU	Need to See You [*Online dialog*]
NTD	Negative to Date [*Medicine*] (MELL)

NTE	Neutral Thermal Environment [*Medicine*] (MELL)
NTF	Notify
NTI	National Toxics Inventory [*Environmental science*] (EPAT)
NTIA	Netia Holdings ADS [*NASDAQ symbol*] (SG)
NTLI	NTL, Inc. [*NASDAQ symbol*] (SG)
NTOP	Net2Phone [*NASDAQ symbol*] (SG)
NTPA	Netopia, Inc. [*NASDAQ symbol*] (SG)
NTV	Neurotransmitter Vesicle [*Medicine*] (MELL)
NTX	Naltrexone [*Medicine*] (MELL)
NUC	Nonspecific Ulcerative Colitis [*Medicine*] (MELL)
nuc.	Nuclear (MILB)
NUC	Nulliparous Uterine Cervix [*Medicine*] (MELL)
NUCMC	National Union Catalog of Manuscript Collections (GEAB)
NUS	Nu Skin Enterprises'A' [*NYSE symbol*] (SG)
NUT	Nonobstructive Urinary Tract [*Medicine*] (MELL)
NV	Near Vision (MELL)
NV	Norwalk Virus [*Medicine*] (MELL)
NVH	Natl R.V.Holdings [*NYSE symbol*] (SG)
NVIS	Night Vision Imaging System
NVL	No Visible Lesion [*Medicine*] (MELL)
NVMA	Nebraska Veterinary Medical Association (GVA)
NWC	Navy Widow's Certificate (GEAB)
NWD	Normal Well Developed (MELL)
NWDL	Modular Well-Differentiated Lymphocytic Lymphoma [*Medicine*] (MELL)
NWGS	North Wall of the Gulf Stream (QUAC)
NWSS	National Women's Scuba Society (EA)
NWWIIGPA	National World War II Glider Pilots Association (EA)
Nx	Nephrectomy [*Medicine*] (MELL)
NXB	Non-X-Ray Background
NXCD	NextCard, Inc. [*NASDAQ symbol*] (SG)
NXLK	NEXTLINK Communications'A' [*NASDAQ symbol*] (SG)
NXRA	Nextera Enterprises'A' [*NASDAQ symbol*] (SG)
NYE	Nycomed Amersham ADS [*NYSE symbol*] (SG)
NYG	New York Giants [*National Football League*] [*1925-present*] (NFLA)
NYJ	New York Jets [*National Football League*] [*1963-present*] (NFLA)
NYLA	New York Library Association
NYM	NYMAGIC, Inc. [*NYSE symbol*] (SG)
NYT	New York Titans [*National Football League*] [*1960-62*] (NFLA)
NYY	New York Yanks [*National Football League*] [*1950-51*] (NFLA)
NZTB	New Zealand Tourism Board (EA)
NZUNINET	New Zealand University Network
NZVA	New Zealand Veterinary Association (GVA)

O

By Acronym

O	Oath (GEAB)
O	Oman (MILB)
O	Osteocyte (MELL)
OA	Obstructive Apnea [*Medicine*] (MELL)
OA	Ocular Albinism [*Medicine*] (MELL)
OA	Opioid Analgesics [*Medicine*] (MELL)
OA	Oral Administration (MELL)
OAA	Oglethorpe Astronomical Association [*Savannah, Georgia*]
Oac	On Approval of Credit
OAD	Obstructive Arterial Disease [*Medicine*] (MELL)
OADP	Organisation de l'Action Democratique et Populaire [*Morocco*]
Oak	Oakland Raiders [*National Football League*] [*1960-81*] (NFLA)
OAM	Oblique Abdominal Muscle [*Medicine*] (MELL)
O&L	Osteoporosis and Leukemia [*Medicine*] (MELL)
OAP	Ortho-Amino-Phenols [*Medicine*] (MELL)
OAP	Orthosorb Absorbable Pin [*Medicine*] (MELL)
OaR	Oakland Raiders [*National Football League*] [*1995-present*] (NFLA)
OAR	Ottawa Ankle Rules
OAR	Overall Rate of Return [*Business term*]
OARnet	Ohio Academic Research Network
OAS	Opiate Abstinence Syndrome [*Medicine*] (MELL)
OAW	Oral Airways (MELL)
OAWO	Opening Abductory Wedge Osteotomy [*Medicine*] (MELL)
OB	Obliterative Bronchiolitis [*Medicine*] (MELL)
OB	Olecranon Bursitis [*Medicine*] (MELL)
OBF	Open Book Fracture [*Medicine*] (MELL)
ob gene	Obese Gene [*Medicine*] (MELL)
OBP	Osteoporosis and Back Pain [*Medicine*] (MELL)
OBR	Osteoporosis from Bed Rest [*Medicine*] (MELL)
OBRO	Or Best Reasonable Offer
obs.	Observation (MILB)
OC	Optical Carrier
OCB	Obsessive-Compulsive Behavior (MELL)
OCD	Organ-Confined Disease [*Medicine*] (MELL)
OCD	Outer Canthal Distance [*Medicine*] (MELL)
OCIS	Oncology Center Information System (MELL)
OCM	Ocean Circulation Model (QUAC)
ocn.	Ocean (BEE)
OCOGC	Official Centennial Olympic Games Club (EA)
OCPD	Obsessive-Compulsive Personality Disorder (MELL)
OCRD	Oculocerebrorenal Disease [*Medicine*] (MELL)
OCS	Occipital Condyle Syndrome [*Medicine*] (MELL)
OCS	Occult Congenital Syphilis [*Medicine*] (MELL)
OCS	Oral Contraceptive Steroid [*Medicine*] (MELL)
OCS	Orifice of Coronary Sinus [*Medicine*] (MELL)
OD	Opioid Dependence [*Medicine*] (MELL)
OD	Orphan Drug [*Medicine*] (MELL)
ODan	Old Danish (BEE)
ODD	Oxalate Deposition Disease [*Medicine*] (MELL)
ODP	Offspring of Diabetic Parent [*Medicine*] (MELL)
ODR	Oil Droplet Reflex [*Medicine*] (MELL)
ODS	Orbiter Docking System [*NASA*]
ODSG	Ophthalmic Doppler Sonogram [*Medicine*] (MELL)
ODSI	ODS Networks [*NASDAQ symbol*] (SG)
OE	Old England (GEAB)
OE	Optical Engineering
OEMA	Oregon Educational Media Association
OEP	Office of Extramural Programs (MELL)
OET	Oral Esophageal Tube [*Medicine*] (MELL)
OET	Organ Extract Therapy [*Medicine*] (MELL)
OETT	Oral Endotracheal Tube (MELL)
OF	Open Fracture [*Medicine*] (MELL)
Of	Osmond Tape Exchange [*An association*] (EA)
OFC	Corporate Office Prop Tr SBI [*NYSE symbol*] (SG)
off	Official (MILB)
OFI	Overflow Incontinence [*Medicine*] (MELL)
OFM	Open Face Mask [*Medicine*] (MELL)
OFR	Offer
oft	Often (GEAB)
OGC	On-Going Care [*Medicine*] (MELL)
OGH	Opera-Glass Hand (MELL)
OGP	Oncogenic Potential (MELL)
OGS	Osteogenic Sarcoma (MELL)
OGS	Osteogenic Scoliosis (MELL)
OGS	Oxford Glycosciences
OH	Ocular Hypertension (MELL)
OHH	Orthopedia Head Halter (MELL)
OhioLINK	Ohio Library and Information Network
OHS	Ocular Hypofusion Syndrome (MELL)
OI	Obturator Internus [*Muscle*] (MELL)
OI	Occult Injury (MELL)
OI	Opportunistic Illness (MELL)
OI	Otitis Interna [*Medicine*] (MELL)
OI	Ovarian Insufficiency [*Medicine*] (MELL)
OIFC	Osmonds International Fan Club (EA)
OILD	Occupational Immunologic Lung Disease (MELL)
OIS	Oxygen Isotope Stage (QUAC)
OIT	Oil Immersion Test (MELL)
OITP	Ohio Industrial Training Program
OJ	Obstructive Jaundice [*Medicine*] (MELL)
OK	Old Kent Finl. [*NYSE symbol*] (SG)
OLCA	Orifice of Left Coronary Artery [*Medicine*] (MELL)
OLS	Optical Line Scanner (EOSA)
OLTS	On-Line Tracking System [*Environmental Protection Agency*] (EPAT)
OM	Organized Militia (GEAB)
OMAC	Otitis Media, Acute Catarrhal [*Medicine*] (MELL)
OMC	Opel Motorsport Club (EA)
OME	Omega Protein [*NYSE symbol*] (SG)
OMH	Omohyoid [*Muscle*] (MELL)
OMM	Orbicular Muscle of Mouth (MELL)
OMNTS	Over Mountains (WEAT)
OMO	Oral Malodor [*Medicine*] (MELL)
OMP	Obstetrical Measuring Plate [*Medicine*] (MELL)
OMS	Opsocionus-Myoclonus Syndrome [*Medicine*] (MELL)
OMS	Oral Morphine Sulfate [*Medicine*] (MELL)
OMT	Oriental Movement Therapy (MELL)
ON	Obstructive Nephropathy [*Medicine*] (MELL)
ONB	Obturator Nerve Block [*Medicine*] (MELL)
OND	Organic Nervous Disease [*Medicine*] (MELL)
ONE	Bank One Corp. [*NYSE symbol*] (SG)
ONet	Ontario Network [*Canada*]
ONHN	OnHealth Network [*NASDAQ symbol*] (SG)
ONST	On Stage Entertainment [*NASDAQ symbol*] (SG)
OOC	OEC Compression [*AMEX symbol*] (SG)
OOF	Orbiting Quarantine Facility [*A proposed Earth-orbiting laboratory*]
OORA	Oligoarticular Onset Rheumatoid Arthritis [*Medicine*] (MELL)
OOW	Out of Wedlock (MELL)
OP	Obstructive Pancreatitis [*Medicine*] (MELL)
OP&CMIA	Operative Plasterers and Cement Masons International Association
OPC	Outpatient Catheterization [*Medicine*] (MELL)
OPGA	Outpatient General Anesthesia (MELL)
OPO	Oropharyngeal Candidiasis [*Medicine*] (MELL)
op/ops	Operational/Operations (MILB)
OPP	Organophosphorous Poisoning [*Medicine*] (MELL)
OPS	Optical Sensor (EOSA)
OPT	Open Pneumothorax [*Medicine*] (MELL)
OR	Oral Rehydration [*Medicine*] (MELL)
OR	Orienting Reflex [*Medicine*] (MELL)
ORA	Opiate Receptor Agonist [*Medicine*] (MELL)
ORB	Online Reference Book for Medieval Studies [*Internet resource*]
ORCH	Orchiectomy [*Medicine*] (MELL)
ORD	Oral Radiation Death (MELL)
ord	Ordained (GEAB)
ORF	Open Reading Frame (MELL)
org	Organization (GEAB)
orig	Original (BEE)
Orig	Original
ORN	Osteoradionecrosis [*Medicine*] (MELL)
ornithol.	Ornithology (BEE)
ORP	Opioid-Resistant Pain [*Medicine*] (MELL)
ORS	Ovarian Remnant Syndrome [*Medicine*] (MELL)
ORSA	Operational Research System Analysts
OSCRO	Oglala Sioux Civil Rights Organization [*South Dakota*]
OSD	Osgood-Schlatter Disease
OSE	Office Server Extension
OSE	Osage Systems Group [*AMEX symbol*] (SG)
OSEA	Oregon School Employees Association
OSI	Open Society Institute
OSp	Old Spanish (BEE)
OSPARCOM	Oslo-Paris Commission
OSRAP	Optimum Stockage Requirements Analysis Program
OST	Occlusal Splint Therapy [*Medicine*] (MELL)

OSTI............. Office of Science and Technology
OT................ Oxygen Therapy (MELL)
OTA.............. Ovarian Tumor-Associated Antigen [*Medicine*] (MELL)
OTABN........ Ortho-Tolueno-Azo-Beta-Naphthol [*Medicine*] (MELL)
OTC.............. Online Training Center (MELL)
OTEA............ Office of Trade & Economic Analysis [*U.S. Department of Commerce*] [*Internet resource*]
OTHG.......... Over the Hill Gang, International (EA)
OTL.............. Opportunity to Learn
OTR............. Organ Transplant Rejection [*Medicine*] (MELL)
OTR............. Ozone Transport Region [*Environmental Protection Agency*] (EPAT)
OVC............. Ovarian Cancer (MELL)

OVLA........... Oblique Vein of Left Atrium [*Medicine*] (MELL)
OVX............. Ovariectomy [*Medicine*] (MELL)
OW................ Oval Window (MELL)
OWB........... Oscillating Waterbed (MELL)
OWCL.......... Old World Cutaneous Leishmaniasis [*Medicine*] (MELL)
OWERP........ Open Window Early Retirement Plans
OWLT.......... One-Way Light Time
OX................ Optic Chiasma [*Medicine*] (MELL)
OX................ Oxacillin [*Medicine*] (MELL)
OX................ Oxytocin [*Medicine*] (MELL)
OXP............ Oxypressin [*Medicine*] (MELL)
OXT.............. Oxytocin [*Medicine*] (MELL)
OXZ............. Oxazepam [*Medicine*] (MELL)

P

By Acronym

P .... Pancreas (MELL)
P .... Passenger [*Automotive tire designation*]
P .... Patella (MELL)
P .... Pellagra [*Medicine*] (MELL)
P .... Peritoneum [*Medicine*] (MELL)
P .... Pharynx (MELL)
P .... Pollicis (MELL)
p .... Populus (GEAB)
P .... Precursor (MELL)
P .... Prions [*Medicine*] (MELL)
P .... Prolactin (MELL)
P .... Pulmonary (MELL)
PA .... pancreatic Ascites [*Medicine*] (MELL)
PA .... Panniculus Adiposus [*Medicine*] (MELL)
PA .... Parenteral Alimentation [*Medicine*] (MELL)
PA .... Performance Appraisal
PA .... Periodontal Abscess [*Medicine*] (MELL)
PA .... Peritoneal Adhesions [*Medicine*] (MELL)
PA .... Personnel Assistant
PA .... Personnel Association
PA .... Phobics Anonymous (MELL)
PA .... Placenta Accreta [*Medicine*] (MELL)
PA .... Power Antenna [*Automotive term*]
PA .... Psoriatic Arthritis
PAA .... Peri-Appendicular Abscess [*Medicine*] (MELL)
PAA .... Plains All Amer Pipeline [*NYSE symbol*] (SG)
PAa .... Plasma Angiotensinase Activity [*Medicine*] (MELL)
PAA .... Polyammino Acid [*Medicine*] (MELL)
PAAMS .... Principal Anti-Air Missile System (MILB)
PAB .... Pes Anserinus Bursa [*Medicine*] (MELL)
PABA .... Para-Aminobenzoic Acid [*Medicine*] (MELL)
PABD .... Predeposited Autologous Blood Donation [*Medicine*] (MELL)
PAC .... Periapical Cyst [*Medicine*] (MELL)
PACCOM ..... Pacific Computer Communications
PACE .... Paper, Allied-Industrial, Chemical and Energy Workers International
PACE .... Personalizaed Acquisition Center Exchange [*Military*]
PACP .... Pulmonary Alveolar-Capillary Permeability [*Medicine*] (MELL)
PACT .... Partnership for Capacity Building in Africa
PAD .... Physician-Assisted Death (MELL)
PAD .... Pitless Adapter Division
PAE .... Peace Arch Entertainment'B' [*AMEX symbol*] (SG)
PAE .... Positive Affect Enhancement (MELL)
PAE .... Postantibiotic Effect [*Medicine*] (MELL)
PAEMST ...... Presidential Awards for Excellence in Math and Science Teaching
PAFTA .... Pacific Free Trade Area
PAG .... Pneumatic Antishock Garment (MELL)
PAG .... Pregnancy-Associated Globulin [*Medicine*] (MELL)
PAGE .... Paging Network [*NASDAQ symbol*] (SG)
PAH .... Polynuclear Aromatic Hydrocarbons (MELL)
PAHVC .... Pulmonary Alveolar Hypoxic Vasoconstrictor [*Medicine*] (MELL)
PAI .... Platelet Accumulation Index [*Medicine*] (MELL)
PAI .... Polar Area Index [*Palynology*] (QUAC)
PAI .... Pure Active Ingredient (EPAT)
PAIR .... Personnel Administration and Industrial Relations
PAIRS .... Pain and Impairment Relationship Scale (MELL)
PAIT .... Passive Adoptive Immunotherapy [*Medicine*] (MELL)
PAL .... Plasma Ammonia Level [*Medicine*] (MELL)
Paleontol ..... Paleontology (BEE)
PAM .... Pesticide Analytical Manual (EPAT)
PAMD .... Prelingually Acquired Meningitic Deafness [*Medicine*] (MELL)
PAMS .... Photochemical Assessment Monitoring Stations (EPAT)
PAN .... Periaortic Nodes [*Medicine*] (MELL)
P&C .... Precautions and Contraindications [*Medicine*] (MELL)
P&C .... Property or Casualty
P&E .... Pneumonia and Empyema (MELL)
P & I .... Pneumonia and Influenza (MELL)
PANESS ...... Physical and Neurologic Examination for Soft Signs [*Medicine*] (MELL)
PANFERT ..... Pregnancy After Infertility [*Medicine*]
PANS .... Peripheral Autonomic Nervous System [*Medicine*] (MELL)
PAOD .... Peripheral Arterial Occlusive Disease [*Medicine*] (MELL)
PAP .... Passive-Agressive Personality (MELL)
PAPD .... Passive-Agressive Personality Disorder (MELL)
par .... Parish (GEAB)
para .... Paratroop (MILB)
PAR-Q .... Physical Activity Readiness Questionnaire

Parres plot... Partial Residual Plot
PAS .... Phosphatase Acid Serum [*Medicine*] (MELL)
PAS .... Pulmonary Aspiration Syndrome [*Medicine*] (MELL)
PASS .... Professional Airways Systems Specialists Division [*An association*] (EA)
pat .... Patent (GEAB)
PAT .... Platelet Aggregation Test [*Medicine*] (MELL)
PATC .... Pain-Anxiety-Tension Cycle (MELL)
PATI .... Penetrating Abdominal Trauma Index (MELL)
PATS .... Pesticide Action Tracking System (EPAT)
PAW .... Florida Panthers Hlds [*NYSE symbol*] (SG)
PAX .... Paxson Communications 'A' [*AMEX symbol*] (SG)
PAZ .... Pollen Assemblage Zone (QUAC)
PB .... Pony Baseball/Softball [*An association*] (EA)
PBA .... Partial-Birth Abortion (MELL)
PBA .... Preliminary Benefit Analysis [*Environmental Protection Agency*] (EPAT)
PBA .... Pudendal Block Anesthesia [*Medicine*] (MELL) ·
PBAR .... Post-Balloon Angioplasty Restenosis [*Medicine*] (MELL)
PBC .... Progestin-Binding Complement [*Medicine*] (MELL)
PBCC .... Pigmented Basal Cell Carcinoma [*Medicine*] (MELL)
PBD .... Pigeon Breeder's Disease [*Medicine*] (MELL)
PBD .... Primary Blistering Disorder [*Medicine*] (MELL)
PBL .... Peripheral Blood Lymphocyte [*Medicine*] (MELL)
PBL .... Pigeon Breeder's Lung [*Medicine*] (MELL)
PBMV .... Percutaneous Balloon Mitral Valvoplasty [*Medicine*] (MELL)
PBND .... Pollybeak Nasal Deformity [*Medicine*] (MELL)
PBP .... Postural Back Pain (MELL)
PBR .... Patient's Bill of Rights (MELL)
PBRS .... Prison Behavior Rating Scale
PBx .... Prostate Biopsy [*Medicine*] (MELL)
PBY .... Postgraduate Year (MELL)
PC .... Paccinian Corpuscle [*Medicine*] (MELL)
PC .... Pain Control (MELL)
PC .... Pancreatic Carcinoma [*Medicine*] (MELL)
PC .... Pancreatic Cholera [*Medicine*] (MELL)
PCA .... Papillary Cystadenoma [*Medicine*] (MELL)
PCAD .... Premature Coronary Artery Disease (MELL)
PCAN .... Potential Child Abuse and Neglect (MELL)
PCB .... Paracolon Bacilli [*Medicine*] (MELL)
PCB .... Placebo [*Medicine*] (MELL)
PCBZ .... Polychlorobenzene [*Medicine*] (MELL)
PCC .... Pericardial Constriction [*Medicine*] (MELL)
PCC .... Permanently Crewed Capability
PCC .... Perry Como Circle (EA)
PCC/I/O/R/H... Patrol Craft, Coastal/Inshore/Offshore/Riverine/Harbour (MILB)
PCDT .... Pacific Coast Dog Tick (MELL)
PCE .... Pericardial Effusion [*Medicine*] (MELL)
PCE .... Posterior Chamber of Eye [*Medicine*] (MELL)
PCF .... Posterior Cervical Fusion [*Medicine*] (MELL)
PCF .... Procoagulant Factor [*Medicine*] (MELL)
PCFC .... Phil Collins Information [*Formerly, Phil Collins Fan Club*] (EA)
PCG .... Primary Congenital Glaucoma (MELL)
pchd .... Purchased (GEAB)
PCI .... Pulverised Coal Injection [*Coal industry*]
PCIS .... Post-Cardiac Injury Syndrome (MELL)
PCKRR .... Pine Creek Railroad [*An association*] (EA)
PCL .... Plasma Cholesterol Level (MELL)
PCL .... Precancerous Lesion (MELL)
PCLD .... Polycystic Liver Disease (MELL)
PCLN .... priceline.com, Inc. [*NASDAQ symbol*] (SG)
PCL-R .... Psychopathy Checklist-Revised
PCM .... Plasma Cell Myeloma [*Medicine*] (MELL)
PCM .... Pneumococcal Meningitis [*Medicine*] (MELL)
PCN .... Pameco Corp'A' [*NYSE symbol*] (SG)
PCN .... Policy Criteria Notice [*Environmental Protection Agency*] (EPAT)
PCNV .... Postchemotherapy Nausea and Vomiting [*Medicine*] (MELL)
PCOR .... pcOrder.com, Inc.'A' [*NASDAQ symbol*] (SG)
PCP .... Partial Cleft Palate (MELL)
PCP .... Pericardial Pressure [*Medicine*] (MELL)
PCP .... Plasma Cell Pneumonia [*Medicine*] (MELL)
PCPF .... Percutaneous Pin Fixation [*Medicine*] (MELL)
PCR .... Postinfarction Cardiac Rehabilitation [*Medicine*] (MELL)
PCS .... Pelvic Congestion Syndrome [*Medicine*] (MELL)
PCSP .... Polar Continental Shelf Project [*Canada*] (QUAC)
PCT .... Painful Cervical Trauma [*Medicine*] (MELL)

PCT............ Patient Care Technician (MELL)
PCT............ Prepared Childbirth Training (MELL)
PCTA.......... Percutaneous Transluminal Angioplasty [*Medicine*] (MELL)
PCV............ Polychlorinated Vinyl (MELL)
PCV system... Positive Crankcase Ventilation System
PD............. Panic Disorder (MELL)
PD............. Papillary Duct [*Medicine*] (MELL)
PD............. Partial Denture (MELL)
PD............. Personality Disorder (MELL)
PD............. Perthes' Disease (MELL)
PD............. Peyronie's Disease (MELL)
PD............. Plastic Drum Institute
PD............. Porsche Design
pd............. Potential Difference (MELL)
PDA........... Parenteral Drug Association (MELL)
PDA........... Periodontal Abscess (MELL)
PDA........... Polydrug Abuse (MELL)
PDA........... Prescription Drug Abuse (MELL)
PDAS......... Pulmonary Disease-Anemia Syndrome (MELL)
PDB........... Paget's Disease of Bone (MELL)
PDB........... Power Disc Brakes [*Automotive term*]
PDCA......... Posterior Descending Coronary Artery [*Medicine*] (MELL)
PDCA......... Primary Degenerative Cerebral Disease [*Medicine*] (MELL)
PDCI.......... Product Data Call-In (EPAT)
PDD........... Percent Depth Dose [*Medicine*] (MELL)
PDD........... Peridontal Disease (MELL)
PDD........... Progressive Diaphyseal Dysplasia [*Medicine*] (MELL)
PDE........... Progressive Dialysis Encephalopathy [*Medicine*] (MELL)
PDEGF....... Platelet-Derived Epidermal Growth Factor [*Medicine*] (MELL)
PDF........... Pigmented Dermatofibroma [*Medicine*] (MELL)
PDHI.......... Palmer Drought Hydrological Index
PDK........... Polycystic Kidney Disease (MELL)
PDL........... Power Door Locks
PDL........... Progressively Diffused Leukoencephalopathy [*Medicine*] (MELL)
PDLR......... Power Deck Lid Release
PDR........... Pendaries Petroleum [*AMEX symbol*] (SG)
PDR........... Peripheral Diabetic Retinopathy [*Medicine*] (MELL)
pdr............ Pounder (MILB)
PDR........... Power Deck Release
PDS........... Poly-P-Dioxanone
PE............. Performance Evaluation
Pe............. Peru (MILB)
PE............. Pulled Elbow (MELL)
PE............. Pulmonary Emphysema [*Medicine*] (MELL)
PE............. Pyramidal Eminence [*Medicine*] (MELL)
PEAK......... Pricing Electronic Access to Knowledge
PEARL....... Pupils Equal and React to Light [*Medicine*] (MELL)
PEC........... Pelvic Cramps [*Medicine*] (MELL)
PECT......... Progestin-Estrogen Cyclic Therapy [*Medicine*] (MELL)
PEF........... Pharyngo-Epiglottic Fold [*Medicine*] (MELL)
Peff........... Effective Filtration Pressure [*Medicine*] (MELL)
PEH........... Papillary Endothelial Hyperplasia [*Medicine*] (MELL)
PEN........... Pentegra Dental Group [*AMEX symbol*] (SG)
Penin......... Peninsula (BEE)
PENS......... Percutaneous Electrical Nerve Stimulation
peo........... People (GEAB)
PEO-C3S...... Program Executive Office, Command, Control, and Communications Systems [*Army*]
PEO-STAMIS... Program Executive Office, Standard Army Management Information Systems
PEP........... Paper Electrophoresis (MELL)
PEP........... Patient Educational Program (MELL)
PEP........... Pigmentation, Edema and Plasma Cell Dyscrasia (MELL)
PEP........... Pole-Equator-Pole (QUAC)
PEP........... Pupil Evaluation Program
PER........... Perot Systems'A' [*NYSE symbol*] (SG)
PER........... Pronated External Rotation [*Medicine*] (MELL)
perh.......... Perhaps (GEAB)
Pers.......... Persian (BEE)
PERSCOM.... Personnel Command [*Army*]
PERV......... Porcine Endogenous Retrovirus
PERY......... Ellis, Perry, Intl. [*NASDAQ symbol*] (SG)
PESA......... Percutaneous Epididymal Sperm Aspiration [*Medicine*] (MELL)
PEST......... Planning and Evaluation of Sequential Trials [*Statistics*]
PET........... Polyethylene Tubing [*Medicine*] (MELL)
PET........... Program Evaluation Test
petr.......... Petitioner (GEAB)
PEX........... PetroCorp, Inc. [*AMEX symbol*] (SG)
PF............. Pacemaker Failure (MELL)
PF............. Pen Fanciers (EA)
PF............. Piedmont Fracture (MELL)
PF............. Pipkin Fracture (MELL)
PF............. Pott's Fracture [*Medicine*] (MELL)
PFA........... Alliance Forest Prod [*NYSE symbol*] (SG)
PFC........... Patellofemoral Chondrosis [*Medicine*] (MELL)
PFC........... Perfluorocarbon
PFC........... Press-Fit Component (MELL)
PFCWKS...... Pogo Fan Club and Walt Kelly Society (EA)
pfd........... Preferred
PFES......... Pelvic Floor Electrical Stimulation [*Medicine*] (MELL)
PFF........... Pluto Express Mission [*Space exploration*]
PFID.......... Perturbed Free Induction Decay
PFP........... Peripheral Facial-Paralysis [*Medicine*] (MELL)
PFT........... Plant Functional Type (QUAC)
PFT........... Platelet-Fibrin-Thrombi [*Medicine*] (MELL)

PG............. Pelvic Girdle [*Medicine*] (MELL)
PG............. Powerglide [*Automatic transmission*]
PGB........... Paravertebral Ganglion Block [*Medicine*] (MELL)
PGE........... Posterior Gastroenterostomy [*Medicine*] (MELL)
PGLAF........ Progen Industries [*NASDAQ symbol*] (SG)
PGP........... Progressive General Paralysis (MELL)
PGS........... Postsurgical Gastroparesis Syndrome [*Medicine*] (MELL)
PGS........... Product Generation System (EOSA)
PGU........... Peripheral Glucose Uptake [*Medicine*] (MELL)
PGWV........ Persian Gulf War Veteran (MELL)
PH............. Partial Hysterectomy [*Medicine*] (MELL)
PH............. Postural Hypotension [*Medicine*] (MELL)
PHA........... Potentially Hazardous Asteroids
PHACO....... Phacoemulsification [*Medicine*] (MELL)
PHAP......... Phytohemagglutinin Protein [*Medicine*] (MELL)
PHCM........ Phone.com,Inc. [*NASDAQ symbol*] (SG)
PHI........... Past History of Illness (MELL)
Phi........... Philadelphia Eagles [*National Football League*] [*1933-42, 1944-present*] (NFLA)
PHI........... Pre-Harvest Interval (EPAT)
PHIA......... Profoundly Hearing Impaired Adult (MELL)
PhiKaps...... Phi Kappa Theta National (EA)
phil.......... Philanthropic (PROS)
Philos....... Philosophy (BEE)
PHL........... Planet Hollywood Intl'A' [*NYSE symbol*] (SG)
Pho........... Phoenix Cardinals [*National Football League*] [*1988-93*] (NFLA)
Phot......... Photography (BEE)
PHP........... Pooled Human Plasma (MELL)
PHR........... Professional in Human Resources
PHS........... ProVantage Health Svcs. [*NYSE symbol*] (SG)
PHSC........ Posterior Horn of Spinal Cord [*Medicine*] (MELL)
PHV........... Prosthetic Heart Valve (MELL)
Physiol...... Physiology (BEE)
PI............. Paleo-Indian (QUAC)
PI............. Parainfluenza (MELL)
PI............. Passive Immunity [*Medicine*] (MELL)
Pi............. Philippines (MILB)
PIF........... Prostatic Interstitial Fluid [*Medicine*] (MELL)
PIFA......... Pain-Inhibition Fear Avoidance [*Medicine*] (MELL)
PIFG......... Poor Intrauterine Fetal Growth [*Medicine*] (MELL)
PIGI.......... Pregnancy-Induced Glucose Intolerance [*Medicine*] (MELL)
PIH........... Post-Inflammatory Hyperpigmentation [*Medicine*] (MELL)
PIK........... Potsdam Institute for Climate Impact Research
PiLam........ Pi Lambda Phi (EA)
PIMS......... Pesticide Incident Monitoring System [*Environmental Protection Agency*] (EPAT)
PIN........... AMF Bowling [*NYSE symbol*] (SG)
PIN........... Prostatic Intraepithelial Neoplasia [*Medicine*] (MELL)
PINS......... Patient in Need of Supervision (MELL)
PIO........... Pioneer Corp ADR [*NYSE symbol*] (SG)
PIOCA....... Peruvian Inca Orchid Dog Club of America (EA)
pion.......... Pioneer (GEAB)
PIP........... Positive Inspiratory Pressure [*Medicine*] (MELL)
PIP........... Postinfusion Phlebitis [*Medicine*] (MELL)
PISI.......... Palmar Intercalated Segmental Instability [*Medicine*] (MELL)
PIT........... Permit Improvement Team [*Environmental science*] (EPAT)
Pit........... Pittsburgh Steelers [*National Football League*] [*1941-42, 1945-present*] (NFLA)
PIU........... Performance and Innovation Unit
PIV........... Primate Immunodeficiency Virus [*Medicine*] (MELL)
PIVH......... Peripheral Intravenous Hyperalimentation [*Medicine*] (MELL)
PIVI.......... Parainfluenza Virus Infection [*Medicine*] (MELL)
PIWT......... Partially Impacted Wisdom Tooth (MELL)
PIX........... Avenue Entertainment Grp [*AMEX symbol*] (SG)
PJ............. Pancreatic Juice [*Medicine*] (MELL)
PJ............. Porcelain Jacket [*Dentistry*] (MELL)
PJP........... Probate Judge of the Peace (GEAB)
PKA........... Prekallikrein Activator [*Medicine*] (MELL)
PKD........... Pyruvate Kinase Deficiency [*Medicine*] (MELL)
Pke........... Pike (PROS)
PKF........... Permanent Kidney Failure (MELL)
PKSI.......... Primus Knowledge Solutions [*NASDAQ symbol*] (SG)
PKTR........ Packeteer, Inc. [*NASDAQ symbol*] (SG)
pl............. Platoon (MILB)
Pl............. Poland (MILB)
PLB........... Amer Italian Pasta'A' [*NYSE symbol*] (SG)
Plc........... Public Limited Company
PLCE......... Children's Place Retail Stores [*NASDAQ symbol*] (SG)
PLDD......... Percutaneous Laser Disc Decompression
PLH........... Posterior Lobe of Hypophysis [*Medicine*] (MELL)
PLL........... Posterior Longitudinal Ligament [*Medicine*] (MELL)
PLMS......... Periodic Limb Movement when Sleeping (MELL)
PLN........... Pancreatic Lymph Nodes [*Medicine*] (MELL)
PLN........... Pudendal Lymph Nodes [*Medicine*] (MELL)
PLND......... Pelvic Lymph Node Dissection [*Medicine*] (MELL)
PLP........... Parathyroidlike Protein [*Medicine*] (MELL)
PLP........... Phantom Limb Pain (MELL)
PLP........... Power Law Process
PLS........... Plastic Surgery (MELL)
PLT........... Platelet [*Medicine*] (MELL)
plz........... Plaza (BEE)
PLZF......... Promyelocytic Leukaemia Zinc-Finger
PM............. Partial Mastectomy (MELL)
PM............. Power Mirrors
PM............. Product Manager

PMAS..........	Photochemical Assessment Monitoring Stations (EPAT)
PMB..........	Papillomacular Bundle [Medicine] (MELL)
PMC..........	Post-Ministerial Conference [ASEAN]
PMC..........	Pressure-Modulator Cell (EOSA)
PMCI..........	Postmyocardial Infarct [Medicine] (MELL)
PMCIS........	Post-Myocardial Infarction Syndrome [Medicine] (MELL)
PMCPE......	Prime Capital [NASDAQ symbol] (SG)
PMDI..........	Palmer Drought Severity Index
PME..........	Premature Ejaculation [Medicine] (MELL)
PME..........	Progressive Myoclonus Epilepsy [Medicine] (MELL)
PMGV........	Postmeal Glucose Value [Medicine] (MELL)
PMH..........	Previous Medical History (MELL)
PMH..........	Pseudomyocardial Hypertrophy [Medicine] (MELL)
PM-HTV......	Program Manager for Heavy Tactical Vehicles [Military]
PMI..........	Patient Medication Information
PMI..........	Perioperative Myocardial Infarction [Medicine] (MELL)
PMI..........	Place of Maximal Impulse [Medicine] (MELL)
PMIR..........	Pressure Modulator Infrared Radiometer (EOSA)
PMO..........	Product Management Office [Army]
PMO-MTV...	Project Manager's Office, Medium Tactical Vehicles [Army]
PMP..........	Plantar Metatarsal Padding [Medicine] (MELL)
PMP..........	Postmastectomy Pain (MELL)
PMR..........	Pacemaker Rhythm [Medicine] (MELL)
PMR..........	Patellar Medial Retinaculum [Medicine] (MELL)
PMR..........	Progressive Muscle Relaxation (MELL)
PMS..........	Particle Measurement System
PMS..........	Passive Maternal Smoking (MELL)
PMS..........	Personnel Management Services
PMSEIC......	Prime Minister's Science, Engineering and Innovation Council [Australia]
PMSU........	Peripheral Motor-Sensory Unit (MELL)
PMW..........	Post-Menopausal Women (MELL)
PMW..........	Premenopausal Women (MELL)
PMWI..........	PageMart Wireless 'A' [NASDAQ symbol] (SG)
PNAS........	Proceedings of the National Academy of Sciences [A publication]
PNE..........	Copene-Petroquimica ADS [NYSE symbol] (SG)
PNED........	Peaceful Nuclear Explosive Device
PNG..........	Penn-America Group [NYSE symbol] (SG)
pnk..........	Pinl
PNM..........	Peripheral Nerve Myelin [Medicine] (MELL)
PNP..........	Pan Pacific Retail Prop. [NYSE symbol] (SG)
PNPB........	Positive-Negative Pressure Breathing (MELL)
PNSL..........	Papulonodular Skin Lesion [Medicine] (MELL)
POBP..........	Preoperative Bowel Preparation [Medicine] (MELL)
POBT..........	Postoperative Bleeding Time [Medicine] (MELL)
POC..........	Para-Ovarian Cyst [Medicine] (MELL)
POC..........	Postoperative Complication [Medicine] (MELL)
POC..........	Probability of Chance (MELL)
POD..........	Postobstructive Diuresis [Medicine] (MELL)
POE..........	Pediatric Orthopedic Examination (MELL)
POEM........	Polar-Orbiting Earth Mission [European Space Agency] (EOSA)
POEMS......	Positron Electron Magnetic Spectrometer (EOSA)
POF..........	Physician's Order Form (MELL)
PoF..........	Physics of Failure [Program]
POF..........	Premature Ovarian Failure [Medicine]
POH..........	Personal Oral Hygiene (MELL)
POHA........	Preoperative Holding Area [Medicine] (MELL)
POI..........	Postoperative Instructions [Medicine] (MELL)
POI..........	Proof of Illness (MELL)
Pol..........	Polish (BEE)
POLES........	Polar Exchange at the Sea Surface (EOSA)
Polytech......	Polytechnic (PROS)
PON..........	Passive Optical Network
POP..........	Postoperative Pain [Medicine] (MELL)
POP..........	SCI-FI Society of Long Island [Formerly, Patrexes of the Panopticon] (EA)
POPIN........	Population Information Network [United Nations] [Internet resource]
POPS........	Principal Oscillation Patterns Analysis
Por..........	Portsmouth Spartans [National Football League] [1930-33] (NFLA)
POS..........	Patella Overload Syndrome [Medicine] (MELL)
Pos..........	Positive Ground
Poss..........	Possession (BEE)
POT..........	Pulmonary Oxygen Transfer [Medicine] (MELL)
POTA........	Planet of the Apes [Movie title]
PPA..........	Pediatric Pain Assessment (MELL)
PPAA........	Palynological and Palaeobotanical Association of Australia (QUAC)
PPAS........	Postpolio Atrophy Syndrome [Medicine] (MELL)
PPB..........	Prepatellar Bursitis [Medicine] (MELL)
PPBE........	Postpartum Breast Engorgement [Medicine] (MELL)
PPCM........	Postpartum Cardiomyopathy [Medicine] (MELL)
PPCS........	Postpericardiotomy Syndrome [Medicine] (MELL)
PPDR........	Preproliferative Diabetic Retinopathy [Medicine] (MELL)
PPE..........	Park Place Entertainment [NYSE symbol] (SG)
PPE..........	Preparticipation Physical Exam
PPGD........	Pelvic Plane of Greatest Dimension [Medicine] (MELL)
PPGS........	Postpartum Glomerulosclerosis [Medicine] (MELL)
PPH..........	Postlumbar Puncture Headache [Medicine] (MELL)
PPI..........	Permanent Pacemaker Implantation [Medicine] (MELL)
PPIC..........	Pesticide Programs Information Center (EPAT)
PPICC........	Plasma Proinflammatory Cytokine Concentration [Medicine] (MELL)
PPIS..........	Pollution Prevention Inventives for States (EPAT)
PPK..........	Programmable Power Key [Computer science]
PPLOV......	Painless Progressive Loss of Vision (MELL)
PPLV..........	Pars Plana Lensectomy-Vitrectomy [Medicine] (MELL)
Ppm..........	Parts per Million

PPP..........	Palmar-Plantar Pustulosis
P-P plot.......	Probability-Probability Plot [Statistics]
PPR..........	Physician-Patient Relation (MELL)
PPr..........	Pittsburgh Pirates [National Football League] [1933-40] (NFLA)
PQUA..........	Preliminary Quantitative Usage Analysis [Environmental science] (EPAT)
PR..........	Partial (WEAT)
PR..........	Precipitation Radar (EOSA)
pr..........	Probated (GEAB)
Pr..........	Proof [Numismatic term]
PRA..........	Postrenal Azotemia [Medicine] (MELL)
PRAREE......	Precise Range and Rate Equipment-Extended Version (EOSA)
PRATS........	Pesticides Regulatory Action Tracking System (EPAT)
PRC..........	Photo Receptor Cell [Medicine] (MELL)
PRC..........	Proximal Row Carpectomy [Medicine] (MELL)
PRCGT......	Confederacion Generale Trabajadores de Puerto Rico
PRCL..........	Confederacion Laborista de Puerto Rico
PRCP..........	Percutaneous Renal Cyst Puncture [Medicine] (MELL)
PRCUI........	Congreso Uniones Industriales de Puerto Rico
PRDPC......	Pooled Random Donor Platelet Concentrates [Medicine] (MELL)
PRESSFR....	Pressure Falling Rapidly [Meteorology] (WEAT)
PRESSRR....	Pressure Rising Rapidly [Meteorology] (WEAT)
PRFM........	Prolonged Rupture of Fetal Membranes [Medicine] (MELL)
PRFPT........	Federacion Puertorriqueno de Trabajadores
PRG..........	Peer Review Group (MELL)
PRGY..........	Prodigy Communications [NASDAQ symbol] (SG)
PRH..........	Preretinal Hemorrhage [Medicine] (MELL)
PRICEMMM...	Protection, Rest, Ice, Compression, and Elevation
prin..........	Principal (PROS)
PRL..........	Prolong International [AMEX symbol] (SG)
PRMF..........	Preretinal Macular Fibrosis [Medicine] (MELL)
PRMSS........	Pregnancy-Related Mortality Surveillance System (MELL)
PRND..........	Prophylactic Regional Node Dissection [Medicine] (MELL)
pro..........	Probate (GEAB)
PRO BIKE....	Bicycle Federation of America (EA)
prof..........	Professor (PROS)
prov..........	Provencal (BEE)
PRP..........	Penicillinase-Resistant Penicillin [Medicine] (MELL)
PRP..........	Procedure-Related Pain (MELL)
prpl..........	Purple
PRS..........	Personality Rating Scale (MELL)
PRS..........	Pierre Robin Syndrome (MELL)
PRS..........	Prolonged Respiratory Support (MELL)
Prsbytn......	Presbyterian (BEE)
PRSF..........	Portal Software [NASDAQ symbol] (SG)
PRSPT........	Sindicato de Obreros Unidos del Sur de Puerto Rico
PRSPT........	Sindicato Puertorriqueno de Trabajadores
PRTA..........	Proximal Renal Tubular Acidosis [Medicine] (MELL)
PRZ..........	Pressoreceptor Zone [Medicine] (MELL)
PS..........	Pacemaker Syndrome [Medicine] (MELL)
PS..........	Paranoid Schizophrenia [Medicine] (MELL)
PS..........	Partial Seizure (MELL)
PS..........	Passive Smoke (MELL)
PS..........	Phrenic Stimulation [Medicine] (MELL)
PS..........	Physiologic Saline [Medicine] (MELL)
PS..........	Pressure Sore (MELL)
PS..........	Primary Syphilis (MELL)
PS..........	Prostatic Secretion [Medicine] (MELL)
PSA..........	Poly-Substance Abuse [Medicine] (MELL)
PSA..........	Prepseudoarthrosis [Medicine] (MELL)
PSACO........	Papillary Serous Adenocarcinoma of Ovary [Medicine] (MELL)
PSAD..........	Prostate-Specific Antigen Density [Medicine] (MELL)
PSAT..........	Prostate-Specific Antigen Test [Medicine] (MELL)
PSC..........	Palynological Society of China (QUAC)
PSC..........	Papillary Serous Cyst [Medicine] (MELL)
PSC..........	Principal Surface Combatant (MILB)
PSC..........	Program Site Coordinator [Environmental science] (EPAT)
PSCC..........	Posterior Subcapsular Cataract [Medicine] (MELL)
PSCNet........	Pittsburgh Supercomputing Center Network [Pennsylvania]
PSCT..........	Peripheral Stem Cell Transplant [Medicine] (MELL)
PSD..........	Partial Sleep Deprivation (MELL)
PSD..........	Poststenotic Dilatation [Medicine] (MELL)
PSD..........	Postsurgical Distress [Medicine] (MELL)
PSDA..........	Psychoactive Substance Dependence and Abuse (MELL)
PSE..........	Passive Smoke Exposure (MELL)
PSE..........	Pi Sigma Epsilon (EA)
pseud..........	Pseudonym (BEE)
PSFC/HIMH...	Buzzcocks Fan Club/Harmony in My Head (EA)
PSI..........	Pressure per Square Inch (EPAT)
PSIFC..........	Pat Shea International Fan Club (EA)
PSIG..........	Pressure per Square Inch Gauge (EPAT)
PSJ..........	Palynological Society of Japan (QUAC)
PSJ..........	Petsec Energy ADS [NYSE symbol] (SG)
PSLA..........	Pennsylvania School Librarians Association
PSLD..........	Parasympatholytic Drug [Medicine] (MELL)
PSLV..........	Polar Space Launch Vehicle [Indian Space Research]
PSM..........	Portal-Systemic Myelopathy [Medicine] (MELL)
PSM..........	Purse-String Mouth (MELL)
PSMA..........	Progressive Streptococcal Muscular Atrophy [Medicine] (MELL)
PSN..........	Packet Switch Node
PSO..........	Project Science Office (EOSA)
PSP..........	Palynological Society of Poland (QUAC)
PSP..........	Prone Sleeping Position (MELL)
PSPCA........	Pennsylvania Society for the Prevention of Cruelty to Animals
PSPS..........	Postsurgical Pain Syndrome (MELL)

PSR .... Portal Systemic Resistance [*Medicine*] (MELL)
PSS .... Painful Shoulder Syndrome (MELL)
PSSI .... PSS World Medical [*NASDAQ symbol*] (SG)
PST .... Platelet Survival Time [*Medicine*] (MELL)
PSU .... Practical Salinity Unit
PSVT .... Paroxysmal Supraventricular Tachycardia [*Medicine*]
Psychoanal... Psychoanalysis (BEE)
PT .... Part-Time
PT .... Patch Test [*Medicine*] (MELL)
PT .... Performance Testing
PT .....,......... Peroneal Tendonitis [*Medicine*] (MELL)
PT .... Pigeon-Toed (MELL)
PTA .... Penn Treaty American [*NYSE symbol*] (SG)
PTA .... Pure Tone Audiometry (MELL)
PTBD .... Percutaneous Transluminal Balloon Dilatation [*Medicine*] (MELL)
PTCL .... Pakistan Telecommunication Company Limited
PTD .... Personality Trait Disorder (MELL)
PTD .... Prior to Delivery (MELL)
PTE .... Post-Traumatic Epilepsy (MELL)
PTE .... Potentially Toxic Element
ptf .... Plaintiff (GEAB)
PTHS .... Profile Total Hip System (MELL)
PTL .... Pain Tolerance Level (MELL)
PTM .... Patient Monitored (MELL)
PTM .... Post-Traumatic Meningitis [*Medicine*] (MELL)
PTNB .... Preterm Newborn (MELL)
PTPD .... Post-Traumatic Personality Defect (MELL)
PTPI .... Post-Traumatic Pulmonary Insufficiency [*Medicine*] (MELL)
PTR .... Patient to Return (MELL)

PTR .... Prothrombin Time Ratio [*Medicine*] (MELL)
PTT .... Patellar Tendon Transfer [*Medicine*] (MELL)
PTVL .... Preview Travel [*NASDAQ symbol*] (SG)
PTW .... Pork Tapeworm [*Medicine*] (MELL)
PU .... Pickup
publ .... Public (MILB)
publ .... Published (PROS)
PuD .... Pulmonary Disorder [*Medicine*] (MELL)
pulm .... Pulmonary (MELL)
PV .... Paravertebral [*Medicine*] (MELL)
p/v .... Pool View
PVI .... Placental Villus Inflammation [*Medicine*] (MELL)
PVI .... Post-Vaccination Immunity [*Medicine*] (MELL)
PVM .... Preventive Medicine (MELL)
PVOD .... Pulmonary Vascular Obstructive Disease [*Medicine*] (MELL)
PVP .... Polyvinylpyridine
PVR .... Portal Venous Pressure [*Medicine*] (MELL)
PVS .... Private Vocational Schools
pvt .... Private (GEAB)
PW .... Penetrating Wound (MELL)
PW .... Puncture Wound (MELL)
PWA .... Premiumwear, Inc. [*NYSE symbol*] (SG)
PWA .... Professional Women's Association
Py .... Paraguay (MILB)
pymt .... Payment (GEAB)
PZ .... Proliferative Zone (MELL)
PZA .... Pyrazinoic Acid (MELL)
PZE .... PennzEnergy Co. [*NYSE symbol*] (SG)
PZL .... Pennzoil-Quaker State [*NYSE symbol*] (SG)
PZN .... Prison Realty Trust [*NYSE symbol*] (SG)

Q

By Acronym

Q................. Qatar (MILB)
QADI............ QAD,Inc. [*NASDAQ symbol*] (SG)
Q & O .... Quinidine and Quinine [*Medicine*] (MELL)
QBTU .... Quadrillion British Thermal Unit (EPAT)
QED .... Queer Resources Directory [*Internet resource*]
QEEG .... Quantitative Electroencephalography [*Medicine*] (MELL)
QELS........... Quantum Electronics and Laser Science
QFT.............. Quantum Field Theory
QJSA............ Qualified Joint and Survivor Annuity

QL................ Quantification Limit (EPAT)
QM.............. Queensland Museum [*Australia*]
QMI............. Q-Wave Myocardial Infraction [*Medicine*] (MELL)
QPSA .... Qualified Preretirement Survivor Annuity
Q-Q plot....... Quantile-Quantile Plot
QR .... Quiet Room (MELL)
QTB............. Quadriceps Tendon Bearing [*Medicine*] (MELL)
QUA .... Qualitative Use Assessment (EPAT)
QUIPE......... Quarterly Update for Inspector in Pesticide Enforcement (EPAT)
QWST .... Qwest Communications [*NASDAQ symbol*] (SG)

R

By Acronym

r................. Radius (MELL)
R................. Recapitulation (MELL)
r................. Recombinant (MELL)
r................. Rector (GEAB)
R................. Remission (MELL)
R................. Replication (MELL)
R................. Residue (MELL)
R................. Rubella (MELL)
RA............... Radiographic Absorptiometry [*Medicine*] (MELL)
RA............... Regression Analysis (MELL)
RA............... Restaurant Associates
RA............... Ruptured Appendix [*Medicine*] (MELL)
RAAA......... Ruptured Abdominal Aortic Aneurysm [*Medicine*] (MELL)
RAAG......... Rheumatoid Arthritis Agglutination [*Medicine*] (MELL)
RAAM......... Renin-Angiotensin-Aldosterone Mechanism [*Medicine*] (MELL)
RA & AS..... Rheumatoid Arthritis and Ankylosing Spondylitis [*Medicine*] (MELL)
RA & H........ Rheumatoid Arthritis and Hypersplenism [*Medicine*] (MELL)
RAB .... Risk Assessed By [*Medicine*] (MELL)
RAD .... Reactive Attachment Disorder [*Medicine*] (MELL)
RADAR........ Regional Alcohol and Drug Awareness Resources (MELL)
Radarsat...... Canadian Synthetic Aperture Radar Satellite (EOSA)
RADCA........ Right Anterodescending Coronary Artery [*Medicine*] (MELL)
RADS .... Rapid Assay Delivery System [*Medicine*] (MELL)
RAF............ Rapid Atrial Fibrillation [*Medicine*] (MELL)
RAH-66 .... Reconnaissance and Attack Helicopter [*Military*]
RAIR.......... Rectoanal Inhibitory Reflex [*Medicine*] (MELL)
RALN .... Retro-Auricular Lymph Node [*Medicine*] (MELL)
RANA .... Rheumatoid Agglutinin Nuclear Antigen [*Medicine*] (MELL)
R & B .... Risks and Benefits [*Medicine*] (MELL)
R & C .... Referral and Consultation (MELL)
R & C .... Risks and Complications (MELL)
R & D .... Risk and Death (MELL)
RAP .... Recurrent Abdominal Pain (MELL)
RAPID......... Reorganized Army Plains Infantry Division (MILB)
RAPID......... Research and Public Information Dissemination
RAS .... Resource Asset Invstmt. [*AMEX symbol*] (SG)
RAS .... Routine Analytical Service (EPAT)
RASS .... Radar Altimeter Speedometer Sounder
rat.............. Rated (GEAB)
RAVC .... Retrograde Atrioventricular Conduction [*Medicine*] (MELL)
RAVV .... Right Atrioventricular Valve [*Medicine*] (MELL)
RAZF........... Razorfish,Inc.'A' [*NASDAQ symbol*] (SG)
RB............. Radiation Burn (MELL)
RB............. Record Book
RB............. Request for Bid (EPAT)
RBA .... Ritchie Bros. Auctioneers [*NYSE symbol*] (SG)
RBAK .... Redback Networks [*NASDAQ symbol*] (SG)
RBD .... Randomized Block Design
RBD .... Relative Biologic Dose (MELL)
RBD .... Round-Back Deformity (MELL)
RBF........... Rat Bite Fever (MELL)
RBG .... Random Blood Glucose (MELL)
RBLT.......... Rebuilt [*Automobile*]
RBMG......... Resource Bancshares Mtg. Gp. [*NASDAQ symbol*] (SG)
RBN .... Robbins & Myers [*NYSE symbol*] (SG)
RBO .... RiboGene,Inc. [*AMEX symbol*] (SG)
RBV .... Resource Bankshares [*AMEX symbol*] (SG)
RCA .... Relative Chemotactic Activity [*Medicine*] (MELL)
RCAST .... Research Centre for Advanced Science and Technology
RCC .... Rickets and Chronic Cough (MELL)
RCC .... Right Common Carotid [*Medicine*] (MELL)
RCCK .... Rock Financial [*NASDAQ symbol*] (SG)
RCD .... Renal Cystic Disease [*Medicine*] (MELL)
RCD .... Right Crus of Diaphragm [*Medicine*] (MELL)
RCD .... Rotator Cuff Disease [*Medicine*] (MELL)
RCE .... Right Carotid Endarterectomy [*Medicine*] (MELL)
RCF........... Rica Foods [*AMEX symbol*] (SG)
RCF........... Root Canal Filling [*Dentistry*] (MELL)
RCG .... Radiocardiography [*Medicine*] (MELL)
RCGS .... Royal Canadian Geographical Society (QUAC)
RCHSA........ Radiation Control for Health and Safety Act (MELL)
RCI........... Radiocarpal Joint [*Medicine*] (MELL)
RCIFC .... Roy Clark International Fan Club (EA)
RCII.......... Rent-A-Center [*NASDAQ symbol*] (SG)
RCL.......... Renal Clearance [*Medicine*] (MELL)
RCM........... Regional Climate Model (QUAC)

RCM........... Retinal Capillary Microaneurysm [*Medicine*] (MELL)
RCME........ Racing Champions Mint Editions [*Toy collection*]
RCO .... Regional Compliance Officer [*Environmental science*] (EPAT)
RCP .... Research Centers Program (EPAT)
RCSM .... Royal College of Surgeon's Museum [*London, England*]
RCT............ Rotator Cuff Tear [*Medicine*] (MELL)
RD .... Rectal Dysfunction [*Medicine*] (MELL)
RD .... Recurrent Depression (MELL)
RD .... Release of Dower Rights (GEAB)
rd............. Road (BEE)
RDC .... Raytheon Demilitarization Company
rdg............. Ridge (BEE)
RDL .... Riddell Sports [*AMEX symbol*] (SG)
RDN .... Radian Group [*NYSE symbol*] (SG)
Rdstr.......... Roadster
RDV .... Reference Dose Values [*Environmental science*] (EPAT)
re.............. Regarding (GEAB)
recce .... Reconnaissance (MILB)
REDA .... Recycling Economic Development Advocate (EPAT)
redr........... Recorder (GEAB)
REENIC .... Russian and East European Network Information Center
reg............ Register (GEAB)
reg............ Regular (BEE)
REGI .... Renaissance Worldwide [*NASDAQ symbol*] (SG)
regt........... Regiment (MILB)
rehab .... Rehabilitation (PROS)
REI........... Reliant Energy [*NYSE symbol*] (SG)
REI........... Restricted Entry Interval [*Environmental Protection Agency*] (EPAT)
rel............ Religious (PROS)
reld........... Relieved (GEAB)
rels............ Relations (PROS)
ren............ Renunciation (GEAB)
REOC .... Royal Enfield Owners Club (EA)
rep............ Reprinted (GEAB)
Repbl......... Republican (PROS)
RePEc .... Research Papers in Economics
repl........... Replaced (GEAB)
repud......... Repudiated (GEAB)
res............ Residence (BEE)
RESAC .... Regional Earth Science Applications Center [*NASA*]
Rev........... Revised
Rev........... Revolutionary War (GEAD)
REX........... Rexx Environmental [*AMEX symbol*] (SG)
RFC........... New York Rangers Fan Club [*Formerly, Rangers Fan Club*] (EA)
RFH........... Richfood Hldgs. [*NYSE symbol*] (SG)
RFM........... Red-Fronted Macaw [*Bird*]
RFMD .... RF Micro Devices [*NASDAQ symbol*] (SG)
RG .... Registered Genealogist (GEAB)
RH .... Rottlund Co. [*AMEX symbol*] (SG)
RHA .... Rhodia ADS [*NYSE symbol*] (SG)
RHB .... RehabCare Group [*NYSE symbol*] (SG)
RHC .... Rao-Hartley-Cochran Method
RHRS.......... Revised Hazard Ranking System [*Environmental science*] (EPAT)
RIA .... Regional Integration Arrangement
RIC .... Richmont Mines [*AMEX symbol*] (SG)
RIM .... Research in Motion
ring............ Relinquished (GEAB)
RIP .... Reproductive Immunophynotype [*Medicine*]
RIS........... Reflector in Space (EOSA)
RJI .... Reeds Jewelers [*AMEX symbol*] (SG)
RJI .... Royal Jordanian Investments
rkt............. Rocket (MILB)
RKY .... Coors (Adolph)Cl'B' [*NYSE symbol*] (SG)
RL............ Polo Ralph Lauren'A' [*NYSE symbol*] (SG)
RL............ Red Line [*Automotive tire designation*]
RL............ Red Lines [*Toy collection*]
RLS........... Rick's Loyal Supporters [*An association*] (EA)
RMG .... Ragen Mackenzie Grp. [*NYSE symbol*] (SG)
rmP........... Returning Polar Maritime Airmass [*Meteorology*] (WEAT)
RMS........... Ride Motion Simulator
RMSD .... Root Mean Square Difference
RMY .... Delco Remy Intl.'A' [*NYSE symbol*] (SG)
RNT .... Aaron Rents [*NYSE symbol*] (SG)
ROAC .... Rock of Ages'A' [*NASDAQ symbol*] (SG)
ROC curves... Receiver Operating Characteristic Curves
ROCLF .... Royal Olympic Cruise Line [*NASDAQ symbol*] (SG)

Rolex.......... Horology Exquisite
Rom............. Roman (BFF)
ROP............ Rate of Progress (EPAT)
ROP............ Roper Industries [*NYSE symbol*] (SG)
ROPA.......... Realising Our Potential Award
ROPA.......... Register of Professional Archaeologists
ROS............ Rostelecom Telecommun ADS [*NYSE symbol*] (SG)
ROSA........... Regional Ozone Study Area [*Environmental Protection Agency*] (EPAT)
ROWE........ RoweCom,Inc. [*NASDAQ symbol*] (SG)
RPC............ Roberts Pharmaceutical [*AMEX symbol*] (SG)
RPC............ Russian Palynological Commission (QUAC)
RPGA.......... Role Playing Game Association Network (EA)
RPI.............. Roberts Realty Investors [*AMEX symbol*] (SG)
RPL............. Recurrent Pregnancy Loss [*Medicine*]
Rpm............. Revolutions per Minute
RR.............. Real Riders [*Toy collection*]
RR.............. Resource Record
RRC............ Rapid-Reaction Corps (MILB)
RRD............ Rose Rosette Disease
RRRR.......... Rare Medium Group [*NASDAQ symbol*] (SG)
RRSS......... Research Resources for the Social Sciences [*Internet resource*]
RS.............. Rally Sport
RS.............. Registration Standard (EPAT)
RS.............. Rumble Seat

RSA............ Recurrent Spontaneous Abortion [*Medicine*]
RSG............ Republic Services [*NYSE symbol*] (SG)
RSI............. Repetitive Stress Injury
RSI............. Revenue Systems, Inc.
RSIFC........ Ricky Skaggs International Fan Club (EA)
rsl.............. Relative Sea Level (QUAC)
RSLC......... RSL Communications 'A' [*NASDAQ symbol*] (SG)
RSLN......... Roslyn Bancorp [*NASDAQ symbol*] (SG)
RSM........... Royal Scottish Museum [*Edinburgh*]
rss............. Root-Sum-Square (EOSA)
RTA............ Ready to Assemble
RTA............ Religious and Theological Abstracts [*A publication*]
RTC............ Riviera Tool [*AMEX symbol*] (SG)
RTDF......... Remediation Technologies Development Forum (EPAT)
RTHM......... Rhythms NetConnections [*NASDAQ symbol*] (SG)
RTI............. Read the Instructions [*Online dialog*]
RTO............ RTO Enterprises [*Toronto Stock Exchange symbol*] (SG)
Russ........... Russian (BEE)
RVW........... Rving Women [*ASO*] (EA)
Rwa............ Rwanda (MILB)
Rwl............. Raised White Letter
RWY........... Rent-Way, Inc. [*NYSE symbol*] (SG)
RYAAY........ Ryanair Holdings ADS [*NASDAQ symbol*] (SG)
RYD............ DECS Trust II 6.875% 2000 [*NYSE symbol*] (SG)
RYG............ Royal Group Tech. [*NYSE symbol*] (SG)
RZT............ ResortQuest Intl. [*NYSE symbol*] (SG)

S
By Acronym

S .... Sacral Vertebra (MELL)
S .... Scapula (MELL)
S .... Schizophrenia (MELL)
S .... Shingles [Medicine] (MELL)
S .... Skeleton (MELL)
S .... Skull (MELL)
s .... Soldier (GEAB)
S .... Soluble (MELL)
S .... Spleen (MELL)
S .... Sternum (MELL)
S .... Stomach (MELL)
S .... Succinylcholine (MELL)
S .... Supine (MELL)
S .... Syndrome [Medicine] (MELL)
S .... Systolic [Medicine] (MELL)
S-7 .... Super Seven [Aircraft]
SA .... Sand in Suspension in the Air (WEAT)
SA .... Seasonal Allergy (MELL)
SA .... Semen Albumin [Medicine] (MELL)
SA .... Sensory Aphasia [Medicine] (MELL)
SA .... Skin Absorption (MELL)
SA .... Sleep Apnea (MELL)
SA .... Solitary Adenomas [Medicine] (MELL)
SA .... Speech Audiometry (MELL)
SA .... Spontaneous Abortion (MELL)
SA .... Spousal Abuse (MELL)
SA .... Stable Angina [Medicine] (MELL)
SA .... Sustainable Agriculture
SAA .... Strategia Corp. [AMEX symbol] (SG)
SAA .... Subareolar Abscess [Medicine] (MELL)
SAAFTI .... Society of Asset Allocators & Fund Timers Inc.
SAAT .... Serum Aspartate Aminotransferase [Medicine] (MELL)
SAB .... Sinoauricular Block [Medicine] (MELL)
SAB .... Subacromial Bursa [Medicine] (MELL)
SAC .... S-allylcysteine
SAC .... Standardized Assessment of Concussion
SACCWEST ... Swedish American Chamber of Commerce of the Western United States (EA)
SADS .... Sudden Arrhythmia Death Syndrome [Medicine] (MELL)
SAE .... Specific Action Exercise (MELL)
SAE .... Super-Sol Ltd.ADS [NYSE symbol] (SG)
SAE .... Supported Arm Exercise (MELL)
SAEB .... Sinoatrial Entrance Block [Medicine] (MELL)
SAF .... Serum Accelerator Factor [Medicine] (MELL)
SAF .... Small Abattoir Federation (GVA)
SAF .... Superior Articular Facet (MELL)
SAFE .... Self-Abuse Finally Ends [Medical treatment unit]
SAFIRE .... Spectroscopy of the Atmosphere Using Far Infrared Emission (EOSA)
SAGE III ...... Stratospheric Aerosol and Gas Experiment III (EOSA)
SAH .... Sonic Automotive'A' [NYSE symbol] (SG)
SAI .... Security Assoc.Intl. [AMEX symbol] (SG)
SAL .... Salisbury Bancorp [AMEX symbol] (SG)
SAL .... Saudi Arabian Light [Crude oil]
SAL .... Suction-Assisted Lipectomy [Medicine] (MELL)
SALM .... Salem Communications'A' [NASDAQ symbol] (SG)
SAM .... Serratus Anterior Muscle [Medicine] (MELL)
SAM .... Sportsman's Alliance of Maine
SAMANA ...... Sheet Metal and Air Conditioning Contractors National Association, Inc.
SAMC .... S-allymercaptocysteine
SAMI........... Southern Appalachian Mountains Initiative (EPAT)
SAN .... Storage Area Network
S&R .... Search and Rescue (EOSA)
S&S .... Stewart & Stevenson Services, Inc.
SAOAS .... Staff Association of the Organization of American States (EA)
SAP .... SAP Aktiengesellschaft ADS [NYSE symbol] (SG)
SAP .... Standard Assessment of Personality (MELL)
SAP .... Standard Auto Plan [Insurance]
SAP .... Systolic Arterial Pressure [Medicine] (MELL)
SAPHO .... Synovitis, Acne Pustulosis, Hyperostosis and Osteomyelitis
SAPV .... Superior Articular Process of Vertebra [Medicine] (MELL)
SAR .... Seasonal Allergic Rhinitis [Medicine] (MELL)
SAS .... Scalenus Anterior Syndrome [Medicine] (MELL)
SAS .... Special Analytical Service (EPAT)
SAS .... Suicide and Aggression Survey (MELL)
SASA .... Sex Abuse Survivors Anonymous (MELL)

SASBLIA ...... South African Stud Book and Livestock Improvement Association (GVA)
SASSI-2 .... Substance Abuse Subtle Screening Inventory-2
SAT .... Asia Satellite Telecom ADS [NYSE symbol] (SG)
SAT .... Streptococcal Antibody Test [Medicine] (MELL)
Sau .... Saudi Arabia (MILB)
SAVA .... South African Veterinary Association (GVA)
SAVMA .... Student American Veterinary Medical Association (GVA)
SAVS .... Subaortic Valvular Stenosis [Medicine] (MELL)
SB .... Sitz Bath (MELL)
SB .... Surface Biopsy (MELL)
SBA .... Saddle Block Anesthesia [Medicine] (MELL)
SBA .... Sideroblastic Anemia [Medicine] (MELL)
SBA .... Simulation Based Acquisition [Army]
SBA .... Standby Angioplasty [Medicine] (MELL)
SBAC .... SBA Communications'A' [NASDAQ symbol] (SG)
SBC .... Single Breath Cannister (EPAT)
SBCCOM ...... Soldier and Biological Chemical Command [Army]
SBD .... Spinal Bone Density [Medicine] (MELL)
SBDS .... Social Breakdown Syndrome (MELL)
SBI .... Serious Bacterial Infection (MELL)
SBI .... Silicone Breast Implant (MELL)
SBI .... Subsidiary Body on Implementation
SBIFC.......... Sawyer Brown International Fan Club (EA)
SBIRS .... Spaced-Based Infrared Sensor [Military]
SBO .... Spina Bifida Occulta [Medicine] (MELL)
SBOT .... Single-Breath Oxygen Test (MELL)
SBP .... Banco Santander-Puerto Rico [NYSE symbol] (SG)
SBP .... Systemic Biopsy of Prostate [Medicine] (MELL)
SBRN .... Superficial Branch of Radial Nerve [Medicine] (MELL)
SBS .... Short Bowel Syndrome [Medicine] (MELL)
SBS .... Smart Battery Systems
SBS .... Straight Back Syndrome [Medicine] (MELL)
SBSTA .... Subsidiary Body for Scientific and Technical Advice
SBTT .... Simplate Bleeding Time Test [Medicine] (MELL)
SBTV .... SBS Broadcasting [NASDAQ symbol] (SG)
SC .... Schwann Cell [Medicine] (MELL)
SC .... Sebaceous Cyst [Medicine] (MELL)
SC .... Senile Cataract [Medicine] (MELL)
SC .... Sodium Citrate (MELL)
Sc .... Stratocumulus (WEAT)
SCA .... Steroidal-Cell Antibody [Medicine] (MELL)
SCAI........... Sanchez Computer Assoc. [NASDAQ symbol] (SG)
Scand .... Scandinavian (BEE)
SCANSCAT ... Scanning Scatterometer (EOSA)
SCar .... South Carolina (BEE)
SCARABE ..... Scanning Radiation Budget Experiment (EOSA)
SCB .... Community Bankshares S.C. [AMEX symbol] (SG)
SCB .... Shallow Coin Biopsy [Medicine] (MELL)
SCBE .... Single Contrast Barium Enema [Medicine] (MELL)
SCC .... Security Capital Corp'A' [AMEX symbol] (SG)
SCC .... Semicircular Canal [Medicine] (MELL)
SCC .... Serum Cholesterol Concentration [Medicine] (MELL)
SCC .... Spinal Cord Compression [Medicine] (MELL)
SCCD .... Subacute Corticoid Cerebellar Degeneration [Medicine] (MELL)
SCCS .... Spinal Cord Compression Syndrome [Medicine] (MELL)
SCCT .... Severe Cerebrocranial Trauma [Medicine] (MELL)
SCD .... Shepherd's Crook Deformity [Medicine] (MELL)
SCF .... Subcapital Fracture [Medicine] (MELL)
SCF .... Supracondylar Fracture [Medicine] (MELL)
SCFS .... Seacoast Finl.Svcs. [NASDAQ symbol] (SG)
SCH .... Squamous Cell Hyperplasia [Medicine] (MELL)
SCH .... Supracervical Hysterectomy [Medicine] (MELL)
SCI .... SCI Systems [nyse symbol] (SG)
SCI .... Staphylococcal Infection [Medicine] (MELL)
SCI .... Streptococcal Infection [Medicine] (MELL)
SCID .... Structured Clinical Interview for Diagnosis
SCIRI .... Supreme Council of the Islamic Revolution in Iraq
SCIU .... Spinal Cord Injury Unit (MELL)
SCJ .... Sternocostal Joint [Medicine] (MELL)
SCLD .... Severe Chronic Liver Disease (MELL)
SCM .... Subcutaneous Mastectomy [Medicine] (MELL)
SCMC .... SCM Microsystems [NASDAQ symbol] (SG)
SCMM .... Sternocleidomastoid Muscle [Medicine] (MELL)
SCN .... Sickle Cell Nephropathy [Medicine] (MELL)
SCNA .... Saab Club of North America (EA)

SCO	SCOR ADS [*NYSE symbol*] (SG)
Scot	Scottish (BEE)
SCOT	Scottish Annuity & Life Hldgs. [*NASDAQ symbol*] (SG)
ScotGael	Scottish Gaelic (BEE)
SCPPB	Subcutaneous Prepatellar Bursa [*Medicine*] (MELL)
SCS	Small-Capacity Syndrome (MELL)
SCS	Spinal Cord Syndrome (MELL)
SCS	Splenocaval Shunt [*Medicine*] (MELL)
SCS	Spur-Cell Syndrome [*Medicine*] (MELL)
SCSL	Steelcase Inc,'A' [*NYSE symbol*] (SG)
SCSL	Stratocumulus Standing Lenticular Cloud (WEAT)
SCT	Scattered Cloud (WEAT)
SCT	Sertoli Cell Tumor [*Medicine*] (MELL)
SCT	Sweat Chloride Test (MELL)
SCTT	Scott Technologies [*NASDAQ symbol*] (SG)
SCUCP	Small Cell Undifferentiated Carcinoma of Prostate [*Medicine*] (MELL)
SCV	Small Cardiac Vein [*Medicine*] (MELL)
SCV	Squamous Cancer of Vagina [*Medicine*] (MELL)
SCW	Swiss Classic Watches
SCWIST	Society for Canadian Women in Science and Technology (QUAC)
SCZ	Security Capital Grp'B'. (SG)
SD	San Diego Chargers [*National Football League*] [*1961-present*] (NFLA)
SD	Schistosome Dermatitis [*Medicine*] (MELL)
SD	Seborrheic Dermatitis [*Medicine*] (MELL)
SD	Selective Decontamination (MELL)
SD	Simply Divoon - Jayne Mansfield Fan Club (EA)
SD	Sleep Disorder (MELL)
SD	Small Date [*Numismatic term*]
SD	Streeter Dysplasia [*Medicine*] (MELL)
SD	Substance Dependence (MELL)
SD	Swallowing Disorder (MELL)
SDA	Sialodacryoadenitis [*Medicine*] (MELL)
SDA	Surface of the Drainage Area
SDAP	Single Donor Apheresis Platelets [*Medicine*] (MELL)
SDB	Second-Degree Burn (MELL)
SDC	Santa Fe Intl. [*NYSE symbol*] (SG)
SDD	Sclerodermoid Dermatitis [*Medicine*] (MELL)
SDD	Selective Decontamination of the Digestive Tract (MELL)
SDDD	Spinal Degenerative Disk Disease (MELL)
SDH	Sodexho Marriott Svcs. [*NYSE symbol*] (SG)
SDM	Sensing and Diagnostic Module
Sdn	Sudan (MILB)
SDNA	Sedona Corp. [*NASDAQ symbol*] (SG)
SDP	Single-Donor Platelets [*Medicine*] (MELL)
SDPD	Self-Defeating Personality Disorder (MELL)
SDR	Spontaneous Discharge Rate (MELL)
SDRSC	Single-Dose Radiation Survival Curve (MELL)
SDS	Salivary Duct Strictures [*Medicine*] (MELL)
SDS	SunGard Data Systems [*NYSE symbol*] (SG)
SDS	Surfactant Deficiency Syndrome (MELL)
SDSCnet	San Diego Supercomputer Center [*California*]
SD-SEO	South Dakota State Employees Organization
SDT	Sensory Decision Theory (MELL)
SDX	Sigma Delta Chi Foundation (EA)
SE	Staphylococcal Endotoxin [*Medicine*] (MELL)
Sea	Seattle Seahawks [*National Football League*] [*1976-present*] (NFLA)
SEAC	SeaChange Intl. [*NASDAQ symbol*] (SG)
SEAD	Small Economic Activity Development
SEANC	State Employees Association of North Carolina, Inc.
SEC	Science Executive Committee (EOSA)
sec	Security
SEC	Specialty Equipment [*NYSE symbol*] (SG)
SecNav	Secretary of the Navy
secy	Secretary (PROS)
SEDA	Spinal Epidural Abscess [*Medicine*] (MELL)
SEG	StanCorp Financial Group [*NYSE symbol*] (SG)
SEGIP	State Environmental Goals and Improvement Project (EPAT)
SEH	Spinal Epidural Hematoma [*Medicine*] (MELL)
SEI	Substance-Exposed Infant (MELL)
SEM	Smart Enterprise Model
SEM	Subacute Encephalomyelopathy [*Medicine*] (MELL)
sen	Senator (PROS)
Sen	Senegal (MILB)
SEP	Serum Electrophoresis [*Medicine*] (MELL)
SEP	System Enhancement Program
SEPA	Scottish Environmental Protection Agency (GVA)
Sept	September (BEE)
serg	Sergeant (GEAB)
serv	Service (GEAB)
SES	Sick Euthyroid Syndrome [*Medicine*] (MELL)
SES	Standard Electrolyte Solution (MELL)
SESQUINET	Texas Sesquicentennial Network
SETS	Statewide Education Technology Services
sett	Settler (GEAB)
SEU	Social Exclusion Unit
SEV	Seven Seas Petroleum [*AMEX symbol*] (SG)
Sey	Seychelles (MILB)
SF	San Francisco 49ers [*National Football League*] [*1950-present*] (NFLA)
SF	Saturated Fat (MELL)
SF	Scapular Fracture [*Medicine*] (MELL)
SF	Simple Fracture (MELL)
SF	Skull Fracture (MELL)
SF	Slice Fracture (MELL)
SF	Stress Fracture (MELL)
SF	Swine Fever (MELL)
SFDS	Sanitary Facility Data System (EPAT)
SFE	Supply Function Equilibrium
SFH	Serum-Free Hemoglobin [*Medicine*] (MELL)
SFLOC	Sferic Location (WEAT)
SFO	Sonic Foundry [*AMEX symbol*] (SG)
SFP	Salton, Inc. [*NYSE symbol*] (SG)
SFP	Standard Fire Policy [*Insurance*]
SFR	Spot-Film Radiography [*Medicine*] (MELL)
SFS	Santa Fe Snyder [*NYSE symbol*] (SG)
SFT	Stratesec,Inc. [*AMEX symbol*] (SG)
SFTP	Simple File Transfer Protocol
SFTP	Soft Top [*Automobile*]
SFTT	Skin-Fold-Thickness Test (MELL)
SFTW-LISC	Stamps for the Wounded [*Affiliated with Lions International Stamp Club*] (EA)
SFU	Surgical Follow-Up (MELL)
SFWMD	South Florida Water Management District
SFX	SFX Entertainment'A' [*NYSE symbol*] (SG)
SG	Palestine Study Group (EA)
SG	Salivary Gland (MELL)
SG	Scientific Games Hldgs. [*NYSE symbol*] (SG)
SGA	Sweat Gland Adenoma [*Medicine*] (MELL)
SGAH	Second-Generation Antihistamine [*Medicine*] (MELL)
SGBI	Silicone Gel Breast Implant [*Medicine*] (MELL)
SGC	Superior Uniform Group [*AMEX symbol*] (SG)
S-GCOS	Space-Based Global Change Observation System (EOSA)
SGE	Stage Stores [*NYSE symbol*] (SG)
SGG	SGL Carbon AG ADS [*NYSE symbol*] (SG)
Sgp	Singapore (MILB)
SGR	Shaw Group [*NYSE symbol*] (SG)
Sgr A*	Sagittarius A* [*Astronomy*]
SGRM	Stimson Gravity Reduction Maneuver [*Medicine*] (MELL)
SGU	Star Gas Ptnrs L.P. [*NYSE symbol*] (SG)
SGV	Society of Greyhound Veterinarians (GVA)
SH	Sexual History (MELL)
sh	Ship (GEAB)
SH	Spinal Headache (MELL)
SHA	Superior Hypophyseal Artery [*Medicine*] (MELL)
SHARE	Supporting Hospitals Abroad with Resources and Equipment (MELL)
SHCS	Second Hand Cigarette Smoke (MELL)
SHD	Syphilitic Heart Disease (MELL)
SHF	Schuff Steel [*AMEX symbol*] (SG)
SHGC	Solar Heat Gain Coefficient
SHI	Severe Head Injury (MELL)
SHL	Sudden Hearing Loss (MELL)
SHLN	Suprahyoid Lymph Node [*Medicine*] (MELL)
SHO	Showpower, Inc. [*AMEX symbol*] (SG)
SHP	Schein Pharmaceutical [*NYSE symbol*] (SG)
SHPIC	Specialized Health Prods Intl. [*NASDAQ symbol*] (SG)
SHRP	Sharper Image [*NASDAQ symbol*] (SG)
SHS	Sauer, Inc. [*NYSE symbol*] (SG)
SHS	Second-Hand Smoke (MELL)
SHS	Shoulder-Hand Syndrome (MELL)
SHTS	Second-Hand Tobacco Smoke (MELL)
SI	Second Infertility [*Medicine*]
SI	Sexual Infantilism (MELL)
SI	Solar Influences (EOSA)
SI	Straddle Injury (MELL)
SI	Streptococcal Infection [*Medicine*] (MELL)
SI	Surveillance Index (EPAT)
SI	Swimmer's Itch (MELL)
SIA	Sulfite-Induced Asthma (MELL)
SIBC	Serum Iron-Binding Capacity (MELL)
SIC	Self Intermittent Catheterization [*Medicine*] (MELL)
SIC	Soil Inorganic Carbon (QUAC)
SICB	Sodium Ion Channel Blocker [*Medicine*] (MELL)
SID	Comp Siderurgica Nacional ADS [*NYSE symbol*] (SG)
SID	Severe Iron Deficiency (MELL)
SIDPERS-3	Standard Army Installation and Division Personnel System Version 3.0
SIDS	Small Island Developing States
SIE	Sigma Iota Epsilon (EA)
SIFEE	Securities Industry Foundation for Economic Education
sigs	Signals (MILB)
SIGYY	Signet Group ADR [*NASDAQ symbol*] (SG)
SIIA	Software & Information Industry Association
SIL	Apex Silver Mines [*AMEX symbol*] (SG)
SIM	Space Interferometry Mission
SIMV	Spontaneous Intermittent Mandatory Ventilation [*Medicine*] (MELL)
SIN	Spinal Interneuron [*Medicine*] (MELL)
SIND	Synthetic Industries [*NASDAQ symbol*] (SG)
SIP	Stroke in Progression (MELL)
SIP	Sutured in Place [*Medicine*] (MELL)
SIR	Secondary Immune Response (MELL)
SIR	Subcutaneous Inguinal Ring [*Medicine*] (MELL)
SIR-C	Shuttle Imaging Radar-C (EOSA)
SIS	Shaken Impact Syndrome (MELL)
sis	Sister (GEAB)
SIS	Structured Interview for Schizotypy (MELL)
SIT	Saline Infusion Test [*Medicine*] (MELL)
SiTr	Silent Treatment [*Medicine*] (MELL)
SITS	Soccer in the Streets [*An association*]
SIZ	Shanxi Institute of Zoology [*China*]

SJ	Saddle Joint [*Medicine*] (MELL)
SJ	Synovial Joint [*Medicine*] (MELL)
Ska	Sri Lanka (MILB)
SKI	Amer Skiing [*NYSE symbol*] (SG)
SKM	SK Telecom ADS [*NYSE symbol*] (SG)
SKP	SCPIE Holdings [*NYSE symbol*] (SG)
SKS	Saks, Inc. [*NYSE symbol*] (SG)
SKX	Skechers U.S.A. Cl'A' [*NYSE symbol*] (SG)
SKYT	SkyTel Communications [*NASDAQ symbol*] (SG)
SL	Short Leg (MELL)
SL	Sign Language (MELL)
SL	Simian Line (MELL)
SL	Small Letters [*Numismatic term*]
SLA	Superior Laryngeal Artery [*Medicine*] (MELL)
SLAP	Scientific, Literary, Artistic, or Political
SLAP	Standard Light Antarctic Precipitation (QUAC)
SLB	Suspensory Ligament of Breast [*Medicine*] (MELL)
SLCC	Society of Lincoln Cent Collectors (EA)
SLD	Specific Learning Disability (MELL)
SLG	SL Green Realty [*NYSE symbol*] (SG)
SLI	SLI,Inc. [*NYSE symbol*] (SG)
SLIES	Stratospheric Limb Infrared Emission Spectrometer (EOSA)
SLMS	School Library Media Specialist
SLN	Salt-Losing Nephritis [*Medicine*] (MELL)
SLN	Special Local Need (EPAT)
SLN	Subclavian Lymph Node [*Medicine*] (MELL)
SLORC	State Law and Order Council [*China*]
SLT	Sri Lanka Telecom Limited
Slvk	Slovakia (MILB)
Slvn	Slovenia (MILB)
SLW	St. Laurent Paperboard [*NYSE symbol*] (SG)
SLW	Straight Leg Walker [*Doll collecting*]
SM	Scale Manufacturers Association
SM	Scarlet Macaw [*Bird*]
SM	Segmental Mastectomy [*Medicine*] (MELL)
SM	Skeletal Muscle (MELL)
SM	Sports Medicine (MELL)
SM	Sulzer Medica ADS [*NYSE symbol*] (SG)
SM	Syringomyelia [*Medicine*] (MELL)
SMART	Simulation and Modeling for Acquisition, Requirements, and Training [*Army*]
SMC	Selenomethylnorcholesterol [*Medicine*] (MELL)
SMC	Systemic Mastocytosis [*Medicine*] (MELL)
SMC	System Management Center (EOSA)
SMCD	Senile Macular Chorioretinal Degeneration [*Medicine*] (MELL)
SMDS	Secondary Myelodysplastic Syndrome [*Medicine*] (MELL)
SME	Severe Myoclonic Epilepsy [*Medicine*] (MELL)
Sme	Suriname (MILB)
SMGS	SEMCO Energy [*NASDAQ symbol*] (SG)
SMI	Starfleet Marines International (EA)
SMI	Sulfate-Methane Interface (QUAC)
SMIPG	Seromuscular Intestinal Patch Graft [*Medicine*] (MELL)
SML	Sphenomandibular Ligament [*Medicine*] (MELL)
SML	Stylomandibular Ligament [*Medicine*] (MELL)
SMM	Society of Marine Mammalogists (GVA)
SMMP	Society for Mineral Museum Professionals
SMN	Second Malignant Neoplasm [*Medicine*] (MELL)
SMNS	Seminis,Inc.'A' [*NASDAQ symbol*] (SG)
SMO	Sample Management Office [*Environmental Protection Agency*] (EPAT)
SMP	State Management Plan (EPAT)
SMS	Scalded Mouth Syndrome (MELL)
SMS	Self-Mutilation Syndrome (MELL)
SMS	Shared Medical Sys. [*NYSE symbol*] (SG)
SMS	Smith-Magenis Syndrome [*Medicine*]
SMS/GOES	Synchronous Meteorological Satellite/Geostationary Operational Environmental Satellite (EOSA)
SMT	Spinal Manipulative Therapy [*Medicine*] (MELL)
SMTI	SMTEK Intl. [*NASDAQ symbol*] (SG)
SMTO	St. Maarten Tourist Information Office (EA)
SMURFS	Southern Michigan Unorganized Regional Festival of Stargazers
SMW	Standard Meteorological Week
SN	Snow (WEAT)
SN	Space Network (EOSA)
snafu	Situation Normal, All Fouled Up
SNAP	Score of Neonatal Acute Physiology [*Medicine*] (MELL)
SNB	Sacral Nerve Block [*Medicine*] (MELL)
SNB	Spinal Nerve Block [*Medicine*] (MELL)
SNB	Sunburst Hospitality [*NYSE symbol*] (SG)
SNC	Swan-Neck Catheter [*Medicine*] (MELL)
SNCAC	Statewide Nontraditional Career Assistance Center
SNCL	Sinus Node Cycle Length [*Medicine*] (MELL)
SNDT	Sand Technology Sys Intl'A' [*NASDAQ symbol*] (SG)
SNHY	Sun Hydraulics [*NASDAQ symbol*] (SG)
SNINCR	Snow Increasing Rapidly (WEAT)
SNMG	Supernumerary Mammary Gland [*Medicine*] (MELL)
SNMJ	Skeletal Neuromuscular Junction [*Medicine*] (MELL)
SNP	Space Nuclear Power
SNRF	Sunroof
SO	Survivors' Originals (GEAB)
SOAR	Searchable Online Archive of Recipes
SOBE	Short of Breath on Exertion (MELL)
SoC	Sense of Control
SOCC	Satellite Operation Command and Control (EOSA)
Sociol	Sociology (BEE)

SODA	Sportsplex Operators and Developers of America (EA)
SoFAMMS	South Florida Atmospheric Mercury Monitoring Study
SOFN	Softnet Systems [*NASDAQ symbol*] (SG)
SOI	Solutia,Inc. [*NYSE symbol*] (SG)
SOJA	Systemic Onset Juvenile Arthritis [*Medicine*] (MELL)
SOLSTICE	Solar Stellar Irradiance Comparison Experiment (EOSA)
SOM	Senior Officials Meeting [*Dublin*]
SOM	Suppurative Otitis Media [*Medicine*] (MELL)
SOMR	Source-Oriented Medical Record (MELL)
SOMTI	Senior Officials Meeting on Trade and Investment [*Brussels*]
SONE	Security First Technologies [*NASDAQ symbol*] (SG)
SOOC	Spiral Organ of Corti [*Medicine*] (MELL)
SOS	Suboptimal Surgery (MELL)
SOSA	Starfleet Operations International [*Formerly, Starfleet Operations*] (EA)
SOT	Systemic Oxygen Transport (MELL)
Sp	Spain (MILB)
SpaceDrums	Dynamically Responding Ultrasonic Matix System [*Commercial research facility*]
SPALS	Subsequent Pregnancy After a Loss Support
SPC	Statistical Quality Control
Spd	Speed
Specs	Specifications
SPF	South Polar Feature
SPHR	Senior Professional in Human Resources
SPI	Scottish Power ADS [*NYSE symbol*] (SG)
SPI	Standardized Precipitation Index
SPII	Society of the Plastics Industry, Inc.
Spkrs	Speakers
SPLN	Sportsline USA [*NASDAQ symbol*] (SG)
SPLR	Spoiler
SPN	Security of Pennsylvania Finl. [*AMEX symbol*] (SG)
Spncr	Spencer (BEE)
spr	Sponsor (GEAB)
spr	Spring
SPSO	Science Processing Support Office (EOSA)
spt	Support (MILB)
SqFt	Square Foot
SqIn	Square Inch
sqn	Squadron (MILB)
SR	Somali Republic (MILB)
SR	Special Review [*Environmental Protection Agency*] (EPAT)
SR	Species Richness
SRC	Survey Research Center
SRE	Sempra Energy [*NYSE symbol*] (SG)
SRI	Stoneridge,Inc. [*NYSE symbol*] (SG)
SRK	SeraCare,Inc. [*AMEX symbol*] (SG)
SRP	Special Review Procedure [*Environmental Protection Agency*] (EPAT)
SRR	Second Round Review [*Environmental Protection Agency*] (EPAT)
SRS	ARV Assisted Living [*AMEX symbol*] (SG)
SRT	StarTek,Inc. [*NYSE symbol*] (SG)
SS	Sandstorm (WEAT)
SSA	Saatchi & Saatchi ADS [*NYSE symbol*] (SG)
SSAB	Society for the Study of Animal Breeding (GVA)
SSALT	Solid-State Radar Altimeter (EOSA)
SSC	Suspended Sediment Concentration
SSCC	Smurfit-Stone Container [*NASDAQ symbol*] (SG)
SSCC	Snowmobile Safety & Certification Committee, Inc..
SSD	Simpson Manufacturing [*NYSE symbol*] (SG)
SSFC	Street Sharks Fan Club (EA)
SSIMS	Stainless Steel International Metallurgical Society
SSLM	Southern Sudan Liberation Movement
SSM	School Science and Mathematics [*A publication*]
SSM/I	Special Sensor Microwave/Imager (EOSA)
SSN	Sonus Corp. [*AMEX symbol*] (SG)
SSP	Sea Surface Productivity (QUAC)
SSPEI	Special Study Panel on Education Indicators [*1991*]
SSPSA	Social Studies Provincial Specialist Association
SSR	Software Safety Release
SSSI	Sites of Special Scientific Interest [*Geology*]
sst	Sea Surface Temperature (QUAC)
SSUV	Shuttle Solar Ultraviolet
ST	Star Trek [*Television program*]
St	Stratus Cloud (WEAT)
STA	Stormwater Treatment Area
STAF	StaffMark,Inc. [*NASDAQ symbol*] (SG)
STAR	Study of Tamoxifen and Raloxifene
stat	Statistics (BEE)
StC	St. Louis Cardinals [*National Football League*] [*1960-87*] (NFLA)
STC	Swedish Trade Council (EA)
STD	Banco Santander Cent Hispano ADS [*NYSE symbol*] (SG)
Std	Standard
STE	STERIS Corp. [*NYSE symbol*] (SG)
ste	Suite (BEE)
STEP	Small Towns Environment Program
StG	St. Louis Gunners [*National Football League*] [*1934*] (NFLA)
STGC	Startec Global Communic. [*NASDAQ symbol*] (SG)
STHLY	Stet Hellas Telecomm ADS [*NASDAQ symbol*] (SG)
STII	Sigma Theta Tau International (EA)
STIKSCAT	Stick Scatterometer (EOSA)
StL	St. Louis Rams [*National Football League*] [*1995-present*] (NFLA)
STNR	Steiner Leisure [*NASDAQ symbol*] (SG)
str	Strength (MILB)
STRM	StarMedia Network [*NASDAQ symbol*] (SG)
STRX	STAR Telecommunications [*NASDAQ symbol*] (SG)

STSR .... Spatiotemporal Stochastic Resonance
STVM .... Society for Tropical Veterinary Medicine (GVA)
STWS .... Storm Tide Warning Service (WEAT)
STY .... Star Data Systems [*Toronto Stock Exchange symbol*] (SG)
SU .... Soviet Urals [*Crude oil*]
SUB .... Supplemental Unemployment Compensation Benefit Trusts
SUCCESS ..... Subsonic Aircraft: Contrail and Cloud Effects Special Study [*NASA project*]
SULEV .... Super Low Emission Vehicle
SUM .... Successive Unsharp Masking
sum .... Summer
SUNET .... Swedish Network
SUR .... CNA Surety [*NYSE symbol*] (SG)
surg .... Surgeon (GEAB)
Surg .... Surgery (BEE)
SUT .... Superior Telecom [*NYSE symbol*] (SG)
SUV .... Sons of Union Veterans (GEAB)
SUV .... Sport-Utility Vechicle
s/v .... Sea View
SV .... Significant Violater [*Environmental Protection Agency*] (EPAT)
SVE .... Service Experts [*NYSE symbol*] (SG)
SVEPM .... Society for Veterinary Epidemiology and Preventive Medicine (GVA)
SVEV .... 7-Eleven,Inc. [*NASDAQ symbol*] (SG)
SVHFC .... Sweet Valley High Fan Club (EA)
SVI .... Scott Values Inventory
SVI .... SVI Holdings [*AMEX symbol*] (SG)
SVME .... Society for Veterinary Medical Ethics (GVA)
SVP .... Society of Vertebrate Palaeontology (QUAC)
SVR .... Silverleaf Resorts [*NYSE symbol*] (SG)
SVS .... Sheep Veterinary Society (GVA)

SVS .... State Veterinary Service [*British*] (GVA)
SW .... Star Wars [*Movie title*]
SWAN .... Solar Wind Anisotroples
SWAP .... Source Water Assessment Program [*Environmental Protection Agency*] (EPAT)
SWC .... Southwest Athletic Conference (EA)
SWC .... Stillwater Mining [*AMEX symbol*] (SG)
SWCA .... Self Winding Clock Association (EA)
SWD .... Shorewood Packaging [*NYSE symbol*] (SG)
SWIR .... Short-Wavelength Infrared (EOSA)
SWIRLS .... Stratospheric Wind Infrared Limb Sounder (EOSA)
SWITCH .... Switzerland Network
SWLDY .... Smallworldwide ADS [*NASDAQ symbol*] (SG)
SWORD .... Short-Range Missile Defense with Optimized Radar Distribution [*Military weapon system*]
SWPA .... Source Water Protection Area [*Environmental Protection Agency*] (EPAT)
SWQPPP ...... Source Water Quality Protection Partnership Petitions (EPAT)
SWS .... Southwest Securities Grp. [*NYSE symbol*] (SG)
sy .... Security (MILB)
SYBB .... SYNSORB Biotech [*NASDAQ symbol*] (SG)
SYC .... Sybron Chemicals [*AMEX symbol*] (SG)
SYI .... SY Bancorp [*AMEX symbol*] (SG)
SYK .... Stryker Corp. [*NYSE symbol*] (SG)
SYNOP .... Synoptic Report [*Meteorology*] (WEAT)
SYNT .... Syntel,Inc. [*NASDAQ symbol*] (SG)
SYOL .... See You Online [*Online dialog*]
SYS .... CPS Systems [*AMEX symbol*] (SG)
SYX .... Systemax,Inc. [*NYSE symbol*] (SG)
SZA .... Suiza Foods [*NYSE symbol*] (SG)

T
By Acronym

tac .... Tactical (MILB)
TAC .... Total Atmospheric Carbon (QUAC)
Tach .... Tachometer
TACOM .... Tank-Automotive and Armaments Command [Army]
TACOM-ARDEC... Tank Automotive and Armaments Command's Armament Research, Development, and Engieering Center [Army]
TAD .... Technical Assistance Document [Environmental Protection Agency] (EPAT)
TAE .... Transportable Applications Executive (EOSA)
TAFTA .... Transatlantic Free Trade Area
TAG .... Tag-It Pacific [AMEX symbol] (SG)
TAG .... Timneh African Grey [Bird]
TALK .... Talk.com,Inc. [NASDAQ symbol] (SG)
TAM .... Tropical Asian Monsoon (QUAC)
TAMR .... Teen Association of Model Railroaders (EA)
T&E .... Test and Evaluation
TAP .... Troutwine Athletic Profile
TAR .... Threshold Autoregression
TARR .... Tarragon Realty Investors [NASDAQ symbol] (SG)
TAS .... Tolerance Assessment System (EPAT)
TASC........... Treatment Alternatives for Safe Commission [Illinois project]
TB .... Tampa Bay Buccaneers [National Football League] [1976-present] (NFLA)
TBB .... Teenie Beanie Babies [Ty, Inc.]
TBC .... Technology Business Council
TBFC .... Telebanc Financial [NASDAQ symbol] (SG)
TC .... Technology and Culture [A publication]
TCA .... Traditional Cat Association (EA)
TCC .... Trammell Crow [NYSE symbol] (SG)
TCC .... Transmission Congestion Contract
TCLP .... Total Concentrate Leachate Procedure (EPAT)
TCLPZ .... TC Pipelines L.P. [NASDAQ symbol] (SG)
TCM .... Tropical Cyclone Motion
TCN .... Tele Norte Celular Part ADS [NYSE symbol] (SG)
TCP............. Turkish Committee for Palynology (QUAC)
TCPS........... Twentieth Century Petroleum Statistics [1997] [A publication]
TCR .... Cornerstone Realty Income Tr [NYSE symbol] (SG)
TD50 .... Tumorigenic Dose 50
TDR .... TRICOM SA ADR [NYSE symbol] (SG)
TDX............. Thermedics Detection [AMEX symbol] (SG)
TECII .... Total Environmental Concern Interaction Index
TEK .... Traditional Environmental Knowledge (QUAC)
Tel & Tel .... Telephone and Telegraph (PROS)
Telecomm ... Telecommunications (BEE)
TEMO .... Training, Exercises, and Military Operations [Army]
TEMPO......... Temporarily (WEAT)
tempy .... Temporary (MILB)
Ten .... Tennessee Titans [National Football League] [1999-present] (NFLA)
TENF........... TenFold Corp. [NASDAQ symbol] (SG)
TEO .... Tel Argentina-France Tel'B'ADS [NYSE symbol] (SG)
TeO .... Tennessee Oilers [National Football League] [1997-98] (NFLA)
TER............. Tau Epsilon Rho Law Society (EA)
terr............. Territory (BEE)
TERSE.......... Tunable Etalon Remote Sounder of Earth (EOSA)
TES .... Tropospheric Emission Spectrometer
TESE .... Testicular Sperm Extraction [Medicine]
test .... Testament (GEAB)
TET .... Technical Evaluation Testing
TEVRO .... Tennessee Equine Veterinary Research Organization (GVA)
TEXM .... Texas Micro [NASDAQ symbol] (SG)
TFAP .... Trade Facilitation Action Plan [Singapore]
TFR............. Tefron Ltd. [NYSE symbol] (SG)
Tg .... Togo (MILB)
TGAI........... Technical Grade of the Active Ingredient (EPAT)
TGI............. Triumph Group [NYSE symbol] (SG)
TGL............. Triangle Bancorp [NYSE symbol] (SG)
TGLO .... theglobe.com [NASDAQ symbol] (SG)
TGNT .... Teligent,Inc.'A' [NASDAQ symbol] (SG)
TGO .... Teleglobe,Inc. [NYSE symbol] (SG)
TGP............. Technical Grade Product (EPAT)
Th .... Thailand (MILB)
TH............... Treasure Hunt [Toy collection]
Theol .... Theology (BEE)
THQI .... THQ,Inc. [NASDAQ symbol] (SG)
THT .... Todhunter Intl. [AMEX symbol] (SG)
TIAC........... Thrift Institution Advisory Council

TIB .... Temple Index Bureau (GEAB)
TICCC.......... Terlingua International Championship Chili Cook-Off [An association] (EA)
Tiel............. Cockatiel [Bird]
TIGER .... Trans-Iron Galactic Element Recorder
TIM .... FIRSTPLUS Finl 7.25%'TIMES' [AMEX symbol] (SG)
TiO............. Titanium Oxide
TIS .... Tolerance Index System [Environmental science] (EPAT)
TIWI............ Telesystem Intl.Wireless [NASDAQ symbol] (SG)
Tjk .... Tajikistan (MILB)
TJS .... Texas Journal of Science [A publication]
tk .... Tank (MILB)
TK .... Traditional Knowledge (QUAC)
Tkm .... Turkmenistan (MILB)
tkr .... Tanker (MILB)
TLA .... Texas Library Association
TLCF........... Team Leader Computing Facility (EOSA)
TLE .... Two-Line Elements
TLIFC.......... Tracy Lynne International Fan Club (EA)
TLM .... Talisman Energy [NYSE symbol] (SG)
TM .... Total Moisture [Coal industry]
TMC .... Technical Manufacturing Corporation
TMC .... Terminate, Monitor, and Control
TMP .... Tompkins Trustco [AMEX symbol] (SG)
Tn .... Tunisia (MILB)
TND .... Tele Nordeste Cel Partici ADS [NYSE symbol] (SG)
TNE .... Tele Norte Leste Partici ADS [NYSE symbol] (SG)
TNHC .... Texas Natural History Collection [Austin]
TNS .... Technology Needs Survey
TNT .... A.O. Tatneft ADS [NYSE symbol] (SG)
TNZR .... Tranz Rail Hlds ADS [NASDAQ symbol] (SG)
TOCR .... Total Ownership Cost Reduction
TOMUIS ...... 3-Dimensional Ozone Mapping with Ultraviolet Imaging Spectrometer (EOSA)
Too .... Cockatoo [Bird]
top .... Topographical (GEAB)
TOPS .... Treatment Outcome Prospective Study
torp............. Torpedo (MILB)
TOY .... Thinking of You [Online dialog]
TP .... Technical Product (EPAT)
TP .... Textile Processors, Service Trades, Health Care Professional, and Technical Em ployees International Union
TP .... TNT Post Group ADS [NYSE symbol] (SG)
Tp .... Township (GEAB)
tp .... Troop (MILB)
TPC .... Testing Priorities Committee [Environmental science] (EPAT)
TPC .... Top Air Mfg. [AMEX symbol] (SG)
TPC .... Tropical Prediction Center
TPN .... TownPagesNet.com ADS [AMEX symbol] (SG)
TPS .... Temporary Protected Status
tpt .... Transport (MILB)
TPW .... Total Precipitable Water
tr .... Trillion (MILB)
TRAC .... Tolerance Review Assessment Committee [EPA]
Trans .... Transportation (BEE)
transcr......... Transcribed (GEAB)
transl.......... Translation (GEAB)
trg .... Training (MILB)
TRIB............ Temple Records Index Bureau (GEAB)
TRI-FED ...... USA Triathlon [An association] (EA)
Trig............. Trigonometry (BEE)
TRO .... Tele Centro Oeste Partici ADS [NYSE symbol] (SG)
TRT .... Trio-Tech Intl. [AMEX symbol] (SG)
trust............ Trustee (PROS)
TRV .... Thousand Trails [AMEX symbol] (SG)
TS .... Total Sulphur [Coal industry]
TSD .... Tele Sudeste Celular Part ADS [NYSE symbol] (SG)
TSE .... Tokyo Stock Exchange
TSFC........... Three Stooges Fan Club (EA)
TSFW .... TSI Intl.Software [NASDAQ symbol] (SG)
TSI .... Thermal System Insulation (EPAT)
TSN .... Tyson Foods Cl'A' [NYSE symbol] (SG)
TSP............. Telesp Participacoes ADS [NYSE symbol] (SG)
TSP............. Texas Star Party
TSR............. Thermal and Solar Radiometer
TSU............. Tele Celular Sul Partici ADS [NYSE symbol] (SG)

TT	Technology Team
TTA	Treasure Hunting Research and Information Center [*Formerly, Treasure Trove Archives*] (EA)
TTCL	Tanzania Telecommunications Corporation Ltd.
TTI	TETRA Technologies [*NYSE symbol*] (SG)
TTNT	Till the Next Time [*Online dialog*]
Tu	Turkey (MILB)
TUI	Transportation Components [*NYSE symbol*] (SG)
TUNE	TCI Music'A' [*NASDAQ symbol*] (SG)
TUTS	Tut Systems [*NASDAQ symbol*] (SG)
TVC	Tenn Val Auth'PARRS' 'D' [*NYSE symbol*] (SG)
TVE	Tenn Val Auth'PARRS'2029 [*NYSE symbol*] (SG)
TVGIA	TV Guide'A' [*NASDAQ symbol*] (SG)
TVI	Temporary Veterinary Inspector [*British*] (GVA)
TVMA	Texas Veterinary Medical Association (GVA)
TVOC	Total Volatile Organic Compound (EPAT)
TVRCCNA	TVR Car Club North America (EA)
TWE	TD Waterhouse Group [*NYSE symbol*] (SG)
TWH	Transworld HealthCare [*AMEX symbol*] (SG)
TWLB	Twinlab Corp. [*NASDAQ symbol*] (SG)
twn	Town (GEAB)
twp	Township (BEE)
TWP	Trex Co. [*NYSE symbol*] (SG)
TWR	Tower Automotive [*NYSE symbol*] (SG)
TWRS	Crown Castle Intl. [*NASDAQ symbol*] (SG)
TWS	Transient Water System (EPAT)
TWV	Tactical Wheeled Vehicle [*Military*]
TWVRMO	Tactical Wheeled Vehicle Requirements Management Office [*Army*]
ty	Territory (GEAB)
TYL	Tyler Technologies [*NYSE symbol*] (SG)
Tz	Tanzania (MILB)
TZA	TV Azteca,S.A. ADS [*NYSE symbol*] (SG)

U

By Acronym

U2 .... Umbrella Cockatoo [*Bird*]
UAF .... Union of Feminine Action [*Morocco*]
UAI .... Unistar Financial Svc. [*AMEX symbol*] (SG)
UAMM .... University of Arizona Mineral Museum
UAOSTE ...... United Association of Office, Sales, and Technical Employees
UAWIU .... General Service Employees Union Local 73 (EA)
UBB .... Unibanco Banc/Unibanco Hld GDS [*NYSE symbol*] (SG)
UBCF .... United Burmese Cat Fanciers (EA)
UBL .... United Bank Limited [*Pakistan*]
UBP .... Urstadt Biddle Properties [*NYSE symbol*] (SG)
UBPPA .... Uni-Bell Pipe Association
UCCC .... United Council of Corvette Clubs (EA)
UCMP .... University of California Museum of Paleontology
UCP .... UniCapital Corp. [*NYSE symbol*] (SG)
UDG .... Unidigital,Inc. [*AMEX symbol*] (SG)
UDM .... United Domin Rlty Tr 8.50 Percent Nts [*NYSE symbol*] (SG)
UDP .... Under-Drive Pulley [*Automotive term*]
Uga .... Uganda (MILB)
UGS .... Unigraphics Solutions'A' [*NYSE symbol*] (SG)
UGSOA .... United Government Security Officers of America
UH .... University of Hertfordshire [*England*]
UHIE .... Urban Heat Island Effect [*Meteorology*] (WEAT)
UIS .... Universal Infinity-Corrected Objective
UKB .... UK Brent [*Crude oil*]
UKERF .... University of Kentucky Equine Research Foundation (GVA)
Ukr .... Ukraine (MILB)
ULDB .... Ultra Long Duration Balloon
UMR .... Uniform Mixture Ratio
UMS .... University Musical Society
Un .... United (PROS)
UNA .... UNOVA,Inc. [*NYSE symbol*] (SG)
UNAC .... United Nurses Associations of California
UNAM .... National Autonomous University of Mexico
UNAVEM I .... Unlted Nations Angola Verification Mission
Unc .... Uncirculated [*Numismatic term*]
UniS .... University of Surrey
unm .... Unmarried (GEAB)
unorg .... Unorganized (GEAB)
UPCOY .... United Pan-Euro Commun ADS [*NASDAQ symbol*] (SG)
UPEA .... Utah Public Employees Association
UPFC .... United PanAm Finl. [*NASDAQ symbol*] (SG)
Uph .... Upholstery
UPM .... UPM-Kymmene Corp.ADS [*NYSE symbol*] (SG)

UR .... Unidad Revolucionario [*Cuban political movement*]
URI .... United Rentals [*NYSE symbol*] (SG)
Ury .... Uruguay (MILB)
USAA .... United Services Automobile Association
USAB .... U.S.A Boxing [*An association*] (EA)
USA GYM .... U.S.A Gymnastics [*An association*] (EA)
USAH .... U.S.A. Hockey [*An association*] (EA)
USAI .... USA Networks [*NASDAQ symbol*] (SG)
USANA .... United Sportsmans Association of North America (EA)
USARC .... United States Arctic Research Commission (QUAC)
USATF .... U.S.A. Track and Field [*An association*] (EA)
USATT .... U.S.A. Table Tennis [*An association*] (EA)
USAUF .... United States of America Underwater Federation (EA)
USB .... U.S. Bancorp [*NYSE symbol*] (SG)
USBF .... U.S.A. Baseball [*An association*] (EA)
US Chess .... United States Chess Federation (EA)
USDCAT ...... U.S. Deaf Cycling Association (EA)
USDel .... United States Delegation
USDOL .... U.S. Department of Labor
USEA .... Utah School Employees Association
USG .... Uniform Selection Guidelines
USISA .... United States International Speedskating Association (EA)
USIT .... Unit Share Investment Trust
USIX .... USinternetworking, Inc. [*NASDAQ symbol*] (SG)
USL .... US Liquid [*AMEX symbol*] (SG)
USLASA .... United States les Autres Sports Association (EA)
US/MC .... United States/Memorandum of Conversation
USOA .... Underwater Society of America (EA)
USON .... US Oncology [*NASDAQ symbol*] (SG)
USPL .... U.S. Plastic Lumber [*Stock market symbol*]
USRowing .... United States Rowing Association (EA)
USSF .... United States Sailing Foundation (EA)
USSS .... United States Synchronized Swimming [*An association*] (EA)
USSTF .... United States Ski Team Foundation (EA)
USU .... USEC, Inc. [*NYSE symbol*] (SG)
USWA .... United States Windsurfing Association (EA)
USWB .... USWeb Corp. [*NASDAQ symbol*] (SG)
UTI .... Urinary Tract Infection [*Medicine*]
utl .... Utility (MILB)
u/w/o .... Under the Will Of (PROS)
UWS .... Urban Wildlife Society (GVA)
UXP .... U.S. Exploration [*AMEX symbol*] (SG)
Uz .... Uzbekistan (MILB)

V

By Acronym

V .... Varying (WEAT)
VAa .... Alveolar Ventilation Rate for Experimental Animal Species
VAAJ .... Veterinary Association for Arbitration and Jurisprudence (GVA)
VAh .... Alveolar Ventilation Rate for Human
VALT .... Variable-Stress Accelerated Life Testing Trials
VAN .... Value Added Network
VAR .... Varian Medical Systems [*NYSE symbol*] (SG)
VATS .... Video-Assisted Thoracic Spine Surgery
VBF .... Veterinary Benevolent Fund (GVA)
VC .... Vinegar Connoiseurs (EA)
VCA .... Vizsla Club of America (EA)
VCAS .... Vermont Comprehensive Assessment System
VCD .... Vocal Cord Dysfunction [*Medicine*]
vchmn .... Vice Chairman (PROS)
VCO .... Voltage Controlled Oscillator
VCOA .... Vespa Club of America (EA)
VCP .... Voluntary Cleanup Program [*Environmental science*] (EPAT)
VDAT .... Visual Data [*NASDAQ symbol*] (SG)
VDCE .... Virtual Distributed Collaborative Environment
VDS .... Veterinary Deer Society (GVA)
Ve .... Venezuela (MILB)
VEB .... Veba Corp.ADS [*NYSE symbol*] (SG)
veh .... Vehicle (MILB)
VEI .... Vista Energy Resources [*AMEX symbol*] (SG)
VERnet........ Virginia Education and Research Network
VERT........... VerticalNet,Inc. [*NASDAQ symbol*] (SG)
VHEVPG ...... Vehicle and Heavy Equipment Virtual Proving Ground
VHS .... Veterinary History Society (GVA)
VIBES.......... Virtual International Business and Economics Sources [*Internet resource*]
VIC.............. Very Inexpensive Computer
VIDI .... Vidikron Technologies Group [*NASDAQ symbol*] (SG)
VIGN .... Vignette Corp. [*NASDAQ symbol*] (SG)
VIRS .... Visible Infrared Scanner (EOSA)

VIRSR.......... Visible Infrared Scanning Radiometer (EOSA)
Visc .... Viscount (GEAB)
VISI............. Volar Intercalary Segment Instability
VIU............. Venice International University [*Italy*]
VIZ............. Visualization
VL............... Vlasic Foods,Intl. [*NYSE symbol*] (SG)
VLTS........... Valentis [*Stock market symbol*]
VMHA .... Veterinary Meat Hygiene Adviser (GVA)
VMS........... Vertical Marketing System
VN............. Veterinary Nurse (GVA)
Vn............. Vietnam (MILB)
VNT........... Compania Cervecerias Unidas ADS [*NYSE symbol*] (SG)
VNWK .... Visual Networks [*NASDAQ symbol*] (SG)
VOAR .... Mount Pearl, NF [*AM radio station call letters*] (BROA)
VOCL .... VocalTec Commun. Ltd. [*NASDAQ symbol*] (SG)
VOL............ Volt Info Sciences [*NYSE symbol*] (SG)
VOO .... Vornado Operating [*AMEX symbol*] (SG)
VOS .... Vehicle Operating Survey (EPAT)
VOYN .... Voyager.net [*NASDAQ symbol*] (SG)
VPG .... Virtual Proving Ground
VPHA.......... Veterinary Public Health Association (GVA)
VPMA......... Veterinary Practice Management Association (GVA)
VPS............ Vermont Pure Hldgs. Ltd. [*AMEX symbol*] (SG)
VRIO........... Verio,Inc. [*NASDAQ symbol*] (SG)
VRSN......... VeriSign,Inc. [*NASDAQ symbol*] (SG)
VS............. Video Services [*AMEX symbol*] (SG)
VSA/1800..... Volvo Sports America Registry (EA)
VSCRFC ...... Vince Smith and Carol Redo Fan Club (EA)
VSF .... Vita Food Products [*AMEX symbol*] (SG)
VSOHP........ Visual Satellite Observer's Home Page
VTR............ Ventas,Inc. [*NYSE symbol*] (SG)
VUSA.......... Value America [*NASDAQ symbol*] (SG)
VVMA......... Virginia Veterinary Medical Association (GVA)
VWD .... Veterinary Written Direction (GVA)
VYSI........... Vysis,Inc. [*NASDAQ symbol*] (SG)

W

By Acronym

w .... West (GEAB)
WA .... Western Atlantic (QUAC)
WAAT .... Olyphant, PA [*AM radio station call letters*] (BROA)
WABC-DT .... New York, NY [*Television station call letters*] (BROA)
WABG-TV .... Greenwood, MS [*Television station call letters*] (BROA)
WACA .... Wheaton, MD [*AM radio station call letters*] (BROA)
WACL-FM .... Elkton, VA [*FM radio station call letters*] (BROA)
WACQ-FM .... Tallassee, AL [*FM radio station call letters*] (BROA)
WADB .... Asbury Park, NJ [*AM radio station call letters*] (BROA)
WAEF-FM .... Cordele, GA [*FM radio station call letters*] (BROA)
WAFAC .... Wide-Angle Free-Air Chamber
WAFN-FM .... Arab, AL [*FM radio station call letters*] (BROA)
wag .... Wagoner (GEAB)
WAGA-DT .... Atlanta, GA [*Television station call letters*] (BROA)
WAGC .... World Amateur Golf Council (EA)
WAHI .... Knoxville, TN [*AM radio station call letters*] (BROA)
WAJM-FM .... Atlantic City, NJ [*FM radio station call letters*] (BROA)
WAKC-FM .... Pittsfield, IL [*FM radio station call letters*] (BROA)
WAKV .... Otsego, MI [*AM radio station call letters*] (BROA)
WAKX-FM .... Narragansett Pier, RI [*FM radio station call letters*] (BROA)
WALC-FM .... Charleston, SC [*FM radio station call letters*] (BROA)
WAMI-TV ..... Hollywood, FL [*Television station call letters*] (BROA)
WAMJ-FM .... Roswell, GA [*FM radio station call letters*] (BROA)
WAMO-FM .... Beaver Falls, PA [*FM radio station call letters*] (BROA)
WAMX-FM .... Milton, WV [*FM radio station call letters*] (BROA)
W&S .... Wage & Salary
WANG-FM .... Havelock, NC [*FM radio station call letters*] (BROA)
WAOY-FM .... Gulfport, MS [*FM radio station call letters*] (BROA)
WAQD-FM .... Alberta, VA [*FM radio station call letters*] (BROA)
WARD-FM .... Charlotte Amalie, VI [*FM radio station call letters*] (BROA)
WARN-FM .... Culpepper, VA [*FM radio station call letters*] (BROA)
Was .... Washington Redskins [*National Football League*] [*1937-present*]
                     (NFLA)
WASM-FM .... Natchez, MS [*FM radio station call letters*] (BROA)
WASW-FM .... Waycross, GA [*FM radio station call letters*] (BROA)
WATU-FM .... Port Gibson, MS [*FM radio station call letters*] (BROA)
WATY-FM .... Folkston, GA [*FM radio station call letters*] (BROA)
WAUT-FM .... Tullahoma, TN [*FM radio station call letters*] (BROA)
WAUV-FM .... Ripley, TN [*FM radio station call letters*] (BROA)
WAUZ-FM .... Greensburg, IN [*FM radio station call letters*] (BROA)
WAVE .... World Association of Veterinary Educators (GVA)
WAVG .... Jeffersonville, IN [*AM radio station call letters*] (BROA)
WAVO .... WAVO Corp. [*NASDAQ symbol*] (SG)
WAVT-FM .... Pottsville, PA [*FM radio station call letters*] (BROA)
WAVW-FM .... Gifford, FL [*FM radio station call letters*] (BROA)
WAWV .... World Association of Wildlife Veterinarians (GVA)
WAXD .... Adel, GA [*AM radio station call letters*] (BROA)
WAXK .... Jewett, NY [*FM radio station call letters*] (BROA)
WAXP .... Warner Robins, GA [*AM radio station call letters*] (BROA)
WAXU-FM .... Troy, AL [*FM radio station call letters*] (BROA)
WAYD-FM .... Islesboro, ME [*FM radio station call letters*] (BROA)
WAYG-FM .... Grand Rapids, MI [*FM radio station call letters*] (BROA)
WAYH-FM .... Port Wentworth, GA [*FM radio station call letters*] (BROA)
WAYI-FM .... Thomaston, AL [*FM radio station call letters*] (BROA)
WAYR-FM .... Brunswick, GA [*FM radio station call letters*] (BROA)
WAYU .... Rochester, NH [*AM radio station call letters*] (BROA)
WAZA-FM .... Liberty, MS [*FM radio station call letters*] (BROA)
WAZD-FM .... Savannah, TN [*FM radio station call letters*] (BROA)
WAZG .... Myrtle Beach, SC [*AM radio station call letters*] (BROA)
WAZI .... Sussex, WI [*AM radio station call letters*] (BROA)
WAZJ .... Atlanta, GA [*AM radio station call letters*] (BROA)
WAZO-FM .... Shallotte, NC [*FM radio station call letters*] (BROA)
WAZP-FM .... Cape Charles, VA [*FM radio station call letters*] (BROA)
WAZU-FM .... Circleville, OH [*FM radio station call letters*] (BROA)
WAZV-FM .... Norwood, NY [*FM radio station call letters*] (BROA)
WAZW .... Antigo, WI [*Television station call letters*] (BROA)
WAZY .... Lafayette, IN [*AM radio station call letters*] (BROA)
WAZZ .... Fayetteville, NC [*AM radio station call letters*] (BROA)
WB .... Warbirds of America [*An association*] (EA)
WB .... Welcome Back [*Online dialog*]
WBA .... World Bocce Association (EA)
WBAH .... Elizabeth, NJ [*AM radio station call letters*] (BROA)
WBAL-DT .... Baltimore, MD [*Television station call letters*] (BROA)
WBBB-FM .... Raleigh, NC [*FM radio station call letters*] (BROA)
WBBE-FM .... Vero Beach, FL [*FM radio station call letters*] (BROA)
WBBF-FM .... Rochester, NY [*FM radio station call letters*] (BROA)

WBBI-FM ..... Endwell, NY [*FM radio station call letters*] (BROA)
WBBM-DT .... Chicago, IL [*Television station call letters*] (BROA)
WBBN-FM .... Laurel, MS [*FM radio station call letters*] (BROA)
WBCD-FM .... Headland, AL [*FM radio station call letters*] (BROA)
WBCS-FM .... Jasper, GA [*FM radio station call letters*] (BROA)
WBCY-FM .... Archbold, OH [*FM radio station call letters*] (BROA)
WBDCS .... Wide-Band Data Collection System (EOSA)
WBDI .... Highland, IL [*AM radio station call letters*] (BROA)
WBDM-FM .... Canton, IL [*FM radio station call letters*] (BROA)
WBDO .... Palm City, FL [*AM radio station call letters*] (BROA)
WBDQ-FM .... Cross Hill, SC [*FM radio station call letters*] (BROA)
WBDS-FM .... Norlina, NC [*FM radio station call letters*] (BROA)
WBDW-FM .... Knoxville, IL [*FM radio station call letters*] (BROA)
WBDY .... Bluefield, VA [*AM radio station call letters*] (BROA)
WBEH-FM .... Norris, TN [*FM radio station call letters*] (BROA)
WBEO-FM .... Machias, ME [*AM radio station call letters*] (BROA)
WBEP-FM .... Siren, WI [*FM radio station call letters*] (BROA)
WBEU-FM .... Brookville, PA [*FM radio station call letters*] (BROA)
WBFA-FM .... Smiths, AL [*FM radio station call letters*] (BROA)
WBFE-FM .... Barron, WI [*FM radio station call letters*] (BROA)
WBFG-FM .... Parker's Crossroads, TN [*FM radio station call letters*] (BROA)
WBFK-FM .... Roann, IN [*FM radio station call letters*] (BROA)
WBFW-FM .... Flora, IL [*FM radio station call letters*] (BROA)
WBFY-FM .... Pinehurst, NC [*FM radio station call letters*] (BROA)
WBFZ-FM .... Selma, AL [*FM radio station call letters*] (BROA)
WBGB-FM .... Ponte Vedra Beach, FL [*FM radio station call letters*] (BROA)
WBGI-FM .... Mantoo, NC [*FM radio station call letters*] (BROA)
WBGJ-FM .... Sylvan Beach, NY [*FM radio station call letters*] (BROA)
WBGK-FM .... Old Forge, NY [*FM radio station call letters*] (BROA)
WBGP-FM .... Pensacola, FL [*FM radio station call letters*] (BROA)
WBGQ-FM .... Bulls Gap, TN [*FM radio station call letters*] (BROA)
WBGY-FM .... Naples, FL [*FM radio station call letters*] (BROA)
WBHB-FM .... New Market, VA [*FM radio station call letters*] (BROA)
WBHE .... Charlotte, NC [*AM radio station call letters*] (BROA)
WBHR .... Saulk Rapids, MN [*AM radio station call letters*] (BROA)
WBHU-FM .... Bayboro, NC [*FM radio station call letters*] (BROA)
WBHZ-FM .... Elkins, WV [*FM radio station call letters*] (BROA)
WBIA-FM .... Shelbyville, TN [*AM radio station call letters*] (BROA)
WBID-FM .... Wilmington, NC [*FM radio station call letters*] (BROA)
WBIE-FM .... Delphos, OH [*FM radio station call letters*] (BROA)
WBIS .... Annapolis, MD [*AM radio station call letters*] (BROA)
WBIX-FM .... New York, NY [*FM radio station call letters*] (BROA)
WBJZ-FM .... Berlin, WI [*FM radio station call letters*] (BROA)
WBKS-FM .... Greenwood, IN [*FM radio station call letters*] (BROA)
WBKT-FM .... Norwich, NY [*FM radio station call letters*] (BROA)
WBKX-FM .... Yankeetown, FL [*FM radio station call letters*] (BROA)
WBLO-FM .... Charlestown, IN [*FM radio station call letters*] (BROA)
WBMR-FM .... Telford, PA [*FM radio station call letters*] (BROA)
WBMZ-FM .... Metter, GA [*FM radio station call letters*] (BROA)
WBNN-FM .... Dillwyn, VA [*FM radio station call letters*] (BROA)
WBNS-DT .... Columbus, OH [*Television station call letters*] (BROA)
WBNS-FM .... Columbus, OH [*FM radio station call letters*] (BROA)
WBOB .... Florence, KY [*AM radio station call letters*] (BROA)
WBQW-FM .... Scarborough, ME [*FM radio station call letters*] (BROA)
WBRK-FM .... Pittsfield, MA [*FM radio station call letters*] (BROA)
WBRO-FM .... Kankakee, IL [*FM radio station call letters*] (BROA)
WBT-FM ...... Chester, SC [*FM radio station call letters*] (BROA)
WBTJ-FM .... Hubbard, OH [*FM radio station call letters*] (BROA)
WBTN-FM .... Bennington, VT [*FM radio station call letters*] (BROA)
WBTR .... Carrollton, GA [*AM radio station call letters*] (BROA)
WBTV-DT .... Charlotte, NC [*Television station call letters*] (BROA)
WBUB .... Washington Court (BROA)
WBUR .... West Yarmouth, MA [*AM radio station call letters*] (BROA)
WBUS-FM .... Boalsburg, PA [*FM radio station call letters*] (BROA)
WBVA .... Bayside, VA [*AM radio station call letters*] (BROA)
WBVS-FM .... Coal City, IL [*FM radio station call letters*] (BROA)
WBXX-TV .... Crossville, TN [*Television station call letters*] (BROA)
WBXY-FM .... Newberry, FL [*FM radio station call letters*] (BROA)
WBYM .... Hampton, VA [*AM radio station call letters*] (BROA)
WBZ-DT ...... Boston, MA [*Television station call letters*] (BROA)
WBZL .... Miami, FL [*Television station call letters*] (BROA)
WBZV-FM .... Christianburg, VA [*FM radio station call letters*] (BROA)
WCA .... Water Conservation Area
WCAA-FM .... Newark, NJ [*FM radio station call letters*] (BROA)
WCAL-FM .... Northfield, MN [*FM radio station call letters*] (BROA)
WCAN-FM .... Canajoharie, NY [*FM radio station call letters*] (BROA)

WCAT-FM .... Athol, MA [*FM radio station call letters*] (BROA)
WCAU-DT .... Philadelphia, PA [*Television station call letters*] (BROA)
WCAV-FM .... Brockton, MA [*FM radio station call letters*] (BROA)
WCBE-FM .... Columbus, OH [*FM radio station call letters*] (BROA)
WCBJ-FM .... Campton, KY [*FM radio station call letters*] (BROA)
WCBS-DT .... New York, NY [*Television station call letters*] (BROA)
WCC .... Watson's Collectors' Club (EA)
WCC .... WESCO International [*NYSE symbol*] (SG)
WCCB-DT .... Charlotte, NC [*Television station call letters*] (BROA)
WCCL-FM .... Punta Rassa, FL [*FM radio station call letters*] (BROA)
WCH .... Working Class Hero Beatles Club (EA)
WCHA-FM .... Greencastle, PA [*FM radio station call letters*] (BROA)
WCHK-FM .... Talking Rock, GA [*FM radio station call letters*] (BROA)
WCHR .... Trenton, NJ [*AM radio station call letters*] (BROA)
WCLB .... West Coast Lumber Inspection Bureau
WCLU-FM .... Munfordville, KY [*FM radio station call letters*] (BROA)
WCLX-FM .... McArthur, OH [*FM radio station call letters*] (BROA)
WCMB-FM .... Oscoda, MI [*FM radio station call letters*] (BROA)
WCOL-FM .... Columbus, OH [*FM radio station call letters*] (BROA)
WCPI-FM .... McMinnville, TN [*FM radio station call letters*] (BROA)
WCPO-DT .... Cincinnati, OH [*Television station call letters*] (BROA)
WCPX .... Chicago, IL [*Television station call letters*] (BROA)
WCQL-FM .... Glens Fall, NY [*FM radio station call letters*] (BROA)
WCRQ-FM .... Dennysville, ME [*FM radio station call letters*] (BROA)
WCRS-FM .... Greenwood, SC [*FM radio station call letters*] (BROA)
WCSP-FM .... Washington, DC [*FM radio station call letters*] (BROA)
WCTA-FM .... San German, PR [*FM radio station call letters*] (BROA)
WCTD-FM .... Dallas, PA [*FM radio station call letters*] (BROA)
WCTP-FM .... Carbondale, PA [*FM radio station call letters*] (BROA)
WCVB-DT .... Boston, MA [*Television station call letters*] (BROA)
WCVC-FM .... Wise, VA [*FM radio station call letters*] (BROA)
WCVI-TV .... Christiansted, VI [*Television station call letters*] (BROA)
WCVT-FM .... Stowe, VT [*FM radio station call letters*] (BROA)
WCWB .... Pittsburgh, PA [*Television station call letters*] (BROA)
WCYK .... Crozet, VA [*AM radio station call letters*] (BROA)
WCZZ-FM .... London, OH [*FM radio station call letters*] (BROA)
wd .... Widow (GEAB)
WDCD-FM .... Clifton Park, NY [*FM radio station call letters*] (BROA)
WDCQ .... University Center, MI [*Television station call letters*] (BROA)
WDCZ .... Rochester, NY [*AM radio station call letters*] (BROA)
WDEO .... Saline, MI [*AM radio station call letters*] (BROA)
WDHP .... Frederiksted, VI [*AM radio station call letters*] (BROA)
WDID .... Shelbyville, IL [*AM radio station call letters*] (BROA)
WDIN-FM .... Camuy, PR [*FM radio station call letters*] (BROA)
WDIV-DT .... Detroit, MI [*Television station call letters*] (BROA)
WDIZ .... Panama City, FL [*AM radio station call letters*] (BROA)
WDJA .... West Palm Beach, FL [*AM radio station call letters*] (BROA)
WDKS-FM .... Newburgh, IN [*FM radio station call letters*] (BROA)
WDLS-FM .... Old Forge, NY [*FM radio station call letters*] (BROA)
WDLT .... Fairhope, AL [*AM radio station call letters*] (BROA)
WDLX .... Washington, NC [*AM radio station call letters*] (BROA)
WDLZ-FM .... Murfreesboro, NC [*FM radio station call letters*] (BROA)
WDMN .... Toledo, OH [*AM radio station call letters*] (BROA)
WDOT .... Plattsburgh, NY [*AM radio station call letters*] (BROA)
WDR .... Waddell & Reed Fin'l 'A' [*NYSE symbol*] (SG)
WDRE-FM .... Westhampton, NY [*FM radio station call letters*] (BROA)
WDRF .... Woodruff, SC [*AM radio station call letters*] (BROA)
WDRL-TV .... Danville, VA [*Television station call letters*] (BROA)
WDRV-FM .... Pittsburgh, PA [*FM radio station call letters*] (BROA)
WDTJ-FM .... Detroit, MI [*FM radio station call letters*] (BROA)
WDTL-TV .... Greenville, MS [*Television station call letters*] (BROA)
WDZD-FM .... Ocean Isle Beach, NC [*FM radio station call letters*] (BROA)
WDZK .... Bloomfield, CT [*AM radio station call letters*] (BROA)
WDZN-FM .... Romney, WV [*FM radio station call letters*] (BROA)
WDZY .... Colonial Heights, VA [*AM radio station call letters*] (BROA)
WEA .... Westfield America [*NYSE symbol*] (SG)
WEAE .... Pittsburgh, Pa [*AM radio station call letters*] (BROA)
WEAL .... Greensboro, NC [*AM radio station call letters*] (BROA)
WECT .... World Encyclopedia of Contemporary Theatre [*A publication*]
WEDA-FM .... Homewood, AL [*FM radio station call letters*] (BROA)
WEEK-FM .... Eureka, IL [*FM radio station call letters*] (BROA)
WEEO-FM .... McConnellsburg, PA [*FM radio station call letters*] (BROA)
WEGE-FM .... Westerville, OH [*FM radio station call letters*] (BROA)
WEGH-FM .... Northumberland, PA [*FM radio station call letters*] (BROA)
WEHR-FM .... Elberton, GA [*FM radio station call letters*] (BROA)
WEJC-FM .... White Star, MI [*FM radio station call letters*] (BROA)
WEL .... Boots&Coots Intl. Well Control [*AMEX symbol*] (SG)
WELL-FM .... Dadeville, AL [*FM radio station call letters*] (BROA)
WELS-FM .... Kinston, NC [*FM radio station call letters*] (BROA)
WEMA .... Wisconsin Educational Media Association
WEMY-FM .... Green Bay, WI [*FM radio station call letters*] (BROA)
WERI-FM .... Block Island, RI [*FM radio station call letters*] (BROA)
WESH-DT .... Daytona Beach, FL [*Television station call letters*] (BROA)
WESK-FM .... Loudon, TN [*FM radio station call letters*] (BROA)
WESR-FM .... Onley-Onancock, VA [*FM radio station call letters*] (BROA)
WETA-DT .... Washington, DC [*Television station call letters*] (BROA)
WEVA .... World Equine Veterinary Association (GVA)
WEWS-DT .... Cleveland, OH [*Television station call letters*] (BROA)
WEXP-FM .... Brandon, VT [*FM radio station call letters*] (BROA)
WEZC .... Neon, KY [*AM radio station call letters*] (BROA)
WEZI .... Harrisonburg, VA [*AM radio station call letters*] (BROA)
WEZN .... Birmingham, AL [*AM radio station call letters*] (BROA)
WEZO .... Rochester, NY [*AM radio station call letters*] (BROA)
WEZU .... Stillwater, MN [*AM radio station call letters*] (BROA)
WFAA-DT .... Dallas, TX [*Television station call letters*] (BROA)
WFAL-FM .... Falmouth, VA [*FM radio station call letters*] (BROA)
WFCG-FM .... Franklinton, LA [*FM radio station call letters*] (BROA)
WFCM .... Smyrna, TN [*AM radio station call letters*] (BROA)
WFFX .... Meridian, MS [*AM radio station call letters*] (BROA)
WFGE-FM .... Murray, KY [*FM radio station call letters*] (BROA)
WFGF-FM .... Lima, OH [*FM radio station call letters*] (BROA)
WFI .... Winton Financial [*AMEX symbol*] (SG)
WFJO-FM .... St. Petersburg, FL [*FM radio station call letters*] (BROA)
WFJY-FM .... Pontage, PA [*FM radio station call letters*] (BROA)
WFLD-DT .... Chicago, IL [*Television station call letters*] (BROA)
WFLX-DT .... West Palm Beach, FL [*Television station call letters*] (BROA)
WFMZ-DT .... Allentown, PA [*Television station call letters*] (BROA)
WFMZ-FM .... Hertford, NC [*FM radio station call letters*] (BROA)
WFNC-FM .... Lumberton, NC [*FM radio station call letters*] (BROA)
WFOR-DT .... Miami, FL [*Television station call letters*] (BROA)
WFPC2 .... Wide Field and Planetary Camera 2
WFPF-FM .... Aurora, NC [*FM radio station call letters*] (BROA)
WFRF .... Tallahassee, FL [*AM radio station call letters*] (BROA)
WFRI-FM .... Winamac, IN [*FM radio station call letters*] (BROA)
WFTC .... Working Families Tax Credit
WFTS-DT .... Tampa, FL [*Television station call letters*] (BROA)
WFXN-FM .... Ironton, OH [*FM radio station call letters*] (BROA)
WFXS .... Wittenberg, WI [*Television station call letters*] (BROA)
WFXT-DT .... Boston, MA [*Television station call letters*] (BROA)
wg .... White Gold [*Watch*]
WG .... Willbros Group [*NYSE symbol*] (SG)
wg .... Wing (MILB)
WGBG-FM .... Seaford, DE [*FM radio station call letters*] (BROA)
WGBH-DT .... Boston, MA [*Television station call letters*] (BROA)
WGBX-DT .... Boston, MA [*Television station call letters*] (BROA)
WGCU-FM .... Fort Myers, FL [*FM radio station call letters*] (BROA)
wgf .... White Gold Filled [*Watch*]
WGFY .... Charlotte, NC [*AM radio station call letters*] (BROA)
WGH-FM .... Newport News, VA [*FM radio station call letters*] (BROA)
WGIN .... Rochester, HN [*AM radio station call letters*] (BROA)
WGIP .... Exeter, NH [*AM radio station call letters*] (BROA)
WGKL-FM .... Gladstone, MI [*FM radio station call letters*] (BROA)
WGLL .... Auburn, IN [*AM radio station call letters*] (BROA)
WGLN-FM .... Galion, OH [*FM radio station call letters*] (BROA)
WGmc .... West Germanic (BEE)
WGMN .... Roanoke, VA [*AM radio station call letters*] (BROA)
WGNG-FM .... Belzoni, MS [*FM radio station call letters*] (BROA)
WGNR .... Anderson, IN [*AM radio station call letters*] (BROA)
WGNX-DT .... Atlanta, GA [*Television station call letters*] (BROA)
WGOL .... Russellville, AL [*AM radio station call letters*] (BROA)
wgs .... White Gold Shell [*Watch*]
WGSA .... Baxley, GA [*Television station call letters*] (BROA)
WHAN .... Ashland, VA [*AM radio station call letters*] (BROA)
WHCG .... Metter, GA [*AM radio station call letters*] (BROA)
WHDH-DT .... Boston, MA [*Television station call letters*] (BROA)
WHDI-FM .... Sister Bay, WI [*FM radio station call letters*] (BROA)
WH DIV .... Wage and Hour Division
WHFX-FM .... St. Simons Island, GA [*FM radio station call letters*] (BROA)
WHGB-FM .... Murrell's Inlet, SC [*FM radio station call letters*] (BROA)
WHGN-FM .... Inglis, FL [*FM radio station call letters*] (BROA)
WHHA-FM .... Willard, OH [*FM radio station call letters*] (BROA)
WHIM .... Apopka, FL [*AM radio station call letters*] (BROA)
WHJI .... Whitehall Jewellers [*NASDAQ symbol*] (SG)
WHKB-FM .... Houghton, MI [*FM radio station call letters*] (BROA)
WHK-FM .... Canton, OH [*FM radio station call letters*] (BROA)
WHKT .... Portsmouth, VA [*AM radio station call letters*] (BROA)
WHND-FM .... Sister Bay, WI [*FM radio station call letters*] (BROA)
WHP .... Wellhead Protection Program [*Environmental Protection Agency*] (EPAT)
WHSH-DT .... Marlborough, MA [*Television station call letters*] (BROA)
WHSR .... Pompano Beach, FL [*AM radio station call letters*] (BROA)
WHTE .... Johnston City, IL [*AM radio station call letters*] (BROA)
WHUT-TV .... Washington, DC [*Television station call letters*] (BROA)
WHYM .... Lake City, SC [*AM radio station call letters*] (BROA)
WHYT .... Marine City, MI [*AM radio station call letters*] (BROA)
WIA .... Worker Investment Act
WIAT .... Birmingham, AL [*Television station call letters*] (BROA)
WIBD-FM .... Gray, GA [*FM radio station call letters*] (BROA)
WIBH .... Anna, IL [*AM radio station call letters*] (BROA)
WIBM .... Jackson, MI [*AM radio station call letters*] (BROA)
WIC .... Woodwork Institute of California
WICA-FM .... Traverse City, MI [*FM radio station call letters*] (BROA)
WIDE .... Widely Integrated Distributed Environment
WIFE-FM .... Connersville, IN [*FM radio station call letters*] (BROA)
WIFL-FM .... Tavenier, FL [*FM radio station call letters*] (BROA)
WIGH-FM .... Lexington, TN [*FM radio station call letters*] (BROA)
WIHM .... Taylorville, IL [*AM radio station call letters*] (BROA)
WILP-FM .... Freeland, PA [*FM radio station call letters*] (BROA)
WIMZ .... Knoxville, TN [*AM radio station call letters*] (BROA)
WISE .... World Islam Study Enterprise [*Tampa, Florida*]
WISH-DT .... Indianapolis, IN [*Television station call letters*] (BROA)
WISY-FM .... Canandaigua, NY [*FM radio station call letters*] (BROA)
WIT .... Winnebago-Itasca Travelers (EA)
wit .... Witness (GEAB)
WITC .... Wit Capital Group [*Stock market symbol*]
WITF-DT .... Harrisburg, PA [*Television station call letters*] (BROA)
WITW .... Women in the Wind [*An association*] (EA)
WIVR .... Mayfield, KY [*AM radio station call letters*] (BROA)
WIVR-FM .... Mayfield, KY [*FM radio station call letters*] (BROA)
WIVT .... Binghamton, NY [*Television station call letters*] (BROA)

WJBK-DT ..... Detroit, MI [*Television station call letters*] (BROA)
WJBQ-FM .... Portland, ME [*FM radio station call letters*] (BROA)
WJBW .... Jupiter, FL [*AM radio station call letters*] (BROA)
WJBZ .... Knoxville, TN [*AM radio station call letters*] (BROA)
WJCG-FM .... Monee, IL [*FM radio station call letters*] (BROA)
WJCO .... Wesley Jessen VisionCare [*NASDAQ symbol*] (SG)
WJDX .... Jackson, MS [*AM radio station call letters*] (BROA)
WJES-FM ..... Saluda, SC [*FM radio station call letters*] (BROA)
WJFJ .... Tryon, NC [*AM radio station call letters*] (BROA)
WJIC-FM ..... Zanesville, OH [*FM radio station call letters*] (BROA)
WJKS-FM .... Canton, NJ [*FM radio station call letters*] (BROA)
WJLA-DT ..... Washington, DC [*Television station call letters*] (BROA)
WJLG .... Savaannah, GA [*AM radio station call letters*] (BROA)
WJNI-FM .... Ladson, SC [*FM radio station call letters*] (BROA)
WJNV-FM .... Jonesville, VA [*FM radio station call letters*] (BROA)
WJNZ .... Ada, MI [*AM radio station call letters*] (BROA)
WJOK-FM .... Kentland, IN [*FM radio station call letters*] (BROA)
WJOT .... Wabash, IN [*AM radio station call letters*] (BROA)
WJOT-FM ..... Wabash, IN [*FM radio station call letters*] (BROA)
WJRC-FM .... Lewistown, PA [*FM radio station call letters*] (BROA)
WJRV-FM .... Richmond, VA [*FM radio station call letters*] (BROA)
WJSJ-FM ..... Sumrall, MS [*FM radio station call letters*] (BROA)
WJUS .... Marion, AL [*AM radio station call letters*] (BROA)
WJVA .... South Bend, IN [*AM radio station call letters*] (BROA)
WJWB .... Jacksonville, FL [*Television station call letters*] (BROA)
WJWK .... Seaford, DE [*AM radio station call letters*] (BROA)
WJWL .... Georgetown, DE [*AM radio station call letters*] (BROA)
WJWZ-FM .... Wetumpka, AL [*FM radio station call letters*] (BROA)
WJXM-FM .... De Kalb, MS [*FM radio station call letters*] (BROA)
WJYI .... Milwaukee, WI [*AM radio station call letters*] (BROA)
WJYT .... Attleboro, MA [*AM radio station call letters*] (BROA)
WJZ-DT .... Baltimore, MD [*Television station call letters*] (BROA)
WKAJ .... Saratoga Springs, NY [*AM radio station call letters*] (BROA)
WKBH-FM .... West Salem, WI [*FM radio station call letters*] (BROA)
WKDH .... Houston, MS [*Television station call letters*] (BROA)
WKDY .... Spartanburg, SC [*AM radio station call letters*] (BROA)
WKFS-FM .... Milford, OH [*FM radio station call letters*] (BROA)
WKFT-DT .... Fayetteville, NC [*Television station call letters*] (BROA)
WKGE .... East Point, GA [*AM radio station call letters*] (BROA)
WKGJ .... Auburn, NY [*AM radio station call letters*] (BROA)
WKGL-FM .... Russellville, AL [*FM radio station call letters*] (BROA)
WKHI-FM .... Exmore, VA [*FM radio station call letters*] (BROA)
WKI .... Walter Koenig International (EA)
WKIB-FM .... Anna, IL [*FM radio station call letters*] (BROA)
WKIK-FM .... California, MD [*FM radio station call letters*] (BROA)
WKJK .... Louisville, KY [*AM radio station call letters*] (BROA)
WKJS-FM .... Crewe, VA [*FM radio station call letters*] (BROA)
WKJT-FM .... Teutopolis, IL [*FM radio station call letters*] (BROA)
WKLR-FM .... Williamsburg, VA [*FM radio station call letters*] (BROA)
WKLX-FM .... Beaver Dam, KY [*FM radio station call letters*] (BROA)
WKLZ .... Kalamazoo, MI [*AM radio station call letters*] (BROA)
WKMG-TV .... Orlando, FL [*Television station call letters*] (BROA)
WKNJ .... Lakeside, NJ [*AM radio station call letters*] (BROA)
WKOW-DT ... Madison, WI [*Television station call letters*] (BROA)
WKOY-FM .... Princeton, WV [*FM radio station call letters*] (BROA)
WKQS-FM .... Negaunee, MI [*FM radio station call letters*] (BROA)
WKQY-FM .... Tazewell, VA [*FM radio station call letters*] (BROA)
WKRC .... Cincinnati, OH [*AM radio station call letters*] (BROA)
WKRE .... Monroe, NC [*AM radio station call letters*] (BROA)
WKRK-FM .... Detroit, MI [*fm radio station call letters*] (BROA)
WKSL-FM .... Germantown, TN [*FM radio station call letters*] (BROA)
WKSY-FM .... Picayune, MS [*FM radio station call letters*] (BROA)
WKTU-FM .... Lake Success, NY [*FM radio station call letters*] (BROA)
WKXH-FM .... St. Johnsbury, VT [*FM radio station call letters*] (BROA)
WKXS-FM .... Jackson, MS [*FM radio station call letters*] (BROA)
WKYC-DT .... Cleveland, OH [*Television station call letters*] (BROA)
WKYZ-FM .... Key Colony Beach, FL [*FM radio station call letters*] (BROA)
WKZS-FM .... Covington, IN [*FM radio station call letters*] (BROA)
WKZW-FM .... Bay Springs, MS [*FM radio station call letters*] (BROA)
WL .... Worldloppet/American Birkebeiner [*An association*] (EA)
WLCE-FM .... Buffalo, NY [*FM radio station call letters*] (BROA)
WLCG .... Macon, GA [*AM radio station call letters*] (BROA)
WLCG-FM .... Warner Robins, GA [*FM radio station call letters*] (BROA)
WLDI-FM ..... Fort Pierce, FL [*FM radio station call letters*] (BROA)
WLFC .... Willis Lease Finance [*NASDAQ symbol*] (SG)
WLFF-FM .... Brookston, IN [*FM radio station call letters*] (BROA)
WLGH-FM .... Leroy Township, MI [*FM radio station call letters*] (BROA)
WLHJ .... Mount Airy, NC [*AM radio station call letters*] (BROA)
WLHR-FM .... Panama City, FL [*FM radio station call letters*] (BROA)
WLJH-FM .... Glens Falls, NY [*FM radio station call letters*] (BROA)
WLJI-FM ..... Summerton, SC [*FM radio station call letters*] (BROA)
WLJM .... Lima, OH [*AM radio station call letters*] (BROA)
WLK .... Waterlink,Inc. [*NYSE symbol*] (SG)
WLKM-FM ... Three Rivers, MI [*FM radio station call letters*] (BROA)
WLKY .... Louisville, KY [*AM radio station call letters*] (BROA)
WLL .... Willamette Indus. [*NYSE symbol*] (SG)
WLLD-FM .... Holmes Beach, FL [*FM radio station call letters*] (BROA)
WLLR-FM .... Davenport, IA [*FM radio station call letters*] (BROA)
WLLZ .... Monroe, MI [*AM radio station call letters*] (BROA)
WLMA .... Washington Library Media Association
WLMX .... Rossville, GA [*AM radio station call letters*] (BROA)
WLNF-FM .... Lumberton, MS [*FM radio station call letters*] (BROA)
WLNK-FM .... Charlotte, NC [*FM radio station call letters*] (BROA)
WLPDIA .... Western Lath/Plaster/Drywall Industries Association
WLPX-TV .... Charleston, WV [*Television station call letters*] (BROA)
WLQR .... Toledo, OH [*AM radio station call letters*] (BROA)
WLRY-FM .... Rushville, OH [*FM radio station call letters*] (BROA)
WLS-DT .... Chicago, IL [*Television station call letters*] (BROA)
WLSR-FM .... Galesburg, IL [*FM radio station call letters*] (BROA)
WLSY-FM .... New Albany, IN [*FM radio station call letters*] (BROA)
WLT .... Wildlife Land Trust
WLTA .... Alpharetta, GA [*AM radio station call letters*] (BROA)
WLTB-FM .... Owego, NY [*FM radio station call letters*] (BROA)
WLTF-FM .... Englewood, FL [*FM radio station call letters*] (BROA)
WLTI-FM ..... Syracuse, NY [*FM radio station call letters*] (BROA)
WLTM-FM .... Sturgeon Bay, WI [*FM radio station call letters*] (BROA)
WLTY-FM .... Cayce, SC [*FM radio station call letters*] (BROA)
WLWJ-FM .... Masontown, PA [*FM radio station call letters*] (BROA)
WLWT-DT .... Cincinnati, OH [*Television station call letters*] (BROA)
WLXP-FM .... Savannah, GA [*FM radio station call letters*] (BROA)
WLYT-FM .... Hickory, NC [*FM radio station call letters*] (BROA)
WM .... Washington Mutual [*NYSE symbol*] (SG)
WMAA .... Columbus, MS [*Television station call letters*] (BROA)
WMAI .... Cleveland, MS [*Television station call letters*] (BROA)
WMAR-DT .... Baltimore, MD [*Television station call letters*] (BROA)
WMBX-FM ... Jensen Beach, FL [*FM radio station call letters*] (BROA)
WMDC-FM ... Mayville, WI [*FM radio station call letters*] (BROA)
WMDE-FM ... Saegertown, PA [*FM radio station call letters*] (BROA)
WMDM .... Lexington Park, MD [*AM radio station call letters*] (BROA)
WMFD-DT .... Mansfield, OH [*Television station call letters*] (BROA)
WMFL-FM .... Florida City, FL [*FM radio station call letters*] (BROA)
WMGO-FM .... Yazoo City, MS [*FM radio station call letters*] (BROA)
WMHG .... Muskegon, MI [*AM radio station call letters*] (BROA)
WMHX-FM ... Louisville, KY [*FM radio station call letters*] (BROA)
WMIB .... Marco Island, FL [*AM radio station call letters*] (BROA)
WMIW-FM ... North Myrtle Beach, SC [*FM radio station call letters*] (BROA)
WMJR .... Winchester, KY [*AM radio station call letters*] (BROA)
WMKI .... Birmingham, AL [*AM radio station call letters*] (BROA)
WMKO-FM ... Marco, FL [*FM radio station call letters*] (BROA)
WML .... Wireless Markup Language
WMLF .... Columbus, GA [*AM radio station call letters*] (BROA)
WMLV-FM ... Stonewall, MS [*FM radio station call letters*] (BROA)
WMML .... Glens Falls, NY [*AM radio station call letters*] (BROA)
WMMP .... Charleston, SC [*Television station call letters*] (BROA)
WMMZ-FM ... Meridian, MS [*FM radio station call letters*] (BROA)
WMNG-FM ... Christiansted, VI [*FM radio station call letters*] (BROA)
WMNW-FM ... Atlanta, IL [*FM radio station call letters*] (BROA)
WMO .... Wausau-Mosinee Paper [*NYSE symbol*] (SG)
WMOC-FM ... Lumber City, GA [*FM radio station call letters*] (BROA)
WMOM-FM ... Pentwater, MI [*FM radio station call letters*] (BROA)
WMOV-FM ... Ravenswood, WV [*FM radio station call letters*] (BROA)
WMPL-FM ... Hancock, MI [*FM radio station call letters*] (BROA)
WMPS-FM ... Tunica, MS [*FM radio station call letters*] (BROA)
WMPX-TV ... Waterville, ME [*Television station call letters*] (BROA)
WMRE .... Charles Town, WV [*AM radio station call letters*] (BROA)
WMRZ-FM ... Cuthbert, GA [*FM radio station call letters*] (BROA)
WMSR-FM ... Waynesboro, TN [*FM radio station call letters*] (BROA)
WMTX-FM ... Sandusky, OH [*FM radio station call letters*] (BROA)
WMUR-DT ... Manchester, NH [*Television station call letters*] (BROA)
WMWX-FM ... Auburn, ME [*FM radio station call letters*] (BROA)
WMXH-FM ... Luray, VA [*FM radio station call letters*] (BROA)
WMXP-FM ... Callaway, FL [*FM radio station call letters*] (BROA)
WMXQ-FM ... Jacksonville, FL [*FM radio station call letters*] (BROA)
WMXV-FM ... Holidaysburg, PA [*FM radio station call letters*] (BROA)
WMYC .... Yazoo City, MS [*Television station call letters*] (BROA)
WNAI .... Newburg, KY [*AM radio station call letters*] (BROA)
WNAN-FM .... Nantucket, MA [*FM radio station call letters*] (BROA)
WNBQ-FM .... Mansfield, PA [*FM radio station call letters*] (BROA)
WNBX .... Springfield, VT [*AM radio station call letters*] (BROA)
WNDU-DT .... South Bend, IN [*Television station call letters*] (BROA)
WNFC .... William McNamara Fan Club (EA)
WNFT .... Boston, MA [*AM radio station call letters*] (BROA)
WNGE-FM .... Negaunee, MI [*FM radio station call letters*] (BROA)
WNGN-FM ... Argyle, NY [*FM radio station call letters*] (BROA)
WNGU-FM ... Dahlonega, GA [*FM radio station call letters*] (BROA)
WNJO-FM ... Trenton, NJ [*FM radio station call letters*] (BROA)
WNKT-FM .... St. George, SC [*FM radio station call letters*] (BROA)
WNLC-FM .... East Lyme, CT [*FM radio station call letters*] (BROA)
WNMA .... Miami Springs, FL [*AM radio station call letters*] (BROA)
WNMLA .... Winmill & Co,'A' [*NASDAQ symbol*] (SG)
WNMT .... Nashwauk, MN [*AM radio station call letters*] (BROA)
WNND-FM ... Chicago, IL [*FM radio station call letters*] (BROA)
WNNL-FM .... Fuquay-Varina, NC [*FM radio station call letters*] (BROA)
WNNN .... Salem, NJ [*AM radio station call letters*] (BROA)
WNOX .... Knoxville, TN [*AM radio station call letters*] (BROA)
WNPX .... Cookerville, TN [*Television station call letters*] (BROA)
WNRQ-FM ... Nashville, TN [*FM radio station call letters*] (BROA)
WNSG .... Nashville, TN [*AM radio station call letters*] (BROA)
WNSR .... Brentwood, TN [*AM radio station call letters*] (BROA)
WNTC-FM .... Drakesboro, KY [*FM radio station call letters*] (BROA)
WNTF .... Bithlo, FL [*AM radio station call letters*] (BROA)
WNVI .... North Vernon, IN [*AM radio station call letters*] (BROA)
WNWC .... Sun Prairie, WI [*AM radio station call letters*] (BROA)
WNWI .... Oak Lawn, IL [*AM radio station call letters*] (BROA)
WNWO-DT .... Toledo, OH [*Television station call letters*] (BROA)
WNWZ .... Grand Rapids, MI [*AM radio station call letters*] (BROA)
WNYW-DT ... New York, NY [*Television station call letters*] (BROA)
W/o .... Without
WOBE-FM .... Crystal Falls, MI [*FM radio station call letters*] (BROA)
WOC .... Women's Outdoor Challenges [*An association*] (EA)

WOCE-FM .... Benton, TN [*FM radio station call letters*] (BROA)
WOCY-FM .... Carrabelle, FL [*FM radio station call letters*] (BROA)
WOIO-DT ..... Shaker Heights, OH [*Television station call letters*] (BROA)
WOKL-FM .... Thomasville, GA [*FM radio station call letters*] (BROA)
WOLF-FM .... Oswego, NY [*FM radio station call letters*] (BROA)
WOLF-TV .... Hazleton, PA [*Television station call letters*] (BROA)
WOLG-FM .... Carlinville, IL [*FM radio station call letters*] (BROA)
WOLT-FM .... Greer, SC [*FM radio station call letters*] (BROA)
WOOM .... Millington, TN [*AM radio station call letters*] (BROA)
WOOX .... Bedford, PA [*AM radio station call letters*] (BROA)
WOPX .... Melbourne, FL [*Television station call letters*] (BROA)
WORC-FM .... Webster, MA [*FM radio station call letters*] (BROA)
WorLD .... World Links for Development [*Program*]
WoS .... Web of Science
WOSB-FM .... Marion, OH [*FM radio station call letters*] (BROA)
WOTT-FM .... Henderson, NY [*FM radio station call letters*] (BROA)
WOWW .... Germantown, TN [*AM radio station call letters*] (BROA)
WPAR-FM .... Salem, VA [*FM radio station call letters*] (BROA)
WPBC .... Decatur, GA [*AM radio station call letters*] (BROA)
WPBG-FM .... Peoria, IL [*FM radio station call letters*] (BROA)
WPBS-TV ..... Watertown, NY [*Television station call letters*] (BROA)
WPCK-FM .... Kaukauna, WI [*FM radio station call letters*] (BROA)
WPCL-FM .... Spangler, PA [*FM radio station call letters*] (BROA)
WPCN-FM .... Point Pleasant, WV [*FM radio station call letters*] (BROA)
WPDQ-FM .... Freehold Township, NJ [*FM radio station call letters*] (BROA)
WPEA .... Washington Public Employees Association
WPER-FM .... Culpepper, VA [*FM radio station call letters*] (BROA)
WPFM .... Darlington, SC [*AM radio station call letters*] (BROA)
WPHI-FM ..... Jenkintown, PA [*FM radio station call letters*] (BROA)
WPI .... Watson Pharmaceuticals [*NYSE symbol*] (SG)
WPIN .... Dublin, VA [*AM radio station call letters*] (BROA)
WPIR-FM ..... Hickory, NC [*FM radio station call letters*] (BROA)
WPKK-FM .... St. Marys, PA [*FM radio station call letters*] (BROA)
WPLG-DT ..... Miami, FL [*Television station call letters*] (BROA)
WPLT-FM .... Detroit, MI [*FM radio station call letters*] (BROA)
WPMA-FM ... Sparta, GA [*FM radio station call letters*] (BROA)
wpn .... Weapon (MILB)
WPNT-FM .... Brookfield, WI [*FM radio station call letters*] (BROA)
WPPD-FM .... Frederiksted, VI [*FM radio station call letters*] (BROA)
WPPG-FM .... Macon, GA [*FM radio station call letters*] (BROA)
WPRN-FM .... Lisman, AL [*FM radio station call letters*] (BROA)
WPRW-FM ... Naples, FL [*FM radio station call letters*] (BROA)
WPSK .... Narrows, VA [*AM radio station call letters*] (BROA)
WPSM .... Warfighter Physiological Status Monitoring [*Army*]
WPTC-FM .... Williamsport, PA [*FM radio station call letters*] (BROA)
WPTQ-FM .... Cave City, KY [*FM radio station call letters*] (BROA)
WPTT .... Mckeesport, PA [*AM radio station call letters*] (BROA)
WPUR-FM .... Atlantic City, NJ [*FM radio station call letters*] (BROA)
WPVI-DT ..... Philadelphia, PA [*Television station call letters*] (BROA)
WPVMS .... West Point Veterinary Medical Society (GVA)
WPXD .... Ann Arbor, MI [*Television station call letters*] (BROA)
WPXI-DT ...... Pittsburgh, PA [*Television station call letters*] (BROA)
WPXL .... New Orleans, FL [*Television station call letters*] (BROA)
WPXM .... Miami, FL [*Television station call letters*] (BROA)
WPXN-TV .... New York, NY [*Television station call letters*] (BROA)
WPXO .... Minden, LA [*Television station call letters*] (BROA)
WPXP .... Lake Worth, FL [*Television station call letters*] (BROA)
WPXQ .... Block Island, RI [*Television station call letters*] (BROA)
WPXU .... Decatur, IL [*Television station call letters*] (BROA)
WPXV .... Norfolk, VA [*Television station call letters*] (BROA)
WPXX-TV .... Memphis, TN [*Television station call letters*] (BROA)
WQAR-FM .... Stillwater, NY [*FM radio station call letters*] (BROA)
WQCMB .... Water Quality and Contaminant Modeling Branch
WQEM-FM ... Nanticoke, PA [*FM radio station call letters*] (BROA)
WQFM .... Nanicoke, PA [*FM radio station call letters*] (BROA)
WQIX-FM .... Knoxville, TN [*FM radio station call letters*] (BROA)
WQJZ-FM .... Ocean Pines, MD [*FM radio station call letters*] (BROA)
WQKC-FM .... Seymour, IN [*FM radio station call letters*] (BROA)
WQLD-FM .... Luveme, AL [*FM radio station call letters*] (BROA)
WQLL-FM .... Bedford, NH [*FM radio station call letters*] (BROA)
WQPC-FM .... Prairie du Chien, WI [*FM radio station call letters*] (BROA)
WQSH-FM .... Clarksville, IN [*FM radio station call letters*] (BROA)
WQUA-FM .... Citronelle, AL [*FM radio station call letters*] (BROA)
WR .... Women's Participation Ratio
WRAL-DT ..... Raleigh, NC [*Television station call letters*] (BROA)
WRAN-FM .... Tower Hill, IL [*FM radio station call letters*] (BROA)
WRBF .... Kendall, FL [*AM radio station call letters*] (BROA)
WRBG-FM .... Ocean View, DE [*FM radio station call letters*] (BROA)
WRBK-FM .... Richburg, SC [*FM radio station call letters*] (BROA)
WRBN-FM .... Clayton, GA [*FM radio station call letters*] (BROA)
WRBO-FM .... New Albany, MS [*FM radio station call letters*] (BROA)
WRBP .... Warren, OH [*AM radio station call letters*] (BROA)
WRBT-FM .... Harrisburg, PA [*FM radio station call letters*] (BROA)
WRBV-FM .... Warner Robins, GA [*FM radio station call letters*] (BROA)
WRCC .... Battle Creek, MI [*AM radio station call letters*] (BROA)
WRC-DT .... Washington, DC [*Television station call letters*] (BROA)
WRCL-FM .... Richmond, VA [*FM radio station call letters*] (BROA)
WRDQ .... Orlando, FL [*Television station call letters*] (BROA)
WRECA .... Water Resources Engineering and Construction Agency [*Nigeria*]
WREQ-FM .... Ridgebury, PA [*FM radio station call letters*] (BROA)
WRGF-FM .... Greenfield, IN [*FM radio station call letters*] (BROA)
WRGX-FM .... Sturgeon Bay, WI [*FM radio station call letters*] (BROA)
WRHK-FM .... Danville, IL [*FM radio station call letters*] (BROA)
WRHS .... Western Reserve Historical Society (GEAB)
WRKG-FM .... High Springs, FL [*FM radio station call letters*] (BROA)
WRKU-FM .... Forestville, WI [*FM radio station call letters*] (BROA)
WRLU-FM .... Algoma, WI [*FM radio station call letters*] (BROA)
WRNB-FM .... Troy, OH [*FM radio station call letters*] (BROA)
WRNI .... Providence, RI [*AM radio station call letters*] (BROA)
WRPN .... Ripon, WI [*AM radio station call letters*] (BROA)
WRPRC .... Wisconsin Regional Primate Research Center (GVA)
WRPT .... Ashland, MA [*AM radio station call letters*] (BROA)
WRPX .... Rocky Mountain, NC [*Television station call letters*] (BROA)
WRQT-FM .... La Crosse, WI [*FM radio station call letters*] (BROA)
WRSB .... Canandaigua, NY [*AM radio station call letters*] (BROA)
WRSR-FM .... Owosso, MI [*FM radio station call letters*] (BROA)
WRTE-FM .... Chicago, IL [*FM radio station call letters*] (BROA)
WRTR-FM .... Tuscaloosa, AL [*FM radio station call letters*] (BROA)
WRTV-DT ..... Indianapolis, IN [*Television station call letters*] (BROA)
WRUO-FM ... Mayaguez, PR [*FM radio station call letters*] (BROA)
WRVB-FM .... Marietta, OH [*FM radio station call letters*] (BROA)
WRVI-FM ..... Valley Station, KY [*FM radio station call letters*] (BROA)
WRVJ .... Wildlife Rescue Veterinarian Association of Japan (GVA)
WRVW-FM ... Lebanon, TN [*FM radio station call letters*] (BROA)
WRVX-FM ... Lynchburg, VA [*FM radio station call letters*] (BROA)
WRXF-FM .... Lapeer, MI [*FM radio station call letters*] (BROA)
WRZK-FM .... Colonial Heights, TN [*FM radio station call letters*] (BROA)
WS .... Work Status (EPAT)
WSAX-FM .... Pleasantville, NJ [*FM radio station call letters*] (BROA)
WSB-DT .... Atlanta, GA [*Television station call letters*] (BROA)
WSDL-FM .... Ocean City, MD [*FM radio station call letters*] (BROA)
WSEA-FM .... Atlantic Beach, SC [*FM radio station call letters*] (BROA)
WSFN .... Brunswick, GA [*AM radio station call letters*] (BROA)
WSGY-Fm .... Somerset, PA [*FM radio station call letters*] (BROA)
WSHI-FM ..... Columbia City, IN [*FM radio station call letters*] (BROA)
WSIS-FM ..... Springfield, GA [*FM radio station call letters*] (BROA)
WSJC .... Magee, MS [*AM radio station call letters*] (BROA)
WSJZ-FM ..... Boston, MA [*FM radio station call letters*] (BROA)
WSKY-FM .... Micanopy, FL [*FM radio station call letters*] (BROA)
WSMR-FM .... Sarasota, FL [*FM radio station call letters*] (BROA)
WSMS .... Warrior Systems Modernization Strategy [*Military*]
WSNI-FM ..... Colfax, IL [*FM radio station call letters*] (BROA)
WSOC-DT .... Charlotte, NC [*Television station call letters*] (BROA)
WSOX-FM .... Red Lion, PA [*FM radio station call letters*] (BROA)
WSPE .... World Standard Printed English
WSPX-TV ..... Syracuse, NY [*Television station call letters*] (BROA)
WSRA-FM .... Central City, PA [*FM radio station call letters*] (BROA)
WSRV-FM .... Deltaville, VA [*FM radio station call letters*] (BROA)
WSSE .... World Standard Spoken English
WSSH-FM .... Marlboro, VT [*FM radio station call letters*] (BROA)
WSSI-FM ..... Carthage, MS [*FM radio station call letters*] (BROA)
WSSR-FM .... Clearwater, FL [*FM radio station call letters*] (BROA)
WST .... West Pharmaceutical Services [*NYSE symbol*] (SG)
WSTE-FM .... Toccoa, GA [*FM radio station call letters*] (BROA)
WSTK .... Jacksonville, NC [*AM radio station call letters*] (BROA)
WSTN-FM .... Mount Olive, IL [*FM radio station call letters*] (BROA)
WSUM-FM .... Madison, WI [*FM radio station call letters*] (BROA)
WSUSA .... Wheelchair Sports, USA [*An association*] (EA)
WSVMA .... Washington State Veterinary Medical Association (GVA)
WSVN-DT .... Miami, FL [*Television station call letters*] (BROA)
WSVP-FM .... Emporia, VA [*FM radio station call letters*] (BROA)
WTA .... WTA Tour Players Association (EA)
WTAL-FM .... Monticello, FL [*FM radio station call letters*] (BROA)
W/tax .... Witholding Tax
WTB .... Wanted to Buy
WTBB-FM .... Gadsden, AL [*FM radio station call letters*] (BROA)
WTBC .... Tuscaloosa, AL [*AM radio station call letters*] (BROA)
WTBC-FM .... Williston, VT [*FM radio station call letters*] (BROA)
WTBF-FM .... Brundidge, AL [*FM radio station call letters*] (BROA)
WTCD-FM .... Indianola, MS [*FM radio station call letters*] (BROA)
WTCV .... San Juan, PR [*Television station call letters*] (BROA)
WTDA .... Madison, WI [*AM radio station call letters*] (BROA)
WTECE .... Warrantech Corp. [*NASDAQ symbol*] (SG)
WTEL .... Red Springs, NC [*AM radio station call letters*] (BROA)
WTGG-FM .... Amite, LA [*FM radio station call letters*] (BROA)
WTHM .... Red Lion, PA [*AM radio station call letters*] (BROA)
WTHR-DT .... Indianapolis, IN [*Television station call letters*] (BROA)
WTIC-FM ..... Hartford, CT [*FM radio station call letters*] (BROA)
WTIM-FM .... Taylorville, IL [*FM radio station call letters*] (BROA)
WTJK .... South Beloit, IL [*AM radio station call letters*] (BROA)
WTKB-FM .... Atwood, TN [*FM radio station call letters*] (BROA)
WTKT .... Georgetown, KY [*AM radio station call letters*] (BROA)
WTLI-FM ..... Bear Creek Township, MI [*FM radio station call letters*] (BROA)
WTLX-FM .... Columbus, WI [*FM radio station call letters*] (BROA)
WTMG-FM ... Williston, FL [*FM radio station call letters*] (BROA)
WTMM .... Rensselaer, NY [*AM radio station call letters*] (BROA)
WTMS .... Melbourne, FL [*AM radio station call letters*] (BROA)
WTMV-FM ... Youngsville, PA [*FM radio station call letters*] (BROA)
wtn .... Witness (GEAB)
WTND-FM .... Poughkeepsie, NY [*FM radio station call letters*] (BROA)
WTNH-DT .... New Haven, CT [*Television station call letters*] (BROA)
WTNX-FM .... Sharpsville, PA [*FM radio station call letters*] (BROA)
WTOP-FM .... Warrenton, VA [*FM radio station call letters*] (BROA)
WTRT-FM .... Benton, KY [*FM radio station call letters*] (BROA)
WTRV-FM .... Walker, MI [*FM radio station call letters*] (BROA)
WTRY-FM .... Rotterdam, NY [*FM radio station call letters*] (BROA)
WTSP-DT .... St. Petersburg, FL [*Television station call letters*] (BROA)
WTTG-DT .... Washington, DC [*Television station call letters*] (BROA)
WTVD-DT .... Durham, NC [*Television station call letters*] (BROA)
WTW .... Westower Corp. [*AMEX symbol*] (SG)

WTXF-DT ..... Philadelphia, PA [*Television station call letters*]   (BROA)
WTZK .... Black Mountain, NC [*AM radio station call letters*]   (BROA)
WUAB-DT .... Lorain, OH [*Television station call letters*]   (BROA)
WUGR .... Nicholasville, KY [*AM radio station call letters*]   (BROA)
WUSA-DT .... Washington, DC [*Television station call letters*]   (BROA)
WUZZ .... Watertown, NY [*AM radio station call letters*]   (BROA)
WUZZ-FM .... Lima, OH [*FM radio station call letters*]   (BROA)
WV .... Water Vapor
WV .... Workplace Violence
WVA .... World Veterinary Association   (GVA)
WVBO-FM .... Winneconne, WI [*FM radio station call letters*]   (BROA)
WVCV .... Orange, VA [*AM radio station call letters*]   (BROA)
WVFX .... Clarksburg, WV [*Television station call letters*]   (BROA)
WVGM .... Lynchburg, VA [*AM radio station call letters*]   (BROA)
WVIC-FM .... Charlotte, MI [*FM radio station call letters*]   (BROA)
WVIS-FM .... Vieques, PR [*FM radio station call letters*]   (BROA)
WVJZ-FM .... Charlotte Amalie, VI [*FM radio station call letters*]   (BROA)
WVKL-FM .... Norfolk, VA [*FM radio station call letters*]   (BROA)
WVLT-TV .... Knoxville, TN [*Television station call letters*]   (BROA)
WVMC .... Mount Carmel, IL [*AM radio station call letters*]   (BROA)
WVMQ-FM ... Key West, FL [*FM radio station call letters*]   (BROA)
WVMV-FM .... Detroit, MI [*FM radio station call letters*]   (BROA)
WVMX-FM ... Cincinnati, OH [*FM radio station call letters*]   (BROA)
WVNET .... West Virginia Network
WVOM-FM .... Howland, ME [*FM radio station call letters*]   (BROA)
WVOQ-FM .... Mexico, NY [*FM radio station call letters*]   (BROA)
WVOZ .... San Juan, PR [*AM radio station call letters*]   (BROA)
WVOZ-FM .... Carolina, PR [*FM radio station call letters*]   (BROA)
WVPI-FM ..... Charlotte Amalie, VI [*FM radio station call letters*]   (RROA)
WVXA-FM .... Rogers City, MI [*Television station call letters*]   (BROA)
WVYB-FM .... Holly Hill, FL [*FM radio station call letters*]   (BROA)
WWAZ-TV .... Madisonville, KY [*Television station call letters*]   (BROA)
WWBA .... Pinellas Park, FL [*AM radio station call letters*]   (BROA)
WWBR-FM .... Mount Clemens, MI [*FM radio station call letters*]   (BROA)
WWF .... World Wrestling Federation
WWFX-FM .... Lacrosse, FL [*FM radio station call letters*]   (BROA)
WWHW-FM .... Jeffersonville, NY [*FM radio station call letters*]   (BROA)
WWJD-FM .... Pippa Passes, KY [*FM radio station call letters*]   (BROA)
WWJ-DT .... Detroit, MI [*Television station call letters*]   (BROA)
WWJY .... New London, CT [*AM radio station call letters*]   (BROA)
WWKN-FM .... Marshall, MI [*FM radio station call letters*]   (BROA)
WWKO-FM .... Belleview, FL [*FM radio station call letters*]   (BROA)
WWKR-FM .... Pentwater, MI [*FM radio station call letters*]   (BROA)
WWMO-FM .... Asheboro, NC [*FM radio station call letters*]   (BROA)
WWND-FM .... Raleigh, NC [*FM radio station call letters*]   (BROA)
WWPB .... Western Women Professional Bowlers   (EA)
WWQM .... Wetland Water Quality Model
WWSH-FM .... White River Junction, VT [*FM radio station call letters*]   (BROA)
WWSN-FM .... Waycross, GA [*FM radio station call letters*]   (BROA)
WWTU .... Wastewater Treatment Unit [*Environmental Protection Agency*]   (EPAT)
WWUZ-FM .... Bowling Green, VA [*FM radio station call letters*]   (BROA)
WWVT .... Christiansburg, WA [*AM radio station call letters*]   (BROA)
WWVV-FM .... Bluffton, SC [*FM radio station call letters*]   (BROA)
WWWB .... Lakeland, FL [*Television station call letters*]   (BROA)
WWWE .... Carrollton, GA [*AM radio station call letters*]   (BROA)
WWWFC ...... Kitty Wells-Johnny Wright-Bobby Wright International Fan Club   (EA)
WWWJ .... Galax, VA [*AM radio station call letters*]   (BROA)

WWYY-FM ... Belvidere, NJ [*FM radio station call letters*]   (BROA)
WWZB-FM ... Burnside, KY [*FM radio station call letters*]   (BROA)
WWZK-FM ... Villas, NJ [*FM radio station call letters*]   (BROA)
WWZY-FM ... Long Branch, NJ [*FM radio station call letters*]   (BROA)
Wx .... Weather   (WEAT)
WXBH .... Cobleskill, NY [*AM radio station call letters*]   (BROA)
WXBV .... Kentwood, MI [*AM radio station call letters*]   (BROA)
WXCT-FM .... Baton Rouge, LA [*FM radio station call letters*]   (BROA)
WXIA-DT .... Atlanta, GA [*Television station call letters*]   (BROA)
WXII .... Eden, NC [*AM radio station call letters*]   (BROA)
WXIX-DT .... Newport, KY [*Television station call letters*]   (BROA)
WXKO-FM .... Pana, IL [*FM radio station call letters*]   (BROA)
WXKT-FM .... Signal Mountain, TN [*FM radio station call letters*]   (BROA)
WXLN-FM .... Shepherdsville, KY [*FM radio station call letters*]   (BROA)
WXMG-FM .... Upper Arlington, OH [*FM radio station call letters*]   (BROA)
WXOX-FM .... Attica, NY [*FM radio station call letters*]   (BROA)
WXPX .... Bradenton, FL [*Television station call letters*]   (BROA)
WXQD-FM .... Roanoke Rapids, NC [*FM radio station call letters*]   (BROA)
WXRD-FM .... Crown Point, IN [*FM radio station call letters*]   (BROA)
WXRP .... Hanceville, AL [*AM radio station call letters*]   (BROA)
WXSS-FM .... Wauwatosa, WI [*FM radio station call letters*]   (BROA)
WXST-FM .... Delaware, OH [*FM radio station call letters*]   (BROA)
WXTM-FM .... Jerseyville, IL [*FM radio station call letters*]   (BROA)
WXXC-FM .... Truxton, NY [*FM radio station call letters*]   (BROA)
WXXE-FM .... Fenner, NY [*FM radio station call letters*]   (BROA)
WXXP-FM .... Calverton-Roanoke, NY [*FM radio station call letters*]   (BROA)
WXXR-FM .... Holly Pond, AL [*FM radio station call letters*]   (BROA)
WXXS-FM .... Lancaster, NH [*FM radio station call letters*]   (BROA)
WXXY-FM .... Highland Park, IL [*FM radio station call letters*]   (BROA)
WXYZ-DT .... Detroit, MI [*Television station call letters*]   (BROA)
WYAA-FM .... Crete, IL [*FM radio station call letters*]   (BROA)
WYAM-FM .... Addison, AL [*FM radio station call letters*]   (BROA)
WYBC .... New Haven, CT [*AM radio station call letters*]   (BROA)
WYG .... Wyman-Gordon [*NYSE symbol*]   (SG)
WYHI .... Fernandina Beach, FL [*AM radio station call letters*]   (BROA)
WYJZ-FM .... Lebanon, IN [*FM radio station call letters*]   (BROA)
WYKL-FM .... Benton Harbor, MI [*FM radio station call letters*]   (BROA)
WYLI .... Marietta, OH [*AM radio station call letters*]   (BROA)
WYLX-FM .... Lebanon, OH [*FM radio station call letters*]   (BROA)
WYSK .... Fredericksburg, WA [*AM radio station call letters*]   (BROA)
WYST-FM .... Harwichport, MA [*FM radio station call letters*]   (BROA)
WYSX-FM .... Ogdensburg, NY [*FM radio station call letters*]   (BROA)
WYUM-FM .... Mount Vernon, GA [*FM radio station call letters*]   (BROA)
WYXX-FM .... Morris, IL [*FM radio station call letters*]   (BROA)
WYYW-FM .... Marion, MS [*FM radio station call letters*]   (BROA)
WYYX-FM .... Bonifay, FL [*FM radio station call letters*]   (BROA)
WZAZ-FM .... Marysville, OH [*AM radio station call letters*]   (BROA)
WZDE .... Carolina, PR [*Television station call letters*]   (BROA)
WZEC-FM .... Hoosick Falls, NY [*FM radio station call letters*]   (BROA)
WZEN-FM .... Farmington, NH [*FM radio station call letters*]   (BROA)
WZIO-FM .... South Webster, OH [*FM radio station call letters*]   (BROA)
WZJT-FM .... Dora, AL [*FM radio station call letters*]   (BROA)
WZKR-FM .... Kosciusko, MS [*FM radio station call letters*]   (BROA)
WZKT-FM .... Charleroi, PA [*FM radio station call letters*]   (BROA)
WZRQ-FM .... Biltmore Forest, NC [*FM radio station call letters*]   (BROA)
WZSP-FM .... Nocatee, FL [*FM radio station call letters*]   (BROA)
WZUM .... Carnegie, PA [*AM radio station call letters*]   (BROA)
WZYY-FM .... Renovo, PA [*FM radio station call letters*]   (BROA)
WZZW .... Milton, WV [*AM radio station call letters*]   (BROA)

X-Y-Z
By Acronym

X-CAB.......... Extended Cab [*Automotive term*]
x-d.............. Ex-Dividend
XF.............. Extremely Fine [*Numismatic term*]
XFPB............ Extra-Fast Patrol Boat (MILB)
XIE.............. X-Ray Imaging Experiment (EOSA)
XL................ XL Capital Ltd'A' [*NYSE symbol*] (SG)
XLG.............. Excel Legacy [*AMEX symbol*] (SG)
XLSW........... Excel Switching [*NASDAQ symbol*] (SG)
XMAT.......... Explosives Management Alternatives Team [*Army*]
XMCM.......... XOOM.com,Inc. [*NYSE symbol*] (SG)
XP................ Experimental Test Pilot [*Army*]
Xr................ Christian (GEAB)
XRT.............. X-Ray Telescope
Xt................ Christ (GEAB)
Xtian........... Christian (GEAB)
Xty.............. Christianity (GEAB)
xw................ Ex-Warrants
YATS........... Youth Attitude Tracking Study
YCC............. Yankee Candle, Inc. [*NYSE symbol*] (SG)
YCM............. Yellow Collared Macaw [*Bird*]
Ye.............. Yemen, Republic of (MILB)
YFM............. Big City Radio 'A' [*AMEX symbol*] (SG)

yg................ Yellow Gold [*Watch*]
ygf.............. Yellow Gold Filled [*Watch*]
ygs............... Yellow Gold Shell [*Watch*]
yld.............. Yield
YMHA........ Young Men's Hebrew Association (PROS)
YNA............ Yellow Naped Amazon [*Bird*]
YNR............ Young & Rubicam [*NYSE symbol*] (SG)
YOCM.......... YOCREAM Intl. [*NASDAQ symbol*] (SG)
yORF.......... Yeast Open Reading Frame
YOW........... Your Own World [*Internet service*]
YUNAC........ Yugoslav Academic and Research Network
YWCA.......... Young Women's Christian Association (PROS)
YWHA........ Young Women's Hebrew Association (PROS)
YZC............. Yanzhou Coal Mining ADS [*NYSE symbol*] (SG)
Z................. Zambia (MILB)
ZDZ............ Ziff-Davis ZDNet [*NYSE symbol*] (SG)
ZIP.............. Zero-Inflated Poisson Regression [*Statistics*]
ZLC............. Zale Corp. [*NYSE symbol*] (SG)
ZNH............ China Southern Airlines'H' ADS [*NYSE symbol*] (SG)
ZSI.............. Zoological Survey of India [*Calcutta, West Bengal*]
ZSSD.......... Zoological Society of San Diego
Zw.............. Zimbabwe (MILB)
ZZTIFC........ ZZ Top International Fan Club (EA)

Numerics
By Meaning

3-Dimensional Ozone Mapping with Ultraviolet Imaging Spectrometer (EOSA) .... TOMUIS
4th Infantry Division [*Army*] 4ID
7-Eleven,Inc. [*NASDAQ symbol*] (SG) .... SVEV
18 Square Meter Sailing Association (EA) .... ESMSA

A
By Meaning

Aaron Rents [*NYSE symbol*] (SG) .... RNT
Abacus Direct [*NASDAQ symbol*] (SG) .... ABDR
Abbey (GEAB) .... ab
Abbott Consortium for Technology .... ACT
Abbreviated Tracking and Reporting Form (IUSS) .... ATARF
ABC-Naco Inc. [*NASDAQ symbol*] (SG) .... ABCR
Abdicated (GEAB) .... abd
Aberdeen, SD [*FM radio station call letters*] (BROA) .... KBFO-FM
Aberdeen Test Center .... ATC
Abilene, TX [*AM radio station call letters*] (BROA) .... KGMM
Abilene, TX [*AM radio station call letters*] (BROA) .... KMPC
Abilene, TX [*FM radio station call letters*] (BROA) .... KULL-FM
Abitibi-Consolidated [*NYSE symbol*] (SG) .... ABY
ABM Industries, Inc. [*NYSE symbol*] (SG) .... ABM
ABN AMRO Holding ADS [*NYSE symbol*] (SG) .... AAN
Aboriginal and Torres Strait Islander Commission [*Australia*] ... ATSIC
About (BEE) .... ab
About Good [*Numismatic term*] .... AG
About Uncirculated [*Numismatic term*] .... AU
About.com, Inc. [*NASDAQ symbol*] (SG) .... BOUT
Above Sea Level (QUAC) .... asl
Above-Threshold Dissociation .... ATD
Abridgement .... ab
Absolute Cryogenic Radiometer .... ACR
Abstract (GEAB) .... abs
Abu Dhabi Investment Company .... ADIC
Academia de Ciencias de Cuba (GEOI) .... ACC
Academic Press Print and Electronic Access License .... APPEAL
Academie de Medecine Veterinaire du Quebec (GVA) .... AMVQ
Academy of Veterinary Emergency & Critical Care Technicians
    (GVA) .... AVECCT
Academy of Veterinary Homeopathy (GVA) .... AVH
Acceptance Test Procedure (IUSS) .... ATP
Accessories .... Acc
Account (GEAB) .... acco
Accountable Area [*Environmental science*] (EPAT) .... AA
Accountant (PROS) .... acct
Accumulated Deductible Employee Contributions .... ADEC
Accuracy Improvement Program (IUSS) .... AIP
Accurate (GEAB) .... accu
Acid Rain Advisory Committee [*Environmental Protection Agency*]
    (EPAT) .... ARAC
Acid Rain National Early Warning Systems (EPAT) .... ARNEWS
Ackerley Group [*NYSE symbol*] (SG) .... AK
Acknowledged (GEAB) .... ackd
Acoustic (IUSS) .... ACC
Acoustic Data Base Management System (IUSS) .... ADBMS
Acoustic Data Base System (IUSS) .... ADBSS
Acoustic Data Relay (IUSS) .... ADR
Acoustic Database (IUSS) .... ADB
Acoustic Display Console (IUSS) .... ADC
Acoustic Intercept System (IUSS) .... AIS
Acoustic Performance Prediction Program (IUSS) .... APPP
Acoustic Performance Prediction System (IUSS) .... APPS
Acquisition Civilian Record Brief [*Army*] .... ACRB
Acquisition Command [*Army*] .... AC
Acquisition Coordinating Group (IUSS) .... ACG
Acquisition Education, Training, and Experience [*Army*] .... AETE
Acquisition Engineer [*Military*] (IUSS) .... AE
Acquisition Management Branch [*Army*] .... AMB
Acquisition Planning Conference (IUSS) .... APC
Acquisition Planning System (IUSS) .... APS
Acquisition Policy Working Group (IUSS) .... APWG
Acquisition Program Review Board (IUSS) .... APRB
Acquisition Program Sponsor (IUSS) .... APS
Acquisition Project Officer (IUSS) .... APO
Acquisition Request (IUSS) .... AR
Acquisition Review Council (IUSS) .... ARC
Acquisition Streamlining Initiative (IUSS) .... ASI
Acquisition Team (IUSS) .... AT
Acquisition Workforce Support Specialist [*Army*] .... AWSS
Acrodermatitis Chronica Atrophicans [*Dermatology*] .... ACA
Acting (GEAB) .... actg
Action Leakage Rate [*Environmental science*] (EPAT) .... ALR
Active Area .... AA
Active Change Initiating Document (IUSS) .... ACID

Active Control Equivalence Studies .... ACES
Active Control Station (IUSS) .... ACS
Active Electronic Countermeasures (IUSS) .... AECCM
Active Emitter File (IUSS) .... AEF
Active Fleet Ships (IUSS) .... AFS
Active Galactic Nuclei .... AGN
Active Long-Term Archive (EOSA) .... ALTA
Active Microwave Imager Synthetic Aperture Radar (GEOI) ... AMISAR
Active to Inert Conversion [*Environmental science*] (EPAT) ..... AIC
Actual Commitment (EPAT) .... AC
Ada, MI [*AM radio station call letters*] (BROA) .... WJNZ
Ada, OK [*FM radio station call letters*] (BROA) .... KTGS-FM
Adams Golf [*NASDAQ symbol*] (SG) .... ADGO
Adaptable Hydrologic Data Acquisition System (GEOI) ...... AHDAS
Adaptive Broadband [*NASDAQ symbol*] (SG) .... ADAP
Adaptive Detection, Estimation, and Correlation (IUSS) ..... ADEC
Adaptive Fire Control System [*Military*] (IUSS) .... AFCS
Adaptive Phased Array [*Military*] (IUSS) .... APA
Adaptive Planning System (GEOI) .... APS
Adaptive Triangular Mesh (GEOI) .... ATM
Addison, AL [*FM radio station call letters*] (BROA) .... WYAM-FM
Adel, GA [*AM radio station call letters*] (BROA) .... WAXD
AdForce, Inc. [*NASDAQ symbol*] (SG) .... ADFC
Adjusted (MILB) .... adj
Adjusted Acceptable Daily Intake .... AADI
Adjusted Mapping Support Data (GEOI) .... AMSD
Adjutant (GEAB) .... adj
Administaff, Inc. [*NYSE symbol*] (SG) .... ASF
Administrator (GEAB) .... admin
Admiralty (GEOI) .... Adm
Admission (GEAB) .... adm
Admissions per Thousand [*Hospitalization*] .... APT
Adolf Schild .... AS
Adolf Stieler (GEOI) .... AdSt
Adolph Schild, S.A. .... ASSA
Adtran, Inc. [*NASDAQ symbol*] (SG) .... ADTN
Advance Spaceborne Thermal Emission and Reflectance Radiometer ..... ASTER
Advance Tracker Prototype (IUSS) .... ATP
Advanced Acoustic Decoy [*Military*] (IUSS) .... AAD
Advanced Aerial Fire Support System [*Military*] (IUSS) ...... AAFS
Advanced Along-Track Scanning Radiometer (EOSA) .... AATSR
Advanced Array Sensor [*Military*] (IUSS) .... AAS
Advanced Cartographic Environment (GEOI) .... ACE
Advanced Cartographic Equipment (GEOI) .... ACE
Advanced Cartographic Systems (GEOI) .... ACS
Advanced Communications Grp. [*NYSE symbol*] (SG) .... ADG
Advanced Concept Excursion [*Army*] .... ACE
Advanced Concepts and Engineering [*Military*] (IUSS) .... AC&E
Advanced Data Technologies, Inc. (GEOI) .... ADT
Advanced Development Phase (IUSS) .... ADP
Advanced Development Program (IUSS) .... ADP
Advanced Early Warning System [*Military*] (IUSS) .... AEWS
Advanced Earth Observing Satellite (GEOI) .... ADEO
Advanced Earth Resources Satellite (GEOI) .... AERS
Advanced Elect Support Pds [*NASDAQ symbol*] (SG) .... AESP
Advanced Fibre Communication [*NASDAQ symbol*] (SG) ..... AFCI
Advanced Force Commander (IUSS) .... AFC
Advanced Humionics Platform [*Military*] .... AHP
Advanced Mach Vision Ci'A' [*NASDAQ symbol*] (SG) .... AMVC
Advanced Marine Airborne Signal Intelligence System (IUSS) ..... AMASS
Advanced Matis Group [*NQS*] .... ADMG
Advanced Medium Resolution Infrared Radiometer .... AMRIR
Advanced Microwave Sounding Unit-A (EOSA) .... AMSU-A
Advanced Moisture and Temperature Sounder (EOSA) .... AMTS
Advanced Particles and Fields Observer (EOSA) .... APAFO
Advanced Passive Sensors [*Military*] (IUSS) .... APAS
Advanced Program Management Course [*Army*] .... APMC
Advanced Radar Altimeter (EOSA) .... ADALT
Advanced Radio Telecom [*NASDAQ symbol*] (SG) .... ARTT
Advanced Reconnaissance Sensor [*Military*] (IUSS) .... ADRES
Advanced Research Project Agency Measurement Radar (IUSS) ... AMRAD
Advanced Scatterometer (EOSA) .... A-SCAT
Advanced Scientific Array Processors (GEOI) .... ASAP
Advanced Secondary Treatment [*Environmental science*] (EPAT) ..... AST
Advanced Sensor Exploration [*Military*] (IUSS) .... ASE
Advanced Spaceborne Computer Module (IUSS) .... ASCM

Advanced Spaceborne Thermal Emission and Reflection Radiometer (EOSA) ... ASTER
Advanced Strategic Computing Initiative [*Department of Energy*] ... ASCI
Advanced Submarine Combat System [*Military*] (IUSS) ... ASCS
Advanced Surface/Air Missile (IUSS) ... ASAM
Advanced Surveillance Workstation [*Military*] (IUSS) ... ASWS
Advanced Synthetic Aperture Radar (EOSA) ... A-SAR
Advanced Tactical Radar System (IUSS) ... ATRS
Advanced Technical Products [*NASDAQ symbol*] (SG) ... ATPX
Advanced Technical Workstation (IUSS) ... ATW
Advanced Technology Classroom (IUSS) ... ATC
Advanced Testing Technology (IUSS) ... ATT
Advanced Tissue Sciences [*NASDAQ symbol*] (SG) ... ATIS
Advanced Underwater Weapons System [*Military*] (IUSS) ... AUWS
Advanced Visible/InfraRed Imaging Spectrometer (GEOI) ... AVIRIS
Advanced Web Creations ... AWC
Advanced X-Ray Astrophysics Facility-Imaging [*NASA*] ... AXAF-I
Advantage Marketing System [*AMEX symbol*] (SG) ... AMM
Advertising Cup and Mug Collectors of America (EA) ... ACMCA
Advisory Committee on Agricultural Product Health and Safety [*European Union*] (GVA) ... ACAPHS
Advisory Committee on Animal Feedingstuffs (GVA) ... ACAF
Advisory Committee on the Microbiological Safety of Food (GVA) ... ACMSV
Advisory Committee on Veterinary Training [*European Union*] (GVA) ... ACVT
Aegis Realty [*AMEX symbol*] (SG) ... AER
AEGON N.V. Ord [*NYSE symbol*] (SG) ... AEG
Aerial Cartographics of America (GEOI) ... ACA
Aerial Communications [*NASDAQ symbol*] (SG) ... AERL
Aerial Data Reduction Associates, Inc. (GEOI) ... ADR
Aerial Experimental Component [*Military*] (IUSS) ... AEC
Aerial Locations of Hazardous Atmospheres (GEOI) ... ALOHA
Aerial Photography Contract Management System (GEOI) ... APCM
Aerial Photography Information System (GEOI) ... APIS
Aerial Photography Micrographic Index (GEOI) ... APMI
Aerial Photography Progress Summary Report (GEOI) ... APPSR
Aerial Photography Quad File (GEOI) ... APQF
Aerial Photography Summary Record (GEOI) ... APSR
Aerial Photography Summary Record System (GEOI) ... APSRS
Aerial Profiling of Terrain System (GEOI) ... APTS
Aerocentury Corp. [*AMEX symbol*] (SG) ... ACY
Aero-Metric Engineering, Inc. (GEOI) ... AME
Aeronautical Charting Division (GEOI) ... ADC
Aeronautics (BEE) ... Aeron
Aerosol-Cloud Interactions (QUAC) ... ACI
Aero-Triangulation (GEOI) ... AT
Affairs (PROS) ... Aff
Affidavit (GEAB) ... af
Affiliated Computer Services 'A' [*NYSE symbol*] (SG) ... ACS
Affiliated Data Center (EOSA) ... ADC
Affiliated Distributed Active Archive Center (EOSA) ... ADAAC
Affiliated Managers Grp [*NYSE symbol*] (SG) ... AMG
Affiliation (PROS) ... affil
Affirmative Action Clause ... AAC
Affirmative Action Officer ... AAO
Afghanistan (MILB) ... Afg
Afloat Contingency Command Center [*Military*] (IUSS) ... ACCC
Afloat Cryptologic Support System [*Military*] (IUSS) ... ACCS
African-American (BEE) ... Afro-Amer
After-Death Communication ... ADC
Aftermarket Technology [*NASDAQ symbol*] (SG) ... ATAC
Agenzia Spaziale Italiana [*Italy*] (EOSA) ... ASI
Agribrands Intl. [*NYSE symbol*] (SG) ... AGX
Agricultural Colony (GEOI) ... COL
Agricultural Drainage Well (GEOI) ... ADW
Agricultural Non-Point Source [*Environmental science*] ... AGNPS
Agricultural Sciences Advisory Panel (GEOI) ... ASAP
Agriculture (BEE) ... Agric
Agriculture Control Program [*Environmental Protection Agency*] (EPAT) ... ACP
Agriculture Network Information Center [*Internet resource*] ... AgDB
Agritope, Inc. [*NASDAQ symbol*] (SG) ... AGTO
Ahold Ltd. ADR [*NYSE symbol*] (SG) ... AHO
AHT Corp. [*NASDAQ symbol*] (SG) ... AHTC
AimGlobal Technologies [*AMEX symbol*] (SG) ... AGT
Aiming and Guidance [*Military*] (IUSS) ... A&G
Air Campaign Planning Tool [*Military*] (IUSS) ... ACPT
Air Command Acoustic Processing (IUSS) ... ACAP
Air Conditioner ... Air
Air Conditioning ... A/C
Air Control Supervisor [*Military*] (IUSS) ... ACS
Air Force Base/Station (MILB) ... AFB/S
Air Force Center (IUSS) ... AFC
Air Force Intelligent System (IUSS) ... AFIS
Air Force Phillips Laboratory ... AFPL
Air Force Satellite (IUSS) ... AFSAT
Air Force Studies and Analysis (IUSS) ... AF/SA
Air Management Oversight System [*Environmental science*] (EPAT) ... AMOS
Air Operations Control Center (IUSS) ... AOCC
Air Operations Officer [*Military*] (IUSS) ... AOO
Air Quality Control Program [*Environmental Protection Agency*] (EPAT) ... AQCP
Air Resources Element Coordinator (IUSS) ... AREC
Air Tour Management Plan ... ATMP
Air Traffic Control System (IUSS) ... ATCS
Air Unit Risk [*Environmental Science*] ... AUR
Air Warfare Simulation Model [*Military*] (IUSS) ... AWSIM
Airborne Anti-Submarine Warfare Coordination Aircraft (IUSS) ... AACA
Airborne Anti-Submarine Warfare Tactical Coordinator (IUSS) ... AATC
Airborne Anti-Submarine-Launched Ballistic Missile [*Military*] (IUSS) ... AASLBM
Airborne Corps (IUSS) ... ABC
Airborne Early Warning Control Center [*Military*] (IUSS) ... AEWCC
Airborne Imagery Transmission [*Military*] (IUSS) ... ABIT
Airborne Integrated Mapping System (GEOI) ... AIMS
Airborne Link Segment [*Military*] (IUSS) ... ALS
Airborne Missions and Applications Division [*Ames Research Center*] (GEOI) ... AMAD
Airborne Relay [*Military*] (IUSS) ... ABR
Airborne Remote Mapping (GEOI) ... ARM
Airborne/Shipboard Universal Recovery Device (IUSS) ... ABSURD
Airborne Strategic Communication System (IUSS) ... ASCS
Airboss of America [*Toronto Stock Exchange symbol*] (SG) ... BOS
Aircraft Reports (WEAT) ... Aireps
Airdance, Inc. [*Formerly, Bellanca-Champion Club*] (EA) ... BCC
Air-Deployable Array Sonobuoy [*Military*] (IUSS) ... ADAS
Airglow Measurements of Infrared Measurements Emissions (GEOI) ... AMIF
Airglow Solar Spectrometer Instrument ... ASSI
AirNet Systems [*NYSE symbol*] (SG) ... ANS
Airport Systems Intl. [*AMEX symbol*] (SG) ... ASY
Air-Quality Management Plan [*Environmental Protection Agency*] (EPAT) ... AQMP
Air-to-Air Missile/Refuelling (MILB) ... AAM/R
AirTran Hldgs [*NASDAQ symbol*] (SG) ... AAIR
Alabama (BEE) ... Ala
Alabama Virtual Library ... AVL
Alaris Medical [*NASDAQ symbol*] (SG) ... ALRS
Alaska (BEE) ... Alsk
Alaska Anthropological Association (QUAC) ... AAA
Alaska Department of Fish and Game (GEOI) ... ADFG
Alaska Department of Natural Resources (GEOI) ... ADNR
Alaska Department of Transportation and Public Facilities (GEOI) ... ADOTPF
Alaska Division of Policy Development and Planning (GEOI) ... ADPDP
Alaska High-Altitude Aerial Photography (GEOI) ... AHAP
Alaska Land and Resources System (GEOI) ... ALARS
Alaska Native Regional Corp. (GEOI) ... ANRC
Alaska Native Village (GEOI) ... ANV
Alaska Native Village Statistical Area (GEOI) ... ANVSA
Alaska Society of Professional Land Surveyors (GEOI) ... ASPLS
Alaskan Arctic National Wildlife Refuge (EPAT) ... AANWR
Alberta Bureau of Surveying and Mapping [*Canada*] (GEOI) ... ABSM
Alberta Geological Survey [*Canada*] (GEOI) ... AGS
Alberta Research Council [*Canada*] (QUAC) ... ARC
Alberta, VA [*FM radio station call letters*] (BROA) ... WAQD-FM
Albin, WY [*FM radio station call letters*] (BROA) ... KKAW-FM
Albuquerque, NM [*AM radio station call letters*] (BROA) ... KHTZ
Alcoa, Inc. [*NASDAQ symbol*] (SG) ... AA
Alcohol, Tobacco, and Other Drugs ... ATOD
Alderman (GEAB) ... ald
Alert Pending [*Military*] (IUSS) ... A/P
Alexander Zakreski (GEOI) ... AZ
Alexandria Digital Library (GEOI) ... ADL
Alexandria Drafting Company (GEOI) ... ADC
Alexandria, LA [*FM radio station call letters*] (BROA) ... KEDG-FM
Alexandria R.E. Equities [*NYSE symbol*] (SG) ... ARE
Algebra (BEE) ... Alg
Algeria (MILB) ... Ag
Algoma, WI [*FM radio station call letters*] (BROA) ... WRLU-FM
Algonquian (BEE) ... Algon
Algos Pharmaceutical [*NASDAQ symbol*] (SG) ... ALGO
Alias (GEAB) ... als
Alien Life-Form ... ALF
All About Marilyn [*An association*] (EA) ... AAM
All Nippon Airways ... ANA
All Purpose Tracker [*Military*] (IUSS) ... APT
Allaire Corp. [*NASDAQ symbol*] (SG) ... ALLR
Allegheny Teledyne [*NYSE symbol*] (SG) ... ALT
Allegiance (GEAB) ... alleg
Allegiance Telecom [*NASDAQ symbol*] (SG) ... ALGX
Allen Osborne Associates, Inc. (GEOI) ... ADA
Allen Telecom [*NYSE symbol*] (SG) ... ALN
Allentown, PA [*Television station call letters*] (BROA) ... WFMZ-DT
Alliance Atlantis Communic'B' [*NASDAQ symbol*] (SG) ... AACB
Alliance for Environmental Education (GEOI) ... AEF
Alliance Forest Prod [*NYSE symbol*] (SG) ... PFA
Alliant Energy [*NYSE symbol*] (SG) ... LNT
Allied Capital [*NASDAQ symbol*] (SG) ... ALLC
Allied Data Publication (IUSS) ... ADATP
Allied Healthcare Prod [*NASDAQ symbol*] (SG) ... AHPI
Allied Holdings [*NYSE symbol*] (SG) ... AHI
Allied Operational Center [*Military*] (IUSS) ... AOC
Allied Telesyn International Corp. ... ATI
Allied Waste Ind [*NYSE symbol*] (SG) ... AW
Allowance Change Request-Fixed (IUSS) ... ACR-F
Allowance Components List (IUSS) ... ACL
Allowance Quantity (IUSS) ... AQ
Allowance Support Code (IUSS) ... ASC
Allowance Tracking System [*Environmental science*] (EPAT) ... ATS
Allscripts, Inc. [*NASDAQ symbol*] (SG) ... MDRX
All-Source Imagery Processing System [*Marine Corps*] (IUSS) ... ASIP
All-Source Information Center (IUSS) ... ASIC
Allstar Systems [*NASDAQ symbol*] (SG) ... ALLS
Alltrista Corp. [*NYSE symbol*] (SG) ... ALC
Alopecia Universalis [*Dermatology*] ... AU
Alpha Beta Gamma International (EA) ... ABG

Alpha Chi (EA) ... AX
Alpha Indus [*NASDAQ symbol*] (SG) ... AHAA
Alpha Phi Delta (EA) ... APD
Alpharetta, GA [*AM radio station call letters*] (BROA) ... WLTA
Alpine Group [*NYSE symbol*] (SG) ... AGI
ALSTOM ADS [*NYSE symbol*] (SG) ... ALS
Alteration (BEE) ... alter
Alternate Logistic Control Number (IUSS) ... ALCN
Alternate National Military Command Center Software Directorate (IUSS) ... ANMCCSD
Alternate Proficiency Assessments ... APA
Alternating Conditional Expectation ... ACE
Alternating Hemiplegia of Childhood [*Medicine*] ... AHC
Alternating Magnetic (IUSS) ... AM
Alternation Installation Requirements (IUSS) ... AIR
Alternative (BEE) ... alt
Alternative Risk Transfer [*Finance*] ... ART
Alterra Healthcare [*AMEX symbol*] (SG) ... ALI
Altocumulus Castellenas Cloud (WEAT) ... AcCast
Altocumulus Lenticularis Cloud (WEAT) ... AcLent
Altocumulus Standing Lenticular Cloud (WEAT) ... ACSI
Alton, IL [*FM radio station call letters*] (BROA) ... KATZ-FM
Altos Hornos de Mexico ADS [*NYSE symbol*] (SG) ... IAM
Altostratus Cloud (WEAT) ... As
Aluminum ... Alum
Aluminum, Brick, and Glass Workers International Union ... ABG
Aluminum Four-Barrel [*Automotive term*] ... AFB
Alveolar Ventilation Rate for Experimental Animal Species ... VAa
Alveolar Ventilation Rate for Human ... VAh
Amarillo, TX [*FM radio station call letters*] (BROA) ... KAVW-FM
Amarillo, TX [*FM radio station call letters*] (BROA) ... KNSY-FM
Amarillo, TX [*FM radio station call letters*] (BROA) ... KPQZ-FM
Amateur Radio Network (EA) ... AR-Net
Amateur Speedskating Union of the United States (EA) ... ASU-USA
Amazon.com [*NASDAQ symbol*] (SG) ... AMZN
AMB Property [*NYSE symbol*] (SG) ... AMB
Ambac Financial Group [*NYSE symbol*] (SG) ... ARK
Ambassador at Large ... AL
Ambiguity Function Technique (GEOI) ... AFT
AMC Pacer Club (EA) ... AMCPC
Amdocs Ltd. [*NYSE symbol*] (SG) ... DOX
Amer Acess Technologies [*NASDAQ symbol*] (SG) ... AATK
Amer Aircarriers Support [*NASDAQ symbol*] (SG) ... AIRS
Amer Axle & Manufacturing [*NYSE symbol*] (SG) ... AXL
Amer Bank Note Holographics [*NYSE symbol*] (SG) ... ABH
Amer Bankers Insur Grp [*NYSE symbol*] (SG) ... ABI
Amer Capital Strategies [*NASDAQ symbol*] (SG) ... ACAS
Amer Community Properties Tr [*AMEX symbol*] (SG) ... APO
Amer Eco [*NASDAQ symbol*] (SG) ... ECGO
Amer Greetings Cl'A' [*NYSE symbol*] (SG) ... AM
Amer Health Pro [*NYSE symbol*] (SG) ... AHE
Amer Heritage Life [*NYSE symbol*] (SG) ... AHL
Amer Home Products [*NYSE symbol*] (SG) ... AHP
Amer Ins Mtge Inv L.P. [*AMEX symbol*] (SG) ... AIA
Amer Ins Mtge Inv Ser 85 [*AMEX symbol*] (SG) ... AII
Amer Ins Mtge Inv Ser 86 [*AMEX symbol*] (SG) ... AIJ
Amer Ins Mtge Inv Ser 88 [*AMEX symbol*] (SG) ... AIK
Amer Intl. Group [*NYSE symbol*] (SG) ... AIG
Amer Italian Pasta'A' [*NYSE symbol*] (SG) ... PLB
Amer Medical Security Grp [*NYSE symbol*] (SG) ... AMZ
Amer Mgmt Systems [*NASDAQ symbol*] (SG) ... AMSY
Amer Natl Can Group [*NYSE symbol*] (SG) ... CAN
Amer Power Conversion [*NASDAQ symbol*] (SG) ... APCC
Amer Precision Indus [*NYSE symbol*] (SG) ... APR
Amer Residential Inv Trust [*NYSE symbol*] (SG) ... INV
Amer Retirement [*NYSE symbol*] (SG) ... ACR
Amer Safety Ins Grp [*NYSE symbol*] (SG) ... ASI
Amer Science & Engr [*AMEX symbol*] (SG) ... ASE
Amer Skiing [*NYSE symbol*] (SG) ... SKI
Amer States Water [*NYSE symbol*] (SG) ... AWR
Amer Tower'A' [*NYSE symbol*] (SG) ... AMT
Amer Vanguard [*AMEX symbol*] (SG) ... AVD
Amerada Hess [*NYSE symbol*] (SG) ... AHC
Ameren Corp. [*NYSE symbol*] (SG) ... AEE
America First Mtg Investments [*NYSE symbol*] (SG) ... MFA
America West Holdings'B' [*NYSE symbol*] (SG) ... AWA
American Academy of Veterinary Disaster Medicine (GVA) ... AAVDM
American Academy of Veterinary Informatics (GVA) ... AAVI
American Accreditation Health Care Commission ... AAHC
American Antiquarian Society Proceedings (GEAB) ... AASP
American Association of Cat Enthusiasts (EA) ... AACE
American Association of Cereal Chemists ... AACCH
American Association of Food Hygiene Veterinarians (GVA) ... AAFHV
American Association of Petroleum Geologists (QUAC) ... AAPG
American Association of Professional Apiculturalists (QUAC) ... AAPA
American Association of Public Health Veterinarians (GVA) ... AAPHV
American Association of State Highway and Transportation Officials (GEOI) ... ASHTD
American Association of Veterinary Immunologists (GVA) ... AAVI
American Athletic Trainers Association and Certification Board (EA) ... AATA
American Autoduel Association (EA) ... AADA
American Belgian Malinois Club (EA) ... ABMC
American Cartographer [*A publication*] (GEOI) ... AC
American Cat Fanciers Association (EA) ... ACFA
American Chamber of Commerce for Brazil-Sao Paulo (EA) ... AMCHAM-Sao Paulo
American Chamber of Commerce in Argentina (EA) ... AmCham-Argentina
American Chamber of Commerce in Belgium (EA) ... AMCHAM
American Chamber of Commerce in France (EA) ... ACCF
American Chamber of Commerce in Italy [*An association*] ... AmCham
American Chamber of Commerce in Korea (EA) ... AMCHAM KOREA
American Chamber of Commerce in New Zealand (EA) ... AMCHAM
American Chamber of Commerce in Okinawa (EA) ... AMCHAM
American Chamber of Commerce in the Netherlands (EA) ... AMCHAM
American Chamber of Commerce of El Salvador (EA) ... AMCHAM EL SALVADOR
American Chamber of Commerce of Peru (EA) ... AMCHAM PERU
American Chamber of Commerce-Egypt (EA) ... AMCHAM Egypt
American Committee on Laboratory Animal Diseases (GVA) ... ACLAD
American Community Survey (GEOI) ... ACS
American Deaf Volleyball Association (EA) ... ADVBA
American Depositary Receipts ... ADRS
American Ferret Association (GVA) ... AFA
American Hardboard Association ... AHBA
American Indian (BEE) ... AmerInd
American Indian/Alaska Native Area (GEOI) ... AI/ANA
American Indian Lands Environmental Support Project (GEOI) ... AILESP
American Indian Policy Review Commission ... AIPRC
American Indian Reservation (GEOI) ... AIR
American Industry Government Emissions Research Consortium ... AIGER
American Institute for Management ... AIM
American Institute of Chemical Engineers ... AICHE
American Mathematical Monthly [*A publication*] ... AMM
American Museum of Natural History ... AMNH
American Muslim Council ... AMC
American Oceanographic Organization (GEOI) ... AOO
American Order of Pioneers (GEAB) ... AOP
American Ordnance Limited Liability Corporation ... AO LLC
American Pre-Veterinary Medical Association (GVA) ... APVMA
American Public Water Works Association (GEOI) ... APWWA
American Roque and Croquet Association [*Formerly, American Roque League*] (EA) ... ARL
American Running & Fitness Association ... ARFA
American Sailing Association Foundation (EA) ... ASF
American/Saudi Business Roundtable (EA) ... ASBR
American Society for Personnel Administration Accreditation Institute ... AAI
American Society for Testing Materials (GEOI) ... ASTM
American Spanish (BEE) ... AmerSp
American Stock Exchange ... Amex
American Veterinary Chiropractic Association (GVA) ... AVCA
American Veterinary Dental College (GVA) ... AVDC
American Veterinary Medical Foundation (GVA) ... AVMF
American Watchmakers-Clockmakers Institute ... AWI
American Wire Producers Association ... AWP
American Women's Association of Rome [*Italy*] ... AWAR
American-Hellenic Chamber of Commerce (EA) ... AHCC
Americans for Medical Progress (GVA) ... AMP
Americans in Milan [*An association*] ... AIM
AmeriTrade Holding'A' [*NASDAQ symbol*] (SG) ... AMTD
AmerUs Life Holdings'A' [*NYSE symbol*] (SG) ... AMH
Ames, IA [*FM radio station call letters*] (BROA) ... KLTI-FM
Ames, IA [*Television station call letters*] (BROA) ... KPWB-TV
Ames Research Center [*NASA*] (GEOI) ... ARC
Ames Satellite Communications Facility (GEOI) ... ASCF
AMF Bowling [*NYSE symbol*] (SG) ... PIN
AMFM, Inc. [*NYSE symbol*] (SG) ... AFM
Amite, LA [*FM radio station call letters*] (BROA) ... WTGG-FM
Amkor Technology [*NASDAQ symbol*] (SG) ... AMKR
Ammoniacal Copper Quaternary ... ACQ
Ampal-Amer Israel'A' [*AMEX symbol*] (SG) ... AIS
Amphibious Air Traffic Control/Direct Altitude and Identity Readout [*Military*] (IUSS) ... AATC/DAIR
Amphibious Armoured Vehicle (MILB) ... AAV
Amphibious Assault Oceanographic Reconnaissance System [*Military*] (IUSS) ... AAORS
Amphibious Control Center [*Military*] (IUSS) ... ACC
Amphibious Operations [*Military*] (IUSS) ... AO
Amplifier Control Cabinet [*Military*] (IUSS) ... ACC
Amplifier Interface Group (IUSS) ... AIG
Amplitude Line Integration (IUSS) ... ALI
Amplitudes/Hour ... A/H
AMRESCO Capital Tr [*NASDAQ symbol*] (SG) ... AMCT
Amry's Acquisition Workforce ... AAW
AmTec, Inc. [*AMEX symbol*] (SG) ... ATC
AMVESCAP PLC ADS [*NYSE symbol*] (SG) ... AVZ
Amyloid Precursor Protein ... APP
ANADIGICS, Inc. [*NASDAQ symbol*] (SG) ... ANAD
Analysis of Mobility Platform [*Military*] (IUSS) ... AMP
Analytical Detection Methods for the Irradiation Treatment of Foods ... ADMIT
Analytical Methods/Inorganic ... AMI
Analytical Methods/Organic ... AMO
Analytical Methods/Partial ... AMP
Analytical Plotter (GEOI) ... AP
Analytical Surveys, Inc. (GEOI) ... ASI
Analyzer/Classifier (IUSS) ... A/C
Ancestor Chart [*Genealogy*] (GEAB) ... AC
Ancestry (GEAB) ... anc
Anchorage, AK [*FM radio station call letters*] (BROA) ... KAFC-FM
Anchorage, AK [*FM radio station call letters*] (BROA) ... KFAT-FM
Anchorage, AK [*AM radio station call letters*] (BROA) ... KTZN

Anderson Exploration [*Toronto Stock Exchange symbol*] (SG) ...... AXL
Anderson, IN [*AM radio station call letters*] (BROA) ...... WGNR
Andrew [*Stock market symbol*] ...... ANDR
Angel Flight/Silverwings [*An association*] (EA) ...... AnF/SW
Angle Cell [*Military*] (IUSS) ...... ANGCEL
Anglo-American Cataloguing Committee for Cartographic Materials
    (GEOI) ...... AACCCM
Anglogold Ltd. ADS [*NYSE symbol*] (SG) ...... AU
Angwin, CA [*FM radio station call letters*] (BROA) ...... KNDL-FM
Animal Health and Veterinary Group [*British*] (GVA) ...... AHVG
Animal Health/Emerging Animal Diseases (GVA) ...... AHEAD
Animal Medicines Training and Regulatory Authority (GVA) ...... AMTRA
Animal Procedures Committee (GVA) ...... APC
Animal Test Certificate (GVA) ...... ATC
Animal Treatment Center (GVA) ...... ATC
Animal Welfare Foundation (GVA) ...... AWF
Animal Welfare, Science, Ethics, and Law Veterinary Association
    (GVA) ...... AWSELVA
Ankeny, IA [*FM radio station call letters*] (BROA) ...... KYSY-FM
Ann Arbor, MI [*Television station call letters*] (BROA) ...... WPXD
Anna, IL [*AM radio station call letters*] (BROA) ...... WIBH
Anna, IL [*FM radio station call letters*] (BROA) ...... WKIB-FM
Annaly Mortgage Mgmt [*NYSE symbol*] (SG) ...... NLY
Annapolis, MD [*AM radio station call letters*] (BROA) ...... WBIS
Annotated (GEAB) ...... annot
Annual Real Growth (IUSS) ...... ARG
Annual Records of Tropical Systems (QUAC) ...... ARTS
Annual Review of Progress ...... ARP
Annual to Decadal Variability in Climate in Europe (QUAC) ...... ADVICE
Annuity & Life Re [*NASDAQ symbol*] (SG) ...... ALRE
Annular Proton Telescope ...... APT
Anomalous Propagation [*Meteorology*] (WEAT) ...... ANAPROP
Anonymous (BEE) ...... Anon
Another (GEAB) ...... ano
Another World Fan Club (EA) ...... AWFC
ANSYS, Inc. [*NASDAQ symbol*] (SG) ...... ANSS
Antarctic Meteorology Research Center ...... AMRC
Antarctic Space Analog Program [*NASA*] ...... ASAP
Anterior Neural Boundary Organizer ...... ANB
Anterior Visceral Endodermal ...... AVE
Anthracite Capital [*NYSE symbol*] (SG) ...... AHR
Anti-Air Weapon Control System [*Military*] (IUSS) ...... AAWCS
Antigen Binding Fragments (MELL) ...... FAB
Antigo, WI [*Television station call letters*] (BROA) ...... WAZW
Antigua and Barbuda (MILB) ...... AB
Anti-Ovarian Antibody [*Medicine*] ...... AVA
Anti-Personnel Land-Mine (MILB) ...... APL
Anti-Phopholipid Antibody [*Medicine*] ...... APA
Antiquary (GEAB) ...... ant
Antique Engine, Tractor, and Toy Association (EA) ...... AETTA
Antique Souvenir Collectors (EA) ...... ASC
Antiquities (GEAB) ...... antiq
Anti-Roll Bar ...... ARB
Anti-Sperm Antibody [*Medicine*] ...... ASA
Anti-Spoofing (GEOI) ...... AS
Anti-Submarine Warfare Command, Control, and Communications
    Systems [*Military*] (IUSS) ...... ASWCCS
Anti-Submarine Warfare Module [*Military*] (IUSS) ...... ASWM
Anti-Submarine Warfare Operations Center-Tape Operation Systems
    [*Military*] (IUSS) ...... ATOS
Anti-Submarine Warfare School [*Military*] (IUSS) ...... ASWS
Anti-Submarine Warfare/Search and Rescue [*Military*] (IUSS) ...... ASW/SAR
Anti-Submarine Warfare Surveillance System [*Military*] (IUSS) ...... ARIADNE
Anti-Submarine Warfare Systems Project [*Military*] (IUSS) ...... ASWSP
Anti-Submarine Warfare Tactical Support Center [*Military*] (IUSS) ...... ASTAC
Antonio Castro (GEOI) ...... AC
Antonio Castro (GEOI) ...... CA
Anworth Mortgage Asset [*AMEX symbol*] (SG) ...... ANH
Any Credible Evidence [*Environmental science*] (EPAT) ...... ACE
Any Willing Provider [*Insurance*] ...... AWP
ANZ Exch Pfd Tr [*NYSE symbol*] (SG) ...... ANU Pr
A.O. Tatneft ADS [*NYSE symbol*] (SG) ...... TNT
APAC Customer Services [*NASDAQ symbol*] (SG) ...... APAC
Apex, Inc. [*NASDAQ symbol*] (SG) ...... APEX
Apex Mortgage Capital [*NYSE symbol*] (SG) ...... AXM
Apex Silver Mines [*AMEX symbol*] (SG) ...... SIL
Apogee (GEOI) ...... Apo
Apopka, FL [*AM radio station call letters*] (BROA) ...... WHIM
Appalachian Development Highway System ...... ADHS
Apparently (BEE) ...... appar
Appeared (GEAB) ...... apprd
Apple Octopus Now [*An association*] (EA) ...... AOFC
Apple Orthodontix'A' [*AMEX symbol*] (SG) ...... AOI
Application Control Center ...... ACC
Application for State School Aid ...... ASSA
Applications and Research Involving Space Technologies Observing the
    Earth's Field from a Low Earth Orbiting Satellite (EOSA) ...... ARISTOTELES
Applications Interface (IUSS) ...... AIF
Applications Network Software (IUSS) ...... ANS
Applied Analytical Industries [*NASDAQ symbol*] (SG) ...... AAII
Applied Digital Solutions [*NASDAQ symbol*] (SG) ...... ADSX
Applied Graphics Tech [*NASDAQ symbol*] (SG) ...... AGTX
Applied Indus Technologies [*NYSE symbol*] (SG) ...... APZ
Applied Mapping, Inc. (GEOI) ...... AMI
Applied Micro Circuits [*NASDAQ symbol*] (SG) ...... AMCC

Applied Quaternary Studies (QUAC) ...... AQR
Applied Research Laboratory/University of Texas (IUSS) ...... ARL/UT
AppliedTheory Corp. [*NASDAQ symbol*] (SG) ...... ATHY
Appreciation ...... app
Approved for Operational Use (IUSS) ...... AOU
Approved Training Center (GVA) ...... ATC
Approximately (GEAB) ...... approx
Apria Healthcare Grp [*NYSE symbol*] (SG) ...... AHG
April (BEE) ...... Apr
APT Satellite Hldg Ltd ADS [*NYSE symbol*] (SG) ...... ATS
Aqua Alliance'A' [*AMEX symbol*] (SG) ...... AAI
Arab, AL [*FM radio station call letters*] (BROA) ...... WAFN-FM
Arabic (BEE) ...... Ar
Arabic Sciences and Philosophy [*A publication*] ...... ASP
Arbeitsgemeinschaft fuer Osteosynthesefragen North America (GVA) ...... AONA
Arbeitsgemeinschaft fuer Osteosynthesefragen-Association for the Study
    of Internal Fixation (GVA) ...... AO/ASIF
Arbitrageur [*Business term*] ...... arb
Arboreal Pollen (QUAC) ...... AP
Arc Digitized Raster Graphics (GEOI) ...... ADRG
Arc Facilities Manager (GEOI) ...... ArcFM
Arc View Marine Spill Analysis System (GEOI) ...... AWMSAS
Arcadia Financial Ltd. [*NYSE symbol*] (SG) ...... AAC
Arch Chemicals [*NYSE symbol*] (SG) ...... ARJ
Arch Coal [*NYSE symbol*] (SG) ...... ACI
Archaeological Survey of Alberta [*Canada*] (QUAC) ...... ASA
Archaeological Survey of Canada (QUAC) ...... ASC
Archbishop (GEAB) ...... Abp
Archbold, OH [*FM radio station call letters*] (BROA) ...... WBCY-FM
Archeology (BEE) ...... Archeol
Archer-Daniels-Midland [*NYSE symbol*] (SG) ...... ADM
Archive for History of Exact Sciences [*A publication*] ...... AHES
Arctic Logistics Information Access Service (QUAC) ...... ALIAS
Arctic Monitoring and Assessment Program (GEOI) ...... AMAP
Arden Realty [*NYSE symbol*] (SG) ...... ARI
Argentaria Banco Hipotecario ADS [*NYSE symbol*] (SG) ...... AGR
Argonaut Group [*NASDAQ symbol*] (SG) ...... AGII
Argonne Tandem Linear Accelerator System ...... ATLAS
Argos Data Collection and Location System [*France*] (EOSA) ...... ARGOS
Argosy Gaming [*NYSE symbol*] (SG) ...... AGY
Argyle, NY [*FM radio station call letters*] (BROA) ...... WNGN-FM
Ariba, Inc. [*NASDAQ symbol*] (SG) ...... ARBA
Arid Climate, Adaptation, and Cultural Innovation in Africa (QUAC) ...... ACACIA
Arizona (BEE) ...... Ariz
Arizona Cardinals [*National Football League*] [*1994-present*] (NFLA) ...... Ari
Arizona Department of Transportation (GEOI) ...... ADOT
Arizona Department of Water Resources (GEOI) ...... ADWR
Arizona Geographic Information Council (GEOI) ...... AGIC
Arizona Mapping Advisory Council (GEOI) ...... AzMAP
Arizona Poison and Drug Information Center ...... APDIC
Arizona Resources Information System (GEOI) ...... ARIS
Arizona Vegetation Resource Inventory (GEOI) ...... AVRI
Arkansas (BEE) ...... Ark
Arkansas Association of Registered Land Surveyors (GEOI) ...... AARLS
Arkansas City, KS [*FM radio station call letters*] (BROA) ...... KLPQ-FM
Arkansas Geological Commission (GEOI) ...... AGC
Arkansas Resource Management Information System (GEOI) ...... ARMIS
Arkansas Society of Professional Surveyors (GEOI) ...... ASPS
Arlington, TX [*Television station call letters*] (BROA) ...... KPXD
Arlington, TX [*FM radio station call letters*] (BROA) ...... KWRD-FM
ARM Financial Grp'A' [*NYSE symbol*] (SG) ...... ARM
ARM Holdings ADS [*NASDAQ symbol*] (SG) ...... ARMHY
Arm-Disarm [*Military*] (IUSS) ...... A-D
Armed for Anti-Personnel Attack (MILB) ...... AP
Armor Holdings [*NYSE symbol*] (SG) ...... AH
Armored (MILB) ...... armd
Armored Cavalry Regiment ...... Armd Cav Regt
Arms Control Proposal [*Military*] (IUSS) ...... ACP
Armstrong World Ind 7.45% 'QUIBS' [*NYSE symbol*] (SG) ...... AKK
Army Acquisition Workforce ...... AAW
Army Development Test Command ...... ADTC
Army Materiel Systems Analysis Activity ...... AMSAA
Army Modeling and Simulation Office ...... AMSO
Army Operational Test Command ...... AOTC
Army Tank Contractor ...... ATC
Army Transportation Command (IUSS) ...... ATC
Army Warfighting Experiments ...... AWE
Army Year of Values Scales ...... AYVS
Array Gain (IUSS) ...... AG
Array Position Message (IUSS) ...... APM
Ars Orientalis: The Arts of Islam and the East [*A publication*] ...... AO
Artesyn Technologies [*NASDAQ symbol*] (SG) ...... ATSN
Arthur, ND [*FM radio station call letters*] (BROA) ...... KOCL-FM
Artillery (MILB) ...... arty
Artillery, Mortars, Cruise Missiles, Antiradiation Missiles [*Military*] ...... ARM
Arts, Bachelor of (PROS) ...... AB
Arts Create Excellent Schools [*Program*] ...... ACES
ARV Assisted Living [*AMEX symbol*] (SG) ...... SRS
Arvin, CA [*FM radio station call letters*] (BROA) ...... KBDS-FM
As a Matter of Fact [*Online dialog*] ...... AAMOF
As Received ...... AR
ASAHI/America [*NASDAQ symbol*] (SG) ...... ASAM
Asbestos-Containing Waste Material (EPAT) ...... ACWM
Asbestos-Covered Frame Building (GEOI) ...... ASBCI
Asbury Park, NJ [*AM radio station call letters*] (BROA) ...... WADB

Ascertain (GEAB) .... ascert
ASE Test Ltd. [*NASDAQ symbol*] (SG) .... ASTSF
Ash Fusion Temperature [*Coal industry*] .... AFT
Asheboro, NC [*FM radio station call letters*] (BROA) .... WWMO-FM
Ashland, MA [*AM radio station call letters*] (BROA) .... WRPT
Ashland, VA [*AM radio station call letters*] (BROA) .... WHAN
Ashore Navigation Center [*Military*] (IUSS) .... ANC
Ashtech Office Suite for Survey (GEOI) .... AOSS
Asia Pacific Development Information Programme .... APDIP
Asia Pacific Wire & Cable [*NYSE symbol*] (SG) .... AWC
Asia Satellite Telecom ADS [*NYSE symbol*] (SG) .... SAT
Asia-Europe Meeting .... ASEM
Asian Association on Remote Sensing (GEOI) .... AARS
Asian Conference on Remote Sensing (GEOI) .... ACRS
Asian Regional Remote Sensing Training Centre (GEOI) ... ARRSTC
Asiatic Parrot Society of America (EA) .... APSA
ASK Jeeves [*NASDAQ symbol*] (SG) .... ASKJ
ASM Intl. N.V. [*NASDAQ symbol*] (SG) .... ASMI
ASM Lithography Hldg NV [*NASDAQ symbol*] (SG) .... ASML
Asociacion Mexicana de Medicos Veterinarios Especialistas en Pequenas
  Especies [*Mexican Small Animal Veterinary Association*] (GVA) .... AMMVEPE
Asociation de Juventud Rebelde [*Association of Rebel Youth*] .... AJR
Asperger's Syndrome [*Medicine*] .... AS
Asphalt Roofing Manufacturers Association .... ARM
Assault (MILB) .... aslt
Assessment of Long-Range Fleet Architecture [*Military*] (IUSS) .... ALFA
Assessor (GEAB) .... asr
Assigned (GEAB) .... asgd
Assistant Program Manager (IUSS) .... APM
Assistant Secretary of the Army for Acquistion, Logistics, and
  Technology .... ASAALT
Assistant Secretary of the Army for Installations, Logistics and
  Environment .... ASA(ILE)
Assisted Reproductive Technology [*Medicine*] .... ART
Associacao Brasileira de Buiatria [*Brazilian Veterinary Cattle Association*]
  (GVA) .... ABB
Associacao Brasileira de Veterinarios de Animais Selvagens [*Brazilian
  Small Animal Veterinary Association*] (GVA) .... ABRAVAS
Associacion Mexicana Automovilistica (GEOI) .... AMA
Associated Actors and Artistes of America (EA) .... 4A's
Associated Service Organization .... ASO
Associates (BEE) .... assocs
Associates for Research into the Science of Enjoyment .... ARISE
Association (GEOI) .... Ass
Association (PROS) .... Assn
Association Canadienne des Palynologues (QUAC) .... ACP
Association Democratique des Femmes du Maroc [*Morocco*] .... ADFM
Association for Educational Communications & Technology .... AECT
Association for Environmental Archaeology (QUAC) .... AEA
Association for Geographic Information [*London, England*] (GEOI) .... AGI
Association for Protection of Jewish Immigrants (GEAB) .... APJI
Association for the Study of Literature and the Environment (QUAC) .... ASLE
Association for Veterinary Clinical Pharmacology and Therapeutics
  (GVA) .... AVCPT
Association for Veterinary Informatics (GVA) .... AVI
Association Internationale de Palynologie Africaine [*International
  Association of African Palynology*] (QUAC) .... AIPA
Association of American Battery Manufacturers, Inc. .... AABM
Association of Bay Area Governments [*California*] (GEOI) .... ABAG
Association of British Dogs' Homes (GVA) .... ABDH
Association of Canadian Land Surveyors (GEOI) .... ACLS
Association of Canadian Map Libraries (GEOI) .... ACML
Association of Certified Survey Technicians and Technologists of Ontario
  [*Canada*] (GEOI) .... ACSTTO
Association of Chartered Physiotherapists in Animal Therapy (GVA) .... ACPAT
Association of Coffee Mill Enthusiasts (EA) .... ACME
Association of Computing Machinery Geographic Information Systems
  (GEOI) .... ACMGIS
Association of Computing Machinery Special Interest Group on Graphics
  (GEOI) .... ACM-SIGGRAPH
Association of Container Reconditioners .... NABADA
Association of Earth Science Editors (GEOI) .... AESE
Association of Ontario Land Surveyors [*Canada*] (GEOI) .... AOLS
Association of Pet Behavior Counsellors (GVA) .... APBC
Association of Polish Geomorphologists (QUAC) .... APG
Association of Reptilian & Amphibian Veterinarians (GVA) .... ARAV
Association of State Veterinary Officers (GVA) .... ASVO
Association of Veterinarians for Animal Rights (GVA) .... AVAR
Association of Veterinarians in Industry (GVA) .... AVI
Association of Veterinary Consultants (GVA) .... AVC
Association of Veterinary Surgeons Practicing in Northern Ireland
  (GVA) .... AVSPNI
Association of Veterinary Teachers and Research Workers (GVA) .... AVT&RW
Associative Ionization .... AI
Asteroid Detection System .... ADS
Asteroid Negation System .... ANS
Astoria, OR [*AM radio station call letters*] (BROA) .... KCHT
AstraZeneca ADR [*NYSE symbol*] (SG) .... AZN
Astronomical Data Center .... ADC
Astrophysical, Planetary, and Atmospheric Sciences .... APAS
Asymmetric Maximum Likelihood [*Statistics*] .... AML
Asymmetric Maximum Liklihood .... AML
Asynchronous Channel Multiplexer (IUSS) .... ACM
Asynchronous Communication Channel Multiplexer (IUSS) .... ACCM
At Entertainment, Inc. [*NASDAQ symbol*] (SG) .... ATEN

At Home Corp.'A' [*NASDAQ symbol*] (SG) .... ATHM
At Sea Tactical Exercises [*Military*] (IUSS) .... ASTE
Atalanta/Sosnoff Capital [*NYSE symbol*] (SG) .... ATL
AT&T Canada'B' [*NASDAQ symbol*] (SG) .... ATTC
AT&T Capital 8.25% 'PINES' [*NYSE symbol*] (SG) .... NCD
AT&T Capital 8.125% 'PINES' [*NYSE symbol*] (SG) .... NCF
Atchinson, Topeka, & Santa Fe Railway Co. .... ASTF
Atchison Casting [*NYSE symbol*] (SG) .... FDY
Athol, MA [*FM radio station call letters*] (BROA) .... WCAT-FM
Atkins, AR [*FM radio station call letters*] (BROA) .... KBHY-FM
Atlanta Falcons [*National Football League*] [*1966-present*] (NFLA) .... Atl
Atlanta, GA [*Television station call letters*] (BROA) .... WAGA-DT
Atlanta, GA [*AM radio station call letters*] (BROA) .... WAZJ
Atlanta, GA [*Television station call letters*] (BROA) .... WGNX-DT
Atlanta, GA [*Television station call letters*] (BROA) .... WSB-DT
Atlanta, GA [*Television station call letters*] (BROA) .... WXIA-DT
Atlanta, IL [*FM radio station call letters*] (BROA) .... WMNW-FM
Atlantic Beach, SC [*FM radio station call letters*] (BROA) .... WSEA-FM
Atlantic City, NJ [*FM radio station call letters*] (BROA) .... WAJM-FM
Atlantic City, NJ [*FM radio station call letters*] (BROA) .... WPUR-FM
Atlantic Climate Change .... ACC
Atlantic Coast Airlines Hldgs [*NASDAQ symbol*] (SG) .... ACAI
Atlantic Data Coverage .... ADC
Atlantic Premium Brands [*AMEX symbol*] (SG) .... ABR
Atlantic Richfield [*NYSE symbol*] (SG) .... ARC
Atlantic Tele-Network [*AMEX symbol*] (SG) .... ANK
Atlantic Telephone & Telegraph .... AT&T
Atlantis Plastics [*AMEX symbol*] (SG) .... AGH
Atlas Air [*NYSE symbol*] (SG) .... CGO
ATMI, Inc. [*NASDAQ symbol*] (SG) .... ATMI
Atmospheric and Environmental Research (EOSA) .... AER
Atmospheric and Oceanographic Image Processing System (GEOI) .... AOIPS
Atmospheric Emitted Radiance Interferometer .... AERI
Atmospheric Explorer Mission (GEOI) .... AEM
Atmospheric Lyman Alpha Emissions (GEOI) .... ALAE
Atmospheric Mesoscale Campaigns (QUAC) .... AMC
Atomic, Molecular, and Optical .... AMO
Attach Center [*Military*] (IUSS) .... AC
Attachment Disorder [*Medicine*] .... AD
Attack Group [*Military*] (IUSS) .... AG
Attack Group Commander [*Military*] (IUSS) .... AGC
Attica, NY [*FM radio station call letters*] (BROA) .... WXOX-FM
Attitude Measurement Sensor (GEOI) .... AMS
Attitudes, Interests, and Opinions .... AIO
Attleboro, MA [*AM radio station call letters*] (BROA) .... WJYT
Atwood Oceanics [*NYSE symbol*] (SG) .... ATW
Atwood, TN [*FM radio station call letters*] (BROA) .... WTKB-FM
Auburn, CA [*AM radio station call letters*] (BROA) .... KSMH
Auburn, IN [*AM radio station call letters*] (BROA) .... WGLL
Auburn, ME [*FM radio station call letters*] (BROA) .... WMWX-FM
Auburn, NY [*AM radio station call letters*] (BROA) .... WKGJ
Audio Book Club (SG) .... KLB
Audio Switching Matrix (IUSS) .... ASM
Audio/Visual Object (GEOI) .... AVO
Audio-Visual and Cartographic Archives Division [*National Archives of
  Canada*] (GEOI) .... AVCA
Auditor (GEAB) .... aud
Audits of Data Quality [*Environmental science*] (EPAT) .... ADQ
Augmentative (BEE) .... aug
August (BEE) .... Aug
Auguste Reymond, SA .... ARSA
Aurora Foods [*NYSE symbol*] (SG) .... AOR
Aurora, NC [*FM radio station call letters*] (BROA) .... WFPF-FM
Auroral Imaging Observatory (EOSA) .... AURIO
Austin, TX [*Television station call letters*] (BROA) .... KLRU-DT
Australasian Data Exchange Centre (GEOI) .... AUSDEC
Australasian Regional Association of Zoological Parks and Aquaria
  (GVA) .... ARAZPA
Australasian Urban and Regional Information Systems Association
  (GEOI) .... AURISA
Australia (MILB) .... Aus
Australia New Zealand Land Information Council (GEOI) .... ANZLIC
Australia School Library Association .... ASLA
Australian (BEE) .... Aust
Australian and New Zealand Council for the Care of Animals in Research
  and Teaching (GVA) .... ANZCCART
Australian Animal Health Council (GVA) .... AAHC
Australian Animal Health Laboratory .... AAHL
Australian Association of Veterinary Conservation Biologists (GVA) .... AAVCB
Australian Bat Lyssavirus .... ABL
Australian Bureau of Statistics (GEOI) .... ABS
Australian Companion Animal Health Foundation (GVA) .... ACAHF
Australian Institute of Cartographers (GEOI) .... AIC
Australian Mammal Society (GVA) .... AMS
Australian Map Grid (GEOI) .... AMG
Australian National Antarctic Research Expeditions (GEOI) .... ANARE
Australian Remote Sensing Conference (GEOI) .... ARSC
Australian Science and Technology Council .... ASTEC
Australian Small Animal Veterinary Association (GVA) .... ASAVA
Australian Survey Office (GEOI) .... ASO
Australian Surveying and Land Information Group (GEOI) .... AUSLIG
Australian Veterinary Association (GVA) .... AVA
Authorized Development Deviation (IUSS) .... ADD
Authorized Replacement Parts List (IUSS) .... ARPL
Auto House (GEOI) .... A

Auto in Basement (GEOI)	A IN B
Auto-Alerting (IUSS)	AA
Autoallergic Myositis [Dermatology]	AM
AutoBond Acceptance [AMEX symbol] (SG)	ABD
autobytel.com, Inc. [NASDAQ symbol] (SG)	ABTL
AutoCAD Data Extension (GEOI)	ADE
Autoclaved Aerated Concrete	AAC
Autoliv, Inc. [NYSE symbol] (SG)	ALV
Automated Cartographic Information Center [University of Minnesota Library] (GEOI)	ACIC
Automated Cartographic Systems (GEOI)	ACS
Automated Census Mapping System (GEOI)	ACMS
Automated Chart Production System (GEOI)	ACAPS
Automated Command and Control Message Processing System [Military] (IUSS)	ACCMPS
Automated Data Processing Standardization Working Group (IUSS)	ADPSWG
Automated Data Processing Standards Policy Group (IUSS)	ASPG
Automated Data System-Development Plan (IUSS)	ADDS-DP
Automated Detection/Computer-Aided Classification (IUSS)	AD/CAC
Automated Geographic Information System (GEOI)	AGIS
Automated Graphics Digitizing System (GEOI)	AGDS
Automated Integrated Language (IUSS)	AIL
Automated Integrated Language System Identification Number (IUSS)	AILSIN
Automated Land Information System (GEOI)	ALIS
Automated Lands Project (GEOI)	ALP
Automated Mapping System (GEOI)	AMS
Automated Message Processing Equipment (IUSS)	AMPE
Automated Package Test System (IUSS)	APTS
Automated Product Development Framework	APDF
Automated Tactical Information Display System (IUSS)	ATIDS
Automated Tactical Information System (IUSS)	ATIS
Automated Technical Manual (IUSS)	ATM
Automated Technical Systems (GEOI)	ATS
Automated Text Message Handling System (IUSS)	ATMHS
Automated Voice Switching System (IUSS)	AVSS
Automatic Beam Forming [Military] (IUSS)	ABF
Automatic Bearing Instrumentation (IUSS)	ABI
Automatic Electronic Intelligence Emitter Location System (IUSS)	AEELS
Automatic Experimental Monitoring (IUSS)	AEM
Automatic Facilities Control Subsystem (IUSS)	AFCS
Automatic Key Distribution Center (IUSS)	AKDC
Automatic Musical Instrument Collectors Association International (EA)	AMICA
Automatic Reporting System (IUSS)	ARS
Automatic Secure Voice Communications Network, Phase II (IUSS)	AUTOSEVCOMII
Automatic Sprinklers (GEOI)	AS
Automatic Telecommunications Program (IUSS)	ATP
Automatic Transmission	ATX
Automatic Transmission	Auto
Automatic Transmission	AUTO
Automobile Club of Southern California (GEOI)	ACSC
Automotive Youth Employment Services	AYES
Automovil Club Argentino (GEOI)	ACA
AutoNation, Inc. [NYSE symbol] (SG)	AN
Autonomous System Number	ASN
Autoweb.com, Inc. [NASDAQ symbol] (SG)	AWEB
Autralasian Quaternary Association (QUAC)	AQUA
Auxiliary Interface Cabinet (IUSS)	AIC
Avado Brands [NASDAQ symbol] (SG)	AVDO
Avalon, CA [Television station call letters] (BROA)	KBJO
Avalon Holdings'A' [AMEX symbol] (SG)	AWX
Avenue (GEOI)	Av
Avenue Entertainment Grp [AMEX symbol] (SG)	PIX
Average Circulated [Numismatic term]	AVG
Average on Board	AOB
Average Percent Complete (IUSS)	APC
Aviation (MILB)	avn
Aviation Management Information System (GEOI)	AMIS
Aviation Sales [NYSE symbol] (SG)	AVS
Aviation Weather Center	AWC
Avionics Maintenance Trainer [Military] (IUSS)	AMT
Avis Rent A Car [NYSE symbol] (SG)	AVI
Avista, Corp. [NYSE symbol] (SG)	AVA
AxyS Pharmaceuticals [NASDAQ symbol] (SG)	AXPH
Azerbaijan (MILB)	Az
Aztec Mfg Co. [NYSE symbol] (SG)	AZZ
Azurix Corp. [NYSE symbol] (SG)	AZX

B

By Meaning

Babe Ruth Baseball/Softball [*An association*] (EA) .... BRB
Bachelor (GEAB) .... ba
Bachelor (GEAB) .... bach
Back at Keyboard [*Online dialog*] .... BAK
Back to the Future, the Fan Club (EA) .... BTTFTFC
Background Air Pollution Monitoring (QUAC) .... BAPMON
BackWeb Technologies [*NASDAQ symbol*] (SG) .... BWEB
Bacteriology (BEE) .... Bacteriol
Badan Pembinaan dan Penerapan Teknologi [*Indonesia*] (GEOI) .... BPPT
Bagdad, AZ [*FM radio station call letters*] (BROA) .... KBJU-FM
Bahamas Billfish Championship .... BBC
Bahamas Lands and Surveys Department (GEOI) .... BLS
Bahrain (MILB) .... Brn
Baker, Michael [*AMEX symbol*] (SG) .... BKR
Baker, MT [*FM radio station call letters*] (BROA) .... KJJM-FM
Bakery, Confectionary, Tobacco Workers, and Grain Millers International
  Union .... BCTGM
Balanced Care [*AMEX symbol*] (SG) .... BAL
Balanced Incomplete Repeated Measures Design .... BIRMD
Ball, LA [*FM radio station call letters*] (BROA) .... KHFX-FM
Ballard Power Systems [*NASDAQ symbol*] (SG) .... BLDP
Ballistic Electron Emission Spectroscopy .... BEEM
Bally Total Fitness Holding [*NYSE symbol*] (SG) .... BFT
Baltic Sea Experiment (QUAC) .... BALTEX
Baltimore Colts [*National Football League*] [*1950, 1953-83*] (NFLA) .... Bal
Baltimore, MD [*Television station call letters*] (BROA) .... WBAL-DT
Baltimore, MD [*Television station call letters*] (BROA) .... WJZ-DT
Baltimore, MD [*Television station call letters*] (BROA) .... WMAR-DT
Baltimore Ravens [*National Football League*] [*1996-present*] (NFLA) .... BRv
Banc Galicia-Buenos AiresADR [*NASDAQ symbol*] (SG) .... BGALY
Banco BHIF ADS [*NYSE symbol*] (SG) .... BB
Banco Nacional de Obras y Servicios Publicos [*Mexico*] (GEOI) .... Banobras
Banco Rio De La Plata ADS [*NYSE symbol*] (SG) .... BRS
Banco Santander Cent Hispano ADS [*NYSE symbol*] (SG) .... STD
Banco Santander Central Hispano [*Spain*] .... BSCH
Banco Santander-Puerto Rico [*NYSE symbol*] (SG) .... SBP
BancorpSouth [*NYSE symbol*] (SG) .... BXS
BancWest Corp. [*NYSE symbol*] (SG) .... BWE
Band Interleaved by Pixel (GEOI) .... BIP
Band Sequential (GEOI) .... BSQ
Bandwidth Compression (GEOI) .... BWC
Bandwith Expansion (GEOI) .... BWE
Bangladesh (MILB) .... Bng
Bank of America [*NYSE symbol*] (SG) .... BAC
Bank of Ireland Governor & Co ADS [*NYSE symbol*] (SG) .... IRE
Bank of New York .... BONY
Bank One Corp. [*NYSE symbol*] (SG) .... ONE
Bank United 'A' [*NYSE symbol*] (SG) .... BNKU
BankAtlantic Bancorp 'A' [*NYSE symbol*] (SG) .... BBX
BankBoston Corp. [*NYSE symbol*] (SG) .... BKB
Bankfull (QUAC) .... bkf
Banta Corp. [*NYSE symbol*] (SG) .... BN
Baptism (GEAB) .... bap
Baptized (GEAB) .... bpt
Bar Code Information System (GEOI) .... BARCIS
Bar Harbor Bankshares [*AMEX symbol*] (SG) .... BHB
Barbados (MILB) .... Bds
Barbara Eden's Official Fan Club (EA) .... BEOFC
Bare Eyed Cockatoo [*Bird*] BE2
barnesandnoble.com, Inc.'A' [*NASDAQ symbol*] (SG) .... BNBN
Barr Laboratories [*NYSE symbol*] (SG) .... BRL
Barrel [*Automotive term*] .... Bbl
Barron, WI [*FM radio station call letters*] (BROA) .... WBFE-FM
Base Spatial Unit (GEOI) .... BSU
Base Topo (GEOI) .... BT
Baseball .... BB
Basic Land and Property Unit (GEOI) .... BLPU
Basic Order Agreement .... BOA
Basile, LA [*FM radio station call letters*] (BROA) .... KQIS-FM
Basket .... Bas
Basketball .... bskb
Bastrop, LA [*FM radio station call letters*] (BROA) .... KAXV-FM
Bastrop, TX [*FM radio station call letters*] (BROA) .... KYCM-FM
Batesville, AR [*FM radio station call letters*] (BROA) .... KBTA-FM
Bathymetric Navigation Planning Chart (GEOI) .... BNPC
Batman the Animated Series [*Television program*] .... BTAS

Baton Rouge, LA [*FM radio station call letters*] (BROA) ...... WXCT-FM
Battalion (MILB) .... bn
Battery (MILB) .... bty
Battle Creek, MI [*AM radio station call letters*] (BROA) .... WRCC
Battle Point Astronomical Association .... BPAA
Baume & Mercier .... BM
Baxley, GA [*Television station call letters*] (BROA) .... WGSA
Bay Area Automated Mapping Association (GEOI) .... BAAMA
Bay Area Digital GeoResource (GEOI) .... BADGER
Bay Conservation and Development Commission (GEOI) .... BCDC
Bay Springs, MS [*FM radio station call letters*] (BROA) ...... WKZW-FM
Bay State Bancorp [*AMEX symbol*] (SG) .... BYS
Bay View Capital [*NYSE symbol*] (SG) .... BVC
Bayboro, NC [*FM radio station call letters*] (BROA) .... WBHU-FM
Baycorp Holdings [*AMEX symbol*] (SG) .... MWH
Bayside, VA [*AM radio station call letters*] (BROA) .... WBVA
BB&T Corp. [*NYSE symbol*] (SG) .... BBT
BCE Mobile Communic [*NYSE symbol*] (SG) .... BCX
BCT.TELUS Communications [*Toronto Stock Exchange symbol*] (SG) .... BTS
BE Semiconductor Indus [*NASDAQ symbol*] (SG) .... BESI
BEA Systems [*NASDAQ symbol*] (SG) .... BEAS
Beach Boys Fan Club (EA) .... BBFC
Bear Creek Township, MI [*FM radio station call letters*] (BROA) .... WTLI-FM
Beatles Fan Club: Good Day Sunshine (EA) .... BFCGDS
Beaufort and Arctic Storms Experiment (QUAC) .... BASE
Beaufort Force (WEAT) .... Bf
Beaumont, TX [*AM radio station call letters*] (BROA) .... KRCM
Beaver Dam, KY [*FM radio station call letters*] (BROA) .... WKLX-FM
Beaver Falls, PA [*FM radio station call letters*] (BROA) ...... WAMO-FM
BEC Energy [*NYSE symbol*] (SG) .... BSE
Became (GEAB) .... bec
Beckman Coulter [*New York City*] (SG) .... BEC
Bedford, NH [*FM radio station call letters*] (BROA) .... WQLL-FM
Bedford, PA [*AM radio station call letters*] (BROA) .... WOOX
Bedliner .... BDLNR
Before Upper Dead Center .... BUDC
BEI Technologies [*NASDAQ symbol*] (SG) .... BEIQ
Beijing Astronomical Observatory [*China*] .... BAO
Beijing Underground-Network Information System [*China*] (GEOI) .... BUPNIS
Beijing Yanhua Petrochem'H' ADS [*NYSE symbol*] (SG) .... BYH
Bel .... B
Bel Fuse, Inc.'A' [*NASDAQ symbol*] (SG) .... BELFA
Belarus (MILB) .... Bel
Belgian Veterinary Computer Association (GVA) .... BCVA
Belgium (MILB) .... Be
Belize (MILB) .... Bze
Bell Canada Intl. [*NASDAQ symbol*] (SG) .... BCICF
Bell Labs Layered Space-Time .... BLAST
Bellaire, TX [*AM radio station call letters*] (BROA) .... KILE
Belle Plaine, IA [*FM radio station call letters*] (BROA) .... KZAT-FM
Belleek Collectors' International Society (EA) .... BCS
Belleview, FL [*FM radio station call letters*] (BROA) .... WWKO-FM
Bellevue, WA [*Television station call letters*] (BROA) .... KWPX
Bellview, MN [*FM radio station call letters*] (BROA) .... KBGP-FM
Below Datum (QUAC) .... bd
Below Surface (QUAC) .... bs
Belvidere, NJ [*FM radio station call letters*] (BROA) .... WWYY-FM
Belzoni, MS [*FM radio station call letters*] (BROA) .... WGNG-FM
Bemidji, MN [*FM radio station call letters*] (BROA) .... KKZY-FM
Benchmark Electronics [*NYSE symbol*] (SG) .... BHE
Benckiser N.V.'B' [*NYSE symbol*] (SG) .... BNV
Bengston, DeBell, Elkin & Titus Ltd. (GEOI) .... BDET
Benguet Corp.Cl'B' [*NYSE symbol*] (SG) .... BE
Benin (MILB) .... Bn
Bennington, VT [*FM radio station call letters*] (BROA) .... WBTN-FM
Bent Knee Walker [*Doll collecting*] .... BKW
Benthos, Inc. [*NASDAQ symbol*] (SG) .... BTHS
Benton Harbor, MI [*FM radio station call letters*] (BROA) ...... WYKL-FM
Benton, KY [*FM radio station call letters*] (BROA) .... WTRT-FM
Benton Oil & Gas [*NYSE symbol*] (SG) .... BNO
Benton, TN [*FM radio station call letters*] (BROA) .... WOCE-FM
Benvenuto Club [*Milan, Italy*] .... BV
Berkeley Internet Name Domain [*California*] .... BIND
Berkeley-Illinois-Maryland Array .... BIMA
Berkley, W.R. [*NASDAQ symbol*] (SG) .... BKLY
Berlin Kommandatura Commandents' Letter .... BKC/L

Berlin Quadripartite Document ... BQD
Berlin Task Force ... BTF
Berlin, WI [*FM radio station call letters*] (BROA) ... WBJZ-FM
Bernhard, Eisenbraun and Associates (GEOI) ... BEA
Best Buy [*NYSE symbol*] (SG) ... BBY
Best Conventional Pollutant Control Technology (EPAT) ... BCPCT
Best Demonstrated Achievable Technology [*Environmental science*] (EPAT) ... BDAT
Best Demonstrated Control Technology [*Environmental science*] (EPAT) ... BDCT
Best Qualified ... BQ
Bestfoods [*NYSE symbol*] (SG) ... BFO
Beta Kappa Chi (EA) ... BKX
Beta-Site Amyloid Precursor Protein-Cleaving Enzyme ... BACE
Better Assessment Science Integrating Point and Nonpoint Systems (GEOI) ... BASINS
Beyond.com Corp. [*NASDAQ symbol*] (SG) ... BYND
BFX Hospitality Group [*AMEX symbol*] (SG) ... BFX
BG plc ADS [*NYSE symbol*] (SG) ... BRG
BHA Group [*NASDAQ symbol*] (SG) ... BHAG
Bibliography (GEAB) ... bl
Bicuculline ... Bicuc
Bicycle Federation of America (EA) ... PRO BIKE
Big City Radio 'A' [*AMEX symbol*] (SG) ... YFM
Big Evil Grin [*Online dialog*] ... BEG
Big Flower Holdings [*NYSE symbol*] (SG) ... BGF
Big Lake, TX [*FM radio station call letters*] (BROA) ... KWTR-FM
Big Spring, TX [*FM radio station call letters*] (BROA) ... KBCX-FM
Big Ten Conference (EA) ... BTC
Bilateral Hilar Adenopathy [*Dermatology*] ... BHA
Billing Concepts [*NASDAQ symbol*] (SG) ... BILL
Billings, MT [*FM radio station call letters*] (BROA) ... KBEX-FM
Billings, MT [*AM radio station call letters*] (BROA) ... KBUL
Billings, MT [*FM radio station call letters*] (BROA) ... KCMT-FM
Billy Blanton Fan Club International (EA) ... BBFCI
Biltmore Forest, NC [*FM radio station call letters*] (BROA) ... WZRQ-FM
Binary Digit Eight ... byte
Binary Line Generalization (GEOI) ... BLG
Binghamton, NY [*Television station call letters*] (BROA) ... WIVT
BioChem Pharma [*NASDAQ symbol*] (SG) ... BCHE
Biodegradation, Hydrolysis and Photolysis ... BHP
Biodiversity Mapping for Protection and Sustainable Use of Natural Resources (GEOI) ... BIOMAPS
Biological and Toxin Weapons Convention ... BTWC
Biological Chemicals of Concern [*Environmental science*] ... BCC
Biological Values ... BV
Biomatrix, Inc. [*NYSE symbol*] (SG) ... BXM
Biomedical Research Education Trust (GVA) ... BRET
Bioremediation Action Committee [*Environmental science*] (EPAT) ... BAC
Biosphere-Atmosphere Trace Gas Exchange in the Tropics (QUAC) ... BATGE
Biosphere-Atmosphere Transfers and Ecological Research in Situ Studies in Amazonia (QUAC) ... BATERISTA
Bird Clubs of America (EA) ... BCA
Birds and Wildlife ... B&W
Birmingham, AL [*AM radio station call letters*] (BROA) ... WEZN
Birmingham, AL [*Television station call letters*] (BROA) ... WIAT
Birmingham, AL [*AM radio station call letters*] (BROA) ... WMKI
Birth Certificate (GEAB) ... bcer
Birth Date (GEAB) ... bdt
Birthplace (GEAB) ... bp
Birthplace (GEAB) ... bpl
Bishop (GEAB) ... bish
Bismarck, ND [*Television station call letters*] (BROA) ... KBME-DT
Bismarck, ND [*Television station call letters*] (BROA) ... KNDX
Bithlo, FL [*AM radio station call letters*] (BROA) ... WNTF
Bivariate Normal Probability Density (GEOI) ... BNPD
BJ Services [*NYSE symbol*] (SG) ... BJS
BJ's Wholesale Club [*NYSE symbol*] (SG) ... BJ
Black and White ... B/W
Black Mountain, NC [*AM radio station call letters*] (BROA) ... WTZK
Blackfoot, ID [*AM radio station call letters*] (BROA) ... KBLI
Blackhawk Standbys [*An association*] (EA) ... BSI
Blacksburg Electronic Village ... BEV
Blackwall [*Automotive term*] ... BW
Blanchard, LA [*FM radio station call letters*] (BROA) ... KRVQ-FM
BLC Financial Svcs [*AMEX symbol*] (SG) ... BCL
Blimpie Int'l. [*AMEX symbol*] (SG) ... BLM
Block Island, RI [*FM radio station call letters*] (BROA) ... WERI-FM
Block Island, RI [*Television station call letters*] (BROA) ... WPXQ
Blocked Impurity Band ... BIB
Blood Lead ... BL
Bloomfield (BEE) ... Blmfld
Bloomfield, CT [*AM radio station call letters*] (BROA) ... WDZK
Bloomington (BEE) ... Bton
Blown Head Gasket [*Automotive term*] ... BHG
Blue and Gold Macaw [*Bird*] ... B&G
Blue Crown Conure [*Bird*] ... BC
Blue Fronted Amazon [*Bird*] ... BFA
Blue Square-Israel ADS [*NYSE symbol*] (SG) ... BSI
Bluefield, VA [*AM radio station call letters*] (BROA) ... WBDY
Bluffton, SC [*FM radio station call letters*] (BROA) ... WWVV-FM
B-Lymphocyte Chemoattractant ... BLC
BMW Car Club of America (EA) ... BMW CCA
BMW Riders Association (EA) ... BMW RA
Boalsburg, PA [*FM radio station call letters*] (BROA) ... WBUS-FM
Board of Coast and Geodetic Survey [*Philippines*] (GEOI) ... BCGS
Board of Registration for Professional Engineers and Land Surveyors [*California*] (GEOI) ... BORPELS
Bob Crane Memorial Fan Club (EA) ... BCMFC
Bob Dylan Newsletter [*An association*] (EA) ... BDN
BOC Group ADS [*NYSE symbol*] (SG) ... BOX
Bofors Optronic Fire Control Instrument (MILB) ... BOFI
Boggs and Lewis (GEOI) ... B&L
Boise, ID [*FM radio station call letters*] (BROA) ... KBSX-FM
Bolt Technology [*AMEX symbol*] (SG) ... BTJ
Bomber (MILB) ... bbr
Bondsman (GEAB) ... bndsmn
Bonifay, FL [*FM radio station call letters*] (BROA) ... WYYX-FM
Bonnie Lou Bishop International Fan Club (EA) ... BLBIFC
Bonsai ... Bon
Book Item Contribution Identifer (GEOI) ... BICI
Books and Open-File Report Section (GEOI) ... BOFRS
Boonville, MO [*FM radio station call letters*] (BROA) ... KBHO-FM
Boonville, MO [*FM radio station call letters*] (BROA) ... KCLR-FM
Boots&Coots Intl. Well Control [*AMEX symbol*] (SG) ... WEL
Bore and Stroke ... B&S
Boron LePore & Assoc [*NASDAQ symbol*] (SG) ... BLPG
Borough (BEE) ... Boro
Bosnia-Herzegovina (MILB) ... BiH
Boston Braves [*National Football League*] [*1932*] (NFLA) ... BBr
Boston Bruins Hockey Fan Club (EA) ... BBFC
Boston Harbor Software, Inc. (GEOI) ... BHS
Boston, MA [*Television station call letters*] (BROA) ... WBZ-DT
Boston, MA [*Television station call letters*] (BROA) ... WCVB-DT
Boston, MA [*Television station call letters*] (BROA) ... WFXT-DT
Boston, MA [*Television station call letters*] (BROA) ... WGBH-DT
Boston, MA [*Television station call letters*] (BROA) ... WGBX-DT
Boston, MA [*Television station call letters*] (BROA) ... WHDH-DT
Boston, MA [*AM radio station call letters*] (BROA) ... WNFT
Boston, MA [*FM radio station call letters*] (BROA) ... WSJZ-FM
Boston Patriots [*National Football League*] [*1960-70*] (NFLA) ... Bos
Boston Properties [*NYSE symbol*] (SG) ... BXP
Boston Redskins [*National Football League*] [*1933-36*] (NFLA) ... BRd
Boston Survey Consultants (GEOI) ... BSC
Boston Yanks [*National Football League*] [*1944-48*] (NFLA) ... BYk
Botany (BEE) ... Bot
Botswana (MILB) ... Btwa
Botswana Ministry Agriculture (GEOI) ... BMA
Boulder City, NV [*FM radio station call letters*] (BROA) ... KSTJ-FM
Boulder, CO [*AM radio station call letters*] (BROA) ... KVCU
Boulevard (GEOI) ... Bl
Boundless Corp. [*AMEX symbol*] (SG) ... BND
Bouygues Offshore ADS [*NYSE symbol*] (SG) ... BWG
Bowhunters of America (EA) ... BWC
Bowl America Cl'A' [*AMEX symbol*] (SG) ... BWLA
Bowlin Outdoor Adv/Travel [*AMEX symbol*] (SG) ... BWN
Bowling Green, VA [*FM radio station call letters*] (BROA) ... WWUZ-FM
Bowne & Co. [*NYSE symbol*] (SG) ... BNE
Box Hill Systems [*NYSE symbol*] (SG) ... BXH
Boyds Collection [*NYSE symbol*] (SG) ... FOR
Boykin Lodging [*NYSE symbol*] (SG) ... BOY
Bozeman, MT [*FM radio station call letters*] (BROA) ... KZLO-FM
BP Amoco ADS [*NYSE symbol*] (SG) ... BPA
Bradenton, FL [*Television station call letters*] (BROA) ... WXPX
Brady Corp.'A' [*NYSE symbol*] (SG) ... BRC
Bragg Crystal Spectrometer ... BCS
Branched-Chain Amino Acid ... BCAA
Brandon, MB [*FM radio station call letters*] (BROA) ... CKX-FM
Brandon, VT [*FM radio station call letters*] (BROA) ... WEXP-FM
Brawley, CA [*AM radio station call letters*] (BROA) ... KKSC
Brazil (MILB) ... Br
Brazilian National Development Bank ... BNDES
Brazilian Purpuric Fever [*Medicine*] ... BPF
Breckenridge, TX [*FM radio station call letters*] (BROA) ... KLXK-FM
Breckenridge, TX [*AM radio station call letters*] (BROA) ... KROO
Brentwood, TN [*AM radio station call letters*] (BROA) ... WNSR
Bret Hart Fan Club (EA) ... BHFC
Brick Enclosed Elevator (GEOI) ... BE
Bricklin International Owners Club (EA) ... BIOC
Bridgeport, TX [*FM radio station call letters*] (BROA) ... KBFR-FM
Bridgestreet Accomodations [*AMEX symbol*] (SG) ... BDS
Brigade (MILB) ... bde
Brigade Headquarters ... Brig Hq
Brigham City, UT [*FM radio station call letters*] (BROA) ... KRAR-FM
Brigham City, UT [*AM radio station call letters*] (BROA) ... KXOL
Brightness Value Unit (GEOI) ... BVU
Brilliant Digital Entertain't [*AMEX symbol*] (SG) ... BDE
Brinkley, AR [*FM radio station call letters*] (BROA) ... KTRQ-FM
Bristol Hotel & Resorts [*NYSE symbol*] (SG) ... BH
British (GEAB) ... Br
British (BEE) ... Brit
British Aerospace ... BAE
British and Irish Committee for Map Information and Cataglogue Systems (GEOI) ... BRICMICS
British Antarctic Survey (QUAC) ... BAR
British Association for Veterinary Ophthalmology (GVA) ... BrAVO
British Association of Feed Supplement and Additives Manufacturers (GVA) ... BAFSAM
British Cattle Movement Service (GVA) ... BCMS
British Chamber of Commerce for Italy ... BCCI
British Columbia Agency ... BCCA

British Columbia Cancer Foundation .... BCCF
British Columbia Cancer Research Centre .... BCCRC
British Dog Breeders' Council (GVA) .... BDBC
British Holistic Veterinary Medicine Association (GVA) .... BHVMA
British Horse Industry Confederation (GVA) .... BHIC
British Horseracing Board (GVA) .... BHB
British House Rabbit Association (GVA) .... BHRA
British Journal for the History of Science [A publication] .... BJHS
British Micropalaeontological Society (QUAC) .... BMS
British Nuclear Fuels .... BNFL
British Pig Association (GVA) .... BPA
British Sedimentological Research Group (QUAC) .... BSRG
British Society of Animal Science (GVA) .... BSAS
British Veterinary Camelid Association (GVA) .... BVCA
British Veterinary Dental Association (GVA) .... BVDA
Broadband Cable System .... BCS
Broadcom Corp.'A' [NASDAQ symbol] (SG) .... BRCM
Broadway Stores Wrrt [NYSE symbol] (SG) .... BWY WS
Brocade Communic Sys [NASDAQ symbol] (SG) .... BRCD
Brockton, MA [FM radio station call letters] (BROA) .... WCAV-FM
Broken Cloud (WEAT) .... BKN
Bromeliad Society (EA) .... BSI
Bromine Monoxide (EOSA) .... BrO
Bronson, KS [FM radio station call letters] (BROA) .... KBJQ-FM
Brookfield Properties [NYSE symbol] (SG) .... BPO
Brookfield, WI [FM radio station call letters] (BROA) .... WPNT-FM
Brookline Bancorp [NASDAQ symbol] (SG) .... BRKL
Brooklyn Dodgers [National Football League] [1930-43] (NFLA) .... BkD
Brooklyn Tigers [National Football League] [1044] (NFLA) .... BkI
Brookston, IN [FM radio station call letters] (BROA) .... WLFF-FM
Brooktrout, Inc. [NASDAQ symbol] (SG) .... BRKT
Brookville, PA [FM radio station call letters] (BROA) .... WBEU-FM
Brother (GEAB) .... br
Brotherhood Railway Carmen Division/Transportation Communications
    Union (EA) .... BRC/TCU
Brown & Brown [NYSE symbol] (SG) .... BRO
Brown Shoe [NYSE symbol] (SG) .... BWS
Brownwood, TX [FM radio station call letters] (BROA) .... KPBE-FM
Brundidge, AL [FM radio station call letters] (BROA) .... WTBF-FM
Brunei (MILB) .... Bru
Brunson Electronic Triangulation System (GEOI) .... BETS
Brunswick, GA [FM radio station call letters] (BROA) .... WAYR-FM

Brunswick, GA [AM radio station call letters] (BROA) .... WSFN
Brush, CO [FM radio station call letters] (BROA) .... KPRB-FM
Bryan, TX [FM radio station call letters] (BROA) .... KXBK
Buckle, Inc. [NYSE symbol] (SG) .... BKE
Budget (MILB) .... bdgt
Budget Group 'A' [NYSE symbol] (SG) .... BD
Buffalo Bills [National Football League] [1960-present] (NFLA) .... Buf
Buffalo, NY [FM radio station call letters] (BROA) .... WLCE-FM
Buffalo, WY [FM radio station call letters] (BROA) .... KBUW-FM
Building Omission Area (GEOI) .... BOA
Bulgaria (MILB) .... Bg
Bull Run [NASDAQ symbol] (SG) .... BULL
Bulletin of the Australian Mathematical Society [A publication] .... BAMS
Bulletin of the Institute of Mathematics and Its Applications
    [A publication] .... BIMA
Bulletin of the Metals Museum [A publication] [Sendai, Japan] .... BMM
Bullous Ichthyosis [Dermatology] .... BI
Bulls Gap, TN [FM radio station call letters] (BROA) .... WBGQ-FM
Bunzl PLC ADS [NYSE symbol] (SG) .... BNL
Bureau Mineral Resources [Austalia] (GEOI) .... BMR
Bureau of Economic Geology [Texas] (GEOI) .... BEG
Bureau of Mines and Geosciences [Philippines] (GEOI) .... BMG
Bureau of Planning and Entitlement Grants .... BPEG
Bureau of Printing (GEOI) .... BOP
Bureau of Statistics [Japan] (GEOI) .... BS
Bureau of the Census (GEOI) .... BOC
Buried (GEAB) .... bd
Buried (GEAB) .... bur
Burney, CA [FM radio station call letters] (BROA) .... KRRX-FM
Burns Intl. Services [NYSE symbol] (SG) .... BOR
Burnside, KY [FM radio station call letters] (BROA) .... WWZB-FM
Burundi (MILB) .... Bu
Business & Legal Reports, Inc. .... BLR
Business Card Museum [An association] (EA) .... BCM
Business Geographics Conference (GEOI) .... BGC
Business Objects ADS [NASDAQ symbol] (SG) .... BOBJ
Business Periodicals Index .... BPI
But You Knew That [Online dialog] .... BYKT
Butterfly .... Bfly
Buttes Watch Co. .... BWC
Buzzcocks Fan Club/Harmony In My Head (EA) .... PSFC/HIMH
Bye Bye for Now [Online dialog] .... BBFN
Bypass (BEE) .... byp

By Meaning

C
By Meaning

Cabana .... cba
Cable & Wireless ADS [*NYSE symbol*] (SG) .... CWP
Cable & Wireless Communic ADS [*NYSE symbol*] (SG) .... CWZ
Cable & Wireless HKT ADR [*NYSE symbol*] (SG) .... HKT
Cable Design Technologies [*NYSE symbol*] (SG) .... CDT
Cable Twister Orthosis [*Medicine*] (MELL) .... CTO
Cabot Industrial Tr [*NYSE symbol*] (SG) .... CTR
Cache Array Routing Protocol [*Computer science*] .... CARP
Cadillac Fairview [*NYSE symbol*] (SG) .... CDF
CAE, Inc. [*Toronto Stock Exchange symbol*] (SG) .... CAE
Cagle's Inc.'A' [*AMEX symbol*] (SG) .... CGLA
CAIS Internet [*NASDAQ symbol*] (SG) .... CAIS
Calcaneal Spur (MELL) .... CS
Calcaneal Tendon Reflex [*Medicine*] (MELL) .... CTR
Calcaneus Fracture (MELL) .... CF
Calcarine Fissure (MELL) .... CF
Calcifying Odontogenic Cyst [*Medicine*] (MELL) .... COC
Calcium Citrate Malate (MELL) .... CCM
Calcium Compensation Depth (QUAC) .... CCD
Calcium Ion Concentration (MELL) CIC
Calcium Oxalate (MELL) .... CO
Calcium Oxalate Dihydrate Urinary Calculi [*Medicine*] (MELL) .... CODUC
Calcium Oxalate Stone [*Medicine*] (MELL) .... COS
Calcium Pyrophosphate Deposition [*Medicine*] (MELL) .... CPD
Calcium Store Disease [*Medicine*] (MELL) .... CSD
Calculated Mean Organism (MELL) .... CMO
Caldwell-Luc Operation [*Medicine*] (MELL) .... CLO
Caledonia, MN [*FM radio station call letters*] (BROA) .... KSFF-FM
Calgary, AB [*FM radio station call letters*] (BROA) .... CHKF-FM
Calgary, AB [*FM radio station call letters*] (BROA) .... CJSI-FM
Calibration (MILB) .... cal
Calibration Base Line (GEOI) .... CBL
Calibration/Validation (EOSA) .... Cal/Val
Calif Water Svc Grp [*NYSE symbol*] (SG) .... CWT
California Civil Addict Program .... CAP
California Council of Civil Engineers and Land Surveyors (GEOI) .... CCCELS
California Department of Conservation (GEOI) .... CDC
California Department of Fish and Game (GEOI) .... CDFG
California Department of Forestry (GEOI) .... CDF
California Department of Water Resources (GEOI) .... CDWR
California Digital Library (GEOI) .... CDL
California Division of Mines and Geology (GEOI) .... CDMG
California Encephalitis Virus [*Medicine*] (MELL) .... CEV
California Environmental Resource Evaluation System (GEOI) .... CERES
California Institute of Technology .... Caltech
California Integrated Remote Sensing System (GEOI) .... CIRSS
California Land Surveyors Association (GEOI) .... CLSA
California Map Society (GEOI) .... CMS
California, MD [*FM radio station call letters*] (BROA) .... WKIK-FM
California Medical Association (MELL) .... CMA
California Regional Primate Research Center (GVA) .... CRPRC
California Remote Sensing Council (GEOI) .... CRSC
California School Library Association .... CSLA
Callaway, FL [*FM radio station call letters*] (BROA) .... WMXP-FM
Called .... cld
Callisburg, TX [*FM radio station call letters*] (BROA) .... KPFC-FM
Callon Petroleum [*NYSE symbol*] (SG) .... CPE
Calverton-Roanoke, NY [*FM radio station call letters*] (BROA) ...... WXXP-FM
Cambodia (MILB) .... Cam
Cambridge, ON [*FM radio station call letters*] (BROA) .... CIZN-FM
Cambridge Research Instrumentation .... CRI
Camden National [*AMEX symbol*] (SG) .... CAC
Cameroon (MILB) .... Crn
Campaign for the Protection of Hunted Animals (GVA) .... CPHA
Campbell, MO [*FM radio station call letters*] (BROA) .... KFEB-FM
Campton, KY [*FM radio station call letters*] (BROA) .... WCBJ-FM
Camuy, PR [*FM radio station call letters*] (BROA) .... WDIN-FM
Can We Meet [*Online dialog*] .... CWM
Canada (MILB) .... Ca
Canada Centre for Mapping (GEOI) .... CCM
Canada Foundation for Innovation .... CFI
Canada Land Use Monitoring Program (GEOI) .... CLUMP
Canada Map Office (GEOI) .... CMO
Canadex Resources [*Toronto Stock Exchange symbol*] (SG) ...... CDX
Canadian 88 Energy [*AMEX symbol*] (SG) .... EEE
Canadian Active Control System (GEOI) .... CACS

Canadian Air and Precipitation Monitoring Network (EPAT) .... CAPMoN
Canadian Air Mail Collectors Club (EA) .... CAN
Canadian Archaeological Radiocarbon Database (QUAC) .... CARD
Canadian Association of Provincial and Territorial Archaeologists
    (QUAC) .... CAPTA
Canadian Association of Public Data Users (GEOI) .... CAPDU
Canadian Association of Veterinary Ophthalmology (GVA) ...... CAVO
Canadian Biodiversity Information Network (QUAC) .... CBIN
Canadian Botanical Conservation Network (QUAC) .... CBCN
Canadian Business Periodicals Index .... CBPI
Canadian Climate Program (QUAC) .... CCP
Canadian Climate Research Network (QUAC) .... CCRN
Canadian Committee for the Bibliographic Control of Cartographic
    Materials (GEOI) .... CCBCCM
Canadian Council on Geographic Education (GEOI) .... CCGE
Canadian Digital Elevation Data (GEOI) .... CDED
Canadian Food Inspection Agency (GVA) .... CFIA
Canadian Geoscience Information Centre (GEOI) .... CGIC
Canadian Geospatial Data Infrastructure (GEOI) .... CGDI
Canadian Global Change Program (EOSA) .... CGCP
Canadian Imperial Blk Commerce [*NYSE symbol*] (SG) .... BCM
Canadian Institute for Climate Studies (QUAC) .... CICS
Canadian Journal of Earth Sciences [*A publication*] (QUAC) ...... CJES
Canadian Medical Association Journal [*A publication*] (MELL) ...... CMAJ
Canadian Museum of Civilization (QUAC) .... CMC
Canadian Museum of Nature (QUAC) .... CMN
Canadian Natl Railway [*NYSE symbol*] (SG) .... CNI
Canadian Natural Resources [*Toronto Stock Exchange symbol*] (SG) ...... CNQ
Canadian Options for Greenhouse Gas Emissions Reduction
    (QUAC) .... COGGER
Canadian Road Network (GEOI) .... CRN
Canadian Spatial Reference System (GEOI) .... CSRS
Canadian Swine Breeders Association (GVA) .... CSBA
Canadian Synthetic Aperture Radar Satellite (EOSA) .... Radarsat
Canadian Water Resources Program (GEOI) .... CWRA
Canajoharie, NY [*FM radio station call letters*] (BROA) .... WCAN-FM
Canandaigua, NY [*FM radio station call letters*] (BROA) ...... WISY-FM
Canandaigua, NY [*AM radio station call letters*] (BROA) .... WRSB
Cancer Chemotherapy [*Medicine*] (MELL) .... CCT
Cancer of Unknown Primary Site [*Medicine*] (MELL) .... CUPS
Cancer Pain Treatment (MELL) .... CPT
Cancer Procoagulant [*Medicine*] (MELL) .... CP
Cancer-Prone Family (MELL) .... CPF
Candies, Inc. [*NASDAQ symbol*] (SG) .... CANDE
Canine Health Schemes Management Group [*British*] (GVA) ...... CHSMG
Canmore, AB [*FM radio station call letters*] (BROA) .... CJMT-FM
Cannon (MILB) .... can
Cannon Express [*AMEX symbol*] (SG) .... AB
Canon City, CO [*FM radio station call letters*] (BROA) .... KTLC-FM
Canon, Inc. ADR [*NASDAQ symbol*] (SG) .... CANNY
Canonical Correspondence Analysis (QUAC) .... CCA
Canton, IL [*FM radio station call letters*] (BROA) .... WBDM-FM
Canton, NJ [*FM radio station call letters*] (BROA) .... WJKS-FM
Canton, OH [*FM radio station call letters*] (BROA) .... WHK-FM
Canton, SD [*FM radio station call letters*] (BROA) .... KYBB-FM
CanWest Global Commun [*NYSE symbol*] (SG) .... CWG
Cape Charles, VA [*FM radio station call letters*] (BROA) ..... WAZP-FM
Cape York Peninsula (GEOI) .... CYP
Cape York Peninsula Land Use Strategy (GEOI) .... CYPLUS
Capillary Drainage [*Medicine*] (MELL) .... CD
Capillary Filling Time [*Medicine*] (MELL) .... CFT
Capillary Fragility Test [*Medicine*] (MELL) .... CFT
Capillary Hemorrhage [*Medicine*] (MELL) .... CH
Capillary Lumen [*Medicine*] (MELL) CL
Capillary Refill Test [*Medicine*] (MELL) .... CRT
Capillary-Like Space [*Medicine*] (MELL) .... CLS
Capital Alliance Income Tr [*AMEX symbol*] (SG) .... CAA
Capital Automotive REIT [*NASDAQ symbol*] (SG) .... CARS
Capital City Bank Grp [*NASDAQ symbol*] (SG) .... CCBG
Capital Federal Financial [*NASDAQ symbol*] (SG) .... CFFN
Capital Properties [*AMEX symbol*] (SG) .... CPI
Capital Senior Living [*NYSE symbol*] (SG) .... CSU
Capital Trust 'A' [*NYSE symbol*] (SG) .... CT
Capitation .... Cap
Capsaicin-Related Drug (MELL) .... CRD
Captec Net Lease Realty [*NASDAQ symbol*] (SG) .... CRRR

Captured (GEAB) .... capt
Carbohydrate Addict's Diet .... CAD
Carbohydrate Deficient Glycoprotein Syndrome [*Medicine*] .... CDGS
Carbohydrate Utilization Test [*Medicine*] (MELL) .... CUT
Carbon Dioxide Intercalibration Experiment (QUAC) .... CARBICE
Carbon Dioxide LASER Therapy [*Medicine*] (MELL) .... CDLT
Carbon Dioxide Membrane Lung [*Medicine*] (MELL) .... CDML
Carbon Monoxide Hemoglobin [*Medicine*] (MELL) .... HbCO
Carbon Monoxide Poisoning (MELL) .... CMP
Carbon, Oxygen, Nitrogen, Phosphorus, and Sulphur (QUAC) .... CONPS
Carbon Tetrachloride Intoxication (MELL) .... CTI
Carbon Tetrachloride Poisoning [*Medicine*] (MELL) .... CTCP
Carbonaceous Mass Fraction (QUAC) .... CMF
Carbon-Carbon Bond (MELL) .... CCB
Carbondale, PA [*FM radio station call letters*] (BROA) .... WCTP-FM
Carbon-Hydrogen Bond (MELL) .... CHB
Carboxyhemoglobin [*Medicine*] (MELL) .... HbCO
Carcinoid-Like Syndrome [*Medicine*] (MELL) .... CLS
Carcinoma in Situ [*Medicine*] (MELL) .... CIS
Carcinoma in Situ of Cervix [*Medicine*] (MELL) .... CISC
Carcinoma in Situ of Vagina [*Medicine*] (MELL) .... CISV
Carcinomatous Neuromyopathy [*Medicine*] (MELL) .... CNM
Cardarelli's Sign [*Medicine*] (MELL) .... CS
Cardiac Dysrhythmia [*Medicine*] (MELL) .... CD
Cardiac Embolism [*Medicine*] (MELL) .... CE
Cardiac Hypertrophy [*Medicine*] (MELL) .... CH
Cardiac Lipomas [*Medicine*] (MELL) CL
Cardiac Muscle [*Medicine*] (MELL) .... CM
Cardiac Output Estimation [*Medicine*] (MELL) .... COE
Cardiac Pacemaker (MELL) .... CPM
Cardiac Pump Function [*Medicine*] (MELL) .... CPF
Cardiac Purkinje Fiber [*Medicine*] (MELL) .... CPF
Cardiac Risk Index [*Medicine*] (MELL) .... CRI
Cardiac T Rapid Assay [*Medicine*] (MELL) .... CTRA
Cardiac Tamponade (MELL) .... CT
Cardiac Volume [*Medicine*] (MELL) CV
Cardiopulmonary Bypass [*Medicine*] (MELL) .... CPBP
Cardiopulmonary Disease (MELL) .... CPD
Cardiopulmonary Support [*Medicine*] (MELL) .... CPS
Cardiorenal Failure [*Medicine*] (MELL) .... CRF
Cardiorespiratory Failure [*Medicine*] (MELL) .... CRF
Cardiotech Intl. [*AMEX symbol*] (SG) .... CTE
Cardiovascular Adverse Effects [*Medicine*] (MELL) .... CVAE
Cardiovascular Failure [*Medicine*] (MELL) .... CVF
Card-Pitt [*National Football League*] [*1944*] (NFLA) .... CaP
Caregiver Stress (MELL) .... CGS
CareInsite, Inc. [*NASDAQ symbol*] (SG) .... CARL
CareMatrix Corp. [*NASDAQ symbol*] (SG) .... CMDC
Careside, Inc. [*AMEX symbol*] (SG) .... CSA
Carey Diversified LLC [*NYSE symbol*] (SG) .... CDC
Caribbean Tourism Organization, American Branch (EA) .... CTO
Caries Susceptible [*Medicine*] (MELL) .... CS
Carlinville, IL [*FM radio station call letters*] (BROA) .... WOLG-FM
Carlsbad, CA [*FM radio station call letters*] (BROA) .... KMSX-FM
Carlsbad, NM [*FM radio station call letters*] (BROA) .... KBFV-FM
Carnegie Museum of Natural History .... CMNH
Carnegie, PA [*AM radio station call letters*] (BROA) .... WZUM
Carolina (BEE) .... Car
Carolina Brahman Breeders Association (GVA) .... CBBA
Carolina Panthers [*National Football League*] [*1995-present*] (NFLA) .... Car
Carolina, PR [*FM radio station call letters*] (BROA) .... WVOZ-FM
Carolina, PR [*Television station call letters*] (BROA) .... WZDE
Carotid Chemoreflex [*Medicine*] (MELL) .... CCR
Carotid Doppler Ultrasonography [*Medicine*] (MELL) .... CDUS
Carotid Pulse [*Medicine*] (MELL) .... CP
Carotid Sinus Syndrome [*Medicine*] (MELL) .... CSS
Carotid Sympathetic Plexus [*Medicine*] (MELL) .... CSP
Carpal-Tarsal Osteolysis [*Medicine*] (MELL) .... CTO
Carpometacarpal Articulation [*Medicine*] (MELL) .... CMA
Carpometacarpal Joint Dislocation [*Medicine*] (MELL) .... CMJD
Carpometacarpal Ligament [*Medicine*] (MELL) .... CMCL
Carrabelle, FL [*FM radio station call letters*] (BROA) .... WOCY-FM
Carrier Replacement [*Insurance*] .... CR
Carrollton, GA [*AM radio station call letters*] (BROA) .... WBTR
Carrollton, GA [*AM radio station call letters*] (BROA) .... WWWE
Carson City, NV [*FM radio station call letters*] (BROA) .... KBUL-FM
Carthage, MS [*FM radio station call letters*] (BROA) .... WSSI-FM
Cartier Ebel Christalor .... CEC
Cartilage Hair Dysplasia (MELL) .... CHD
Cartographer Development Program (GEOI) .... CDP
Cartographic Catalog (GEOI) CC
Cartographic Data Visualizer (GEOI) .... CDV
Cartographic Feature File (GEOI) .... CFF
Cartographic Material Order and Tracking System (GEOI) .... CMOTS
Cartographic Operations Management Information System (GEOI) .... COMIS
Cartographic Perspectives [*A publication*] (GEOI) .... CP
Cartographic Publishing House [*China*] (GEOI) .... CPH
Cartographic Reproduction and Interactive Graphic Editing System (GEOI) .... CRAIGES
Cartographic Research Laboratory (GEOI) .... CRI
Cartographic Technology Laboratory (GEOI) .... CTL
Cartographic Workstation (GEOI) .... CWS
Cartography (GEOI) C
Cartography and Geographic Information Science [*A publication*] (GEOI) .... CaGIS
Cartography and Geographic Information Society (GEOI) .... CAGIS
Cartography and Geographic Information Systems [*A publication*] (GEOI) .... CaGIS
Cartography Special Group [*Association of American Geographers*] (GEOI) .... CSG
Cartometric Operations (GEOI) .... CO
Cartwheel Fracture (MELL) .... CWF
Case History [*Medicine*] (MELL) .... CH
Caseouslike Necrosis Cervical Lymph Node [*Medicine*] (MELL) .... CLN
Casey Jones Railroad Unit [*An association*] (EA) .... CJRRU
Casino Reinvestment Development Authority .... CRDA
Casoni Intradermal Test [*Medicine*] (MELL) .... CIT
Casper, WY [*Television station call letters*] (BROA) .... KCWY
Casper, WY [*FM radio station call letters*] (BROA) .... KHOC-FM
Casper, WY [*AM radio station call letters*] (BROA) .... KMCG
Casper, WY [*FM radio station call letters*] (BROA) .... KWYY-FM
Cassette Player .... CASS
Cast Iron Soil Pipe Institute .... CISP
Castana, IA [*FM radio station call letters*] (BROA) .... KMAP-FM
Castlegar, BC [*FM radio station call letters*] (BROA) .... CKQR-FM
Casualty Evacuation (MILB) .... casevac
Catalog of Environmental Resource Data (GEOI) .... CERD
Catalogue (GEAB) .... catal
Catastrophic Health (MELL) .... CHIP
Categorical Exclusion (EPAT) .... CE
Category (MILB) .... Cat
Catheter-Induced Infection [*Medicine*] (MELL) CII
Catheter-Related Bloodstream Infection [*Medicine*] (MELL) .... CRBSI
Catheter-Related Sepsis [*Medicine*] (MELL) .... CRS
Cat-Scratch Bacillus [*Medicine*] (MELL) .... CSB
Cattle Tracing System (GVA) .... CTS
Cauda Equina Syndrome [*Medicine*] (MELL) .... CES
Caudal Dysplasia Syndrome [*Medicine*] (MELL) .... CDS
Cause Undetermined [*Medicine*] (MELL) .... CU
Cave City, KY [*FM radio station call letters*] (BROA) .... WPTQ-FM
Cave Creek, AZ [*AM radio station call letters*] (BROA) .... KFNX
Cavernous Sinus [*Medicine*] (MELL) CV
Cavernous Sinus Infiltration [*Medicine*] (MELL) .... CSI
Cavernous Sinus Syndrome [*Medicine*] (MELL) .... CSS
Cavum Conchal Cartilage Graft [*Medicine*] (MELL) .... CCCG
Cavus Foot (MELL) .... CF
Cawker City, KS [*FM radio station call letters*] (BROA) .... KZDY-FM
Cayce, SC [*FM radio station call letters*] (BROA) .... WLTY-FM
Cayman Golf Association (EA) .... CGA
Cayuga Syndrome [*Reproductive disturbance in fish*] .... CS
C-COR.net Corp [*NASDAQ symbol*] (SG) .... CCBL
Cedar City, UT [*Television station call letters*] (BROA) .... KCSG
Cedar Falls, IA [*AM radio station call letters*] (BROA) .... KDNZ
Cedar Rapids, IA [*Television station call letters*] (BROA) .... KPXR
Cedar Rapids, IA [*AM radio station call letters*] (BROA) .... KTOF
Cedar Rapids, IA [*FM radio station call letters*] (BROA) .... KZIA-FM
Cefazolin Sodium (MELL) .... CZS
Celestial Ephemeris Pole (GEOI) .... CEP
Celestica, Inc. [*NYSE symbol*] (SG) .... CLS
Celiac Plexus [*Medicine*] (MELL) .... CP
Celiac Syndrome [*Medicine*] (MELL) .... CS
Cell Recovery System [*Medicine*] (MELL) .... CRS
Cell Therapy [*Medicine*] (MELL) .... CT
Cell-Mediated Cytotoxicity [*Medicine*] (MELL) .... CMC
Cell-Mediated Toxicity [*Medicine*] (MELL) .... CMT
Cellulitic Phlegmasia [*Medicine*] (MELL) .... CP
Cement Block [*Construction*] (GEOI) .... CB
Cement Kiln Dust (EPAT) .... CKD
Cement Kiln Recycling Coalition (EPAT) .... CKRC
Cemetery (GEAB) .... cem
Cemetery (GEOI) .... Cem
Census (GEAB) .... cen
Census Designated Place (GEOI) .... CDP
Census Feature Class Code (GEOI) .... CFCC
Census Statistical Area Committee (GEOI) .... CSAC
Census Tract (GEOI) .... CT
Center (BEE) .... cntr
Center for Advanced Computation [*University of Illinois*] (GEOI) .... CAAD
Center for Advanced Land Management Information Technologies [*University of Nebraska-Lincoln*] (GEOI) .... CALMIT
Center for Advanced Telecommunications Systems and Services .... CATTS
Center for Agricultural, Resource, and Environmental Systems [*University of Missouri*] (GEOI) .... CARES
Center for Bioethics (MELL) .... CFB
Center for Health Effects of Environmental Contamination [*University of Iowa*] (GEOI) .... CHEEC
Center for Human Genome Studies [*Internet resource*] .... CHGS
Center for Integration of Natural Disaster Information (GEOI) .... CINDI
Center for Medical Devices and Radiologic Health (MELL) .... CMDRH
Center for Patient Advocacy (MELL) .... CPA
Center for Statistical Consultation and Research .... CSCAR
Center for the Assessment and Monitoring of Forest and Environmental Resources [*University of California, Berkeley*] (GEOI) .... CAMFER
Center for the Education of Women .... CEW
Center for the Integrative Study of Animal Behavior (GVA) .... CISAB
Center for the Reproduction of Endangered Species .... CRES
Center Line Data (GEOI) .... CLD
Center Trust [*NYSE symbol*] (SG) .... CTA
CenterPoint Prop TrSBI [*NYSE symbol*] (SG) .... CNT
Central (BEE) .... cen
Central Auditory Processing Disorder [*Medicine*] .... CAPD

Central City, PA [*FM radio station call letters*] (BROA) ... WSRA-FM
Central Conduction Time (MELL) ... CCT
Central Contractor Register ... CCR
Central Core Disease (MELL) ... CCD
Central Fracture Dislocation [*Medicine*] (MELL) ... CFD
Central Geographic Data Base (GEOI) ... CGDB
Central Inhibition [*Medicine*] (MELL) ... CIN
Central Limit Order Book [*Singapore*] ... CLOB
Central Mapping Agency [*New South Wales*] (GEOI) ... CMA
Central Nervous System Dysfunction [*Medicine*] (MELL) ... CNSD
Central Obesity (MELL) ... CO
Central Office of Statistics [*Malta*] (GEOI) ... COS
Central Parking [*NYSE symbol*] (SG) ... CPC
Central Pocket Whorl [*Fingerprint*] (MELL) ... CPW
Central Region (GEOI) ... CR
Central Science Laboratory (GVA) ... CSL
Central Serous Retinopathy [*Medicine*] (MELL) ... CSR
Central Sleep Apnea [*Medicine*] (MELL) ... CSA
Central United States Earthquake Consortium (GEOI) ... CUSEC
Central Venous Infusions [*Medicine*] (MELL) ... CVI
Central VT Pub Svc [*NYSE symbol*] (SG) ... CV
Centralny Urzad Geodezji i Kartografil [*Poland*] (GEOI) ... CUGiK
Centre de Recherche Informatique de Montreal [*Canada*] ... CRIM
Centre de Recherches Biologiques Tropicales [*Algeria*] (GEOI) ... CRBT
Centre d'Ecologie des Ressources Renouvelables [*France*] (GEOI) ... CERR
Centre d'Etudes et de Realisations Cartographiques Geographiques [*France*] (GEOI) ... CERCG
Centre d'Information Sur les Sciences de la Terre [*Canada*] (GEOI) ... CIST
Centre for Advanced Spatial Analysis [*University College, London*] (GEOI) ... CASA
Centre for Analysis of Social Exclusion [*Great Britain*] ... CASE
Centre National de la Recherche Scientifique et Technologique [*Burkina Faso*] (GEOI) ... CNRST
Centre National de Recherches Geomorphologiques [*Belgium*] (GEOI) ... CNRG
Centre National d'Informations Toxicologiques Veterinaires (GVA) ... CNITV
Centre National pour l'Exploitation des Oceans [*France*] (GEOI) ... CNEXO
Centre on Juvenile and Criminal Justice ... CJCJ
Centris Group [*NYSE symbol*] (SG) ... CGE
Centro de Investigacion y Aplicacion de Sensores Remotos [*Bolivia*] (GEOI) ... CIACER
Centro de Observacao Astronomica no Algarve ... COAA
Centro de Recursos Naturales [*El Salvador*] (GEOI) ... CENREN
Centro Informatico Cientifico de Andalucia [*Group of eight universities in Spain*] ... CICA
Centro Nacional de Reconhecimento e Ordenamento Agrario [*Portugal*] (GEOI) ... CNROA
Centro Nacional de Tecnologia Agropecuaria [*El Salvador*] (GEOI) ... CENTA
Century (GEAB) ... cent
Century Business Svcs [*NASDAQ symbol*] (SG) ... CBIZ
Century Tel, Inc. [*NYSE symbol*] (SG) ... CTL
Cerclage Wire (MELL) ... CW
Cerebellar Cortical Degeneration [*Medicine*] (MELL) ... CCD
Cerebellar Degeneration [*Medicine*] (MELL) ... CD
Cerebral Cortical Degeneration [*Medicine*] (MELL) ... CCD
Cerebral Edema Syndrome [*Medicine*] (MELL) ... CES
Cerebral Embolism [*Medicine*] (MELL) ... CE
Cerebral Embolism of Unknown Source [*Medicine*] (MELL) ... CEUS
Cerebral Fissure [*Medicine*] (MELL) ... CF
Cerebral Gigantism [*Medicine*] (MELL) ... CG
Cerebral Hemisphere [*Medicine*] (MELL) ... CH
Cerebral Lateral Sulcus [*Medicine*] (MELL) ... CLS
Cerebral Longitudinal Fissure [*Medicine*] (MELL) ... CLF
Cerebral Percutaneous Transluminal Angioplasty [*Medicine*] (MELL) ... CPTA
Cerebral Transient Ischemic Attack [*Medicine*] (MELL) ... CTIA
Cerebro-Costo-Mandibular Syndrome [*Medicine*] (MELL) ... CCMS
Cerebrohepatorenal [*Medicine*] (MELL) ... CHR
Cerebro-Oculo-Facio-Skeletal Syndrome [*Medicine*] (MELL) ... COFSS
Cerebrovascular [*Medicine*] (MELL) ... CV
Cerebrovascular Incident [*Medicine*] (MELL) ... CVI
Ceres Group [*NASDAQ symbol*] (SG) ... CERG
Ceridian Corp. [*NYSE symbol*] (SG) ... CEN
Certificate (GEAB) ... cer
Certificate in Veterinary Practice Management (GVA) ... CVPM
Certificate of Coverage [*Insurance*] ... COC
Certified Cardiographic Technician (MELL) ... CCT
Certified Degree of Indian Blood (GEAB) ... CBID
Certified Drug Counselor (MELL) ... CDC
Certified Health Education Specialist ... CHES
Certified Literate Community Program ... CLCP
Certified Mortgage Banker ... CMB
Certified Real Estate Brokerage Manager ... CRB
Cervical Biopsy [*Medicine*] (MELL) ... CxBx
Cervical Collar (MELL) ... CS
Cervical Degenerative Disk Disease [*Medicine*] (MELL) ... CDDD
Cervical Disk Disease [*Medicine*] (MELL) ... CDD
Cervical Disk Syndrome [*Medicine*] (MELL) ... CDS
Cervical Dysplasia [*Medicine*] (MELL) ... CD
Cervical Intraepithelial Neoplasia [*Medicine*] (MELL) ... CIEN
Cervical Intraepithelial Neoplasia [*Mild*] [*Medicine*] (MELL) ... CIN I
Cervical Intraepithelial Neoplasia [*Moderate*] [*Medicine*] (MELL) ... CIN II
Cervical Pain Syndrome [*Medicine*] (MELL) ... CPS
Cervical Plexus [*Medicine*] (MELL) ... CP
Cervical Rib Syndrome [*Medicine*] (MELL) ... CRS
Cervical Smear (MELL) ... CS
Cervical Spine Hyperextension-Flexion Injury [*Medicine*] (MELL) ... CSHFI
Cervical Spine Injury [*Medicine*] (MELL) ... CSI
Cervical Sponge (MELL) ... CS
Cervical Traction [*Medicine*] (MELL) ... CxTx
Cervicofacial Actinomycosis [*Medicine*] (MELL) ... CFA
Cervico-Oculo-Acoustic Syndrome [*Medicine*] (MELL) ... COAS
Cervicovaginal Fistula [*Medicine*] (MELL) ... CVF
Cervicovaginal Fluid [*Medicine*] (MELL) ... CVF
CFS Bancorp [*NASDAQ symbol*] (SG) ... CITZ
CGI Group [*NYSE symbol*] (SG) ... GIB
C.H. Robinson Worldwide [*NASDAQ symbol*] (SG) ... CHRW
Chad (MILB) ... Cha
Chaddock's Toe Sign [*Medicine*] (MELL) ... CTS
Chairperson (PROS) ... chp
Chairwoman (PROS) ... chwn
Championship Auto Racing [*NYSE symbol*] (SG) ... MPH
Championship Auto Racing Teams [*An association*] (EA) ... IndyCar
Chanarin Syndrome [*Medicine*] ... CS
Chancery (GEAB) ... chan
Chancroid Ulcer Disease [*Medicine*] (MELL) ... CUD
Channell Commercial [*NASDAQ symbol*] (SG) ... CHNL
Chapter (PROS) ... Chap
Charcot Joint (MELL) ... CJ
Charleroi, PA [*FM radio station call letters*] (BROA) ... WZKT-FM
Charles Town, WV [*AM radio station call letters*] (BROA) ... WMRE
Charleston Museum [*South Carolina*] ... CHM
Charleston, SC [*FM radio station call letters*] (BROA) ... WALC-FM
Charleston, SC [*Television station call letters*] (BROA) ... WMMP
Charleston, WV [*Television station call letters*] (BROA) ... WLPX-TV
Charlestown, IN [*FM radio station call letters*] (BROA) ... WBLO-FM
Charley-Horse [*Spasm*] (MELL) ... CH
Charlotte Amalie, VI [*FM radio station call letters*] (BROA) ... WARD-FM
Charlotte Amalie, VI [*FM radio station call letters*] (BROA) ... WVJZ-FM
Charlotte Amalie, VI [*FM radio station call letters*] (BROA) ... WVPI-FM
Charlotte, MI [*FM radio station call letters*] (BROA) ... WVIC-FM
Charlotte, NC [*AM radio station call letters*] (BROA) ... WBHE
Charlotte, NC [*Television station call letters*] (BROA) ... WBTV-DT
Charlotte, NC [*Television station call letters*] (BROA) ... WCCB-DT
Charlotte, NC [*AM radio station call letters*] (BROA) ... WGFY
Charlotte, NC [*FM radio station call letters*] (BROA) ... WLNK-FM
Charlotte, NC [*Television station call letters*] (BROA) ... WSOC-DT
Charter Muni Mtg Acceptance [*AMEX symbol*] (SG) ... CHC
Chartwell Re [*NYSE symbol*] (SG) ... CWL
Chase Industries [*NYSE symbol*] (SG) ... CSI
Chateau Communities [*NYSE symbol*] (SG) ... CPJ
Cheap Tickets [*NASDAQ symbol*] (SG) ... CTIX
Check Engine Light [*Automotive term*] ... CEL
Check Plotter (GEOI) ... CK-PL
Check Point Software Tech [*NASDAQ symbol*] (SG) ... CHKP
Check Technology [*NASDAQ symbol*] (SG) ... CTCQ
Chemdex Corp. [*NASDAQ symbol*] (SG) ... CMDX
Chemfab Corp. [*NYSE symbol*] (SG) ... CFA
ChemFirst, Inc. [*NYSE symbol*] (SG) ... CEM
Chemical Dependence Profile [*Medicine*] (MELL) ... CDP
Chemical Dependency (MELL) ... CD
Chemical Sampling Information ... CH
Chemical Vocabulary (EPAT) ... CV
Chemically Assembled Electronic Nanocomputers ... CAEN
Chemical-Vapour-Deposited ... CVD
Chemistry and Physics on Stamps Study Unit [*An association*] (EA) ... CPOSSU
Chemohormonal Therapy [*Medicine*] (MELL) ... CHT
Chemoprophylaxis [*Medicine*] (MELL) ... CP
Chemoreceptor [*Medicine*] (MELL) ... CR
Chemotactic Activity [*Medicine*] (MELL) ... CTA
Chemotactic Agent [*Medicine*] (MELL) ... CTA
Chequemate Intl. [*AMEX symbol*] (SG) ... DDD
Cherry-Red Spot [*Tay's sign*] [*Medicine*] (MELL) ... CRS
Cherryville, OR [*FM radio station call letters*] (BROA) ... KLVP-FM
Chesapeake Energy [*NYSE symbol*] (SG) ... CHK
Chest Pain of Undetermined Etiology [*Medicine*] (MELL) ... CPUE
Chest Pain Syndrome [*Medicine*] (MELL) ... CPS
Chest Roentgenogram [*Medicine*] (MELL) ... CRG
Chest Wall Pain (MELL) ... CWP
Chester, CA [*FM radio station call letters*] (BROA) ... KBNF-FM
Chester, SC [*FM radio station call letters*] (BROA) ... WBT-FM
Cheyenne, WY [*FM radio station call letters*] (BROA) ... KZCY-FM
Cheyne-Stokes Breathing [*Medicine*] (MELL) ... CSB
Chiari Osteotomy [*Medicine*] (MELL) ... CO
Chicago and Northwestern Railway Co. ... CNW
Chicago Bears [*National Football League*] [*1922-present*] (NFLA) ... Chi
Chicago Bridge & Iron N.V. [*NYSE symbol*] (SG) ... CBI
Chicago Cardinals [*National Football League*] [*1920-59*] (NFLA) ... ChC
Chicago, IL [*Television station call letters*] (BROA) ... WBBM-DT
Chicago, IL [*Television station call letters*] (BROA) ... WCPX
Chicago, IL [*Television station call letters*] (BROA) ... WFLD-DT
Chicago, IL [*Television station call letters*] (BROA) ... WLS-DT
Chicago, IL [*FM radio station call letters*] (BROA) ... WNND-FM
Chicago, IL [*FM radio station call letters*] (BROA) ... WRTE-FM
Chicago Staleys [*National Football League*] [*1921*] (NFLA) ... ChS
Chicago Title [*NYSE symbol*] (SG) ... CTZ
Chickasha, OK [*FM radio station call letters*] (BROA) ... KTUZ-FM
Chico, CA [*Television station call letters*] (BROA) ... KNVN
Chief Executive Officer (PROS) ... ceo
Chief Financial Officer (PROS) ... cfo
Chief Hydrologist (GEOI) ... CH
Chief Operating Officer (PROS) ... coo

Chief Resident [*Medicine*] (MELL)	CR
Chief School Administrator	CSA
Chief, Topographic Division (GEOI)	CTD
Child of a Deaf Adult	CODA
Child of a Substance Abuser	COSA
Child Personality Scale [*Medicine*] (MELL)	CPS
Child Resistant Device (MELL)	CRD
Child Sexual Abuse (MELL)	CSA
Childhood Epileptic Encephalopathy [*Medicine*] (MELL)	CEE
Childhood Language Disorder (MELL)	CLD
Childhood Sexual Abuse (MELL)	CSA
Children (GEAB)	ch
Children (GEAB)	chldn
Children's Broadcasting [*NASDAQ symbol*] (SG)	FILM
Children's Place Retail Stores [*NASDAQ symbol*] (SG)	PLCE
Child-Resistant Packaging (EPAT)	CRP
Chile (MILB)	Chl
Chilhood-Onset Insomnia [*Medicine*] (MELL)	COI
Chills and Fever (MELL)	C & F
Chimney Sweeps Cancer [*Medicine*] (MELL)	CSC
China Eastern Airlines ADS [*NYSE symbol*] (SG)	CEA
China Energy Resources [*AMEX symbol*] (SG)	CHG
China Meteorological Administration	CMA
China Southern Airlines'H' ADS [*NYSE symbol*] (SG)	ZNH
China Telecom Hong Kong ADS [*NYSE symbol*] (SG)	CHL
China.com Corp. [*NASDAQ symbol*] (SG)	CHINA
Chinese Communist	ChiCom
Chinese Ecological Research Network (QUAC)	CERN
Chinese Liver Fluke [*Medicine*] (MELL)	CLF
Chip Fracture (MELL)	CF
Chi-Square Test (MELL)	CST
Chittenden Corp. [*NYSE symbol*] (SG)	CHZ
Chloriazepoxide [*Medicine*] (MELL)	CDX
Chlorine Dioxide (MELL)	ClO
Chlorine Institute, Inc.	CHI
Chlorine Monoxide (EOSA)	ClO
Chloroquine and Primaquine [*Medicine*] (MELL)	C & P
Chlorpropamide [*Medicine*] (MELL)	CPA
Choice Hotels Intl. [*NYSE symbol*] (SG)	CHH
ChoicePoint, Inc. [*NYSE symbol*] (SG)	CPS
Cholecalciferol [*Medicine*] (MELL)	D3
Cholelithiasis (MELL)	CL
Cholesterol Ester Ratio [*Medicine*] (MELL)	CER
Cholesterol-Lowering Therapy [*Medicine*] (MELL)	CLT
Cholinergic Receptor Site [*Medicine*] (MELL)	CRS
Chondrodysplasia Punctata [*Medicine*] (MELL)	CDP
Chondrodystrophic Myotonia [*Medicine*] (MELL)	CDM
Chondroitin Sulfate Protein (MELL)	CSP
Chopart Joint (MELL)	CJ
Chorda Equina of Spinal Cord [*Medicine*] (MELL)	CESC
Chorionic Villi [*Medicine*] (MELL)	CV
Chowchilla, CA [*FM radio station call letters*] (BROA)	KSKD-FM
Christ (GEAB)	Xt
Christened (GEAB)	chr
Christian (GEAB)	Xr
Christian (GEAB)	Xtian
Christian Periodical Index [*A publication*]	CPI
Christian Veterinary Mission (GVA)	CVM
Christian Veterinary Missions of Canada (GVA)	CVMC
Christianburg, VA [*FM radio station call letters*] (BROA)	WBZV-FM
Christianity (GEAB)	Xty
Christiansburg, WA [*AM radio station call letters*] (BROA)	WWVT
Christiansted, VI [*Television station call letters*] (BROA)	WCVI-TV
Christiansted, VI [*FM radio station call letters*] (BROA)	WMNG-FM
Chromosome Eight Trisomy Syndrome [*Medicine*] (MELL)	CETS
Chromosome Eighteen Trisomy Syndrome [*Medicine*] (MELL)	CETS
Chromosome Mapping [*Medicine*] (MELL)	CM
Chronic Catarrhal Colitis [*Medicine*] (MELL)	CCC
Chronic Catarrhal Tonsillitis [*Medicine*] (MELL)	CCT
Chronic Cigarette Cough (MELL)	CCC
Chronic Constrictive Pericarditis [*Medicine*] (MELL)	CCP
Chronic Destructive Periodontitis [*Medicine*] (MELL)	CDP
Chronic Dialysis [*Medicine*] (MELL)	CD
Chronic Diarrhea [*Medicine*] (MELL)	CD
Chronic Dislocating Shoulder [*Medicine*] (MELL)	CDS
Chronic Disseminated Candidiasis [*Medicine*] (MELL)	CDC
Chronic Eosinophilic Pneumonia [*Medicine*] (MELL)	CEP
Chronic Exertional Compartment Syndrome [*Medicine*] (MELL)	CECS
Chronic Fibrous Thyroiditis [*Medicine*] (MELL)	CFT
Chronic Follicular Gastritis [*Medicine*] (MELL)	CFG
Chronic Foot Dermatitis [*Medicine*] (MELL)	CFD
Chronic Hepatic Encephalopathy [*Medicine*] (MELL)	CHE
Chronic Hepatitis (MELL)	CH
Chronic Hypertension (MELL)	CH
Chronic Hypertrophic Emphysema [*Medicine*] (MELL)	CHE
Chronic Idiopathic Megacolon [*Medicine*] (MELL)	CIM
Chronic Inflammatory Cell [*Medicine*] (MELL)	CIC
Chronic Intermittent Peritoneal Dialysis [*Medicine*] (MELL)	CIPD
Chronic Intestinal Ischemia [*Medicine*] (MELL)	CII
Chronic Intestinal Pseudoobstruction [*Medicine*] (MELL)	CIP
Chronic Intractable Shoulder Pain (MELL)	CISP
Chronic Irritant Contact Dermatitis (MELL)	CICD
Chronic Ischemic Heart Disease [*Medicine*] (MELL)	CIHD
Chronic Maxillary Sinusitis [*Medicine*] (MELL)	CMS
Chronic Monocytic Leukemia [*Medicine*] (MELL)	CMOL

Chronic Mucopurulent Bronchitis [*Medicine*] (MELL)	CMPB
Chronic Myelodysplastic Syndrome [*Medicine*] (MELL)	CMS
Chronic Myelogenous Leukemia [*Medicine*]	CML
Chronic Narrow Angle Glaucoma (MELL)	CNAG
Chronic Neutrophilic Leukemia [*Medicine*] (MELL)	CNL
Chronic Nonspecific Diarrhea of Childhood [*Medicine*] (MELL)	CNDC
Chronic Obstructive Uropathy [*Medicine*] (MELL)	COU
Chronic Opioid Medication [*Medicine*] (MELL)	COM
Chronic Osteomyelitis [*Medicine*] (MELL)	COM
Chronic Pain Center (MELL)	CPC
Chronic Pain Disorder (MELL)	CPD
Chronic Paroxysmal Hemicrania [*Medicine*] (MELL)	CPH
Chronic Pelvic Pain (MELL)	CPP
Chronic Peritoneal Dialysis [*Medicine*] (MELL)	CPD
Chronic Pharyngitis [*Medicine*] (MELL)	CP
Chronic Pigmented Purpura [*Medicine*] (MELL)	CPP
Chronic Pleurisy (MELL)	CP
Chronic Polyarthritis [*Medicine*] (MELL)	CP
Chronic Progressive Myelopathy [*Medicine*] (MELL)	CPM
Chronic Prostatitis Syndrome [*Medicine*] (MELL)	CPS
Chronic Protein Deprivation [*Medicine*] (MELL)	CPD
Chronic Radiodermatitis [*Medicine*] (MELL)	CRD
Chronic Rejection (MELL)	CR
Chronic Relapsing Demyelinating Inflammatory Polyneuropathy [*Medicine*] (MELL)	CRDIP
Chronic Respiratory Alkalosis [*Medicine*] (MELL)	CRA
Chronic Respiratory Insufficiency [*Medicine*] (MELL)	CRI
Chronic Rheumatoid Arthritis (MELL)	CRA
Chronic Smoke Inhalation (MELL)	CSI
Chronic Subdural Hematoma [*Medicine*] (MELL)	CSDH
Chronic Tension Headache (MELL)	CTH
Chronic Thrombotic Pulmonary Vascular Obstruction [*Medicine*] (MELL)	CTPVO
Chronic Ulcerative Stomatitis [*Medicine*]	CUS
Chronic Valvular Heart Disease [*Medicine*] (MELL)	CVHD
Chronotherapeutics (MELL)	CT
Chrysler Data Visualizer	CDV
Chubbuck, ID [*AM radio station call letters*] (BROA)	KRTK
Church (BEE)	chr
Church Records Archives (GEAB)	CRA
Chylomicrons (MELL)	CM
CIBER, Inc. [*NYSE symbol*] (SG)	CBR
CIENA Corp. [*NASDAQ symbol*] (SG)	CIEN
Cincinnati Bengals [*National Football League*] [*1968-present*] (NFLA)	Cin
Cincinnati, OH [*Television station call letters*] (BROA)	WCPO-DT
Cincinnati, OH [*AM radio station call letters*] (BROA)	WKRC
Cincinnati, OH [*Television station call letters*] (BROA)	WLWT-DT
Cincinnati, OH [*FM radio station call letters*] (BROA)	WVMX-FM
Cincinnati Reds [*National Football League*] [*1933-34*] (NFLA)	CiR
Cingulate Motor Area [*Part of brain's cortex*]	CMA
Circa (GEAB)	cir
Circadian Rhythm (MELL)	CR
Circadian Rhythm Disorder [*Medicine*] (MELL)	CRD
Circle International Group [*NASDAQ symbol*] (SG)	CRCL
Circle of Willis [*Medicine*] (MELL)	COW
Circleville, OH [*FM radio station call letters*] (BROA)	WAZU-FM
Circuit City Strs-CarMx Grp [*NYSE symbol*] (SG)	KMX
Circuit City Strs-CrctCty Grp [*NYSE symbol*] (SG)	CC
Circuity Upgrade	CU
Circulating Immune-Complex Disease [*Medicine*] (MELL)	CICD
Circumcision (MELL)	Circ
Circumpolar Arctic Paleo Environments (QUAC)	CAPE
Circumvallate Papilla [*Medicine*] (MELL)	CVP
Cirrhosis of Liver [*Medicine*] (MELL)	CL
Cirrocumulus Cloud (WEAT)	Cc
Cirrocumulus Standing Lenticular Cloud (WEAT)	CCSL
Cirrostratus Cloud (WEAT)	Cs
Cirrus Cloud (WEAT)	Ci
CIT Group 'A' [*NYSE symbol*] (SG)	CIT
Citadel Communications [*NASDAQ symbol*] (SG)	CITC
Citigroup, Inc. [*NYSE symbol*] (SG)	C
Citronelle, AL [*FM radio station call letters*] (BROA)	WQUA-FM
City Graphic (GEOI)	CITYG
City of Portland Bureau of Planning [*Oregon*] (GEOI)	COP/BOP
City Real Property Database (GEOI)	CRPD
City View	c/v
Civil (GEAB)	civ
Civil Engineering Data	CED
Civil War (GEAB)	CW
Civilian Police (MILB)	civ pol
Clarent Corp. [*NASDAQ symbol*] (SG)	CLRN
Clarion Commercial Hldgs'A' [*NYSE symbol*] (SG)	CLR
Clarksburg, WV [*Television station call letters*] (BROA)	WVFX
Clarksville, IN [*FM radio station call letters*] (BROA)	WQSH-FM
Class Identifier (GEOI)	CLID
Class Size Reduction	CSR
Classic Bicycle and Whizzer Club (EA)	CBWCA
Classic Chevy Club International (EA)	CCI
Classification and Regression Tree Technique [*Statistics*]	CART
Classified Image Editor (GEOI)	CIE
Classroom Teacher Network	CTN
Claw Hand Deformity (MELL)	CHD
Clay Shoveler's Fracture [*Medicine*] (MELL)	CSF
Clayton, GA [*FM radio station call letters*] (BROA)	WRBN-FM
Clean Catch Urinalysis [*Medicine*] (MELL)	CCUA

Clean Development Mechanism ... CDM
Clean Midstream Urine [*Specimen*] [*Medicine*] (MELL) ... CMSU
Clean Water Restoration Act (MELL) ... CWRA
Clear Cell Adenocarcinoma [*Medicine*] (MELL) ... CCAC
Clear Cell Carcinoma [*Medicine*] (MELL) ... CCC
Clear Lake, SD [*FM radio station call letters*] (BROA) ... KBGV-FM
Clearwater, FL [*FM radio station call letters*] (BROA) ... WSSR-FM
Cleco Corp. [*NYSE symbol*] (SG) ... CNL
Cleft Lip (MELL) ... CL
Cleft Uvula [*Medicine*] (MELL) ... CU
Clerk (GEOI) ... Clk
Clerk (GEAB) ... clk
Cleveland Browns [*National Football League*] [*1999-present*] (NFLA) ... ClB
Cleveland Browns [*National Football League*] [*1950-95*] (NFLA) ... Cle
Cleveland, MS [*Television station call letters*] (BROA) ... WMAI
Cleveland, OH [*Television station call letters*] (BROA) ... WEWS-DT
Cleveland, OH [*Television station call letters*] (BROA) ... WKYC-DT
Cleveland Rams [*National Football League*] [*1937-45*] (NFLA) ... ClR
Cleveland, TX [*FM radio station call letters*] (BROA) ... KKTL-FM
Clever Fellows Innovation Consortium ... CFIC
Click2Send Safe Deposit Box [*Digital storage*] ... CSDB
Clifton Park, NY [*FM radio station call letters*] (BROA) ... WDCD-FM
Climate and Global Change ... CGC
Climate Change Action Plan [*Environmental Protection Agency*] (EPAT) ... CCAP
Climate Interest Group (GEOI) ... CIG
Climate Variability ... CLIVAR
Climatological Data (EPAT) ... CD
Clinical Death (MELL) ... CD
Clinical Ecological Illness (MELL) ... CEI
Clinical Studies Trust Fund (GVA) ... CSTF
Clinical Toxicology and Commercial Products (MELL) ... CTCP
Clinically Observed Seizures (MELL) ... COS
Clinton, IA [*FM radio station call letters*] (BROA) ... KZEG-FM
Clipping Injury Fracture (MELL) ... CIF
Cloquet's Lymph Node [*Medicine*] (MELL) ... CLN
Closed Cerebral Trauma (MELL) ... CCT
Closed Chest Massage [*Medicine*] (MELL) ... CCM
Closed Cup ... CC
Closed Drainage System [*Medicine*] (MELL) ... CDS
Closed Intramedullary Pinning [*Medicine*] (MELL) ... CIMP
Closed Observation Room (MELL) ... COR
Closed Thoracotomy [*Medicine*] (MELL) ... CT
Closed Urinary Drainage System [*Medicine*] (MELL) ... CUDS
Close-Quarter Marksmanship ... CQM
Clot Dissolving Drug [*Medicine*] (MELL) ... CDD
Clotting Factor [*Medicine*] (MELL) ... CF
Clotting Time [*Medicine*] (MELL) ... CLT
Cloud Ceiling Height (WEAT) ... CIG
Cloud to Air Lightning (WEAT) ... CA
Cloud to Cloud Lightning (WEAT) ... CC
Clovis, CA [*AM radio station call letters*] (BROA) ... KBEG
Clovis, CA [*AM radio station call letters*] (BROA) ... KOOR
Clovis, NM [*FM radio station call letters*] (BROA) ... KKYC-FM
Club Zoologico [*Universiti Putra Malaysia*] [*University student group*] (GVA) ... CZ
Clublink Corp. [*Toronto Stock Exchange symbol*] (SG) ... LNK
CMGI, Inc. [*NASDAQ symbol*] (SG) ... CMGI
CMI Corp. Cl'A' [*NYSE symbol*] (SG) ... CMI
CNA Surety [*NYSE symbol*] (SG) ... SUR
CNET, Inc. [*NASDAQ symbol*] (SG) ... CNET
CNF Transportation [*NYSE symbol*] (SG) ... CNF
Coach USA [*NYSE symbol*] (SG) ... CUI
Coal City, IL [*FM radio station call letters*] (BROA) ... WBVS-FM
Coal Reserves Data Base ... CRDB
Coalition Against On-Line Forms ... CAOF
Coalition for the Defense of Human Rights Under Islam ... CDHRUI
Coalition of Essential Schools ... CES
Coastal Change Analysis Project (QUAC) ... CCAP
Coastal Mapping Program (GEOI) ... CMP
Coastal Ocean Management, Planning, and Assessment System (GEOI) ... COMPAS
Cobleskill, NY [*AM radio station call letters*] (BROA) ... WXBH
Cocaine Hydrochloride [*Medicine*] (MELL) ... CHCl
Cocaine-Induced Respiratory Failure [*Medicine*] (MELL) ... CIRF
Coccidioidomycosis [*Medicine*] (MELL) ... COCCID
Cochlear Occlusion [*Medicine*] (MELL) ... CO
Cochlear Ossification [*Medicine*] (MELL) ... CO
Cockatiel [*Bird*] ... Tiel
Cockatoo [*Bird*] ... Too
Code Red (MELL) ... CR
Coeur d'Alene, ID [*FM radio station call letters*] (BROA) ... KBIH-FM
Coexisting Illness (MELL) ... CEI
Coffee Worker's Lung (MELL) ... CWL
Cognition Disorder (MELL) ... CD
Cognitive Strategies Questionnaire (MELL) ... CSQ
Coil Spring Brace [*Medicine*] (MELL) ... CSB
Coin Lesion (MELL) ... CL
Colby, KS [*FM radio station call letters*] (BROA) ... KWGB-FM
Cold Air Induction ... CAT
Cold Cup Biopsy [*Medicine*] (MELL) ... CCB
Cold War International History Project [*Woodrow Wilson International Center for Scholars*] [*Internet resource*] ... CWIHP
Coldwater Creek [*NASDAQ symbol*] (SG) ... CWTR
Colfax, IL [*FM radio station call letters*] (BROA) ... WSNI-FM
Collaborative Environment ... CE
Collagen Replacement Therapy [*Medicine*] (MELL) ... CRT
Collection Insertion Map (GEOI) ... CIM
College Mathematics Journal [*A publication*] ... CMJ
College of American Pathology ... CAP
College of Architecture and Urban Planning ... CAUP
College of Engineering ... CoE
Collegiate Gymnastics Association (EA) ... CGA
Collingwood, ON [*FM radio station call letters*] (BROA) ... CKCB-FM
Colombia (MILB) ... Co
Colonel (GEAB) ... col
Colonial Gas [*NYSE symbol*] (SG) ... CLG
Colonial Heights, TN [*FM radio station call letters*] (BROA) ... WRZK-FM
Colonial Heights, VA [*AM radio station call letters*] (BROA) ... WDZY
Colonic Polyposis [*Medicine*] (MELL) ... CP
Colony (BEE) ... col
Colony Count for Diarrhea [*Medicine*] (MELL) ... CCD
Colony-Forming Assay [*Medicine*] (MELL) ... CFA
Color and Temperature [*Medicine*] (MELL) ... C & T
Color Imaging Systems (GEOI) ... CIS
Color Scanner (GEOI) ... CS
Colorado Department of Agriculture (GEOI) ... CDA
Colorado Division of Planning (GEOI) ... CDP
Colorado Division of Wildlife (GEOI) ... CDOW
Colorado Educational Media Association ... CEMA
Colorado Plateau Field Station (GEOI) ... CPFS
Colorado State Forest Service (GEOI) ... CSFS
Colorado Student Assessment Program ... CSAP
Colorado Tick Fever Virus (MELL) ... CTFV
Colorectal Surgery [*Medicine*] (MELL) ... CRS
COLT Telecom Group ADS [*NASDAQ symbol*] (SG) ... COLT
Columbia City, IN [*FM radio station call letters*] (BROA) ... WSHI-FM
Columbia Energy Group [*NYSE symbol*] (SG) ... CG
Columbia, IL [*FM radio station call letters*] (BROA) ... KMJM-FM
Columbia Region Association of Governments (GEOI) ... CRAG
Columbia Sportswear [*NASDAQ symbol*] (SG) ... COLM
Columbus (BEE) ... Colmbs
Columbus, GA [*AM radio station call letters*] (BROA) ... WMLF
Columbus, MS [*Television station call letters*] (BROA) ... WMAA
Columbus, OH [*Television station call letters*] (BROA) ... WBNS-DT
Columbus, OH [*FM radio station call letters*] (BROA) ... WBNS-FM
Columbus, OH [*FM radio station call letters*] (BROA) ... WCBE-FM
Columbus, OH [*FM radio station call letters*] (BROA) ... WCOL-FM
Columbus SoPwr 7.92% Sub Db [*NYSE symbol*] (SG) ... CJA
Columbus, WI [*FM radio station call letters*] (BROA) ... WTLX-FM
Column Builder (GEOI) ... CB
Com21, Inc. [*NASDAQ symbol*] (SG) ... CMTO
Comanche Portable Cockpit [*Army*] ... CPC
Comanche, TX [*FM radio station call letters*] (BROA) ... KOXZ-FM
Comanding General, United States, Army, Atlantic ... CGUSARLANT
Combat (MILB) ... cbt
Combat-Capable Trainer (MILB) ... CCT
Combination Drug Therapy (MELL) ... CDT
Combined Hormonal Therapy [*Medicine*] (MELL) ... CHT
Combining Conditional Expectations and Residuals Plot ... CERES plot
Comfort Systems USA [*NYSE symbol*] (SG) ... FIX
Comision de Estudios del Territorio Nacional [*Mexico*] (GEOI) ... CETENAL
Command (MILB) ... comd
Command, Control, Communications, Computers, and Intelligence ... C4I
Command, Control, Communications, Computers, Intelligence, Electronic Warfare, and Sensors [*Army*] ... C4IEWS
Command Ship (MILB) ... CMDS
Commander (GEAB) ... com
Commander, Air Force Task Force ... COMAFTASKOR
Commanding (GEOI) ... Comdg
Commando (MILB) ... cdo
Commerce Bancorp [*NYSE symbol*] (SG) ... CBH
Commerce One [*NASDAQ symbol*] (SG) ... CMRC
Commercial Space Centers ... CSC
Commission (GEOI) ... Com
Commission (PROS) ... commn
Commission for Environmental Cooperation [*Environmental Protection Agency*] (EPAT) ... CEC
Commission Geologique du Canada (GEOI) ... CGC
Commission on Education and Training (GEOI) ... CET
Commission on Food, Environment, and Renewable Resources [*National Association of State Universities and Land-Grant Colleges*] (GVA) ... CFERR
Commission on Map Use and Spatial Data Use (GEOI) ... CMSDU
Commission on National and Regional Atlases (GEOI) ... CNRA
Commissioner (PROS) ... commnr
Commissioners (GEAB) ... comm
Committee (PROS) ... comm
Committee for the Advancement of Role-Playing Games (EA) ... CAR=PGa
Committee Investigating Cartographic Entity, Definitions, and Standards (GEOI) ... CICAEDAS
Committee on Data Management, Archiving, and Computation (EOSA) ... CODMAC
Committee on Marine Surveying and Mapping (GEOI) ... CMSM
Committee on Natural Resource Information Management [*Alaska*] (GEOI) ... CONRIM
Committee on Southern Map Libraries (GEOI) ... COSMI
Committee on Southern Map Libraries (GEOI) ... CSML
Committee on the Exchange of Digital Data (GEOI) ... CEDD
Committee on the Federal Procurement of Architect and Engineer Services (GEOI) ... COFPAES
Committee on the Status of Endangered Wildlife in Canada (QUAC) ... COSEWIC
Common (BEE) ... com

Common Fund for Commodities ... CFC
Common Iliac Artery [*Medicine*] (MELL) ... CIA
Common Iliac Catheter [*Medicine*] (MELL) ... CIC
Common Iliac Lymph Node [*Medicine*] (MELL) ... CILN
Common Land Data Base (GEOI) ... CLDB
Common Ragweed (MELL) ... CRW
Common Sense Initiative [*Environmental science*] (EPAT) ... CSI
Common Wart (MELL) ... CW
Commonwealth of Virginia Information Systems (GEOI) ... COVIS
Commonwealth Tel Enterp [*NASDAQ symbol*] (SG) ... CTCO
Commscope, Inc. [*NYSE symbol*] (SG) ... CTV
Communication (BEE) ... comm
Communication, Culture, and Technology Program ... CCT
Communications (MILB) ... comms
Communications and Broadcasting Engineering Test Satellite ... COMETS
Communications and Data Handling (GEOI) ... CDH
Communications & Measurement Technologies Ltd. (GEOI) ... C&MT
Communications for North Carolina Education, Research, and Technology Network ... CONCERT
Community Bank System [*NYSE symbol*] (SG) ... CBU
Community Bankshares S.C. [*AMEX symbol*] (SG) ... SCB
Community Base Station (GEOI) ... CBS
Community Based Environmental Project (EPAT) ... CBEP
Community Capital [*AMEX symbol*] (SG) ... CYL
Community Health Onsite Information Centers [*New York Public Library*] ... CHOICES
Community Independent Bank [*AMEX symbol*] (SG) ... INB
Community Perspectives on Land and Agrarian Reform [*South Africa*] (GEOI) ... CPLAR
Community Resources Against Street Hoodlums [*An association*] ... CRASH
Community Service Learning ... CSL
Community-Based Environmental Protection (GEOI) ... CBEP
Comp Cervelaria Brahma Pfd ADS [*NYSE symbol*] (SG) ... BRH
Comp Paranaense Energia'B' ADS [*NYSE symbol*] (SG) ... ELP
Comp Siderurgica Nacional ADS [*NYSE symbol*] (SG) ... SID
Compact-Flash [*Computer science*] ... CF
Compagnie Genl Geophy ADS [*NYSE symbol*] (SG) ... GGY
Companhia Brasileira ADS [*NYSE symbol*] (SG) ... CBD
Compania Cervecerias Unidas ADS [*NYSE symbol*] (SG) ... CU
Compania Cervecerias Unidas ADS [*NYSE symbol*] (SG) ... VNT
Companion Animal Welfare Council (GVA) ... CAWC
Company (GEAB) ... comp
Company (MILB) ... coy
Company Services Advisory Committee [*British*] (GVA) ... CSAC
Compaq Networking Management Software [*Computer science*] ... CNMS
Comparative (BEE) ... compar
Comparative Performance Exploratory Analysis ... CPEA
Comparative Respiratory Society (GVA) ... CRS
Compartmental Knee Prosthesis (MELL) ... CKP
Compass and Inclinometer (GEOI) ... CI
Compassion in World Farming (GVA) ... CWF
Competative Cooperative Agreements Program (GEOI) ... CCAP
Competitive Medical Organization (MELL) ... CMO
Complete Business Solutions [*NASDAQ symbol*] (SG) ... CBSI
Complete Cleft Palate (MELL) ... CCP
Complete Occupational Therapy Evaluation (MELL) ... COTE
Complete Testicular Feminization Syndrome (MELL) ... CTFS
Completely Healed (MELL) ... CH
Composite Healthcare System (MELL) ... CHS
Composites Institute ... CINS
Compound Myopic Astigmatism [*Medicine*] (MELL) ... CMA
Comprehensive Care Clinic (MELL) ... CCC
Comprehensive Drug Abuse Prevention and Control Act (MELL) ... CDAPCA
Comprehensive Economic Data Atlas of China (GEOI) ... CEDAC
Comprehensive Educational Improvement and Financing Act ... CEIFA
Comprehensive Health Care (MELL) ... CHC
Comprehensive Healthcare Clinic (MELL) ... CHCC
Comprehensive School Reform Demonstration ... CSRD
Compressed Aeronautical Chart (GEOI) ... CAAD
Compressed Digital Terrain Elevation Data (GEOI) ... CDTED
Comptroller (PROS) ... comptr
CompuCredit Corp. [*NASDAQ symbol*] (SG) ... CCRT
Computed Tomography Angiographic Portography [*Medicine*] (MELL) ... CTAP
Computer Aided Mapping (GEOI) ... CAM
Computer Assisted Land Survey System (GEOI) ... CALS
Computer Assisted Thermography (GEOI) ... CAT
Computer Display Terminal (GEOI) ... CDT
Computer Graphics World [*A publication*] (GEOI) ... CGW
Computer Network Security Response Team ... CNSRT
Computer Scatter Tomography (MELL) ... CST
Computer Sciences Corporation (GEOI) ... CSC
Computer Security Resource and Response Center ... CSRC
Computer Systems Information Network (GEOI) ... CSIN
Computer-Aided Drafting, Mapping, and Photogrammetry (GEOI) ... CADMAP
Computer-Aided Machining ... CAM
Computer-Aided Three-Dimensional Interactive Application ... CATIA
Computerized Optimization Model for Predicting and Analyzing Support Structures [*Army*] ... COMPASS
Computerized Renal Tomography [*Medicine*] (MELL) ... CRT
Computron Software [*AMEX symbol*] (SG) ... CFW
CompX Intl.'A' [*NYSE symbol*] (SG) ... CIX
Comtech Telecommns [*NASDAQ symbol*] (SG) ... CMTL
Concentric Network [*NASDAQ symbol*] (SG) ... CNCX
Conceptual Design and Cost Review (EOSA) ... CDCR
Concert (BEE) ... con
Conchologists of America (EA) ... COA
Concord Communications [*NASDAQ symbol*] (SG) ... CCRD
Concrete Block Enclosed Elevator (GEOI) ... CBET
Concrete, Lime, Cinder or Cement Brick (GEOI) ... CBR
Conditioned Escape Response [*Medicine*] (MELL) ... CES
Condor Tech Solutions [*NASDAQ symbol*] (SG) ... CNDR
Conduction System Disease [*Medicine*] (MELL) ... CSD
Conductive Deafness (MELL) ... CD
Conductive Hearing Loss (MELL) ... CHL
Condylar Fracture (MELL) ... CF
Condylar Process of Mandible [*Medicine*] (MELL) ... CPM
Condylocephalic Nail (MELL) ... CCN
Conectiv, Inc. [*NYSE symbol*] (SG) ... CIV
Conexant Systems [*NASDAQ symbol*] (SG) ... CNXT
Confederacion de Trabajadores Cubanos [*Confederation of Cuban Workers*] ... CTC
Confederacion Generale Trabajadores de Puerto Rico ... PRCGT
Confederacion Laborista de Puerto Rico ... PRCL
Confederation (PROS) ... confed
Conference Nationale des Veterinaires Specialises en Petits Animaux [*France*] (GVA) ... CNVSPA
Conference on Information Knowledge Management (GEOI) ... CIKM
Conference on Remote Sensing Education (GEOI) ... CORSE
Conferred (GEAB) ... confer
Confidential Letters of Map Amendment (GEOI) ... CLOMA
Confirmatory Factor Analysis ... CFA
Confluence (GEOI) ... CNFL
Conformal Space Projection (GEOI) ... CSP
Congenital Cardiovascular Malformation [*Medicine*] (MELL) ... CCVM
Congenital Dacryocystocele [*Medicine*] (MELL) ... CDC
Congenital Deafness (MELL) ... CD
Congenital Defect (MELL) ... CD
Congenital Dislocation of Knee (MELL) ... CDK
Congenital Dysplastic Hip (MELL) ... CDH
Congenital Facial Diplegia [*Medicine*] (MELL) ... CFD
Congenital Glaucoma (MELL) ... CG
Congenital Hip Subluxation [*Medicine*] (MELL) ... CHS
Congenital Hypoventilation Syndrome [*Medicine*] (MELL) ... CHS
Congenital Ichtyosisform Erythroderma [*Dermatology*] ... CIE
Congenital Intestional Aganglionosis [*Medicine*] (MELL) ... CIA
Congenital Lactase Deficiency [*Medicine*] (MELL) ... CLD
Congenital Lobar Emphysema [*Medicine*] (MELL) ... CLE
Congenital Myasthenia Gravis [*Medicine*] (MELL) ... CMG
Congenital Nephrotic Syndrome [*Medicine*] (MELL) ... CNS
Congenital Nonspherocytic Hemolytic Anemia [*Medicine*] (MELL) ... CNHA
Congenital Polycystic Disease [*Medicine*] (MELL) ... CPD
Congenital Red Cell Anemia [*Medicine*] (MELL) ... CRCA
Congenital Retinal Telangiectasia [*Medicine*] (MELL) ... CRT
Congenital Rubella [*Medicine*] (MELL) ... CR
Congenital Rubella Deafness [*Medicine*] (MELL) ... CRD
Congenital Sensory Neuropathy [*Medicine*] (MELL) ... CSN
Congenital Vertical Talus [*Medicine*] (MELL) ... CVT
Congenital-Kyphosis [*Medicine*] (MELL) ... CK
Congestive Cardiomyopathy [*Medicine*] (MELL) ... COCM
Congestive Hepatomegaly [*Medicine*] (MELL) ... CHM
Congestive Mastitis [*Medicine*] (MELL) ... CM
Conglutinogen Activating Factor [*Medicine*] (MELL) ... KAF
Congo African Grey [*Bird*] ... CAG
Congreso Uniones Industriales de Puerto Rico ... PRCUI
Congress of Cartographic Information Specialist Associations (GEOI) ... CCISA
Conjecture (GEAB) ... conject
Conjoined Twins (MELL) ... CT
Conjoint Family Therapy (MELL) ... CFT
Conjugal Rights (MELL) ... CR
Conjugated Estrogen Substance [*Medicine*] (MELL) ... CES
Conjunctival Intraepithelial Neoplasia [*Medicine*] (MELL) ... CIEN
Connected Network Backup [*CMP*] ... CNB
Connecticut Geological and Natural History Survey (GEOI) ... CGNHS
Connecticut Union of Telephone Workers ... CUTW
Connecticut United for Research Excellence (GVA) ... CURE
Connective Tissue Activating Peptide [*Medicine*] (MELL) ... CTAP
Connersville, IN [*FM radio station call letters*] (BROA) ... WIFE-FM
Conrad Veidt Society (EA) ... CVS
Conroe, TX [*AM radio station call letters*] (BROA) ... KCHC
Conroe, TX [*Television station call letters*] (BROA) ... KTBU
Consanguineous Marriage (MELL) ... CM
Conscript Ratio in the Air Forces ... CRAF
Consejo Revolucionario Cubano [*Cuban Revolutionary Council*] ... CRC
Consejo Superior de Investigaciones Cientificas [*Spain*] (GEOI) ... CSIC
Conselho Federal de Medicina Veterinaria [*Brazil*] (GVA) ... CFMV
Conselho Regional de Medicina Veterinaria de Sao Paulo (GVA) ... CRMV-SP
Conselho Regional de Medicina Veterinaria do Rio de Janeiro (GVA) ... CRMV-RJ
Consequences Assessment Tool Set (GEOI) ... CATS
Conservation Breeding Specialist Group (GVA) ... CBSG
Conservation of Arctic Flora and Fauna (GEOI) ... CAFF
Consol Delivery & Logistics [*AMEX symbol*] (SG) ... CDV
CONSOL Energy [*NYSE symbol*] (SG) ... CNX
Consolidated Ed 7.35%'PINES' [*NYSE symbol*] (SG) ... EPI
Consolidated Graphics [*NYSE symbol*] (SG) ... CGX
Consortium for Equity in Standards and Testing ... CTEST
Consortium for Risk Evaluation with Stakeholder Participation (GEOI) ... CRESP
Consortium of Aquariums, Universities, and Zoos (GVA) ... CAUZ
Consortium of North American Veterinary Interactive New Concept Education (GVA) ... CONVINCE

Constant (WEAT)	CONS
Constellation Energy Group [*NYSE symbol*] (SG)	CEG
Constrained Delaunay Triangulation (GEOI)	CDT
Constrictive Pericarditis [*Medicine*] (MELL)	CPC
Consultant (PROS)	Consult
Consulting Engineers and Land Surveyors of California (GEOI)	CELSOC
Consulting Engineers Council of Washington (GEOI)	CECW
Consumer Consortium on Assisted Living	CCAL
Consumer Health Care (MELL)	CHC
Consumer Product Safety Commission (MELL)	CPS
Consumer Unity & Trust Society	CUTS
Contact Lens (MELL)	CL
Content Standard for Digital Geospatial Metadata (GEOI)	CSDGM
Continental Kennel Club (GVA)	CKC
Continental Polluted Air Mass (QUAC)	CPAM
Continental Scale International Project (GEOI)	CSIP
Continucare Corp. [*AMEX symbol*] (SG)	CNU
Continued Stay Review [*Medicine*] (MELL)	CSR
Continues to Improve (MELL)	CTI
Continuing Disability Review (MELL)	CDR
Continuous Area Pattern Mapping (GEOI)	COMAP
Continuous Insulin Infusion [*Medicine*] (MELL)	CII
Continuous Intravenous Insulin Infusion [*Medicine*] (MELL)	CIVII
Continuous Lumbar Epidural [*Medicine*] (MELL)	CLE
Continuous Mandatory Ventilation (MELL)	CMV
Continuous Mixed Venous Oximetry (MELL)	CMVO
Continuous Radon (EPAT)	CR
Continuous Subcutaneous Infusion [*Medicine*] (MELL)	CSI
Continuous Wave [*Radar*]	CW
Continuous Wave	cw
Continuously Operated Reference Station (GEOI)	CORS
Contl Airlines'B' [*NYSE symbol*] (SG)	CAL
Contl Information Sys [*NASDAQ symbol*] (SG)	CISC
Contour Interpolation Program (GEOI)	CIP
Contour to Grid (GEOI)	CTOG
Contract (GEAB)	contr
Contract Addenda Committee	CAC
Contrast Ventriculography [*Medicine*] (MELL)	CV
Control Group [*Medicine*] (MELL)	CG
Controladora Comer'l Mex GDS [*NYSE symbol*] (SG)	MCM
Controlled Flights into Terrain [*Aviation*]	CFIT
Controlled Image Base (GEOI)	CIB
Controlled Medical Assistance Drug List (MELL)	CMADL
Controlled Multispectral Image Base (GEOI)	CMIB
Controlled-Release Tablet Corrected [*Medicine*] (MELL)	CRT
Controller (PROS)	contr
Conus Medullaris (MELL)	CM
Conventional Air-Launched Cruise Missile (MILB)	CALCM
Conventional Insulin Therapy (MELL)	CIT
Conventionally Armed Stand-Off Missiles (MILB)	CASM
Convergent Communications [*NASDAQ symbol*] (SG)	CONV
Convergys Corp. [*NYSE symbol*] (SG)	CVG
Convertible Slip Knot (MELL)	CSK
Convex (MELL)	Cx
Con-way Central Express	CCX
Con-way Intergrated Services	CIS
Con-way Southern Express	CSE
Con-way Truckload Services	CWT
Con-way Western Express	CWX
Cook Islands Department of Survey (GEOI)	CISD
Cookerville, TN [*Television station call letters*] (BROA)	WNPX
Cooper Cameron [*NYSE symbol*] (SG)	CAM
Cooper Cos. [*NYSE symbol*] (SG)	COO
Cooper Mtn Networks [*NASDAQ symbol*] (SG)	CMTN
Cooperation for Open Systems	COS
Cooperative Agreements Program (GEOI)	CAP
Cooperative Base Network (GEOI)	CBN
Cooperative Polygyny	CP
Coordinates, Definitions, and Notations (GEOI)	CDN
Coordinating Committee for Intercontinental Research	CCIRN
Coors (Adolph)Cl'B' [*NYSE symbol*] (SG)	RKY
Copene-Petroquimica ADS [*NYSE symbol*] (SG)	PNE
Copernican (BEE)	Cop
Coracohumeral Ligament (MELL)	CHL
Cordant Technologies [*NYSE symbol*] (SG)	CDD
Cordele, GA [*FM radio station call letters*] (BROA)	WAEF-FM
Cordiant Communic Grp ADS [*NYSE symbol*] (SG)	CDA
Core Automated Virtual Environment	CAVE
Core Curriculum Content Standards	CCCS
Core Curriculum Content Standards Aid	CCSA
Core Labortories N.V. [*NYSE symbol*] (SG)	CLB
Core Materials [*AMEX symbol*] (SG)	CME
Corel Corp. [*NASDAQ symbol*] (SG)	CORL
Corixa Corp. [*NASDAQ symbol*] (SG)	CRXA
Corn Blight Watch Experiment (GEOI)	CBWE
Corn Products Intl. [*NYSE symbol*] (SG)	CPO
Corn Refiners Association, Inc.	CR
Corn Residue Equivalents [*Environmental science*]	CRE
Corneal Grafting (MELL)	CG
Cornell Corrections [*NYSE symbol*] (SG)	CRN
Corner Brook, NF [*FM radio station call letters*] (BROA)	CKXX-FM
Cornerstone Bancorp [*AMEX symbol*] (SG)	CBN
Cornerstone Properties [*NYSE symbol*] (SG)	CPP
Cornerstone Realty Income Tr [*NYSE symbol*] (SG)	TCR
Corona Radiata [*Medicine*] (MELL)	CR
Coronado 15 Association (EA)	CFA
Coronal Diagnostic Spectrometer	CDS
Coronary Dilatation Catheter [*Medicine*] (MELL)	CDC
Coronary Force (MELL)	CF
Coroner (BEE)	cor
Coronoid Process of Mandible [*Medicine*] (MELL)	CPM
Corporal (GEAB)	corp
Corporal Veno-Occlusive Dysfunction [*Medicine*] (MELL)	CVOD
Corporate Executive Board [*NASDAQ symbol*] (SG)	EXBD
Corporate Office Prop Tr SBI [*NYSE symbol*] (SG)	OFC
Corporate Venturing [*Business term*]	CV
Corpus Luteum Cyst [*Medicine*] (MELL)	CLC
Corpus Luteum Hormone [*Medicine*] (MELL)	CLH
Corpuscle of Meissner [*Medicine*] (MELL)	COM
Corrected Line Length (GEOI)	CLL
Corrected Report (WEAT)	COR
Correctional Properties Tr [*NYSE symbol*] (SG)	CPV
Corrective Osteotomy [*Medicine*] (MELL)	CO
Correspond (GEAB)	crspd
Corruption-Perception Index	CPI
Corsicana, TX [*FM radio station call letters*] (BROA)	KDXX-FM
Cort Business Services [*NYSE symbol*] (SG)	CBZ
Cortebert Watch Company	CWC
Cortical Evoked Response [*Medicine*] (MELL)	CER
Corticoid Suppression Test (MELL)	CST
Corticotropic Hormone [*Medicine*] (MELL)	CTH
Corticotropin-Releasing Hormone [*Medicine*] (MELL)	CPH
Corvallis Microtechnology, Inc. (GEOI)	CMI
Corvallis Microtechnology, Inc. (GEOI)	CMT
Cosmic Exposure Dating (QUAC)	CED
Cosmic Hot Interstellar Plasma Spectrometer [*NASA*]	CHIPS
Cosmic Ray Satellite-B [*European Space Agency*]	COS-B
Cost Account Managers	CAM
Cost and Economic Assessment (EPAT)	CEA
Cost Avoidance to Total Investment Ratio	CVIR
Cost Reduction/Technical Excellence	CR/TE
Costa Rican-American Chamber of Commerce (EA)	AmCham
Costco Cos. [*NASDAQ symbol*] (SG)	COST
Costoclavicular Maneuver [*Medicine*] (MELL)	CCM
Costovertebral Joint (MELL)	CVJ
Cote d'Ivoire (MILB)	CI
Cottage Grove, OR [*FM radio station call letters*] (BROA)	KEUG-FM
Cotton Fracture (MELL)	CF
Cotton-Spot Macular Edema [*Medicine*] (MELL)	CSME
Cougar Club of America (EA)	CCOA
Cough and Expectoration (MELL)	C & E
Cough Frequency (MELL)	CF
Coulter Pharmaceutical [*NASDAQ symbol*] (SG)	CLTR
Council (PROS)	Counc
Council for Science and Technology [*Buenas Aires, Argentina*]	CONICET
Council of British Geography (GEOI)	COBRIG
Council of Canadian Personnel Associations	CCPA
Council of Ivy Group Presidents (EA)	CIGP
Council of the Americas (EA)	CoA
Council on Indoor Air Quality [*Environmental Protection Agency*] (EPAT)	CIAQ
Counsel (PROS)	couns
Counsellor (GEAB)	couns
Counselor of Real Estate	CRE
Counterirritants (MELL)	CIs
Countryside Council for Wales (GVA)	CCW
County Judge (GEAB)	CJ
Coupe	Cpe
Court-Ordered Examination [*Medicine*] (MELL)	COE
Courtyard	c/y
Cousin (GEAB)	c
Cousin (GEAB)	cous
Covad Communications Grp [*NASDAQ symbol*] (SG)	COVD
Covance, Inc. [*NYSE symbol*] (SG)	CVD
Covenant (GEAB)	coven
Coventry Health Care [*NASDAQ symbol*] (SG)	CVTY
Covington, IN [*FM radio station call letters*] (BROA)	WKZS-FM
Cow's Milk Protein (MELL)	CMP
Cow's Milk, Protein-Free (MELL)	CMPF
Cox Radio 'A' [*NYSE symbol*] (SG)	CXR
Coxa Vera [*Medicine*] (MELL)	CV
C-Phone Corp. [*NASDAQ symbol*] (SG)	CFON
CPS Systems [*AMEX symbol*] (SG)	SYS
Crab Lice (MELL)	CL
Cranial Electrical Stimulation [*Medicine*] (MELL)	CES
Cranial Nerve I [*Olfactory nerve*] [*Medicine*] (MELL)	cranial I
Cranial Nerve II [*Optic nerve*] [*Medicine*] (MELL)	cranial II
Cranial Nerve III [*Oculomotor nerve*] [*Medicine*] (MELL)	cranial III
Cranial Nerve IV [*Trochlear nerve*] [*Medicine*] (MELL)	cranial IV
Cranial Nerve IX [*Glossopharyngeal nerve*] [*Medicine*] (MELL)	cranial IX
Cranial Nerve Palsy [*Medicine*] (MELL)	CNP
Cranial Nerve Syndrome [*Medicine*] (MELL)	CNS
Cranial Nerve V [*Trigeminal nerve*] [*Medicine*] (MELL)	cranial V
Cranial Nerve VI [*Abducent nerve*] [*Medicine*] (MELL)	cranial VI
Cranial Nerve VII [*Facial nerve*] [*Medicine*] (MELL)	cranial VII
Cranial Nerve VIII [*Vestibulocochlear nerve*] [*Medicine*] (MELL)	cranial VIII
Cranial Nerve X [*Vagus nerve*] [*Medicine*] (MELL)	cranial X
Cranial Spinal Irradiation [*Medicine*] (MELL)	CSI
Craniofacial Dysostosis [*Medicine*] (MELL)	CFD
Craniospinal Defect [*Medicine*] (MELL)	CSD
Crater (GEOI)	CRTR

Crease .... crs
Creatinine Clearance (MELL) .... CrCl
Credicorp Ltd. [*NYSE symbol*] (SG) .... BAP
Creedmoor, TX [*AM radio station call letters*] (BROA) .... KQQA
Creepy Crawlers Fan Club (EA) .... CCFC
Cremaster Reflex [*Medicine*] (MELL) .... CR
Crescendo Murmur [*Medicine*] (MELL) .... CM
Crestar Energy [*Toronto Stock Exchange symbol*] (SG) .... CRS
Crestline Capital [*NYSE symbol*] (SG) .... CLJ
Creston, IA [*FM radio station call letters*] (BROA) .... KSIB-FM
Cretaceous-Tertiary .... K-T
Crete, IL [*FM radio station call letters*] (BROA) .... WYAA-FM
Crewe, VA [*FM radio station call letters*] (BROA) .... WKJS-FM
Cricothyroid Lymph Node [*Medicine*] (MELL) .... CTLN
Crisis Intervention Center (MELL) CIC
Crisp Uncirculated [*Numismatic term*] .... CrUnc
Critical Assessment of Methods of Protein Structure Prediction .... CASP
Critical Care Nursing (MELL) .... CCN
Critical Care Ventilator (MELL) CCV
Critical Path [*NASDAQ symbol*] (SG) .... CPTH
Critical Point Drying (MELL) .... CPD
Croatia (MILB) .... Cr
Cronos Group [*NASDAQ symbol*] (SG) .... CRNS
Crop Simulation Model .... CSM
Cross Cl'A' [*AMEX symbol*] (SG) .... ATX
Cross Hill, SC [*FM radio station call letters*] (BROA) .... WBDQ-FM
Cross Leg Flap (MELL) .... CLF
Cross-Content Workplace Readiness .... CCWR
Cross-Modality Matching (MELL) .... CMM
Crossville, TN [*Television station call letters*] (BROA) .... WBXX-TV
Crown Castle Intl. [*NASDAQ symbol*] (SG) .... TWRS
Crown Point, IN [*FM radio station call letters*] (BROA) .... WXRD-FM
Crozet, VA [*AM radio station call letters*] (BROA) .... WCYK
Cruciate Ligament [*Medicine*] (MELL) CL
Crucible Swell Number .... CSN
Cruciform Ligament [*Medicine*] (MELL) CL
Cruise Control [*Automotive term*] CC
Crush Kidney [*Medicine*] (MELL) .... CK
Crush Syndrome [*Medicine*] (MELL) .... CF
Cryogenic Surgery [*Medicine*] (MELL) .... CGS
CryoLife, Inc. [*NYSE symbol*] (SG) .... CRY
Cryospheric System (EOSA) .... CRYSYS
Cryotherapy [*Medicine*] (MELL) .... CT
Cryptococcal Pneumonitis [*Medicine*] (MELL) .... CCP
Crystal Falls, MI [*FM radio station call letters*] (BROA) .... WOBE-FM
Crystal Gas Storage [*AMEX symbol*] (SG) .... COR
Crystallex Intl. [*AMEX symbol*] (SG) .... KRY
CSK Auto [*NYSE symbol*] (SG) .... CAO
CTC Communications [*NASDAQ symbol*] (SG) .... CPTL
CTG Resources [*NYSE symbol*] (SG) .... CTG
Cuba, MO [*FM radio station call letters*] (BROA) .... KFXE-FM

Cuban Expeditionary Force .... CEF
Cubic Feet .... Cu Ft
Cubic Inch .... Cu In
Cubital Fossa [*Medicine*] (MELL) .... CF
Cullen/Frost Bankers [*NYSE symbol*] (SG) .... CFR
Culminating Demonstration .... CD
Culp, Inc. [*NYSE symbol*] (SG) .... CFI
Culpepper, VA [*FM radio station call letters*] (BROA) .... WARN-FM
Culpepper, VA [*FM radio station call letters*] (BROA) .... WPER-FM
Cultural Property Implementation Act .... CPIA
Culture Collection of Entomogenous Bacteria (MELL) .... CCEB
Cumulative Dose [*Medicine*] (MELL) .... CD
Cumulative Hydrologic Impact Assessment (GEOI) .... CHIA
Cumulonimbus Mamatus Cloud (WEAT) .... CbMam
Cumulus Cloud (WEAT) .... Cu
Cumulus Congestus Cloud (WEAT) .... CuCon
Cumulus Humilis Cloud (WEAT) .... CuHu
Cumulus Media 'A' [*NASDAQ symbol*] (SG) .... CMLS
Cumulus Medicoris Cloud (WEAT) .... CuMed
Cuneonavicular Joint (MELL) .... CNJ
Current (PROS) .... curr
Current Meter Digitizer (GEOI) .... CMD
Curriculum, Accreditation and Registration Committee (GEOI) .... CAR
Curved Calapinto Needle [*Medicine*] (MELL) .... CCN
Cushieri Maneuver [*Medicine*] (MELL) .... CM
Customer (PROS) .... cust
Customer Representative .... CR
CustomTracks Corp. [*NASDAQ symbol*] (SG) .... CUST
Cutaneous Larva Migrans [*Medicine*] (MELL) .... CLM
Cutaneous Leukocytoclastic Vasculitis [*Medicine*] (MELL) CLV
Cutaneous Lichen Amyloidosis [*Medicine*] (MELL) .... CLA
Cutaneous Occupational Infection [*Medicine*] (MELL) .... COI
Cuthbert, GA [*FM radio station call letters*] (BROA) .... WMRZ-FM
Cutis Laxa [*Loose skin*] (MELL) CL
CVF Technologies [*AMEX symbol*] (SG) .... CNV
Cybershop Intl. [*NASDAQ symbol*] (SG) .... CYSP
CyberSource [*Stock market symbol*] .... CYBS
Cyclin-Dependent Kinases .... CDK
Cylinder .... Cyl
Cymer, Inc. [*NASDAQ symbol*] (SG) .... CYMI
Cypros Pharmaceutical [*AMEX symbol*] (SG) .... CYP
Cyprus (MILB) .... Cy
Cystic Duct Stump Syndrome [*Medicine*] (MELL) .... CDSS
Cystic Fibrosis Association (MELL) .... CFA
Cystic Fibrosis Chest Pain [*Medicine*] (MELL) .... CFCP
Cystine Deficiency [*Medicine*] (MELL) .... CD
Cystourethrocele [*Medicine*] (MELL) .... CUC
Cytomegalovirus-Induced Thrombocytopenia and Hemolysis [*Medicine*]
(MELL) .... CITH
Czech Republic (MILB) .... Cz
Czechoslovak Academy of Sciences (GEOI) .... CSAV

D
By Meaning

Dacryoadenitis [*Medicine*] (MELL) .... DA
Dadeville, AL [*FM radio station call letters*] (BROA) .... WELL-FM
Daft, McCune, Walker (GEOI) .... DMW
Dahlonega, GA [*FM radio station call letters*] (BROA) .... WNGU-FM
Daily Permissible Intake [*Medicine*] (MELL) .... DPI
Daimler Chrysler Aerospace .... DASA
Daimler-Benz 5.75% Sub Notes [*NYSE symbol*] (SG) .... DAJ
DaimlerChrysler AG [*NYSE symbol*] (SG) .... DCX
Daimler-Chrysler Corporation .... DCC
Dain Rauscher [*NYSE symbol*] (SG) .... DRC
Dairy & Food Industries Supply Association, Inc. 3-A
Dairy Industry Federation (GVA) .... DIF
Dairy Mart Conven Str'B' [*AMEX symbol*] (SG) .... DMCB
Dallas Cowboys [*National Football League*] [*1960-present*] (NFLA) .... Dal
Dallas; PA [*FM radio station call letters*] (BROA) .... WCTD-FM
Dallas Texans [*National Football League*] [*1952*] (NFLA) .... DaT
Dallas Texans [*National Football League*] [*1960-62*] (NFLA) .... DTx
Dallas, TX [*Television station call letters*] (BROA) .... KDFW-DT
Dallas, TX [*AM radio station call letters*] (BROA) .... KDXX
Dallas, TX [*AM radio station call letters*] (BROA) .... KLUV
Dallas, TX [*Television station call letters*] (BROA) .... WFAA-DT
Dal-Tile Intl. [*NYSE symbol*] (SG) .... DTL
Dalton (MELL) .... D
Dan River 'A' [*NYSE symbol*] (SG) .... DRF
Danbury Mint .... DM
Dandruff (MELL) .... DD
Dandy-Walker Syndrome [*Medicine*] (MELL) .... DWS
Danmarks Geologiske Undersogelse (GEOI) .... DGU
Danube View .... d/v
Danville, IL [*FM radio station call letters*] (BROA) .... WRHK-FM
Danville, VA [*Television station call letters*] (BROA) .... WDRL-TV
Dark Shadows Official Fan Club (EA) .... DSOFC
Darling International [*AMEX symbol*] (SG) .... DAR
Darlington, SC [*AM radio station call letters*] (BROA) .... WPFM
Dashboard Fracture [*Medicine*] (MELL) .... DBF
Dassault Systems ADS [*NASDAQ symbol*] (SG) .... DASTY
Data Acquisitions and Systems Maintenance (GEOI) .... DA&SM
Data and Information System (EOSA) .... DIS
Data Archive and Distribution System (EOSA) .... DADS
Data Base Population Planning Working Group (GEOI) .... DBPPWG
Data Base Population Working Group (GEOI) .... DBPWG
Data Base Specifications (GEOI) .... DBS
Data Collection and Analysis (GEOI) .... DC&A
Data Collection System Receiving Site Equipment (GEOI) .... DCS/RSE
Data Collection System Tape (GEOI) .... DCST
Data Descriptive Area (GEOI) .... DDA
Data Descriptive File (GEOI) .... DDF
Data Descriptive Record (GEOI) .... DDR
Data Extraction (GEOI) .... DE
Data Extraction Segment (GEOI) .... DE/S
Data Information Delivery (GEOI) .... DID
Data Information Description (GEOI) .... DID
Data Integration Program (GEOI) .... DIP
Data Liberation Initiative [*Canada*] (GEOI) .... DLI
Data Logging (GEOI) .... DL
Data Management Segment Interface [*Control Document*] (GEOI) .... DMSI
Data Processing Environment (GEOI) .... DPE
Data Programming Language (GEOI) .... DPL
Data Review Record [*Environmental Protection Agency*] (EPAT) .... DRR
Database Publishing Systems Limited .... DPSL
Date of Birth (MELL) .... db
Date of Conception (MELL) .... DOC
Date of Discharge [*Medicine*] (MELL) .... DOD
Date of Illness (MELL) .... DOI
Date of Implant (MELL) .... DOI
Date of Investigation (MELL) .... DOI
Date of Last Drink [*Medicine*] (MELL) .... DLD
Date Rape (MELL) .... DR
Date-Time-Group .... DTG
Daughter (GEAB) .... dau
Daughter (GEAB) .... dtr
Dave & Buster's [*NYSE symbol*] (SG) .... DAB
Dave Durham Fan Club .... DDFC
Davenport, IA [*FM radio station call letters*] (BROA) .... WLLR-FM
Davenport, WA [*FM radio station call letters*] (BROA) .... KKRS-FM
David Birney International Fan Club (EA) .... DBIFC

David Copperfield International Fan Club (EA) .... DCIFC
David's Bridal [*NASDAQ symbol*] (SG) .... DABR
Day of Delivery [*Medicine*] (MELL) .... DD
Day One [*First day seen for treatment*] [*Medicine*] (MELL) D1
Day Surgery Unit (MELL) .... DSU
Day-Care Home (MELL) .... DCH
Days after Birth (MELL) .... DAB
Days Post Coitum [*Medicine*] (MELL) .... DPC
Dayton Superior 'A' [*NYSE symbol*] (SG) .... DSD
Dayton, WA [*FM radio station call letters*] (BROA) .... KZZM-FM
Daytona Beach, FL [*Television station call letters*] (BROA) .... WESH-DT
DBT Online [*NYSE symbol*] (SG) .... DBT
De Kalb, MS [*FM radio station call letters*] (BROA) .... WJXM-FM
De Novo Inflammatory Growth [*Medicine*] (MELL) .... DNIG
Deacon (GEAB) .... dea
Dead Fetus Syndrome (MELL) .... DFS
Dead on Arrival Despite Resuscitation Attempt (MELL) .... DOA-DRA
Dead-Arm Syndrome [*Medicine*] (MELL) .... DAS
Deafness and Goiter (MELL) .... D & G
Deafness, Diabetes, Photomyoclonus and Nephropathy [*Medicine*]
    (MELL) .... DDPN
Deafness, Hyperprolinuria, and Ichthyosis [*Medicine*] (MELL) .... DHI
Deafness Sensorineural, Recessive Profound [*Medicine*] (MELL) .... DS-RP
Death after Resuscitation (MELL) .... DAR
Death and Dignity (MELL) .... D & D
Death Place (GEAB) .... dpl
Debrancher Enzyme Deficiency [*Medicine*] (MELL) .... DED
Debt Coverage Ratio [*Business term*] .... DCR
Decamethonium (MELL) .... D
Decatur, GA [*AM radio station call letters*] (BROA) .... WPBC
Decatur, IL [*Television station call letters*] (BROA) .... WPXU
Decatur Staleys [*National Football League*] [*1920*] (NFLA) .... Dec
Decision (GEAB) .... decis
Decision-Oriented Resource Information System [*Ventura County, CA*]
    (GEOI) .... DORIS
Declination (GEOI) .... dec
Decompression Sickness (MELL) .... DS
Decrease (MELL) .... d
Decreased Sensory Perception (MELL) .... DSP
DECS Trust 8.50% 2000 [*NYSE symbol*] (SG) .... DET
DECS Trust II 6.875% 2000 [*NYSE symbol*] (SG) .... RYD
Dededo, GU [*FM radio station call letters*] (BROA) .... KGUM-FM
Dedham Pottery Collectors Society (EA) .... DPCS
Deep Infrapatellar Bursa [*Medicine*] (MELL) .... DIPB
Deep Inguinal Ring [*Medicine*] (MELL) .... DIR
Deep Sedative (MELL) .... DS
Deep Sky Exploration .... DSE
Deep Sleep (MELL) .... DS
Deer Lodge, MT [*FM radio station call letters*] (BROA) .... KQRV-FM
Deer River, MN [*FM radio station call letters*] (BROA) .... KBAJ-FM
Defective Glucose Counterregulation [*Medicine*] (MELL) .... DGCR
Defence Engineering and Science Group .... DESG
Defense (MILB) .... def
Defense Automated Addressing System Center (GEOI) .... DAASC
Defense Automated Message Exchange Service (GEOI) .... DAMES
Defense Data Network Security Coordination Center .... DDN SCC
Defense Dissemination Program Office (GEOI) .... DDPO
Defense Hydrographic Initiative (GEOI) .... DHI
Defense Mapping Agency Feature File (GEOI) .... DMAFF
Defense Mapping Agency Inter-American Geodetic Survey (GEOI) .... DMAIAGS
Defense Mapping Agency Special Program Office for Exploitation
    Modernization (GEOI) .... DMASPOEM
Defense Mapping School Operations Office (GEOI) .... DMSO
Defense Mapping Unit [*Singapore*] (GEOI) .... DMU
Defense Mobilization Ship (MILB) .... DMS
Defense Systems Affordability Council .... DSAC
Defensive Medicine (MELL) .... DM
Deferent Duct [*Medicine*] (MELL) .... DD
Deferent Duct Tumor [*Medicine*] (MELL) .... DDT
Deferoxamine Infusion Test [*Medicine*] (MELL) .... DIT
Defined Dollar Benefit .... DDB
Definite Brain Damage (MELL) .... DBD
Definition (MILB) .... defn
Definitive Host (MELL) .... DH
Degenerated Disk [*Medicine*] (MELL) .... DD
Degenerative Facet Disease [*Medicine*] (MELL) .... DFD

Degree (GEAB) ... degr
Del Castillo Syndrome [*Medicine*] (MELL) ... DCS
Del Monte Foods [*NYSE symbol*] (SG) ... DLM
Delaware Assocation of Surveyors (GEOI) ... DAS
Delaware Geological Survey (GEOI) ... DGS
Delaware, OH [*FM radio station call letters*] (BROA) ... WXST-FM
Delaware State Testing Program ... DSTP
Delayed after Depolarization [*Medicine*] (MELL) ... DAP
Delayed Hypersensitivity [*Medicine*] (MELL) ... DHS
Delayed Sleep Phase (MELL) ... DSP
Delayed Sleep-Phase Disorder (MELL) ... DSPD
Delayed Traumatic Intracerebral Hematoma [*Medicine*] (MELL) ... DTICH
Delayed-Action Preparation [*Medicine*] (MELL) ... DAP
Delayed-Onset Muscle Soreness ... DOMS
Delco Remy Intl.'A' [*NYSE symbol*] (SG) ... RMY
Delegate (PROS) ... del
Delerium/Confusional State [*Medicine*] (MELL) ... DCS
dELiAs, Inc. [*NASDAQ symbol*] (SG) ... DLIA
Deliberate Self-Harm Syndrome [*Medicine*] (MELL) ... DSHS
Delineation (GEOI) ... del
Delineator (GEOI) ... delt
Delirium, Infection, Atrophic Urethritis, Pharmaceuticals, Psychologic Depressi on, Excessive Urination, Restricted Mobility, and Stool Impaction [*Causes of transient urinary incontinence*] [*Medicine*] (MELL) ... DIAPPERS
Delivery Date [*Medicine*] (MELL) ... DD
Dell Rapids, SD [*FM radio station call letters*] (BROA) ... KSOB-FM
Delphi Automotive Systems [*NYSE symbol*] (SG) ... DPH
Delphi Fin'l Group 'A' [*NYSE symbol*] (SG) ... DFG
Delphian Node [*Medicine*] (MELL) ... DN
Delphos, OH [*FM radio station call letters*] (BROA) ... WBIE-FM
Delta Air Lines 8.125% Nts [*NYSE symbol*] (SG) ... DNT
Delta, CO [*FM radio station call letters*] (BROA) ... KPRU-FM
Delta Epsilon Sigma (EA) ... DES
Delta Financial [*NYSE symbol*] (SG) ... DFC
Deltaville, VA [*FM radio station call letters*] (BROA) ... WSRV-FM
Deltic Timber [*NYSE symbol*] (SG) ... DEL
Delusional Disorder [*Medicine*] (MELL) ... DD
Demand Pacemaker (MELL) ... DP
Dementia Associated with Alcoholism (MELL) ... DAA
Dementia Associated with Alcoholism [*Medicine*] (MELL) ... DDA
Democratic Republic of Afghanistan ... DRA
Democratic Republic of Congo (MILB) ... DROC
Demonstrably Effective Program Aid ... DEPA
Demonstrated Reserve Base ... DRB
Den Danske Dyrlaegeforening [*Danish Veterinary Association*] (GVA) ... DDD
Denbury Resources [*NYSE symbol*] (SG) ... DNR
Denervated Muscle Atrophy [*Medicine*] (MELL) ... DMA
Dengue Fever [*Medicine*] (MELL) ... DF
Denison-Sherman, TX [*AM radio station call letters*] (BROA) ... KKLF
Denison-Sherman, TX [*AM radio station call letters*] (BROA) ... KTBK
Denmark (MILB) ... Da
Dennis Miller Fan Club (EA) ... DMFC
Dennysville, ME [*FM radio station call letters*] (BROA) ... WCRQ-FM
Dental Caries (MELL) ... DC
Dental Decay (MELL) ... DD
Dental Plaque (MELL) ... DP
Dentino-Osseous Dysplasia [*Medicine*] (MELL) ... DOD
Denver Broncos [*National Football League*] [*1960-present*] (NFLA) ... Den
Denver, CO [*AM radio station call letters*] (BROA) ... KBJD
Denver, CO [*Television station call letters*] (BROA) ... KPXC-TV
Deoxyadenosine (MELL) ... DA
Deoxy-D-Glucose (MELL) ... DDG
Deoxyribose (MELL) ... DR
Deoxyribose Nucleic Acid ... DNA
Departamento Administrativo Nacional de Estadstica [*Colombia*] (GEOI) ... DANE
Department (GEOI) ... Dpt
Department of Civil Aviation ... DCA
Department of Community Affairs [*Montana*] (GEOI) ... DCA
Department of Energy Laboratory Accreditation Program ... DOELAP
Department of Environment, Transport, and the Regions ... DETR
Department of Environmental Protection (GEOI) ... DEP
Department of Fish and Game (GEOI) ... DFG
Department of Fish and Wildlife (GEOI) ... DFW
Department of Game and Fish (GEOI) ... DGF
Department of Geological Survey and Exploration [*Burma*] (GEOI) ... DGSF
Department of Indian Affairs (GEOI) ... DIA
Department of International Affairs (GEOI) ... DIA
Department of Land and Natural Resources (GEOI) ... DLNR
Department of Land and Water Conservation (GEOI) ... DLCW
Department of Land and Water Conservation [*Australia*] (GEOI) ... DLWC
Department of Lands and Survey [*Guyana*] (GEOI) ... DLS
Department of Mineral Resources of Thailand (GEOI) ... DMRT
Department of Mines and Energy [*Nova Scotia*] (GEOI) ... DME
Department of Natural Resource Protection ... DNRP
Department of Natural Resources and Conservation [*Montana*] (GEOI) ... DNRC
Department of Natural Resources and Environmental Protection [*Kentucky*] (GEOI) ... DNREP
Department of Planning and Economic Development (GEOI) ... DPED
Department of Primary Industries and Energy [*Australia*] (GEOI) ... DPIE
Department of Public Safety [*Arizona*] ... DPS
Department of State Telegram ... Deptel
Department of Survey and Land Information [*New Zealand*] (GEOI) ... DOSLI
Department of the Environment, Transport, and the Regions ... DETR
Dependence and Tolerance (MELL) ... D & T
Dependent Edema [*Medicine*] (MELL) ... DE
Depomed, Inc. [*AMEX symbol*] (SG) ... DMI
Depository Distribution Information System (GEOI) ... DDIS
Depot (GEAB) ... dep
Depreciation ... depr
Depressed, Cognitively Normal [*Medicine*] (MELL) ... DCN
Depressed Fracture [*Medicine*] (MELL) ... DF
Depressive Personality and Allied Disorders (MELL) ... DP & AD
Depth Below Datum (QUAC) ... dbd
Depth Below Surface (QUAC) ... dbs
Deputy Assistant Chief Hydrologist (GEOI) ... DACH
Deputy Clerk (GEAB) ... DC
Deputy Director for Acquisition Career Management [*Army*] ... DDACM
Deputy Foreign Minister ... DepFonMin
Deputy Ministry for Mineral Resources [*Saudi Arabia*] (GEOI) ... DMMR
Dermal Regeneration Template [*Medicine*] (MELL) ... DRT
Dermatofibroma [*Medicine*] (MELL) ... DF
Dermoid Cyst [*Medicine*] (MELL) ... DC
Des Arc, AR [*FM radio station call letters*] (BROA) ... KBDO-FM
Des Moines, IA [*AM radio station call letters*] (BROA) ... KBGG
Des Moines, IA [*FM radio station call letters*] (BROA) ... KLNQ-FM
Descemet's Membrane [*Medicine*] (MELL) ... DM
Descendant (GEAB) ... desc
Descendant (GEAB) ... dsct
Descendants of Colonial Governors (GEAB) ... DCG
Descending Perineum Syndrome [*Medicine*] (MELL) ... DPS
Descriptor Differential Scale [*Medicine*] (MELL) ... DDS
Desert Inn ... DI
Design Concept Review (GEOI) ... DCR
Design Data, Inc. (GEOI) ... DDI
Design Institute of America ... DIA
Designer Drug [*Medicine*] (MELL) ... DD
Desktop Digital Photogrammetry System (GEOI) ... DDPS
Desktop Mapping Technologies, Inc. (GEOI) ... DMTI
Desmoid Tumor [*Medicine*] (MELL) ... DT
Desmoplastic Small Round-Cell Tumor [*Medicine*] (MELL) ... DSRCT
Desquamation and Regeneration [*Medicine*] (MELL) ... D & R
Destructive Nerve Block [*Medicine*] (MELL) ... DNB
Detached Retina (MELL) ... DR
Detachment (MILB) ... det
Detainees Parents' Support Committee ... DPSC
Detector Test System ... DTS
Detergent Worker's Lung [*Medicine*] (MELL) ... DWL
Determination d'Orbite et Radiopositionement Integre par Satellite (EOSA) ... DORIS
Determination of Need (MELL) ... DON
Determined Osteogenic Precursor Cell [*Medicine*] (MELL) ... DOPC
Detroit Edison 7.54% 'QUIDS' [*NYSE symbol*] (SG) ... DTB
Detroit Edison 7.375% 'QUIDS' [*NYSE symbol*] (SG) ... DTH
Detroit Lions [*National Football League*] [*1934-present*] (NFLA) ... Det
Detroit, MI [*Television station call letters*] (BROA) ... WDIV-DT
Detroit, MI [*FM radio station call letters*] (BROA) ... WDTJ-FM
Detroit, MI [*Television station call letters*] (BROA) ... WJBK-DT
Detroit, MI [*fm radio station call letters*] (BROA) ... WKRK-FM
Detroit, MI [*FM radio station call letters*] (BROA) ... WPLT-FM
Detroit, MI [*FM radio station call letters*] (BROA) ... WVMV-FM
Detroit, MI [*Television station call letters*] (BROA) ... WWJ-DT
Detroit, MI [*Television station call letters*] (BROA) ... WXYZ-DT
Deutsche Agentur fur Raumfahrtangelegenheiten [*Germany*] (EOSA) ... DARA
Deutsche Telekom ADS [*NYSE symbol*] (SG) ... DT
Deutsche Veterinaermedizinische Gesellschaft [*German Veterinary Association*] (GVA) ... DVG
Deutsches Krebsforschungszentrum [*Germany*] ... dkfz
Deutsches Primatenzentrum GmbH Goettingen [*German Primate Center*] (GVA) ... DPZ
Deutsches Zentrum Fuer Luft- und Raumfahrt ... DLR
Development and Discretionary Grants Bureau ... DDG
Development Dysplasia of Hip [*Medicine*] (MELL) ... DDH
Developmental Dyslexia [*Medicine*] (MELL) ... DD
Device Upgrade ... DU
Devils Fan Club (EA) ... DFC
Devised (GEAB) ... devis
Dewey Decimal (GEOI) ... DD
Deworming (MELL) ... DW
Dextroamphetamine Phosphate [*Medicine*] (MELL) ... DAP
Dextrose in Normal Solution [*Medicine*] (MELL) ... DNS
Diabetes Nutritional Assessment (MELL) ... DNA
Diabetic Acidosis [*Medicine*] (MELL) ... DA
Diabetic Encephalopathy [*Medicine*] (MELL) ... DEP
Diabetic Foot Ulcer [*Medicine*] (MELL) ... DFU
Diabetic Hyperosmolar State [*Medicine*] (MELL) ... DHS
Diabetic Ketoacidosis [*Medicine*] (MELL) ... DK
Diabetic Nephropathy [*Medicine*] (MELL) ... DN
Diabetic Proximal Neuropathy [*Medicine*] (MELL) ... DPN
Diagnostic and Statistical Manual, 4th Edition [*A publication*] ... DSMIV
Diagnostic Error [*Medicine*] (MELL) ... DE
Diagnostic Interview for Personality Disorders (MELL) ... DIPD
Diagnostic Peritoneal Lavage [*Medicine*] (MELL) ... DPL
Diagnostic Radiographic Quality (MELL) ... DRQ
Dial Divisions per Minute ... ddpm
Dialectical Behavior Therapy [*Medicine*] (MELL) ... DBT
Dialog Corp. ADS [*NASDAQ symbol*] (SG) ... DIAL
Dialysis Osteomalacia Syndrome [*Medicine*] (MELL) ... DOS
Diamond-Blackfan Syndrome [*Medicine*] (MELL) ... DBS
DIAMONDS Trust, Series 1 [*AMEX symbol*] (SG) ... DIA

Diamond-Shaped Murmur [*Medicine*] (MELL) .... DSM
Diaper Rash (MELL) .... DR
Diarthrodial Joint (MELL) .... DAI
Diastolic (MELL) .... D
Diastolic Arterial Pressure [*Medicine*] (MELL) .... DAP
Diastolic Heart Failure [*Medicine*] (MELL) .... DHF
Diastolic Left Ventricular Dysfunction [*Medicine*] (MELL) .... DLVD
Diba Consulting Software Engineers (MELL) .... DCSF
Dictionary of American Biography [*A publication*] (GEAB) .... DAB
Dideoxy Finger-Printing (MELL) .... DDF
Died in Emergency Department (MELL) .... DIED
Died in Emergency Room (MELL) .... DIER
Died in Hospital (MELL) .... DIH
Died Young (GEAB) .... dy
Diesel Exhaust Particulates [*Medicine*] (MELL) .... DEP
Diet Therapy (MELL) .... DT
Dietary Chaos (MELL) .... DC
Dietary Risk Evaluation System [*Environmental Protection Agency*] (EPAT) .... DRES
Differential Corrections, Inc. (GEOI) .... DCI
Differential Global Positioning Satellite (GEOI) .... DGPS
Differential White Cell Count [*Medicine*] (MELL) .... DWCC
Differentiated Adenomatous Carcinoma [*Medicine*] (MELL) .... DAC
Difficulty Falling Asleep (MELL) .... DFA
Diffuse Alveolar Consolidation [*Medicine*] (MELL) .... DAC
Diffuse Alveolar Hemorrhage [*Medicine*] (MELL) .... DAH
Diffuse Brain Damage (MELL) .... DBD
Diffuse Cutaneous Scleroderma [*Medicine*] (MELL) .... DCS
Diffuse Interstitial Fibrosing Pneumonitis [*Medicine*] (MELL) .... DIFP
Diffuse Interstitial Lung Disease [*Medicine*] (MELL) .... DILD
Diffuse Interstitial Pulmonary Fibrosis [*Medicine*] (MELL) .... DIPF
Diffuse Myalgia [*Medicine*] (MELL) .... DM
Diffuse Non-Hodgkin's Lymphoma [*Medicine*] (MELL) .... DNHL
Diffuse Nontoxic Goiter [*Medicine*] (MELL) .... DNG
Diffuse Scleroderma [*Medicine*] (MELL) .... DS
Diffuse Sound Field (MELL) .... DSF
Diffuse Spasm of Esophagus [*Medicine*] (MELL) .... DSE
Diffuse Systemic Sclerosis .... dSSc
Diffuse Toxic Goiter [*Medicine*] (MELL) .... DTG
Diffusing Capacity of Carbon Monoxide (MELL) .... DCCO
Diffusing Capacity of Lung for Carbon Monoxide (MELL) .... DCLCO
DiGeorge Syndrome (MELL) .... DiG
Digestive Disorder (MELL) .... DD
Digex Inc.'A' [*NASDAQ symbol*] (SG) .... DIGX
Digi International [*NASDAQ symbol*] (SG) .... DGII
Digital Airborne Topographic Imaging System (GEOI) .... DATIS
Digital Assisted Data Base System (GEOI) .... DADS
Digital Bathymetry Data Base (GEOI) .... DBDB
Digital Cartographic Data Standards Task Force (GEOI) .... DCDSTF
Digital Cartographic File (GEOI) .... DCF
Digital Cartographic Production (GEOI) .... DCP
Digital Cartographic Production Segment (GEOI) .... DCPS
Digital Cartographic Software System (GEOI) .... DCASS
Digital Cartography Section (GEOI) .... DCS
Digital Catalog (GEOI) .... DIGCAT
Digital Chart Update Manual (GEOI) .... DCHUM
Digital Clubbing (MELL) .... DC
Digital Data Editing System (GEOI) .... DDES
Digital Editing Station (GEOI) .... DES
Digital Elevation Matrix (GEOI) .... DEM
Digital Elevation Model Verify (GEOI) .... DEMVFY
Digital Elevation Model-Graphic (GEOI) .... DEM-G
Digital Elevation Model-Planar (GEOI) .... DEM-P
Digital Flight Information Publication (GEOI) .... DFIIP
Digital Geospatial Data Files (GEOI) .... DGDF
Digital Graphic Product (GEOI) .... DGP
Digital Image (GEOI) .... DI
Digital Image Data (GEOI) .... DID
Digital Image Enhancement System (GEOI) .... DIES
Digital Image Matching (GEOI) .... DIM
Digital Intravenous Subtraction Angiography [*Medicine*] (MELL) .... DISA
Digital Island [*NASDAQ symbol*] (SG) .... ISLD
Digital Lava [*AMEX symbol*] (SG) .... DGV
Digital Lightwave [*NASDAQ symbol*] (SG) .... DIGL
Digital Line Graph to Digital Elevation Model (GEOI) DLG2DEM
Digital Line Graph-Enhanced (GEOI) .... DLG-E
Digital Line Graph-Framework (GEOI) .... DLGF
Digital Line Graph-Optional (GEOI) .... DLG-O
Digital Model Assembly (GEOI) .... DMA
Digital Nautical Chart (GEOI) .... DNC
Digital Number (GEOI) .... DN
Digital Ortho (GEOI) .... DO
Digital Orthophoto Quadrangle (GEOI) .... DOQ
Digital Orthophoto Quarter Quadrangle (GEOI) .... DOQQ
Digital Orthophoto System (GEOI) .... DOS
Digital Photogrammetry (GEOI) .... DP
Digital Point Positioning Data Base (GEOI) .... DPPDB
Digital Power [*AMEX symbol*] (SG) .... DPW
Digital Production System (GEOI) .... DPS
Digital Property Rights Language .... DPRL
Digital Rights Management .... DRM
Digital Subtraction Phlebography (MELL) .... DSP
Digitalis Intoxication [*Medicine*] (MELL) .... DI
Digitalis-Like Substance [*Medicine*] (MELL) .... DLS
Dignified Dying (MELL) .... DD

Dilatation Catheter [*Medicine*] (MELL) .... DC
Dilated (MELL) .... D
Dilator Naris Muscle [*Medicine*] (MELL) .... DNM
Dillard's Cap Tr 7.50% Cap Sec [*NYSE symbol*] (SG) .... DDT
Dillard's Inc.'A' [*NYSE symbol*] (SG) .... DDS
Dillon, MT [*FM radio station call letters*] (BROA) .... KBEV-FM
Dillwyn, VA [*FM radio station call letters*] (BROA) .... WBNN-FM
Dilution (MELL) .... D
Dimercaprol [*Medicine*] (MELL) .... DMP
Dinas Hidro Oceanografi [*Indonesia*] (GEOI) .... DISHIDROS
Dinuba, CA [*FM radio station call letters*] (BROA) .... KSOF-FM
Diocesan Registry (GEAB) .... DR
Diocese (GEAB) .... dio
Diphencyprone [*Medicine*] .... DCP
Diptheria and Tetanus Toxoids Combined with Acellular Pertussis Vaccine [*Medicine*] (MELL) .... DTaP
Direccion de Geologia, Minas y Petrolio [*Costa Rica*] (GEOI) .... DGMP
Direccion General de Estadistica y Censos [*Costa Rica*] (GEOI) .... DGEC
Direccion General de Geologia y Minas [*Colombia*] (GEOI) .... DGGM
Direccion General de Integracion y Analisis de la Informacion [*Mexico*] (GEOI) .... DGIAI
Direccion General de la Produccion Agraria [*Spain*] (GEOI) .... DGPA
Direccion General de Minas y Geologia [*Venezuela*] (GEOI) .... DGMG
Direccion General de Oceanografia [*Mexico*] (GEOI) .... DGO
Direccion General de Recursos Minerales [*Panama*] (GEOI) .... DGRM
Direccion Nacional de Mineria y Geologia [*Uruguay*] (GEOI) .... DMMG
Direccion Nacional de Topografia [*Uruguay*] (GEOI) .... DNT
Direct Aerosol Radiative Forcing (QUAC) .... DARF
Direct and Consensual (MELL) .... D & C
Direct Ascent Nonnuclear Antisatellite .... DANNASAT
Direct Ascent Nuclear Antisatellite .... DANASAT
Direct Bronchoscopy [*Medicine*] (MELL) .... DB
Direct Coombs [*Test*] [*Medicine*] (MELL) .... DC
Direct Current Electrical Stimulation (MELL) .... DCES
Direct Diagnosis [*Medicine*] (MELL) .... DD
Direct Geodetic Constraint (GEOI) .... DGC
Direct Geodetic Constraint Method (GEOI) .... DGCM
Direct Illumination Component (MELL) .... DIC
Direct Intra-Peritoneal Insemination [*Medicine*] .... DIPI
Direct Mechanical Ventricular Actuator [*Medicine*] (MELL) .... DMVA
Direct Platelet Count [*Medicine*] (MELL) .... DPC
Direct Sounding Broadcast (EOSA) .... DSB
Direct State Services .... DSS
Direct Visualization of Vocal Cords (MELL) .... DVC
Direct-Acting Carcinogen [*Medicine*] (MELL) .... DAC
Direction Changing Positional Nystagmus [*Medicine*] (MELL) .... DCPN
Direction de l'Amernagement du Territoire et de la Protection de l'Environnement [*Haiti*] (GEOI) .... DATPE
Direction National de Production Cartographique et Topographique [*Mali*] (GEOI) .... DNPCT
Direction Topographique et du Cadastre [*Congo*] (GEOI) .... DCT
Directional Neighbourhoods Approach .... DNA
Directives .... DR
Directorate of Presidential Affairs .... DPA
Directory Information Services Infrastructure .... DISI
Directory of Nursing Homes [*A publication*] (MELL) .... DNH
Directory of Physicians in the United States [*A publication*] (MELL) .... DPUS
Direktorat Geologi [*Indonesia*] (GEOI) .... DGI
Disability (MELL) .... dis
Disability Rating Scale (MELL) .... DRS
Disabled Collectors' Correspondence Club (EA) .... DCCC
Disarticulation of Hip (MELL) .... DAH
Disarticulation of Knee (MELL) .... DAK
Disaster Medical Assistance Team (MELL) .... DMAT
Discharge (GEAB) .... dis
Discharge and Advise [*Medicine*] (MELL) .... D & A
Discharge Diagnosis [*Medicine*] (MELL) .... DD
Discharge Summary [*Medicine*] (MELL) .... DS
Discharged against Medical Advice (MELL) .... DAMA
Discipline (GEAB) .... discip
Disease (MELL) .... dis
Disease-Disability Scale [*Medicine*] (MELL) .... DDS
Disk Unseen Object .... DUO
Dislocated Civilian .... DC
Dislocation of Patella [*Medicine*] (MELL) .... DLP
Disorders of Sleep-Wake Schedule (MELL) .... DSWS
Disorganized Schizophrenia [*Medicine*] (MELL) .... DS
Displaced Child Syndrome [*Medicine*] (MELL) .... DCS
Disposable Surgical Mask (MELL) .... DSM
Disruptive Behavior Disorder (MELL) .... DBD
Dissecting Aneurysm [*Medicine*] (MELL) .... DA
Disseminated Discoid Lupus Erythematosus [*Medicine*] (MELL) .... DDLE
Disseminated Kaposi Sarcoma [*Medicine*] (MELL) .... DKS
Dissociative Hysteria [*Medicine*] (MELL) .... DH
Distal Metastases [*Medicine*] (MELL) .... DM
Distal Muscular Dystrophy [*Medicine*] (MELL) .... DMD
Distal Phalanx [*Medicine*] (MELL) .... DP
Distal Renal Tubular Acidosis [*Medicine*] (MELL) .... DRT
Distal Third [*Medicine*] (MELL) D/3
Distal Tingling on Pressure [*Medicine*] (MELL) .... DTP
Distal Transverse Crease (MELL) .... DTC
Distant (WEAT) .... DSNT
Distended Abdomen (MELL) .... DA
Distolic Murmur [*Medicine*] (MELL) .... DM
Distribucion y Servico ADS [*NYSE symbol*] (SG) .... DYS

Distributed Ocean Data System .... DODS
Distributed Satellite Telemetry Data Handling System (GEOI) .... DISTDAHS
Distribution Management System (GEOI) .... DMS
Distributive Data Environment .... DDE
Distributor (PROS) .... Distr
District Chief (GEOI) .... DC
District of Columbia (GEOI) .... DC
District of Columbia Veterinary Medical Association (GVA) .... DCVMA
District Report of Transported Resident Students .... DRTRS
Ditigal Geographic Information Working Group (GEOI) .... DGIWG
Diuretic Therapy [Medicine] (MELL) .... DT
Diurnal Insulin Resistance [Medicine] (MELL) .... DIR
Diversified Corp. Resources [AMEX symbol] (SG) .... HIR
Diversified Energy Services, Inc. (GEOI) .... DESI
Diversinet Corp. [NASDAQ symbol] (SG) .... DVNT
Division of Grants and Contracts Management (MELL) .... DGCM
Divisional Veterinary Manager (GVA) .... DVM
Divorced (GEAB) .... div
Dizygotic (MELL) .... DZT
Djibouti (MILB) .... Dj
Doctor at Bedside (MELL) .... DBS
Doctor-Assisted Suicide (MELL) .... DAS
Document Object Identifier (GEOI) .... DOI
Documents Data Miner (GEOI) .... DDM
Dog Tick (MELL) .... DT
Doghouse Disease (MELL) .... DHD
Doing Well (MELL) .... DW
Dole Food $2.7475'TRACES' [AMEX symbol] (SG) .... DLA
Dollar Gen'l 8.50%'STRYPES' [NYSE symbol] (SG) .... DGS
Dollar Thrifty Auto Grp [NYSE symbol] (SG) .... DTG
Dollar Tree Stores [NASDAQ symbol] (SG) .... DLTR
Dollywood Foundation (EA) .... DWF
Domestic Abuse and Violence (MELL) .... DAV
Domestic Data Service .... DDS
Domestic Geographic Name (GEOI) .... DGN
Domestic Geographic Names Report (GEOI) .... DGNR
Dominant Juvenile Optic Atrophy [Medicine] (MELL) .... DJOA
Dominant Trait (MELL) .... DT
Dominican Republic (MILB) .... DR
Donald, Luf & Jen-DLJdirect [NYSE symbol] (SG) .... DIR
DONCASTERS plc ADS [NYSE symbol] (SG) .... DCS
Donna Karan Intl. [NYSE symbol] (SG) .... DK
Donnacona, PQ [FM radio station call letters] (BROA) .... CKNU-FM
Donnelly Corp.Cl'A' [NYSE symbol] (SG) .... DON
Donny Osmond International Network (EA) .... DOIN
Donor (PROS) .... don
Donor Eggs [Medicine] .... DE
Donor-Recipient Matching [Medicine] (MELL) .... DRM
Door .... Dr
Dopamine [Medicine] (MELL) .... DPM
Dopamine Agonist [Medicine] (MELL) .... DA
Doppler Effect (MELL) .... DE
Doppler Lidar (EOSA) .... DOPLID
Doppler Method of Diagnosis [Medicine] (MELL) .... DMD
Doppler on Wheels .... DOW
Doppler Perfusion Index [Medicine] (MELL) .... DPI
Doppler Wind Sensor (EOSA) .... DWS
Dora, AL [FM radio station call letters] (BROA) .... WZJT-FM
Dorel Industries'B' [NASDAQ symbol] (SG) .... DIIBF
Dorsal Artery of Penis [Medicine] (MELL) .... DAP
Dorsal Cell Column (MELL) .... DCC
Dorsal Lithotomy Position [Medicine] (MELL) .... DLP
Dorsal Nerve Root [Medicine] (MELL) .... DNR
Dorsal Nucleus of Lateral Lemniscus [Medicine] (MELL) .... DNLL
Dorsal Penis Vein [Medicine] (MELL) .... DPV
Dorsal Root Damage (MELL) .... DRD
Dorsal Uterine Artery [Medicine] (MELL) .... DUA
Double .... Dbl
Double Diffusion Test [Medicine] (MELL) .... DDT
Double Loop Whorl [Fingerprint] (MELL) .... DLW
Double Lumen Tube [Medicine] (MELL) .... DLT
Double Pneumonia (MELL) .... DP
Double Whammy Syndrome [Medicine] (MELL) .... DWS
Double Yellow Headed Amazon [Bird] .... DYH
Double-Blind Test [Medicine] (MELL) .... DBT
Double-Blind Trial [Medicine] (MELL) .... DBT
DoubleClick, Inc. [NASDAQ symbol] (SG) .... DCLK
Double-Contrast Study (MELL) .... DCS
Double-Current Catheter [Medicine] (MELL) .... DCC
Double-Lung Transplantation [Medicine] (MELL) .... DLT
Doublesex .... dsx
Douglas, AZ [Television station call letters] (BROA) .... KBGF
Dover Downs Entertainment [NYSE symbol] (SG) .... DVD
Dowager's Hump [Medicine] (MELL) .... DH
Downey Financial [NYSE symbol] (SG) .... DSL
Drainage (MELL) .... drg
Drainage (MELL) .... DRGE
Drakesboro, KY [FM radio station call letters] (BROA) .... WNTC-FM
Dream Anxiety Attack (MELL) .... DAA
Dressing Change [Medicine] (MELL) .... DC
Dressler's Syndrome [Medicine] (MELL) .... DS
Drifting (WEAT) .... DR
Drill Hole (GEOI) .... DH
Dril-Quip, Inc. [NYSE symbol] (SG) .... DRQ
Drip Infusion Cholangiography [Medicine] (MELL) .... DIC

Driving Under the Influence of Drugs (MELL) .... DUID
drkoop.com, Inc. [NASDAQ symbol] (SG) .... KOOP
Drop Foot Splint (MELL) .... DFS
Drug Abuse (MELL) .... DA
Drug Abuse Screening Test (MELL) .... DAST
Drug Combination [Medicine] (MELL) .... DC
Drug Dependence (MELL) .... DD
Drug Dependence Treatment Center (MELL) .... DDTC
Drug Dependence Treatment Program (MELL) .... DDTP
Drug Dose-Response Curve [Medicine] (MELL) .... DDRC
Drug Free (MELL) .... DF
Drug Intoxication (MELL) .... DI
Drug of Choice (MELL) .... DOC
Drug Overdose (MELL) .... DO
Drug Overdose (MELL) .... DOD
Drug Oxidation (MELL) .... DO
Drug Receptor (MELL) .... DR
Drug Residue (MELL) .... DR
Drug Resistance (MELL) .... DR
Drug Screening (MELL) .... DS
Drug Therapy (MELL) .... DT
Drug Toxicity (MELL) .... DT
Drug Use Forecast (MELL) .... DUF
Drug-Abuse Reporting (MELL) .... DAR
Drug-Free Workplace (MELL) .... DFW
Drug-Free Zone (MELL) .... DFZ
Drug-Induced (MELL) .... DI
Drug-Induced Aplastic Anemia [Medicine] (MELL) .... DIAA
Drug-Induced Constipation [Medicine] (MELL) .... DIC
Drug-Induced Headache [Medicine] (MELL) .... DIH
Drug-Induced Hepatic Encephalopathy [Medicine] (MELL) .... DIHE
Drug-Induced Movement Disorder [Medicine] (MELL) .... DIMD
Drug-Induced Thrombocytopenia [Medicine] (MELL) .... DIT
Drug-Related Admission (MELL) .... DRA
Drug-Related Dementia (MELL) .... DRD
Drug-Related Problem (MELL) .... DRP
drugstore.com, Inc. [NASDAQ symbol] (SG) .... DSCM
Dry Dock Shelter (MILB) .... DDS
Dry Heaves [Medicine] (MELL) .... DH
Dry Ice (MELL) .... DI
Dry Skin Eczema (MELL) .... DSE
Dry Socket [Medicine] (MELL) .... DS
Dry Sterile Dressing [Medicine] (MELL) .... DSR
Dry Sterile Gauze (MELL) .... DSG
DSP Communications [NYSE symbol] (SG) .... DSP
Dual Choice [Insurance] .... DC
Dual Diagnosis [Medicine] (MELL) .... DD
Dual Disorder [Medicine] (MELL) .... DD
Dual Energy Photon Absorptiometry (MELL) .... DEPA
Dual-Use .... DU
Dual-Use Applications Program .... DUAP
Duane Reade [NYSE symbol] (SG) .... DRD
Duane's Retraction Syndrome [Medicine] (MELL) .... DRS
Dubai Airport Free Zone .... DAFZ
Dublin, TX [FM radio station call letters] (BROA) .... KSTV-FM
Dublin, VA [AM radio station call letters] (BROA) .... WPIN
Ducati Motor Hldg ADS [NYSE symbol] (SG) .... DMH
Duck Embryo Rabies Vaccine (MELL) .... DERV
Duck Waddle Test (MELL) .... DWT
Duck-Billed Speculum [Medicine] (MELL) .... DBS
Ducommun, Inc. [NYSE symbol] (SG) .... DCO
Ductus Reuniens (MELL) .... DR
Duke Energy 6.60% Sr Notes'C' [NYSE symbol] (SG) .... DUT
Duke-Weeks Realty [NYSE symbol] (SG) .... DRE
Dumbbell Tumor [Medicine] (MELL) .... DBT
Duncan, OK [AM radio station call letters] (BROA) .... KKEN
Duncan, OK [FM radio station call letters] (BROA) .... KKEN-FM
Dunn Computer [NASDAQ symbol] (SG) .... DNCC
Duodenal Atresia [Medicine] (MELL) .... DA
Duodenal Flexure [Medicine] (MELL) .... DF
Duodenal Peptic Ulcer Disease [Medicine] (MELL) .... DPUD
Duodenal Ulcer Diet [Medicine] (MELL) .... DUD
Duplicate Coverage Inquiry [Insurance] .... DCI
DuPont Photomasks [NASDAQ symbol] (SG) .... DPMI
Duquesne Light 7.375% Bonds [NYSE symbol] (SG) .... DQZ
Dura Automotive Sys'A' [NASDAQ symbol] (SG) .... DRRA
Durango, CO [Television station call letters] (BROA) .... KBEI
Durango, CO [FM radio station call letters] (BROA) .... KPTE-FM
Durham, NC [Television station call letters] (BROA) .... WTVD-DT
Dust in Suspension in the Air (WEAT) .... DU
Dutch Association of Safety Experts .... DASE
Duty to Warn (MELL) .... DTW
DVI, Inc. [NYSE symbol] (SG) .... DVI
Dwelling (GEOI) .... D
Dwelling, Building, and Contents .... DB&C
Dying Patient (MELL) .... DP
Dynamex, Inc. [AMEX symbol] (SG) .... DDN
Dynamic Limb Sounder (EOSA) .... DLS
Dynamically Responding Ultrasonic Matix System [Commercial research
  facility] .... SpaceDrums
Dynex Capital [NYSE symbol] (SG) .... DX
Dysesthetic Pain Syndrome [Medicine] (MELL) .... DPS
Dysosteosclerosis [Medicine] (MELL) .... DOS
Dysphagia and Dysphonia [Medicine] (MELL) .... D & D
Dysplasia Epiphysalis Multiplex [Medicine] (MELL) .... DEM

Dysplastic Melanocytic Nevi [*Medicine*] .... DMN
Dystrophic Cardiac Calcinosis [*Medicine*] (MELL) .... DCC

E
By Meaning

E Trade Group [*NASDAQ symbol*] (SG) .... EGRP
E4L, Inc. [*NYSE symbol*] (SG) .... ETV
Early After-Depolarization [*Medicine*] (MELL) .... EAD
Early Amniocentesis [*Medicine*] (MELL) .... EA
Early Childhood Program Aid .... ECPA
Early China .... EC
Early Defibrillation/Advanced Care [*Medicine*] (MELL) .... EDAC
Early Diastolic Relaxation [*Medicine*] (MELL) .... EDR
Early Gastric Carcinoma [*Medicine*] (MELL) .... EGC
Early Glottic Carcinoma [*Medicine*] (MELL) .... EGC
Early Infantile Autism [*Medicine*] (MELL) .... EIA
Early Infantile Epileptic Encephalopathy [*Medicine*] (MELL) .... EIEE
Early Melanoma [*Medicine*] (MELL) .... EM
Early Morning Specimen of Urine (MELL) .... EMSU
Early Morning Stiffness (MELL) .... EMS
Early Morning Urine (MELL) .... EMU
Early Morning Urine Specimen (MELL) .... EMUS
Early Mortality Syndrome [*Reproductive disturbance in fish*] .... EMS
Early Neonatal Death (MELL) .... END
Early Neurobehavioral Score (MELL) .... ENBS
Early Ovarian Cancer (MELL) .... EOC
Early Retirement for Disability (MELL) .... ERD
Early Ventricular Repolarization Syndrome [*Medicine*] (MELL) .... EVRS
Early-Labeled Bilirubin [*Medicine*] (MELL) .... ELB
Early-Onset Breast Cancer (MELL) .... EOBC
Early-Onset Endocarditis [*Medicine*] (MELL) .... EOEC
Earned Value Management System .... EVMS
Earth Observations International Coordination Working Group (EOSA) .... EO-ICWG
Earth Observing Scanner Polarimeter .... EOSP
Earth Observing Scanning Polarimeter (EOSA) .... EOSP
Earth Resources Technology Satellite-1 (EOSA) ERTS-1
Earth Science and Applications Division [*NASA*] (EOSA) .... ESAD
Earth System History (QUAC) .... ESH
Earthlink Network [*NASDAQ symbol*] (SG) .... ELNK
EarthShell Corp. [*NASDAQ symbol*] (SG) .... ERTH
EarthWeb, Inc. [*NASDAQ symbol*] (SG) .... EWBX
Earwax (MELL) .... EW
East Lyme, CT [*FM radio station call letters*] (BROA) .... WNLC-FM
East Moline, IL [*FM radio station call letters*] (BROA) .... KUUL-FM
East Point, GA [*AM radio station call letters*] (BROA) .... WKGE
Eastern Equine Virus (MELL) .... EEV
Easyriders, Inc. [*AMEX symbol*] (SG) .... EZR
Eating Disorder (MELL) .... ED
Eaton Vance [*NYSE symbol*] (SG) .... EV
Ebauches Electronic Marin .... EEM
eBay, Inc. [*NASDAQ symbol*] (SG) .... EBAY
Ebola Virus [*Medicine*] (MELL) .... EV
Ebola Virus Disease [*Medicine*] (MELL) .... EVD
Echelon International [*NYSE symbol*] (SG) .... EIN
Echinococcus Antibody [*Medicine*] (MELL) .... ECA
Echo Virus Antibody [*Medicine*] (MELL) .... EVA
Echo-Encephalography [*Medicine*] (MELL) .... EEG
Echovirus [*Medicine*] (MELL) .... EV
Eco Soil Systems [*NASDAQ symbol*] (SG) .... ESSL
Ecological Monitoring and Assessment Network [*Canada*] (QUAC) .... EMAN
Ecology (BEE) .... ecol
Economic Community for Africa (EPAT) .... ECA
Economic Swiss Time Holding .... ESTH
Economics (BEE) .... econ
Economics Minister .... EconMin
Ecosystem Restoration [*Environmental Protection Agency*] (EPAT) .... ER
ECsoft Group ADR [*NASDAQ symbol*] (SG) .... ECSGY
Ectopia Cordis [*Medicine*] (MELL) .... EC
Ectopia Lentis [*Medicine*] (MELL) .... EL
Ectopic Abdominal Pregnancy (MELL) .... EAP
Ectopic Implantation [*Medicine*] (MELL) .... EI
Ectopic Pacemaker (MELL) .... EP
Ectopic-Hypercalcemia Syndrome [*Medicine*] (MELL) .... EHS
Ecuador (MILB) .... Ec
Edema, Erythema, and Exudate [*Medicine*] (MELL) .... EEE
Edema, Proteinuria, and Hypertension [*Medicine*] (MELL) .... EPH
Edematous Pancreatitis [*Medicine*] (MELL) .... EP
Eden, NC [*AM radio station call letters*] (BROA) .... WXII
Eden Prairie, MN [*FM radio station call letters*] (BROA) .... KZNZ-FM
Edetic Acid (MELL) .... EA
Edetic Acid Eugenics [*Medicine*] (MELL) .... EAE
Edge X-Ray Absorption Fine Structure .... EXAFS
Edible .... Ed
Edinburgh Veterinary Zoological Society (GVA) .... EVZS
Edmonton, AB [*Television station call letters*] (BROA) .... CKEM-TV
Edmonton, AB [*FM radio station call letters*] (BROA) .... CKER-FM
Edmonton, AB [*FM radio station call letters*] (BROA) .... CKUA-FM
Edna, TX [*FM radio station call letters*] (BROA) .... KGUL-FM
EDP-Electricidade Portugal ADS [*NYSE symbol*] (SG) .... EDP
EdperBrascan Corp.'A' [*AMEX symbol*] (SG) .... EBC
Edrophonium [*Medicine*] (MELL) .... EDR
Education (BEE) .... ed
Education (BEE) .... edu
Education Management [*NASDAQ symbol*] (SG) .... EDMC
Educational Media Association of New Jersey .... EMANJ
Educational Video Conferencing [*NASDAQ symbol*] (SG) .... EVCI
EduTrek Intl.'A' [*NASDAQ symbol*] (SG) .... EDUT
Edward Mulhare's Foundations (EA) .... EMFF
Edwards(AG), Inc. [*NYSE symbol*] (SG) .... AGE
eFax.com, Inc. [*AMEX symbol*] (SG) .... EFAX
EFC Bancorp [*AMEX symbol*] (SG) .... EFC
Effective Core Potential .... ECP
Effective Filtration Pressure [*Medicine*] (MELL) .... Peff
Efferent Glomerular Arteriole [*Medicine*] (MELL) .... EGA
Efferent Lymphatic Vessel [*Medicine*] (MELL) .... ELV
Efferent Nerve [*Medicine*] (MELL) .... EN
Efficient Networks [*NASDAQ symbol*] (SG) .... EFNT
Egg Marketing Inspectorate (GVA) .... EMI
Egghead.com, Inc. [*NASDAQ symbol*] (SG) .... EGGS
eGlobe, Inc. [*NASDAQ symbol*] (SG) .... EGLO
Egypt (MILB) .... Et
Egypt Suez [*Crude oil*] .... ES
Egyptian (BEE) .... Egypt
Eidos PLC ADR [*NASDAQ symbol*] (SG) .... EIDSY
Einstein/Noah Bagel [*NASDAQ symbol*] (SG) .... ENBX
Ejaculatory Dysfunction [*Medicine*] (MELL) .... ED
Ejection Time Index (MELL) .... ETI
Ekco Group [*AMEX symbol*] (SG) .... EKO
El Dorado, AR [*FM radio station call letters*] (BROA) .... KHBX-FM
El Dorado, AR [*Television station call letters*] (BROA) .... KKYK-TV
El Dorado, KS [*FM radio station call letters*] (BROA) .... KBTL-FM
El Paso, TX [*FM radio station call letters*] (BROA) .... KATH-FM
El Paso, TX [*AM radio station call letters*] (BROA) .... KBIV
El Paso, TX [*Television station call letters*] (BROA) .... KKWB
El Salvador (MILB) .... EIS
El Toro International Yacht Racing Association (EA) .... ETIYRA
Elastic Back Strap (MELL) .... EBS
Elastic Stockings (MELL) .... ES
Elastomyofibrosis [*Medicine*] (MELL) .... EMF
Elberton, GA [*FM radio station call letters*] (BROA) .... WEHR-FM
Elbow Dislocation (MELL) .... ED
Elder Abuse (MELL) .... EA
Elderly and Mentally Infirmed (MELL) .... EMI
ElderTrust SBI [*NYSE symbol*] (SG) .... ETT
Electra, TX [*FM radio station call letters*] (BROA) .... KOLI-FM
Electric Boat Association of the Americas (EA) .... EBAA
Electric Lightwave'A' [*NASDAQ symbol*] (SG) .... ELIX
Electric Resonance Optothermal Spectrometer .... EROS
Electric Shock Protector (MELL) .... ESP
Electric Shocklike Pain (MELL) .... ESLP
Electrical (BEE) .... elect
Electrical Overstress/Electrostatic Discharge Association, Inc. .... ESD
Electrical Status Epilepticus during Sleep [*Medicine*] (MELL) .... ESES
Electricity (BEE) .... electr
Electro-Acupuncture Analgesia [*Medicine*] (MELL) .... EAA
Electroarteriography [*Medicine*] (MELL) .... EAG
Electrocardiagraphic Monitoring [*Medicine*] (MELL) .... ECGM
Electrocardiography [*Medicine*] (MELL) .... ECG
Electrocardiography [*Medicine*] (MELL) .... EKG
Electrocautery [*Medicine*] (MELL) .... EC
Electrocautery Unit [*Medicine*] (MELL) .... ECU
Electrochemical Fabrication .... EFAB
Electrochemical Ind (1952) [*AMEX symbol*] (SG) .... EIL
Electrode Catheter [*Medicine*] (MELL) .... EC
Electrode Catheter Ablation [*Medicine*] (MELL) .... ECA
Electrogastrography [*Medicine*] (MELL) .... EGG

Electromyelogram [*Medicine*] (MELL) ... EMG
Electromyocardial Dissociation [*Medicine*] (MELL) ... EMD
Electron Beam Computed Tomography ... EBCT
Electron Beam Instrumentation (MELL) ... EBI
Electron Microscopy [*Medicine*] (MELL) ... EM
Electron Pulse Radiolysis System [*Medicine*] (MELL) ... EPRS
Electronic Box ... E-box
Electronic Commerce Modeling Language ... ECML
Electronic Data Exchange (EPAT) ... EDX
Electronic Data Interchange and Electronic Data Access ... EDI/EDA
Electronic Data Systems [*NYSE symbol*] (SG) ... EDS
Electronic Fetal Monitoring [*Medicine*] (MELL) ... EMF
Electronic Food and Beverage Exchange ... EFDEX
Electronic Information for Libraries Direct ... EIFL Direct
Electronic Publishing Initiative at Columbia ... EPIC
Electronic Trading Systems [*Finance*] ... ECNS
Electronics Boutique Hldgs [*NASDAQ symbol*] (SG) ... ELBO
Electro-Optic Phase Modulation (EOSA) ... EOPM
Electrophoretic Immunoblotting [*Medicine*] (MELL) ... EIB
Electrophoretic Type [*Medicine*] (MELL) ... ET
Electroresection [*Medicine*] (MELL) ... ER
Electroshock Wave Lithotripsy [*Medicine*] (MELL) ... ESWL
Electrosource, Inc. [*NASDAQ symbol*] (SG) ... ELSI
Electrosurgical Unit (MELL) ... ESU
Element (MILB) ... elm
Elementary School Proficiency Assessment ... ESPA
Elementary School Proficiency Test ... ESPA
Elephant Managers Association (GVA) ... EMA
Elevated Plasma Cholesterol (MELL) ... EPC
Elevated Prostate-Specific Antigen [*Medicine*] (MELL) ... EPSA
Elevated Prostate-Specific Antigen Level [*Medicine*] (MELL) ... EPSAL
Elizabeth, NJ [*AM radio station call letters*] (BROA) ... WBAH
Elkins, WV [*FM radio station call letters*] (BROA) ... WBHZ-FM
Elkton, VA [*FM radio station call letters*] (BROA) ... WACL-FM
Ellensburg, WA [*FM radio station call letters*] (BROA) ... KCSH-FM
Ellensburg, WA [*FM radio station call letters*] (BROA) ... KCWU-FM
Elliot Lake, ON [*FM radio station call letters*] (BROA) ... CKNR-FM
Elliott-Larsen Civil Rights Act [*Michigan*] ... ELCRA
Ellis, Perry, Intl. [*NASDAQ symbol*] (SG) ... PERY
E-Loan, Inc. [*NASDAQ symbol*] (SG) ... EELN
Elvis Presley Memorial Society (EA) ... EMS
Elvisnet Elvis Presley Fan Club (EA) ... ElvisNet EPFC
Ely, NV [*Television station call letters*] (BROA) ... KBJN
Ely, NV [*FM radio station call letters*] (BROA) ... KCLS-FM
Ely, NV [*FM radio station call letters*] (BROA) ... KHIX-FM
Embasy ... Emb
Embasy Office ... EmbOff
Embedded (WEAT) ... EMBD
Embratel Participacoes ADS [*NYSE symbol*] (SG) ... EMT
Embryo (MELL) ... emb
Embryo Toxic Factor [*Medicine*] ... ETF
Embryo Toxicity Assay [*Medicine*] ... ETA
Embryo-Fetal Alcohol Syndrome (MELL) ... EFAS
Embryonic Antibody [*Medicine*] (MELL) ... EA
Embryonic Stem [*Medicine*] (MELL) ... ES
Embryonic System [*Medicine*] ... ES
Emergency Bypass Surgery (MELL) ... EBS
Emergency Department Physician (MELL) ... EDP
Emergency Laparotomy [*Medicine*] (MELL) ... EL
Emergency Laparotomy Drain [*Medicine*] (MELL) ... ELD
Emergency Medical Identification (MELL) ... EMI
Emergency Medical Indentification Symbol (MELL) ... EMIS
Emergency Medical Team (MELL) ... EMT
Emergency Physician (MELL) ... EP
Emergency Planning District [*Environmental science*] (EPAT) ... EPD
Emergency Response System (MELL) ... ERS
Emergency Room Triage (MELL) ... ERT
Emergency Treatment Record (MELL) ... ETR
Emirates (BEE) ... em
Emissary Vein [*Medicine*] (MELL) ... EV
Emissions Tracking System [*Environmental Protection Agency*] (EPAT) ... ETS
Emitter Current Programmer (MELL) ... ECP
Emotional Intelligence (MELL) ... EI
Emotional Stress (MELL) ... ES
Emotionally Unstable (MELL) ... EU
Employee Assistance Program Association ... EAPA
Employee Health Service (MELL) ... EHS
Employee Stock Ownership Association ... ESOA
Employment (PROS) ... empl
Employment Practices Liability Insurance ... EPLI
Emporia, VA [*FM radio station call letters*] (BROA) ... WSVP-FM
Empresa Nac'l De El Chile, ADS [*NYSE symbol*] (SG) ... EOC
EMS Technologies [*NASDAQ symbol*] (SG) ... ELMG
Encal Energy [*NYSE symbol*] (SG) ... ECA
Encapsulated Lymph Node [*Medicine*] (MELL) ... ELN
Enchondromatosis [*Medicine*] (MELL) ... ECM
End Child Prostitution and Trafficking [*An association*] ... ECPAT
End of Lecture [*Online dialog*] ... EOL
End of Pipe (EPAT) ... EOP
End Positive-Pressure Breathing (MELL) ... EPPB
End-Diastolic Load [*Medicine*] (MELL) ... EDL
End-Diastolic Thickness [*Medicine*] (MELL) ... EDT
End-Expiratory Lung Volume [*Medicine*] (MELL) ... EELV
Endocardial Hemorrhage [*Medicine*] (MELL) ... ECH
Endocervical Aspiration [*Medicine*] (MELL) ... ECA
Endocervical Aspirator [*Medicine*] (MELL) ... ECA
Endocrine Gland [*Medicine*] (MELL) ... ECG
Endocrine Therapy [*Medicine*] (MELL) ... ET
End-of-Life Care (MELL) ... EOLC
Endogenous (MELL) ... E
Endogenous Reninangiotensin System [*Medicine*] (MELL) ... ERAS
Endolymphatic Duct [*Medicine*] (MELL) ... ELD
Endolymphatic Sac [*Medicine*] (MELL) ... ELS
Endometrial Ablation [*Medicine*] (MELL) ... EA
Endometrial Biopsy [*Medicine*] ... EB
Endometrial Cancer [*Medicine*] (MELL) ... EMC
Endometrial Carcinoma [*Medicine*] (MELL) ... EMC
Endometrial Curettage [*Medicine*] (MELL) ... EMC
Endometrial Hyperplasia [*Medicine*] (MELL) ... EH
Endometrial Intraepithelial Neoplasia [*Medicine*] (MELL) ... EIEN
Endometrial Intraepithelial Neoplasia [*Medicine*] (MELL) ... EIN
Endometrial Stromal Meiosis [*Medicine*] (MELL) ... ESM
Endometrioid Endocarcinoma of Ovary [*Medicine*] (MELL) ... EACOA
Endometritis, Salpingitis, and Peritonitis [*Medicine*] (MELL) ... ESP
Endomyocardial Biopsy [*Medicine*] (MELL) ... EMCB
Endorex Corp. [*AMEX symbol*] (SG) ... DOR
End-Organ Dysfunction [*Medicine*] (MELL) ... EOD
Endoscopic Band Ligation (MELL) ... EBL
Endoscopic Carpal Tunnel Release [*Medicine*] (MELL) ... ECTR
Endoscopic Mucosal Resection [*Medicine*] (MELL) ... EMR
Endoscopic Mucosectomy (MELL) ... EMS
Endoscopic Pancreatocholangiography [*Medicine*] (MELL) ... EPC
Endoscopy [*Medicine*] (MELL) ... EN
Endosseous Dental Implant (MELL) ... EDI
Endotracheal Airway [*Medicine*] (MELL) ... ETA
Endotracheal Anesthesia [*Medicine*] (MELL) ... ETA
Endotracheal Catheter [*Medicine*] (MELL) ... EC
Endotracheal Intubation [*Medicine*] (MELL) ... ETI
End-Stage Kidney Disease (MELL) ... ESKD
End-Stage Liver Failure (MELL) ... ESLF
End-to-End Ureteral Anastomosis [*Medicine*] (MELL) ... EEUA
End-Use Product (EPAT) ... EUP
Endwell, NY [*FM radio station call letters*] (BROA) ... WBBI-FM
Enema of Choice [*Medicine*] (MELL) ... EOC
Energis PLC ADS [*NASDAQ symbol*] (SG) ... ENGSY
Energy East [*NYSE symbol*] (SG) ... NEG
Energy Information Agency ... EIA
Energy Research [*AMEX symbol*] (SG) ... ERC
Energy Search [*NASDAQ symbol*] (SG) ... EGAS
Enesco Group [*NYSE symbol*] (SG) ... ENC
Enforcement Case Review [*Environmental science*] (EPAT) ... ECR
Engage Technologies [*NASDAQ symbol*] (SG) ... ENGA
Engineer (PROS) ... engr
Engineering (BEE) ... Engin
Engineering Design Agreement ... EDA
Engineering Design Simulator ... EDS
Englewood, FL [*FM radio station call letters*] (BROA) ... WLTF-FM
English (BEE) ... Eng
Enhanced Blue Fluorescent Protein ... EBFP
Enhanced Counter Air Capability [*Military*] ... ECAC
Enhanced Yellow Fluorescent Protein ... EYFP
Enhancing Factor of Allergy [*Medicine*] (MELL) ... EFA
Enid, OK [*AM radio station call letters*] (BROA) ... KBFQ
Enlisted Aviation Warfare Specialist ... EAWS
Enough (GEAB) ... eno
Ensign (GEAB) ... ens
Ensuing (GEAB) ... ensu
Entercom Communications'A' [*NYSE symbol*] (SG) ... ETM
Enteric Coated Aspirin (MELL) ... ECA
Enteric Fistula [*Medicine*] (MELL) ... EF
Enteric Gram Negative Bacteria [*Medicine*] (MELL) ... EGNB
Enteric Viral Pathogens [*Medicine*] (MELL) ... EVP
Entering Diagnosis [*Medicine*] (MELL) ... ED
Enteritis Necroticans [*Medicine*] (MELL) ... EN
Enteroinvasive E. coli [*Medicine*] (MELL) ... EIEC
Enterotoxin (MELL) ... ET
Enterovaginal Fistula [*Medicine*] (MELL) ... EVF
Enteroviral Meningitis in Childhood [*Medicine*] (MELL) ... EVMC
Enteroviruses [*Medicine*] (MELL) ... EV
Enterprise Information Portals ... EIP
Enterprise Products Partners [*NYSE symbol*] (SG) ... EPD
Entertainment Properties Tr [*NYSE symbol*] (SG) ... EPR
Entomology (BEE) ... Entomol
Entotic Sound [*Medicine*] (MELL) ... ES
Entrapment Neuropathy [*Medicine*] (MELL) ... EN
Entrust Technologies [*NASDAQ symbol*] (SG) ... ENTU
Entry Age Normal with Frozen Initial Past Service Liability [*Business term*] ... EIPSL
Enveloping Layer ... EVL
Environmental Concern Interaction Score ... ECIS
Environmental Council of the States (EPAT) ... ECOS
Environmental Effects Assessment Panel ... EEAP
Environmental Hypersensitivity Disease [*Medicine*] (MELL) ... EHD
Environmental Monitoring Testing Site (EPAT) ... EMTS
Environmental Performance Agreement (EPAT) ... EnPA
Environmental Preference Inventory ... EPI
Environmental Quality Technology ... EQT
Environmental Safeguards [*AMEX symbol*] (SG) ... EVV
Environmental Technology Integrated Process Team ... ETIPT
Environmental Technology Technical Council ... ETTC

Environmental Technology Verification Program (EPAT) ..... ETV
Environmental Tobacco Smoke (MELL) ..... ETS
Environmental Treaties and Resource Indicators [Internet resource] ..... ENTRI
Environment-Mapped Bump Mapping [Computer science] ..... EMBM
Enzyme Pancreatic Secretion [Medicine] (MELL) ..... EPS
Enzyme Replacement Therapy [Medicine] (MELL) ..... ERT
Enzyme-Dependent Reaction [Medicine] (MELL) ..... EDR
Enzyme-Linked Immunoassay (MELL) ..... ELIA
Enzyme-Releasing Peptide (MELL) ..... ERP
Ephedrine, Theophylline and Phenobarbital [Medicine] (MELL) ..... ETP
Ephelis (MELL) ..... E
Ephemera Society of America (EA) ..... EPHSOC
Epicardial Hemorrhage [Medicine] (MELL) ..... ECH
Epicondylar Fracture [Medicine] (MELL) ..... EF
Epicor Software [NASDAQ symbol] (SG) ..... EPIC
Epidemic Kaposi's Sarcoma [Medicine] (MELL) ..... EKS
Epidemic Listeriosis [Medicine] (MELL) ..... EL
Epidemic Threshold (MELL) ..... ET
Epidemiological, Graphics, Estimation, and Testing [Program] ..... EGRET
Epidermal Abscess [Medicine] (MELL) ..... EDA
Epidermal Nevus Syndrome [Medicine] ..... ENS
Epidermolysis Bullosa Hereditaria [Dermatology] ..... EBH
Epidermolytic Hyperkeratosis [Dermatology] ..... EH
Epidural Abscess [Medicine] (MELL) ..... EA
Epidural Anesthesia [Medicine] (MELL) ..... EDA
Epidural Hematoma [Medicine] (MELL) ..... EH
Epidural Spinal Cord Compression [Medicine] (MELL) ..... ESCC
Epidural Steroid Injection [Medicine] (MELL) ..... ESI
Epiglottic Cartilage [Medicine] (MELL) ..... EGC
Epilepsy Monitoring Unit [Medicine] (MELL) ..... EMU
Epileptic Intentional Deficit Disorder (MELL) ..... EIDD
Epinephrine Tolerance Test [Medicine] (MELL) ..... ETT
Epiphyseal Ossification Center [Medicine] (MELL) ..... EOC
Epiphyseal Plate [Medicine] (MELL) ..... EPP
Episcleral Venous Pressure [Medicine] (MELL) ..... EVP
Episode Free Day [Medicine] (MELL) ..... EFD
Episodic Cluster Headache (MELL) ..... ECH
Episodic Paroxysmal Hemicrania [Medicine] (MELL) ..... EPH
Epithelial Cell Vacuolization [Medicine] (MELL) ..... ECV
Epithelial Corneal Dystrophy [Medicine] (MELL) ..... ECD
Epithelial Ovarian Cancer (MELL) ..... EOC
Epstein-Barr Virus (MELL) ..... EBv
Epstein-Barr Virus Type 1 (MELL) EBV-1
Epstein-Barr Virus Type 2 (MELL) EBV-2
Equal Breath Sounds (MELL) ..... EBS
Equality Bancorp [AMEX symbol] (SG) ..... EBI
EQUANT N.V. ADS [NYSE symbol] (SG) ..... ENT
Equatorial Guinea (MILB) ..... EG
Equine Tetanus Immune Globulin (MELL) ..... ETIG
Equipment (MILB) ..... eqpt
Equity Inns [NYSE symbol] (SG) ..... ENN
Equity One [NYSE symbol] (SG) ..... EQY
Equivalent Dose (QUAC) ..... ED
Equivalent Field Office [Environmental Protection Agency] (EPAT) ..... EFO
Erath, LA [FM radio station call letters] (BROA) ..... KRXZ-FM
Erb Disease [Medicine] (MELL) ..... ED
Erb Paralysis [Medicine] (MELL) ..... EP
Erectile Dysfunction [Medicine] (MELL) ..... ED
Erector Spinae Muscle [Medicine] (MELL) ..... ESM
Ergonomics ..... ER
Ergonovine Maleate Test [Medicine] (MELL) ..... EMT
Ergot Poisoning (MELL) ..... EP
Erich Lacher Co. ..... LACO
Ericsson, L.M., Tel'B'ADS [NASDAQ symbol] (SG) ..... ERICY
Eritrea (MILB) ..... Er
Erlenmeyer Flask Deformity [Medicine] (MELL) ..... EFD
Erogenous Zone (MELL) ..... EZ
Erosion and Ulcer [Medicine] (MELL) ..... E & U
Erupted Wisdom Teeth (MELL) ..... EWT
Erythema Infectiosum [Medicine] (MELL) ..... EI
Erythema Migrans [Medicine] (MELL) ..... EM
Erythema Multiforme [Medicine] (MELL) ..... EMD
Erythrityl Tetranitrate [Medicine] (MELL) ..... ETN
Erythrocyte Antiserum [Medicine] (MELL) ..... EA
Erythrocyte Fragility Test [Medicine] (MELL) ..... EFT
Erythrocyte Receptor [Medicine] (MELL) ..... ER
Esat Telecom Group ADS [NASDAQ symbol] (SG) ..... ESAT
Escape Beat [Medicine] (MELL) ..... EB
Escape Rhythm [Medicine] (MELL) ..... ER
Escherichia Coli 0157 [Virulent strain of the bacterium E. coli] [Medicine] (MELL) ECO157
Escision (MELL) ..... exc
ESG Re Ltd [NASDAQ symbol] (SG) ..... ESREF
E-Sim Ltd. [AMEX symbol] (SG) ..... EIM
Esophageal Chalasia [Medicine] (MELL) ..... EC
Esophageal Diverticulum [Medicine] (MELL) ..... ED
Esophageal Myotonia Dystrophica [Medicine] (MELL) ..... EMD
Esophageal Reflux [Medicine] (MELL) ..... ER
Esophageal Spasm [Medicine] (MELL) ..... ES
Esophageal Variceal Bleeding [Medicine] (MELL) ..... EVB
Esophagocardiomyotomy [Medicine] (MELL) ..... ECM
Espace d'Interpellation Democratique [Forum for Democratic Consultation] [Mali] ..... EID
Esparto, CA [FM radio station call letters] (BROA) ..... KTTA-FM
Espatriate Turin [Italy] [An association] ..... ESPRIT

e.spire Communications [NASDAQ symbol] (SG) ..... ESPI
Esquire (BEE) ..... esq
Essential High Blood Pressure (MELL) ..... EHBP
Essential Hypertension (MELL) ..... EHT
Essential Mixed Cryoglobulinemia [Medicine] (MELL) ..... EMC
Essential Monoclonal Gammopathy [Medicine] (MELL) ..... EMG
Essential-Familial Tremor [Medicine] (MELL) ..... EFT
Essentially Negative (MELL) ..... EN
Establishment (GEAB) ..... establ
Estate (GEAB) ..... est
Esterified Estrogen [Medicine] (MELL) ..... EE
Estes Park, CO [AM radio station call letters] (BROA) ..... KEZZ
Estimated (GEAB) ..... estd
Estimated Renal Plasma Flow [Medicine] (MELL) ..... ERPF
Estimated Time of Arrival (MELL) ..... ETOA
Estimated Weight Loss (MELL) ..... EWL
Estonia (MILB) ..... Ea
Estradiol Receptor Assay [Medicine] (MELL) ..... ERA
Estrogen Gel [Medicine] (MELL) ..... EG
Estrogen Patch (MELL) ..... EP
Etiology Unknown [Medicine] (MELL) ..... EU
eToys, Inc. [NASDAQ symbol] (SG) ..... ETYS
Euchromatin and Heterochromatin [Medicine] (MELL) ..... E & H
Eugene Meylan, SA ..... EMSA
Eugene, OR [FM radio station call letters] (BROA) ..... KKTT-FM
Euglobulin Lysis Test [Medicine] (MELL) ..... ELT
Eureka, IL [FM radio station call letters] (BROA) ..... WEEK-FM
Euro Banking Association ..... EBA
Euro-Nevada Mining [Toronto Stock Exchange symbol] (SG) ..... EN
Europe Network ..... EUnet
European Association of Establishments for Veterinary Education (GVA) ..... EAEVE
European Association of Petroleum Geologists (QUAC) ..... EAPG
European Association of State Veterinary Officers (GVA) ..... EASVO
European Association of Zoo and Wildlife Veterinary Surgeons (GVA) ..... EAZWVS
European Biomedical Research Association (GVA) ..... EBRA
European Board of Veterinary Specialisation (GVA) ..... EBVS
European Centre for Earth Observation (GEOI) ..... CEO
European College for Animal Reproduction (GVA) ..... ECAR
European College for Veterinary Public Health, Population Medicine, and Food Scince (GVA) ..... ECVPH-PM-FS
European College of Veterinary Anaesthesia (GVA) ..... ECVA
European College of Veterinary and Comparative Nutrition (GVA) ..... ECVCN
European College of Veterinary Internal Medicine-Companion Animals (GVA) ..... ECVIM-CA
European College of Veterinary Ophthalmologists (GVA) ..... ECVO
European College of Veterinary Pathologists (GVA) ..... ECVP
European College of Veterinary Surgeons (GVA) ..... ECVS
European Council of American Chambers of Commerce (EA) ..... ECACC
European Feed Additives Manufacturers Association (GVA) ..... FEFANA
European Journal of Physics [A publication] ..... EJP
European Lake Coring Project (QUAC) ..... ELCP
European Lake Drilling Program (QUAC) ..... ELDP
European North Atlantic Margin (QUAC) ..... ENAM
European Polar Satellite ..... EPS
European Polar-Orbiting Platform (EOSA) ..... EPOP
European Pollen Database (QUAC) ..... EPD
European Radiation Dosimetry Group ..... EURADOS
European Research Group for Alternatives in Toxicity Testing (GVA) ..... ERGATT
European Society of Feline Medicine (GVA) ..... ESFM
European Society of Toxicology in Vitro (GVA) ..... ESTIV
European Society of Veterinary Orthopaedics and Traumatology (GVA) ..... ESVOT
European Space Research and Space Technology Centre (EOSA) ..... ESTEC
European Veterinary Dental College (GVA) ..... EVDC
European Veterinary Libraries Group (GVA) ..... EVLG
European Veterinary Society for the Study of Small Animal Reproduction (GVA) ..... EVSSAR
Eustachian Tube Dysfunction [Medicine] (MELL) ..... ETD
Evaluate and Advise [Medicine] (MELL) ..... E & A
Evaluated Nuclear Data Library ..... ENDL
Evaluation Analysis Center [Army] ..... EAC
Evaluation and Follow-Up [Medicine] (MELL) ..... EFU
Evans, Inc. [NASDAQ symbol] (SG) ..... EVANE
Eveleth, MN [AM radio station call letters] (BROA) ..... KRBT
Evening School for Foreign Born ..... EFB
EVEREN Capital [NYSE symbol] (SG) ..... EVR
Everglades Agricultural Area ..... EAA
Everglades Forever Act ..... EFA
Everglades National Park ..... ENP
Every Other Day ..... eod
Evidence-Based Medicine ..... EBM
Evoked Visual Response [Medicine] (MELL) ..... EVP
Exabyte Corp. [NASDAQ symbol] (SG) ..... EXBT
Exacerbating-Remitting Multiple Scelrosis (MELL) ..... ERMS
Excel Legacy [AMEX symbol] (SG) ..... XLG
Excel Maritime Carriers [AMEX symbol] (SG) ..... EXM
Excel Switching [NASDAQ symbol] (SG) ..... XLSW
Excellent ..... Exc
Excimer Laser [Medicine] (MELL) ..... EL
Excisional Biopsy [Medicine] (MELL) ..... EB
Excitation-Contraction [Medicine] (MELL) ..... EC
Excludes (MILB) ..... excl
Excretory Urography [Medicine] (MELL) ..... EUG

By Meaning

Ex-Dividend .... x-d
Executive Committee for Humanitarian Affairs [*United Nations*] .... ECHA
Executive Master's in Technology Management .... EMTM
Executone Info Sys [*NASDAQ symbol*] (SG) .... ELOT
Executrix (GEAB) .... exox
Executrix (GEAB) .... exx
Exercise-Induced Myocardial Ischemia [*Medicine*] (MELL) .... EIMI
Exercise-Related Anaphylaxis [*Medicine*] (MELL) .... ERA
Exertional Muscle Pain Syndrome [*Medicine*] (MELL) .... EMPS
Exeter, NH [*AM radio station call letters*] (BROA) .... WGIP
Exfoliation Glaucoma [*Medicine*] (MELL) .... EG
Exmore, VA [*FM radio station call letters*] (BROA) .... WKHI-FM
Exodus Communications [*NASDAQ symbol*] (SG) .... EXDS
Exogenous Antigen Disease [*Medicine*] (MELL) .... EAD
Exophoria [*Medicine*] (MELL) .... EXO
Expected Value .... E
Expenditure (MILB) .... exp
Experimental Lidar (EOSA) .... E-LIDAR
Experimental Product (EPAT) .... EP
Experimental Repair Ship [*Military*] (IUSS) .... ARX
Experimental Storage Ring .... ESR
Experimental Test Pilot [*Army*] .... XP
Expiratory Time (MELL) .... ET
Exploratory Laparotomy [*Medicine*] (MELL) .... EL
Explosives Management Alternatives Team [*Army*] .... XMAT
Expoloratory [*Medicine*] (MELL) .... EXP
Exposure Radical Mastectomy (MELL) .... ERM
Exposure-Related Hypothermic Death (MELL) .... ERHD
Expression-Linked Copy (MELL) .... ELC
Ex-Smoker (MELL) .... ExS
Exstrophy of Bladder [*Medicine*] (MELL) .... EOB
Extended Cab [*Automotive term*] .... X-CAB
Extended Endocardial Resection Procedure [*Medicine*] (MELL) ...... EERP
Extended Field (MELL) .... EF
Extended Service Program .... ESP
Extended Stay Amer. [*NYSE symbol*] (SG) .... ESA
Extended-Release Tablets [*Medicine*] (MELL) .... ERT
Extendicare, Inc. [*NASDAQ symbol*] (SG) .... EXEA
Extensor Proprius Hallucis [*Medicine*] (MELL) .... EPH
Extent of Disease (MELL) .... EOD
Exterior .... Ext

External Cardiopulmonary Resuscitation [*Medicine*] (MELL) .... ECPR
External Carotid Artery [*Medicine*] (MELL) .... ECA
External Counterpressure Device [*Medicine*] (MELL) .... ECPD
External Ear (MELL) .... EE
External Iliac Vein (MELL) .... EIV
External Jugular Vein (MELL) .... EJN
External Mammary Lymph Node Group [*Medicine*] (MELL) .... EMLNG
External Oblique Aponeurosis [*Medicine*] (MELL) .... EOA
External Occipital Protuberance [*Medicine*] (MELL) .... EOP
External Ostomy Appliance [*Medicine*] (MELL) .... EOA
External Pudendal Vein [*Medicine*] (MELL) .... EPV
External Vacuum Therapy (MELL) .... EVT
Extra-Articular Fracture [*Medicine*] (MELL) .... EAF
Extracapsular Fracture [*Medicine*] (MELL) .... ECF
Extracardiac Obstructive Shock [*Medicine*] (MELL) .... ECOS
Extracellular Mass [*Medicine*] (MELL) .... ECM
Extracellular Matrix [*Medicine*] (MELL) .... EM
Extracorporeal Membrane Oxidation [*Medicine*] (MELL) .... ECMO
Extra-Fast Patrol Boat (MILB) .... XFPB
Extrahepatic Obstructive Jaundice [*Medicine*] (MELL) .... EOJ
Extra-Mural Rotations (GVA) .... EMR
Extra-Mural Studies (GVA) .... EMS
Extraocular Movement [*Medicine*] (MELL) .... EOM
Extraocular Muscle Palsy [*Medicine*] (MELL) .... EMP
Extrapyramidal Hypertonia [*Medicine*] (MELL) .... EPH
Extrarespiratory .... ER
Extra-Strength (MELL) .... ExS
Extrasystolic Atrial Tachycardia [*Medicine*] (MELL) .... ESAT
Extrathoracic .... ET
Extrauterine Pregnancy (MELL) .... EUP
Extreme Intervertebral Disk Collapse [*Medicine*] (MELL) .... EIDC
Extreme Networks [*NASDAQ symbol*] (SG) .... EXTR
Extreme Somatosensory Evoked Potential [*Medicine*] (MELL) ..... ESEP
Extremely Fine [*Numismatic term*] .... XF
Extrinsic Allergic Alveolitis [*Medicine*] (MELL) .... EAA
Extroverted Personality (MELL) .... EVP
Extubation [*Medicine*] (MELL) .... EXTUB
Ex-Warrants .... xw
EXX, Inc.'A' [*AMEX symbol*] (SG) .... EXXA
Eye and Ear (MELL) .... E & E
E-Z EM, Inc.'A' [*AMEX symbol*] (SG) .... EZMA

F
By Meaning

Fabry's Disease [*Medicine*] (MELL) .... FD
Face Lift (MELL) .... FL
Facet Joint Syndrome (MELL) .... FJS
Facial Canal (MELL) .... FC
Facial Dyskinesias [*Medicine*] (MELL) .... FD
Facial Pain (MELL) .... FP
Facial Vein (MELL) .... FV
Facility for Access Control and Security [*RadWare*] .... FACS
Factory 2-U Stores [*NYSE symbol*] (SG) .... FTUS
Factory Mutual Engineering & Research Corp. .... FMERC
Factory Service Manual .... FSM
FactSet Research Systems [*NYSE symbol*] (SG) .... FDS
Fahnestock Viner Hldgs'A' [*NYSE symbol*] (SG) .... FVH
Failed Back Surgery Syndrome [*Medicine*] (MELL) .... FBSS
Failed Back Syndrome (MELL) .... FBS
Failed to Keep Appointment (MELL) .... FTKA
Failure to Thrive Syndrome [*Medicine*] (MELL) .... FTTS
Fair [*Numismatic term*] .... Fr
Fair Rate .... f/r
Fairbanks, AK [*FM radio station call letters*] (BROA) .... KKED-FM
Fairbanks, AK [*Television station call letters*] (BROA) .... KTVF-DT
Fairbanks Dysostosis [*Medicine*] (MELL) .... FD
Fairbault, MN [*FM radio station call letters*] (BROA) .... KBGY-FM
Fairhope, AL [*AM radio station call letters*] (BROA) .... WDLT
Faisalabad Electric Supply Company [*Pakistan*] .... FESCO
Falfurrias, TX [*FM radio station call letters*] (BROA) .... KDFM-FM
Fall Color .... fc
Fall River Gas [*AMEX symbol*] (SG) .... FAL
Fallopian Tube Carcinoma [*Medicine*] (MELL) .... FTC
Fallopian Tube Ligation Ring [*Medicine*] (MELL) .... FTLR
Fallopian Tube Papilloma [*Medicine*] (MELL) .... FTP
Fallopian Tube Sarcoma [*Medicine*] (MELL) .... FTS
Falmouth, VA [*FM radio station call letters*] (BROA) .... WFAL-FM
False Positive Rate (MELL) .... FPR
False-Positive Error [*Medicine*] (MELL) .... FPE
Familial Alzheimer's Dementia (MELL) .... FAD
Familial Benign Chronic Pemphigus [*Medicine*] (MELL) .... FBCP
Familial Benign Hypocalciuric Hypercalcemia [*Medicine*] (MELL) .... FBHH
Familial Dysbetalipoproteinemia [*Medicine*] (MELL) .... FDBLP
Familial Exudative Vitreoretinopathy [*Medicine*] (MELL) .... FEVR
Familial Fat-Induced Hyperlipemia [*Medicine*] (MELL) .... FFIH
Familial Intestinal Polyposis [*Medicine*] (MELL) .... FIP
Familial Juvenile Polyposis [*Medicine*] (MELL) .... FJP
Familial Lipoprotein Lipase Deficiency [*Medicine*] (MELL) .... FLLD
Familial Melanoma [*Medicine*] (MELL) .... FM
Familial Metaphyseal Dysplasia [*Medicine*] (MELL) .... FMD
Familial Neonatal Hypoglycemia [*Medicine*] (MELL) .... FNH
Familial Orthostatic Hypotension [*Medicine*] (MELL) .... FOH
Familial Osseous Dystrophy [*Medicine*] (MELL) .... FOD
Familial Polyposis [*Medicine*] (MELL) .... FP
Familial Polyposis Registry (MELL) .... FPR
Familial Visceral Neuropathy [*Medicine*] (MELL) .... FVN
Family (GEAB) .... fam
Family Auto Plan .... FAP
Family Campers and Rivers [*An association*] (EA) .... FCRV
Family Group Record Archives [*Genealogy*] (GEAB) .... FGRA
Family History Center [*Genealogy*] (GEAB) .... FHC
Family History Library [*Genealogy*] (GEAB) .... FHL
Family Physician (MELL) .... FP
Family Registry (GEAB) .... FR
Fans and Friends of Ray Price [*An association*] (EA) .... FFRP
Fantom Technologies [*NASDAQ symbol*] (SG) .... FTMTF
Fargo, ND [*FM radio station call letters*] (BROA) .... KFBN-FM
Fargo, ND [*AM radio station call letters*] (BROA) .... KQWB
Farm Animal Welfare Council (GVA) .... FAWC
Farm Family Holdings [*NYSE symbol*] (SG) .... FFH
Farmer's Lung (MELL) .... FL
Farmersville, TX [*AM radio station call letters*] (BROA) .... KTUB
Farmersville, TX [*FM radio station call letters*] (BROA) .... KXEZ-FM
Farming and Rural Conservation Agency (GVA) .... FRCA
Farmington, NH [*FM radio station call letters*] (BROA) .... WZEN-FM
Farmington, NM [*AM radio station call letters*] (BROA) .... KNNT
Farmington, NM [*Television station call letters*] (BROA) .... KOFT
Farwell, TX [*Television station call letters*] (BROA) .... KBGD
Fascia (MELL) .... F
Fasciculation [*Medicine*] (MELL) .... FASC
Fasciocutaneous Flap [*Medicine*] (MELL) .... FCF
Fasting Gastrin Level [*Medicine*] (MELL) .... FGL
Fasting Glucose Value [*Medicine*] (MELL) .... FGV
Fasting Hemoglobin [*Medicine*] (MELL) .... FH
Fasting Plasma Lipids [*Medicine*] (MELL) .... FPL
Fat Cell (MELL) .... FC
Fat Embolism (MELL) .... FE
Fat Pad (MELL) .... FP
Fat Tolerance Test [*Medicine*] (MELL) .... FTT
Fatal Childhood Diarrhea [*Medicine*] (MELL) .... FCD
Fatal Facts .... FF
Fatal Hyponatremic Encephalopathy [*Medicine*] (MELL) .... FHE
Fatal Pulmonary Embolism [*Medicine*] (MELL) .... FPE
Fat-Free Diet (MELL) .... FFD
Father (GEAB) .... f
Father (GEAB) .... fa
Fatigue and Sleep (MELL) .... F & S
Fatigue Factor (MELL) .... FF
Fatigue Fracture (MELL) .... FF
Fat-Restricted Diet (MELL) .... FRD
Fat-Soluble Vitamins (MELL) .... FSV
Fatty Liver and Kidney Syndrome (MELL) .... FLKS
Fatty Liver Cell (MELL) .... FLC
Fauna and Flora International .... FFI
Fayetteville, NC [*AM radio station call letters*] (BROA) .... WAZZ
Fayetteville, NC [*Television station call letters*] (BROA) .... WKFT-DT
FBL Financial Group'A' [*NYSE symbol*] (SG) .... FFG
FDX Corp. [*NYSE symbol*] (SG) .... FDX
Febrile Antigen Agglutination [*Medicine*] (MELL) .... FAA
Febrile Nonhemolytic Reaction [*Medicine*] (MELL) .... FNHR
Fecal Reducing Substance [*Medicine*] (MELL) .... FRS
Fecal Trypsin [*Medicine*] (MELL) .... FT
Federacion Puertorriqueno de Trabajadores .... PRFPT
Federal Agricultural Mtge'A' [*NYSE symbol*] (SG) .... AGMA
Federal Coordinating Committee on Science .... FCCSET
Federal Highway Administration Office of Highway Safety .... FHWA
Federal Pay Comparability Act of 1970 .... FPCA
Federal Pollution Prevention Act (EPAT) .... FPPA
Federal Republic of Germany .... FedRep
Federal Republic of Yugoslavia (MILB) .... FRY
Federal Reserve Board .... Fed
Federal Tax Rate .... FEDRT
Federated Investors 'B' [*NYSE symbol*] (SG) .... FII
Federation of European Companion Animal Veterinary Associations (GVA) .... FECAVA
Federation of European Equine Veterinary Associations (GVA) .... FEEVA
Federation of Historical Bottle Collectors (EA) .... FOHBC
Federation of Petanque U.S.A. (EA) .... FPUSA
Feeding Pump (MELL) .... FP
Fellow American Society of Genealogists (GEAB) .... FASG
Female Reproductive System (MELL) .... FRS
Femoral Hernia [*Medicine*] (MELL) .... FH
Femoral Nerve Traction Test [*Medicine*] (MELL) .... FNTT
Femoral Valgus Osteotomy [*Medicine*] (MELL) .... FVO
Femur (MELL) .... F
Fenner, NY [*FM radio station call letters*] (BROA) .... WXXE-FM
Fernandina Beach, FL [*AM radio station call letters*] (BROA) .... WYHI
Ferndale, WA [*AM radio station call letters*] (BROA) .... KCCF
Ferric Chloride Test [*Medicine*] (MELL) .... FCT
Fertilled Egg (MELL) .... FE
Fetal Cocaine Syndrome [*Medicine*] (MELL) .... FCS
Fetal Cytomegalovirus Syndrome [*Medicine*] (MELL) .... FCMVS
Fetal Danger Zone (MELL) .... FDZ
Fetal Death (MELL) .... FD
Fetal Distress (MELL) .... FD
Fetal Estrogen-Binding Protein (MELL) .... FEBP
Fetal Fibronectin [*Medicine*] (MELL) .... FFN
Fetal Heart Rate Acceleration (MELL) .... FHRA
Fetal Hemoglobin [*Medicine*] (MELL) .... FH
Fetal Medicine (MELL) .... FM
Fetal Membranes (MELL) .... FM
Fetal Monitor (MELL) .... FM
Fetal Movement Count (MELL) .... FMC
Fetal Presentation [*Medicine*] (MELL) .... FP
Fetal Radiation Syndrome [*Medicine*] (MELL) .... FRS
Fetal Rubella Syndrome [*Medicine*] (MELL) .... FRS

Fetal Scalp Sampling [*Medicine*] (MELL) .... FSS
Fetal Solvent Syndrome [*Medicine*] (MELL) .... FSS
Fetal Syphilis Syndrome [*Medicine*] (MELL) .... FSS
Fetal Tobacco Syndrome [*Medicine*] (MELL) .... FTS
Fetal-Maternal Exchange [*Medicine*] (MELL) .... FME
Fetus and Neonate (MELL) .... F & N
Fever (MELL) .... F
Fever and Chills (MELL) .... F & C
Fever Blister (MELL) .... FB
Fever, Chills, and Sweating (MELL) .... FCS
Fever Without Localizing Signs (MELL) .... FWLS
FFP Marketing [*AMEX symbol*] (SG) .... FMM
Fiber Optic Isolated Spherical Dipole Antenna (EPAT) ...... FOISD
Fiber Optic Sigmoidoscope [*Medicine*] (MELL) .... FOS
FiberMark, Inc. [*NYSE symbol*] (SG) .... FMK
Fiberoptic Sigmoidoscopy [*Medicine*] (MELL) .... FOS
Fiber-Rich Diet (MELL) .... FRD
Fibroadenoma of Breast [*Medicine*] (MELL) .... F
Fibroblast (MELL) .... F
Fibrocystic Breast Disease [*Medicine*] (MELL) ...... FCBD
Fibrocystic Breast Syndrome [*Medicine*] (MELL) ...... FBS
Fibrocystic Disorder of Breast [*Medicine*] (MELL) ...... FCDB
Fibrocytoma of Ovary [*Medicine*] (MELL) .... FCO
Fibroepithelial Polyp [*Medicine*] (MELL) .... FEP
Fibromyalgia (MELL) .... FM
Fibromyalgia Syndrome [*Medicine*] .... FMA
Fibromyalgia Syndrome [*Medicine*] .... FMS
Fibrotic Lung Disease (MELL) .... FLD
Fibrous Dysplasia (MELL) .... FD
Fibula (MELL) .... F
Fibula (MELL) .... FI
Fibula Fracture (MELL) .... FF
Fidelity (GEAB) .... fidel
Fidelity Natl Finl [*NYSE symbol*] (SG) .... FNF
Field (MILB) .... fd
Field Support Terminal (EOSA) .... FST
Field-Emitter Arrays .... FEA
Field-Emitter Displays .... FEDS
Fighter (MILB) .... ftr
Fiji (MILB) .... Fji
Filiform Papilla [*Medicine*] (MELL) .... FFP
Fill in the Blank [*Online dialog*] .... FITB
Filtration-Resistant Glaucoma (MELL) .... FRG
Filum Terminale [*Medicine*] (MELL) .... FT
Financial Federal [*NYSE symbol*] (SG) .... FIF
Financial Management Assistance Project [*Environmental Protection Agency*] (EPAT) .... FMAP
Financial Management Rate of Return [*Business term*] ...... FMRR
Financial Supervisory Agency [*Japan*] .... FSA
Finet.com, Inc. [*NASDAQ symbol*] (SG) .... FNCM
Finger Joint Size (MELL) .... FJS
Finger Tip (MELL) .... FT
Fingerprick Blood Glucose [*Medicine*] (MELL) .... FPBG
Fingerstick Blood Glucose [*Medicine*] (MELL) .... FSBG
Finger-to-Finger Test [*Medicine*] (MELL) .... FFT
Finger-to-Nose Test (MELL) .... FNT
Finger-Trap Phenomenon [*Medicine*] (MELL) .... FTP
Fini Sec Assurance 6.95%Sr'QUIDS' [*NYSE symbol*] (SG) ..... FSE
Finite Real Estate Investment Trust .... FRIET
Finning Intl. [*Toronto Stock Exchange symbol*] (SG) ...... FTT
Finnish Game and Fisheries Research Institute .... FGFRI
Finnish Laboratory Animal Scientists (GVA) .... FinLAS
Finnish Veterinary Association (GVA) .... FVA
Fire Weather Index (QUAC) .... FWI
Firearm Injury (MELL) .... FI
Firearm-Related Injury (MELL) .... FRI
Fire-Broken Rock [*Archaeology*] (QUAC) .... fbr
First Alliance 'A' [*NASDAQ symbol*] (SG) .... FACO
First Appearance (QUAC) .... FAP
First Appearance of Date (QUAC) .... FAD
First Bancorp [*NYSE symbol*] (SG) .... FBP
First Digitized Division [*Army*] .... FDD
First Health Group [*NASDAQ symbol*] (SG) .... FHCC
First National Corp. [*AMEX symbol*] (SG) .... FNC
First Occurence of Date (QUAC) .... FOD
First Tenn Natl [*NYSE symbol*] (SG) .... FTN
First Trimester of Pregnancy (MELL) .... FTOP
First Wash Realty Trust [*NYSE symbol*] (SG) .... FRW
First-Degree Burn (MELL) .... FDB
First-Dollar Coverage [*Insurance*] (MELL) .... FDC
FirstFed Amer Bancorp [*AMEX symbol*] (SG) .... FAB
First-Generation Antihistamine [*Medicine*] (MELL) ...... FGAH
First-Morning Urine (MELL) .... FMU
FIRSTPLUS Finl 7.25%'TIMES' [*AMEX symbol*] (SG) ...... TIM
FirstSpartan Financial [*NASDAQ symbol*] (SG) .... FSPT
Fiscal Year (MELL) .... FY
Fishmeal Information Network (GVA) .... FIN
Fissured Tongue (MELL) .... FT
Fissured Tongue Syndrome [*Medicine*] (MELL) .... FTS
Five-Speed [*Manual transmission*] 5-SPD
Five-Year Survival (MELL) .... FYS
Fixed Action Potential (MELL) .... FAP
FJ United States [*An association*] (EA) .... FJUS
Flabby Back Syndrome [*Medicine*] (MELL) .... FBS
Flagstar Bancorp [*NASDAQ symbol*] (SG) .... FLGS

Flail Chest (MELL) .... FC
Flandreau, SD [*FM radio station call letters*] (BROA) ...... KSQB-FM
FlashNet Communications [*NASDAQ symbol*] (SG) ...... FLAS
Flavin Monooxygenases .... FMO
Fleet Patrol Ship (MILB) .... FPS
Flexible Fiberoptic Sigmoidoscopy [*Medicine*] (MELL) ...... FFS
Flexible Video Laparoscopy [*Medicine*] (MELL) ...... FVL
Flexion (MELL) .... F
Flexion Body Cast (MELL) .... FBC
Flexion-Rotation Drawer Test (MELL) .... FRDT
Flextronics Intl. [*NASDAQ symbol*] (SG) .... FLEX
Flight (MILB) .... flt
Flight Control System Integration Laboratory [*Army*] ...... FCSIL
Flight Test Simulation Station .... FTSS
flightserv.com [*AMEX symbol*] (SG) .... FSW
Flint Colon Injury Scale [*Medicine*] (MELL) .... FCIS
Flint's Murmur [*Medicine*] (MELL) .... FM
Floaters (MELL) .... F
Floating Arm Keyboard (MELL) .... FAK
Floor (PROS) .... Fl
Floppy Infant Syndrome [*Medicine*] (MELL) .... FIS
Floppy Valve Syndrome [*Medicine*] (MELL) .... FVS
Flora, IL [*FM radio station call letters*] (BROA) ...... WBFW-FM
Floral Variant of Follicular Lymphoma [*Medicine*] (MELL) ...... FFL
Florence, KY [*AM radio station call letters*] (BROA) ...... WBOB
Florence, OR [*FM radio station call letters*] (BROA) ...... KLFO
Floresville, TX [*FM radio station call letters*] (BROA) ...... KLEY-FM
Florida City, FL [*FM radio station call letters*] (BROA) ...... WMFL-FM
Florida Comprehensive Achievement Test .... FCAT
Florida Internet Center for Understanding Sustainability ...... FICUS
Florida P&L 7.05% CABCO Tr Debs [*NYSE symbol*] (SG) ...... ELB
Florida Panthers Hlds [*NYSE symbol*] (SG) .... PAW
Florida Rock Indus [*NYSE symbol*] (SG) .... FRK
Flour City Intl. [*NASDAQ symbol*] (SG) .... FCIN
Flow Cytometric Immunophenotyping [*Medicine*] (MELL) ...... FCI
Flow Cytometry [*Medicine*] (MELL) .... FC
Flow Regime .... FR
Flower .... flw
Flower-Spray Nerve Ending (MELL) .... FSNE
Flowserve Corp. [*NYSE symbol*] (SG) .... FLS
Fludaradine [*Medicine*] (MELL) .... FA
Fluid Restriction (MELL) .... FR
Fluid Retention (MELL) .... FR
Fluorescent Cytoprint Assay (MELL) .... FCA
Fluorescent Treponemal Antibody Absorption Test [*Medicine*] (MELL) ...... FTAAT
Fluorescent-Labeled Antibody [*Medicine*] (MELL) .... FLA
Fluoride Treatment (MELL) .... FT
Fluoro-Assisted Lumbar Puncture [*Medicine*] (MELL) ...... FALP
Fluorscent Antinuclear Antibody Test (MELL) .... FAAT
Flurazepam Hydrochloride [*Medicine*] (MELL) .... FLZ
Flycast Communications [*NASDAQ symbol*] (SG) ...... FCST
Focal Communications [*NASDAQ symbol*] (SG) .... FCOM
Focal Macular Choroidopathy [*Medicine*] (MELL) .... FMC
Focal Segmental Sclerosis [*Medicine*] (MELL) ...... FSS
Fog Fever (MELL) .... FF
Folacin (MELL) .... F
Folate Deficiency (MELL) .... FD
Folic Acid Injection (MELL) .... FAI
Folkston, GA [*FM radio station call letters*] (BROA) ...... WATY-FM
Follicular Center Cell Lymphoma [*Medicine*] (MELL) ...... FCCL
Follicular Fluid (MELL) .... FF
Fomento Economico ADS [*NYSE symbol*] (SG) .... FMX
Fonix Corp. [*NASDAQ symbol*] (SG) .... FONX
Fontanel (MELL) .... F
Food Allergy (MELL) .... FA
Food Allergy Insomnia (MELL) .... FAI
Food Animal Practitioners Club [*Ohio State University*] (GVA) ...... FAPC
Food Chemical Intolerance (MELL) .... FCI
Food Intolerance (MELL) .... FI
Food Safety Promotion Board [*Ireland*] (GVA) .... FSPB
Food Standards Agency (GVA) .... FSA
Foodborne Illness (MELL) .... FBI
Foodborne Listeriosis [*Medicine*] (MELL) .... FL
Foot Compartment Syndrome (MELL) .... FCS
Foot Pad (MELL) .... FP
Football .... FB
Football Finger (MELL) .... FBF
Footdrop (MELL) .... FD
Footling Breech [*Medicine*] (MELL) .... FB
Footling Breech Presentation [*Medicine*] (MELL) .... FBP
For the Benefit Of (PROS) .... f/b/o
Foramen Cecum of Tongue [*Medicine*] (MELL) .... FCT
Force XXI Land Warrior [*Military*] .... FXXILW
Forced Duction Test (MELL) .... FDT
Forced Expiration (MELL) .... FE
Forced Inspiratory Spirogram [*Medicine*] (MELL) .... FIS
Forced Inspiratory Vital Capacity (MELL) .... FIVC
Forced Inspiratory Volume (MELL) .... FIV
Ford Foundation .... ff
Ford Motor Company .... Fomoco
Ford Motor Company .... FORD
Foreign Body Reaction (MELL) .... FBR
Foreign Born Doctor (MELL) .... FBD
Foreign Military Assistance/Financing/Sales (MILB) ...... FMA/F/S
Foreign Minister .... FonMin

Foreign Office ..... FonOff
Foreign Purchase Acknowledgement Statements (EPAT) ..... FPAS
Foreign Substance Inhalation [Medicine] (MELL) ..... FSI
Foreign-Body Sarcoma [Medicine] (MELL) ..... FBS
Forest Ecology Network ..... FEN
Forest Oil [NYSE symbol] (SG) ..... FST
Forestville, WI [FM radio station call letters] (BROA) ..... WRKU-FM
Forging Industry Association ..... FIAS
Formaldehyde, Acetic Acid, and Alcohol (MELL) ..... FAA
Forme Fruste of Chickenpox (MELL) ..... FFCP
Former Soviet Union ..... fsu
Forrester Research [NASDAQ symbol] (SG) ..... FORR
Fort (PROS) ..... Ft
Fort Bridger, WY [FM radio station call letters] (BROA) ..... KNYN-FM
Fort McMurray, AB [FM radio station call letters] (BROA) ..... CKYX-FM
Fort Myers, FL [FM radio station call letters] (BROA) ..... WGCU-FM
Fort Nelson, BC [FM radio station call letters] (BROA) ..... CKRX-FM
Fort Pierce, FL [FM radio station call letters] (BROA) ..... WLDI-FM
Fort Worth, TX [AM radio station call letters] (BROA) ..... KBCM
Fort Worth, TX [Television station call letters] (BROA) ..... KTVT-DT
Fort Worth, TX [Television station call letters] (BROA) ..... KXAS-DT
Fort Worth, TX [AM radio station call letters] (BROA) ..... KZMP
Fortune Natural Res [AMEX symbol] (SG) ..... FPX
Fossa (MELL) ..... F
Fossa of Vestibule of Vagina [Medicine] (MELL) ..... FVV
Foster Care (MELL) ..... FC
Foundation (BEE) ..... fdn
Foundation for the Study of the Arts and Crafts Movement at Roycroft
(EA) ..... FSA/CM
Foundation Health Systems'A' [NYSE symbol] (SG) ..... FHS
Founder (PROS) ..... fdr
Fountain Powerboat Ind [NASDAQ symbol] (SG) ..... FPWR
Four Seasons Hotels [NYSE symbol] (SG) ..... FS
Four Times a Day [Medicine] (MELL) 4/d
Four-Cylinder [Engine] 4CYL
Four-Door [Automobile] 4-DR
Fourier Transform Infrared ..... FTIR
Fourier Transform Microwave ..... FTM
Fourier Transform Microwave Spectroscopy ..... FTMS
Fourier Transform-Infrared Reflection Absorption Spectroscopy ..... FT-IRAS
Fourth World Documentation Project [Center for World Indigenous Studies]
[Internet resource] ..... FWDP
Fovea Centralis (MELL) ..... FC
Fox Entertainment Grp 'A' [NYSE symbol] (SG) ..... FOX
Fox Farm, WY [AM radio station call letters] (BROA) ..... KKWY
Foxhound Club of North America (EA) ..... FCNA
FPIC Insurance Grp [NASDAQ symbol] (SG) ..... FPIC
Fractional Tubular Reabsorption [Medicine] (MELL) ..... FTR
Fractocumulus Cloud (WEAT) ..... Fc
Fractostratus Cloud (WEAT) ..... Fs
Fracture (MELL) ..... Fx
Fracture Site (MELL) ..... FS
Fragile X Foundation (MELL) ..... FXF
Fragrant ..... Fra
France Telecom ADS [NYSE symbol] (SG) ..... FTE
Franchise Mtge Acceptance [NASDAQ symbol] (SG) ..... FMAX
Frank Breech Presentation [Medicine] (MELL) ..... FBB
Frank Orthogonal System [Medicine] (MELL) ..... FOS
Franklin Electric [NASDAQ symbol] (SG) ..... FELE
Franklin Mint ..... FM
Franklin Telecommunications [AMEX symbol] (SG) ..... FCM
Franklin, TX [FM radio station call letters] (BROA) ..... KZTR-FM
Franklinton, LA [FM radio station call letters] (BROA) ..... WFCG-FM
FREDDIE MAC 6.688%'98 Debs [NYSE symbol] (SG) ..... FWG
Fredericksburg, TX [Television station call letters] (BROA) ..... KBEJ
Fredericksburg, WA [AM radio station call letters] (BROA) ..... WYSK
Frederiksted, VI [AM radio station call letters] (BROA) ..... WDHP
Frederiksted, VI [FM radio station call letters] (BROA) ..... WPPD-FM
Fredonia, KS [FM radio station call letters] (BROA) ..... KGGF-FM
Free and Full Range of Motion (MELL) ..... FFROM
Free Erythrocyte Protoporphyrin [Medicine] (MELL) ..... FEB

Free Gingiva (MELL) ..... FG
Free Tendon Graft [Medicine] (MELL) ..... FTG
Free Testosterone (MELL) ..... FT
Free Tissue Transfer [Medicine] (MELL) ..... FTT
Free Vascularized Bone Graft [Medicine] (MELL) ..... FVBG
Free-Air Carbon Dioxide Enrichment (QUAC) ..... FACE
Freedom from Relapse (MELL) ..... FFR
Freedom Securities [NYSE symbol] (SG) ..... FSI
Freehold Township, NJ [FM radio station call letters] (BROA) ..... WPDQ-FM
Freeland, PA [FM radio station call letters] (BROA) ..... WILP-FM
Freeman (GEAB) ..... freem
Freeserve plc ADS [NASDAQ symbol] (SG) ..... FREE
Freeze-Fracturing ..... FF
Fremont, CA [FM radio station call letters] (BROA) ..... KLDZ-FM
Fremont Genl [NYSE symbol] (SG) ..... FMT
French (BEE) ..... Fr
Frequency-Selective Saturation [Medicine] (MELL) ..... FSS
Frequentative (BEE) ..... freq
Fresenius Medical AG ADS [NYSE symbol] (SG) ..... FMS
Fresh Del Monte Produce [NYSE symbol] (SG) ..... FDP
Fresh Water (MELL) ..... fw
Fresno, CA [FM radio station call letters] (BROA) ..... KALZ-FM
Friede Goldman Intl. [NYSE symbol] (SG) ..... FGI
Friedman Billings Ramsey Gp'A' [NYSE symbol] (SG) ..... FBR
Friends' Health Connection (EA) ..... FHC
Friends of Julio International (EA) ..... FOJI
Friends of Mineralogy ..... FM
Friends of the Cassidys [An association] (EA) ..... FOCFC
Frog Leg Position [Medicine] (MELL) ..... FLP
Front Motor Mount [Automotive term] ..... FMM
Frontal Lobe of Cerebrum [Medicine] (MELL) ..... FLC
Frontier Oil [NYSE symbol] (SG) ..... FTO
Frontozygomatic Suture [Medicine] (MELL) ..... FZS
Frostbite (MELL) ..... FB
Frost-Free Season (QUAC) ..... FFS
Frozen Embryo Transfer [Medicine] ..... FET
Frozen Shoulder (MELL) ..... FS
Fructooligosaccharides [Type of carbohydrate] ..... FOS
Fructose Intolerance (MELL) ..... FI
Fruits ..... frs
FTI Consulting [AMEX symbol] (SG) ..... FCN
Fudan University [China] ..... FU
Full Knee Extension (MELL) ..... FKE
Full Lower Denture (MELL) ..... FLD
Full Range of Movements (MELL) ..... FROM
Full Upper Denture (MELL) ..... FUD
Full-Term Pregnancy (MELL) ..... FTP
Full-Term Spontaneous Delivery [Medicine] (MELL) ..... FTSD
Full-Text Retrieval System (MELL) ..... FTRS
Full-Thickness Burn (MELL) ..... FTB
Full-Time Outservice (MELL) ..... FTOS
Fulminating Infection [Medicine] (MELL) ..... FI
Fulminating Meningococcemia [Medicine] (MELL) ..... FMC
Functional Acquisition Specialist [Army] ..... FAS
Functional Assessment of Cancer Therapy (MELL) ..... FACT
Functional Bladder Syndrome [Medicine] (MELL) ..... FBS
Functional Residual Capacity (MELL) ..... FRC
Fund for Appalachian Industrial Restraining ..... FAIR
Fundus (MELL) ..... F
Fungal Immunodiffusion [Medicine] (MELL) ..... FID
Fungal Infection (MELL) ..... FI
Fungiform Papilla [Medicine] (MELL) ..... FFP
Fungiform Papilla [Medicine] (MELL) ..... FP
Funnel Chest (MELL) ..... FC
Fuquay-Varina, NC [FM radio station call letters] (BROA) ..... WNNL-FM
Furnishing (BEE) ..... furn
Furuncular Myiasis [Medicine] (MELL) ..... FM
Fused Apophyseal Joint [Medicine] (MELL) ..... FAJ
Fused Deposition Modeling ..... FDM
Future Scout and Cavalry System [Army] ..... FSCS
FVC.com, Inc. [NASDAQ symbol] (SG) ..... FVCX

G
By Meaning

g02net, Inc. [*NASDAQ symbol*] (SG) ... GNET
Gabelli Asset Management'A' [*NYSE symbol*] (SG) ... GBL
Gabon (MILB) ... Gbn
Gadsden, AL [*FM radio station call letters*] (BROA) ... WTBB-FM
Gaelic (BEE) ... Gael
Gainesville, TX [*FM radio station call letters*] (BROA) ... KDOS-FM
Galactic Cosmic Ray [*Astronomy*] ... GCR
Galax, VA [*AM radio station call letters*] (BROA) ... WWWJ
GalaxiWorld.com [*NASDAQ symbol*] (SG) ... GLXW
Galaxy Evolution Explorer ... GALEX
Galea Aponeurotica (MELL) ... GA
Galeazzi Fracture-Dislocation [*Medicine*] (MELL) ... GFD
Galena, KS [*FM radio station call letters*] (BROA) ... KBGZ-FM
Galesburg, IL [*FM radio station call letters*] (BROA) ... WLSR-FM
Galileo Intl. [*NYSE symbol*] (SG) ... GLC
Galileo Technology [*NASDAQ symbol*] (SG) ... GALT
Galion, OH [*FM radio station call letters*] (BROA) ... WGLN-FM
Gallaher Group ADS [*NYSE symbol*] (SG) ... GLH
Gallon ... Gal
Gallons per Minute ... Gpm
Gallup, NM [*FM radio station call letters*] (BROA) ... KBFF-FM
Gambia (MILB) ... Gam
Gamekeeper Thumb (MELL) ... GT
Gamma Alpha (EA) ... GA
Gamma Globulinemia [*Medicine*] (MELL) ... GG
Gamma Sigma Delta (EA) ... GSD
Gamma-Ray Large Area Space Telescope ... GLAST
Gamma-Site Amyloid Precursor Protein-Cleaving Enzyme ... GACE
Gangliocytic Paraganglioma [*Medicine*] (MELL) ... GP
Ganglion of Facial Nerve [*Medicine*] (MELL) ... GFN
Garaged [*Automobile*] ... GAR
Garden (BEE) ... gar
Garden City, MO [*FM radio station call letters*] (BROA) ... KGAR-FM
Gardeners of America (EA) ... GOA
Gardner Denver [*NYSE symbol*] (SG) ... GDI
Gardner-Wells Tongs (MELL) ... GWT
Gas Chemical Sterlization (MELL) ... GCS
Gas Gangrene (MELL) ... GG
Gas Imaging Spectrometer ... GIS
Gas Insufflation (MELL) ... GI
Gas-Bloat Syndrome [*Medicine*] (MELL) ... GBS
Gas-Forming Bacteria (MELL) ... GFB
Gastric Acid (MELL) ... GA
Gastric Bypass Surgery (MELL) ... GBS
Gastric Lavage [*Medicine*] (MELL) ... GL
Gastric Lymph Node [*Medicine*] (MELL) ... GLN
Gastric Polyp [*Medicine*] (MELL) ... GP
Gastric Tonometry [*Medicine*] (MELL) ... GT
Gastric Vertical Stapling [*Medicine*] (MELL) ... GVS
Gastrin-Releasing Factor [*Medicine*] (MELL) ... GRF
Gastrocolic Ligament [*Medicine*] (MELL) ... GCL
Gastroduodenal Artery (MELL) ... GDA
Gastroepiploic Artery Graft [*Medicine*] (MELL) ... GEAG
Gastrointestinal Anthrax [*Medicine*] (MELL) ... GIA
Gastrointestinal Bleeding from Aspirin (MELL) ... GIBA
Gastrointestinal Disease (MELL) ... GID
Gastrointestinal Disorder (MELL) ... GID
Gastrointestinal Fistula [*Medicine*] (MELL) ... GIF
Gastrointestinal Myiasis [*Medicine*] (MELL) ... GIM
Gastrointestinal Obstruction [*Medicine*] (MELL) ... GIO
Gastrophrenic Ligament (MELL) ... GPL
Gastrulation (MELL) ... G
Gatesville, TX [*FM radio station call letters*] (BROA) ... KBDE-FM
Gateway, Inc. [*NYSE symbol*] (SG) ... GTW
Gateway Western Railway Co. ... GWWR
Gaucher's Disease (MELL) ... GD
Gauze Dressing (MELL) ... GD
Gay Airline and Travel Club (EA) ... GATC
Gay and Homosexually Active ... GHA
Gay and Lesbian History Stamp Club (EA) ... GLHSC
Gay and Lesbian Veterinary Association [*Australia*] (GVA) ... GALVA
Gays and Lesbians in Foreign Affairs [*An association*] (EA) ... GLFA
Gel Diffusion Precipitin [*Medicine*] (MELL) ... GDF
Gem Artists of North America ... GANA
Gemstar Intl. Group [*NASDAQ symbol*] (SG) ... GMST
Gender (MELL) ... g
Gene Expression Regulation [*Medicine*] (MELL) ... GER
Gene Pitney International Fan Club (EA) ... GPIFC
Gene Therapy (MELL) ... GT
Gene Therapy Advisory Committee (GVA) ... GTAC
Genealogical Library Catalog (GEAB) ... GLC
Genealogical Periodical Annual Index (GEAB) ... GPAI
General Aviation Recovery Devices ... GARD
General Body Weakness (MELL) ... GBW
General Dynamics Ordnance Systems ... GDOS
General Occupational Classification ... GOC
General Packet Radio Service ... GPRS
General Physician (MELL) ... GP
General Purpose Channel Interface ... GPCI
General Service Employees Union Local 73 (EA) ... UAWIU
General Watch Co. ... GWC
Generalized Autoregressive Conditional Heteroskedasticy Process ... GARCH
Generalized Lymphoid Hyperplasia [*Medicine*] (MELL) ... GLH
Generalized Mixed Models ... GMM
Generalized Nash-Equilibrium [*Game*] ... GNE
Generalized Thyroid Hormone Resistance [*Medicine*] (MELL) ... GTHR
Generalized Tonic-Clonic Seizure [*Medicine*] (MELL) ... GTCS
Generalized Work Distress Scale (MELL) ... GWDS
Generals Dynamics Land Systems ... GDLS
Generic Data Exemption (EPAT) ... GDE
Geneseo, IL [*FM radio station call letters*] (BROA) ... KQLI-FM
Genesis Microchip [*NASDAQ symbol*] (SG) ... GNSS
Genesys Telecommunications [*NASDAQ symbol*] (SG) ... GCTI
Genetic Code (MELL) ... GC
Genetic Counseling (MELL) ... GC
Genetic Disorder (MELL) ... GD
Genetic Linkage Map [*Medicine*] (MELL) ... GLM
Genetic Recombination [*Medicine*] (MELL) ... GR
Genetic Screening (MELL) ... GS
Genetic Screening Test (MELL) ... GST
Genetic Transduction (MELL) ... GT
Genetically Determined Immunodeficiency Disease (MELL) ... GDID
Genetically Engineered Drug (MELL) ... GED
Genetronics Biomedical [*Toronto Stock Exchange symbol*] (SG) ... GEB
Geniohyoid Muscle (MELL) ... GHM
Genital Warts (MELL) ... GW
Genitofemoral Nerve [*Medicine*] (MELL) ... GFN
Genitourinary Tract [*Medicine*] (MELL) ... GUT
Genome Analysis (MELL) ... GA
Genome Sequence Centre ... GSC
Genomic Imprinting (MELL) ... GI
Genomic Library (MELL) ... GL
Genset ADR [*NASDAQ symbol*] (SG) ... GENXY
GenTek, Inc. [*NYSE symbol*] (SG) ... GK
Genu Valgum (MELL) ... GV
Genu Varum (MELL) ... GV
Geographic Information Systems Interest Group (GEOI) ... CISIG
Geographic Tongue [*Medicine*] (MELL) ... GT
Geographical Analysis Machine ... GAM
Geological Association of Canada (QUAC) ... GAC
Geology (BEE) ... Geol
Geomagnetic Observing System (EOSA) ... GOS
Geometric Mean Titer of Controls (MELL) ... GMTC
Geometry (BEE) ... Geom
Geomorphic Response Unit (QUAC) ... GRU
Georgetown, DE [*AM radio station call letters*] (BROA) ... WJWL
Georgetown, KY [*AM radio station call letters*] (BROA) ... WTKT
Georgia Kindergarten Assessment Program ... GKAP
Geoscience Laser Altimeter System (EOSA) ... GLAS
Geoscience Laser Ranging System-Altimeter (EOSA) ... GLRS-A
Geoscience Laser Ranging System-Ranger (EOSA) ... GLRS-R
Geosphere-Biosphere Models (QUAC) ... GBM
Geosphere-Biosphere Observatories (QUAC) ... GBO
Geosynchronous Meteorology Satellite (EOSA) ... METEOSAT
Gerber Childrenswear [*NYSE symbol*] (SG) ... GCW
Gerdau S.A. ADS [*NYSE symbol*] (SG) ... GGB
Geriatric Assessment (MELL) ... GA
Geriatric Medicine (MELL) ... GM
Gering, NE [*FM radio station call letters*] (BROA) ... KOLT-FM
Germ Cell Cancer (MELL) ... GCC
Germ Line [*Medicine*] (MELL) ... GL
German Measles (MELL) ... GM

Germanic (BEE) .... Gmc
Germantown, TN [*FM radio station call letters*] (BROA) .... WKSL-FM
Germantown, TN [*AM radio station call letters*] (BROA) .... WOWW
Germany (MILB) .... Ge
Germ-Free Life (MELL) .... GFL
Gesellschaft fuer Biotechnologische Forschung mbH [*Germany*] .... GBF
Gestational Carbohydrate Intolerance [*Medicine*] (MELL) .... GCI
Gestational Diabetes (MELL) .... GD
Gestational Edema with Proteinuria and Hypertension [*Medicine*] (MELL) .... GEPH
Gestational Glaucoma (MELL) .... GG
Gestational Hypotension [*Medicine*] (MELL) .... GH
Gestational Stress Incontinence [*Medicine*] (MELL) .... GSI
Gestational Trophoblastic Carcinoma [*Medicine*] (MELL) .... GTC
Gestational Trophoblastic Tumor [*Medicine*] (MELL) .... GTT
Getty Petroleum Mktg. [*NYSE symbol*] (SG) .... GPM
Getty Realty [*NYSE symbol*] (SG) .... GTY
Ghana (MILB) .... Gha
Ghost Surgery (MELL) .... GS
Giant Cell Pneumonia [*Medicine*] (MELL) .... GCP
Giant Follicular Cell Lymphoma [*Medicine*] (MELL) .... GFCL
Giant Intestinal Fluke [*Medicine*] (MELL) .... GIF
Giant Pyramidal Cell (MELL) .... GPC
Giant Urticaria [*Medicine*] (MELL) .... GU
Giant-Cell Sarcoma (MELL) .... GCS
Gibsland, LA [*FM radio station call letters*] (BROA) .... KBEF-FM
Gifford, FL [*FM radio station call letters*] (BROA) .... WAVW-FM
Gigahertz .... GHz
Gildan Activewear'A' [*AMEX symbol*] (SG) .... GIL
Gingival Fibromatosis [*Medicine*] (MELL) .... GF
Gingival Hyperplasia [*Medicine*] (MELL) .... GH
Gingival Index (MELL) .... GI
Gingivectomy [*Medicine*] (MELL) .... GV
Girard-Perregaux .... GP
Girdwood, AK [*FM radio station call letters*] (BROA) .... KEUL-FM
Girls in National Alliance [*An association*] .... GINA
Glacial Acetic Acid Test (MELL) .... GAAT
Gladstone, MI [*FM radio station call letters*] (BROA) .... WGKL-FM
Gland (MELL) .... G
Gland (MELL) .... GL
Glandular Cancer (MELL) .... GC
Glandular Fever [*Medicine*] (MELL) .... GF
Glasgow University Veterinary Medical Association (GVA) .... GUVMA
Glasgow University Veterinary Zoological Society (GVA) .... GUVZS
Glassblower's Cataract (MELL) .... GBC
Glassy Cell Carcinoma (MELL) .... GCC
Glendale, AZ [*FM radio station call letters*] (BROA) .... KWCY-FM
Glendo, WY [*FM radio station call letters*] (BROA) .... KUUY-FM
Glenoid Fossa [*Medicine*] (MELL) .... GF
Glens Fall, NY [*FM radio station call letters*] (BROA) .... WCQL-FM
Glens Falls, NY [*FM radio station call letters*] (BROA) .... WLJH-FM
Glens Falls, NY [*AM radio station call letters*] (BROA) .... WMML
Global Change Category (EOSA) .... GCC
Global Change Research Information Office (QUAC) .... GCRIO
Global Computer Model (WEAT) .... GCM
Global Crossing Ltd. [*NASDAQ symbol*] (SG) .... GBLX
Global Defense Initiative .... GDI
Global Employer's Network, Inc. .... GENI
Global Environmental Research (QUAC) .... GER
Global Food Animal Residue Avoidance Databank (GVA) .... gFARAD
Global Gecko Association (GVA) .... GGA
Global Imager (EOSA) .... GLI
Global Light Telecommun. [*AMEX symbol*] (SG) .... GBT
Global Mean Water Line (QUAC) .... GMWL
Global Positioning System Demonstration Receiver (EOSA) .... GPSDR
Global Remedy for the Environment and Energy Use--Technology Information Exchange .... GREENTIE
Global Services Management Platform [*Newbridge Network*] .... GSMP
Global TeleSystems Grp. [*NASDAQ symbol*] (SG) .... GTSG
Global Tropospheric Chemistry Experiment (EOSA) .... GTCE
Global Vacation Grp. [*NYSE symbol*] (SG) .... GVG
Global Warming (QUAC) .... GW
Global-Tech Appliances [*NYSE symbol*] (SG) .... GAI
Globe, AZ [*FM radio station call letters*] (BROA) .... KDDJ-FM
Glucagonoma Syndrome [*Medicine*] (MELL) .... GS
Glucose Intolerance (MELL) .... GI
Glucose Monophosphate [*Medicine*] (MELL) .... GMP
Glucose Uptake [*Medicine*] (MELL) .... GU
Glucose-Blood Level [*Medicine*] (MELL) .... GBL
Glucose-Fatty Acid Cycle (MELL) .... GFAC
Glucose-Lactase Tolerance Test [*Medicine*] (MELL) .... GLTT
Glutamate Dehydrogenase [*Medicine*] (MELL) .... GMD
Glutathione Reductase [*Medicine*] (MELL) .... GSR
Gluteus Compartment Syndrome (MELL) .... GCS
Gluteus Maximus Muscle (MELL) .... GMM
Glycerol Tolerant Gel [*Medicine*] (MELL) .... GTG
Glyceryl Trinitrate [*Medicine*] (MELL) .... GT
Glycocalyx [*Medicine*] (MELL) .... GC
Glycogen Synthesis [*Medicine*] (MELL) .... GS
Glycogen Synthetase Deficiency [*Medicine*] (MELL) .... GSD
Glycophorins (MELL) .... GP
Glycosylation Inhibition Factor [*Medicine*] (MELL) .... GIF
Goal of Treatment [*Medicine*] (MELL) .... GOT
Goat Veterinary Society (GVA) .... GVS
Goblet Cells [*Medicine*] (MELL) .... GC
Godfather (GEAB) .... godf
Godmother (GEAB) .... godm
Gold Filled [*Watch*] .... gf
Gold Inlay (MELL) .... GI
Gold Line [*Automotive tires*] .... GL
Gold Steel Titanium .... GST
Golden State Bancorp [*NYSE symbol*] (SG) .... GSB
Golden Triangle Ind. [*NASDAQ symbol*] (SG) .... GTLL
Goldman Sachs Group [*NYSE symbol*] (SG) .... GS
Gold-Veneer Crown (MELL) .... GVC
Goleta, CA [*FM radio station call letters*] (BROA) .... KKSB-FM
Golf Entertainment [*NASDAQ symbol*] (SG) .... GECC
Golf Trust of America [*AMEX symbol*] (SG) .... GTA
Gonorrheal Vaginitis [*Medicine*] (MELL) .... GV
Gordon's Biological Test (MELL) .... GBT
GoTo.com, Inc. [*NASDAQ symbol*] (SG) .... GOTO
Gouty Arthritis (MELL) .... GA
Gouty Nephropathy [*Medicine*] (MELL) .... GN
Gouty Node [*Medicine*] (MELL) .... GN
Gouverneur Bancorp [*AMEX symbol*] (SG) .... GOV
Government Computer Sales, Inc. .... GCSI
Government Information Sharing Project [*Internet resource*] .... GISP
Government of Argentina .... GOA
Government of Brazil .... GOB
Government of Cuba .... GOC
Government of France .... GOF
Government of Sri Lanka .... GOSL
Governor's Council on Alcoholism and Drug Abuse [*New Jersey*] .... GCADA
Gower's Muscular Dystrophy [*Medicine*] (MELL) .... GMD
GP Strategies [*NYSE symbol*] (SG) .... GPX
Grade Eight Proficiency Assessment .... GEPA
Graduate (GEAB) .... gr
Graduate Driver Licensing .... GDL
Graduate Realtors Institute .... GRI
Graduate Student Instructor .... GSI
Graduate Student Research Assistant .... GSRA
Graduate Student Staff Assistant .... GSSA
Graft-Versus Host Disease [*Medicine*] .... GVHD
Gram Negative Cocci [*Medicine*] (MELL) .... GNC
Gram Parsons Foundation (EA) .... GPF
Gram Stain [*Medicine*] (MELL) .... GS
Gram-Negative Diplococci [*Medicine*] (MELL) .... GNDC
Gram-Negative Infection [*Medicine*] (MELL) .... GNI
Gram-Negative Sepsis [*Medicine*] (MELL) .... GNS
Gram-Positive Bacilli (MELL) .... GPB
Gram-Positive Bacteria (MELL) .... GPB
Grand Canyon Visibility Transport Commission (EPAT) .... GCVTC
Grand Isle, LA [*FM radio station call letters*] (BROA) .... KBIL-FM
Grand Junction, CO [*FM radio station call letters*] (BROA) .... KBFE-FM
Grand Junction, CO [*AM radio station call letters*] (BROA) .... KKGJ
Grand Junction, CO [*Television station call letters*] (BROA) .... KRMJ
Grand Mal Convulsive Disorder [*Medicine*] (MELL) .... GMCD
Grand Rapids, MI [*FM radio station call letters*] (BROA) .... WAYG-FM
Grand Rapids, MI [*AM radio station call letters*] (BROA) .... WNWZ
Grandchildren (GEAB) .... gch
Grandfather (GEAB) .... grf
Grandmother (GEAB) .... gm
Grandmother (GEAB) .... grmo
Grandson (GEAB) .... grs
Granite Construction [*NYSE symbol*] (SG) .... GVA
Grant Funding Order (EPAT) .... GFO
Grants, NM [*FM radio station call letters*] (BROA) .... KQLV-FM
Granular Activated Carbon Treatment (EPAT) .... GACT
Granulocyte (MELL) .... G
Granulocytic Sarcoma [*Medicine*] (MELL) .... GS
Granulocytopenia [*Medicine*] (MELL) .... GCP
Granuloma Inguinale [*Medicine*] (MELL) .... GI
Granulomatous Lung Disease (MELL) .... GLD
Granulosa Lutein Cell [*Medicine*] (MELL) .... GLC
Granulose Cell Tumor (MELL) .... GCV
Gravitational Constant (MELL) .... g
Gravity Stress Test (MELL) .... GST
Gray, GA [*FM radio station call letters*] (BROA) .... WIBD-FM
Great (GEAB) .... g
Great Adductor Muscle [*Medicine*] (MELL) .... GAM
Great Bend, KS [*FM radio station call letters*] (BROA) .... KBDA-FM
Great Cephalic Vein [*Medicine*] (MELL) .... GCV
Great Falls, MT [*AM radio station call letters*] (BROA) .... KQDI
Great Internet Mersenne Prime Search .... GIMPS
Great Lakes REIT [*NYSE symbol*] (SG) .... GL
Great Lakes-St. Lawrence Basin (QUAC) .... GLSLB
Great Plains Software [*NYSE symbol*] (SG) .... GPSI
Great Plains Veterinary Educational Center [*University of Nebraska*] (GVA) .... GPVEC
Greater Palatine Foramen (MELL) .... GPF
Greater Pectoral Muscle (MELL) .... GPM
Greater Sciatic Foramen [*Medicine*] (MELL) .... GSF
Greater Sciatic Notch [*Medicine*] (MELL) .... GSN
Greater Sulphur Crested Cockatoo [*Bird*] .... GSC
Greater-Vestibular Gland (MELL) .... GVG
Grebe Syndrome [*Medicine*] (MELL) .... GS
Greece (MILB) .... Gr
Greek (BEE) .... Gk
Green Bay Packers [*National Football League*] [*1921-present*] (NFLA) .... BG
Green Bay, WI [*FM radio station call letters*] (BROA) .... WEMY-FM

Green Cheeked Conure [*Bird*] .... GC
Green River, WY [*FM radio station call letters*] (BROA) .... KFRZ-FM
Greencastle, PA [*FM radio station call letters*] (BROA) .... WCHA-FM
Greenfield, IN [*FM radio station call letters*] (BROA) .... WRGF-FM
Greenhouse Effect Detection Experiment (EOSA) .... GEDEX
Greenhouse Gases .... GHG
Greensboro, NC [*AM radio station call letters*] (BROA) .... WEAL
Greensburg, IN [*FM radio station call letters*] (BROA) .... WAUZ-FM
Greenstick Fracture [*Medicine*] (MELL) .... GF
Greenstick Fracture [*Medicine*] (MELL) .... GSF
Greenville, MS [*Television station call letters*] (BROA) .... WDTL-TV
Greenwood, IN [*FM radio station call letters*] (BROA) .... WBKS-FM
Greenwood, MS [*Television station call letters*] (BROA) .... WABG-TV
Greenwood, SC [*FM radio station call letters*] (BROA) .... WCRS-FM
Greer, SC [*FM radio station call letters*] (BROA) .... WOLT-FM
Gregory, TX [*FM radio station call letters*] (BROA) .... KBHD-FM
Gross Air Dried .... GAD
Gross as Received .... GAR
Gross Income Multiplier [*Business term*] .... GIM
Ground Frost (WEAT) .... GF
Ground Substance [*Medicine*] (MELL) .... GS
Ground Surface Temperature Histories (QUAC) .... GSTH
Groundwater Protection Strategy [*Environmental science*] (EPAT) .... GWPS
Group (MELL) .... g
Group 1 Automotive [*NYSE symbol*] (SG) .... GPI
Group Army (MILB) .... GA
Group Legal Services Organization .... GLSO
Grove Property Trust [*NYSE symbol*] (SG) .... GVE
Grover City, CA [*FM radio station call letters*] (BROA) .... KQJZ-FM
Growth Factor Receptors (MELL) .... GFR
Growth Failure (MELL) .... GF

Growth Hormone Inhibiting Hormone (MELL) .... GHIH
Growth Plate (MELL) .... GP
Growth Plate Injury (MELL) .... GPI
Gruma S.A. ADS [*NYSE symbol*] (SG) .... GMK
GSE Systems [*AMEX symbol*] (SG) .... GVP
GST Telecommunications [*NASDAQ symbol*] (SG) .... GSTX
GTO Association of America (EA) .... GTOAA
Guard (MILB) .... gd
Guardian (GEAB) .... gdn
Guardian Royal Exchange [*Great Britain*] .... GRE
Guatemala (MILB) .... Gua
Guess, Inc. [*NYSE symbol*] (SG) .... GES
Guest Supply [*NYSE symbol*] (SG) .... GSY
Guidaut Defibrillator [*Medicine*] (MELL) .... GDF
Guide Catheter [*Medicine*] (MELL) .... GC
Guide to Available Mathematical Software [*Internet resource*] .... GAMS
Guinea (MILB) .... Gui
Guinea-Bissau (MILB) .... GuB
Guitar Center [*NASDAQ symbol*] (SG) .... GTRC
Gulf Indonesia Resources [*NYSE symbol*] (SG) .... GRL
Gulfport, MS [*FM radio station call letters*] (BROA) .... WAOY-FM
Gulfstream Aeorspace [*NYSE symbol*] (SG) .... GAC
Gundle/SLT Environmental [*NYSE symbol*] (SG) .... GSE
Gun-Launch to Space .... GLTS
Gunshot Fracture [*Medicine*] (MELL) .... GSF
Gunstock Deformity [*Medicine*] (MELL) .... GSD
Gurkha Ex-Servicemen's Organisation .... GESO
Guyana (MILB) .... Guy
Gym Itch (MELL) .... GI
Gymnast's Wrist (MELL) .... GW
Gynecologic Oncology Group (MELL) .... GOG

By Meaning

H
By Meaning

Habib Bank Limited [*Pakistan*] .... HBL
Hagler Bailly [*NASDAQ symbol*] (SG) .... HBIX
Haglund Deformity [*Medicine*] (MELL) .... HD
Hahns Macaw [*Bird*] .... HM
Hain Food Group [*Toronto Stock Exchange symbol*] (SG) .... HAIN
Hair (MELL) .... H
Hair Follicle (MELL) .... HF
Hairy Leukemia (MELL) .... HL
Half Disappearance Time (MELL) .... HDT
Hallettsville, TX [*FM radio station call letters*] (BROA) .... KTXM-FM
Hallucis (MELL) .... H
Hallux Valgus Orthosis [*Medicine*] (MELL) .... HVO
HA-LO Industries [*NYSE symbol*] (SG) .... HMK
Halo Test [*Medicine*] (MELL) .... HT
Halothane Anesthia [*Medicine*] (MELL) .... HA
Hambrecht & Quist Group [*NYSE symbol*] (SG) .... HQ
Hamilton, MT [*FM radio station call letters*] (BROA) .... KBEB-FM
Hamilton, ON [*FM radio station call letters*] (BROA) .... CIOI-FM
Hamman-Rich Syndrome [*Medicine*] (MELL) .... HRS
Hammered Aluminum Collectors Association (EA) .... HACA
Hampton, VA [*AM radio station call letters*] (BROA) .... WBYM
Hamster Egg Penetration Assay .... HEPA
Hamstring (MELL) .... HS
Hanceville, AL [*AM radio station call letters*] (BROA) .... WXRP
Hancock, MI [*FM radio station call letters*] (BROA) .... WMPL-FM
Handage (MELL) .... H
Handlebar Palsy [*Medicine*] (MELL) .... HBP
Hand-Schueller-Christlan Disease (MELL) .... HSCD
Hanging Arm Cast (MELL) .... HAC
Hanging Cast (MELL) .... HC
Hangman's Fracture [*Medicine*] (MELL) .... HF
Hank's Dilator [*Medicine*] (MELL) .... HD
Hannah's Prayer [*Christian infertility/pregnancy loss group*] .... HP
Hanover Capital Mtg. [*AMEX symbol*] (SG) .... HCM
Hanover Compressor [*NYSE symbol*] (SG) .... HC
Haploidentical Bone Marrow Transplantation [*Medicine*] (MELL) .... HBMT
Harbour View .... h/v
Hard Cancer (MELL) .... HC
Hard Palate [*Medicine*] (MELL) .... HP
Hard to Find [*Collectibles*] .... HTF
Hardgrove Grindability Index .... HGI
Hardtop .... HDTP
Hardware (BEE) .... hdwr
Harker Heights, TX [*FM radio station call letters*] (BROA) .... KYUL-FM
Harrisburg, AR [*FM radio station call letters*] (BROA) .... KBGQ-FM
Harrisburg, PA [*Television station call letters*] (BROA) .... WITF-DT
Harrisburg, PA [*FM radio station call letters*] (BROA) .... WRBT-FM
Harrison, AR [*Television station call letters*] (BROA) .... KWBM
Harrisonburg, VA [*AM radio station call letters*] (BROA) .... WEZI
Hartford, CT [*FM radio station call letters*] (BROA) .... WTIC-FM
Hartford Finl Svcs Gp. [*NYSE symbol*] (SG) .... HIG
Hartford Life 'A' [*NYSE symbol*] (SG) .... HLI
Hartnup Disease [*Medicine*] (MELL) .... HD
Harvard Medical School .... HMS
Harvard Pump [*Medicine*] (MELL) .... HP
Harvard School of Public Health (MELL) .... HSPH
Harwichport, MA [*FM radio station call letters*] (BROA) .... WYST-FM
Harwood, ND [*FM radio station call letters*] (BROA) .... KRKH-FM
Hastings, NE [*FM radio station call letters*] (BROA) .... KBGT-FM
Hastings, NE [*FM radio station call letters*] (BROA) .... KROR-FM
Hatchback .... HBK
Hatchback .... HTBK
Hatfield, AR [*FM radio station call letters*] (BROA) .... KBII-FM
Havelock, NC [*FM radio station call letters*] (BROA) .... WANG-FM
Hawaii (BEE) .... Haw
Hayden, CO [*FM radio station call letters*] (BROA) .... KBDU-FM
Haygarth's Node [*Medicine*] (MELL) .... HN
Hazardous Air Pollutant (QUAC) .... HAP
Hazardous Substance (MELL) .... HS
Hazleton, PA [*Television station call letters*] (BROA) .... WOLF-TV
HCR Manor Care [*NYSE symbol*] (SG) .... HCR
Head Balter Traction (MELL) .... HHT
Head Injury Unit (MELL) .... HIU
Head of Epididymis [*Medicine*] (MELL) .... HOE
Head of Fetus (MELL) .... HF
Headland, AL [*FM radio station call letters*] (BROA) .... WBCD-FM

Heads of European Veterinary Regulatory Agencies (GVA) .... HEVRA
Health and Safety Laboratory .... HSL
Health Care Worker (MELL) .... HCW
Health Insurance Plan (MELL) .... HIP
Health Insurance Portability & Accountability Act .... HIPAA
Health Insurance Portability and Accountability Act of 1996 .... HIPAA
Health Maintenance Program (MELL) .... HMP
Health Scientist Administrator (MELL) .... HSA
Health Security Act (MELL) .... HSA
Health-Care Power of Attorney [*Medicine*] (MELL) .... HCPA
Healthcare Recoveries [*NASDAQ symbol*] (SG) .... HCRI
Hearing and Speech (MELL) .... H & S
Hearne, TX [*FM radio station call letters*] (BROA) .... KVJM-FM
Hearst, ON [*FM radio station call letters*] (BROA) .... CINN-FM
Heart Catheterization (MELL) .... HC
Heart Sounds Normal [*Medicine*] (MELL) .... HSN
Heartburn (MELL) .... HB
Hearts in Harmony - World Family of John Denver [*An association*]
  (EA) .... HIH-WFJD
Heat Capacity Mapping Mission/Applications Explorer Mission-1
  (EOSA) HCMM/AEM-1
Heat Coagulation Test (MELL) .... HCT
Heat Exhaustion (MELL) .... HE
Heat Rash (MELL) .... HR
Heat Therapy (MELL) .... HT
Heat Transfer Division .... HTD
Heated Serum Reagin [*Medicine*] (MELL) .... HSR
Heat-Labile Enterotoxin [*Medicine*] (MELL) .... HLE
Heavener, OK [*FM radio station call letters*] (BROA) .... KPRV-FM
Heavy (MILB) .... hy
Heavy Armored Combat Vehicle (MILB) .... HACV
Heavy Chain Deposition [*Medicine*] (MELL) .... HCD
Heavy Chain Gene Rearrangement [*Medicine*] (MELL) .... HCGR
Heavy Equipment Recovery Combat Utility Lift and Evacuation System
  [*Military*] .... HERCULES
Heavy Metal Poisoning (MELL) .... HMP
Heavy-Duty Diesel Truck (EPAT) .... HDDT
Heavy-Duty Gasoline Truck (EPAT) .... HDGT
Hebronville, TX [*FM radio station call letters*] (BROA) .... KEKO-FM
Hectopascals (WEAT) .... hPa
Hector Communications [*AMEX symbol*] (SG) .... HCT
Heel Pain Syndrome (MELL) .... HPS
Heimlich Maneuver [*Medicine*] (MELL) .... HM
Heineke-Mikulicz Pyloroplasty [*Medicine*] (MELL) .... HMP
Heiress (GEAB) .... h
Helena, MT [*Television station call letters*] (BROA) .... KMTF
Helicobacter Pylori [*Medicine*] (MELL) .... HBP
Helicopter (MILB) .... hel
Heller Financial 'A' [*NYSE symbol*] (SG) .... HF
Heloma Molle [*Medicine*] (MELL) .... HM
Helsinki Commission .... HELCOM
Hemadsorbent (MELL) .... HA
Hematologic Disorder [*Medicine*] (MELL) .... HD
Hematologic Toxin [*Medicine*] (MELL) .... HT
Hematopoietic Cell Transplantation [*Medicine*] (MELL) .... HCT
Hemifacial Microsomia (MELL) .... HM
Hemispherx BioPharma [*AMEX symbol*] (SG) .... HEB
Hemizona Assay Index [*Medicine*] (MELL) .... HZI
Hemofiltration (MELL) .... HF
Hemoglobin Dissociation Curve [*Medicine*] (MELL) .... HDC
Hemoglobin Gene Loci [*Medicine*] (MELL) .... HGL
Hemolytic Disease [*Medicine*] (MELL) .... HD
Hemopexin [*Medicine*] (MELL) .... Hpx
Hemorrhage and Shock (MELL) .... H & S
Hemorrhagic Fever with Renal Stones [*Medicine*] (MELL) .... HFRS
Hemorrhoid (MELL) .... H
Hemothorax [*Medicine*] (MELL) .... HT
Hemothorax [*Medicine*] (MELL) .... HTX
Henderson, NV [*AM radio station call letters*] (BROA) .... KDOX
Henderson, NV [*FM radio station call letters*] (BROA) .... KMXB-FM
Henderson, NY [*FM radio station call letters*] (BROA) .... WOTT-FM
Henderson-Jones Chondromatosis [*Medicine*] (MELL) .... HJC
Henoch-Schonlein Purpura Nephritis [*Medicine*] (MELL) .... HSPN
Hensen's Node [*Medicine*] (MELL) .... HN
Heparin [*Medicine*] (MELL) .... H
Heparin Cofactor [*Medicine*] (MELL) .... HC

Hepatic Agenesis (MELL)	HA
Hepatic Angiosarcoma [Medicine] (MELL)	HAS
Hepatic Candidiasis [Medicine] (MELL)	HC
Hepatic Disease [Medicine] (MELL)	HD
Hepatic Fibrosis [Medicine] (MELL)	HF
Hepatic Hydatid Cyst [Medicine] (MELL)	HHC
Hepatic Hydatidosis [Medicine] (MELL)	HH
Hepatic Reticuloendothelial [Medicine] (MELL)	HRE
Hepatitis and Cirrhosis (MELL)	H & C
Hepatitis E Virus (MELL)	HEV
Hepatogastric Ligament [Medicine] (MELL)	HGM
Hepatoportal Sclerosis [Medicine] (MELL)	HPS
Herbalife Intl'A' [NASDAQ symbol] (SG)	HERBA
Hereditary Angioedema [Medicine] (MELL)	HAE
Hereditary Breast Ovarian Cancer (MELL)	HBOC
Hereditary Chronic Nephritis [Medicine] (MELL)	HCN
Hereditary Hemolytic Syndrome [Medicine] (MELL)	HHS
Hereditary Motor and Sensory Neuropathy [Medicine] (MELL)	HMSN
Hereditary Non-Polyposis Colorectal Cancer (MELL)	HNPCC
Hereditary, Sensory, and Autonomic Neuopathy [Medicine] (MELL)	HSAN
Herfindahl-Hirschmann Index [Economics]	HHI
Herniated Cervical Disk [Medicine] (MELL)	HCD
Herpes Simplex, Type 1 [Medicine]	HSV1
Herpes Simplex, Type 2 [Medicine]	HSV2
Herpes Simplex Virus Type 2	HSV2
Herpes Virus Sensitivity [Medicine] (MELL)	HVS
Herpes Zoster Acute Neuralgia [Medicine] (MELL)	HZAN
Herpes Zoster Infection [Medicine] (MELL)	HZI
Herpes Zoster Lesion [Medicine] (MELL)	HZL
Herpetic Whitlow [Medicine] (MELL)	HW
Hersha Hospitality Trust [AMEX symbol] (SG)	HT
Hertford, NC [FM radio station call letters] (BROA)	WFMZ-FM
Hertz Corp'A' [NYSE symbol] (SG)	HRZ
Heterologous (MELL)	HE
Heterologous Antibody Disease [Medicine] (MELL)	HAD
Heterosexual Male (MELL)	HSM
Heterotopic Kidney Transplant (MELL)	HKT
Hickory, NC [FM radio station call letters] (BROA)	WLYT-FM
Hickory, NC [FM radio station call letters] (BROA)	WPIR-FM
High Altitude Hypertrophic Cardiomyopathy Syndrome [Medicine] (MELL)	HHCS
High Altitude Syncope [Medicine] (MELL)	HAS
High Apgar Score [Medicine] (MELL)	HAS
High Energy Astrophysics Branch [NASA]	HEAB
High Energy Solar Spectroscopic Imager	HESSI
High Heels [Doll collecting]	HH
High Molecular Weight Component (MELL)	HMWC
High Neonatal Morality (MELL)	HNM
High Output Failure [Medicine] (MELL)	HOF
High Output Renal Failure [Medicine] (MELL)	HORF
High Oxygen Affinity (MELL)	HOA
High Performance	HiPerf
High Pressure Liquid Chromatographic	HPLC
High Red Cell Phosphatidylcholine Anemia [Medicine] (MELL)	HPCHA
High Resolution Interferometer Sounder (EOSA)	HIS
High Resolution Mirror Assembly	HRMA
High Resolution Optical Instrument (EOSA)	HROI
High Resolution Video (EOSA)	HRV
High School Proficiency Assessment	HSPA
High School Proficiency Test	HSPT
High Speed Access [NASDAQ symbol] (SG)	HSAC
High Speed Photometer	HSP
High Springs, FL [FM radio station call letters] (BROA)	WRKG-FM
High Touch Therapy (MELL)	HTT
High Tracheostomy [Medicine] (MELL)	HT
High-Altitude Retinopathy [Medicine] (MELL)	HAR
High-Calorie Diet (MELL)	HCD
High-Dose Chemotherapy [Medicine] (MELL)	HDC
High-Energy Radio Frequency	HERF
Higher Education Funding Council for Wales (GVA)	HEFCW
High-Grade Squamous Intraepithelial Lesion [Medicine] (MELL)	HGSIL
High-Grade Squamous Intraepithelial Lesions [Medicine]	HGSIL
Hig-Hinge Abduction Brace [Medicine] (MELL)	HHAB
Highland, IL [AM radio station call letters] (BROA)	WBDI
Highland Park, IL [FM radio station call letters] (BROA)	WXXY-FM
Highlands and Islands Veterinary Services Scheme (GVA)	HIVSS
High-Pitched Murmur [Medicine] (MELL)	HPM
High-Resolution Computed Tomography (MELL)	HRCT
High-Resolution Dynamics Limb Sounder (EOSA)	HIRDLS
High-Resolution Microwave Spectrometer Sounder (EOSA)	HIMSS
High-Risk Pregnancy (MELL)	HRP
High-Risk Premature Infant (MELL)	HRPI
Highway Miles	HWY MI
Hilar Cell Tumor [Medicine] (MELL)	HCL
Hilo, HI [Television station call letters] (BROA)	KHVO-DT
Hilum of Kidney (MELL)	HOK
Himalayan Climate Centre (QUAC)	HCC
Himalayan Interdisciplinary Paleoclimate Project (QUAC)	HIPP
Hindustani (BEE)	Hind
Hines Horticulture [NASDAQ symbol] (SG)	HORT
Hinged Knee Replacement Prosthesis (MELL)	HKRP
Hinged Penile Prosthesis [Medicine] (MELL)	HPP
Hip Dislocation (MELL)	HD
Hip Fracture (MELL)	HF
Hip Osteoarthritis [Medicine] (MELL)	HAO

Hip Prosthesis (MELL)	HP
Hippocratic Oath (MELL)	HO
Hippuric Acid (MELL)	HA
Hirsutism-Virilizing Syndromes [Medicine] (MELL)	HVS
Hispanic Male (MELL)	HM
Histamine Challenge [Medicine] (MELL)	HC
Histidinemethemoglobin [Medicine] (MELL)	H
Histiocytic Necrotizing Lymphadenitis [Medicine] (MELL)	HNL
Historia Mathematica [A publication]	
Historian (GEAB)	hist
Historical Canadian Climate Dataset (QUAC)	HCCD
Histrionic Personality Disorder [Medicine] (MELL)	HPD
Hoisington, KS [Television station call letters] (BROA)	KBDK
Holbrook, AZ [Television station call letters] (BROA)	KBCZ
Holevilla, AZ [FM radio station call letters] (BROA)	KUYI-FM
Holidaysburg, PA [FM radio station call letters] (BROA)	WMXV-FM
Holly Hill, FL [FM radio station call letters] (BROA)	WVYB-FM
Holly Pond, AL [FM radio station call letters] (BROA)	WXXR-FM
Hollywood Casino'A' [AMEX symbol] (SG)	HWD
Hollywood Entertainment [NASDAQ symbol] (SG)	HLYW
Hollywood, FL [Television station call letters] (BROA)	WAMI-TV
Hollywood Park [NYSE symbol] (SG)	HPK
Holmes Beach, FL [FM radio station call letters] (BROA)	WLLD-FM
Holmes-Adie Syndrome [Medicine] (MELL)	HAS
Holosystolic Murmur [Medicine] (MELL)	HM
Home Apnea Monitoring [Medicine] (MELL)	HAM
Home Health Services (MELL)	HHS
Home Incapacity Scale (MELL)	HIS
Home Infusion Therapy (MELL)	HIT
Home Intravenous Antibiotic Therapy (MELL)	HIVAT
Home Intravenous Therapy (MELL)	HIT
Home Phoneline Networking Alliance	HPNA
Home Prothrombin Time Monitoring [Medicine] (MELL)	HPTM
Home Security Intl. [AMEX symbol] (SG)	HSI
Home Service [British] (MILB)	HS
Home-Automated Peritoneal Dialysis [Medicine] (MELL)	HAPD
HomeBase, Inc. [NYSE symbol] (SG)	HBI
Homer, LA [FM radio station call letters] (BROA)	KYLA-FM
Homewood, AL [FM radio station call letters] (BROA)	WEDA-FM
Homologous (MELL)	HO
Homologous Blood Transfusion (MELL)	HBT
Homologous Restriction Factor [Medicine] (MELL)	HRF
Honduras (MILB)	Hr
Honeybees	Hon
Hong Kong Influenza (MELL)	HKI
Hong Kong Trade Development Council (EA)	HKTDC
Honolulu, HI [Television station call letters] (BROA)	KITV-DT
Honolulu, HI [FM radio station call letters] (BROA)	KMKP-FM
Honorable (GEAB)	hon
Honorably (GEAB)	honor
Honorary (GEAB)	honor
Hooks, TX [FM radio station call letters] (BROA)	KPWW-FM
Hookworm (MELL)	HW
Hoosick Falls, NY [FM radio station call letters] (BROA)	WZEC-FM
Hoover's Inc. [NASDAQ symbol] (SG)	HOOV
Horizon Mission Methodology [NASA]	HMM
Horizon Pharmacies [!AMX] (SG)	HZP
Horizontal Plane (MELL)	HP
Hormone Receptor (MELL)	HR
Horology Exquisite	Rolex
Horseshoe Abscess [Medicine] (MELL)	HSA
Horseshoe Kidney [Medicine] (MELL)	HSK
Hospice (MELL)	H
Hospital Arrival Time (MELL)	HAT
Hospital-Acquired Meningitis (MELL)	HAM
Hospital-Acquired Pneumonia (MELL)	HAP
Hospital-Acquired Respiratory Infection (MELL)	HARI
Hospital-Based Organ Procurement Agency (MELL)	HOPA
Hospitality Worldwide Svcs. [AMEX symbol] (SG)	HWS
Hospitalization not Indicated (MELL)	HNI
Host Cell Reactivation [Medicine] (MELL)	HCR
Host Defense Mechanism [Medicine] (MELL)	HDM
Host Terminal Data Server	HTDS
Hostile Cervical Mucus [Medicine] (MELL)	HCM
Hot Compress (MELL)	HC
Hot Cross Bun Skull (MELL)	HCBS
Hot Flashes (MELL)	HF
Hot Springs, AR [FM radio station call letters] (BROA)	KLXQ-FM
Hot Tub Lung (MELL)	HTL
Hot Wet Pack (MELL)	HWP
Hot Wheels [Mattel]	HW
Houghton, MI [FM radio station call letters] (BROA)	WHKB-FM
Houma, LA [FM radio station call letters] (BROA)	KUMX-FM
Housemaid's Knee (MELL)	HMK
Houston, AK [FM radio station call letters] (BROA)	KJHA-FM
Houston Industries 7 Percent,'ACES' [NYSE symbol] (SG)	HXT
Houston, MS [Television station call letters] (BROA)	WKDH
Houston Oilers [National Football League] [1960-96] (NFLA)	Hou
Houston, TX [AM radio station call letters] (BROA)	KBME
Houston, TX [Television station call letters] (BROA)	KHOU-DT
Houston, TX [Television station call letters] (BROA)	KPRC-DT
Houston, TX [Television station call letters] (BROA)	KRIV-DT
Houston, TX [Television station call letters] (BROA)	KTRK-DT
Hoverclub of America (EA)	HCA
Howitzer (MILB)	how

Howland, ME [*FM radio station call letters*] (BROA) .... WVOM-FM
Howmet International [*NYSE symbol*] (SG) .... HWM
HSB Group [*NYSE symbol*] (SG) .... HSB
HSBC Holdings ADS [*NYSE symbol*] (SG) .... HBC
Hubbard, OH [*FM radio station call letters*] (BROA) .... WBTJ-FM
Hudson River Bancorp [*NASDAQ symbol*] (SG) .... HRBT
Hudson United Bancorp [*NYSE symbol*] (SG) .... HU
Hudson's Bay Company Archives [*Canada*] (QUAC) .... HBCA
Hugoton Royalty Trust [*NYSE symbol*] (SG) .... HGT
Humalog (MELL) .... H
Human Albumin (MELL) .... HA
Human Fertilization Embryo Authority [*Great Britain*] .... HFEA
Human Genome [*Medicine*] (MELL) .... HG
Human Genome Management Information System .... HGMIS
Human Glucose Monitoring [*Medicine*] (MELL) .... HGM
Human Growth Hormone (MELL) .... HUGH
Human Neurophysin [*Medicine*] (MELL) .... HNP
Human Papillomavirus [*Medicine*] (MELL) .... HPVI
Human Platelet Suspension [*Medicine*] (MELL) .... HPS
Human T-cell Leukemia (MELL) .... HTL
Human Use Committee .... HUC
Humboldt, KS [*FM radio station call letters*] (BROA) .... KINZ-FM
Humeroscapular Periarthritis [*Medicine*] (MELL) .... HP
Humidity Mask (MELL) .... HM
Hummingbird .... Hum
Hummingbird Communications [*NASDAQ symbol*] (SG) .... HUMC
Hunchback (MELL) .... HB
Hundred (GEAB) .... hund
Hungary (MILB) .... Hu
Huntsville, MO [*FM radio station call letters*] (BROA) .... KROW-FM
Huntsville, TX [*AM radio station call letters*] (BROA) .... KHCH
Huntsville, TX [*FM radio station call letters*] (BROA) .... KUST-FM
Hurthle Cell Cancer (MELL) .... HCC
Husband (GEAB) .... hus
Husband-Coached Childbirth (MELL) .... HCC
Hussmann Intl. [*NYSE symbol*] (SG) .... HSM
Hutchinson, KS [*FM radio station call letters*] (BROA) .... KLSI-FM
Hutchinson, KS [*Television station call letters*] (BROA) .... KSCC
Hutto, TX [*FM radio station call letters*] (BROA) .... KQQQ-FM
Hydatid Cyst (MELL) .... HC
Hydesville, CA [*FM radio station call letters*] (BROA) .... KBHN-FM
Hydration (MELL) .... HYD
Hydrocarbon-Induced Neoplasm [*Medicine*] (MELL) .... HCIN
Hydrochloric Acid (MELL) .... HCl
Hydrocortisone Hemisuccinate [*Medicine*] (MELL) .... HCHS
Hydrofluorocarbon .... HFC
Hydrogen Breath Test (MELL) .... HBT
Hydrogen Ion Concentration [*Medicine*] (MELL) .... HIC
Hydrogen Peroxide (MELL) .... HP
Hydrogenated Starch Hydrolysates [*Medicine*] (MELL) .... HSH
Hydronephrosis [*Medicine*] (MELL) .... HN
Hydrostatic Permeability Edema [*Medicine*] (MELL) .... HPE
Hydroureter [*Medicine*] (MELL) .... HU
Hydroxyarachidonic Acid (MELL) .... HETE

Hydroxycorticoid (MELL) .... HOC
Hydroxysteroid Oxidoreductase [*Medicine*] (MELL) .... HSOR
Hygiene Assessment System [*British*] (GVA) .... HAS
Hyoglossus Muscle [*Medicine*] (MELL) .... HGM
Hyoid Bone (MELL) .... HB
Hyperactive Child (MELL) .... HAC
Hyperadrenocorticism [*Medicine*] (MELL) .... HAC
Hypercalcemic Nephropathy [*Medicine*] (MELL) .... HCN
Hypercarbic Respiratory Failure (MELL) .... HCRF
Hypercom Corp. [*NYSE symbol*] (SG) .... HYC
Hyperion Telecommunications 'A' [*NASDAQ symbol*] (SG) .... HYPT
Hyperkeratosis [*Medicine*] (MELL) .... HK
Hyperlipemia [*Medicine*] (MELL) .... HL
Hypernasal Speech (MELL) .... HNS
Hyperosmolar Coma (MELL) .... HOC
Hyperosmolar Nonacidotic Diabetes [*Medicine*] (MELL) .... HNAD
Hyperosmolar Nonketotic Coma [*Medicine*] (MELL) .... HNKC
Hyperostosis [*Medicine*] (MELL) .... HO
Hyperostosis Corticalis Deformans Invenilis [*Medicine*] (MELL) .... HCDJ
Hyperostosis Frontalis Interna [*Medicine*] (MELL) .... HFI
Hyperperistalsis [*Medicine*] (MELL) .... HP
Hyperplasia [*Medicine*] (MELL) .... HP
Hyperplastic Polyps [*Medicine*] (MELL) .... HPP
Hyper-Real-Time Simulation .... HRTS
Hypersensitive Carotid Sinus Syndrome (MELL) .... HCSS
Hypersensitivity Glomerular Disease [*Medicine*] (MELL) .... HGD
Hypertension (MELL) .... H
Hypertension, Anemia, Renal, Malabsorption [*Medicine*] (MELL) .... HARM
Hypertensive Arteriosclerotic Heart Disease (MELL) .... HASHD
Hypertensive Cardiovascular Disease (MELL) .... HTCVD
Hypertensive Intracranial Hemorrhage [*Medicine*] (MELL) .... HICH
Hypertonic Uterine Dysfunction [*Medicine*] (MELL) .... HUD
Hypertrophic Cicatrix [*Medicine*] (MELL) .... HTC
Hyperuricemic Nephropathy [*Medicine*] (MELL) .... HUN
Hypervitamintosis A [*Medicine*] (MELL) .... HVA
Hypocalcemia and Seizures (MELL) .... H & S
Hypoglossal Nerve [*Medicine*] (MELL) .... HGN
Hypokalemia [*Medicine*] (MELL) .... HK
Hypokalemic Alkalosis [*Medicine*] (MELL) .... HKA
Hypokalemic Periodic Paralysis [*Medicine*] (MELL) .... HPP
Hypophosphatemic Rickets [*Medicine*] (MELL) .... HPR
Hypoplastic Acute Leukemia [*Medicine*] (MELL) .... HAL
Hypothalamic Releasing Factor [*Medicine*] (MELL) .... HRF
Hypothalamic-Pituitary Dsyfunction [*Medicine*] (MELL) .... HPD
Hypothalamo-Hypophyseal Tract [*Medicine*] (MELL) .... HHT
Hypothenar Eminence [*Medicine*] (MELL) .... HTE
Hypotonic Uterine Dysfunction [*Medicine*] (MELL) .... HUD
Hypotropia [*Medicine*] (MELL) .... Hot
Hypoventilation and Cyanosis [*Medicine*] (MELL) .... H & C
Hypovolemic Shock [*Medicine*] (MELL) .... HVS
Hypoxic Pulmonary Vasoconstriction [*Medicine*] (MELL) .... HPVC
Hysteria and Repression (MELL) .... H & R
Hysterical Convulsions (MELL) .... HC
Hysterical Gait Disorder [*Medicine*] (MELL) .... HGD

By Meaning

I

By Meaning

I-Band (MELL) I
Iceland (MILB) Icl
ICG Communications [*NASDAQ symbol*] (SG) .... ICGX
ICH Corp. [*AMEX symbol*] (SG) .... IH
Ichthyosis Simplex [*Medicine*] (MELL) .... IS
Ictal Fear [*Medicine*] (MELL) .... IF
Idabel, OK [*FM radio station call letters*] (BROA) ...... KQIB-FM
Idacorp, Inc. [*NYSE symbol*] (SG) .... IDA
Idaho (BEE) .... Ida
Idiopathic Ankylosing Spondylitis [*Medicine*] (MELL) .... IAS
Idiopathic Aplastic Bone Marrow [*Medicine*] (MELL) ..... IABM
Idiopathic Autonomic Insufficiency [*Medicine*] (MELL) ... IAI
Idiopathic Central Nervous System Hypersommia [*Medicine*] (MELL) ...... ICNSH
Idiopathic Diffuse Fibrosis [*Medicine*] (MELL) .... IDF
Idiopathic Hirsutism [*Medicine*] (MELL) .... IH
Idiopathic Interstitial Pneumonitis [*Medicine*] (MELL) ... IIP
Idiopathic Juvenile Osteoporosis [*Medicine*] (MELL) ..... IJO
Idiopathic Neurologic Syndrome [*Medicine*] (MELL) ...... INS
Idiopathic Parkinsonism [*Medicine*] (MELL) .... IP
Idiopathic Pulmonary Hemosiderosis [*Medicine*] (MELL) .. IDP
Idiopathic Rapidly Progressive Glomerulonephritis [*Medicine*] (MELL) ...... IRPGN
Idiotype (MELL) .... ID
Ikon Office Solutions [*NYSE symbol*] (SG) .... IKN
Ileocecal Valve [*Medicine*] (MELL) ICV
Iliac Artery Aneurysm [*Medicine*] (MELL) .... IAA
Iliac Bone Graft [*Medicine*] (MELL) .... IBG
Iliac Crest [*Medicine*] (MELL) IC
Iliac Wing Fracture [*Medicine*] (MELL) .... IWF
Iliohypogastric Nerve [*Medicine*] (MELL) .... IHN
Iliolumbar Ligament [*Medicine*] (MELL) ILL
Illinois (BEE) Ill
Illinois Digital Academic Library .... IDAL
Illinois Goal Assessment Program .... IGAP
Illinois State Museum (QUAC) .... ISM
Illinois State Veterinary Medical Association (GVA) .... ISVMA
Illiterate (BEE) .... Illit
Illness Behavior Questionnaire (MELL) .... IBQ
Illuminated Nasal Speculum [*Medicine*] (MELL) .... INS
Ilwaco, WA [*FM radio station call letters*] (BROA) ...... KBKH-FM
ILX Resorts [*AMEX symbol*] (SG) ILX
Image Analysis Computer (MELL) .... IAC
Image Reduction and Analysis Facility .... IRAF
Imaging Photon Detector (QUAC) .... IPD
ImaginOn, Inc. [*NASDAQ symbol*] (SG) .... IMON
i-Mall, Inc. [*NASDAQ symbol*] (SG) .... IMAL
Imation Corp. [*NYSE symbol*] (SG) .... IMN
Imax Corp. [*NASDAQ symbol*] (SG) .... IMAX
Iminoglycinuria [*Medicine*] (MELL) .... IGU
Imitative (BEE) .... imit
Immature Oocyte Retrieval [*Medicine*] .... IOR
Immediate Asthma Reaction (MELL) .... IAR
Immediate Care [*Medicine*] (MELL) IC
Immediate Pigment Darkening [*Medicine*] (MELL) .... IPM
Immoblization of Ankle Joint (MELL) .... IAJ
Immune Complex Nephritis [*Medicine*] (MELL) .... ICN
Immune Dot-Blot Test [*Medicine*] (MELL) .... IDBT
Immune Response Modifier [*Medicine*] (MELL) .... IRM
Immune-Suppression Drug (MELL) .... ISD
Immunoadsorbent [*Medicine*] (MELL) .... IA
Immunocompromised [*Medicine*] (MELL) IC
Immunocompromised Patient [*Medicine*] (MELL) .... ICP
Immunoconjugate [*Medicine*] (MELL) IC
Immunofixation [*Medicine*] (MELL) .... IF
Immunoradioassay [*Medicine*] (MELL) .... IRA
Immunoreactive Cholecystokinin [*Medicine*] (MELL) ... ICCK
Immunosuppressive Therapy [*Medicine*] (MELL) .... IST
Impacted Embolism [*Medicine*] (MELL) .... IE
Impacted Tooth [*Medicine*] (MELL) .... IT
Impacted Wisdom Tooth (MELL) .... IWT
Impaired Glucose Tolerance [*Medicine*] (MELL) .... ICT
Impaired Hepatic Uptake [*Medicine*] (MELL) .... IHU
Impaired Intellect (MELL) II
Impaired Renal Tubular Reabsorption [*Medicine*] (MELL) .... IRTR
Impending Myocardial Infarction [*Medicine*] (MELL) .... IMI
Imperforate Hymen [*Medicine*] (MELL) .... IH
Imperial Bancorp [*NYSE symbol*] (SG) .... IMP

Imperial Credit Comm'l Mtg. [*NASDAQ symbol*] (SG) .... ICMI
Imperial Klingon Embassy/Star Trek [*An association*] (EA) .... IKE
Imperial Sugar [*AMEX symbol*] (SG) .... IHK
Imperial Tobacco Grp ADS [*NYSE symbol*] (SG) .... ITY
Impetigo Contagiosa [*Medicine*] (MELL) IC
Implant Failure [*Medicine*] (MELL) .... IF
Implant Resection Arthroplasty [*Medicine*] (MELL) .... IRA
Implantable Automatic Cardioverter-Defibrillator [*Medicine*] (MELL) ... IACD
Implantable Cardioverter Defibrillator Catheter [*Medicine*] (MELL) ...... ICDC
Implantable Defibrillator Insertion [*Medicine*] (MELL) ... IDI
Implantation (MELL) .... IOB
Implantation of Blastocyst [*Medicine*] (MELL) .... IOB
Implanted Electrode Stimulation Therapy [*Medicine*] (MELL) .... IEST
Importation (GEAB) .... imp
Improved (MILB) .... imp
Improved Atmospheric Sounding Interferometer (EOSA) ... IASI
Impulse Control Disorder (MELL) .... ICD
IMRglobal Corp. [*NASDAQ symbol*] (SG) .... IMRS
In No Apparent Distress [*Medicine*] (MELL) .... INAD
In Situ Plasma Vitrification .... ISPV
InaCom Corp. [*NYSE symbol*] (SG) .... ICO
Inactivated Pepsin [*Medicine*] (MELL) .... IP
Inappropriate Disability (MELL) .... ID
Inborn Error of Development (MELL) .... IBED
Inborn Errors of Organic Acid Metabolism [*Medicine*] (MELL) ... IEOAM
Incapacitating Illness (MELL) II
Incapacitating Injury (MELL) II
Incision (MELL) I
Incisional Hernia [*Medicine*] (MELL) .... IH
Incompetent Cervix [*Medicine*] (MELL) IC
Incompetent Patient (MELL) .... IP
Incomplete Pulmonary Infarction [*Medicine*] (MELL) ... IPIS
Incompletely Healed [*Medicine*] (MELL) .... IH
Incoordinate Uterine Dysfunction [*Medicine*] (MELL) ... IUD
Incumbent Local Exchange Carriers .... ILECS
Incurable Problem Drinker (MELL) .... IPD
Independent (MILB) .... indep
Independent Front Suspension .... Ifs
Independent Organ Procurement Agency [*Medicine*] (MELL) .... IOPA
Independent Pilots Association .... IPA
Independent Rear Suspension .... Irs
Independent System Operator .... ISO
Independent Transportation Network .... ITN
India (MILB) .... Ind
Indian Ocean Experiment [*National Science Foundation project*] ... INDOEX
Indiana (BEE) .... Ind
Indiana Network .... INet
Indiana Statewide Testing for Educational Progress ...... ISTEP
Indianapolis (BEE) .... Indpls
Indianapolis Colts [*National Football League*] [*1984-present*] (NFLA) ... Ind
Indianapolis, IN [*Television station call letters*] (BROA) ... WISH-DT
Indianapolis, IN [*Television station call letters*] (BROA) ... WRTV-DT
Indianapolis, IN [*Television station call letters*] (BROA) ... WTHR-DT
Indianola, MS [*FM radio station call letters*] (BROA) ... WTCD-FM
Indians (GEAB) .... Ind
Indicated Horsepower .... IHP
Indicated Low Forceps [*Medicine*] (MELL) .... ILF
Indicator Dilution Technique [*Medicine*] (MELL) .... IDT
Indigo N.V. [*NASDAQ symbol*] (SG) .... INDG
Indio, CA [*AM radio station call letters*] (BROA) .... KESQ
Indio, CA [*FM radio station call letters*] (BROA) .... KJJZ-FM
Indio, CA [*FM radio station call letters*] (BROA) .... KKUU-FM
Indirect Antiglobulin Test [*Medicine*] (MELL) .... IAGT
Indirect Immunofluorescence Assay [*Medicine*] (MELL) ... IFA
Indirect Platelet Count [*Medicine*] (MELL) .... IPC
Individual Social Security Retirement Account .... ISSRA
Indolic Acid (MELL) .... IA
Indonesia (MILB) .... Indo
Indonesia Minas [*Crude oil*] .... IM
Induced Abortion (MELL) .... IAB
Induced Myocardial Ischemia [*Medicine*] (MELL) ...... IMCI
Induced Vestibular Dysfunction [*Medicine*] (MELL) ... IVD
Industrial Code and Logic ICL
Industrial Data Systems [*AMEX symbol*] (SG) .... IDS
Industrial Democracy Commission .... IDC
Industrial Distribution Grp. [*NYSE symbol*] (SG) .... IDG

Industrial in Vitro Toxicology Group (GVA) .... IIVTG
Industrial Nurse (MELL) .... IN
Industrial Operations Command [*Army*] .... IOC
Industries Perforators Association, Inc. .... IPA
Ineffective Erythropoiesis Syndrome [*Medicine*] (MELL) .... IES
Inet Technologies [*NASDAQ symbol*] (SG) .... INTI
Infant (GEAB) .... inf
Infant Appnea Syndrome [*Medicine*] (MELL) .... IAS
Infant Botulism [*Medicine*] (MELL) .... IB
Infant of Drug-Abusing Mother (MELL) .... IDAM
Infant of Drug-Addicted Mother (MELL) .... IDAM
Infant of Drug-Addicted Mother (MELL) .... IODAM
Infantile Apnea [*Medicine*] (MELL) .... IA
Infantile Arteriosclerosis [*Medicine*] (MELL) .... IAS
Infantile Cortical Hyperostosis [*Medicine*] (MELL) .... ICH
Infantile Glaucoma (MELL) .... IG
Infantile Lobar Emphysema [*Medicine*] (MELL) .... ILE
Infantile Polycystic Disease [*Medicine*] (MELL) .... IPD
Infantile Polycystic Kidney Disease [*Medicine*] (MELL) .... IPKD
Infantile Refsum's Syndrome [*Medicine*] (MELL) .... IRD
Infantry (MILB) .... inf
Infantry Brigade .... Inf Bde
Infarction [*Medicine*] (MELL) .... INF
Infarction Zone [*Medicine*] (MELL) .... IZ
Infared Astronomical Satellite [*Launched in January 1983*] .... IRAS
Infared Liver Scan [*Medicine*] (MELL) .... ILS
Infected Open Wound (MELL) .... IOW
Infection-Associated Hemophagocytic Syndrome [*Medicine*] (MELL) .... IAHS
Infectious Arthritis (MELL) .... IA
Infectious Endocarditis [*Medicine*] (MELL) .... IEC
Infectious Mononucleosis [*Medicine*] (MELL) .... IMN
Infectious Peritonitis Virus [*Medicine*] (MELL) .... IPV
Infectious Polymyositis [*Medicine*] (MELL) .... IPM
Infectious Spondylitis [*Medicine*] (MELL) .... IS
Infective Endocarditis [*Medicine*] (MELL) .... IEC
Infective Thrombosis [*Medicine*] (MELL) .... IT
Infective Thrombus [*Medicine*] (MELL) .... IT
Inferior Cornu of Thyroid Cartilage [*Medicine*] (MELL) .... ICTC
Inferior Esophageal Sphincter [*Medicine*] (MELL) .... IES
Inferior Facet [*Medicine*] (MELL) .... IF
Inferior Mediastinum [*Medicine*] (MELL) .... IM
Inferior Sagittal Sinus [*Medicine*] (MELL) .... ISS
Inferior Vertebral Notch [*Medicine*] (MELL) .... IVN
Inferior Wall Infarct [*Medicine*] (MELL) .... IWI
Infertile Male Syndrome (MELL) .... IMS
Infiltrating Ductal Breast Cancer (MELL) .... IDBC
Inflammatory Exudate [*Medicine*] (MELL) .... IE
Inflammatory Glaucoma (MELL) .... IG
Inflammatory Lung Disease (MELL) .... ILD
Inflatable Tubular Structure .... ITS
Inflatable Tubular Torso Restraint .... ITTR
Influenced (BEE) .... infl
Influenza Type A [*Medicine*] (MELL) .... ITA
Influenza Vaccination [*Medicine*] (MELL) IV
Influenza Virus Vaccine [*Medicine*] (MELL) IVV
INFOCURE Corp. [*NASDAQ symbol*] (SG) .... INCX
Information, Communication, Entertainment, Safety, and Security .... ICES
Information Holdings [*NYSE symbol*] (SG) .... IHI
Information Resources Management Association .... IFMA
Infosys Technologies ADS [*NASDAQ symbol*] (SG) .... INFY
Infra-Abdominal Abscess [*Medicine*] (MELL) .... IAA
Infraorbital Foramen [*Medicine*] (MELL) .... IOF
Infraorbital Nerve [*Medicine*] (MELL) .... ION
Infrapatellar Fat [*Medicine*] (MELL) .... IF
Infrared Atmospheric Sounding Interferometer .... IASI
Infrared Radiation Interferometer Spectrometer .... IRIS
Infrared Thermal Imaging Radiometer (EOSA) .... ITIR
Infundibulum of Hypophysis [*Medicine*] (MELL) .... IOH
Ingalls, KS [*FM radio station call letters*] (BROA) .... KBGU-FM
Ingalls, KS [*FM radio station call letters*] (BROA) .... KBIE-FM
Inglis, FL [*FM radio station call letters*] (BROA) .... WHGN-FM
Ingram, TX [*FM radio station call letters*] (BROA) .... KTXI-FM
Ingrown Toenail (MELL) .... IGTN
Inguinal Lymph Node [*Medicine*] (MELL) .... ILN
Inguinal Syndrome [*Medicine*] (MELL) .... IS
Inhabitant (GEAB) .... inhab
Inhalation Anesthesia (MELL) .... IA
Inhalation Injury (MELL) II
Inhaled Tobacco Smoke (MELL) .... ITS
Inherent Moisture [*Coal industry*] .... IM
Inherited (GEAB) .... inh
Inhibiting Activity Factor [*Medicine*] (MELL) .... IAF
Initial Data Analysis [*Statistics*] .... IDA
Initial Malignant Neoplasm [*Medicine*] (MELL) .... IMN
Initial Visit [*Medicine*] (MELL) IV
Inktomi Corp. [*NASDAQ symbol*] (SG) .... INKT
Inland Boatmen's Union of the Pacific .... IBU
Inmet Mining Toronto Stock Exchange symbol (SG) .... IMN
Inner Ear (MELL) .... IE
Innocent Murmur [*Medicine*] (MELL) .... IM
Innovative Clinical Solutions [*NASDAQ symbol*] (SG) .... ICSL
Innovative Technology Council (EPAT) .... ITC
Inoperable Lung Cancer (MELL) .... IOLC
Inpatient Acute Care (MELL) .... IAC
Insight Communications [*NASDAQ symbol*] (SG) ICCI
InSite Vision [*AMEX symbol*] (SG) .... ISV
Inspiration (MELL) I
Inspiratory and Expiratory [*Medicine*] (MELL) .... I & E
INSpire Insurance Solutions [*NASDAQ symbol*] (SG) .... NSPR
Institut National des Sciences Appliques [*France*] (EOSA) .... INSA
Institute (BEE) .... inst
Institute for Higher Education Policy .... IHEP
Institute for International Cooperation in Animal Biologics (GVA) .... IICAB
Institute for Space and Astronautical Science .... ISAS
Institute of Biology (GVA) .... IOB
Institute of Chemistry and Cell Biology [*Harvard Medical School*] .... ICCB
Institute of Environmental Sciences .... IES
Institute of Experimental Animal Sciences [*Osaka University*] (GVA) .... IEXAS
Institute of International Health (GVA) .... IIH
Instituto Nacional de Pesquisas de Amazonia [*Brazil*] (EOSA) .... INPA
Instituto Nacional de Pesquisas Espaciais [*Brazil*] (EOSA) .... INPE
Instrument Control Facility (EOSA) .... ICF
Instrument Support Terminal (EOSA) .... IST
Instrumental (MELL) .... INST
Insulin (MELL) I
Insulin Autoimmune Syndrome [*Medicine*] (MELL) .... IAS
Insulin Neuritis [*Medicine*] (MELL) .... IN
Insulin Therapy [*Medicine*] (MELL) .... IT
Insulin-Independent Diabetes Mellitus [*Medicine*] (MELL) .... IIDM
InsWeb Corp. [*NASDAQ symbol*] (SG) .... INSW
Intact Bag of Waters [*Medicine*] (MELL) .... IBOW
Integral Vision [*NASDAQ symbol*] (SG) .... INVI
Integrated Atmospheric Deposition Network [*Environmental Protection Agency*] (EPAT) .... IADN
Integrated Color Analysis (QUAC) .... ICA
Integrated Electrical Svcs. [*NYSE symbol*] (SG) .... IEE
Integrated Helicopter Design Tool .... IHDT
Integrated Image Processing (MELL) .... IIP
Integrated Orthopaedics [*AMEX symbol*] (SG) .... IOI
Integrated Shape Imaging System (MELL) .... ISIS
Integrated Trans Ntwk Grp. [*AMEX symbol*] (SG) .... ITR
Intellectual Impairment (MELL) II
Intended Use Plan [*Environmental science*] (EPAT) .... IUP
Intensive (BEE) .... intens
Intentional Injury (MELL) II
Inter Parfums [*NASDAQ symbol*] (SG) .... IPAR
Interagency Working Group on Data Management for Global Change (EOSA) .... IWGDMGC
InterCept Group [*NASDAQ symbol*] (SG) .... ICPT
Intercostal Block [*Medicine*] (MELL) .... ICB
Intercostal Muscle [*Medicine*] (MELL) .... ICM
Interdisciplinary Group (MELL) .... IDG
Interdisciplinary Investigator (EOSA) II
Interdisciplinary Science (EOSA) .... IDS
Interferometric Monitor of Greenhouse Gases (EOSA) .... IMG
Interferon [*Medicine*] (MELL) .... INF
Intergovernmental Oceanographic Commission (EOSA) .... IOC
Interior .... Int
Interliant, Inc. [*NASDAQ symbol*] (SG) .... INIT
Intermediate End Point of Therapy (MELL) .... IEPT
Intermediate Longitudinal Crease [*Medicine*] (MELL) ILC
Intermenstrual Pain (MELL) .... IMP
Intermittent Angle-Closure Glaucoma (MELL) .... IACG
Intermittent Catheterization [*Medicine*] (MELL) .... IMC
Intermittent Catheterization Protocol [*Medicine*] (MELL) .... ICP
Intermittent Heartburn (MELL) .... IHB
Intermittent Traction [*Medicine*] (MELL) .... IT
Internal Audit Group [*British*] (GVA) .... IAG
Internal Cardioverter Defibrillator [*Medicine*] (MELL) .... ICD
Internal Carotid Artery Aneurysm [*Medicine*] (MELL) .... ICAA
Internal Combustion Engine Institute, Inc. .... ICEI
Internal Fetal Scalp Electrode [*Medicine*] (MELL) .... IFSE
Internal Mammary Lymph Node [*Medicine*] (MELL) .... IMLN
Internal Monitor [*Medicine*] (MELL) .... IM
Internal Thoracic Artery [*Medicine*] (MELL) .... ITA
International Academy of Compounding Pharmacists (GVA) .... IACP
International AIDS Vaccine Initative .... IAVA
International Association for Aerobiology (QUAC) .... IAA
International Association of African Palynology (QUAC) .... IAAP
International Association of Duncan Certified Ceramic Teachers (EA) .... IADCCT
International Association of Equine Practitioners (GVA) .... IAEP
International Association of Machinists and Aerospace Workers, Woodworkers District Lodge 1 (EA) .... IAMA
International Association of Skateboard Companies (EA) .... IASC
International Bird Dog Association (EA) .... IBDA
International Boxing Hall of Fame Museum (EA) .... IBHFM
International Brotherhood of Bikers' Teardrops (EA) .... IBBT
International Brotherhood of Boilermakers, Iron Ship Builders, Blacksmiths, Forgers and Helpers (EA) .... BSF
International Buddy Rich Fan Club (EA) .... IBRFC
International Center for Aquaculture and Aquatic Environments (GVA) .... ICAAE
International Christian Cycling Club USA (EA) ICCC
International Climate Change Partnership (EPAT) .... ICCP
International Code of Zoological Nomenclature (QUAC) .... ICZN
International Committee on Archaeological Heritage Management (QUAC) .... ICAHM
International Congress on Animal Reproduction (GVA) .... ICAR
International Connections Manager .... ICM
International Council for Laboratory Animal Science (GVA) .... ICLAS
International Council on Infertility Information Dissemination .... INCIID

International Dark-Sky Association .... IDA
International Decade of East African Lakes (QUAC) .... IDEAL
International Earth Observing System (EOSA) .... IEOS
International Elbow Working Group (GVA) .... IEWG
International Embryo Transfer Society (GVA) .... IET
International Flipper Pinball Association (EA) .... IFPA
International Forum on Chemical Safety (EPAT) .... IFCS
International Fund for Avian Research (GVA) .... IFAR
International Glaciospeleological Society (QUAC) .... IGS
International Global Aerosol Program (EOSA) .... IGAP
International Group of Funding Agencies for Global Change Research (QUAC) .... IGFA
International Herpes Management Forum .... IHMF
International Home Foods [*NYSE symbol*] (SG) .... IHF
International Human Dimensions Program on Global Environmental Change (QUAC) .... IHDP
International Hydrocarbon Intercomparison Committee (QUAC) .... IHIC
International Institute for Sustainable Development (QUAC) .... IISD
International Jack Benny Fan Club (EA) .... IJBFC
International Lighting Commission .... CIE
International Medical Regulatory and Shipping Association (GVA) .... IMRSA
International Medical School Graduate (MELL) .... IMSG
International Mensan Philatelists Society (EA) .... IMPS
International Mistral Class Association (EA) .... IMCA
International Mobile Air Conditioning Association, Inc. .... IMAC
International Nannoplankton Association (QUAC) .... INA
International Network of Somewhere in Time Enthusiasts (EA) .... INSITE
International Organization of Masters, Mates, and Pilots .... IOMM&P
International Palynological Congress (QUAC) .... IPC
International Partner Operations Center (EOSA) .... IPOC
International Pen Friends (EA) .... IPF
International Permafrost Association (QUAC) .... IPA
International Projects Assistance Services .... IPAS
International Society for Anthrozoology (GVA) .... ISAZ
International Society for Performance Improvement .... ISPI
International Society of Veterinary Perinatology (GVA) .... ISVP
International Space Year [*1992*] (EOSA) .... ISY
International Specialty Car Association (EA) .... ISCA
International Sphynx Breeders and Fanciers' Association (EA) .... ISBFA
International Sprout Growers Association .... ISGA
International Staging System [*Medicine*] (MELL) .... ISS
International Thunderbird Club (EA) .... ITC
International Trans-Antarctic Scientific Expedition (QUAC) .... ITASE
International Tropospheric Ozone Year (QUAC) .... ITOY
International Tundra Experiment (QUAC) .... ITEX
International Underwater Foundation (EA) .... IUF
International Union of Biological Sciences (QUAC) .... IUBS
International Union of Journeyman Horseshoers .... IUJH
International Veterinary Nurses and Technicians Association (GVA) .... IVNTA
International Watch and Jewelry Guild .... IWJG
International Watch Co. .... IWC
International Water Management Institute .... IWMI
International Welcome Club .... IWC
International Wheelchair Aviators (EA) .... IWA
International Wildlife Education & Conservation (GVA) .... IWEC
International Willie Nelson Fan Club (EA) .... IWNFC
International Year of the Ocean [*1998*] (QUAC) .... IYO
Internet Caching Service [*Computer science*] .... ICS
Internet Corporation for Assigned Names and Numbers .... ICANN
Internet Corporation of Assigned Names and Numbers .... ICANN
Internet Experimental Note .... IEN
Internet Grateful Med [*Program for assisted searching of MEDLINE*] (MELL) .... IGM
Internet Initiative Japan, Inc. .... IIJ
Internet Monthly Report .... IMR
Internet Public Library [*Established by the University of Michigan in 1995*] .... IPL
Internet Registry .... IR
Internet Technology Series .... ITS
Internist (MELL) .... IN
Interplanetary Dust [*Science*] .... IPD
Inter-Professional Group (GVA) .... IPG
Interred (GEAB) .... int
Inter-Regulatory Risk Management Council [*Environmental science*] (EPAT) .... IRMC
Interstitial Cell Tumor [*Medicine*] (MELL) .... ICT
Interstitial Myocarditis [*Medicine*] (MELL) .... IMC
Intertrochanteric [*Medicine*] (MELL) .... ITO
Interventional Ultrasonography [*Medicine*] (MELL) .... IVUS
Interventricular Septal Defect [*Medicine*] (MELL) .... ISD
Intervertebral Disk Disease [*Medicine*] (MELL) .... IVDD
Intervertebral Foramen [*Medicine*] (MELL) .... IVF
Intervertebral Muscle [*Medicine*] (MELL) .... IVM
Interview [*Medicine*] (MELL) IV
InterVU, Inc. [*NASDAQ symbol*] (SG) .... ITVU
Intestinal Gas (MELL) .... IG
Intestinal Multiple Polyposis and Colorectal Cancer (MELL) .... IMPACC
Intestinal Protective Drug Absorption System [*Medicine*] (MELL) .... IPDAS
Intestinal Stenosis [*Medicine*] (MELL) .... IS
Intestional Ischemia [*Medicine*] (MELL) II
Intra-Arterial Catheter [*Medicine*] (MELL) .... IAC
Intra-Articular Anesthetic Injection [*Medicine*] (MELL) .... IAAI
Intracapsular Volar Wrist Ligament [*Medicine*] (MELL) .... IVWL
Intracartilaginous Ossification [*Medicine*] (MELL) .... ICO
Intracavitary Chemotherapy [*Medicine*] (MELL) .... ICCT
Intracavitary Irradiation [*Medicine*] (MELL) ICI
Intracavitary Radium [*Medicine*] (MELL) .... ICR
Intracellular Volume [*Medicine*] (MELL) ICV
Intracochlear Electrodes [*Medicine*] (MELL) .... ICE
Intracortical Hemorrhage [*Medicine*] (MELL) .... ICH
Intracranial Epidural Abscess [*Medicine*] (MELL) .... ICEDA
Intracranial Hematome [*Medicine*] (MELL) .... IH
Intracranial Hypertension [*Medicine*] (MELL) .... ICH
Intracranial Internal Carotid Artery [*Medicine*] (MELL) .... IICA
Intracranial Microaneurysm [*Medicine*] (MELL) .... ICMA
Intracranial Tumor [*Medicine*] (MELL) .... ICT
Intractable Pelvic Pain [*Medicine*] (MELL) .... IPP
Intractable Seizure Disorder [*Medicine*] (MELL) .... ISD
Intradiskal Injection [*Medicine*] (MELL) .... IDI
Intraductal Papilloma [*Medicine*] (MELL) .... IDP
Intraepithelial Dysplasia [*Medicine*] (MELL) .... IED
Intraocular Implant [*Medicine*] (MELL) .... IOI
Intraocular Lens Implantation [*Medicine*] (MELL) .... IOLI
Intraocular Tumor [*Medicine*] (MELL) .... IOT
Intraoperative Abdominal Lavage [*Medicine*] (MELL) .... IOAL
Intraoperative Cholecystogram [*Medicine*] (MELL) .... IOCG
Intraorbital Foramen [*Medicine*] (MELL) .... IOF
Intraperitoneal Chemotherapy [*Medicine*] (MELL) .... IPC
Intraperitoneal Chemotherapy [*Medicine*] (MELL) .... IPCT
Intraperitoneal Cisplatinum [*Medicine*] (MELL) .... ICP
Intraperitoneal Hyperthermic Perfusion [*Medicine*] (MELL) .... IPHP
Intrapulmonary Interstitial Emphysema [*Medicine*] (MELL) .... IPIE
Intrastromal Corneal Ring [*Medicine*] (MELL) .... ISCR
Intravascular Brachytherapy [*Medicine*] .... IVBT
Intravascular Catheter [*Medicine*] (MELL) IVC
Intravenous Feeding [*Medicine*] (MELL) .... IVF
Intravenous Fluid Therapy [*Medicine*] (MELL) .... IVFT
Intravenous Fluorescein Angiogram [*Medicine*] (MELL) .... IVFA
Intravenous Gamma Globulin [*Medicine*] (MELL) .... IVGG
Intravenous Nutritional Feeding (MELL) .... INF
Intraventricular Delay [*Medicine*] (MELL) .... IVD
Intrawest Corp. [*NYSE symbol*] (SG) .... IDR
Intrinsic Sleep Disorder [*Medicine*] (MELL) .... ISD
Invacare Corp. [*NYSE symbol*] (SG) IVC
Invasion Plasmid Antigens [*Medicine*] (MELL) .... IPA
Inverse Addressing .... IN-ADDR
Inverse Discrete Cosine Transform [*Electronics*] .... iDCT
Inversion Stress Test [*Medicine*] (MELL) .... IST
Investigational New Drug Application (MELL) .... INDA
Investigator of Micro-Biosphere (EOSA) .... IMB
Investment Promotion Action Plan [*Bangkok*] .... IPAP
Investment Tech Group [*NYSE symbol*] (SG) .... ITG
Involuntary Muscle [*Medicine*] (MELL) .... IVM
Iodotyrosine Deiodinase Deficiency [*Medicine*] (MELL) .... IDD
Iomed, Inc. [*AMEX symbol*] (SG) .... IOX
Iomega Corp. [*NYSE symbol*] (SG) .... IOM
Ion Pair Chromatography [*Medicine*] (MELL) .... IPC
IONA Technologies ADR [*NASDAQ symbol*] (SG) .... IONA
Iowa (BEE) .... Ia
Iowa City, IA [*AM radio station call letters*] (BROA) .... KCJK
Iran (MILB) .... Ir
Iranian (BEE) .... Iran
Iraq (MILB) .... Irq
Ireland (MILB) .... Irl
IRI International [*NYSE symbol*] (SG) .... IIR
Iridium World Communications'A' [*NASDAQ symbol*] (SG) .... IRID
Iris (MELL) I
Irish (BEE) .... Ir
Irish Medicines Board (GVA) .... IMB
Irish Veterinary Association (GVA) .... IVA
Irish Veterinary Union (GVA) .... IVU
Iron Mountain [*NYSE symbol*] (SG) .... IRM
Iron Overload [*Medicine*] (MELL) .... IOL
Iron-Storage Disease [*Medicine*] (MELL) .... ISD
Ironton, OH [*FM radio station call letters*] (BROA) .... WFXN-FM
Irritable Stomach Syndrome [*Medicine*] (MELL) .... ISS
Ischemic Muscle Pain (MELL) .... IMP
Ischemic Preconditioning [*Medicine*] (MELL) .... IPC
Ischemic Vascular Disease [*Medicine*] (MELL) .... IVD
Ischemic-Anoxic Brain Damage [*Medicine*] (MELL) .... IABD
Ischiogluteal Bursa [*Medicine*] (MELL) .... IGB
Ischiogluteal Bursitis [*Medicine*] (MELL) .... IGB
Ischium (MELL) I
Islamic Association for Palestine .... IAP
Island Park, ID [*FM radio station call letters*] (BROA) .... KEZQ-FM
Islesboro, ME [*FM radio station call letters*] (BROA) .... WAYD-FM
Islet of Langerhans [*Medicine*] (MELL) .... IOL
Islet-Cell Tumor of Pancreas [*Medicine*] (MELL) .... ITP
Isolated Meconium Ileus [*Medicine*] (MELL) .... IMI
Isolated Perfused Lung [*Medicine*] (MELL) .... IPL
Isolette (MELL) .... ISO
Isometric Strength [*Medicine*] (MELL) .... IS
Isonicotinic Acid Hydrazide [*Medicine*] (MELL) .... IAH
Isotonic Strength [*Medicine*] (MELL) .... IS
ISPAT Intl'A' [*NYSE symbol*] (SG) .... IST
Israel (MILB) Il
Israel Network .... ILAN
ISS Group [*NASDAQ symbol*] (SG) .... ISSX
Istituto Bancario Ital ADS [*NYSE symbol*] (SG) .... IMI
IT Group [*NYSE symbol*] (SG) .... ITX
Italian Academy of Veterinary Informatics (GVA) .... IAVI
Italian Car Registry (EA) .... ICAR

Italian National Institute for Nuclear Physics .... INFN

Italy (MILB) .... It

ITC DeltaCom [*NASDAQ symbol*] (SG) .... ITCD

Iteratively Reweighted Least Squares .... IRLS

ITLA Capital [*NASDAQ symbol*] (SG) .... ITLA

IVC Industries (New) [*NASDAQ symbol*] (SG) .... IVCOD

Ivex Packaging [*NYSE symbol*] (SG) IXX

iVillage, Inc. [*NASDAQ symbol*] (SG) IVIL

IXC Communications [*NASDAQ symbol*] (SG) IIXC

iXL Enterprises [*NASDAQ symbol*] (SG) IIXL

J
By Meaning

J. Alexander's Corp. [*NYSE symbol*] (SG) .... JAX
J D Edwards [*NYSE symbol*] (SG) .... JDEC
Jabil Circuit [*NYSE symbol*] (SG) .... JBL
Jacket Crown (MELL) .... JC
Jackson Development Corporation .... JDC
Jackson, MI [*AM radio station call letters*] (BROA) .... WIBM
Jackson, MS [*AM radio station call letters*] (BROA) .... WJDX
Jackson, MS [*FM radio station call letters*] (BROA) .... WKXS-FM
Jackson, WY [*Television station call letters*] (BROA) .... KBEO
Jackson, WY [*FM radio station call letters*] (BROA) .... KBHJ-FM
Jacksonian Epilepsy [*Medicine*] (MELL) .... JE
Jacksonville, FL [*Television station call letters*] (BROA) .... WJWB
Jacksonville, FL [*FM radio station call letters*] (BROA) .... WMXO-FM
Jacksonville Jaguars [*National Football League*] [*1995-present*] (NFLA) .... Jac
Jacksonville, NC [*AM radio station call letters*] (BROA) .... WSTK
Jacksonville, TX [*FM radio station call letters*] (BROA) .... KLJT-FM
Jaeger LeCoultre .... JLC
Jamaica (MILB) .... Ja
Jamaica Association of Villas and Apartments (EA) .... JRJ
Jamaican Vomiting Sickness (MELL) .... JVS
Japan Academic Inter-University Network .... JAIN
Japan Environmental Agency (QUAC) .... JEA
Japan Planetarium Laboratory .... JPL
Japan Tobacco, Inc. .... JT
Japanese Association for Laboratory Animal Medicine (GVA) .... JALAM
Japanese Chamber of Commerce and Industry of New York (EA) .... JCCINY
Japanese Earth Observing Satellite (EOSA) .... JEOS
Japanese Earth Remote-Sensing Satellite-1 (EOSA) JERS-1
Japanese Earth Resources Satellite .... JERS
Japanese Polar Orbiting Platform (EOSA) .... JPOP
Japanese Society for Laboratory Animal and Environment (GVA) .... JSLAE
Japanese Society of Veterinary Science (GVA) .... JSVS
Jasper, GA [*FM radio station call letters*] (BROA) .... WBCS-FM
Jaundice [*Medicine*] (MELL) .... JD
Javelin Thrower's Elbow (MELL) .... JTE
JCC Holding 'A' [*AMEX symbol*] (SG) .... JAZ
JDS Uniphase Corp. [*NASDAQ symbol*] (SG) .... JDSU
Jeffersonville, IN [*AM radio station call letters*] (BROA) .... WAVG
Jeffersonville, NY [*FM radio station call letters*] (BROA) .... WWHW-FM
Jena, LA [*FM radio station call letters*] (BROA) .... KAYT-FM
Jenkintown, PA [*FM radio station call letters*] (BROA) .... WPHI-FM
Jensen Beach, FL [*FM radio station call letters*] (BROA) .... WMBX-FM
Jerseyville, IL [*FM radio station call letters*] (BROA) .... WXTM-FM
Jet Lag Syndrome (MELL) .... JLS
Jewett, NY [*FM radio station call letters*] (BROA) .... WAXK
JFAX.COM, Inc. [*NASDAQ symbol*] (SG) .... JFAX
Jinpan Intl. [*AMEX symbol*] (SG) .... JST
JLK Direct Distribution 'A' [*NYSE symbol*] (SG) .... JLK
JLM Couture [*NYSE symbol*] (SG) .... JHPC
Job Information Matrix System .... JIMS

Job Ordering Contract .... JOC
Jogger's Heel (MELL) .... JH
Johannesburg, CA [*FM radio station call letters*] (BROA) .... KBHM-FM
Johannesburg, CA [*FM radio station call letters*] (BROA) .... KEDD-FM
John von Neumann Center Network .... JvNCnet
John Wilson Gill Fan Club (EA) .... JWGFC
Johnny Lightnings [*Topper Toys*] .... JL
Johns Hopkins University Press .... JHUP
Johnston City, IL [*AM radio station call letters*] (BROA) .... WHTE
Joint Contracture [*Medicine*] (MELL) .... JC
Joint Food Safety and Standards Group [*British*] (GVA) .... JFSSG
Joint Implementation .... JI
Joint Meeting on Pesticide Residues [*Environmental Protection Agency*] (EPAT) .... JMPR
Joint Partnering Contracting .... JPC
Joint Strategic Airborne Reconnaissance System (MILB) .... JSTARS
Joint Tactical Unmanned Aerial Vehicle .... JTUAV
Joliette, PQ [*FM radio station call letters*] (BROA) .... CJLM-FM
Jones Lang LaSalle [*NYSE symbol*] (SG) .... JLL
Jonesville, VA [*FM radio station call letters*] (BROA) .... WJNV-FM
Jonquiere, PQ [*FM radio station call letters*] (BROA) .... CKAJ-FM
Jordan Airports Duty Free .... JADF
Joshua Slocum Society (EA) .... JSS
Jourdanton, TX [*FM radio station call letters*] (BROA) .... KBOP-FM
Journal of Air Pollution Control Association [*A publication*] (EPAT) .... JAPCA
Journal of American Veterinary Medical Association [*A publication*] (GVA) .... JAVMA
Journal of Negro History [*A publication*] (GEAB) .... JNH
Journal of Quaternary Science [*A publication*] (QUAC) .... JOS
Journal of Small Animal Practice [*A publication*] (GVA) .... JSAP
Journal Register [*NYSE symbol*] (SG) .... JRC
JSB Financial [*NYSE symbol*] (SG) .... JSB
Judicial (GEAB) .... judic
Jugular Venous Distention [*Medicine*] (MELL) .... JVD
Julian, CA [*FM radio station call letters*] (BROA) .... KLVJ-FM
JumboSports, Inc. [*NYSE symbol*] (SG) .... JSI
Jumper's Knee (MELL) .... JK
Junction, TX [*FM radio station call letters*] (BROA) .... KOOK-FM
Junctional Escape Beat [*Medicine*] (MELL) .... JEB
Junctional Nevus [*Medicine*] (MELL) .... JN
Junior (GEAB) .... junr
Junior Tennis Foundation (EA) .... JTF
Juniper Networks [*NASDAQ symbol*] (SG) .... JNPR
Juno Online Svcs. [*NASDAQ symbol*] (SG) .... JWEB
Jupiter, FL [*AM radio station call letters*] (BROA) .... WJBW
Just Kidding [*Online dialog*] .... JK
Juvenile Arthritis (MELL) .... JA
Juvenile Cataract (MELL) .... JC
Juvenile Detention Center .... JDC
Juvenile Psoriatic Arthritis [*Medicine*] (MELL) .... JPA
Juvenile Risk Reduction Initiative .... JRRI

K

By Meaning

Kachina Village, AZ [*FM radio station call letters*] (BROA) .... KFLX-FM
Kagel Exercise (MELL) .... KE
Kalamazoo, MI [*AM radio station call letters*] (BROA) .... WKLZ
Kallmann's Syndrome [*Medicine*] (MELL) .... KS
Kaneohe, HI [*Television station call letters*] (BROA) .... KPXO
Kaneohe, HI [*FM radio station call letters*] (BROA) .... KXME-FM
Kangaroo Care [*Medicine*] (MELL) .... KC
Kankakee, IL [*FM radio station call letters*] (BROA) .... WBRO-FM
Kansas Association for Educational Communications & Technology .... KAECT
Kansas City Chiefs [*National Football League*] [*1963-present*] (NFLA) .... KC
Kansas City, KS [*AM radio station call letters*] (BROA) .... KBJC
Kansas City, MO [*Television station call letters*] (BROA) .... KCPT-DT
Kansas City, MO [*Television station call letters*] (BROA) .... KCWE
Kansas City, MO [*AM radio station call letters*] (BROA) .... KPHN
Kansas City, MO [*Television station call letters*] (BROA) .... KPXE
Kansas Library Association .... KLA
Kansas Veterinary Medical Association (GVA) .... KVMA
Kappa Delta (EA) .... KD
Kasilof, AK [*FM radio station call letters*] (BROA) .... KWJG-FM
Kaukauna, WI [*FM radio station call letters*] (BROA) .... WPCK-FM
Kazakstan (MILB) .... Kaz
Keebler Foods [*NYSE symbol*] (SG) .... KBL
Kehr's Sign [*Medicine*] (MELL) .... KS
Kelley Oil & Gas [*NASDAQ symbol*] (SG) .... KOGCC
Kelling's Test [*Medicine*] (MELL) .... KT
Keloid (MELL) .... K
Kelowna, BC [*FM radio station call letters*] (BROA) .... CHSU-FM
Kendall, FL [*AM radio station call letters*] (BROA) .... WRBF
Kennedy Round .... KR
Kennewick, WA [*FM radio station call letters*] (BROA) .... KBLD-FM
Kenpo Karate International (EA) .... KKI
Kentland, IN [*FM radio station call letters*] (BROA) .... WJOK-FM
Kentucky Instructional Results Information System .... KIRIS
Kentucky Veterinary Medical Association (GVA) .... KVMA
Kentwood, MI [*AM radio station call letters*] (BROA) .... WXBV
Kenya (MILB) .... Kya
Keokuk, IA [*FM radio station call letters*] (BROA) .... KMDY-FM
Keratoglobus [*Medicine*] (MELL) .... KG
Keratometry (MELL) .... K
Kerman, CA [*FM radio station call letters*] (BROA) .... KBHH-FM
Kerner's Test [*Medicine*] (MELL) .... KT
Kernig's Sign [*Medicine*] (MELL) .... KS
Kerrville, TX [*FM radio station call letters*] (BROA) .... KKER-FM
Ketchikan, AK [*Television station call letters*] (BROA) .... KUBD
Ketoaciduria (MELL) .... KA
Ketoglutaric Acid (MELL) .... KGA
Ketosteroid [*Medicine*] (MELL) .... KS
Key Colony Beach, FL [*FM radio station call letters*] (BROA) .... WKYZ-FM
Key West, FL [*FM radio station call letters*] (BROA) .... WVMQ-FM
Kidney Dialysis Unit (MELL) .... KDU
Kidney Function Test [*Medicine*] (MELL) .... KFT
Kidney Ultrasound Biopsy [*Medicine*] (MELL) .... KUB

Kids in Integrated Day Care Settings (MELL) .... KIDS
Killeen, TX [*FM radio station call letters*] (BROA) .... KLNC-FM
Killian's Test [*Medicine*] (MELL) .... KT
Kilocalorie (MELL) .... K
Kilodalton (MELL) .... K
Kilojoule (EOSA) .... kJ
Kiloton (MILB) .... KT
Kilroy Realty [*NYSE symbol*] (SG) .... KRC
Kimball, NE [*FM radio station call letters*] (BROA) .... KBFZ-FM
Kimberking City, MO [*FM radio station call letters*] (BROA) .... KOMC-FM
Kinberg's Test [*Medicine*] (MELL) .... KT
Kinetic Energy (MELL) .... E
King (GEAB) .... k
King City, CA [*FM radio station call letters*] (BROA) .... KBAP-FM
King Power Intl. [*AMEX symbol*] (SG) .... KPG
King's Royal Regiment of New York (GEAB) .... KRRNY
Kingsburg, CA [*FM radio station call letters*] (BROA) .... KLVK-FM
Kinston, NC [*FM radio station call letters*] (BROA) .... WELS-FM
Kirsch Laser Welding Technique [*Medicine*] (MELL) .... KLWT
Kirschner Wire Fixation (MELL) .... KWF
Kirtland, NM [*FM radio station call letters*] (BROA) .... KAZX-FM
Kitty Wells-Johnny Wright-Bobby Wright International Fan Club
(EA) .... WWWFC
KLA-Tencor Corp. [*NASDAQ symbol*] (SG) .... KLAC
Kleine-Levin Syndrome [*Medicine*] (MELL) .... KLS
Klimow's Test [*Medicine*] (MELL) .... KT
Knapp's Test [*Medicine*] (MELL) .... KT
Kneading Massage (MELL) .... KM
Knee-Chest Position (MELL) .... KCP
Knight (GEAB) .... knt
Knot .... kn
Knoxville, IL [*FM radio station call letters*] (BROA) .... WBDW-FM
Knoxville, TN [*AM radio station call letters*] (BROA) .... WAHI
Knoxville, TN [*AM radio station call letters*] (BROA) .... WIMZ
Knoxville, TN [*AM radio station call letters*] (BROA) .... WJBZ
Knoxville, TN [*AM radio station call letters*] (BROA) .... WNOX
Knoxville, TN [*FM radio station call letters*] (BROA) .... WQIX-FM
Knoxville, TN [*Television station call letters*] (BROA) .... WVLT-TV
Kober Test [*Medicine*] (MELL) .... KT
Koch-Weeks Bacillus [*Medicine*] (MELL) .... KWB
Kohler Disease (MELL) .... KD
Koplik's Spots [*Medicine*] (MELL) .... KS
Korea Electric Power Corp. .... KEPCO
Korea Telecom ADS [*NYSE symbol*] (SG) .... KTC
Korn/Ferry Intl. [*NYSE symbol*] (SG) .... KFY
Kosciusko, MS [*FM radio station call letters*] (BROA) .... WZKR-FM
Krackow Suture [*Medicine*] (MELL) .... KS
Kraurosis Vulvae [*Medicine*] (MELL) .... KV
Krause's Furniture [*AMEX symbol*] (SG) .... KFI
Krypton Laser Photocoagulation [*Medicine*] (MELL) .... KLPC
Kuwait (MILB) .... Kwt
Kyrgyzstan (MILB) .... Kgz

L
By Meaning

L-3 Communications Hldgs. [*NYSE symbol*] (SG) ... LLL
La Crosse, WI [*FM radio station call letters*] (BROA) ... WRQT-FM
La Junta, CO [*FM radio station call letters*] (BROA) ... KKIK-FM
La Monte, MO [*FM radio station call letters*] (BROA) ... KPOW-FM
La Sarre, PQ [*FM radio station call letters*] (BROA) ... CKLS-FM
Lab Holdings [*NASDAQ symbol*] (SG) ... LABH
Label Use Information System [*Environmental Protection Agency*] (EPAT) ... LUIS
Labor and Delivery (MELL) ... L/D
Labor Pain (MELL) ... LP
Labor Ready [*NYSE symbol*] (SG) ... LRW
Labor Room (MELL) ... LBR
Laboratoire d'Etudes et de Recherches en Teledetection Spatiale [*France*] (EOSA) ... LFRTS
Laboratory Animal Welfare Training Exchange (GVA) ... LAWTE
Laboratory Audit Inspection [*Environmental Protection Agency*] (EPAT) ... LAI
Laborer (GEAB) ... labr
Labrador City, NF [*FM radio station call letters*] (BROA) ... CBDQ-FM
Labyrinthine Dysfunction [*Medicine*] (MELL) ... LD
Lacrimation Reflex [*Medicine*] (MELL) ... LR
Lacrosse, FL [*FM radio station call letters*] (BROA) ... WWFX-FM
Lactase Deficiency [*Medicine*] (MELL) ... LD
Lactic Acidosis [*Medicine*] (MELL) ... LA
Lactic Peroxidase [*Medicine*] (MELL) ... LP
Lactose Intolerance [*Medicine*] (MELL) ... LI
Lactose Tolerance Test [*Medicine*] (MELL) ... LTT
Lactosuria of Pregnancy (MELL) ... LOP
Ladish Co. [*NASDAQ symbol*] (SG) ... LDSH
Ladson, SC [*FM radio station call letters*] (BROA) ... WJNI-FM
Lafayette, IN [*AM radio station call letters*] (BROA) ... WAZY
Lake City, SC [*AM radio station call letters*] (BROA) ... WHYM
lake Havasu City, AZ [*FM radio station call letters*] (BROA) ... KANG-FM
Lake Havasu City, AZ [*FM radio station call letters*] (BROA) ... KRRK-FM
Lake Providence, LA [*FM radio station call letters*] (BROA) ... KLPL-FM
Lake Success, NY [*FM radio station call letters*] (BROA) ... WKTU-FM
Lake View ... l/v
Lake Village, AR [*FM radio station call letters*] (BROA) ... KZYQ-FM
Lake Worth, FL [*Television station call letters*] (BROA) ... WPXP
Lakeland, FL [*Television station call letters*] (BROA) ... WWWB
Lakeside, NJ [*AM radio station call letters*] (BROA) ... WKNJ
Lakeville, MN [*FM radio station call letters*] (BROA) ... KZNR-FM
Lakewood, WA [*AM radio station call letters*] (BROA) ... KNTB
Lamar Advertising 'A' [*NASDAQ symbol*] (SG) ... LAMR
Lamaze Technique [*Medicine*] (MELL) ... LT
Lambda Delta Lambda (EA) ... LDL
Lamellar Body Density [*Medicine*] (MELL) ... LBD
Lamellar Keratoplasty [*Medicine*] (MELL) ... LK
Laminectomy [*Medicine*] (MELL) ... LAMI
Lampasas, TX [*FM radio station call letters*] (BROA) ... KJFK-FM
Lancaster, NH [*FM radio station call letters*] (BROA) ... WXXS-FM
Land Disposal (EPAT) ... LD
Land Remote Sensing Satellite (EOSA) ... Landsat
Landamerica Financial Grp. [*NYSE symbol*] (SG) ... LFG
Landau-Kleffer Syndrome [*Medicine*] ... LKS
Lander, WY [*Television station call letters*] (BROA) ... KCWC-TV
Landfill Methane Outreach Program [*Environmental Protection Agency*] (EPAT) ... LMOP
Landing Craft, Heavy/Merchanised/Tank/Utility/Vehicles and Personnel (MILB) ... LCH/M/T/U/VP
Landing Platform, Dock/Helicopter (MILB) ... LPD/H
Landing Ship, Dock/Heavy/Medium/Tank (MILB) ... LSD/H/M/T
Landscape Response Unit (QUAC) ... LRU
Lane (PROS) ... Ln
Langley Research Center (EOSA) ... LaRC
Lanthanum (MELL) ... La
Lanugo Hair (MELL) ... LH
Laos (MILB) ... Lao
Laparoscopic Herniorrhaphy [*Medicine*] (MELL) ... LH
Laparoscopic Laser Cholecystectomy [*Medicine*] (MELL) ... LLC
Laparoscopic Surgery (MELL) ... LSS
Lapeer, MI [*FM radio station call letters*] (BROA) ... WRXF-FM
Larcher's Sign [*Medicine*] (MELL) ... LS
Laredo, TX [*AM radio station call letters*] (BROA) ... KLNT
Large (BEE) ... lg
Large Date [*Numismatic term*] ... LD
Large Simple Trial [*Statistics*] ... LST
Larned, KS [*FM radio station call letters*] (BROA) ... KBGL
Larned, KS [*AM radio station call letters*] (BROA) ... KNNS
Larva Migrans Visceralis [*Medicine*] (MELL) ... LMV
Laryngeal Atresia [*Medicine*] (MELL) ... LA
Laryngeal Vestibule [*Medicine*] (MELL) ... LV
Larynx (MELL) ... lx
Las Vegas, NV [*FM radio station call letters*] (BROA) ... KISF-FM
Las Vegas, NV [*Television station call letters*] (BROA) ... KVWB
LaSalle Hotel Properties [*NYSE symbol*] (SG) ... LHO
LaSalle Re Holdings [*NYSE symbol*] (SG) ... LSH
Laser Doppler Velocimetry [*Medicine*] (MELL) ... LDV
Laser Indirect Ophthalmoscope [*Medicine*] (MELL) ... LIO
Laser Iridotomy [*Medicine*] (MELL) ... LI
Laser Mortgage Mgmt. [*NYSE symbol*] (SG) ... LMM
Laser Peripheral Iridectomy [*Medicine*] (MELL) ... LPI
Laser Retroreflector (EOSA) ... LR
Laser Retroreflector Array (EOSA) ... LRA
Laser Surgery (MELL) ... LS
Laser-Assisted Microanastomosis [*Medicine*] (MELL) ... LAMA
Lason, Inc. [*NASDAQ symbol*] (SG) ... LSON
Lassa Fever [*Medicine*] (MELL) ... LF
Last Dose (MELL) ... LD
Last Glacial Stage (QUAC) ... LGS
Last Observation Carried Forward ... LOCF
Last Occurrence of Date (QUAC) ... LOD
Last Spring Frost (QUAC) ... LSF
Late Third Trimester Partial Birth Abortion (MELL) ... LTTPBA
Late-Life Depression (MELL) ... LLD
Latent Syphilis (MELL) ... LS
Late-Onset Hepatic Failure [*Medicine*] (MELL) ... LOHF
Lateral Amyotrophic Sclerosis [*Medicine*] (MELL) ... LAS
Lateral Boundary Value (QUAC) ... LBV
Lateral Capsular Ligament [*Medicine*] (MELL) ... LCL
Lateral Facial Dysplasia [*Medicine*] (MELL) ... LFD
Lateral Geniculate [*Medicine*] (MELL) ... LG
Lateral Horn of Spinal Cord [*Medicine*] (MELL) ... LHSC
Lateral Humeral Epicondylalgia [*Medicine*] (MELL) ... LHE
Lateral Humeral Epicondylitis [*Medicine*] (MELL) ... LHE
Lateral Medullary Syndrome [*Medicine*] (MELL) ... LMS
Lateral Osseous Ampulla [*Medicine*] (MELL) ... LOA
Lateral Sacral Vein [*Medicine*] (MELL) ... LSV
Lateral Spinal Stenosis [*Medicine*] (MELL) ... LSS
Lateral Vastus Muscle [*Medicine*] (MELL) ... LVM
Lateral Ventricle [*Medicine*] (MELL) ... LV
Later-Life Sexuality (MELL) ... LLS
Latex Allergy (MELL) ... LA
Latin (BEE) ... Lat
Latin American Network Information Center [*Internet resource*] ... LANIC
Latin American Paper Money Society (EA) ... LANSA
Latin American Pollen Database (QUAC) ... LAPD
Latino Virus [*Medicine*] (MELL) ... LV
Latvia (MILB) ... Lat
Launch Media [*NASDAQ symbol*] (SG) ... LAUN
Laurel, MS [*FM radio station call letters*] (BROA) ... WBBN-FM
Lauren Robbins International Fan Club (EA) ... LRIFC
Lavage Fluid Analysis [*Medicine*] (MELL) ... LFA
Lavage with Saline [*Medicine*] (MELL) ... LWS
Law (GEAB) ... L
Lawton, OK [*AM radio station call letters*] (BROA) ... KXCA
Laxatives and Cathartics (MELL) ... L & C
Lazy Eye (MELL) ... LE
Lead Agency Attorney (EPAT) ... LAA
Lead Pipe Fracture (MELL) ... LPF
Lead Poisoning (MELL) ... LP
Lead, SD [*FM radio station call letters*] (BROA) ... KCYT-FM
Leader (GEAB) ... ldr
Lead-Time Bias (MELL) ... LTB
League of Independent Ferret Enthusiasts (EA) ... LIFE
Leakey, TX [*FM radio station call letters*] (BROA) ... KBLT-FM
Learn2.com, Inc. [*NYSE symbol*] (SG) ... LTWO
Leasing Solutions [*NYSE symbol*] (SG) ... LSN
Lebanon, IN [*FM radio station call letters*] (BROA) ... WYJZ-FM
Lebanon, OH [*FM radio station call letters*] (BROA) ... WYLX-FM
Lebanon, TN [*FM radio station call letters*] (BROA) ... WRVW-FM
Leber's Optic Atrophy [*Medicine*] (MELL) ... LOA
Lecithin Supplement (MELL) ... LS
Left Anterior Oblique [*Medicine*] (MELL) ... LOA

Left Atrioventricular Valve [*Medicine*] (MELL) .... LAVV
Left Brachial Artery [*Medicine*] (MELL) .... LBA
Left Brachiocephalic Vein [*Medicine*] (MELL) .... LBCV
Left Coronary Artery [*Medicine'*] (MELL) .... LCA
Left Crus of Diaphragm [*Medicine*] (MELL) .... LCD
Left End-Expiratory Pressure [*Medicine*] (MELL) .... LEEP
Left Extracapsular Cataract Extraction (MELL) .... LECCE
Left Gastric Artery [*Medicine*] (MELL) .... LGA
Left Index Finger (MELL) .... LIF
Left Liver Lobe (MELL) LLL
Left Lower Leg (MELL) LLL
Left Lower Lid (MELL) LLL
Left Mentoposterior [*Medicine*] (MELL) .... LMP
Left Sacroposterior [*Medicine*] (MELL) .... LSP
Left Short Leg (MELL) .... LSL
Left Sinus of Valsalva [*Medicine*] (MELL) .... LSV
Left Ventricular Outflow Tract Obstruction [*Medicine*] (MELL) .... LVOTO
Left Ventricular Systolic Output [*Medicine*] (MELL) .... LVSO
Left Without Therapy [*Medicine*] (MELL) .... LWOT
Legg-Perthes Disease [*Medicine*] (MELL) .... LPD
Leichtenstern's Sign [*Medicine*] (MELL) .... LS
Leigh's Disease [*Medicine*] (MELL) .... LD
Leisureplanet Holdings [*NASDAQ symbol*] (SG) .... LPHL
Leisure-Time Physical Activity (MELL) .... LTPA
Length-Time Bias (MELL) .... LTB
Lennox Intl. [*NYSE symbol*] (SG) LII
Lenticular Astigmatism (MELL) .... LA
Leonard Nimoy Club (EA) .... LNC
Leone, AS [*FM radio station call letters*] (BROA) .... KHJP-FM
Leptin (MELL) L
Leroy Township, MI [*FM radio station call letters*] (BROA) .... WLGH-FM
Lesbian & Gay Veterinary Medical Association (GVA) .... LGVMA
Lesbians Organising in Solidarity [*An association*] .... LOIS
Lesotho (MILB) .... Ls
Lesser Curve Gastric Ulcer (MELL) .... LCGU
Lesser Quantity Emission Rates (EPAT) .... LQER
Lesser Sciatic Foramen [*Medicine*] (MELL) .... LSF
Lesser Sciatic Notch [*Medicine*] (MELL) .... LSN
Lesser Sulphur-Crested Cockatoo [*Bird*] LS2
Lethal Dose 50 .... LD50
Lethal Factor (MELL) .... LF
Lethbridge, AB [*Television station call letters*] (BROA) .... CJIL-TV
Let's Just Be Friends [*Online dialog*] .... LJBF
Letter Book Copy (GEAB) .... LBC
Leucinamide (MELL) .... LA
Leucine-Induced Hypoglycemia [*Medicine*] (MELL) .... LIH
Leukocyte (MELL) L
Leukocyte (MELL) .... Lkc
Leukocyte Adhesion Stimulator [*Medicine*] (MELL) .... LAP
Leukocyte Bactericidal Assay Test [*Medicine*] (MELL) .... LBAT
Leukocyte Common Antigen [*Medicine*] (MELL) .... LCA
Leukocyte Esterase (MELL) .... LE
Leukocyte Immunization Therapy [*Medicine*] .... LIT
Leukocyte Inhibiting Factor [*Medicine*] (MELL) .... LIH
Leukodystrophy [*Medicine*] (MELL) .... LD
Leukotactic Factor [*Medicine*] (MELL) .... LF
Levator Ani Muscle (MELL) .... LAM
Levator Muscle of Scapula [*Medicine*] (MELL) .... LMS
Levator Muscle Syndrome [*Medicine*] (MELL) .... LMS
Level 3 Communications [*NASDAQ symbol*] (SG) .... LVLT
Level of Pain (MELL) .... LOP
Lewiston, ID [*FM radio station call letters*] (BROA) .... KVTY-FM
Lewiston, MT [*Television station call letters*] (BROA) .... KABO
Lewistown, PA [*radio station call letters*] (BROA) .... WJRC-FM
Lexford Residential TR SBI [*NYSE symbol*] (SG) .... LFT
Lexington Park, MD [*AM radio station call letters*] (BROA) .... WMDM
Lexington, TN [*FM radio station call letters*] (BROA) .... WIGH-FM
Liberate Technologies [*NASDAQ symbol*] (SG) .... LBRT
Liberia (MILB) .... Lb
Liberty, MS [*FM radio station call letters*] (BROA) .... WAZA-FM
Library (GEAB) .... lib
License (BEE) lic
Lichen Planus (MELL) .... LP
Lichen Sclerosis [*Medicine*] (MELL) .... LS
Lichen Simplex [*Medicine*] (MELL) .... LS
Lidar In-Space Technology Experiment (EOSA) .... LITE
Lidocaine Hydrochloride [*Medicine*] (MELL) .... LH
Lieutenant (GEAB) .... lieut
Life Expectancy (MELL) .... LE
Life-Sustaining Device (MELL) .... LSD
Lift-Drag Ratio [*Aerodynamics*] .... L/D
Ligamenta Flava [*Medicine*] (MELL) .... LF
Light Emission Microscopy (MELL) .... LEM
Light Heavy-Duty Diesel Vehicle (EPAT) .... LHDDV
Lightbridge, Inc. [*NASDAQ symbol*] (SG) .... LTBG
Light-Chain Deposition (MELL) .... LCD
Light-Duty Gasoline Truck (EPAT) .... LDGT
Light-Minute .... lm
Lightning Imaging Sensor (MELL) .... LIS
Lightning Position Analyser (QUAC) .... LPA
Light-Second .... ls
Light-Year .... ly
Lihue-Kauai, HI [*FM radio station call letters*] (BROA) .... KAWV-FM
Like New in Box [*Watch collecting*] .... LNIB
Lima, OH [*FM radio station call letters*] (BROA) .... WFGF-FM

Lima, OH [*AM radio station call letters*] (BROA) .... WLJM
Lima, OH [*FM radio station call letters*] (BROA) .... WUZZ-FM
Limb-Salvage Surgery (MELL) .... LSS
Limited Official Use .... LOU
Limited User Testing .... LUT
Limited-Area Fine Mesh .... LAFM
Limousine .... Limo
Lincoln and Continental Owners Club (EA) .... LCOC
Lincoln, NE [*FM radio station call letters*] (BROA) .... KRKR-FM
Lincoln, NE [*FM radio station call letters*] (BROA) .... KZFX-FM
Linden, TX [*FM radio station call letters*] (BROA) .... KIXK-FM
Lindsay Mfg. [*NYSE symbol*] (SG) .... LNN
Lindsay, ON [*FM radio station call letters*] (BROA) .... CKLY-FM
Line Replaceable Unit .... LRU
Linea Aerea Nacional de Chile .... LanChile
Linea Aspera .... LA
Linear Enamel Hypoplasias (QUAC) .... LEH
Linens'n Things [*NYSE symbol*] (SG) .... LIN
Linguistics (BEE) .... Ling
Linolenic Acid (MELL) .... LA
Lionel Railroaders Club (EA) .... LRRC
Lions Gate Entertainment [*AMEX symbol*] (SG) .... LGF
Lipid Pneumonia (MELL) .... LP
Lipid Storage Disease (MELL) .... LSD
Lipid-Lowering Drug (MELL) .... LLD
Lipodystrophy [*Medicine*] (MELL) .... LD
Liquid Audio [*NASDAQ symbol*] (SG) .... LQID
Lisfranc Dislocation [*Medicine*] (MELL) .... LD
Lisman, AL [*FM radio station call letters*] (BROA) .... WPRN-FM
Literature Online [*Chadwyck-Healey*] .... LION
Lithia Motors'A' [*NYSE symbol*] (SG) .... LAD
Lithuania (MILB) L
Little League Shoulder (MELL) .... LLS
Little Rock, AR [*Television station call letters*] (BROA) .... KKAP
Little Rock, AR [*Television station call letters*] (BROA) .... KYPX
Liver Biopsy [*Medicine*] (MELL) .... LB
Liver Fluke [*Medicine*] (MELL) .... LF
Liver Infarct [*Medicine*] (MELL) LI
Liver Scan [*Medicine*] (MELL) .... LS
Living Relative Transplant Donor (MELL) .... LRTD
Lladro Society (EA) .... LS
LNR Property [*NYSE symbol*] (SG) .... LNR
Loan-to-Value Ratio [*Business term*] .... L/V
Lobster-Claw Deformity (MELL) .... LCD
Local Cerebral Ischemia [*Medicine*] (MELL) LCI
Local Data Acquisition .... LDA
Local Electrical Field Instrument (EOSA) .... LEFI
Local Emergency Response Committee (EPAT) .... LERC
Local Financial [*NASDAQ symbol*] (SG) .... LFIN
Local Government Association (GVA) .... LGA
Local Independently Nucleated Units of Structure (MELL) .... LINUS
Local Officials' Administration Network (EA) .... LOAN
Locked-in Syndrome [*Medicine*] (MELL) .... LIS
Lockjaw (MELL) .... LJ
Locomotor Ataxia [*Medicine*] (MELL) .... LA
Loculated Hydropneumothorax [*Medicine*] (MELL) .... LHPT
Lodgian, Inc. [*NYSE symbol*] (SG) .... LOD
Loews Cineplex Entertain't. [*NYSE symbol*] (SG) .... LCP
Log On America .... LOAX
Logan, UT [*FM radio station call letters*] (BROA) .... KVFX-FM
Logistic (MILB) .... log
London, OH [*FM radio station call letters*] (BROA) .... WCZZ-FM
Loners of America [*An association*] (EA) .... LOA
Long Beach, CA [*AM radio station call letters*] (BROA) .... KKTX
Long Beach, CA [*Television station call letters*] (BROA) .... KSCI
Long Beach Finl'. [*NASDAQ symbol*] (SG) .... LBFC
Long Branch, NJ [*FM radio station call letters*] (BROA) .... WWZY-FM
Long March [*Launch vehicle*] .... LM
Long Process of Incus [*Medicine*] (MELL) .... LPI
Longitudinal Arch of Foot (MELL) .... LAOF
Longitudinal Layer of Muscles of Stomach (MELL) .... LLMS
Long-Leg Cylinder Cast [*Medicine*] (MELL) LLCC
Longmont, CO [*FM radio station call letters*] (BROA) .... KCKK-FM
Long-Term Complication (MELL) .... LTC
Long-Term Consequence (MELL) .... LTC
Long-Term Residential .... LTR
Long-Term Venous Catheter [*Medicine*] (MELL) .... LTVC
Lonoke, AR [*FM radio station call letters*] (BROA) .... KHTE-FM
Lorain, OH [*Television station call letters*] (BROA) .... WUAB-DT
Los Angeles, CA [*Television station call letters*] (BROA) .... KABC-DT
Los Angeles, CA [*Television station call letters*] (BROA) .... KCBS-DT
Los Angeles, CA [*Television station call letters*] (BROA) .... KCET-DT
Los Angeles, CA [*FM radio station call letters*] (BROA) .... KCMG-FM
Los Angeles, CA [*Television station call letters*] (BROA) .... KCOP-DT
Los Angeles, CA [*Television station call letters*] (BROA) .... KNBC-DT
Los Angeles, CA [*Television station call letters*] (BROA) .... KTLA-DT
Los Angeles, CA [*Television station call letters*] (BROA) .... KTTV-DT
Los Angeles, CA [*Television station call letters*] (BROA) .... KWHY-DT
Los Angeles, CA [*AM radio station call letters*] (BROA) .... KXTA
Los Angeles Chargers [*National Football League*] [*1960*] (NFLA) .... LAC
Los Angeles County Museum of Natural History [*California*] .... LACM
Los Angeles Kings Booster Club (EA) .... LAKBC
Los Angeles Raiders [*National Football League*] [*1982-94*] (NFLA) .... LAR
Los Angeles Rams [*National Football League*] [*1946-94*] (NFLA) .... Los
Los Molinos, CA [*FM radio station call letters*] (BROA) .... KTHU-FM

Lost in Space [*Television Program*] .... LOS
Lost in Space Fannish Alliance (EA) .... LISFAN
Lou Christie Official Fan Club (EA) .... LCFC
Lou Gehrig Disease [*Medicine*] (MELL) .... LGD
Loudon, TN [*FM radio station call letters*] (BROA) .... WESK-FM
Louisana Department of Environmental Quality .... LDEQ
Louisiana (BEE) .... La
Louisiana Educational Assessment Program .... LEAP
Louisville, KY [*AM radio station call letters*] (BROA) .... WKJK
Louisville, KY [*AM radio station call letters*] (BROA) .... WLKY
Louisville, KY [*FM radio station call letters*] (BROA) .... WMHX-FM
Loveland, CO [*AM radio station call letters*] (BROA) .... KHPN
Low Apgar Score [*Medicine*] (MELL) .... LAS
Low Background Infrared Radiometry .... LBIR
Low Background Reference System .... LBRS
Low Calorie Diet (MELL) .... LCD
Low Cerebrospinal Fluid Pressure [*Medicine*] (MELL) .... LCSFP
Low Exposure (MELL) .... LE
Low Fiber Diet (MELL) .... LFD
Low Malignant Potential [*Medicine*] (MELL) .... LMP
Low Molecular Weight Dextran [*Medicine*] (MELL) .... lmmd
Low Power Radio .... LPR
Low Renin [*Medicine*] (MELL) .... LR
Low Resolution (QUAC) .... LR
Low Right Sternal Border [*Medicine*] (MELL) .... LRSB
Low Salt Diet (MELL) .... LSD
Low Transverse Cervical [*Medicine*] (MELL) .... LTC
Low Transverse Uterine Incision [*Medicine*] (MELL) .... LTUI
Low Urinary Calcium Exortion [*Medicine*] (MELL) .... LUCE
Low Velocity Intense Source .... LVIS
Low-Dose Ionizing Radiation (MELL) .... LDIR
Lowell, AR [*FM radio station call letters*] (BROA) .... KMXF-FM
Lower East Coast .... LEC
Lower Gastrointestinal [*Medicine*] (MELL) .... LGI
Lower Limb Fracture (MELL) .... LLF
Lower Limit of Normal [*Medicine*] (MELL) .... LLN
Lower Nephron Nephrosis [*Medicine*] (MELL) .... LNN
Lower Quadrant [*Medicine*] (MELL) .... LQ

Lowest Acceptable Daily Dose (EPAT) .... LADD
Lowest Dose Tested [*Environmental science*] (EPAT) .... LDT
Lowest Usual Maintenance Dose [*Medicine*] (MELL) .... LUMD
Low-Level Lead Exposure (MELL) .... LLLE
Low-Residue Diet (MELL) .... LRD
Low-Resolution Picture Transmission (EOSA) .... LRPT
Low-Set Ear (MELL) .... LSE
Lubbock, TX [*AM radio station call letters*] (BROA) .... KDAV
Lucey-Driscoll Syndrome [*Medicine*] (MELL) .... LDS
Lufkin, TX [*FM radio station call letters*] (BROA) .... KAVX-FM
Lumbar Facet Joints [*Medicine*] (MELL) .... LFJ
Lumbar Nerve Block [*Medicine*] (MELL) .... LNB
Lumbar Spinal Stenosis [*Medicine*] (MELL) .... LSS
Lumber City, GA [*FM radio station call letters*] (BROA) .. WMOC-FM
Lumberton, MS [*FM radio station call letters*] (BROA) ..... WLNF-FM
Lumberton, NC [*FM radio station call letters*] (BROA) ..... WFNC-FM
Lumbocostal Ligament [*Medicine*] (MELL) LCL
Lumbosacral Agenesis [*Medicine*] (MELL) .... LSA
Lumbosacral Plexus [*Medicine*] (MELL) .... LSP
Lumbosacral Root Injury (MELL) .... LSRI
Lung Biopsy [*Medicine*] (MELL) .... LB
Lung Fluke [*Medicine*] (MELL) .... LF
Lunula (MELL) .... LA
Lupus Anticoagulant [*Medicine*] (MELL) .... LA
Lupus Anticoagulant Syndrome [*Medicine*] (MELL) .... LAS
Lupus Band Test [*Medicine*] .... LBT
Luray, VA [*FM radio station call letters*] (BROA) .... WMXH-FM
Luveme, AL [*FM radio station call letters*] (BROA) .... WQLD-FM
Luxembourg (MILB) .... Lu
Lyme Arthritis (MELL) .... LA
Lyme Disease and Babesiosis [*Medicine*] (MELL) .... LD & B
Lymph Node Biopsy [*Medicine*] (MELL) .... LNB
Lymphadenosis Benigna Cutis [*Medicine*] .... LABC
Lymphogranuloma [*Medicine*] (MELL) .... LGM
Lymphoproliferative Disorder [*Medicine*] (MELL) .... LPD
Lymphoreticular Tissue [*Medicine*] (MELL) .... LRT
Lymphosarcoma Leukemia [*Medicine*] (MELL) .... LSL
Lynchburg, VA [*FM radio station call letters*] (BROA) ..... WRVX-FM
Lynchburg, VA [*AM radio station call letters*] (BROA) .... WVGM

By Meaning

MacDermid, Inc. [*NYSE symbol*] (SG) .... MRD
Machias, ME [*FM radio station call letters*] (BROA) .... WBEO-FM
Macon, GA [*AM radio station call letters*] (BROA) .... WLCG
Macon, GA [*FM radio station call letters*] (BROA) .... WPPG-FM
Macrofollicular Adenoma [*Medicine*] (MELL) .... MFA
Macrophage (MELL) .... M
Macrophage (MELL) .... MAC
Macrophage (MELL) .... MP
Macrosopic Polyarteritis Nodosa [*Medicine*] (MELL) ...... MPAN
Macula (MELL) .... MAC
Macula Coloboma [*Medicine*] (MELL) .... MC
Macula Lutea (MELL) .... ML
Macula of Saccule [*Medicine*] (MELL) .... MOS
Macula of Utricle [*Medicine*] (MELL) .... MOU
Mad Cow Disease [*Medicine*] (MELL) .... MCD
Madagascar (MILB) .... Mdg
Made from Purchased Materials [*Manufacturing*] .... mfpm
Made in the Same Establihment [*Manufacturing*] .... mitse
Madison, WI [*Television station call letters*] (BROA) .... WKOW-DT
Madison, WI [*FM radio station call letters*] (BROA) ..... WSUM-FM
Madison, WI [*AM radio station call letters*] (BROA) .... WTDA
Madisonville, KY [*Television station call letters*] (BROA) ... WWAZ-TV
Magee, MS [*AM radio station call letters*] (BROA) .... WSJC
Magic Latern Society of the United States and Canada (EA) .... ML Society
Magic of Bewitched Fan Club (EA) .... MBFC
Magnetic Field Gradient (MELL) .... MFG
Magnetic Field Satellite (EOSA) .... Magsat
Magnetic Fusion Energy Network .... MFEnet
Magnum Hunter Resources [*AMEX symbol*] (SG) .... MHR
Magyar TavKozlesi ADS [*NYSE symbol*] (SG) .... MTA
Mail Label .... ML
Mail-Well, Inc. [*NYSE symbol*] (SG) .... MWL
Main Mission Antennas .... MMA
Main Operating Room (MELL) .... MOR
Main Outcome Measure [*Medicine*] (MELL) .... MOM
Maine Veterinary Medical Association (GVA) .... MEVMA
Maintainability Development Test [*Army*] .... MDT
Maintained Anesthesia Care (MELL) .... MAC
Maintenance (MILB) .... maint
Maintenance of Inactive Industrial Facilities .... MIIF
Maintenance of Wakefulness Test (MELL) .... MWT
Maisonneuve Fracture [*Medicine*] (MELL) .... MF
Major (GEAB) .... maj
Major Commands [*Military*] .... MACOM
Major Depression and Bipolar Disorder [*Medicine*] (MELL) ... MD-BD
Major Renal Calix [*Medicine*] (MELL) .... MRC
Major Serologic Antigen [*Medicine*] (MELL) .... MSA
Malabsorption Syndrome (MELL) .... MAS
Malawi (MILB) .... Mlw
Malaysia (MILB) .... Mal
Malaysia Tourism Promotion Board (EA) .... MTPB
Male Development Disorder (MELL) .... MDD
Male Escutcheon [*Medicine*] (MELL) .... ME
Male or Female .... M/F
Malformed Low-Set Ears (MELL) .... MLSE
Malibu Entmt Intl. [*AMEX symbol*] (SG) .... MBE
Malignant Astrocytoma [*Medicine*] (MELL) .... MA
Malignant Bone Pain (MELL) .... MBP
Malignant Carcinoid [*Medicine*] (MELL) .... MC
Malignant Carcinoid Syndrome [*Medicine*] (MELL) .... MCS
Malignant Cystic Neoplasm [*Medicine*] (MELL) .... MCN
Malignant Mixed Mesodermal Tumor [*Medicine*] (MELL) .... MMMT
Malignant Mixed Tumor [*Medicine*] (MELL) .... MMT
Malignant Pericardial Effusion [*Medicine*] (MELL) .... MPE
Malignant Renal Neoplasm [*Medicine*] (MELL) .... MRN
Malleable Penile Prosthesis [*Medicine*] (MELL) .... MPP
Mallet Finger (MELL) .... MF
Mallet Fracture [*Medicine*] (MELL) .... MF
Mallory-Weiss Syndrome [*Medicine*] (MELL) .... MWS
Malposition of Uterus [*Medicine*] (MELL) .... MPU
Malpractice (MELL) .... MP
Malta (MILB) .... M
Mal-Union of Fracture [*Medicine*] (MELL) .... MOF
Mammary Gland Adenoma [*Medicine*] (MELL) .... MGA
Mammary Gland Physiology and Pathology Society (GVA) ...... MPPS
Mammogenic Hormone [*Medicine*] (MELL) .... MGH

Mammography Quality Standards Act .... MQSA
Managed Bandwidth Service .... MBS
Managed Care Program (MELL) .... MCP
Managers Capital Appreciation Fund .... MGCAX
Manchester, NH [*Television station call letters*] (BROA) .... WMUR-DT
M&F Worldwide [*NYSE symbol*] (SG) .... MFW
Mandible (MELL) .... M
Mandibular Foramen [*Medicine*] (MELL) .... MF
Mandibular Nerve Block [*Medicine*] (MELL) .... MNB
Maneuvering Reentry Vehicle .... MaRV
Manganese Poisoning [*Medicine*] (MELL) .... MP
Mangled Extremity Severity Score [*Medicine*] (MELL) ...... MESS
Mangum, OK [*FM radio station call letters*] (BROA) .... KHIM FM
Manic Depressive Disorder (MELL) .... MDD
Manic Episode [*Medicine*] (MELL) .... ME
Manitoba School Library Association .... MSLA
Maniwaki, PQ [*FM radio station call letters*] (BROA) ..... CKMG-FM
Mansfield, OH [*Television station call letters*] (BROA) ... WMFD-DT
Mansfield, PA [*FM radio station call letters*] (BROA) .... WNBQ-FM
Manteo, NC [*FM radio station call letters*] (BROA) .... WBGI-FM
Manual Cervical Traction [*Medicine*] (MELL) .... MCT
Manual Transmission .... MTX
Manufacturer (PROS) .... Mfr
Manufacturing (PROS) .... Mfg
Manufacturing Technical Assistance .... MTA
Maple Bark Disease [*Medicine*] (MELL) .... MBD
Maple-Syrup Disease [*Medicine*] (MELL) .... MSD
MapQuest.com, Inc. [*NASDAQ symbol*] (SG) .... MQST
Marathoner's Toe (MELL) .... MT
Marble Bone Disease [*Medicine*] (MELL) .... MBD
Marble Hill, MO [*FM radio station call letters*] (BROA) .. KBGJ-FM
March (BEE) .... Mar
March Fracture [*Medicine*] (MELL) .... MF
Marchiafava-Bignami Disease [*Medicine*] (MELL) .... MF
Marco, FL [*FM radio station call letters*] (BROA) .... WMKO-FM
Marco Island, FL [*AM radio station call letters*] (BROA) ... WMIB
Marie-Bamberger Disease [*Medicine*] (MELL) .... MBD
Marietta, OH [*FM radio station call letters*] (BROA) ..... WRVB-FM
Marietta, OH [*AM radio station call letters*] (BROA) .... WYLI
Marijuana (MELL) .... M
Marimba, Inc. [*NASDAQ symbol*] (SG) .... MRBA
Marine Channel (GEOI) .... CHNM
Marine City, MI [*AM radio station call letters*] (BROA) .... WHYT
Marine Corps .... MarCorps
Marine Engineers' Beneficial Association/National Maritime Union
(EA) .... MEBA/NMU
Marine Expeditionary Force/Brigade/Unit (MILB) .... MEF/B/U
Marine Limit (QUAC) .... ML
Marine Petrol Tr. [*NASDAQ symbol*] (SG) .... MARPS
Marion, AL [*AM radio station call letters*] (BROA) .... WJUS
Marion, MS [*FM radio station call letters*] (BROA) .... WYYW-FM
Marion, OH [*FM radio station call letters*] (BROA) .... WOSB-FM
Maritime Coastal Defense Vessel (MILB) .... MCDV
Markel Corp. [*NYSE symbol*] (SG) .... MKL
MarketWatch.com [*NYSE symbol*] (SG) .... MKTW
Markov Chain Monte Carlo Method .... MCMC
Marlboro, VT [*FM radio station call letters*] (BROA) ..... WSSH-FM
Marlborough, MA [*Television station call letters*] (BROA) ... WHSH-DT
Married (MELL) .... M
Marrow Graft Rejection [*Medicine*] (MELL) .... MGR
Mars Orbiter Laser Altimeter .... MOLA
Mars Sample Return Mission [*NASA*] .... MSRM
Marshall, MI [*FM radio station call letters*] (BROA) ..... WWKN-FM
Martin Suicide Depression Inventory (MELL) .... MSDI
Marvel Enterprises [*NYSE symbol*] (SG) .... MVL
Marvell, AR [*FM radio station call letters*] (BROA) ...... KVRN-FM
Maryland (BEE) .... Md
Maryland Classified Employees Association .... MCEA
Maryland School Performance Assessment Program .... MSPAP
Maryland Veterinary Medical Association (GVA) .... MDVMA
Marysville, OH [*FM radio station call letters*] (BROA) ... WZAZ-FM
Maserati Club of America (EA) .... MCA
Mason & Hanger Corp. .... MHC
Mason City, IA [*AM radio station call letters*] (BROA) ... KBDC-FM
Mason Fracture Classification System [*Medicine*] (MELL) ... MFCS
Masontown, PA [*FM radio station call letters*] (BROA) .... WLWJ-FM

Massachusetts (BEE) .... Mass
Massachusetts Society for Medical Research (GVA) .... MSMR
Massachusetts Veterinary Medical Association (GVA) .... MAVMA
Masseter [*Medicine*] (MELL) .... MA
Massive Blood Transfusion [*Medicine*] (MELL) .... MBT
MasTec, Inc. [*NYSE symbol*] (SG) .... MTZ
Master Record Identification Number (EPAT) .... MRID
Master's Degree in Public Policy .... MPP
Mastoid Air Cell [*Medicine*] (MELL) .... MAC
Mastoid Process [*Medicine*] (MELL) .... MP
Matav-Cable Sys ADS [*NASDAQ symbol*] (SG) .... MATVY
Matchbox [*Mattel*] .... MB
Matchbox [*Toy collection*] .... MBX
Matchbox Challenge Cars [*Toy collection*] .... MBCC
Matchbox Models of Yesteryear [*Toy collection*] .... MBYY
Matchbox Models of Yesteryear [*Toy collection*] .... MOY
Matchbox Regular Wheels [*Toy collection*] .... MBRW
Matchbox Superfast [*Toy collection*] .... MBSF
Matched Unrelated Donor [*Medicine*] (MELL) .... MUD
Materials Dosimetry Reference Facility .... MDRF
Maternal (MELL) .... M
Maternal (GEAB) .... mat
Maternal and Child Health Bureau (MELL) .... MCHB
Maternal Genetic Disease (MELL) .... MGD
Maternal Heart Rate (MELL) .... MHR
Maternal Weight Gain (MELL) .... MWG
Maternal-Fetal Medicine (MELL) .... MFM
Mathematics Teacher [*A publication*] .... MT
Mature Cataract (MELL) .... MC
Mature Corpus Luteum [*Medicine*] (MELL) .... MCL
Mature Cystic Teratoma [*Medicine*] (MELL) .... MCT
Mature Ovarian Folicle [*Medicine*] (MELL) .... MOF
Mature Vesicular Follicle [*Medicine*] (MELL) .... MVS
Maui Land & Pineapple [*AMEX symbol*] (SG) .... MLP
Maumelle, AR [*FM radio station call letters*] (BROA) .... KSIZ-FM
Maurice Lacroix .... ML
Mauritius (MILB) .... Ms
Max-Delbrueck-Center [*Berlin, Germany*] .... MDC
Maxilla (MELL) .... M
Maxilla Alveolar Process [*Medicine*] (MELL) .... MAP
Maxillary Sinus [*Medicine*] (MELL) .... MS
Maximal Blink Index [*Medicine*] (MELL) .... MBI
Maximal Efficacy [*Medicine*] (MELL) .... ME
Maximal Exercise Ventilation (MELL) .... MEV
Maximal Inspiratory Flow Rate [*Medicine*] (MELL) .... MIFR
Maximal Predicted Heart Rate [*Medicine*] (MELL) .... MPHP
Maximal Pulse Rate [*Medicine*] (MELL) .... MPR
Maximal Urethral Pressure [*Medicine*] (MELL) .... MUP
Maximilian Numismatic and Historical Society (EA) .... MAX SOCIETY
Maximum a Posteriori Estimate .... MAP estimate
Maximum Card Study Unit [*An association*] (EA) .... MACSU
Maximum Inspiratory Force [*Medicine*] (MELL) .... MIF
Maximum Possible Number (EPAT) .... MPN
Maximum Tolerated Pressure (MELL) .... MTP
Maximum-Latewood-Density .... MXD
MAXIMUS, Inc. [*NYSE symbol*] (SG) .... MMS
Mayaguez, PR [*FM radio station call letters*] (BROA) .... WRUO-FM
Mayer-Rokitansky-Kuester-Hauser Syndrome [*Medicine*] (MELL) .... MRKHS
Mayfield, KY [*AM radio station call letters*] (BROA) .... WIVR
Mayfield, KY [*FM radio station call letters*] (BROA) .... WIVR-FM
Mayflower Quarterly [*A publication*] (GEAB) .... MQ
Mayville, WI [*FM radio station call letters*] (BROA) .... WMDC-FM
Mazda Club (EA) .... MC
McAlester, OK [*FM radio station call letters*] (BROA) .... KBCW-FM
McArthur, OH [*FM radio station call letters*] (BROA) .... WCLX-FM
McCall, ID [*FM radio station call letters*] (BROA) .... KDZY-FM
McCamey, TX [*FM radio station call letters*] (BROA) .... KPBM-FM
McConnellsburg, PA [*FM radio station call letters*] (BROA) .... WEEO-FM
McCook, NE [*FM radio station call letters*] (BROA) .... KIOD-FM
McCook, NE [*FM radio station call letters*] (BROA) .... KSWN-FM
McCook, TX [*FM radio station call letters*] (BROA) .... KCAS-FM
McCormick & Co. [*NYSE symbol*] (SG) .... MKC
McGill Pain Assessment Questionnaire (MELL) .... MPAQ
Mckeesport, PA [*AM radio station call letters*] (BROA) .... WPTT
McKinney, TX [*FM radio station call letters*] (BROA) .... KZDF-FM
McMinnville, TN [*FM radio station call letters*] (BROA) .... WCPI-FM
McMoRan Exploration [*NYSE symbol*] (SG) .... MMR
MDC Corp. Cl'A' [*NASDAQ symbol*] (SG) .... MDCA
Mean Absorption Time [*Medicine*] (MELL) .... MAT
Mean and Dispersion Additive Model [*Statistics*] .... MADAM
Mean Effective Pressure .... Mep
Mean High Water Level (QUAC) .... MHWL
Mean Incubation Perios (MELL) .... MIP
Mean Low Water Level (QUAC) .... MLWL
Mean Plasma Concentration [*Medicine*] (MELL) .... MPC
Mean Prognostic Score [*Medicine*] (MELL) .... MPS
Mean Sea Level Pressure (WEAT) .... MSLP
Measles (MELL) .... M
Measurement of Atmospheric Pollution from Satellites (EOSA) .... MAPS
Measurement Quality Assurance .... MQA
Meat Hygiene Inspector (GVA) .... MHI
Meat Hygiene Service (GVA) .... MHS
Meatus (MELL) .... M
MECH Financial [*NASDAQ symbol*] (SG) .... MECH
Mechanical Atherectomy [*Medicine*] (MELL) .... MA
Mechanical Incontinence [*Medicine*] (MELL) .... MI
Mechanical Low Back Pain (MELL) .... MLBP
Mechanical Obstruction (MELL) .... MO
Mechanics (BEE) .... Mech
Mechanized (MILB) .... mech
Media Arts Group [*NYSE symbol*] (SG) .... MDA
Media Guide .... MG
Media Metrix [*NASDAQ symbol*] (SG) .... MMXI
Media Networks, Inc. .... MNI
Medial Canthus (MELL) .... MC
Medial Meniscus Tear [*Medicine*] (MELL) .... MMT
Medial Pterygoid Plate [*Medicine*] (MELL) .... MPP
Medial Thyrohyoid Ligament [*Medicine*] (MELL) .... MTHL
Medial Tibial Stress Syndrome [*Medicine*] (MELL) .... MTSS
Median Arcuate Ligament Syndrome [*Medicine*] (MELL) .... MALS
Median Cleft Face Syndrome [*Medicine*] (MELL) .... MCFS
Median Effective Dose ED50
Median Incisal Diastema [*Medicine*] (MELL) .... MID
Median Nerve Entrapment Syndrome [*Medicine*] (MELL) .... MNES
Median Nerve Neuropathy [*Medicine*] (MELL) .... MNN
Median Nerve Palsy [*Medicine*] (MELL) .... MNP
Median Reaction Time (MELL) .... MRT
Median Relapse Time (MELL) .... MRT
Mediastinal Lymph Node [*Medicine*] (MELL) .... MLN
Mediastinal Paraganglionic Tumor [*Medicine*] (MELL) .... MPGT
Medical Antishock Trausers (MELL) .... MAST
Medical Control, Inc. [*NASDAQ symbol*] (SG) .... MDCLC
Medical Emergency Relief International (MELL) .... MERLIN
Medical Error Reduction (MELL) .... MER
Medical House Officer (MELL) .... MHO
Medical Improvement Expectation (MELL) .... MIE
Medical Power of Attorney (MELL) .... MPOA
Medical Termination of Pregnancy (MELL) .... MTP
Medicare (MELL) .... M
Medicated Feeding Stuff (GVA) .... MFS
Medication Error [*Medicine*] (MELL) .... ME
Medication Use Evaluated (MELL) .... MUE
Medieval (BEE) .... med
Medium Energy Telescope .... MET
Medium Heavy-Duty Diesel Vehicle (EPAT) .... MHDDV
Medulla Oblongata [*Medicine*] (MELL) .... MO
Medullary Cavity [*Medicine*] (MELL) .... MC
Medullary Cystic Renal Disease [*Medicine*] (MELL) .... MCRD
Meeting (BEE) .... mtg
Megachannel Extra-Terrestrial Assay .... META
Megacystis-Megaureter Syndrome [*Medicine*] (MELL) .... MMS
Megakaryocyte [*Medicine*] (MELL) .... MKC
Megaloblastic Anemia [*Medicine*] (MELL) .... MA
Megaloblastic Erythropoiesis [*Medicine*] (MELL) .... MGE
Megalocornea (MELL) .... MC
Megalosperm [*Medicine*] (MELL) .... MS
Megaparseo .... Mpc
Melanocytic Nevus [*Medicine*] (MELL) .... MN
Melatonin (MELL) .... MT
Melbourne, FL [*Television station call letters*] (BROA) .... WOPX
Melbourne, FL [*AM radio station call letters*] (BROA) .... WTMS
Melphenal and Prednisone [*Medicine*] (MELL) .... M&P
Membranous Lupus Nephropathy [*Medicine*] (MELL) .... MLN
Membranous Nephropathy [*Medicine*] (MELL) .... MN
Memorial (PROS) .... Meml
Memory Loss (MELL) .... ML
Memphis, TN [*Television station call letters*] (BROA) .... WPXX-TV
Mena, AR [*FM radio station call letters*] (BROA) .... KBIJ-FM
Meningeal (MELL) .... M
Meningitis [*Medicine*] (MELL) .... MEN
Meningococcal Meningitis [*Medicine*] (MELL) .... MCM
Meningococcal Protein Conjugate [*Medicine*] (MELL) .... MPC
Meningococcus Vaccine [*Medicine*] (MELL) .... MCV
Meningomyelocele [*Medicine*] (MELL) .... MMC
Menkes' Syndrome [*Medicine*] (MELL) .... MS
Menstrual-Associatied Sleep Disorder [*Medicine*] (MELL) .... MASD
Mental Health/Chemical Dependency .... MH/CD
Mental Health/Substance Abuse .... MH/SA
Mentally Stable and Oriented (MELL) .... MSO
Mercury Poisoning [*Medicine*] (MELL) .... MP
Meridian Medical Tech. [*NASDAQ symbol*] (SG) .... MTEC
Meridian, MS [*AM radio station call letters*] (BROA) .... WFFX
Meridian, MS [*FM radio station call letters*] (BROA) .... WMMZ-FM
Meristar Hotels & Resorts [*NYSE symbol*] (SG) .... MMH
Meritor Automotive [*NYSE symbol*] (SG) .... MRS
Merkert American [*NASDAQ symbol*] (SG) .... MERK
Mesa, AZ [*Television station call letters*] (BROA) .... KPNX-DT
Mesa, AZ [*FM radio station call letters*] (BROA) .... KZZP-FM
Mesenchymal Cell Concentration [*Medicine*] (MELL) .... MCC
Mesenteric Venous System [*Medicine*] (MELL) .... MVS
Mesh Plug Hernioplasty [*Medicine*] (MELL) .... MPH
Mesio-Linguo-Occlusal [*Dentistry*] (MELL) .... MLO
Mesquite, NV [*FM radio station call letters*] (BROA) .... KBJG-FM
Metabolic Acidosis [*Medicine*] (MELL) .... MA
Metabolic Bone Disease [*Medicine*] (MELL) .... MBD
Metabolic Renal Disease [*Medicine*] (MELL) .... MRD
Metacarpal Bone [*Medicine*] (MELL) .... MCBs
Metacentric Chromosome [*Medicine*] (MELL) .... MCC
Metachronous Seeding [*Medicine*] (MELL) .... MCS
MetaCreations Corp. [*NASDAQ symbol*] (SG) .... MCRE

Metadata Information Clearinghouse Interactive .... MICI
Metallurgy (BEE) .... Metall
Metals USA [*NYSE symbol*] (SG) .... MUI
Metamor Worldwide [*NASDAQ symbol*] (SG) .... MMWW
Metastases with Unknown Primary Site [*Medicine*] (MELL) .... MUPS
Metastatic Carcinomatous Meningitis [*Medicine*] (MELL) .... MCM
Metastatic Efficiency Index [*Medicine*] (MELL) .... MEI
Metastatic Mixed Mullerian Tumor [*Medicine*] (MELL) .... MMMT
Meteorological Actual Report (WEAT) .... METAR
Meteorological Communications Package (EOSA) .... MCP
Meteorology (BEE) .... Meteorol
Methadone Mainetnance Treatment [*Medicine*] (MELL) .... MMT
Methyl Alcohol Poisoning [*Medicine*] (MELL) .... MAP
Methylene Bisphenyl Isocyanate [*Medicine*] (MELL) .... MBI
Metrika Systems [*AMEX symbol*] (SG) .... MKA
Metris Cos. [*NYSE symbol*] (SG) .... MXT
Metro Information Svcs. [*NASDAQ symbol*] (SG) .... MISI
Metromedia Fiber Network'A' [*NASDAQ symbol*] (SG) .... MFNX
Metter, GA [*FM radio station call letters*] (BROA) .... WBMZ-FM
Metter, GA [*AM radio station call letters*] (BROA) .... WHCG
Mettler-Toledo Intl. [*NYSE symbol*] (SG) .... MTD
Mexican Isthmus [*Crude oil*] .... MI
Mexico Network .... MEXnet
Mexico, NY [*FM radio station call letters*] (BROA) .... WVOQ-FM
Meyer-Betz Disease [*Medicine*] (MELL) .... MBD
Miami Dolphins [*National Football League*] [*1966-present*] (NFLA) .... Mia
Miami, FL [*Television station call letters*] (BROA) .... WBZL
Miami, FL [*Television station call letters*] (BROA) .... WFOR-DT
Miami, FL [*Television station call letters*] (BROA) .... WPLG-DT
Miami, FL [*Television station call letters*] (BROA) .... WPXM
Miami, FL [*Television station call letters*] (BROA) .... WSVN-DT
Miami Springs, FL [*AM radio station call letters*] (BROA) .... WNMA
Micanopy, FL [*FM radio station call letters*] (BROA) .... WSKY-FM
Michelson Interferometric Passive Atmosphere Sounder (EOSA) .... MIPAS
Michigan Alliance Against Hate Crimes .... MIAAHC
Michigan Association for Media in Education .... MAME
Michigan Association of Media Educators .... MAME
Michigan Department of Civil Rights .... MDCR
Michigan Elk Breeders Association (GVA) .... MEBA
Michigan Research Library Network .... MIRLYN
Michigan Society for Medical Research (GVA) .... MISMR
Michigan State University Pre-Veterinary Medical Association (GVA) .... MSU-PVMA
Michigan's Remote Operated Vehicle for Education and Research .... M-ROVER
Micro Ecological Life Support Alternative [*European Space Agency*] .... MELISSA
Micro Therapeutics .... MTIX
Microadenoma [*Medicine*] (MELL) .... MA
Microagglutination Test [*Medicine*] (MELL) .... MAT
Microalbuminuria [*Medicine*] (MELL) .... MAU
Microamperage Electrical Nerve Stimulation [*Medicine*] (MELL) .... MENS
Microbial Pest Control Agent (EPAT) .... MPCA
Microcar and Minicar Club (EA) .... MMC
Microemboli [*Medicine*] (MELL) .... ME
Microfilament (MELL) .... MF
Microfilm Card Catalog (GEAB) .... MCC
MicroFinancial, Inc. [*NYSE symbol*] (SG) .... MFI
Micromuse, Inc. [*NASDAQ symbol*] (SG) .... MUSE
Microprocessor Architecture for Lava Computing .... MAJC
Microscope Assisted Guided Intervention [*Medical technique*] .... MAGI
Microsoft Management Console .... MMC
MicroStrategy Inc'A' [*NASDAQ symbol*] (SG) .... MSTR
Microsurgical Discectomy [*Medicine*] (MELL) .... MSD
Microvascular Decompression [*Medicine*] (MELL) .... MVD
Microwave Anisotropy Probe .... MAP
Microwave Humidity Sounder (EOSA) .... MHS
Microwave Radiation (MELL) .... MWR
Microwave Temperature Sounder (EOSA) .... MTS
Mid Penn Bancorp [*AMEX symbol*] (SG) .... MBP
Midas, Inc. [*NYSE symbol*] (SG) .... MDS
Mid-Atlantic State University .... MASU
Mid-Century Mercury Car Club (EA) .... MCMCC
Midclavicular Plane [*Medicine*] (MELL) .... MCP
Middle and High Latitudes Oceanic Variability Study (EOSA) .... MAHLOVS
Middle Cardiac Vein [*Medicine*] (MELL) .... MCV
Middle Constrictor Muscle of Pharynx [*Medicine*] (MELL) .... MCMP
Middle Cranial Fossa [*Medicine*] (MELL) .... MCF
Middle Cranial Fossa Syndrome [*Medicine*] (MELL) .... MCFS
Middle Dutch (BEE) .... MDu
Middle Ear Ventilation (MELL) .... MEV
Middle East Christian Committee .... MECHRIC
Middle East Network Information Center [*Internet resource*] .... MENIC
Middle High German (GEAB) .... MHG
Middle Lobe of Lung (MELL) .... MLL
Middle Sacral Artery [*Medicine*] (MELL) .... MSA
Middle Turbinate Headache Syndrome [*Medicine*] (MELL) .... MTHS
Middle-Ear Infection (MELL) .... MEI
Midland Co. [*NASDAQ symbol*] (SG) .... MLAN
Midland, TX [*Television station call letters*] (BROA) .... KUPB
Midline Retroperitoneal Syndrome [*Medicine*] (MELL) .... MRPS
Midpalmar Crease [*Medicine*] (MELL) .... MPC
Midstream Urine Specimen [*Medicine*] (MELL) .... MUS
Mid-Systolic Murmur [*Medicine*] (MELL) .... MSM
Midvoid Stream [*Medicine*] (MELL) .... MVS
Midwest Insulation Contractors Association .... MICA
Midwest, WY [*FM radio station call letters*] (BROA) .... KRVK-FM
Midwife (MELL) .... MW
Migraine Headache (MELL) .... MH
Migraine with Interval Headache (MELL) .... MIH
Migrant Education Projects .... MEP
MIH Limited'A' [*NASDAQ symbol*] (SG) .... MIHL
MIIX Group [*NYSE symbol*] (SG) .... MHU
Mike Yager Fan Club (EA) .... MYFC
Milacron, Inc. [*NYSE symbol*] (SG) .... MZ
Milbank, SD [*FM radio station call letters*] (BROA) .... KKSD-FM
Mild Mental Retardation (MELL) .... MMR
Mild Thyroid Failure [*Medicine*] (MELL) .... MTF
Miles per Gallon .... Mpg
Miles per Hour .... Mph
Milestone Scientific [*AMEX symbol*] (SG) .... MS
Milford, OH [*FM radio station call letters*] (BROA) .... WKFS-FM
Military (BEE) .... mil
Military and Police Uniform Association (EA) .... MPUA
Military Education Level One [*Army*] .... MEL 1
Military Land Warrant (GEAB) .... MLW
Military Macaw [*Bird*] .... MM
Military Operations in Urban Terrain .... MOUT
Military Participation Ratio of the Military Age Cohorts .... MPRMAC
Military Spending Working Group .... MSWG
Military Sponsored Air Service .... MSAS
Military Standard .... MIL STD
Milk Development Council (GVA) .... MDC
Milk Letdown (MELL) .... ML
Milk Sugar (MELL) .... MS
Milk-Alkali Disease [*Medicine*] (MELL) .... MAD
Milkmaid's Dislocation [*Medicine*] (MELL) .... MMD
Milkmaid's Elbow [*Medicine*] (MELL) .... MME
Milkman's Syndrome [*Medicine*] (MELL) .... MMS
Millennium Star Atlas [*A publication*] .... MSA
Millington, TN [*AM radio station call letters*] (BROA) .... WOOM
Million Years .... Myr
Milton, WV [*FM radio station call letters*] (BROA) .... WAMX-FM
Milton, WV [*AM radio station call letters*] (BROA) .... WZZW
Milton-Freewater, OR [*FM radio station call letters*] (BROA) .... KTHK-FM
Milwaukee Brace [*Medicine*] (MELL) .... MB
Milwaukee, WI [*AM radio station call letters*] (BROA) .... WJYI
MIM Corp. [*NASDAQ symbol*] (SG) .... MIMS
Minden, LA [*FM radio station call letters*] (BROA) .... KSYR-FM
Minden, LA [*Television station call letters*] (BROA) .... WPXO
Mine Countermeasures/Command and Support Ship (MILB) .... MCM/CS
Minehunter, Coastal/Inshore/Offshore (MILB) .... MHC/I/O
Miner, MO [*FM radio station call letters*] (BROA) .... KBHI-FM
Mineralogy (BEE) .... Mineral
Minerva Jacket [*Medicine*] (MELL) .... MJ
Minesweeper, Coastal/Inshore/Offshore/Riverine (MILB) .... MSC/I/O/R
Minimal Infecting Dose [*Medicine*] (MELL) .... MID
Minimal Irradiation Dose [*Medicine*] (MELL) .... MID
Minimal Perceptible Odor (MELL) .... MPO
Minimal Phototoxic Erythema Dose [*Medicine*] (MELL) .... MPED
Minimal Renal Disease [*Medicine*] (MELL) .... MRD
Minimal Resolvable Temperature .... MRT
Minimally Invasive Direct Coronary Artery Bypass [*Medicine*] (MELL) .... MIDCAB
Minimum Convex Polygon .... MCP
Minimum Distance Probability .... MDP
Minimum Methadone Service [*Medicine*] (MELL) .... MMS
Minister of the Gospel (GEAB) .... MG
Minister President .... MinPres
Minnesota Vikings [*National Football League*] [*1961-present*] (NFLA) .... Min
Minor Head Injury (MELL) .... MHI
Minor Motor Aphasia [*Medicine*] (MELL) .... MMA
Minor Planet Electronic Circular [*A publication*] .... MPEC
Minor Renal Calix [*Medicine*] (MELL) .... MRC
Minorities, Females, Handicapped .... M/F/H
Minority/Female Business Enterprise .... MFBE
Minot, ND [*Television station call letters*] (BROA) .... KXND
Mint in a Mint Box [*Collectibles*] .... MIMB
Mint in a Near Mint Box [*Collectibles*] .... MINMB
Mint in Manufacturer's Packaging [*Collectibles*] .... MIMP
Mint in Mint Package [*Collectibles*] .... MIMP
Mint in Near Mint Package [*Collectibles*] .... MINMP
Mint on a Mint Card [*Collectibles*] .... MOMC
Mint on Card [*Collectibles*] .... MOC
Mint on Mint Card [*Toy collection*] .... MOMC
Mint on Near Mint Card [*Collectibles*] .... MONMC
Mint with Both Mint Tags [*Collectibles*] .... MWBMT
Mint with Mint Tag [*Collectibles*] .... MWMT
Minute Ventilatory Volume for Experimental Animal Species .... MVa
Minute Ventilatory Volume for Human .... MVh
Minute Ventilatory Volume for Human in an Occupational Environment .... MVho
Missile (MILB) .... msl
Missing Completely at Random .... MCAR
Mission, KS [*AM radio station call letters*] (BROA) .... KUPN
Mission Operations Manager (EOSA) .... MOM
Missoula, MT [*FM radio station call letters*] (BROA) .... KMZL-FM
Missouri (BEE) .... Mo
Missouri Assessment Program .... MAP
Missouri Association of School Librarian .... MASL
Missouri Association of School Librarians .... MASL
Mitchell, SD [*Television station call letters*] (BROA) .... KDLV-TV
Mitochrondrial Encephalomyopathy with Acidosis and Stroke [*Medicine*] (MELL) .... MELAS

Mitosis Index [*Medicine*] (MELL) .... MI
Mitral Murmur [*Medicine*] (MELL) .... MM
Mitral Valve Cusps [*Medicine*] (MELL) .... MVC
Mixed Anxiety/Depression Syndrome [*Medicine*] (MELL) .... MADS
Mixed Germ Cell Tumor [*Medicine*] (MELL) .... MGCT
Mixed Gonadal Dysgenesis (MELL) .... MGD
Mixed Uranium Plutonium Oxide .... MOX
MKS Instruments [*NASDAQ symbol*] (SG) .... MKSI
MMC Networks [*NASDAQ symbol*] (SG) .... MMCN
Moapa Valley, NV [*FM radio station call letters*] (BROA) .... KBHQ-FM
Moberly, MO [*FM radio station call letters*] (BROA) .... KBKC-FM
Moberly, MO [*FM radio station call letters*] (BROA) .... KCSX-FM
Mobil Air Conditioner (EPAT) .... MAC
Mobile Calibration Unit .... MCU
MOCON, Inc. [*NASDAQ symbol*] (SG) .... MOCO
Model Energy Code [*Environmental Protection Agency*] (EPAT) .... MEC
Model Year .... M/Y
Modem Media.Poppe Tyson'A' [*NASDAQ symbol*] (SG) .... MMPT
Moderate Resolution Imaging Spectrometer-Nadir (EOSA) .... MODIS-N
Moderate Resolution Imaging Spectrometer-Tilt (EOSA) .... MODIS-T
Moderate Resolution Imaging Spectroradiometer (EOSA) .... MODIS
Moderately Low Birth Weight (MELL) .... MLBW
Modern Red Schoolhouse .... MRSh
Modesto, CA [*AM radio station call letters*] (BROA) .... KANM
Modified Bagshawe Protocol [*Medicine*] (MELL) .... MBP
Modified Immune Serum Globulin [*Medicine*] (MELL) .... MISG
Modified Radical Mastectomy [*Medicine*] (MELL) .... MRM
Modiolus (MELL) .... M
Modis Professional Svcs. [*NYSE symbol*] (SG) .... MPS
Modular Well-Differentiated Lymphocytic Lymphoma [*Medicine*] (MELL) .... NWDL
Moeller-Barlow Disease [*Medicine*] (MELL) .... MBD
Mohawk Industries [*NYSE symbol*] (SG) .... MHK
Molality (MELL) .... m
Molarity (MELL) .... M
Moldova (MILB) .... Mol
Molecular Beam Epitaxy .... MBE
Molt Periosteal Elevator [*Medicine*] (MELL) .... MPEC
Moluccan Cockatoo [*Bird*] M2
Monaco Coach [*NYSE symbol*] (SG) .... MNC
Monee, IL [*FM radio station call letters*] (BROA) .... WJCG-FM
Monetary Control Act .... MCA
Mongolia (MILB) .... Mgl
Monitoring the Future [*University of Michigan project*] .... MtF
Monkeein' Around [*An association*] (EA) .... MA
Monoamine Oxidase (MELL) .... MOA
Monoclonal Antibody Therapy (MELL) .... MCAT
Monoclonal Rheumatoid Factor [*Medicine*] (MELL) .... mRF
Monomorphic Adenoma [*Medicine*] (MELL) .... MA
Monophosphoryl Lipid A [*Medicine*] (MELL) .... MLA
Monosil Manufacturers Association .... MMA
Monosodium Glutamate Headache [*Medicine*] (MELL) .... MGH
Monroe, LA [*AM radio station call letters*] (BROA) .... KBJE
Monroe, MI [*AM radio station call letters*] (BROA) .... WLLZ
Monroe, NC [*AM radio station call letters*] (BROA) .... WKRE
Montana Public Employees Association .... MONT-PEA
Monteggia Fracture-Dislocation [*Medicine*] (MELL) .... MFD
Monticello, FL [*FM radio station call letters*] (BROA) .... WTAL-FM
Montreal, PQ [*FM radio station call letters*] (BROA) .... CBME-FM
Montreal, PQ [*FM radio station call letters*] (BROA) .... CJPX-FM
Montrose, CO [*FM radio station call letters*] (BROA) .... KPRH-FM
MONY Group [*NYSE symbol*] (SG) .... MNY
Moose Lake, MN [*FM radio station call letters*] (BROA) .... KBFH-FM
Morbus Hemolyticus Neonatorum [*Medicine*] (MELL) .... MHN
Morel Syndrome [*Medicine*] (MELL) .... MS
Morgagni Hernia [*Medicine*] (MELL) .... MH
Moro's Reflex [*Medicine*] (MELL) .... MR
Morphology (MELL) .... MOR
Morris, IL [*FM radio station call letters*] (BROA) .... WYXX-FM
Morrison Management Specialists [*NYSE symbol*] (SG) .... MHI
Mortgage (GEAB) .... mtg
Morton Toe (MELL) .... MT
Morton's Neuroma of Toe [*Medicine*] (MELL) .... MNT
Mosaic Wart [*Medicine*] (MELL) .... MW
Mother (GEAB) .... mo
Mothers Offering Maternal Support [*An association*] (MELL) .... MOMS
Motile with Normal Morphology [*Medicine*] (MELL) .... MNM
Motion Base Technologies .... MBT
MotivePower Indus. [*NYSE symbol*] (SG) .... MPO
Motor Company of Botswana .... MCB
Motor Interneuron (MELL) .... MIN
Mount Airy, NC [*AM radio station call letters*] (BROA) .... WLHJ
Mount Carmel, IL [*AM radio station call letters*] (BROA) .... WVMC
Mount Clemens, MI [*FM radio station call letters*] (BROA) .... WWBR-FM
Mount Olive, IL [*FM radio station call letters*] (BROA) .... WSTN-FM
Mount Pearl, NF [*AM radio station call letters*] (BROA) .... VOAR
Mount Vernon, GA [*FM radio station call letters*] (BROA) .... WYUM-FM
Mountain (MILB) .... mtn
Mountain Home, AR [*FM radio station call letters*] (BROA) .... KBFJ-FM
Mountain Waves (WEAT) .... MTW
Mouse Infection Neutralization Test [*Medicine*] (MELL) .... MNT
Mouth-to-Mouth Breathing (MELL) .... MMB
Mouth-to-Mouth Resuscitation (MELL) .... MMR
Movado Zenith Mondia .... MZM
Moved (GEAB) .... mov
Moved (GEAB) .... mvd

Movement of Landless Rural Workers [*Brazil*] .... MST
Movement-Associated Fetal Acceleration [*Medicine*] (MELL) .... MAFA
Moves All Extremities Quite Well [*Medicine*] (MELL) .... MAEQW
MP3.com, Inc. [*NASDAQ symbol*] (SG) .... MPPP
Mpath Interactive [*NASDAQ symbol*] (SG) .... MPTH
MPW Industrial Svcs. [*NASDAQ symbol*] (SG) .... MPWG
MSC.Software Corp. [*NYSE symbol*] (SG) .... MNS
M.T. Bottle Collectors Association (EA) .... MTBCA
MTI Technology .... MTIC
Mucin Clot Prevention [*Medicine*] (MELL) .... MCP
Muckle-Wells Syndrome [*Medicine*] (MELL) .... MWS
Mucocutaneous Candidiasis [*Medicine*] (MELL) .... MCCI
Mucopurulent Bronchitis [*Medicine*] (MELL) .... MPB
Mucopurulent Cervicitis [*Medicine*] (MELL) .... MPC
Mucosa-Associated Lymphoid Tissue Lymphoma [*Medicine*] (MELL) .... MALTL
Mucosal Barrier [*Medicine*] (MELL) .... MB
Mucosal Bleeding [*Medicine*] (MELL) .... MB
Mucus (MELL) .... M
Mullerian Duct Cyst [*Medicine*] (MELL) .... MDC
Mullerian Inhibiting Factor [*Medicine*] (MELL) .... MIFR
Mullet-Channel Plate [*Spectrometry*] .... MCP
Multi-Angle Imaging Spectroradiometer (EOSA) .... MISR
Multichannel Cochlear Implant [*Medicine*] (MELL) .... MCC
Multi-Chemical Sensitivity [*Medicine*] (MELL) .... MCS
Multicystic Ovary [*Medicine*] (MELL) .... MCO
Multidrug-Resistant Infection (MELL) .... MDRI
Multidrug-Resistant Tuberculosis (MELL) .... MDRT
Multifocal Giant Cell Encephalitis [*Medicine*] (MELL) .... MGCE
Multi-Frequency Imaging Microwave Radiometer (EOSA) .... MIMR
Multigraphics, Inc. [*AMEX symbol*] (SG) .... MTI
Multilumen Catheter [*Medicine*] (MELL) .... MLC
Multimedia Internet Mail Extension .... MIME
Multi-Nevoid Basal-Cell Carcinoma Syndrome [*Medicine*] (MELL) .... MNBCCS
Multinucleated Cell [*Medicine*] (MELL) .... MNC
Multiple Antigen Peptide [*Medicine*] (MELL) .... MAP
Multiple Daily Injection [*Medicine*] (MELL) .... MDI
Multiple Embolisms [*Medicine*] (MELL) .... ME
Multiple Endocrin Deficiency [*Medicine*] (MELL) .... MED
Multiple Exostoses [*Medicine*] (MELL) .... ME
Multiple Glomus Tumor [*Medicine*] (MELL) .... MGT
Multiple Indicator Multiple Cause Model .... MIMIC model
Multiple Launch Rocket System .... MLRS
Multiple Oocytes per Disk [*Medicine*] (MELL) .... MOP
Multiple Organ System Failure [*Medicine*] (MELL) .... MOSF
Multiple Pituitary Hormone Deficiency [*Medicine*] (MELL) .... MPHD
Multiple Residue Method [*Medicine*] (MELL) .... MRM
Multiple Subcutaneous Injections [*Medicine*] (MELL) .... MSI
Multiple Tics (MELL) .... MT
Multiple Trace Elements [*Medicine*] (MELL) .... MTE
Multiple Warts [*Medicine*] (MELL) .... MW
Multiple-Agent Chemotherapy [*Medicine*] (MELL) .... MACT
Multiple-Angle Reference System .... MARS
Multiplex Genetic Testing [*Medicine*] (MELL) .... MGT
Multiplex Heteroduplex Analysis [*Medicine*] (MELL) .... MHDA
Multipolar Cell [*Medicine*] (MELL) .... MPC
Multipolar Electrocoagulation [*Medicine*] (MELL) .... MPEC
Multipotent Growth Factor [*Medicine*] (MELL) .... MGF
Multiprocess Wet Cleaning (EPAT) .... MPWC
Multispectral Atmospheric Mapping Sensor .... MAMS
Multitrait-Multimethod Model .... MTMM
Multivariate Adaptive Regression Splines .... MARS
Multivoltage Radiation Therapy (MELL) .... MVRT
Mumps Orchitis [*Medicine*] (MELL) .... MO
Munchausen-by-Proxy Syndrome [*Medicine*] (MELL) .... MBPS
Munchausen's Syndrome [*Medicine*] (MELL) .... MS
Munfordville, KY [*FM radio station call letters*] (BROA) .... WCLU-FM
Munich Image Data Analysis System .... MIDAS
Municipal Civil District (GEAB) .... MCD
Murfreesboro, NC [*FM radio station call letters*] (BROA) .... WDLZ-FM
Murine Typhus Fever [*Medicine*] (MELL) .... MTF
Murray, KY [*FM radio station call letters*] (BROA) .... WFGE-FM
Murrell's Inlet, SC [*FM radio station call letters*] (BROA) .... WHGB-FM
Muscat Securities Market .... MSM
Muscle Adenylate Deaminase [*Medicine*] (MELL) .... MADA
Muscle Strengthening Exercise (MELL) .... MSE
Muscle Testing (MELL) .... MT
Muscle Trauma (MELL) .... MT
Muscles and Tendons (MELL) .... M&T
Musculocutaneous Nerve [*Medicine*] (MELL) .... MCN
Museum (BEE) .... musm
Music Object-Oriented Distributed System .... MOODS
Musical Heritage Network [*Internet resource*] .... MHN
Muskegon, MI [*AM radio station call letters*] (BROA) .... WMHG
Muskogee, OK [*Television station call letters*] (BROA) .... KWBT
Muslim Arab Youth Association .... MAYA
Mutual Climatic Range (QUAC) .... MCR
Myanmar (Burma) (MILB) .... My
Myasthenia Gravis [*Medicine*] (MELL) .... MyG
Mycobacterial Infection (MELL) .... MBI
Mydriacyl and Neosynephrine [*Medicine*] (MELL) .... M&N
Myelinated Nerve Fiber [*Medicine*] (MELL) .... MNF
Myeloproliferative Disorder [*Medicine*] (MELL) .... MPD
Myeloproliferative Reaction [*Medicine*] (MELL) .... MPR
Myelosclerosis (MELL) .... MS
Mylohyoid Nerve [*Medicine*] (MELL) .... MHN

Myocardial Embolism [*Medicine*] (MELL) .... MCE
Myocardial Fascicles [*Medicine*] (MELL) .... MCF
Myocardial Hypertrophy [*Medicine*] (MELL) .... MH
Myocardial Infarction Triage [*Medicine*] (MELL) .... MIT
Myocardial Oxygen Supply [*Medicine*] (MELL) .... MOS

Myocardial-Dysplasia Syndrome [*Medicine*] (MELL) .... MDS
Myositis Ossificans Progressiva [*Medicine*] (MELL) .... MOP
Myrtle Beach, SC [*AM radio station call letters*] (BROA) .... WAZG
Myrtle Point, OR [*FM radio station call letters*] (BROA) .... KTBR-FM
Mythology (BEE) .... Myth

By Meaning

N
By Meaning

N3N Restorers Association (EA) .... NARA
Nabisco Group Holdings [*NYSE symbol*] (SG) .... NGH
Nace International .... NACE
N-Acetyl Aspartate (MELL) .... NAA
Naipahu, HI [*FM radio station call letters*] (BROA) .... KKHN-FM
Naltrexone [*Medicine*] (MELL) .... NTX
Nambia (MILB) .... Nba
Name Server .... NS
Nampa, ID [*FM radio station call letters*] (BROA) .... KFXJ-FM
Nanicoke, PA [*FM radio station call letters*] (BROA) .... WQFM
Nanticoke, PA [*FM radio station call letters*] (BROA) .... WQEM-FM
Nantucket, MA [*FM radio station call letters*] (BROA) .... WNAN-FM
Naples, FL [*FM radio station call letters*] (BROA) .... WRGY-FM
Naples, FL [*FM radio station call letters*] (BROA) .... WPRW-FM
Narcotics (MILB) .... Narcs
Narcotics Anonymous (MELL) .... NarAnon
Narragansett Pier, RI [*FM radio station call letters*] (BROA) .... WAKX-FM
Narrows, VA [*AM radio station call letters*] (BROA) .... WPSK
NASA Ocean Data System (EOSA) .... NODS
NASA Polar Orbiting Platform (EOSA) .... NPOP
Nasal Allergy (MELL) .... NA
Nasal Catheter [*Medicine*] (MELL) .... NC
Nasal Continuous Airway Pressure [*Medicine*] (MELL) .... NCAP
Nasal Point of Conversion [*Medicine*] (MELL) .... NPC
Nashville (BEE) .... Nashvl
Nashville, TN [*FM radio station call letters*] (BROA) .... WNRQ-FM
Nashville, TN [*AM radio station call letters*] (BROA) .... WNSG
Nashwauk, MN [*AM radio station call letters*] (BROA) .... WNMT
Nasion (MELL) .... N
Nasobiliary Catheter [*Medicine*] (MELL) .... NBC
Nasociliary Nerve [*Medicine*] (MELL) .... NCN
Nasogastric Intubation [*Medicine*] (MELL) .... NGI
Nasolabial Distance [*Medicine*] (MELL) .... NLD
Nasolacrimal Duct Impatency [*Medicine*] (MELL) .... NLDI
Nasolacrimal Duct Obstruction [*Medicine*] (MELL) .... NLDO
Nasopancreatic Catheter [*Medicine*] (MELL) .... NPC
Nasopharyngeal Intubation [*Medicine*] (MELL) .... NPI
Nasopharyngeal Radium Irradiation [*Medicine*] (MELL) .... NPRI
Natchez, MS [*FM radio station call letters*] (BROA) .... WASM-FM
Natchitoches, LA [*FM radio station call letters*] (BROA) .... KBIO-FM
National Ability Center (EA) .... NAC
National Aeronca Association (EA) .... NAA
National Agrichemical Retailers Association (EPAT) .... NARA
National Air Pollution Surveillance (EPAT) .... NAPS
National Arbitration & Mediation .... NAM
National Assessment Governing Board .... NAGB
National Association of Cattle Foot Trimmers (GVA) .... NACFT
National Association of Farmers' Markets (GVA) .... NAFM
National Association of Greyhound Owners (GVA) .... NAGO
National Association of Independent Veterinary Practices and
  Practitioners (GVA) .... NAIVPP
National Association of Medical Examiners (MELL) .... NAME
National Association of Name Plate Manufacturers, Inc. .... NAME
National Association of Trade Exchanges .... NATE
National Association of Wheat Weavers (EA) .... NAWW, Inc.
National Attention Deficit Disorder Association .... ADDA
National Autonomous University of Mexico .... UNAM
National Basketball Association Entertainment .... NBAE
National Beef Association (GVA) .... NBA
National Bioethics Advisory Commission .... NBAC
National Bird-Feeding Society (EA) .... NBS
National Board of Boiler & Pressure Vessel Inspectors .... NBBP
National Broadcasting Society-Alpha Epsilon Rho [*Formerly, Alpha Epsilon
  Rho*] (EA) .... AERHO
National Camp Association (EA) .... NCA
National Catfishing Association (EA) .... NCA
National Cattlemen's Beef Association (GVA) .... NCBA
National Center for Education Standards .... NCES
National Center for Fair & Open Testing .... FairTest
National Center for Patient's Rights (MELL) .... NCPR
National Centre for Medium Range Weather Forecasting [*New Delhi,
  India*] .... NCMRWF
National Child Abuse Hotline (MELL) .... NCAH
National Cholesterol Education Program .... NCEP
National Climate Archive (QUAC) .... NCA
National Climate Research Committee (QUAC) .... NCRC

National Coal Resource Assessment .... NCRA
National Coalition for Promoting Physical Activity (MELL) .... NCPPA
National Cockatiel Society (EA) .... NCS
National Collection of Food Bacteria (MELL) .... NCFB
National Commission on Infant Mortality (MELL) .... NCIM
National Conference of States on Building Codes and Standards, Inc. .... NCS
National Dairy Herd Improvement Association (GVA) .... NDHIA
National Demolition Derby Association (EA) .... NDDA
National Drought Mitigation Center .... NDMC
National Employee Union Information Center (EA) .... NEUIC
National Environmental Performance Partnership System .... NEPPS
National Federation of State High School Associations .... NFSH
National Football League Alumni [*An association*] (EA) .... NFL Alumni
National Forest Products Association .... NFOR
National Gambling Impact Study Commission .... NGISC
National Hotline for Missing Children (MELL) .... NHMC
National Human Genome Research Institute .... NHGRI
National Incident Coordination Team [*Environmental science*] (EPAT) .... NICT
National Institute for Clinical Excellence .... NICE
National Institute of Culture .... INC
National Institute of Materials and Chemical Research [*Japan*] .... NIMC
National Institute on Aging's Gerontology Research Center (MELL) .... NIAGRC
National Institutional Delivery System .... NIDS
National Laser Facility .... NLF
National Lupus Erythematosus Association (MELL) .... NLEA
National Military Park .... NMP
National Museum of Racing and Hall of Fame (EA) .... NMR
National Network to Prevent Birth Defects (MELL) .... NNPBD
National Oceanographic Global Atmospheric Prediction System
  (WEAT) .... NOGAPS
National Organization for Rivers (EA) .... NORS
National Organization on Fetal Alcohol Syndrome (MELL) .... NOFAS
National Parent Education Network .... NPIN
National Pat Boone Fan Club (EA) .... NPBFC
National Pesticide Hazard Assessment Program (EPAT) .... NPHAP
National Pet Insurance Association (GVA) .... NPIA
National Preserve .... NPres
National Prevention Information Network [*Internet resource*] .... NPIN
National Printing Equipment & Supply Association, Inc. .... NPESA
National Rehabilitation Center (MELL) .... NRC
National Rotorcraft Technology Center .... NRTC
National Scenic Riverway .... NSR
National Scenic Trail .... NST
National Second Surgical Opinion Program (MELL) .... NSSO
National Sleep Foundation (MELL) .... NSF
National Steeplechase Association (EA) .... NSA
National Stinson Club - 108 Series (EA) .... NSC
National Stolen Property Act .... NSPA
National Student Marketing .... NSM
National System for Emergency Coordination (EPAT) .... NSEC
National System for Emergency Preparedness (EPAT) .... NSEP
National Toxics Inventory [*Environmental science*] (EPAT) .... NTI
National Type Culture Collection (MELL) .... NTCC
National Union Catalog of Manuscript Collections (GEAB) .... NUCMC
National Women's Scuba Society (EA) .... NWSS
National World War II Glider Pilots Association (EA) .... NWWIIGPA
Nationsrent, Inc. [*NYSE symbol*] (SG) .... NRI
Nationwide Finl Svcs'A' [*NYSE symbol*] (SG) .... NFS
Natl Bancshares Texas [*AMEX symbol*] (SG) .... NBT
Natl Equipment Svcs. [*NYSE symbol*] (SG) .... NSV
Natl Health Realty [*AMEX symbol*] (SG) .... NHR
Natl Presto Indus. [*NYSE symbol*] (SG) .... NPK
Natl R.V.Holdings [*NYSE symbol*] (SG) .... NVH
Natural Language Command [*Computer science*] .... NLC
Natural Matrix Standard .... NMS
Natural Resources Conservation Service .... NRCS
Naturalized (GEAB) .... na
Nature of Action Code [*Environmental science*] (EPAT) .... NOAC
Naughton Cardiac Exercise (MELL) .... NCE
Nautical Mile (MILB) .... nm
Naval Aide .... NavAide
Navigant Consulting [*NYSE symbol*] (SG) .... NCI
Navigant International [*Stock market symbol*] .... FLYR
Navy EarthMap Explorer .... NEMO
Navy Widow's Certificate (GEAB) .... NWC
NCI Building Systems [*NYSE symbol*] (SG) .... NCS

NCL Holdings ADS [*NYSE symbol*] (SG)	NRW
NCR Corp. [*NYSE symbol*] (SG)	NCR
Near Vision (MELL)	NV
Nebraska Veterinary Medical Association (GVA)	NVMA
Necrotic Enteritis [*Medicine*] (MELL)	NE
Need to See You [*Online dialog*]	NTCU
Needle Aspiration Biopsy [*Medicine*] (MELL)	NABX
Needle Biopsy of Prostate [*Medicine*] (MELL)	NBP
Needle-Knife Sphincterotomy [*Medicine*] (MELL)	NKS
Neff Corp'A' [*NYSE symbol*] (SG)	NFF
Negative Axillary Node [*Medicine*] (MELL)	NANs
Negative Pressure Ventilation [*Medicine*] (MELL)	NPV
Negative to Date [*Medicine*] (MELL)	NTD
Negaunee, MI [*FM radio station call letters*] (BROA)	WKQS-FM
Negaunee, MI [*FM radio station call letters*] (BROA)	WNGE-FM
Negligible Risk (MELL)	NR
Neighborhood Community Service Centers	NCSC
NeoMagic Corp. [*NASDAQ symbol*] (SG)	NMGC
Neomycin [*Medicine*] (MELL)	NM
Neon, KY [*AM radio station call letters*] (BROA)	WEZC
Neonatal Inclusion Conjunctivitis [*Medicine*] (MELL)	NIC
Neonatal Lupus Erythematosus [*Medicine*] (MELL)	NLE
Neonatal Meningitis [*Medicine*] (MELL)	NM
Neonatal Respiratory Distress Syndrome [*Medicine*] (MELL)	NRDS
Neonatology [*Medicine*] (MELL)	NEO
Neoplasm Staging [*Medicine*] (MELL)	NS
Neosynephrine/Mydriacil Dilation [*Medicine*] (MELL)	NMD
Nepal (MILB)	N
Nephew (GEAB)	n
Nephew (GEAB)	neph
Nephrectomy [*Medicine*] (MELL)	Nx
Nephroblastoma [*Medicine*] (MELL)	NB
Nerve Action Potential [*Medicine*] (MELL)	NAP
Nerve Block [*Medicine*] (MELL)	NB
Nerve Root (MELL)	NR
Nerve Root Block (MELL)	NRB
Nerve Root Canal (MELL)	NRC
Nerve Root Compression (MELL)	NRC
Nerve Root Damage (MELL)	NRD
Nervous Exhaustion (MELL)	NE
Net Perceptions [*NASDAQ symbol*] (SG)	NETP
Net Postprandial Protein Utilization	NPPU
Net Primary Production	NPP
Net2Phone [*NASDAQ symbol*] (SG)	NTOP
Net.Bank [*NASDAQ symbol*] (SG)	NTBK
NetGravity, Inc. [*NASDAQ symbol*] (SG)	NETG
Netherlands (MILB)	NI
Netherlands Centre Alternatives to Animal Use (GVA)	NCA
Netherlands Organization for Agricultural Research (GVA)	DLO-NL
Netia Holdings ADS [*NASDAQ symbol*] (SG)	NTIA
NetObjects, Inc. [*NASDAQ symbol*] (SG)	NETO
Netopia, Inc. [*NASDAQ symbol*] (SG)	NTPA
Netscape, Oracle, IBM, Sun-and Everybody Else	NOISE
NetSpeak Corp. [*NASDAQ symbol*] (SG)	NSPK
Network Access Solutions [*NASDAQ symbol*] (SG)	NASC
Network Applications and Information Center	NAIC
Network Plus [*NASDAQ symbol*] (SG)	NPLS
Network Solutions [*NASDAQ symbol*] (SG)	NSOL
Networked Computer Science Technical Reference Library	NCSTRL
Networked Digital Library of Theses and Dissertations	NDLTD
Networks North [*NASDAQ symbol*] (SG)	NETN
Neuroectodermal Pigmented Tumor [*Medicine*] (MELL)	NPT
Neuroendocrine Transducer [*Medicine*] (MELL)	NET
Neurogenic Bladder [*Medicine*] (MELL)	NGB
Neurogenic Pulmonary Edema [*Medicine*] (MELL)	NGPE
Neurohormone [*Medicine*] (MELL)	NH
Neurologic Clinical Examination [*Medicine*] (MELL)	NCE
Neuromuscular Disease [*Medicine*] (MELL)	NMD
Neuromyodysplasia [*Medicine*] (MELL)	NMD
Neuropathic Pain [*Medicine*] (MELL)	NPP
Neuroperfusion Pump [*Medicine*] (MELL)	NPP
Neurosurgical Examination (MELL)	NSX
Neurotransmitter Vesicle [*Medicine*] (MELL)	NTV
Neuter (BEE)	neut
Neutral Thermal Environment [*Medicine*] (MELL)	NTE
Neutralizing Antibodies [*Medicine*] (MELL)	Nab
Neutron Density	ND
Neutrophil Aggregation Activity (MELL)	NAA
Never Removed from Box [*Doll collecting*]	NRF
Nevi, Atrial Myxoma, Myxoid Neurofibroma, and Ephilides [*Syndrome*] [*Medicine*] (MELL)	NAME
Nevocellular Nevus (MELL)	NN
Nevus (MELL)	N
New Albany, IN [*FM radio station call letters*] (BROA)	WLSY-FM
New Albany, MS [*FM radio station call letters*] (BROA)	WRBO-FM
New Bloomfield, MO [*FM radio station call letters*] (BROA)	KNLG-FM
New Boston, TX [*FM radio station call letters*] (BROA)	KOZL-FM
New Century Energies [*NYSE symbol*] (SG)	NCE
New Century Financial	NCEN
New Drug Approval (MELL)	NDA
New England Journal of Medicine [*A publication*]	NEJM
New England Patriots [*National Football League*] [*1971-present*] (NFLA)	NEON
New Era of Networks [*NASDAQ symbol*] (SG)	NF
New Face [*Collectibles*]	NF
New Hampshire Educational Improvement and Assessment Program	NHEIAP

New Haven, CT [*Television station call letters*] (BROA)	WTNH-DT
New Haven, CT [*AM radio station call letters*] (BROA)	WYBC
New Holland N.V. [*NYSE symbol*] (SG)	NH
New in Box [*Watch collecting*]	NIB
New Initiatives	NI
New Investment Technology	NIT
New Jersey Housing & Mortgage Finance Agency	NJHMFA
New Liskeard, ON [*FM radio station call letters*] (BROA)	CJTT-FM
New London, CT [*AM radio station call letters*] (BROA)	WWJY
New Market, VA [*FM radio station call letters*] (BROA)	WBHB-FM
New Mexico Veterinary Medical Association (GVA)	NMVMA
New Orleans, FL [*Television station call letters*] (BROA)	WPXL
New Orleans Saints [*National Football League*] [*1967-present*] (NFLA)	NO
New Radiometry	NEWRAD
New Testament Abstracts [*A publication*]	NTA
New Transatlantic Agenda	NTA
New York Giants [*National Football League*] [*1925-present*] (NFLA)	NYG
New York Jets [*National Football League*] [*1963-present*] (NFLA)	NYJ
New York Library Association	NYLA
New York, NY [*Television station call letters*] (BROA)	WABC-DT
New York, NY [*FM radio station call letters*] (BROA)	WBIX-FM
New York, NY [*Television station call letters*] (BROA)	WCBS-DT
New York, NY [*Television station call letters*] (BROA)	WNYW-DT
New York, NY [*Television station call letters*] (BROA)	WPXN-TV
New York Rangers Fan Club [*Formerly, Rangers Fan Club*] (EA)	RFC
New York Titans [*National Football League*] [*1960-62*] (NFLA)	NYT
New York Yanks [*National Football League*] [*1950-51*] (NFLA)	NYY
New Zealand Tourism Board (EA)	NZTB
New Zealand University Network	NZUNINET
New Zealand Veterinary Association (GVA)	NZVA
Newark, NJ [*FM radio station call letters*] (BROA)	WCAA-FM
Newberry, FL [*FM radio station call letters*] (BROA)	WBXY-FM
Newborn Intensive Care Unit (MELL)	NBICU
Newburg, KY [*AM radio station call letters*] (BROA)	WNAI
Newburgh, IN [*FM radio station call letters*] (BROA)	WDKS-FM
Newcourt Credit Group [*NYSE symbol*] (SG)	NCT
Newmarket, ON [*FM radio station call letters*] (BROA)	CKDX-FM
New-Onset Diabetes [*Medicine*] (MELL)	NOD
Newport, KY [*Television station call letters*] (BROA)	WXIX-DT
Newport News, VA [*FM radio station call letters*] (BROA)	WGH-FM
Newport, OR [*FM radio station call letters*] (BROA)	KBGX-FM
Newsline II Fan Club (EA)	NFC
Newton, IA [*Television station call letters*] (BROA)	KFPX
NextCard, Inc. [*NASDAQ symbol*] (SG)	NXCD
Nextera Enterprises'A' [*NASDAQ symbol*] (SG)	NXRA
NEXTLINK Communications'A' [*NASDAQ symbol*] (SG)	NXLK
NFO Worldwide [*NYSE symbol*] (SG)	NFO
Niacin (MELL)	nia
NICE-Systems ADR [*NASDAQ symbol*] (SG)	NICE
Nicholasville, KY [*AM radio station call letters*] (BROA)	WUGR
Nicotine and Tobacco (MELL)	N&T
Niger (MILB)	Ngr
Nigeria (MILB)	Nga
Nigerian Bonny [*Crude oil*]	NB
Night Blindness (MELL)	NB
Night Vision Imaging System	NVIS
Nightstick Fracture [*Medicine*] (MELL)	NSF
Nikiski, AK [*FM radio station call letters*] (BROA)	KXBA-FM
Nimbostratus Cloud (WEAT)	Ns
Nipple and Areola [*Medicine*] (MELL)	N&A
NiSource, Inc. [*NYSE symbol*] (SG)	NI
Nitric Acid Burns [*Medicine*] (MELL)	NAB
Nitric Oxide Synthase Inhibitor [*Medicine*] (MELL)	NOSI
N-Methyl-D-Aspartate [*Medicine*] (MELL)	NMDA
NMT Medical [*NASDAQ symbol*] (SG)	NMTI
No Abnormality Seen [*Medicine*] (MELL)	NAS
No Adverse Reaction [*Medicine*] (MELL)	NAR
No Apparent Anesthesia Complication [*Medicine*] (MELL)	NAAC
No Back Cover	NBC
No Brain Damage (MELL)	NBD
No Cardiopulmonary Resuscitation [*Medicine*] (MELL)	No-CPR
No Congenital Abnormalities [*Medicine*] (MELL)	NCA
No Evidence of Malignancy [*Medicine*] (MELL)	NEM
No Evidence of Malignancy [*Medicine*] (MELL)	NEOM
No Family Doctor (MELL)	NFD
No Front Cover	NFC
No Further Treatment [*Medicine*] (MELL)	NFT
No Inflammatory signs [*Medicine*] (MELL)	NIS
No Known Basis (MELL)	NKB
No Mail Label	NML
No Meaningful Improvement (MELL)	NMI
No New Laboratory (MELL)	NNL
No Organisms Seen (MELL)	NOS
No Radiation (MELL)	NR
No Respiration (MELL)	NR
No Sign of Acute Disease (MELL)	NSAD
No Visible Lesion [*Medicine*] (MELL)	NVL
Noble Drilling Corp. [*NYSE symbol*] (SG)	NE
Noble International [*NASDAQ symbol*] (SG)	NOBL
Nocatee, FL [*FM radio station call letters*] (BROA)	WZSP-FM
Nocturnal Leg Cramps [*Medicine*] (MELL)	NLC
Nocturnal Leg Muscle Cramp [*Medicine*] (MELL)	NLMC
Nocturnal Myoclonus [*Medicine*] (MELL)	NM
Nocturnal Paroxysmal Dystonia [*Medicine*] (MELL)	NPD
Nocturnal Penile Tumescence Test [*Medicine*] (MELL)	NPTT

Node-Negative Breast Cancer (MELL)	NNBC
Nodular and Diffuse [*Medicine*] (MELL)	N&D
Nodular Goiter [*Medicine*] (MELL)	NG
Nodular Hyperplasia of Prostate [*Medicine*] (MELL)	NHP
Noise Interference Level (MELL)	NHL
Nome, AK [*AM radio station call letters*] (BROA)	KNOM
Non Recorded [*Genealogy*] (GEAB)	nr
Non-Arboreal Pollen [*Palynology*] (QUAC)	NAP
Nonarticular Rheumatic Disorder [*Medicine*] (MELL)	NARD
Non-Child-Resistant Container (MELL)	NCRC
Nonconducted Premature Atrial Contractions [*Medicine*] (MELL)	NPAC
Noncontact Tonometry (MELL)	NCT
Nonconvulsive Status Epilepticus [*Medicine*] (MELL)	NCSE
Non-Developmental Airlift Aircraft [*Military*]	NDAA
None Minted [*Numismatic term*]	NM
Nonexercise activity thermogenesis	NEAT
Non-Familial Disease (MELL)	NFD
Nonhemoglobin Protein [*Medicine*] (MELL)	NHP
Nonimmune Transfusion Reaction [*Medicine*] (MELL)	NITR
Non-Immunologic Disease [*Medicine*] (MELL)	NID
Noninsulin-Treated Disease [*Medicine*] (MELL)	NITD
Nonmalignant [*Medicine*] (MELL)	NM
Nonnarcotic Analgesics [*Medicine*] (MELL)	NNA
Nonobese Subject (MELL)	NOS
Nonobstructive Urinary Tract [*Medicine*] (MELL)	NUT
Nonocclusive Mesenteric Infarction [*Medicine*] (MELL)	NML
Nonoperative Biopsy Technique [*Medicine*] (MELL)	NOBT
Nonpregnant (MELL)	NPG
Nonprescription Drug (MELL)	NPD
Nonproductive Cough (MELL)	NPC
Nonprofit (PROS)	Nonpr
Nonrestorative Sleep Pattern (MELL)	NRSP
Nonrheumatic Atrial Fibrillation [*Medicine*] (MELL)	NRAF
Non-Seasalt Sulphate (QUAC)	NSS
Nonspecific Infection [*Medicine*] (MELL)	NSI
Nonspecific Ulcerative Colitis [*Medicine*] (MELL)	NUC
Nonstandard (BEE)	nonstand
Nonstreptococcal Infection [*Medicine*] (MELL)	NSI
Nonsystemic Antacid Suspension [*Medicine*] (MELL)	NSAS
Non-X-Ray Background	NXB
Nordic Countries Network	NORDUNet
Norfolk, VA [*Television station call letters*] (BROA)	WPXV
Norfolk, VA [*FM radio station call letters*] (BROA)	WVKL-FM
Norlina, NC [*FM radio station call letters*] (BROA)	WBDS-FM
Normal Adult Male (MELL)	NAM
Normal Coitus and Climax (MELL)	NC&C
Normal Hearing Level (MELL)	NHL
Normal Hormone Level (MELL)	NHL
Normal Libido, Coitus and Climax [*Medicine*] (MELL)	NLC&C
Normal Male Infant (MELL)	NML
Normal Nutrition (MELL)	NN
Normal Postpartum [*Medicine*] (MELL)	NPP
Normal Range of Motion (MELL)	NRM
Normal Saline Enema [*Medicine*] (MELL)	NSE
Normal Size, Shape, and Consistency [*Medicine*] (MELL)	NSSC
Normal Well Developed (MELL)	NWD
Normal-Incidence Monochromator	NIM
Normoglycemia [*Medicine*] (MELL)	NG
Norris, TN [*FM radio station call letters*] (BROA)	WBEH-FM
Nortel Networks [*NYSE symbol*] (SG)	NT
North American Agreement on Environmental Cooperation (EPAT)	NAAEC
North American Blastomycosis [*Medicine*] (MELL)	NAB
North American Cottage Garden Society	NACGS
North American Diecast Toy Collectors Association (EA)	NADTCA
North American Equine Ranching Information Council (GVA)	NAERIC
North American Pollen Database (QUAC)	NAPD
North American Research Strategy for Tropospheric Ozone (EPAT)	NARSTO
North American Rock Garden Society (EA)	NARGS
North American Society for Water and Soil Conservation	NASWSC
North American State Securities Administrators	NASSA
North American Veterinary College Administrators (GVA)	NAVCA
North American Veterinary Technician Association (GVA)	NAVTA
North Atlantic Chemistry Experiment (QUAC)	NATAC
North Atlantic Seaboard Program (QUAC)	NASP
North Carolina Veterinary Medical Association (GVA)	NCVMA
North Central Texas Council of Governments	NCTOG
North Las Vegas, NV [*AM radio station call letters*] (BROA)	KXNT
North Myrtle Beach, SC [*FM radio station call letters*] (BROA)	WMIW-FM
North of Boston Library Exchange	NOBLE
North of England Veterinary Association (GVA)	NEVA
North of Ireland Veterinary Association (GVA)	NIVA
North Salt Lake City, UT [*AM radio station call letters*] (BROA)	KWLW
North Vernon, IN [*AM radio station call letters*] (BROA)	WNVI
North Wall of the Gulf Stream (QUAC)	NWGS
Northeast Pennsylvania Finl. [*AMEX symbol*] (SG)	NEP
Northeast Rat and Mouse Club (EA)	NRMCI
Northeast Research Libraries	NERL
Northeastern Lumber Manufacturers Association	NELM
Northeastern Pennsylvania Industrial Resource Center	NEPIRC
Northern Australian Tropical Transect (QUAC)	NATT
Northern Biosphere Information System (EOSA)	NBIS
Northern Biosphere Observation and Modelling Experiment (EOSA)	NBIOME
Northern Telecom	NORTEL
Northfield, MN [*FM radio station call letters*] (BROA)	WCAL-FM
NorthPoint Communic Grp. [*NASDAQ symbol*] (SG)	NPNT
Northumberland, PA [*FM radio station call letters*] (BROA)	WEGH-FM
NorthWestern Corp. [*NYSE symbol*] (SG)	NOR
Norwalk Virus [*Medicine*] (MELL)	NV
Norway (MILB)	No
Norwegian (BEE)	Norw
Norwegian Council for Africa	NCA
Norwegian Space Center (EOSA)	NSC
Norwegian Trade Council (EA)	NTC
Norwich, NY [*FM radio station call letters*] (BROA)	WBKT-FM
Norwood, NY [*FM radio station call letters*] (BROA)	WAZV-FM
Nose Clip (MELL)	NC
Nosebleed (MELL)	NB
Nosocomial Infection Surveillance System [*Medicine*] (MELL)	NISS
Not at Bedside [*Medicine*] (MELL)	NAB
Not at Risk (MELL)	NAR
Not Available Yet [*Numismatic term*]	NAY
Not Breast Fed (MELL)	NBF
Not in Distress [*Medicine*] (MELL)	NID
Not Online Yet (BEE)	NOY
Not Physically Qualified (MELL)	NPQ
Nothing in Light Microscopy (MELL)	NIL
Notice of Arrival [*Environmental Protection Agency*] (EPAT)	NOA
Notice of Intent to Cancel [*Environmental Protection Agency*] (EPAT)	NOIC
Notice of Intent to Suspend [*Environmental Protection Agency*] (EPAT)	NOIS
Notify	NTF
NOVA Chemicals [*NYSE symbol*] (SG)	NCX
NovaStar Financial [*NYSE symbol*] (SG)	NFI
nSTOR Technologies [*AMEX symbol*] (SG)	NSO
NTL, Inc. [*NASDAQ symbol*] (SG)	NTLI
Nu Skin Enterprises'A' [*NYSE symbol*] (SG)	NUS
Nuclear (MILB)	nuc
Nuclear Antigen (MELL)	NA
Nuclear Medicine Technologist (MELL)	NMT
Nuclear Oncogenes [*Medicine*] (MELL)	NOG
Nuclear-Powered Turbo-Reciprocating Engine	NPTRE
Nulliparous Uterine Cervix [*Medicine*] (MELL)	NUC
Nursing Bottle Caries [*Medicine*] (MELL)	NBC
Nursing Care Technician (MELL)	NCT
Nursing Home Care (MELL)	NHC
Nursing Interim Care (MELL)	NIC
Nutrient Broth (MELL)	NB
Nutrition Disorder (MELL)	ND
Nutritionally Deprived (MELL)	ND
Nycomed Amersham ADS [*NYSE symbol*] (SG)	NYE
NYMAGIC, Inc. [*NYSE symbol*] (SG)	NYM

O

By Meaning

Oak Lawn, IL [*AM radio station call letters*] (BROA) .... WNWI
Oakland, CA [*AM radio station call letters*] (BROA) .... KMKY
Oakland, CA [*Television station call letters*] (BROA) .... KTVU-DT
Oakland Raiders [*National Football League*] [*1960-81*] (NFLA) .... Oak
Oakland Raiders [*National Football League*] [*1995-present*] (NFLA) .... OaR
Oath (GEAB) .... o
Obese Gene [*Medicine*] (MELL) .... ob gene
Oblique Abdominal Muscle [*Medicine*] (MELL) .... OAM
Oblique Vein of Left Atrium [*Medicine*] (MELL) .... OVLA
Obliterative Bronchiolitis [*Medicine*] (MELL) .... OB
Observation (MILB) .... obs
Obsessive-Compulsive Behavior (MELL) .... OCB
Obsessive-Compulsive Personality Disorder (MELL) .... OCPD
Obstetrical Measuring Plate [*Medicine*] (MELL) .... OMP
Obstructive Apnea [*Medicine*] (MELL) .... OA
Obstructive Arterial Disease [*Medicine*] (MELL) .... OAD
Obstructive Jaundice [*Medicine*] (MELL) .... OJ
Obstructive Nephropathy [*Medicine*] (MELL) .... ON
Obstructive Pancreatitis [*Medicine*] (MELL) .... OP
Obturator Internus [*Muscle*] (MELL) .... OI
Obturator Nerve Block [*Medicine*] (MELL) .... ONB
Occipital Condyle Syndrome [*Medicine*] (MELL) .... OCS
Occlusal Splint Therapy [*Medicine*] (MELL) .... OST
Occult Congenital Syphilis [*Medicine*] (MELL) .... OCS
Occult Injury (MELL) .... OI
Occupational Immunologic Lung Disease (MELL) .... OILD
Ocean (BEE) .... ocn
Ocean Circulation Model (QUAC) .... OCM
Ocean City, MD [*FM radio station call letters*] (BROA) .... WSDL-FM
Ocean Isle Beach, NC [*FM radio station call letters*] (BROA) .... WDZD-FM
Ocean Pines, MD [*FM radio station call letters*] (BROA) .... WQJZ-FM
Ocean View, DE [*FM radio station call letters*] (BROA) .... WRBG-FM
Ocular Albinism [*Medicine*] (MELL) .... OA
Ocular Hypertension (MELL) .... OH
Ocular Hypofusion Syndrome (MELL) .... OHS
Oculocerebrorenal Disease [*Medicine*] (MELL) .... OCRD
Odessa, TX [*FM radio station call letters*] (BROA) .... KLVW-FM
Odessa, TX [*FM radio station call letters*] (BROA) .... KMCM-FM
Odessa, TX [*Television station call letters*] (BROA) .... KPXK
ODS Networks [*NASDAQ symbol*] (SG) .... ODSI
OEC Compression [*AMEX symbol*] (SG) .... OOC
Offer .... OFR
Office of Aeronautical Charting and Cartography (GEOI) .... AC&C
Office of Extramural Programs (MELL) .... OEP
Office of Science and Technology .... OSTI
Office of Trade & Economic Analysis [*U.S. Department of Commerce*] [*Internet resource*] .... OTEA
Office Server Extension .... OSE
Official (MILB) .... off
Official Centennial Olympic Games Club (EA) .... OCOGC
Offspring of Diabetic Parent [*Medicine*] (MELL) .... ODP
Often (GEAB) .... oft
Ogden, UT [*Television station call letters*] (BROA) .... KUWB
Ogdensburg, NY [*FM radio station call letters*] (BROA) .... WYSX-FM
Oglala Sioux Civil Rights Organization [*South Dakota*] .... OSCRO
Oglethorpe Astronomical Association [*Savannah, Georgia*] .... OAA
Ohio Academic Research Network .... OARnet
Ohio Industrial Training Program .... OITP
Ohio Library and Information Network .... OhioLINK
Oil Droplet Reflex [*Medicine*] (MELL) .... ODR
Oil Immersion Test (MELL) .... OIT
Oklahoma City, OK [*Television station call letters*] (BROA) .... KPSG
Oklahoma City, OK [*FM radio station call letters*] (BROA) .... KYLV-FM
Old Danish (BEE) .... ODan
Old England (GEAB) .... OE
Old Forge, NY [*FM radio station call letters*] (BROA) .... WBGK-FM
Old Forge, NY [*FM radio station call letters*] (BROA) .... WDLS-FM
Old Kent Finl. [*NYSE symbol*] (SG) .... OK
Old Spanish (BEE) .... OSp
Old World Cutaneous Leishmaniasis [*Medicine*] (MELL) .... OWCL
Olecranon Bursitis [*Medicine*] (MELL) .... OB
Oligoarticular Onset Rheumatoid Arthritis [*Medicine*] (MELL) .... OORA
Olyphant, PA [*AM radio station call letters*] (BROA) .... WAAT
Omaha, NE [*FM radio station call letters*] (BROA) .... KSRZ-FM
Omak, WA [*FM radio station call letters*] (BROA) .... KNCW-FM
Omak, WA [*FM radio station call letters*] (BROA) .... KZBE-FM
Oman (MILB) .... O
Omega Protein [*NYSE symbol*] (SG) .... OME
Omohyoid [*Muscle*] (MELL) .... OMH
On Approval of Credit .... Oac
On Stage Entertainment [*NASDAQ symbol*] (SG) .... ONST
Oncogenic Potential (MELL) .... OGP
Oncology Center Information System (MELL) .... OCIS
One Time a Day [*Medicine*] (MELL) 1/d
One-Way Light Time .... OWLT
On-Going Care [*Medicine*] (MELL) .... OGC
OnHealth Network [*NASDAQ symbol*] (SG) .... ONHN
Onley-Onancock, VA [*FM radio station call letters*] (BROA) .... WESR-FM
Online Reference Book for Medieval Studies [*Internet resource*] .... ORB
On-Line Tracking System [*Environmental Protection Agency*] (EPAT) .... OLTS
Online Training Center (MELL) .... OTC
Ontario, CA [*AM radio station call letters*] (BROA) .... KMSL
Ontario Network [*Canada*] .... ONet
Opel Motorsport Club (EA) .... OMC
Open Book Fracture [*Medicine*] (MELL) .... OBF
Open Face Mask [*Medicine*] (MELL) .... OFM
Open Fracture [*Medicine*] (MELL) .... OF
Open Pneumothorax [*Medicine*] (MELL) .... OPT
Open Reading Frame (MELL) .... ORF
Open Society Institute .... OSI
Open Window Early Retirement Plans .... OWERP
Opening Abductory Wedge Osteotomy [*Medicine*] (MELL) .... OAWO
Opera-Glass Hand (MELL) .... OGH
Operational/Operations (MILB) .... op/ops
Operational Research System Analysts .... ORSA
Operative Plasterers and Cement Masons International Association .... OP&CMIA
Ophthalmic Doppler Sonogram [*Medicine*] (MELL) .... ODSG
Opiate Abstinence Syndrome [*Medicine*] (MELL) .... OAS
Opiate Receptor Agonist [*Medicine*] (MELL) .... ORA
Opioid Analgesics [*Medicine*] (MELL) .... OA
Opioid Dependence [*Medicine*] (MELL) .... OD
Opioid-Resistant Pain [*Medicine*] (MELL) .... ORP
Opportunistic Illness (MELL) .... OI
Opportunity to Learn .... OTL
Opsocionus-Myoclonus Syndrome [*Medicine*] (MELL) .... OMS
Optic Chiasma [*Medicine*] (MELL) .... OX
Optical Carrier .... OC
Optical Engineering .... OE
Optical Line Scanner (EOSA) .... OLS
Optical Sensor (EOSA) .... OPS
Optimum Stockage Requirements Analysis Program .... OSRAP
Or Best Reasonable Offer .... OBRO
Oracle, AZ [*FM radio station call letters*] (BROA) .... KIXD-FM
Oraibi, AZ [*FM radio station call letters*] (BROA) .... KBDT-FM
Oral Administration (MELL) .... OA
Oral Airways (MELL) .... OAW
Oral Contraceptive Steroid [*Medicine*] (MELL) .... OCS
Oral Endotracheal Tube (MELL) .... OETT
Oral Esophageal Tube [*Medicine*] (MELL) .... OET
Oral Malodor [*Medicine*] (MELL) .... OMO
Oral Morphine Sulfate [*Medicine*] (MELL) .... OMS
Oral Radiation Death (MELL) .... ORD
Oral Rehydration [*Medicine*] (MELL) .... OR
Orange, VA [*AM radio station call letters*] (BROA) .... WVCV
Orbicular Muscle of Mouth (MELL) .... OMM
Orbiter Docking System [*NASA*] .... ODS
Orbiting Quarantine Facility [*A proposed Earth-orbiting laboratory*] .... OOF
Orchiectomy [*Medicine*] (MELL) .... ORCH
Orcutt, CA [*FM radio station call letters*] (BROA) .... KGDP-FM
Ordained (GEAB) .... ord
Oregon City, OR [*AM radio station call letters*] (BROA) .... KKSN
Oregon Educational Media Association .... OEMA
Oregon School Employees Association .... OSEA
Organ Extract Therapy [*Medicine*] (MELL) .... OET
Organ Transplant Rejection [*Medicine*] (MELL) .... OTR
Organ-Confined Disease [*Medicine*] (MELL) .... OCD
Organic Nervous Disease [*Medicine*] (MELL) .... OND
Organisation de l'Action Democratique et Populaire [*Morocco*] .... OADP
Organization (GEAB) .... org
Organized Militia (GEAB) .... OM
Organophosphorous Poisoning [*Medicine*] (MELL) .... OPP
Oriental Movement Therapy (MELL) .... OMT

Orienting Reflex [*Medicine*] (MELL) .... OR
Orifice of Coronary Sinus [*Medicine*] (MELL) .... OCS
Orifice of Left Coronary Artery [*Medicine*] (MELL) .... OLCA
Original (BEE) .... orig
Original .... Orig
Orlando, FL [*Television station call letters*] (BROA) .... WKMG-TV
Orlando, FL [*Television station call letters*] (BROA) .... WRDQ
Ornithology (BEE) .... ornithol
Oropharyngeal Candidiasis [*Medicine*] (MELL) .... OPO
Orphan Drug [*Medicine*] (MELL) .... OD
Ortho-Amino-Phenols [*Medicine*] (MELL) .... OAP
Orthopedia Head Halter (MELL) .... OHH
Orthosorb Absorbable Pin [*Medicine*] (MELL) .... OAP
Ortho-Tolueno-Azo-Beta-Naphthol [*Medicine*] (MELL) .... OTABN
Ortonville, MN [*FM radio station call letters*] (BROA) .... KPHR-FM
Osage, IA [*FM radio station call letters*] (BROA) .... KWMM-FM
Osage Systems Group [*AMEX symbol*] (SG) .... OSE
Oscillating Waterbed (MELL) .... OWB
Oscoda, MI [*FM radio station call letters*] (BROA) .... WCMB-FM
Osgood-Schlatter Disease .... OSD
Oslo-Paris Commission .... OSPARCOM
Osmond Tape Exchange [*An association*] (EA) .... Of
Osmonds International Fan Club (EA) .... OIFC
Osteocyte (MELL) .... O
Osteogenic Sarcoma (MELL) .... OGS
Osteogenic Scoliosis (MELL) .... OGS
Osteoporosis and Back Pain [*Medicine*] (MELL) .... OBP
Osteoporosis and Leukemia [*Medicine*] (MELL) .... O&L
Osteoporosis from Bed Rest [*Medicine*] (MELL) .... OBR
Osteoradionecrosis [*Medicine*] (MELL) .... ORN
Oswego, NY [*FM radio station call letters*] (BROA) .... WOLF-FM

Otitis Interna [*Medicine*] (MELL) .... OI
Otitis Media, Acute Catarrhal [*Medicine*] (MELL) .... OMAC
Otsego, MI [*AM radio station call letters*] (BROA) .... WAKV
Ottawa Ankle Rules .... OAR
Out of Wedlock (MELL) .... OOW
Outer Canthal Distance [*Medicine*] (MELL) .... OCD
Outpatient Catheterization [*Medicine*] (MELL) .... OPC
Outpatient General Anesthesia (MELL) .... OPGA
Oval Window (MELL) .... OW
Ovarian Cancer (MELL) .... OVC
Ovarian Insufficiency [*Medicine*] (MELL) .... OI
Ovarian Remnant Syndrome [*Medicine*] (MELL) .... ORS
Ovarian Tumor-Associated Antigen [*Medicine*] (MELL) .... OTA
Ovariectomy [*Medicine*] (MELL) .... OVX
Over Mountains (WEAT) .... OMNTS
Over the Hill Gang, International (EA) .... OTHG
Overall Rate of Return [*Business term*] .... OAR
Overflow Incontinence [*Medicine*] (MELL) .... OFI
Owego, NY [*FM radio station call letters*] (BROA) .... WLTB-FM
Owensville, MO [*FM radio station call letters*] (BROA) .... KBDQ-FM
Owosso, MI [*FM radio station call letters*] (BROA) .... WRSR-FM
Oxacillin [*Medicine*] (MELL) .... OX
Oxalate Deposition Disease [*Medicine*] (MELL) .... ODD
Oxazepam [*Medicine*] (MELL) .... OXZ
Oxford Glycosciences .... OGS
Oxygen Isotope Stage (QUAC) .... OIS
Oxygen Therapy (MELL) .... OT
Oxypressin [*Medicine*] (MELL) .... OXP
Oxytocin [*Medicine*] (MELL) .... OX
Oxytocin [*Medicine*] (MELL) .... OXT
Ozark, MO [*FM radio station call letters*] (BROA) .... KCYO-FM
Ozone Transport Region [*Environmental Protection Agency*] (EPAT) .... OTR

P

By Meaning

Paccinian Corpuscle [*Medicine*] (MELL) .... PC
Pacemaker Failure (MELL) .... PF
Pacemaker Rhythm [*Medicine*] (MELL) .... PMR
Pacemaker Syndrome [*Medicine*] (MELL) .... PS
Pacific Coast Dog Tick (MELL) .... PCDT
Pacific Computer Communications .... PACCOM
Pacific Free Trade Area .... PAFTA
Packet Switch Node .... PSN
Packeteer, Inc. [*NASDAQ symbol*] (SG) .... PKTR
PageMart Wireless 'A' [*NASDAQ symbol*] (SG) .... PMWI
Paget's Disease of Bone (MELL) .... PDB
Paging Network [*NASDAQ symbol*] (SG) .... PAGE
Pago Pago, AS (BROA) .... KHJS-FM
Pain and Impairment Relationship Scale (MELL) .... PAIRS
Pain Control (MELL) .... PC
Pain Tolerance Level (MELL) .... PTL
Pain-Anxiety-Tension Cycle (MELL) .... PATC
Painful Cervical Trauma [*Medicine*] (MELL) .... PCT
Painful Shoulder Syndrome (MELL) .... PSS
Pain-Inhibition Fear Avoidance [*Medicine*] (MELL) .... PIFA
Painless Progressive Loss of Vision (MELL) .... PPLOV
Pakistan Telecommunication Company Limited .... PTCL
Paleo-Indian (QUAC) .... PI
Paleontology (BEE) .... Paleontol
Palestine Study Group (EA) .... SG
Palm City, FL [*AM radio station call letters*] (BROA) .... WBDO
Palmar Intercalated Segmental Instability [*Medicine*] (MELL) .... PISI
Palmar-Plantar Pustulosis .... PPP
Palmer Drought Hydrological Index .... PDHI
Palmer Drought Severity Index .... PMDI
Palynological and Palaeobotanical Association of Australia (QUAC) .... PPAA
Palynological Society of China (QUAC) .... PSC
Palynological Society of Japan (QUAC) .... PSJ
Palynological Society of Poland (QUAC) .... PSP
Pameco Corp'A' [*NYSE symbol*] (SG) .... PCN
Pan Pacific Retail Prop. [*NYSE symbol*] (SG) .... PNP
Pana, IL [*FM radio station call letters*] (BROA) .... WXKO-FM
Panama City, FL [*AM radio station call letters*] (BROA) .... WDIZ
Panama City, FL [*FM radio station call letters*] (BROA) .... WLHR-FM
Pancreas (MELL) .... P
pancreatic Ascites [*Medicine*] (MELL) .... PA
Pancreatic Carcinoma [*Medicine*] (MELL) .... PC
Pancreatic Cholera [*Medicine*] (MELL) .... PC
Pancreatic Juice [*Medicine*] (MELL) .... PJ
Pancreatic Lymph Nodes [*Medicine*] (MELL) .... PLN
Panic Disorder (MELL) .... PD
Panniculus Adiposus [*Medicine*] (MELL) .... PA
Paper, Allied-Industrial, Chemical and Energy Workers International .... PACE
Paper Electrophoresis (MELL) .... PEP
Papillary Cystadenoma [*Medicine*] (MELL) .... PCA
Papillary Duct [*Medicine*] (MELL) .... PD
Papillary Endothelial Hyperplasia [*Medicine*] (MELL) .... PEH
Papillary Serous Adenocarcinoma of Ovary [*Medicine*] (MELL) .... PSACO
Papillary Serous Cyst [*Medicine*] (MELL) .... PSC
Papillomacular Bundle [*Medicine*] (MELL) .... PMB
Papulonodular Skin Lesion [*Medicine*] (MELL) .... PNSL
Para-Aminobenzoic Acid [*Medicine*] (MELL) .... PABA
Paracolon Bacilli [*Medicine*] (MELL) .... PCB
Paraguay (MILB) .... Py
Paraguayan-American Chamber of Commerce (EA) .... AMCHAM Paraguay
Parainfluenza (MELL) .... PI
Parainfluenza Virus Infection [*Medicine*] (MELL) .... PIVI
Parakeet [*Bird*] .... Keet
Paranoid Schizophrenia [*Medicine*] (MELL) .... PS
Para-Ovarian Cyst [*Medicine*] (MELL) .... POC
Parasympatholytic Drug [*Medicine*] (MELL) .... PSLD
Parathyroidlike Protein [*Medicine*] (MELL) .... PLP
Paratroop (MILB) .... para
Paravertebral [*Medicine*] (MELL) .... PV
Paravertebral Ganglion Block [*Medicine*] (MELL) .... PGB
Parenteral Alimentation [*Medicine*] (MELL) .... PA
Parenteral Drug Association (MELL) .... PDA
Paris, TX [*FM radio station call letters*] (BROA) .... KBCV-FM
Parish (GEAB) .... par
Park Hills, MO [*FM radio station call letters*] (BROA) .... KBGM-FM
Park Place Entertainment [*NYSE symbol*] (SG) .... PPE

Park Rapids, MN [*FM radio station call letters*] (BROA) .... KXKK-FM
Parker's Crossroads, TN [*FM radio station call letters*] (BROA) .... WBFG-FM
Paroxysmal Supraventricular Tachycardia [*Medicine*] .... PSVT
Pars Plana Lensectomy-Vitrectomy [*Medicine*] (MELL) .... PPLV
Partial (WEAT) .... PR
Partial Cleft Palate (MELL) .... PCP
Partial Denture (MELL) .... PD
Partial Hysterectomy [*Medicine*] (MELL) .... PH
Partial Mastectomy (MELL) .... PM
Partial Residual Plot .... Parres plot
Partial Seizure (MELL) .... PS
Partial Sleep Deprivation (MELL) .... PSD
Partial-Birth Abortion (MELL) .... PBA
Partially Impacted Wisdom Tooth (MELL) .... PIWT
Particle Measurement System .... PMS
Partnership for Capacity Building in Africa .... PACT
Parts per Million .... Ppm
Part-Time .... PT
Passenger [*Automotive tire designation*] .... P
Passive Adoptive Immunotherapy [*Medicine*] (MELL) .... PAIT
Passive Immunity [*Medicine*] (MELL) .... PI
Passive Maternal Smoking (MELL) .... PMS
Passive Optical Network .... PON
Passive Smoke (MELL) .... PS
Passive Smoke Exposure (MELL) .... PSE
Passive-Agressive Personality (MELL) .... PAP
Passive-Agressive Personality Disorder (MELL) .... PAPD
Past History of Illness (MELL) .... PHI
Pat Shea International Fan Club (EA) .... PSIFC
Patch Test [*Medicine*] (MELL) .... PT
Patella (MELL) .... P
Patella Overload Syndrome [*Medicine*] (MELL) .... POS
Patellar Medial Retinaculum [*Medicine*] (MELL) .... PMR
Patellar Tendon Transfer [*Medicine*] (MELL) .... PTT
Patellofemoral Chondrosis [*Medicine*] (MELL) .... PFC
Patent (GEAB) .... pat
Patient Care Technician (MELL) .... PCT
Patient Educational Program (MELL) .... PEP
Patient in Need of Supervision (MELL) .... PINS
Patient Medication Information (MELL) .... PMI
Patient Monitored (MELL) .... PTM
Patient to Return (MELL) .... PTR
Patient's Bill of Rights (MELL) .... PBR
Patrol Craft, Coastal/Inshore/Offshore/Riverine/Harbour (MILB) .... PCC/I/O/R/H
Paxson Communications 'A' [*AMEX symbol*] (SG) .... PAX
Payment (GEAB) .... pymt
Payson, AZ [*FM radio station call letters*] (BROA) .... KBZG-FM
pcOrder.com, Inc.'A' [*NASDAQ symbol*] (SG) .... PCOR
Peace Arch Entertainment'B' [*AMEX symbol*] (SG) .... PAE
Peaceful Nuclear Explosive Device .... PNED
Pediatric Orthopedic Examination (MELL) .... POE
Pediatric Pain Assessment (MELL) .... PPA
Peer Review Group (MELL) .... PRG
Pellagra [*Medicine*] (MELL) .... P
Pelvic Congestion Syndrome [*Medicine*] (MELL) .... PCS
Pelvic Cramps [*Medicine*] (MELL) .... PEC
Pelvic Floor Electrical Stimulation [*Medicine*] (MELL) .... PFES
Pelvic Girdle [*Medicine*] (MELL) .... PG
Pelvic Lymph Node Dissection [*Medicine*] (MELL) .... PLND
Pelvic Plane of Greatest Dimension [*Medicine*] (MELL) .... PPGD
Pen Fanciers (EA) .... PF
Pendaries Petroleum [*AMEX symbol*] (SG) .... PDR
Penetrating Abdominal Trauma Index (MELL) .... PATI
Penetrating Wound (MELL) .... PW
Penicillinase-Resistant Penicillin [*Medicine*] (MELL) .... PRP
Peninsula (BEE) .... Penin
Penn Treaty American [*NYSE symbol*] (SG) .... PTA
Penn-America Group [*NYSE symbol*] (SG) .... PNG
Pennsylvania School Librarians Association .... PSLA
Pennsylvania Society for the Prevention of Cruelty to Animals .... PSPCA
PennzEnergy Co. [*NYSE symbol*] (SG) .... PZE
Pennzoil-Quaker State [*NYSE symbol*] (SG) .... PZL
Pensacola, FL [*FM radio station call letters*] (BROA) .... WBGP-FM
Pentegra Dental Group [*AMEX symbol*] (SG) .... PEN
Pentwater, MI [*FM radio station call letters*] (BROA) .... WMOM-FM
Pentwater, MI [*FM radio station call letters*] (BROA) .... WWKR-FM

People (GEAB) .... peo
Peoria, IL [*FM radio station call letters*] (BROA) .... WPBG-FM
Percent Depth Dose [*Medicine*] (MELL) .... PDD
Percutaneous Balloon Mitral Valvoplasty [*Medicine*] (MELL) ...... PBMV
Percutaneous Electrical Nerve Stimulation .... PENS
Percutaneous Epididymal Sperm Aspiration [*Medicine*] (MELL) ... PESA
Percutaneous Laser Disc Decompression .... PLDD
Percutaneous Pin Fixation [*Medicine*] (MELL) .... PCPF
Percutaneous Renal Cyst Puncture [*Medicine*] (MELL) .... PRCP
Percutaneous Transluminal Angioplasty [*Medicine*] (MELL) ...... PCTA
Percutaneous Transluminal Balloon Dilatation [*Medicine*] (MELL) ... PTBD
Perfluorocarbon .... PFC
Performance and Innovation Unit .... PIU
Performance Appraisal .... PA
Performance Evaluation .... PE
Performance Testing .... PT
Perhaps (GEAB) .... perh
Periaortic Nodes [*Medicine*] (MELL) .... PAN
Periapical Cyst [*Medicine*] (MELL) .... PAC
Peri-Appendicular Abscess [*Medicine*] (MELL) .... PAA
Pericardial Constriction [*Medicine*] (MELL) .... PCC
Pericardial Effusion [*Medicine*] (MELL) .... PCE
Pericardial Pressure [*Medicine*] (MELL) .... PCP
Peridontal Disease (MELL) .... PDD
Periodic Limb Movement when Sleeping (MELL) .... PLMS
Periodontal Abscess [*Medicine*] (MELL) .... PA
Periodontal Abscess (MELL) .... PDA
Perioperative Myocardial Infarction [*Medicine*] (MELL) .... PMI
Peripheral Arterial Occlusive Disease [*Medicine*] (MELL) .... PAOD
Peripheral Autonomic Nervous System [*Medicine*] (MELL) ...... PANS
Peripheral Blood Lymphocyte [*Medicine*] (MELL) .... PBL
Peripheral Diabetic Retinopathy [*Medicine*] (MELL) .... PDR
Peripheral Facial-Paralysis [*Medicine*] (MELL) .... PFP
Peripheral Glucose Uptake [*Medicine*] (MELL) .... PGU
Peripheral Intravenous Hyperalimentation [*Medicine*] (MELL) ... PIVH
Peripheral Motor-Sensory Unit (MELL) .... PMSU
Peripheral Nerve Myelin [*Medicine*] (MELL) .... PNM
Peripheral Stem Cell Transplant [*Medicine*] (MELL) .... PSCT
Peritoneal Adhesions [*Medicine*] (MELL) .... PA
Peritoneum [*Medicine*] (MELL) .... P
Permanent Kidney Failure (MELL) .... PKF
Permanent Pacemaker Implantation [*Medicine*] (MELL) .... PPI
Permanently Crewed Capability .... PCC
Permit Improvement Team [*Environmental science*] (EPAT) .... PIT
Peroneal Tendonitis [*Medicine*] (MELL) .... PT
Perot Systems'A' [*NYSE symbol*] (SG) .... PER
Perry Como Circle (EA) .... PCC
Perry, OK [*AM radio station call letters*] (BROA) .... KOKP
Perry, OK [*FM radio station call letters*] (BROA) .... KOSB-FM
Persian (BEE) .... Pers
Persian Gulf War Veteran (MELL) .... PGWV
Personal Oral Hygiene (MELL) .... POH
Personality Disorder (MELL) .... PD
Personality Rating Scale (MELL) .... PRS
Personality Trait Disorder (MELL) .... PTD
Personalizaed Acquisition Center Exchange [*Military*] .... PACE
Personnel Administration and Industrial Relations .... PAIR
Personnel Assistant .... PA
Personnel Association .... PA
Personnel Command [*Army*] .... PERSCOM
Personnel Management Services .... PMS
Perthes' Disease (MELL) .... PD
Perturbed Free Induction Decay .... PFID
Peru (MILB) .... Pe
Peruvian Inca Orchid Dog Club of America (EA) .... PIOCA
Pes Anserinus Bursa [*Medicine*] (MELL) .... PAB
Pesticide Action Tracking System (EPAT) .... PATS
Pesticide Analytical Manual (EPAT) .... PAM
Pesticide Incident Monitoring System [*Environmental Protection Agency*]
   (EPAT) .... PIMS
Pesticide Programs Information Center (EPAT) .... PPIC
Pesticides Regulatory Action Tracking System (EPAT) .... PRATS
Petitioner (GEAB) .... petr
PetroCorp, Inc. [*AMEX symbol*] (SG) .... PEX
Petsec Energy ADS [*NYSE symbol*] (SG) .... PSJ
Peyronie's Disease (MELL) .... PD
Pflugerville, TX [*AM radio station call letters*] (BROA) .... KOKE
Phacoemulsification [*Medicine*] (MELL) .... PHACO
Phantom Limb Pain (MELL) .... PLP
Pharyngo-Epiglottic Fold [*Medicine*] (MELL) .... PEF
Pharynx (MELL) .... P
Phi Kappa Theta National (EA) .... PhiKaps
Phil Collins Information [*Formerly, Phil Collins Fan Club*] (EA) ...... PCFC
Philadelphia Eagles [*National Football League*] [*1933-42, 1944-present*]
   (NFLA) .... Phi
Philadelphia, PA [*Television station call letters*] (BROA) ...... KYW-DT
Philadelphia, PA [*Television station call letters*] (BROA) .... WCAU-DT
Philadelphia, PA [*Television station call letters*] (BROA) ..... WPVI-DT
Philadelphia, PA [*Television station call letters*] (BROA) ..... WTXF-DT
Philanthropic (PROS) .... phil
Philippines (MILB) .... Pi
Philosophy (BEE) .... Philos
Phobics Anonymous (MELL) .... PA
Phoenix, AZ [*FM radio station call letters*] (BROA) .... KMXP-FM
Phoenix, AZ [*Television station call letters*] (BROA) .... KNXV-DT

Phoenix, AZ [*Television station call letters*] (BROA) .... KPHO-DT
Phoenix Cardinals [*National Football League*] [*1988-93*] (NFLA) ...... Pho
Phone.com,Inc. [*NASDAQ symbol*] (SG) .... PHCM
Phosphatase Acid Serum [*Medicine*] (MELL) .... PAS
Photo Receptor Cell [*Medicine*] (MELL) .... PRC
Photochemical Assessment Monitoring Stations (EPAT) .... PAMS
Photochemical Assessment Monitoring Stations (EPAT) .... PMAS
Photography (BEE) .... Phot
Phrenic Stimulation [*Medicine*] (MELL) .... PS
Physical Activity Readiness Questionnaire .... PAR-Q
Physical and Neurologic Examination for Soft Signs [*Medicine*]
   (MELL) .... PANESS
Physician-Assisted Death (MELL) .... PAD
Physician-Patient Relation (MELL) .... PPR
Physician's Order Form (MELL) .... POF
Physics of Failure [*Program*] .... PoF
Physiologic Saline [*Medicine*] (MELL) .... PS
Physiology (BEE) .... Physiol
Phytohemagglutinin Protein [*Medicine*] (MELL) .... PHAP
Pi Lambda Phi (EA) .... PiLam
Pi Sigma Epsilon (EA) .... PSE
Picayune, MS [*FM radio station call letters*] (BROA) .... WKSY-FM
Pickup .... PU
Piedmont Fracture (MELL) .... PF
Pierre Robin Syndrome (MELL) .... PRS
Pigeon Breeder's Disease [*Medicine*] (MELL) .... PBD
Pigeon Breeder's Lung [*Medicine*] (MELL) .... PBL
Pigeon-Toed (MELL) .... PT
Pigmentation, Edema and Plasma Cell Dyscrasia (MELL) .... PEP
Pigmented Basal Cell Carcinoma [*Medicine*] (MELL) .... PBCC
Pigmented Dermatofibroma [*Medicine*] (MELL) .... PDF
Pike (PROS) .... Pke
Pillager, MN [*FM radio station call letters*] (BROA) .... KBKK-FM
Pine Creek Railroad [*An association*] (EA) .... PCKRR
Pinehurst, NC [*FM radio station call letters*] (BROA) .... WBFY-FM
Pinellas Park, FL [*AM radio station call letters*] (BROA) .... WWBA
Pinl .... pnk
Pioneer (GEAB) .... pion
Pioneer Corp ADR [*NYSE symbol*] (SG) .... PIO
Pipkin Fracture (MELL) .... PF
Pippa Passes, KY [*FM radio station call letters*] (BROA) ... WWJD-FM
Pismo Beach, CA [*FM radio station call letters*] (BROA) .... KXTZ-FM
Pitless Adapter Division .... PAD
Pittsburgh, PA [*Television station call letters*] (BROA) .... KDKA-DT
Pittsburgh, PA [*Television station call letters*] (BROA) .... WCWB
Pittsburgh, PA [*FM radio station call letters*] (BROA) .... WDRV-FM
Pittsburgh, Pa [*AM radio station call letters*] (BROA) .... WEAE
Pittsburgh, PA [*Television station call letters*] (BROA) .... WPXI-DT
Pittsburgh Pirates [*National Football League*] [*1933-40*] (NFLA) ...... PPr
Pittsburgh Steelers [*National Football League*] [*1941-42, 1945-present*]
   (NFLA) .... Pit
Pittsburgh Supercomputing Center Network [*Pennsylvania*] ... PSCNet
Pittsfield, IL [*FM radio station call letters*] (BROA) .... WAKC-FM
Pittsfield, MA [*FM radio station call letters*] (BROA) .... WBRK-FM
Place of Maximal Impulse [*Medicine*] (MELL) .... PMI
Placebo [*Medicine*] (MELL) .... PCB
Placenta Accreta [*Medicine*] (MELL) .... PA
Placental Villus Inflammation [*Medicine*] (MELL) .... PVI
Plains All Amer Pipeline [*NYSE symbol*] (SG) .... PAA
Plaintiff (GEAB) .... ptf
Plainview, TX [*FM radio station call letters*] (BROA) .... KVOP-FM
Planet Hollywood Intl'A' [*NYSE symbol*] (SG) .... PHL
Planet of the Apes [*Movie title*] .... POTA
Planning and Evaluation of Sequential Trials [*Statistics*] ...... PEST
Plant Functional Type (QUAC) .... PFT
Plantar Metatarsal Padding [*Medicine*] (MELL) .... PMP
Plasma Ammonia Level [*Medicine*] (MELL) .... PAL
Plasma Angiotensinase Activity [*Medicine*] (MELL) .... PAa
Plasma Cell Myeloma [*Medicine*] (MELL) .... PCM
Plasma Cell Pneumonia [*Medicine*] (MELL) .... PCP
Plasma Cholesterol Level (MELL) .... PCL
Plasma Proinflammatory Cytokine Concentration [*Medicine*] (MELL) .... PPICC
Plastic Drum Institute .... PD
Plastic Surgery (MELL) .... PLS
Platelet [*Medicine*] (MELL) .... PLT
Platelet Accumulation Index [*Medicine*] (MELL) .... PAI
Platelet Aggregation Test [*Medicine*] (MELL) .... PAT
Platelet Survival Time [*Medicine*] (MELL) .... PST
Platelet-Derived Epidermal Growth Factor [*Medicine*] (MELL) ... PDEGF
Platelet-Fibrin-Thrombi [*Medicine*] (MELL) .... PFT
Platoon (MILB) .... pl
Plattsburgh, NY [*AM radio station call letters*] (BROA) .... WDOT
Plaza (BEE) .... plz
Pleasantville, NJ [*FM radio station call letters*] (BROA) .... WSAX-FM
Pluto Express Mission [*Space exploration*] .... PFF
Pneumatic Antishock Garment (MELL) .... PAG
Pneumococcal Meningitis [*Medicine*] (MELL) .... PCM
Pneumonia and Empyema (MELL) .... P&E
Pneumonia and Influenza (MELL) .... P & I
Pocatello, ID [*Television station call letters*] (BROA) .... KFXP
Pocatello, ID [*FM radio station call letters*] (BROA) .... KISU-FM
Pocatello, ID [*AM radio station call letters*] (BROA) .... KOUU
Pogo Fan Club and Walt Kelly Society (EA) .... PFCWKS
Point Pleasant, WV [*FM radio station call letters*] (BROA) ... WPCN-FM
Point Reyes Station, CA [*FM radio station call letters*] (BROA) ...... KWMR-FM

Poland (MILB) ... Pl
Polar Area Index [*Palynology*] (QUAC) ... PAI
Polar Continental Shelf Project [*Canada*] (QUAC) ... PCSP
Polar Exchange at the Sea Surface (EOSA) ... POLES
Polar Space Launch Vehicle [*Indian Space Research*] ... PSLV
Polar-Orbiting Earth Mission [*European Space Agency*] (EOSA) ... POEM
Pole-Equator-Pole (QUAC) ... PEP
Policy Criteria Notice [*Environmental Protection Agency*] (EPAT) ... PCN
Polish (BEE) ... Pol
Pollen Assemblage Zone (QUAC) ... PAZ
Pollicis (MELL) ... P
Pollution Prevention Inventives for States (EPAT) ... PPIS
Pollybeak Nasal Deformity [*Medicine*] (MELL) ... PBND
Polo Ralph Lauren'A' [*NYSE symbol*] (SG) ... RL
Polyammino Acid [*Medicine*] (MELL) ... PAA
Polychlorinated Vinyl (MELL) ... PCV
Polychlorobenzene [*Medicine*] (MELL) ... PCBZ
Polycystic Kidney Disease (MELL) ... PDK
Polycystic Liver Disease (MELL) ... PCLD
Polydrug Abuse (MELL) ... PDA
Polyethylene Tubing [*Medicine*] (MELL) ... PET
Polynuclear Aromatic Hydrocarbons (EPAT) ... PAH
Poly-P-Dioxanone ... PDS
Poly-Substance Abuse [*Medicine*] (MELL) ... PSA
Polytechnic (PROS) ... Polytech
Polyvinylpyridine ... PVP
Pompano Beach, FL [*AM radio station call letters*] (BROA) ... WHSR
Pontage, PA [*FM radio station call letters*] (BROA) ... WFJY-FM
Ponte Vedra Beach, FL [*FM radio station call letters*] (BROA) ... WBGB-FM
Pony Baseball/Softball [*An association*] (EA) ... PB
Pool View ... p/v
Pooled Human Plasma (MELL) ... PHP
Pooled Random Donor Platelet Concentrates [*Medicine*] (MELL) ... PRDPC
Poor Intrauterine Fetal Growth [*Medicine*] (MELL) ... PIFG
Population Information Network [*United Nations*] [*Internet resource*] ... POPIN
Populus (GEAB) ... p
Porcelain Jacket [*Dentistry*] (MELL) ... PJ
Porcine Endogenous Retrovirus ... PERV
Pork Tapeworm [*Medicine*] (MELL) ... PTW
Porsche Design ... PD
Port Angeles, WA [*AM radio station call letters*] (BROA) ... KIKN
Port Angeles, WA [*FM radio station call letters*] (BROA) ... KNWP-FM
Port Arthur, TX [*FM radio station call letters*] (BROA) ... KOVE-FM
Port Gibson, MS [*FM radio station call letters*] (BROA) ... WATU-FM
Port Wentworth, GA [*FM radio station call letters*] (BROA) ... WAYH-FM
Portal Software [*NASDAQ symbol*] (SG) ... PRSF
Portal Systemic Resistance [*Medicine*] (MELL) ... PSR
Portal Venous Pressure [*Medicine*] (MELL) ... PVR
Portal-Systemic Myelopathy [*Medicine*] (MELL) ... PSM
Porterville, CA [*Television station call letters*] (BROA) ... KPXF
Portland, ME [*FM radio station call letters*] (BROA) ... WJBQ-FM
Portland, OR [*Television station call letters*] (BROA) ... KATU-DT
Portland, OR [*Television station call letters*] (BROA) ... KGW-DT
Portland, OR [*AM radio station call letters*] (BROA) ... KKGT
Portland, OR [*Television station call letters*] (BROA) ... KOIN-DT
Portland, OR [*AM radio station call letters*] (BROA) ... KUPL
Portland, OR [*FM radio station call letters*] (BROA) ... KXL-FM
Portland, TX [*FM radio station call letters*] (BROA) ... KRMP-FM
Portsmouth Spartans [*National Football League*] [*1930-33*] (NFLA) ... Por
Portsmouth, VA [*AM radio station call letters*] (BROA) ... WHKT
Positive Affect Enhancement (MELL) ... PAE
Positive Crankcase Ventilation System ... PCV system
Positive Ground ... Pos
Positive Inspiratory Pressure [*Medicine*] (MELL) ... PIP
Positive-Negative Pressure Breathing (MELL) ... PNPB
Positron Electron Magnetic Spectrometer (EOSA) ... POEMS
Possession (BEE) ... Poss
Post, TX [*FM radio station call letters*] (BROA) ... KOFR-FM
Postantibiotic Effect [*Medicine*] (MELL) ... PAE
Post-Balloon Angioplasty Restenosis [*Medicine*] (MELL) ... PBAR
Post-Cardiac Injury Syndrome (MELL) ... PCIS
Postchemotherapy Nausea and Vomiting [*Medicine*] (MELL) ... PCNV
Posterior Cervical Fusion [*Medicine*] (MELL) ... PCF
Posterior Chamber of Eye [*Medicine*] (MELL) ... PCE
Posterior Descending Coronary Artery [*Medicine*] (MELL) ... PDCA
Posterior Gastroenterostomy [*Medicine*] (MELL) ... PGE
Posterior Horn of Spinal Cord [*Medicine*] (MELL) ... PHSC
Posterior Lobe of Hypophysis [*Medicine*] (MELL) ... PLH
Posterior Longitudinal Ligament [*Medicine*] (MELL) ... PLL
Posterior Subcapsular Cataract [*Medicine*] (MELL) ... PSCC
Postgraduate Year (MELL) ... PBY
Postinfarction Cardiac Rehabilitation [*Medicine*] (MELL) ... PCR
Post-Inflammatory Hyperpigmentation [*Medicine*] (MELL) ... PIH
Postinfusion Phlebitis [*Medicine*] (MELL) ... PIP
Postlumbar Puncture Headache [*Medicine*] (MELL) ... PPH
Postmastectomy Pain (MELL) ... PMP
Postmeal Glucose Value [*Medicine*] (MELL) ... PMGV
Post-Menopausal Women (MELL) ... PMW
Post-Ministerial Conference [*ASEAN*] ... PMC
Postmyocardial Infarct [*Medicine*] (MELL) ... PMCI
Post-Myocardial Infarction Syndrome [*Medicine*] (MELL) ... PMCIS
Postobstructive Diuresis [*Medicine*] (MELL) ... POD
Postoperative Bleeding Time [*Medicine*] (MELL) ... POBT
Postoperative Complication [*Medicine*] (MELL) ... POC
Postoperative Instructions [*Medicine*] (MELL) ... POI
Postoperative Pain [*Medicine*] (MELL) ... POP
Postpartum Breast Engorgement [*Medicine*] (MELL) ... PPBE
Postpartum Cardiomyopathy [*Medicine*] (MELL) ... PPCM
Postpartum Glomerulosclerosis [*Medicine*] (MELL) ... PPGS
Postpericardiotomy Syndrome [*Medicine*] (MELL) ... PPCS
Postpolio Atrophy Syndrome [*Medicine*] (MELL) ... PPAS
Postrenal Azotemia [*Medicine*] (MELL) ... PRA
Poststenotic Dilatation [*Medicine*] (MELL) ... PSD
Postsurgical Distress [*Medicine*] (MELL) ... PSD
Postsurgical Gastroparesis Syndrome [*Medicine*] (MELL) ... PGS
Postsurgical Pain Syndrome (MELL) ... PSPS
Post-Traumatic Epilepsy (MELL) ... PTE
Post-Traumatic Meningitis [*Medicine*] (MELL) ... PTM
Post-Traumatic Personality Defect (MELL) ... PTPD
Post-Traumatic Pulmonary Insufficiency [*Medicine*] (MELL) ... PTPI
Postural Back Pain (MELL) ... PBP
Postural Hypotension [*Medicine*] (MELL) ... PH
Post-Vaccination Immunity [*Medicine*] (MELL) ... PVI
Potassium Chloride (MELL) ... KCl
Potential Child Abuse and Neglect (MELL) ... PCAN
Potential Difference (MELL) ... pd
Potentially Hazardous Asteroids ... PHA
Potentially Toxic Element ... PTE
Potsdam Institute for Climate Impact Research ... PIK
Pott's Fracture [*Medicine*] (MELL) ... PF
Pottsville, PA [*FM radio station call letters*] (BROA) ... WAVT-FM
Poughkeepsie, NY [*FM radio station call letters*] (BROA) ... WTND-FM
Pounder (MILB) ... pdr
Power Antenna [*Automotive term*] ... PA
Power Deck Lid Release ... PDLR
Power Deck Release ... PDR
Power Disc Brakes [*Automotive term*] ... PDB
Power Door Locks ... PDL
Power Law Process ... PLP
Power Mirrors ... PM
Powerglide [*Automatic transmission*] ... PG
Practical Salinity Unit ... PSU
Prairie du Chien, WI [*FM radio station call letters*] (BROA) ... WQPC-FM
Precancerous Lesion (MELL) ... PCL
Precautions and Contraindications [*Medicine*] (MELL) ... P&C
Precipitation Radar (EOSA) ... PR
Precise Range and Rate Equipment-Extended Version (EOSA) ... PRAREE
Precursor (MELL) ... P
Predeposited Autologous Blood Donation [*Medicine*] (MELL) ... PABD
Preferred ... pfd
Pregnancy After Infertility [*Medicine*] ... PANFERT
Pregnancy-Associated Globulin [*Medicine*] (MELL) ... PAG
Pregnancy-Induced Glucose Intolerance [*Medicine*] (MELL) ... PIGI
Pregnancy-Related Mortality Surveillance System (MELL) ... PRMSS
Pre-Harvest Interval (EPAT) ... PHI
Prekallikrein Activator [*Medicine*] (MELL) ... PKA
Preliminary Benefit Analysis [*Environmental Protection Agency*] (EPAT) ... PBA
Preliminary Quantitative Usage Analysis [*Environmental science*] (EPAT) ... PQUA
Prelingually Acquired Meningitic Deafness [*Medicine*] (MELL) ... PAMD
Premature Coronary Artery Disease (MELL) ... PCAD
Premature Ejaculation [*Medicine*] (MELL) ... PME
Premature Ovarian Failure [*Medicine*] ... POF
Premenopausal Women (MELL) ... PMW
Premiumwear, Inc. [*NYSE symbol*] (SG) ... PWA
Preoperative Bowel Preparation [*Medicine*] (MELL) ... POBP
Preoperative Holding Area [*Medicine*] (MELL) ... POHA
Prepared Childbirth Training (MELL) ... PCT
Preparticipation Physical Exam ... PPE
Prepatellar Bursitis [*Medicine*] (MELL) ... PPB
Preproliferative Diabetic Retinopathy [*Medicine*] (MELL) ... PPDR
Prepseudoarthrosis [*Medicine*] (MELL) ... PSA
Preretinal Hemorrhage [*Medicine*] (MELL) ... PRH
Preretinal Macular Fibrosis [*Medicine*] (MELL) ... PRMF
Presbytarian (BEE) ... Prsbytn
Prescott, AZ [*FM radio station call letters*] (BROA) ... KPUB-FM
Prescription Drug Abuse (MELL) ... PDA
Presidential Awards for Excellence in Math and Science Teaching ... PAEMST
Press-Fit Component (MELL) ... PFC
Pressoreceptor Zone [*Medicine*] (MELL) ... PRZ
Pressure Falling Rapidly [*Meteorology*] (WEAT) ... PRESSFR
Pressure Modulator Infrared Radiometer (EOSA) ... PMIR
Pressure per Square Inch (EPAT) ... PSI
Pressure per Square Inch Gauge (EPAT) ... PSIG
Pressure Rising Rapidly [*Meteorology*] (WEAT) ... PRESSRR
Pressure Sore (MELL) ... PS
Pressure-Modulator Cell (EOSA) ... PMC
Preterm Newborn (MELL) ... PTNB
Preventive Medicine (MELL) ... PVM
Preview Travel [*NASDAQ symbol*] (SG) ... PTVL
Previous Medical History (MELL) ... PMH
priceline.com, Inc. [*NASDAQ symbol*] (SG) ... PCLN
Pricing Electronic Access to Knowledge ... PEAK
Primary Blistering Disorder [*Medicine*] (MELL) ... PBD
Primary Congenital Glaucoma (MELL) ... PCG
Primary Degenerative Cerebral Disease [*Medicine*] (MELL) ... PDCA
Primary Syphilis (MELL) ... PS
Primate Immunodeficiency Virus [*Medicine*] (MELL) ... PIV
Prime Capital [*NASDAQ symbol*] (SG) ... PMCPE
Prime Minister's Science, Engineering and Innovation Council [*Australia*] ... PMSEIC

Primus Knowledge Solutions [*NASDAQ symbol*] (SG) .... PKSI
Princeton, MN [*FM radio station call letters*] (BROA) .... KLCI-FM
Princeton, WV [*FM radio station call letters*] (BROA) .... WKOY-FM
Principal (PROS) .... prin
Principal Anti-Air Missile System (MILB) .... PAAMS
Principal Oscillation Patterns Analysis .... POPS
Principal Surface Combatant (MILB) .... PSC
Prions [*Medicine*] (MELL) .... P
Prior to Delivery (MELL) .... PTD
Prison Behavior Rating Scale .... PBRS
Prison Realty Trust [*NYSE symbol*] (SG) .... PZN
Private (GEAB) .... pvt
Private Vocational Schools .... PVS
Probability of Chance (MELL) .... POC
Probability-Probability Plot [*Statistics*] .... P-P plot
Probate (GEAB) .... pro
Probate Judge of the Peace (GEAB) .... PJP
Probated (GEAB) .... pr
Procedure-Related Pain (MELL) .... PRP
Proceedings of the National Academy of Sciences [*A publication*] .... PNAS
Procoagulant Factor [*Medicine*] (MELL) .... PCF
Prodigy Communications [*NASDAQ symbol*] (SG) .... PRGY
Product Data Call-In (EPAT) .... PDCI
Product Generation System (EOSA) .... PGS
Product Management Office [*Army*] .... PMO
Product Manager .... PM
Professional Airways Systems Specialists Division [*An association*]
   (EA) .... PASS
Professional in Human Resources .... PHR
Professional Women's Association .... PWA
Professor (PROS) .... prof
Profile Total Hip System (MELL) .... PTHS
Profoundly Hearing Impaired Adult (MELL) .... PHIA
Progen Industries [*NASDAQ symbol*] (SG) .... PGLAF
Progestin-Binding Complement [*Medicine*] (MELL) .... PBC
Progestin-Estrogen Cyclic Therapy [*Medicine*] (MELL) .... PECT
Program Evaluation Test .... PET
Program Executive Office, Command, Control, and Communications
   Systems [*Army*] PEO-C3S
Program Executive Office, Standard Army Management Information
   Systems .... PEO-STAMIS
Program Manager for Heavy Tactical Vehicles [*Military*] .... PM-HTV
Program Site Coordinator [*Environmental science*] (EPAT) .... PSC
Programmable Power Key [*Computer science*] .... PPK
Progressive Dialysis Encephalopathy [*Medicine*] (MELL) .... PDE
Progressive Diaphyseal Dysplasia [*Medicine*] (MELL) .... PDD
Progressive General Paralysis (MELL) .... PGP
Progressive Muscle Relaxation (MELL) .... PMR
Progressive Myoclonus Epilepsy [*Medicine*] (MELL) .... PME
Progressive Streptococcal Muscular Atrophy [*Medicine*] (MELL) .... PSMA
Progressively Diffused Leukoencephalopathy [*Medicine*] (MELL) .... PDL
Project Manager's Office, Medium Tactical Vehicles [*Army*] ...... PMO-MTV
Project Science Office (EOSA) .... PSO
Prolactin (MELL) .... P
Proliferative Zone (MELL) .... PZ
Prolong International [*AMEX symbol*] (SG) .... PRL
Prolonged Respiratory Support (MELL) .... PRS
Prolonged Rupture of Fetal Membranes [*Medicine*] (MELL) ...... PRFM
Promyelocytic Leukaemia Zinc-Finger .... PLZF

Pronated External Rotation [*Medicine*] (MELL) .... PER
Prone Sleeping Position (MELL) .... PSP
Proof [*Numismatic term*] .... Pr
Proof of Illness (MELL) .... POI
Property or Casualty .... P&C
Prophylactic Regional Node Dissection [*Medicine*] (MELL) ...... PRND
Prostate Biopsy [*Medicine*] (MELL) .... PBx
Prostate-Specific Antigen Density [*Medicine*] (MELL) .... PSAD
Prostate-Specific Antigen Test [*Medicine*] (MELL) .... PSAT
Prostatic Interstitial Fluid [*Medicine*] (MELL) .... PIF
Prostatic Intraepithelial Neoplasia [*Medicine*] (MELL) .... PIN
Prostatic Secretion [*Medicine*] (MELL) .... PS
Prosthetic Heart Valve (MELL) .... PHV
Protection, Rest, Ice, Compression, and Elevation .... PRICEMMM
Prothrombin Time Ratio [*Medicine*] (MELL) .... PTR
ProVantage Health Svcs. [*NYSE symbol*] (SG) .... PHS
Provencal (BEE) .... prov
Providence, RI [*AM radio station call letters*] (BROA) .... WRNI
Provo, UT [*Television station call letters*] (BROA) .... KUPX
Proximal Renal Tubular Acidosis [*Medicine*] (MELL) .... PRTA
Proximal Row Carpectomy [*Medicine*] (MELL) .... PRC
Pseudomyocardial Hypertrophy [*Medicine*] (MELL) .... PMH
Pseudonym (BEE) .... pseud
Psoriatic Arthritis .... PA
PSS World Medical [*NASDAQ symbol*] (SG) .... PSSI
Psychoactive Substance Dependence and Abuse (MELL) .... PSDA
Psychoanalysis (BEE) .... Psychoanal
Psychopathy Checklist-Revised .... PCL-R
Public (MILB) .... publ
Public Limited Company .... Plc
Published (PROS) .... publ
Pudendal Block Anesthesia [*Medicine*] (MELL) .... PBA
Pudendal Lymph Nodes [*Medicine*] (MELL) .... PLN
Pueblo, CO [*AM radio station call letters*] (BROA) .... KAVA
Pulled Elbow (MELL) .... PE
Pullman, WA [*Television station call letters*] (BROA) .... KBGC
Pulmonary (MELL) .... P
Pulmonary (MELL) .... pulm
Pulmonary Alveolar Hypoxic Vasoconstrictor [*Medicine*] (MELL) ... PAHVC
Pulmonary Alveolar-Capillary Permeability [*Medicine*] (MELL) ... PACP
Pulmonary Aspiration Syndrome [*Medicine*] (MELL) .... PAS
Pulmonary Disease-Anemia Syndrome (MELL) .... PDAS
Pulmonary Disorder [*Medicine*] (MELL) .... PuD
Pulmonary Emphysema [*Medicine*] (MELL) .... PE
Pulmonary Oxygen Transfer [*Medicine*] (MELL) .... POT
Pulmonary Vascular Obstructive Disease [*Medicine*] (MELL) .... PVOD
Pulverised Coal Injection [*Coal industry*] .... PCI
Puncture Wound (MELL) .... PW
Punta Rassa, FL [*FM radio station call letters*] (BROA) .... WCCL-FM
Pupil Evaluation Program .... PEP
Pupils Equal and React to Light [*Medicine*] (MELL) .... PEARL
Purchased (GEAB) .... pchd
Pure Active Ingredient (EPAT) .... PAI
Pure Tone Audiometry (MELL) .... PTA
Purple .... prpl
Purse-String Mouth (MELL) .... PSM
Puyallup, WA [*AM radio station call letters*] (BROA) .... KSUH
Pyramidal Eminence [*Medicine*] (MELL) .... PE
Pyrazinoic Acid (MELL) .... PZA
Pyruvate Kinase Deficiency [*Medicine*] (MELL) .... PKD

Q

By Meaning

QAD,Inc. [*NASDAQ symbol*] (SG) .... QADI
Qatar (MILB) .... Q
Quadriceps Tendon Bearing [*Medicine*] (MELL) .... QTB
Quadrillion British Thermal Unit (EPAT) .... QBTU
Qualified Joint and Survivor Annuity .... QJSA
Qualified Preretirement Survivor Annuity .... QPSA
Qualitative Use Assessment (EPAT) .... QUA
Quantification Limit (EPAT) .... QL
Quantile-Quantile Plot .... Q-Q plot
Quantitative Electroencephalography [*Medicine*] (MELL) .... QEEG

Quantum Electronics and Laser Science .... QELS
Quantum Field Theory .... QFT
Quarterly Update for Inspector in Pesticide Enforcement (EPAT) .... QUIPE
Quebec, PQ [*FM radio station call letters*] (BROA) .... CBVX-FM
Queensland Museum [*Australia*] .... QM
Queer Resources Directory [*Internet resource*] .... QED
Quiet Room (MELL) .... QR
Quincy, WA [*FM radio station call letters*] (BROA) .... KGER-FM
Quinidine and Quinine [*Medicine*] (MELL) .... Q & O
Q-Wave Myocardial Infraction [*Medicine*] (MELL) .... QMI
Qwest Communications [*NASDAQ symbol*] (SG) .... QWST

R

By Meaning

Racing Champions Mint Editions [*Toy collection*] .... RCME
Radar Altimeter Speedometer Sounder .... RASS
Radian Group [*NYSE symbol*] (SG) .... RDN
Radiation Burn (MELL) .... RB
Radiation Control for Health and Safety Act (MELL) .... RCHSA
Radiocardiography [*Medicine*] (MELL) .... RCG
Radiocarpal Joint [*Medicine*] (MELL) .... RCI
Radiographic Absorptiometry [*Medicine*] (MELL) .... RA
Radius (MELL) .... r
Ragen Mackenzie Grp. [*NYSE symbol*] (SG) .... RMG
Raised White Letter .... Rwl
Raleigh, NC [*FM radio station call letters*] (BROA) .... WBBB-FM
Raleigh, NC [*Television station call letters*] (BROA) .... WRAL-DT
Raleigh, NC [*FM radio station call letters*] (BROA) .... WWND-FM
Rally Sport .... RS
Random Blood Glucose (MELL) .... RBG
Randomized Block Design .... RBD
Rao-Hartley-Cochran Method .... RHC
Rapid Assay Delivery System [*Medicine*] (MELL) .... RADS
Rapid Atrial Fibrillation [*Medicine*] (MELL) .... RAF
Rapid-Reaction Corps (MILB) .... RRC
Rare Medium Group [*NASDAQ symbol*] (SG) .... RRRR
Rat Bite Fever (MELL) .... RBF
Rate of Progress (EPAT) .... ROP
Rated (GEAB) .... rat
Ravenswood, WV [*FM radio station call letters*] (BROA) .... WMOV-FM
Rayne, LA [*FM radio station call letters*] (BROA) .... KLTW-FM
Raytheon Demilitarization Company .... RDC
Razorfish,Inc.'A' [*NASDAQ symbol*] (SG) .... RAZF
Reactive Attachment Disorder [*Medicine*] (MELL) .... RAD
Read the Instructions [*Online dialog*] .... RTI
Ready to Assemble .... RTA
Real Riders [*Toy collection*] .... RR
Realising Our Potential Award .... ROPA
Rebuilt [*Automobile*] .... RBLT
Recapitulation (MELL) .... R
Receiver Operating Characteristic Curves .... ROC curves
Recombinant (MELL) .... r
Reconnaissance (MILB) .... recce
Reconnaissance and Attack Helicopter [*Military*] RAH-66
Record Book .... RB
Recorder (GEAB) .... redr
Rectal Dysfunction [*Medicine*] (MELL) .... RD
Rectoanal Inhibitory Reflex [*Medicine*] (MELL) .... RAIR
Rector (GEAB) .... r
Recurrent Abdominal Pain (MELL) .... RAP
Recurrent Depression (MELL) .... RD
Recurrent Pregnancy Loss [*Medicine*] .... RPL
Recurrent Spontaneous Abortion [*Medicine*] .... RSA
Recycling Economic Development Advocate (EPAT) .... REDA
Red Line [*Automotive tire designation*] .... RL
Red Lines [*Toy collection*] .... RL
Red Lion, PA [*FM radio station call letters*] (BROA) .... WSOX-FM
Red Lion, PA [*AM radio station call letters*] (BROA) .... WTHM
Red River, NM [*FM radio station call letters*] (BROA) .... KRDR-FM
Red Springs, NC [*AM radio station call letters*] (BROA) .... WTEL
Redback Networks [*NASDAQ symbol*] (SG) .... RBAK
Redfield, SD [*FM radio station call letters*] (BROA) .... KGIM-FM
Red-Fronted Macaw [*Bird*] .... RFM
Reeds Jewelers [*AMEX symbol*] (SG) .... RJI
Reference Dose Values [*Environmental science*] (EPAT) .... RDV
Referral and Consultation (MELL) .... R & C
Reflector in Space (EOSA) .... RIS
Refugio, TX [*FM radio station call letters*] (BROA) .... KTKY-FM
Regarding (GEAB) .... re
Regiment (MILB) .... regt
Regional Alcohol and Drug Awareness Resources (MELL) .... RADAR
Regional Climate Model (QUAC) .... RCM
Regional Compliance Officer [*Environmental science*] (EPAT) .... RCO
Regional Earth Science Applications Center [*NASA*] .... RESAC
Regional Integration Arrangement .... RIA
Regional Ozone Study Area [*Environmental Protection Agency*] (EPAT) .. ROSA
Register (GEAB) .... reg
Register of Professional Archaeologists .... ROPA
Registered Genealogist (GEAB) .... RG
Registration Standard (EPAT) .... RS

Regression Analysis (MELL) .... RA
Regular (BEE) .... reg
RehabCare Group [*NYSE symbol*] (SG) .... RHB
Rehabilitation (PROS) .... rehab
Relations (PROS) .... rels
Relative Biologic Dose (MELL) .... RBD
Relative Chemotactic Activity [*Medicine*] (MELL) .... RCA
Relative Sea Level (QUAC) .... rsl
Release of Dower Rights (GEAB) .... RD
Reliant Energy [*NYSE symbol*] (SG) .... REI
Relieved (GEAB) .... reld
Religious (PROS) .... rel
Religious and Theological Abstracts [*A publication*] .... RTA
Relinquished (GEAB) .... rinq
Remediation Technologies Development Forum (EPAT) .... RTDF
Remission (MELL) .... R
Remote Sensing Center [*Ecuador*] (GEOI) .... CLIRSEN
Renaissance Worldwide [*NASDAQ symbol*] (SG) .... REGI
Renal Clearance [*Medicine*] (MELL) .... RCL
Renal Cystic Disease [*Medicine*] (MELL) .... RCD
Renin-Angiotensin-Aldosterone Mechanism [*Medicine*] (MELL) .... RAAM
Reno, NV [*FM radio station call letters*] (BROA) .... KNHK-FM
Reno, NV [*AM radio station call letters*] (BROA) .... KPTT
Renovo, PA [*FM radio station call letters*] (BROA) .... WZYY-FM
Rensselaer, NY [*AM radio station call letters*] (BROA) .... WTMM
Rent-A-Center [*NASDAQ symbol*] (SG) .... RCII
Renton, WA [*AM radio station call letters*] (BROA) .... KYIZ
Rent-Way, Inc. [*NYSE symbol*] (SG) .... RWY
Renunciation (GEAB) .... ren
Reorganized Army Plains Infantry Division (MILB) .... RAPID
Repetitive Stress Injury .... RSI
Replaced (GEAB) .... repl
Replication (MELL) .... R
Reprinted (GEAB) .... rep
Reproductive Immunophynotype [*Medicine*] .... RIP
Republic Services [*NYSE symbol*] (SG) .... RSG
Republican (PROS) .... Repbl
Repudiated (GEAB) .... repud
Request for Bid (EPAT) .... RB
Research and Public Information Dissemination .... RAPID
Research Centers Program (EPAT) .... RCP
Research Centre for Advanced Science and Technology .... RCAST
Research in Motion .... RIM
Research Papers in Economics .... RePEc
Research Resources for the Social Sciences [*Internet resource*] .... RRSS
Residence (BEE) .... res
Residue (MELL) .... R
ResortQuest Intl. [*NYSE symbol*] (SG) .... RZT
Resource Asset Invstmt. [*AMEX symbol*] (SG) .... RAS
Resource Bancshares Mtg. Gp. [*NASDAQ symbol*] (SG) .... RBMG
Resource Bankshares [*AMEX symbol*] (SG) .... RBV
Resource Record .... RR
Restaurant Associates .... RA
Restricted Entry Interval [*Environmental Protection Agency*] (EPAT) .. REI
Retinal Capillary Microaneurysm [*Medicine*] (MELL) .... RCM
Retro-Auricular Lymph Node [*Medicine*] (MELL) .... RALN
Retrograde Atrioventricular Conduction [*Medicine*] (MELL) .... RAVC
Returning Polar Maritime Airmass [*Meteorology*] (WEAT) .... rmP
Revenue Systems, Inc. .... RSI
Revised (GEAB) .... Rev
Revised Hazard Ranking System [*Environmental science*] (EPAT) ..... RHRS
Revolutionary Armed Forces of Colombia .... FARC
Revolutionary War (GEAB) .... Rev
Revolutions per Minute .... Rpm
Rexx Environmental [*AMEX symbol*] (SG) .... REX
RF Micro Devices [*NASDAQ symbol*] (SG) .... RFMD
Rheumatoid Agglutinin Nuclear Antigen [*Medicine*] (MELL) .... RANA
Rheumatoid Arthritis Agglutination [*Medicine*] (MELL) .... RAAG
Rheumatoid Arthritis and Ankylosing Spondylitis [*Medicine*] (MELL) .. RA & AS
Rheumatoid Arthritis and Hypersplenism [*Medicine*] (MELL) .... RA & H
Rhodia ADS [*NYSE symbol*] (SG) .... RHA
Rhythms NetConnections [*NASDAQ symbol*] (SG) .... RTHM
RiboGene,Inc. [*AMEX symbol*] (SG) .... RBO
Rica Foods [*AMEX symbol*] (SG) .... RCF
Richburg, SC [*FM radio station call letters*] (BROA) .... WRBK-FM
Richfood Hldgs. [*NYSE symbol*] (SG) .... RFH

Richmond, VA [*FM radio station call letters*] (BROA) .... WJRV-FM
Richmond, VA [*FM radio station call letters*] (BROA) .... WRCL-FM
Richmont Mines [*AMEX symbol*] (SG) .... RIC
Rickets and Chronic Cough (MELL) .... RCC
Rick's Loyal Supporters [*An association*] (EA) .... RLS
Ricky Skaggs International Fan Club (EA) .... RSIFC
Riddell Sports [*AMEX symbol*] (SG) .... RDL
Ride Motion Simulator .... RMS
Ridge (BEE) .... rdg
Ridgebury, PA [*FM radio station call letters*] (BROA) .... WREQ-FM
Right Anterodescending Coronary Artery [*Medicine*] (MELL) .... RADCA
Right Atrioventricular Valve [*Medicine*] (MELL) .... RAVV
Right Carotid Endarterectomy [*Medicine*] (MELL) .... RCE
Right Common Carotid [*Medicine*] (MELL) .... RCC
Right Crus of Diaphragm [*Medicine*] (MELL) .... RCD
Rio Grande City, TX [*Television station call letters*] (BROA) .... KTLM
Ripley, TN [*FM radio station call letters*] (BROA) .... WAUV-FM
Ripon, WI [*AM radio station call letters*] (BROA) .... WRPN
Risk and Death (MELL) .... R & D
Risk Assessed By [*Medicine*] (MELL) .... RAB
Risks and Benefits [*Medicine*] (MELL) .... R & B
Risks and Complications (MELL) .... R & C
Ritchie Bros. Auctioneers [*NYSE symbol*] (SG) .... RBA
Riverside, CA [*FM radio station call letters*] (BROA) .... KSSE-FM
Riviera Tool [*AMEX symbol*] (SG) .... RTC
Riviere du Loup, PQ [*FM radio station call letters*] (BROA) .... CJFP-FM
Road (BEE) .... rd
Roadster .... Rdstr
Roann, IN [*FM radio station call letters*] (BROA) .... WBFK-FM
Roanoke Rapids, NC [*FM radio station call letters*] (BROA) .... WXQD-FM
Roanoke, VA [*AM radio station call letters*] (BROA) .... WGMN
Robbins & Myers [*NYSE symbol*] (SG) .... RBN
Roberts Pharmaceutical [*AMEX symbol*] (SG) .... RPC
Roberts Realty Investors [*AMEX symbol*] (SG) .... RPI
Rochester, HN [*AM radio station call letters*] (BROA) .... WGIN
Rochester, MN [*FM radio station call letters*] (BROA) .... KMSE-FM
Rochester, NH [*AM radio station call letters*] (BROA) .... WAYU
Rochester, NY [*FM radio station call letters*] (BROA) .... WBBF-FM
Rochester, NY [*AM radio station call letters*] (BROA) .... WDCZ
Rochester, NY [*AM radio station call letters*] (BROA) .... WEZO
Rock Financial [*NASDAQ symbol*] (SG) .... RCCK
Rock of Ages'A' [*NASDAQ symbol*] (SG) .... ROAC
Rock Springs, WY [*FM radio station call letters*] (BROA) .... KMKX-FM
Rocket (MILB) .... rkt
Rockport, TX [*FM radio station call letters*] (BROA) .... KBTE-FM
Rocky Mountain, NC [*Television station call letters*] (BROA) .... WRPX
Rogers City, MI [*FM radio station call letters*] (BROA) .... WVXA-FM

Role Playing Game Association Network (EA) .... RPGA
Roman (BEE) .... Rom
Romney, WV [*FM radio station call letters*] (BROA) .... WDZN-FM
Root Canal Filling [*Dentistry*] (MELL) .... RCF
Root Mean Square Difference .... RMSD
Root-Sum-Square (EOSA) .... rss
Roper Industries [*NYSE symbol*] (SG) .... ROP
Rosamond, CA [*FM radio station call letters*] (BROA) .... KOSS-FM
Rose Rosette Disease .... RRD
Rosenberg, TX [*FM radio station call letters*] (BROA) .... KOVA-FM
Roslyn Bancorp [*NASDAQ symbol*] (SG) .... RSLN
Rossville, GA [*AM radio station call letters*] (BROA) .... WLMX
Rostelecom Telecommun ADS [*NYSE symbol*] (SG) .... ROS
Roswell, GA [*FM radio station call letters*] (BROA) .... WAMJ-FM
Rotator Cuff Disease [*Medicine*] (MELL) .... RCD
Rotator Cuff Tear [*Medicine*] (MELL) .... RCT
Rotterdam, NY [*FM radio station call letters*] (BROA) .... WTRY-FM
Rottlund Co. [*AMEX symbol*] (SG) .... RH
Round Rock, TX [*FM radio station call letters*] (BROA) .... KFMK-FM
Round-Back Deformity (MELL) .... RBD
Routine Analytical Service (EPAT) .... RAS
RoweCom,Inc. [*NASDAQ symbol*] (SG) .... ROWE
Roy Clark International Fan Club (EA) .... RCIFC
Royal Canadian Geographical Society (QUAC) .... RCGS
Royal College of Surgeon's Museum [*London, England*] .... RCSM
Royal Enfield Owners Club (EA) .... REOC
Royal Group Tech. [*NYSE symbol*] (SG) .... RYG
Royal Jordanian Investments .... RJI
Royal Netherlands Veterinary Association (GVA) .... KNMvD
Royal Olympic Cruise Line [*NASDAQ symbol*] (SG) .... ROCLF
Royal Scottish Museum [*Edinburgh*] .... RSM
RSL Communications 'A' [*NASDAQ symbol*] (SG) .... RSLC
RTO Enterprises [*Toronto Stock Exchange symbol*] (SG) .... RTO
Rubella (MELL) .... R
Rumble Seat .... RS
Ruptured Abdominal Aortic Aneurysm [*Medicine*] (MELL) .... RAAA
Ruptured Appendix [*Medicine*] (MELL) .... RA
Rushville, OH [*FM radio station call letters*] (BROA) .... WLRY-FM
Russellville, AL [*AM radio station call letters*] (BROA) .... WGOL
Russellville, AL [*FM radio station call letters*] (BROA) .... WKGL-FM
Russian (BEE) .... Russ
Russian and East European Network Information Center .... REENIC
Russian Palynological Commission (QUAC) .... RPC
Ruston, LA [*FM radio station call letters*] (BROA) .... KBDJ-FM
Rving Women [*ASO*] (EA) .... RVW
Rwanda (MILB) .... Rwa
Ryanair Holdings ADS [*NASDAQ symbol*] (SG) .... RYAAY

S
By Meaning

Saab Club of North America (EA) .... SCNA
Saatchi & Saatchi ADS [NYSE symbol] (SG) .... SSA
Sacral Nerve Block [Medicine] (MELL) .... SNB
Sacral Vertebra (MELL) .... S
Sacramento, CA [Television station call letters] (BROA) ..... KMAX-TV
Sacramento, CA [FM radio station call letters] (BROA) .... KNDN-FM
Sacramento, CA [AM radio station call letters] (BROA) .... KTKZ
Saddle Block Anesthesia [Medicine] (MELL) .... SBA
Saddle Joint [Medicine] (MELL) .... SJ
Saegertown, PA [FM radio station call letters] (BROA) .... WMDE-FM
Sagittarius A* [Astronomy] .... Sgr A*
Ste. Anne des Monts, PQ [FM radio station call letters] (BROA) .... CJMC-FM
St. Charles, MN [FM radio station call letters] (BROA) .... KLCX FM
St. George, SC [FM radio station call letters] (BROA) .... WNKT-FM
St. George, UT [FM radio station call letters] (BROA) .... KEOT-FM
St. George, UT [FM radio station call letters] (BROA) .... KSNN-FM
St. George, UT [AM radio station call letters] (BROA) .... KTSP
St. Georges-de-Beauce, PQ [FM radio station call letters] (BROA) .... CKRB-FM
St. James, MN [FM radio station call letters] (BROA) .... KRRW-FM
St. Johnsbury, VT [FM radio station call letters] (BROA) .... WKXH-FM
St. Joseph, MN [FM radio station call letters] (BROA) .... KCML-FM
St. Laurent Paperboard [NYSE symbol] (SG) .... SLW
St. Louis Cardinals [National Football League] [1960-87] (NFLA) ..... StC
St. Louis Gunners [National Football League] [1934] (NFLA) ..... StG
St. Louis, MO [Television station call letters] (BROA) .... KMOV-DT
St. Louis, MO [AM radio station call letters] (BROA) .... KTRS
St. Louis, MO [Television station call letters] (BROA) .... KTVI-DT
St. Louis, MO [AM radio station call letters] (BROA) .... KZJZ
St. Louis Rams [National Football League] [1995-present] (NFLA) ..... StL
St. Maarten Tourist Information Office (EA) .... SMTO
St. Marys, PA [FM radio station call letters] (BROA) .... WPKK-FM
St. Paul, AK [AM radio station call letters] (BROA) .... KUHB
St. Paul, MN [Television station call letters] (BROA) .... KTCI-DT
St. Petersburg, FL [FM radio station call letters] (BROA) ..... WFJO-FM
St. Petersburg, FL [Television station call letters] (BROA) .... WTSP-DT
St. Simons Island, GA [FM radio station call letters] (BROA) ... WHFX-FM
Saipan, MP [FM radio station call letters] (BROA) .... KRNM-FM
Saks, Inc. [NYSE symbol] (SG) .... SKS
Salem Communications'A' [NASDAQ symbol] (SG) .... SALM
Salem, NJ [AM radio station call letters] (BROA) .... WNNN
Salem, OR [Television station call letters] (BROA) .... KPXG
Salem, OR [FM radio station call letters] (BROA) .... KRSK-FM
Salem, VA [FM radio station call letters] (BROA) .... WPAR-FM
Salinas, CA [AM radio station call letters] (BROA) .... KTXX
Saline Infusion Test [Medicine] (MELL) .... SIT
Saline, MI [AM radio station call letters] (BROA) .... WDEO
Salisbury Bancorp [AMEX symbol] (SG) .... SAL
Salivary Duct Strictures [Medicine] (MELL) .... SDS
Salivary Gland (MELL) .... SG
S-allylcysteine .... SAC
S-allymercaptocysteine .... SAMC
Salt Lake City, UT [AM radio station call letters] (BROA) ...... KNRS
Salt Lake City, UT [Television station call letters] (BROA) ..... KTMW
Salt-Losing Nephritis [Medicine] (MELL) .... SLN
Salton, Inc. [NYSE symbol] (SG) .... SFP
Saluda, SC [FM radio station call letters] (BROA) .... WJES-FM
Sample Management Office [Environmental Protection Agency] (EPAT) .... SMO
San Angelo, TX [FM radio station call letters] (BROA) .... KMDX-FM
San Antonio, TX [FM radio station call letters] (BROA) ...... KXXM-FM
San Ardo, CA [FM radio station call letters] (BROA) .... KBDH-FM
San Bernardino, CA [AM radio station call letters] (BROA) .... KKDD
San Diego, CA [Television station call letters] (BROA) .... KGTV-DT
San Diego, CA [FM radio station call letters] (BROA) .... KLNV-FM
San Diego, CA [FM radio station call letters] (BROA) .... KLQV-FM
San Diego, CA [Television station call letters] (BROA) .... KNSD-DT
San Diego, CA [FM radio station call letters] (BROA) .... KPLN-FM
San Diego Chargers [National Football League] [1961-present] (NFLA) ..... SD
San Diego Supercomputer Center [California] .... SDSCnet
San Francisco 49ers [National Football League] [1950-present] (NFLA) ..... SF
San Francisco, CA [Television station call letters] (BROA) .... KBWB
San Francisco, CA [Television station call letters] (BROA) .... KGO-DT
San Francisco, CA [Television station call letters] (BROA) .... KPIX-DT
San Francisco, CA [Television station call letters] (BROA) .... KQED-DT
San Francisco, CA [Television station call letters] (BROA) .... KRON-DT
San German, PR [FM radio station call letters] (BROA) .... WCTA-FM
San Joaquin, CA [FM radio station call letters] (BROA) ...... KVPC-FM

San Jose, CA [AM radio station call letters] (BROA) .... KZSF
San Juan, PR [Television station call letters] (BROA) .... WTCV
San Juan, PR [AM radio station call letters] (BROA) .... WVOZ
San Luis Obispo, CA [Television station call letters] (BROA) .... KTAS
Sanchez Computer Assoc. [NASDAQ symbol] (SG) .... SCAI
Sand Diego, CA [Television station call letters] (BROA) ...... KFMB-DT
Sand in Suspension in the Air (WEAT) .... SA
Sand Technology Sys Intl'A' [NASDAQ symbol] (SG) ...... SNDT
Sandpoint, ID [FM radio station call letters] (BROA) .... KIBR-FM
Sandstorm (WEAT) .... SS
Sandusky, OH [FM radio station call letters] (BROA) .... WMTX-FM
Sandy, UT [AM radio station call letters] (BROA) .... KBJA
Sanger, TX [FM radio station call letters] (BROA) .... KXZN-FM
Sanitary Facility Data System (EPAT) .... SFDS
Santa Ana, CA [AM radio station call letters] (BROA) .... KVNR
Santa Barbara, CA [FM radio station call letters] (BROA) .... KIST-FM
Santa Barbara, CA [Television station call letters] (BROA) ... KPMR
Santa Barbara, CA [AM radio station call letters] (BROA) .... KXXT
Santa Barbara, CA [AM radio station call letters] (BROA) .... KZBN
Santa Clara, CA [AM radio station call letters] (BROA) ...... KVVN
Santa Cruz, CA [FM radio station call letters] (BROA) .... KLSN-FM
Santa Fe Intl. [NYSE symbol] (SG) .... SDC
Santa Fe, NM [FM radio station call letters] (BROA) .... KMMG-FM
Santa Fe, NM [Television station call letters] (BROA) .... KWBQ
Santa Fe Snyder [NYSE symbol] (SG) .... SFS
Santa Paula, CA [FM radio station call letters] (BROA) ...... KCZN-FM
Santa Rosa, NM [FM radio station call letters] (BROA) ...... KRSR-FM
SAP Aktiengesellschaft ADS [NYSE symbol] (SG) .... SAP
Sarasota, FL [FM radio station call letters] (BROA) .... WSMR-FM
Saratoga Springs, NY [AM radio station call letters] (BROA) ... WKAJ
Saskatoon, SK [AM radio station call letters] (BROA) .... CINT
Saskatoon, SK [FM radio station call letters] (BROA) .... CKOM-FM
Satellite Operation Command and Control (EOSA) .... SOCC
Saturated Fat (MELL) .... SF
Saudi Arabia (MILB) .... Sau
Saudi Arabian Light [Crude oil] .... SAL
Sauer, Inc. [NYSE symbol] (SG) .... SHS
Saulk Rapids, MN [AM radio station call letters] (BROA) ..... WBHR
Savaannah, GA [AM radio station call letters] (BROA) .... WJLG
Savannah, GA [FM radio station call letters] (BROA) .... WLXP-FM
Savannah, TN [FM radio station call letters] (BROA) .... WAZD-FM
Sawyer Brown International Fan Club (EA) .... SBIFC
SBA Communications'A' [NASDAQ symbol] (SG) .... SBAC
SBS Broadcasting [NASDAQ symbol] (SG) .... SBTV
Scalded Mouth Syndrome (MELL) .... SMS
Scale Manufacturers Association .... SM
Scalenus Anterior Syndrome [Medicine] (MELL) .... SAS
Scandinavian (BEE) .... Scand
Scanning Radiation Budget Experiment (EOSA) .... SCARABE
Scanning Scatterometer (EOSA) .... SCANSCAT
Scapula (MELL) .... S
Scapular Fracture [Medicine] (MELL) .... SF
Scarborough, ME [FM radio station call letters] (BROA) ..... WBQW-FM
Scarlet Macaw [Bird] .... SM
Scattered Cloud (WEAT) .... SCT
Schein Pharmaceutical [NYSE symbol] (SG) .... SHP
Schistosome Dermatitis [Medicine] (MELL) .... SD
Schizophrenia (MELL) .... S
School Library Media Specialist .... SLMS
School Science and Mathematics [A publication] .... SSM
Schuff Steel [AMEX symbol] (SG) .... SHF
Schwann Cell [Medicine] (MELL) .... SC
SCI Systems [nyse symbol] (SG) .... SCI
Science Executive Committee (EOSA) .... SEC
Science Processing Support Office (EOSA) .... SPSO
Scientific Games Hldgs. [NYSE symbol] (SG) .... SG
Scientific, Literary, Artistic, or Political .... SLAP
SCI-FI Society of Long Island [Formerly, Patrexes of the Panopticon] (EA) .... POP
Sclerodermoid Dermatitis [Medicine] (MELL) .... SDD
SCM Microsystems [NASDAQ symbol] (SG) .... SCMM
SCOR ADS [NYSE symbol] (SG) .... SCO
Score of Neonatal Acute Physiology [Medicine] (MELL) ..... SNAP
Scott City, MO [FM radio station call letters] (BROA) .... KGKS-FM
Scott Technologies [NASDAQ symbol] (SG) .... SCTT
Scott Values Inventory .... SVI
Scottish (BEE) .... Scot

Scottish Annuity & Life Hldgs. [*NASDAQ symbol*] (SG) .... SCOT
Scottish Environmental Protection Agency (GVA) .... SEPA
Scottish Gaelic (BEE) .... ScotGael
Scottish Power ADS [*NYSE symbol*] (SG) .... SPI
SCPIE Holdings [*NYSE symbol*] (SG) .... SKP
Sea Surface Productivity (QUAC) .... SSP
Sea Surface Temperature (QUAC) .... sst
Sea View .... s/v
SeaChange Intl. [*NASDAQ symbol*] (SG) .... SEAC
Seacoast Finl.Svcs. [*NASDAQ symbol*] (SG) .... SCFS
Seaford, DE [*FM radio station call letters*] (BROA) .... WGBG-FM
Seaford, DE [*AM radio station call letters*] (BROA) .... WJWK
Search and Rescue (EOSA) .... S&R
Searchable Online Archive of Recipes .... SOAR
Seaside, OR [*FM radio station call letters*] (BROA) .... KULU-FM
Seasonal Allergic Rhinitis [*Medicine*] (MELL) .... SAR
Seasonal Allergy (MELL) .... SA
Seattle Seahawks [*National Football League*] [*1976-present*] (NFLA) .... Sea
Seattle, WA [*AM radio station call letters*] (BROA) .... KAZJ
Seattle, WA [*Television station call letters*] (BROA) .... KING-DT
Seattle, WA [*Television station call letters*] (BROA) .... KIRO-DT
Seattle, WA [*Television station call letters*] (BROA) .... KOMO-DT
Sebaceous Cyst [*Medicine*] (MELL) .... SC
Seborrheic Dermatitis [*Medicine*] (MELL) .... SD
Second Hand Cigarette Smoke (MELL) .... SHCS
Second Infertility [*Medicine*] .... SI
Second Malignant Neoplasm [*Medicine*] (MELL) .... SMN
Second Round Review [*Environmental Protection Agency*] (EPAT) .... SRR
Secondary Immune Response (MELL) .... SIR
Secondary Myelodysplastic Syndrome [*Medicine*] (MELL) .... SMDS
Second-Degree Burn (MELL) .... SDB
Second-Generation Antihistamine [*Medicine*] (MELL) .... SGAH
Second-Hand Smoke (MELL) .... SHS
Second-Hand Tobacco Smoke (MELL) .... SHTS
Secretary (PROS) .... secy
Secretary of the Navy .... SecNav
Securities Industry Foundation for Economic Education .... SIFEE
Security .... sec
Security (MILB) .... sy
Security Assoc.Intl. [*AMEX symbol*] (SG) .... SAI
Security Capital Corp'A' [*AMEX symbol*] (SG) .... SCC
Security Capital Grp'B'. (SG) .... SCZ
Security First Technologies [*NASDAQ symbol*] (SG) .... SONE
Security of Pennsylvania Finl. [*AMEX symbol*] (SG) .... SPN
Sedona Corp. [*NASDAQ symbol*] (SG) .... SDNA
See You Online [*Online dialog*] .... SYOL
Segmental Mastectomy [*Medicine*] (MELL) .... SM
Selective Decontamination (MELL) .... SD
Selective Decontamination of the Digestive Tract (MELL) .... SDD
Selenomethylnorcholesterol [*Medicine*] (MELL) .... SMC
Self Intermittent Catheterization [*Medicine*] (MELL) .... SIC
Self Winding Clock Association (EA) .... SWCA
Self-Abuse Finally Ends [*Medical treatment unit*] .... SAFE
Self-Defeating Personality Disorder (MELL) .... SDPD
Self-Mutilation Syndrome (MELL) .... SMS
Selma, AL [*FM radio station call letters*] (BROA) .... WBFZ-FM
SEMCO Energy [*NASDAQ symbol*] (SG) .... SMGS
Semen Albumin [*Medicine*] (MELL) .... SA
Semicircular Canal [*Medicine*] (MELL) .... SCC
Seminis,Inc.'A' [*NASDAQ symbol*] (SG) .... SMNS
Sempra Energy [*NYSE symbol*] (SG) .... SRE
Senator (PROS) .... sen
Senegal (MILB) .... Sen
Senile Cataract [*Medicine*] (MELL) .... SC
Senile Macular Chorioretinal Degeneration [*Medicine*] (MELL) .... SMCD
Senior Officials Meeting [*Dublin*] .... SOM
Senior Officials Meeting on Trade and Investment [*Brussels*] .... SOMTI
Senior Professional in Human Resources .... SPHR
Sense of Control .... SoC
Sensing and Diagnostic Module .... SDM
Sensory Aphasia [*Medicine*] (MELL) .... SA
Sensory Decision Theory (MELL) .... SDT
September (BEE) .... Sept
SeraCare,Inc. [*AMEX symbol*] (SG) .... SRK
Sergeant (GEAB) .... serg
Serious Bacterial Infection (MELL) .... SBI
Seromuscular Intestinal Patch Graft [*Medicine*] (MELL) .... SMIPG
Serratus Anterior Muscle [*Medicine*] (MELL) .... SAM
Sertoli Cell Tumor [*Medicine*] (MELL) .... SCT
Serum Accelerator Factor [*Medicine*] (MELL) .... SAF
Serum Aspartate Aminotransferase [*Medicine*] (MELL) .... SAAT
Serum Cholesterol Concentration [*Medicine*] (MELL) .... SCC
Serum Electrophoresis [*Medicine*] (MELL) .... SEP
Serum Iron-Binding Capacity (MELL) .... SIBC
Serum-Free Hemoglobin [*Medicine*] (MELL) .... SFH
Service (GEAB) .... serv
Service Experts [*NYSE symbol*] (SG) .... SVE
Settler (GEAB) .... sett
Seven Seas Petroleum [*AMEX symbol*] (SG) .... SEV
Severe Cerebrocranial Trauma [*Medicine*] (MELL) .... SCCT
Severe Chronic Liver Disease (MELL) .... SCLD
Severe Head Injury (MELL) .... SHI
Severe Iron Deficiency (MELL) .... SID
Severe Myoclonic Epilepsy [*Medicine*] (MELL) .... SME
Seward, AK [*FM radio station call letters*] (BROA) .... KPEN-FM

Sex Abuse Survivors Anonymous (MELL) .... SASA
Sexual History (MELL) .... SH
Sexual Infantilism (MELL) .... SI
Seychelles (MILB) .... Sey
Seymour, IN [*FM radio station call letters*] (BROA) .... WQKC-FM
Sferic Location (WEAT) .... SFLOC
SFX Entertainment'A' [*NYSE symbol*] (SG) .... SFX
SGL Carbon AG ADS [*NYSE symbol*] (SG) .... SGG
Shaken Impact Syndrome (MELL) .... SIS
Shaker Heights, OH [*Television station call letters*] (BROA) .... WOIO-DT
Shakopee, MN [*AM radio station call letters*] (BROA) .... KSMM
Shallotte, NC [*AM radio station call letters*] (BROA) .... WAZO-FM
Shallow Coin Biopsy [*Medicine*] (MELL) .... SCB
Shanxi Institute of Zoology [*China*] .... SIZ
Shared Medical Sys. [*NYSE symbol*] (SG) .... SMS
Sharper Image [*NASDAQ symbol*] (SG) .... SHRP
Sharpsville, PA [*FM radio station call letters*] (BROA) .... WTNX-FM
Shasta Lake City, CA [*FM radio station call letters*] (BROA) .... KISK-FM
Shaw Group [*NYSE symbol*] (SG) .... SGR
Sheep Veterinary Society (GVA) .... SVS
Sheet Metal and Air Conditioning Contractors National Association, Inc. .... SAMANA
Shelby, MT [*FM radio station call letters*] (BROA) .... KBJF-FM
Shelbyville, IL [*AM radio station call letters*] (BROA) .... WDID
Shelbyville, TN [*FM radio station call letters*] (BROA) .... WBIA-FM
Shelton, WA [*FM radio station call letters*] (BROA) .... KRXY
Shepherd's Crook Deformity [*Medicine*] (MELL) .... SCD
Shepherdsville, KY [*FM radio station call letters*] (BROA) .... WXLN-FM
Sheridan, WY [*Television station call letters*] (BROA) .... KBJL
Shingle Springs, CA [*FM radio station call letters*] (BROA) .... KRRE-FM
Shingles [*Medicine*] (MELL) .... S
Shingletown, CA [*FM radio station call letters*] (BROA) .... KBHX-FM
Shingletown, CA [*FM radio station call letters*] (BROA) .... KRDG-FM
Ship (GEAB) .... sh
Shorewood Packaging [*NYSE symbol*] (SG) .... SWD
Short Bowel Syndrome [*Medicine*] (MELL) .... SBS
Short Leg (MELL) .... SL
Short of Breath on Exertion (MELL) .... SOBE
Short-Range Missile Defense with Optimized Radar Distribution [*Military weapon system*] .... SWORD
Short-Wavelength Infrared (EOSA) .... SWIR
Shoulder-Hand Syndrome (MELL) .... SHS
Show Low, AZ [*FM radio station call letters*] (BROA) .... KSNX-FM
Showpower, Inc. [*AMEX symbol*] (SG) .... SHO
Shreveport, LA [*FM radio station call letters*] (BROA) .... KBED-FM
Shuttle Imaging Radar-C (EOSA) .... SIR-C
Shuttle Solar Ultraviolet .... SSUV
Sialodacryoadenitis [*Medicine*] (MELL) .... SDA
Sick Euthyroid Syndrome [*Medicine*] (MELL) .... SES
Sickle Cell Nephropathy [*Medicine*] (MELL) .... SCN
Sideroblastic Anemia [*Medicine*] (MELL) .... SBA
Sigma Delta Chi Foundation (EA) .... SDX
Sigma Iota Epsilon (EA) .... SIE
Sigma Theta Tau International (EA) .... STII
Sign Language (MELL) .... SL
Signal Mountain, TN [*FM radio station call letters*] (BROA) .... WXKT-FM
Signals (MILB) .... sigs
Signet Group ADR [*NASDAQ symbol*] (SG) .... SIGYY
Significant Violater [*Environmental Protection Agency*] (EPAT) .... SV
Silent Treatment [*Medicine*] (MELL) .... SiTr
Silicone Breast Implant (MELL) .... SBI
Silicone Gel Breast Implant [*Medicine*] (MELL) .... SGBI
Silverleaf Resorts [*NYSE symbol*] (SG) .... SVR
Simian Line (MELL) .... SL
Simplate Bleeding Time Test [*Medicine*] (MELL) .... SBTT
Simple File Transfer Protocol .... SFTP
Simple Fracture (MELL) .... SF
Simply Divoon - Jayne Mansfield Fan Club (EA) .... SD
Simpson Manufacturing [*NYSE symbol*] (SG) .... SSD
Simulation and Modeling for Acquisition, Requirements, and Training [*Army*] .... SMART
Simulation Based Acquisition [*Army*] .... SBA
Sindicato de Obreros Unidos del Sur de Puerto Rico .... PRSPT
Sindicato Puertorriqueno de Trabajadores .... PRSPT
Singapore (MILB) .... Sgp
Single Breath Cannister (EPAT) .... SBC
Single Contrast Barium Enema [*Medicine*] (MELL) .... SCBE
Single Donor Apheresis Platelets [*Medicine*] (MELL) .... SDAP
Single-Breath Oxygen Test (MELL) .... SBOT
Single-Donor Platelets [*Medicine*] (MELL) .... SDP
Single-Dose Radiation Survival Curve (MELL) .... SDRSC
Sinoatrial Entrance Block [*Medicine*] (MELL) .... SAEB
Sinoauricular Block [*Medicine*] (MELL) .... SAB
Sinus Node Cycle Length [*Medicine*] (MELL) .... SNCL
Sioux Falls, SD [*Television station call letters*] (BROA) .... KDLT-TV
Sioux Falls, SD [*AM radio station call letters*] (BROA) .... KSFS
Siren, WI [*FM radio station call letters*] (BROA) .... WBEP-FM
Sister (GEAB) .... sis
Sister Bay, WI [*FM radio station call letters*] (BROA) .... WHDI-FM
Sister Bay, WI [*FM radio station call letters*] (BROA) .... WHND-FM
Sites of Special Scientific Interest [*Geology*] .... SSSI
Situation Normal, All Fouled Up .... snafu
Sitz Bath (MELL) .... SB
Six-speed [*Manual transmission*] 6-SPD
SK Telecom ADS [*NYSE symbol*] (SG) .... SKM

Skechers U.S.A. Cl'A' [*NYSE symbol*] (SG) ... SKX
Skeletal Muscle (MELL) ... SM
Skeletal Neuromuscular Junction [*Medicine*] (MELL) ... SNMJ
Skeleton (MELL) ... S
Skin Absorption (MELL) ... SA
Skin-Fold-Thickness Test (MELL) ... SFTT
Skull (MELL) ... S
Skull Fracture (MELL) ... SF
SkyTel Communications [*NASDAQ symbol*] (SG) ... SKYT
SL Green Realty [*NYSE symbol*] (SG) ... SLG
Sleep Apnea (MELL) ... SA
Sleep Disorder (MELL) ... SD
Slice Fracture (MELL) ... SF
SLI,Inc. [*NYSE symbol*] (SG) ... SLI
Slovakia (MILB) ... Slvk
Slovenia (MILB) ... Slvn
Small Abattoir Federation (GVA) ... SAF
Small Cardiac Vein [*Medicine*] (MELL) ... SCV
Small Cell Undifferentiated Carcinoma of Prostate [*Medicine*] (MELL) ... SCUCP
Small Date [*Numismatic term*] ... SD
Small Economic Activity Development ... SEAD
Small Island Developing States ... SIDS
Small Letters [*Numismatic term*] ... SL
Small Towns Environment Program ... STEP
Small-Capacity Syndrome (MELL) ... SCS
Smallworldwide ADS [*NASDAQ symbol*] (SG) ... SWLDY
Smart Battery Systems ... SBS
Smart Enterprise Model ... SEM
Smithfield, UT [*FM radio station call letters*] (BROA) ... KGNT-FM
Smith-Magenic Syndrome [*Medicine*] ... SMS
Smiths, AL [*FM radio station call letters*] (BROA) ... WBFA-FM
SMTEK Intl. [*NASDAQ symbol*] (SG) ... SMTI
Smurfit-Stone Container [*NASDAQ symbol*] (SG) ... SSCC
Smyrna, TN [*AM radio station call letters*] (BROA) ... WFCM
Snow (WEAT) ... SN
Snow Increasing Rapidly (WEAT) ... SNINCR
Snowmobile Safety & Certification Committee, Inc. ... SSCC
Snyder, OK [*FM radio station call letters*] (BROA) ... KBKF-FM
Soccer in the Streets [*An association*] ... SITS
Social Breakdown Syndrome (MELL) ... SBDS
Social Exclusion Unit ... SEU
Social Studies Provincial Specialist Association ... SSPSA
Society for Canadian Women in Science and Technology (QUAC) ... SCWIST
Society for Mineral Museum Professionals ... SMMP
Society for the Study of Animal Breeding (GVA) ... SSAB
Society for Tropical Veterinary Medicine (GVA) ... STVM
Society for Veterinary Epidemiology and Preventive Medicine (GVA) ... SVEPM
Society for Veterinary Medical Ethics (GVA) ... SVME
Society of Asset Allocators & Fund Timers Inc. ... SAAFTI
Society of Greyhound Veterinarians (GVA) ... SGV
Society of Lincoln Cent Collectors (EA) ... SLCC
Society of Marine Mammalogists (GVA) ... SMM
Society of the Plastics Industry, Inc. ... SPII
Society of Vertebrate Palaeontology (QUAC) ... SVP
Sociology (BEE) ... Sociol
Sodexho Marriott Svcs. [*NYSE symbol*] (SG) ... SDH
Sodium Citrate (MELL) ... SC
Sodium Ion Channel Blocker [*Medicine*] (MELL) ... SICB
Soft Top [*Automobile*] ... SFTP
Softnet Systems [*NASDAQ symbol*] (SG) ... SOFN
Software & Information Industry Association ... SIIA
Software Safety Release ... SSR
Soil Inorganic Carbon (QUAC) ... SIC
Solar Heat Gain Coefficient ... SHGC
Solar Influences (EOSA) ... SI
Solar Stellar Irradiance Comparison Experiment (EOSA) ... SOLSTICE
Solar Wind Anisotropies ... SWAN
Soldier (GEAB) ... s
Soldier and Biological Chemical Command [*Army*] ... SBCCOM
Solid-State Radar Altimeter (EOSA) ... SSALT
Solitary Adenomas [*Medicine*] (MELL) ... SA
Soluble (MELL) ... S
Solutia,Inc. [*NYSE symbol*] (SG) ... SOI
Somali Republic (MILB) ... SR
Somerset, PA [*FM radio station call letters*] (BROA) ... WSGY-Fm
Sonic Automotive'A' [*NYSE symbol*] (SG) ... SAH
Sonic Foundry [*AMEX symbol*] (SG) ... SFO
Sons of Union Veterans (GEAB) ... SUV
Sonus Corp. [*AMEX symbol*] (SG) ... SSN
Source Water Assessment Program [*Environmental Protection Agency*] (EPAT) ... SWAP
Source Water Protection Area [*Environmental Protection Agency*] (EPAT) ... SWPA
Source Water Quality Protection Partnership Petitions (EPAT) ... SWQPPP
Source-Oriented Medical Record (MELL) ... SOMR
South African Stud Book and Livestock Improvement Association (GVA) ... SASBLIA
South African Veterinary Association (GVA) ... SAVA
South Beloit, IL [*AM radio station call letters*] (BROA) ... WTJK
South Bend, IN [*AM radio station call letters*] (BROA) ... WJVA
South Bend, IN [*Television station call letters*] (BROA) ... WNDU-DT
South Carolina (BEE) ... SCar
South Carolina Basic Skills Assessment Program ... BSAP
South Dakota State Employees Organization ... SD-SEO
South Florida Atmospheric Mercury Monitoring Study ... SoFAMMS
South Florida Water Management District ... SFWMD
South Padre Island, TX [*FM radio station call letters*] (BROA) ... KESO-FM
South Polar Feature ... SPF
South Webster, OH [*FM radio station call letters*] (BROA) ... WZIO-FM
Southern Appalachian Mountains Initiative (EPAT) ... SAMI
Southern Michigan Unorganized Regional Festival of Stargazers ... SMURFS
Southern Sudan Liberation Movement ... SSLM
Southwest Athletic Conference (EA) ... SWC
Southwest Securities Grp. [*NYSE symbol*] (SG) ... SWS
Soviet Urals [*Crude oil*] ... SU
Space Interferometry Mission ... SIM
Space Network (EOSA) ... SN
Space Nuclear Power ... SNP
Space-Based Global Change Observation System (EOSA) ... S-GCOS
Spaced-Based Infrared Sensor [*Military*] ... SBIRS
Spain (MILB) ... Sp
Spangler, PA [*FM radio station call letters*] (BROA) ... WPCL-FM
Sparta, GA [*FM radio station call letters*] (BROA) ... WPMA-FM
Spartanburg, SC [*AM radio station call letters*] (BROA) ... WKDY
Spatiotemporal Stochastic Resonance ... STSR
Speakers ... Spkrs
Special Analytical Service (EPAT) ... SAS
Special Local Need (EPAT) ... SLN
Special Review [*Environmental Protection Agency*] (EPAT) ... SR
Special Review Procedure [*Environmental Protection Agency*] (EPAT) ... SRP
Special Sensor Microwave/Imager (EOSA) ... SSM/I
Special Study Panel on Education Indicators [*1991*] ... SSPEI
Specialized Health Prods Intl. [*NASDAQ symbol*] (SG) ... SHPIC
Specialty Equipment [*NYSE symbol*] (SG) ... SEC
Species Richness ... SR
Specific Action Exercise (MELL) ... SAE
Specific Learning Disability (MELL) ... SLD
Specifications ... Specs
Spectroscopy of the Atmosphere Using Far Infrared Emission (EOSA) ... SAFIRE
Speech Audiometry (MELL) ... SA
Speed ... Spd
Spencer (BEE) ... Spncr
Sphenomandibular Ligament [*Medicine*] (MELL) ... SML
Spina Bifida Occulta [*Medicine*] (MELL) ... SBO
Spinal Bone Density [*Medicine*] (MELL) ... SBD
Spinal Cord Compression [*Medicine*] (MELL) ... SCC
Spinal Cord Compression Syndrome [*Medicine*] (MELL) ... SCCS
Spinal Cord Injury Unit (MELL) ... SCIU
Spinal Cord Syndrome (MELL) ... SCS
Spinal Degenerative Disk Disease (MELL) ... SDDD
Spinal Epidural Abscess [*Medicine*] (MELL) ... SEDA
Spinal Epidural Hematoma [*Medicine*] (MELL) ... SEH
Spinal Headache (MELL) ... SH
Spinal Interneuron [*Medicine*] (MELL) ... SIN
Spinal Manipulative Therapy [*Medicine*] (MELL) ... SMT
Spinal Nerve Block [*Medicine*] (MELL) ... SNB
Spiral Organ of Corti [*Medicine*] (MELL) ... SOOC
Spleen (MELL) ... S
Splenocaval Shunt [*Medicine*] (MELL) ... SCS
Spoiler ... SPLR
Spokane, WA [*Television station call letters*] (BROA) ... KGPX
Spokane, WA [*Television station call letters*] (BROA) ... KXLY-DT
Sponsor (GEAB) ... spr
Spontaneous Abortion (MELL) ... SA
Spontaneous Discharge Rate (MELL) ... SDR
Spontaneous Intermittent Mandatory Ventilation [*Medicine*] (MELL) ... SIMV
Sports Medicine (MELL) ... SM
Sportsline USA [*NASDAQ symbol*] (SG) ... SPLN
Sportsman's Alliance of Maine ... SAM
Sportsplex Operators and Developers of America (EA) ... SODA
Sport-Utility Vechicle ... SUV
Spot-Film Radiography [*Medicine*] (MELL) ... SFR
Spousal Abuse (MELL) ... SA
Spring ... spr
Springfield, GA [*FM radio station call letters*] (BROA) ... WSIS-FM
Springfield, VT [*AM radio station call letters*] (BROA) ... WNBX
Spur-Cell Syndrome [*Medicine*] (MELL) ... SCS
Squadron (MILB) ... sqn
Squamous Cancer of Vagina [*Medicine*] (MELL) ... SCV
Squamous Cell Hyperplasia [*Medicine*] (MELL) ... SCH
Square Foot ... SqFt
Square Inch ... SqIn
Sri Lanka (MILB) ... Ska
Sri Lanka Telecom Limited ... SLT
Stable Angina [*Medicine*] (MELL) ... SA
Staff Association of the Organization of American States (EA) ... SAOAS
StaffMark,Inc. [*NASDAQ symbol*] (SG) ... STAF
Stage Stores [*NYSE symbol*] (SG) ... SGE
Stainless Steel International Metallurgical Society ... SSIMS
Stamford, TX [*FM radio station call letters*] (BROA) ... KOES-FM
Stamps for the Wounded [*Affiliated with Lions International Stamp Club*] (EA) ... SFTW-LISC
StanCorp Financial Group [*NYSE symbol*] (SG) ... SEG
Standard ... Std
Standard Army Installation and Division Personnel System Version 3.0 ... SIDPERS-3
Standard Assessment of Personality (MELL) ... SAP
Standard Auto Plan [*Insurance*] ... SAP
Standard Electrolyte Solution (MELL) ... SES
Standard Fire Policy [*Insurance*] ... SFP
Standard Light Antarctic Precipitation (QUAC) ... SLAP

Standard Meteorological Week ... SMW
Standardized Assessment of Concussion ... SAC
Standardized Precipitation Index ... SPI
Standby Angioplasty [*Medicine*] (MELL) ... SBA
Staphylococcal Endotoxin [*Medicine*] (MELL) ... SE
Staphylococcal Infection [*Medicine*] (MELL) ... SCI
Star Data Systems [*Toronto Stock Exchange symbol*] (SG) ... STY
Star Gas Ptnrs L.P. [*NYSE symbol*] (SG) ... SGU
STAR Telecommunications [*NASDAQ symbol*] (SG) ... STRX
Star Trek [*Television program*] ... ST
Star Wars [*Movie title*] ... SW
Starfleet Marines International (EA) ... SMI
Starfleet Operations International [*Formerly, Starfleet Operations*] (EA) ... SOSA
StarMedia Network [*NASDAQ symbol*] (SG) ... STRM
Startec Global Communic. [*NASDAQ symbol*] (SG) ... STGC
StarTek,Inc. [*NYSE symbol*] (SG) ... SRT
State Employees Association of North Carolina, Inc. ... SEANC
State Environmental Goals and Improvement Project (EPAT) ... SEGIP
State Law and Order Council [*China*] ... SLORC
State Management Plan (EPAT) ... SMP
State Veterinary Service [*British*] (GVA) ... SVS
Statewide Education Technology Services ... SETS
Statewide Nontraditional Career Assistance Center ... SNCAC
Statistical Quality Control ... SPC
Statistics (BEE) ... stat
Steelcase Inc,'A' [*NYSE symbol*] (SG) ... SCS
Steinbach, MB [*FM radio station call letters*] (BROA) ... CILT-FM
Steiner Leisure [*NASDAQ symbol*] (SG) ... STNR
STERIS Corp. [*NYSE symbol*] (SG) ... STE
Sterling City, TX [*FM radio station call letters*] (BROA) ... KKCN-FM
Sternocleidomastoid Muscle [*Medicine*] (MELL) ... SCMM
Sternocostal Joint [*Medicine*] (MELL) ... SCJ
Sternum (MELL) ... S
Steroidal-Cell Antibody [*Medicine*] (MELL) ... SCA
Stet Hellas Telecomm ADS [*NASDAQ symbol*] (SG) ... STHLY
Stewart & Stevenson Services, Inc. ... S&S
Stick Scatterometer (EOSA) ... STIKSCAT
Stillwater Mining [*AMEX symbol*] (SG) ... SWC
Stillwater, MN [*AM radio station call letters*] (BROA) ... WEZU
Stillwater, NY [*FM radio station call letters*] (BROA) ... WQAR-FM
Stillwater, OK [*FM radio station call letters*] (BROA) ... KVRO-FM
Stimson Gravity Reduction Maneuver [*Medicine*] (MELL) ... SGRM
Stomach (MELL) ... S
Stoneridge,Inc. [*NYSE symbol*] (SG) ... SRI
Stonewall, MS [*FM radio station call letters*] (BROA) ... WMLV-FM
Storage Area Network ... SAN
Storm Tide Warning Service (WEAT) ... STWS
Stormwater Treatment Area ... STA
Stowe, VT [*FM radio station call letters*] (BROA) ... WCVT-FM
Straddle Injury (MELL) ... SI
Straight Back Syndrome [*Medicine*] (MELL) ... SBS
Straight Leg Walker [*Doll collecting*] ... SLW
Strategia Corp. [*AMEX symbol*] (SG) ... SAA
Stratesec,Inc. [*AMEX symbol*] (SG) ... SFT
Stratocumulus (WEAT) ... Sc
Stratocumulus Standing Lenticular Cloud (WEAT) ... SCSL
Stratospheric Aerosol and Gas Experiment III (EOSA) ... SAGE III
Stratospheric Limb Infrared Emission Spectrometer (EOSA) ... SLIES
Stratospheric Wind Infrared Limb Sounder (EOSA) ... SWIRLS
Stratus Cloud (WEAT) ... St
Street Sharks Fan Club (EA) ... SSFC
Streeter Dysplasia [*Medicine*] (MELL) ... SD
Strength (MILB) ... str
Streptococcal Antibody Test [*Medicine*] (MELL) ... SAT
Streptococcal Infection [*Medicine*] (MELL) ... SCI
Streptococcal Infection [*Medicine*] (MELL) ... SI
Stress Fracture (MELL) ... SF
Stroke in Progression (MELL) ... SIP
Structured Clinical Interview for Diagnosis ... SCID
Structured Interview for Schizotypy (MELL) ... SIS
Stryker Corp. [*NYSE symbol*] (SG) ... SYK
Student American Veterinary Medical Association (GVA) ... SAVMA
Study of Tamoxifen and Raloxifene ... STAR
Sturgeon Bay, WI [*FM radio station call letters*] (BROA) ... WLTM-FM
Sturgeon Bay, WI [*FM radio station call letters*] (BROA) ... WRGX-FM
Stylomandibular Ligament [*Medicine*] (MELL) ... SML
Subacromial Bursa [*Medicine*] (MELL) ... SAB
Subacute Corticoid Cerebellar Degeneration [*Medicine*] (MELL) ... SCCD
Subacute Encephalomyelopathy [*Medicine*] (MELL) ... SEM
Subaortic Valvular Stenosis [*Medicine*] (MELL) ... SAVS
Subareolar Abscess [*Medicine*] (MELL) ... SAA
Subcapital Fracture [*Medicine*] (MELL) ... SCF
Subclavian Lymph Node [*Medicine*] (MELL) ... SLN
Subcutaneous Inguinal Ring [*Medicine*] (MELL) ... SIR
Subcutaneous Mastectomy [*Medicine*] (MELL) ... SCM
Subcutaneous Prepatellar Bursa [*Medicine*] (MELL) ... SCPPB
Suboptimal Surgery (MELL) ... SOS
Subsequent Pregnancy After a Loss Support ... SPALS
Subsidiary Body for Scientific and Technical Advice ... SBSTA
Subsidiary Body on Implementation ... SBI
Subsonic Aircraft: Contrail and Cloud Effects Special Study [*NASA project*] ... SUCCESS
Substance Abuse Subtle Screening Inventory-2 ... SASSI-2
Substance Dependence (MELL) ... SD
Substance-Exposed Infant (MELL) ... SEI
Successive Unsharp Masking ... SUM
Succinylcholine (MELL) ... S
Suction-Assisted Lipectomy [*Medicine*] (MELL) ... SAL
Sudan (MILB) ... Sdn
Sudbury, ON [*FM radio station call letters*] (BROA) ... CKLU-FM
Sudden Arrhythmia Death Syndrome [*Medicine*] (MELL) ... SADS
Sudden Hearing Loss (MELL) ... SHL
Suicide and Aggression Survey (MELL) ... SAS
Suite (BEE) ... ste
Suiza Foods [*NYSE symbol*] (SG) ... SZA
Sulfate-Methane Interface (QUAC) ... SMI
Sulfite-Induced Asthma (MELL) ... SIA
Sulphur, OK [*FM radio station call letters*] (BROA) ... KIXO-FM
Sulzer Medica ADS [*NYSE symbol*] (SG) ... SM
Summer ... sum
Summerton, SC [*FM radio station call letters*] (BROA) ... WLJI-FM
Sumrall, MS [*FM radio station call letters*] (BROA) ... WJSJ-FM
Sun Hydraulics [*NASDAQ symbol*] (SG) ... SNHY
Sun Prairie, WI [*AM radio station call letters*] (BROA) ... WNWC
Sun Valley, NV [*FM radio station call letters*] (BROA) ... KHXR-FM
Sun Valley, NV [*FM radio station call letters*] (BROA) ... KXXL-FM
Sunburst Hospitality [*NYSE symbol*] (SG) ... SNB
SunGard Data Systems [*NYSE symbol*] (SG) ... SDS
Sunrise Beach, MO [*FM radio station call letters*] (BROA) ... KCRL-FM
Sunroof ... SNRF
Super Low Emission Vehicle ... SULEV
Super Seven [*Aircraft*] ... S-7
Superficial Branch of Radial Nerve [*Medicine*] (MELL) ... SBRN
Superior Articular Facet (MELL) ... SAF
Superior Articular Process of Vertebra [*Medicine*] (MELL) ... SAPV
Superior Hypophyseal Artery [*Medicine*] (MELL) ... SHA
Superior Laryngeal Artery [*Medicine*] (MELL) ... SLA
Superior, MT [*FM radio station call letters*] (BROA) ... KREO-FM
Superior Telecom [*NYSE symbol*] (SG) ... SUT
Superior Uniform Group [*AMEX symbol*] (SG) ... SGC
Supernumerary Mammary Gland [*Medicine*] (MELL) ... SNMG
Super-Sol Ltd.ADS [*NYSE symbol*] (SG) ... SAE
Supine (MELL) ... S
Supplemental Unemployment Compensation Benefit Trusts ... SUB
Supply Function Equilibrium ... SFE
Support (MILB) ... spt
Supported Arm Exercise (MELL) ... SAE
Supporting Hospitals Abroad with Resources and Equipment (MELL) ... SHARE
Suppurative Otitis Media [*Medicine*] (MELL) ... SOM
Supracervical Hysterectomy [*Medicine*] (MELL) ... SCH
Supracondylar Fracture [*Medicine*] (MELL) ... SCF
Suprahyoid Lymph Node [*Medicine*] (MELL) ... SHLN
Supreme Council of the Islamic Revolution in Iraq ... SCIRI
Surface Biopsy (MELL) ... SB
Surface of the Drainage Area ... SDA
Surfactant Deficiency Syndrome (MELL) ... SDS
Surgeon (GEAB) ... surg
Surgery (BEE) ... Surg
Surgical Follow-Up (MELL) ... SFU
Suriname (MILB) ... Sme
Surveillance Index (EPAT) ... SI
Survey Research Center ... SRC
Survivors' Originals (GEAB) ... SO
Susanville, CA [*FM radio station call letters*] (BROA) ... KHJQ-FM
Suspended Sediment Concentration ... SSC
Suspensory Ligament of Breast [*Medicine*] (MELL) ... SLB
Sussex, WI [*AM radio station call letters*] (BROA) ... WAZI
Sustainable Agriculture ... SA
Sutured in Place [*Medicine*] (MELL) ... SIP
SVI Holdings [*AMEX symbol*] (SG) ... SVI
Swallowing Disorder (MELL) ... SD
Swan-Neck Catheter [*Medicine*] (MELL) ... SNC
Sweat Chloride Test (MELL) ... SCT
Sweat Gland Adenoma [*Medicine*] (MELL) ... SGA
Swedish American Chamber of Commerce of the Western United States (EA) ... SACCWEST
Swedish Network ... SUNET
Swedish Trade Council (EA) ... STC
Sweet Home, OR [*FM radio station call letters*] (BROA) ... KLVU-FM
Sweet Valley High Fan Club (EA) ... SVHFC
Swimmer's Itch (MELL) ... SI
Swine Fever (MELL) ... SF
Swiss Classic Watches ... SCW
Switzerland Network ... SWITCH
SY Bancorp [*AMEX symbol*] (SG) ... SYI
Sybron Chemicals [*AMEX symbol*] (SG) ... SYC
Sylvan Beach, NY [*FM radio station call letters*] (BROA) ... WBGJ-FM
Synchronous Meteorological Satellite/Geostationary Operational Environmental Satellite (EOSA) ... SMS/GOES
Syndrome [*Medicine*] (MELL) ... S
Synoptic Report [*Meteorology*] (WEAT) ... SYNOP
Synovial Joint [*Medicine*] (MELL) ... SJ
Synovitis, Acne Pustulosis, Hyperostosis and Osteomyelitis ... SAPHO
SYNSORB Biotech [*NASDAQ symbol*] (SG) ... SYBB
Syntel,Inc. [*NASDAQ symbol*] (SG) ... SYNT
Synthetic Industries [*NASDAQ symbol*] (SG) ... SIND
Syphilitic Heart Disease (MELL) ... SHD
Syracuse, NY [*FM radio station call letters*] (BROA) ... WLTI-FM
Syracuse, NY [*Television station call letters*] (BROA) ... WSPX-TV
Syringomyelia [*Medicine*] (MELL) ... SM

System Enhancement Program	SEP
System Management Center (EOSA)	SMC
Systemax,Inc. [*NYSE symbol*] (SG)	SYX
Systemic Biopsy of Prostate [*Medicine*] (MELL)	SBP
Systemic Mastocytosis [*Medicine*] (MELL)	SMC
Systemic Onset Juvenile Arthritis [*Medicine*] (MELL)	SOJA
Systemic Oxygen Transport (MELL)	SOT
Systolic [*Medicine*] (MELL)	S
Systolic Arterial Pressure [*Medicine*] (MELL)	SAP

By Meaning

T
By Meaning

Tachometer	Tach
Tactical (MILB)	tac
Tactical Wheeled Vehicle [Military]	TWV
Tactical Wheeled Vehicle Requirements Management Office [Army]	TWVRMO
Tag-It Pacific [AMEX symbol] (SG)	TAG
Tahoe City, CA [FM radio station call letters] (BROA)	KLCA-FM
Tajikistan (MILB)	Tjk
Talisman Energy [NYSE symbol] (SG)	TLM
Talk.com,Inc. [NASDAQ symbol] (SG)	TALK
Talking Rock, GA [FM radio station call letters] (BROA)	WCHK-FM
Tallahassee, FL [AM radio station call letters] (BROA)	WFRF
Tallassee, AL [FM radio station call letters] (BROA)	WACQ-FM
Tampa Bay Buccaneers [National Football League] [1976-present] (NFLA)	TD
Tampa, FL [Television station call letters] (BROA)	WFTS-DT
Tank (MILB)	tk
Tank Automotive and Armaments Command's Armament Research, Development, and Engieering Center [Army]	TACOM-ARDEC
Tank-Automotive and Armaments Command [Army]	TACOM
Tanker (MILB)	tkr
Tanzania (MILB)	Tz
Tanzania Telecommunications Corporation Ltd.	TTCL
Tarragon Realty Investors [NASDAQ symbol] (SG)	TARR
Tau Epsilon Rho Law Society (EA)	TER
Tavenier, FL [FM radio station call letters] (BROA)	WIFL-FM
Taylor, TX [FM radio station call letters] (BROA)	KQBT-FM
Taylorville, IL [AM radio station call letters] (BROA)	WIHM
Taylorville, IL [FM radio station call letters] (BROA)	WTIM-FM
Tazewell, VA [FM radio station call letters] (BROA)	WKQY-FM
TC Pipelines L.P. [NASDAQ symbol] (SG)	TCLPZ
TCI Music'A' [NASDAQ symbol] (SG)	TUNE
TD Waterhouse Group [NYSE symbol] (SG)	TWE
Team Leader Computing Facility (EOSA)	TLCF
Technical Assistance Document [Environmental Protection Agency] (EPAT)	TAD
Technical Evaluation Testing	TET
Technical Grade of the Active Ingredient (EPAT)	TGAI
Technical Grade Product (EPAT)	TGP
Technical Manufacturing Corporation	TMC
Technical Product (EPAT)	TP
Technology and Culture [A publication]	TC
Technology Business Council	TBC
Technology Needs Survey	TNS
Technology Team	TT
Teen Association of Model Railroaders (EA)	TAMR
Teenie Beanie Babies [Ty, Inc.]	TBB
Tefron Ltd. [NYSE symbol] (SG)	TFR
Tehachapi, CA [FM radio station call letters] (BROA)	KKZQ-FM
Tel Argentina-France Tel'B'ADS [NYSE symbol] (SG)	TEO
Tele Celular Sul Partici ADS [NYSE symbol] (SG)	TSU
Tele Centro Oeste Partici ADS [NYSE symbol] (SG)	TRO
Tele Nordeste Cel Partici ADS [NYSE symbol] (SG)	TND
Tele Norte Celular Part ADS [NYSE symbol] (SG)	TCN
Tele Norte Leste Partici ADS [NYSE symbol] (SG)	TNE
Tele Sudeste Celular Part ADS [NYSE symbol] (SG)	TSD
Telebanc Financial [NASDAQ symbol] (SG)	TBFC
Telecommunications (BEE)	Telecomm
Teleglobe,Inc. [NYSE symbol] (SG)	TGO
Telephone and Telegraph (PROS)	Tel & Tel
Telesp Participacoes ADS [NYSE symbol] (SG)	TSP
Telesystem Intl.Wireless [NASDAQ symbol] (SG)	TIWI
Telford, PA [FM radio station call letters] (BROA)	WBMR-FM
Teligent,Inc.'A' [NASDAQ symbol] (SG)	TGNT
Temple Index Bureau (GEAB)	TIB
Temple Records Index Bureau (GEAB)	TRIB
Temporarily (WEAT)	TEMPO
Temporary (MILB)	tempy
Temporary Protected Status	TPS
Temporary Veterinary Inspector [British] (GVA)	TVI
TenFold Corp. [NASDAQ symbol] (SG)	TENF
Tenn Val Auth'PARRS' 'D' [NYSE symbol] (SG)	TVC
Tenn Val Auth'PARRS'2029 [NYSE symbol] (SG)	TVE
Tennessee Equine Veterinary Research Organization (GVA)	TEVRO
Tennessee Oilers [National Football League] [1997-98] (NFLA)	TeO
Tennessee Titans [National Football League] [1999-present] (NFLA)	Ten
Terlingua International Championship Chili Cook-Off [An association] (EA)	TICCC
Terminate, Monitor, and Control	TMC
Terrell, TX [FM radio station call letters] (BROA)	KZDL-FM
Territory (BEE)	terr
Territory (GEAB)	ty
Test and Evaluation	T&E
Testament (GEAB)	test
Testicular Sperm Extraction [Medicine]	TESE
Testing Priorities Committee [Environmental science] (EPAT)	TPC
TETRA Technologies [NYSE symbol] (SG)	TTI
Teutopolis, IL [FM radio station call letters] (BROA)	WKJT-FM
Texarkana, TX [AM radio station call letters] (BROA)	KOWS
Texas Journal of Science [A publication]	IJS
Texas Library Association	TLA
Texas Micro [NASDAQ symbol] (SG)	TEXM
Texas Natural History Collection [Austin]	TNHC
Texas Sesquicentennial Network	SESQUINET
Texas Star Party	TSP
Texas Veterinary Medical Association (GVA)	TVMA
Textile Processors, Service Trades, Health Care Professional, and Technical Em ployees International Union	TP
Thailand (MILB)	Th
theglobe.com [NASDAQ symbol] (SG)	TGLO
Theology (BEE)	Theol
Thermal and Solar Radiometer	TSR
Thermal System Insulation (EPAT)	TSI
Thermedics Detection [AMEX symbol] (SG)	TDX
Thinking of You [Online dialog]	TOY
Thomaston, AL [FM radio station call letters] (BROA)	WAYI-FM
Thomasville, GA [FM radio station call letters] (BROA)	WOKL-FM
Thousand Oaks, CA [AM radio station call letters] (BROA)	KLYF
Thousand Oaks, CA [FM radio station call letters] (BROA)	KMLT-FM
Thousand Palms, CA [AM radio station call letters] (BROA)	KXPS
Thousand Trails [AMEX symbol] (SG)	TRV
THQ,Inc. [NASDAQ symbol] (SG)	THQI
Three Rivers, MI [FM radio station call letters] (BROA)	WLKM-FM
Three Stooges Fan Club (EA)	TSFC
Three Times a Day [Medicine] (MELL)	3/d
Three-Dimensional Computer-Aided Engineering	3-D CAE
Three-Door [Automobile]	3-DR
Threshold Autoregression	TAR
Thrift Institution Advisory Council	TIAC
Tigard, OR [AM radio station call letters] (BROA)	KLVP
Till the Next Time [Online dialog]	TTNT
Tillamook, OR [FM radio station call letters] (BROA)	KJUN-FM
Timneh African Grey [Bird]	TAG
Tipton, CA [FM radio station call letters] (BROA)	KCRZ-FM
Titanium Oxide	TiO
TNT Post Group ADS [NYSE symbol] (SG)	TP
Toccoa, GA [FM radio station call letters] (BROA)	WSTE-FM
Todhunter Intl. [AMEX symbol] (SG)	THT
Togo (MILB)	Tg
Tokyo Stock Exchange	TSE
Toledo, OH [AM radio station call letters] (BROA)	WDMN
Toledo, OH [AM radio station call letters] (BROA)	WLQR
Toledo, OH [Television station call letters] (BROA)	WNWO-DT
Tolerance Assessment System (EPAT)	TAS
Tolerance Index System [Environmental science] (EPAT)	TIS
Tolerance Review Assessment Committee [EPA]	TRAC
Tolleson, AZ [Television station call letters] (BROA)	KPPX
Tompkins Trustco [AMEX symbol] (SG)	TMP
Tooele, UT [AM radio station call letters] (BROA)	KIQN
Top Air Mfg. [AMEX symbol] (SG)	TPC
Topographical (GEAB)	top
Toronto, ON [FM radio station call letters] (BROA)	CBLA-FM
Torpedo (MILB)	torp
Total Atmospheric Carbon (QUAC)	TAC
Total Concentrate Leachate Procedure (EPAT)	TCLP
Total Environmental Concern Interaction Index	TECII
Total Moisture [Coal industry]	TM
Total Ownership Cost Reduction	TOCR
Total Precipitable Water	TPW
Total Sulphur [Coal industry]	TS
Total Volatile Organic Compound (EPAT)	TVOC
Tower Automotive [NYSE symbol] (SG)	TWR
Tower Hill, IL [FM radio station call letters] (BROA)	WRAN-FM
Town (GEAB)	twn

TownPagesNet.com ADS [*AMEX symbol*] (SG) .... TPN
Township (GEAB) .... Tp
Township (BEE) .... twp
Tracy Lynne International Fan Club (EA) .... TLIFC
Trade Facilitation Action Plan [*Singapore*] .... TFAP
Traditional Cat Association (EA) .... TCA
Traditional Environmental Knowledge (QUAC) .... TEK
Traditional Knowledge (QUAC) .... TK
Training (MILB) .... trg
Training, Exercises, and Military Operations [*Army*] .... TEMO
Trammell Crow [*NYSE symbol*] (SG) .... TCC
Transatlantic Free Trade Area .... TAFTA
Transcribed (GEAB) .... transcr
Transient Water System (EPAT) .... TWS
Trans-Iron Galactic Element Recorder .... TIGER
Translation (GEAB) .... transl
Transmission Congestion Contract .... TCC
Transport (MILB) .... tpt
Transportable Applications Executive (EOSA) .... TAE
Transportation (BEE) .... Trans
Transportation Components [*NYSE symbol*] (SG) .... TUI
Transworld HealthCare [*AMEX symbol*] (SG) .... TWH
Tranz Rail Hlds ADS [*NASDAQ symbol*] (SG) .... TNZR
Traverse City, MI [*FM radio station call letters*] (BROA) .... WICA-FM
Treasure Hunt [*Toy collection*] .... TH
Treasure Hunting Research and Information Center [*Formerly, Treasure
     Trove Archives*] (EA) .... TTA
Treatment Alternatives for Safe Commission [*Illinois project*] .... TASC
Treatment Outcome Prospective Study .... TOPS
Trenton, NJ [*AM radio station call letters*] (BROA) .... WCHR
Trenton, NJ [*FM radio station call letters*] (BROA) .... WNJO-FM
Trex Co. [*NYSE symbol*] (SG) .... TWP
Triangle Bancorp [*NYSE symbol*] (SG) .... TGL
TRICOM SA ADR [*NYSE symbol*] (SG) .... TDR
Trigonometry (BEE) .... Trig
Trillion (MILB) .... tr
Trio-Tech Intl. [*AMEX symbol*] (SG) .... TRT

Triumph Group [*NYSE symbol*] (SG) .... TGI
Troop (MILB) .... tp
Tropical Asian Monsoon (QUAC) .... TAM
Tropical Cyclone Motion .... TCM
Tropical Prediction Center .... TPC
Tropospheric Emission Spectrometer .... TES
Troutdale, OR [*AM radio station call letters*] (BROA) .... KPAM
Troutwine Athletic Profile .... TAP
Troy, AL [*FM radio station call letters*] (BROA) .... WAXU-FM
Troy, OH [*FM radio station call letters*] (BROA) .... WRNB-FM
Trustee (PROS) .... trust
Truxton, NY [*FM radio station call letters*] (BROA) .... WXXC-FM
Tryon, NC [*AM radio station call letters*] (BROA) .... WJFJ
TSI Intl.Software [*NASDAQ symbol*] (SG) .... TSFW
Tullahoma, TN [*FM radio station call letters*] (BROA) .... WAUT-FM
Tumor Histocompatibility Antigen [*Medicine*] (MELL) .... MHCA
Tumorigenic Dose 50 .... TD50
Tunable Etalon Remote Sounder of Earth (EOSA) .... TERSE
Tunica, MS [*FM radio station call letters*] (BROA) .... WMPS-FM
Tunisia (MILB) .... Tn
Turkey (MILB) .... Tu
Turkish Committee for Palynology (QUAC) .... TCP
Turkmenistan (MILB) .... Tkm
Tuscaloosa, AL [*FM radio station call letters*] (BROA) .... WRTR-FM
Tuscaloosa, AL [*AM radio station call letters*] (BROA) .... WTBC
Tut Systems [*NASDAQ symbol*] (SG) .... TUTS
TV Azteca,S.A. ADS [*NYSE symbol*] (SG) .... TZA
TV Guide'A' [*NASDAQ symbol*] (SG) .... TVGIA
TVR Car Club North America (EA) .... TVRCCNA
Twentieth Century Petroleum Statistics [*1997*] [*A publication*] .... TCPS
Twinlab Corp. [*NASDAQ symbol*] (SG) .... TWLB
Two Harbors, MN [*FM radio station call letters*] (BROA) .... KZIO-FM
Two Times a Day [*Medicine*] (MELL) 2/d
Two-Door [*Automobile*] 2-DR
Two-Line Elements .... TLE
Tyler Technologies [*NYSE symbol*] (SG) .... TYL
Tyson Foods Cl'A' [*NYSE symbol*] (SG) .... TSN

U

By Meaning

Uganda (MILB)	Uga
UK Brent [*Crude oil*]	UKB
Ukraine (MILB)	Ukr
Ultra Long Duration Balloon	ULDB
Umbrella Cockatoo [*Bird*]	U2
Uncirculated [*Numismatic term*]	Unc
Under the Will Of (PROS)	u/w/o
Under-Drive Pulley [*Automotive term*]	UDP
Underwater Society of America (EA)	USOA
Unibanco Banc/Unibanco Hld GDS [*NYSE symbol*] (SG)	UBB
Uni-Bell Pipe Association	UBPPA
UniCapital Corp. [*NYSE symbol*] (SG)	UCP
Unidad Revolucionario [*Cuban political movement*]	UR
Unidigital,Inc. [*AMEX symbol*] (SG)	UDG
Uniform Mixture Ratio	UMR
Uniform Selection Guidelines	USG
Unigraphics Solutions'A' [*NYSE symbol*] (SG)	UGS
Union of Feminine Action [*Morocco*]	UAF
Unistar Financial Svc. [*AMEX symbol*] (SG)	UAI
Unit Share Investment Trust	USIT
United (PROS)	Un
United Association of Office, Sales, and Technical Employees	UAOSTE
United Bank Limited [*Pakistan*]	UBL
United Burmese Cat Fanciers (EA)	UBCF
United Council of Corvette Clubs (EA)	UCCC
United Domin Rlty Tr 8.50 Percent Nts [*NYSE symbol*] (SG)	UDM
United Government Security Officers of America	UGSOA
United Nations Angola Verification Mission	UNAVEM I
United Nurses Associations of California	UNAC
United PanAm Finl. [*NASDAQ symbol*] (SG)	UPFC
United Pan-Euro Commun ADS [*NASDAQ symbol*] (SG)	UPCOY
United Rentals [*NYSE symbol*] (SG)	URI
United Services Automobile Association	USAA
United Sportsmans Association of North America (EA)	USANA
U.S. Amateur Confederation of Roller Skating (EA)	ARSF
United States Arctic Research Commission (QUAC)	USARC
U.S. Bancorp [*NYSE symbol*] (SG)	USB
United States Base Association (EA)	BASE
U.S. Chamber of Commerce in Ireland (EA)	AMCHAM IRELAND
United States Chess Federation (EA)	US Chess
U.S. Deaf Cycling Association (EA)	USDCAT
United States Delegation	USDel
U.S. Department of Labor	USDOL
U.S. Exploration [*AMEX symbol*] (SG)	UXP
United States International Speedskating Association (EA)	USISA
United States les Autres Sports Association (EA)	USLASA
United States/Memorandum of Conversation	US/MC
United States of America Underwater Federation (EA)	USAUF
U.S. Pan-Asian Chamber of Commerce (EA)	AAACC
U.S. Plastic Lumber [*Stock market symbol*]	USPL
United States Rowing Association (EA)	USRowing
United States Sailing Foundation (EA)	USSF
United States Ski Team Foundation (EA)	USSTF
United States Synchronized Swimming [*An association*] (EA)	USSS
United States Windsurfing Association (EA)	USWA
Universal Infinity-Corrected Objective	UIS
University Center, MI [*Television station call letters*] (BROA)	WDCQ
University Musical Society	UMS
University of Arizona Mineral Museum	UAMM
University of California Museum of Paleontology	UCMP
University of Hertfordshire [*England*]	UH
University of Kentucky Equine Research Foundation (GVA)	UKERF
University of Surrey	UniS
Unmarried (GEAB)	unm
Unorganized (GEAB)	unorg
UNOVA,Inc. [*NYSE symbol*] (SG)	UNA
Upholstery	Uph
UPM-Kymmene Corp.ADS [*NYSE symbol*] (SG)	UPM
Upper Arlington, OH [*FM radio station call letters*] (BROA)	WXMG-FM
Urban Heat Island Effect [*Meteorology*] (WEAT)	UHIE
Urban Wildlife Society (GVA)	UWS
Urinary Tract Infection [*Medicine*]	UTI
Urstadt Biddle Properties [*NYSE symbol*] (SG)	UBP
Uruguay (MILB)	Ury
US Liquid [*AMEX symbol*] (SG)	USL
US Oncology [*NASDAQ symbol*] (SG)	USON
U.S.A. Baseball [*An association*] (EA)	USBF
U.S.A Boxing [*An association*] (EA)	USAB
U.S.A Gymnastics [*An association*] (EA)	USA GYM
U.S.A. Hockey [*An association*] (EA)	USAH
USA Networks [*NASDAQ symbol*] (SG)	USAI
U.S.A. Table Tennis [*An association*] (EA)	USATT
U.S.A. Track and Field [*An association*] (EA)	USATF
USA Triathlon [*An association*] (EA)	TRI-FED
USEC, Inc. [*NYSE symbol*] (SG)	USU
USinternetworking, Inc. [*NASDAQ symbol*] (SG)	USIX
USWeb Corp. [*NASDAQ symbol*] (SG)	USWB
Utah Public Employees Association	UPEA
Utah School Employees Association	USEA
Utility (MILB)	utl
Uvalde, TX [*Television station call letters*] (BROA)	KPXL
Uzbekistan (MILB)	Uz

V

By Meaning

Valdez, AK [*FM radio station call letters*] (BROA) .... KVAK-FM
Valentis [*Stock market symbol*] .... VLTS
Vallejo, CA [*AM radio station call letters*] (BROA) .... KDYA
Valley Station, KY [*FM radio station call letters*] (BROA) .... WRVI-FM
Value Added Network .... VAN
Value America [*NASDAQ symbol*] (SG) .... VUSA
Van Buren, MO [*FM radio station call letters*] (BROA) .... KBIY-FM
Vancouver, WA [*AM radio station call letters*] (BROA) .... KFXX
Vancouver, WA [*FM radio station call letters*] (BROA) .... KKLQ-FM
Variable-Stress Accelerated Life Testing Trials .... VALT
Varian Medical Systems [*NYSE symbol*] (SG) .... VAR
Varo Beach, FL [*FM radio station call letters*] (BROA) .... WBBE-FM
Varying (WEAT) V
Veba Corp.ADS [*NYSE symbol*] (GG) .... VEB
Vehicle (MILB) .... veh
Vehicle and Heavy Equipment Virtual Proving Ground .... VHEVPG
Vehicle Operating Survey (EPAT) .... VOS
Venezuela (MILB) .... Ve
Venice International University [*Italy*] .... VIU
Ventas,Inc. [*NYSE symbol*] (SG) .... VTR
Ventura, CA [*Television station call letters*] (BROA) .... KJLA
Ventura, CA [*AM radio station call letters*] (BROA) .... KXFS
Verio,Inc. [*NASDAQ symbol*] (SG) .... VRIO
VeriSign,Inc. [*NASDAQ symbol*] (SG) .... VRSN
Vermont Comprehensive Assessment System .... VCAS
Vermont Pure Hldgs. Ltd. [*AMEX symbol*] (SG) .... VPS
Vertical Marketing System .... VMS
VerticalNet,Inc. [*NASDAQ symbol*] (SG) .... VERT
Very Inexpensive Computer VIC
Vespa Club of America (EA) .... VCOA
Veterinary Association for Arbitration and Jurisprudence (GVA) .... VAAJ
Veterinary Benevolent Fund (GVA) .... VBF
Veterinary Deer Society (GVA) .... VDS
Veterinary History Society (GVA) .... VHS
Veterinary Meat Hygiene Adviser (GVA) .... VMHA
Veterinary Nurse (GVA) .... VN
Veterinary Practice Management Association (GVA) .... VPMA
Veterinary Public Health Association (GVA) .... VPHA

Veterinary Written Direction (GVA) .... VWD
Vice Chairman (PROS) .... vchmn
Video Services [*AMEX symbol*] (SG) .... VS
Video-Assisted Thoracic Spine Surgery .... VATS
Vidikron Technologies Group [*NASDAQ symbol*] (SG) .... VIDI
Vieques, PR [*FM radio station call letters*] (BROA) .... WVIS-FM
Vietnam (MILB) .... Vn
Vignette Corp. [*NASDAQ symbol*] (SG) .... VIGN
Villas, NJ [*FM radio station call letters*] (BROA) .... WWZK-FM
Vince Smith and Carol Redo Fan Club (EA) .... VSCRFC
Vinegar Connoiseurs (EA) VC
Virginia Education and Research Network .... VERnet
Virginia Veterinary Medical Association (GVA) .... VVMA
Virtual Distributed Collaborative Environment .... VDCE
Virtual International Business and Economics Sources [*Internet
    resource*] .... VIBES
Virtual Proving Ground .... VPG
Viscount (GEAB) .... Visc
Visible Infrared Scanner (EOSA) .... VIRS
Visible Infrared Scanning Radiometer (EOSA) .... VIRSR
Vista Energy Resources [*AMEX symbol*] (SG) .... VEI
Visual Data [*NASDAQ symbol*] (SG) .... VDAT
Visual Networks [*NASDAQ symbol*] (SG) .... VNWK
Visual Satellite Observer's Home Page .... VSOHP
Visualization .... VIZ
Vita Food Products [*AMEX symbol*] (SG) .... VSF
Vizsla Club of America (EA) .... VCA
Vlasic Foods,Intl. [*NYSE symbol*] (SG) VL
Vocal Cord Dysfunction [*Medicine*] .... VCD
VocalTec Commun. Ltd. [*NASDAQ symbol*] (SG) .... VOCL
Volar Intercalary Segment Instability .... VISI
Volt Info Sciences [*NYSE symbol*] (SG) .... VOL
Voltage Controlled Oscillator .... VCO
Voluntary Cleanup Program [*Environmental science*] (EPAT) .... VCP
Volvo Sports America Registry (EA) VSA/1800
Vornado Operating [*AMEX symbol*] (SG) .... VOO
Voyager.net [*NASDAQ symbol*] (SG) .... VOYN
Vysis,Inc. [*NASDAQ symbol*] (SG) .... VYSI

W
By Meaning

Wabash, IN [*AM radio station call letters*] (BROA) .... WJOT
Wabash, IN [*FM radio station call letters*] (BROA) .... WJOT-FM
Waddell & Reed Fin'l 'A' [*NYSE symbol*] (SG) .... WDR
Wage and Hour Division .... WH DIV
Wage & Salary .... W&S
Wagoner (GEAB) .... wag
Wailuku, HI [*Television station call letters*] (BROA) .... KMAU-DT
Wake Village, TX [*FM radio station call letters*] (BROA) .... KBHA-FM
Walhalla, ND [*FM radio station call letters*] (BROA) .... KAUJ-FM
Walker, MI [*FM radio station call letters*] (BROA) .... WTRV-FM
Walker, MN [*FM radio station call letters*] (BROA) .... KQKK-FM
Walla Walla, WA [*AM radio station call letters*] (BROA) .... KUJ-FM
Wallace, ID [*FM radio station call letters*] (BROA) .... KSIL-FM
Walnut Creek, CA [*FM radio station call letters*] (BROA) .... KFJO-FM
Walter Koenig International (EA) .... WKI
Wanted to Buy .... WTB
Warbirds of America [*An association*] (EA) .... WB
Warfighter Physiological Status Monitoring [*Army*] .... WPSM
Warm Springs, OR [*FM radio station call letters*] (BROA) .... KWEG-FM
Warner Robins, GA [*AM radio station call letters*] (BROA) .... WAXP
Warner Robins, GA [*FM radio station call letters*] (BROA) .... WLCG-FM
Warner Robins, GA [*FM radio station call letters*] (BROA) .... WRBV-FM
Warrantech Corp. [*NASDAQ symbol*] (SG) .... WTECE
Warren, OH [*AM radio station call letters*] (BROA) .... WRBP
Warrenton, VA [*FM radio station call letters*] (BROA) .... WTOP-FM
Warrior Systems Modernization Strategy [*Military*] .... WSMS
Washington Court (BROA) .... WBUB
Washington, DC [*FM radio station call letters*] (BROA) .... WCSP-FM
Washington, DC [*Television station call letters*] (BROA) .... WETA-DT
Washington, DC [*Television station call letters*] (BROA) .... WHUT-TV
Washington, DC [*Television station call letters*] (BROA) .... WJLA-DT
Washington, DC [*Television station call letters*] (BROA) .... WRC-DT
Washington, DC [*Television station call letters*] (BROA) .... WTTG-DT
Washington, DC [*Television station call letters*] (BROA) .... WUSA-DT
Washington Library Media Association .... WLMA
Washington, MO [*AM radio station call letters*] (BROA) .... KWMO
Washington Mutual [*NYSE symbol*] (SG) .... WM
Washington, NC [*AM radio station call letters*] (BROA) .... WDLX
Washington Public Employees Association .... WPEA
Washington Redskins [*National Football League*] [*1937-present*] (NFLA) .... Was
Washington State Veterinary Medical Association (GVA) .... WSVMA
Wastewater Treatment Unit [*Environmental Protection Agency*] (EPAT) .... WWTU
Water Conservation Area .... WCA
Water Quality and Contaminant Modeling Branch .... WQCMB
Water Resources Engineering and Construction Agency [*Nigeria*] .... WRECA
Water Vapor (WEAT) .... WV
Waterlink,Inc. [*NYSE symbol*] (SG) .... WLK
Watertown, NY [*Television station call letters*] (BROA) .... WPBS-TV
Watertown, NY [*AM radio station call letters*] (BROA) .... WUZZ
Waterville, ME [*Television station call letters*] (BROA) .... WMPX-TV
Watson Pharmaceuticals [*NYSE symbol*] (SG) .... WPI
Watson's Collectors' Club (EA) .... WCC
Wausau-Mosinee Paper [*NYSE symbol*] (SG) .... WMO
Wauwatosa, WI [*FM radio station call letters*] (BROA) .... WXSS-FM
WAVO Corp. [*NASDAQ symbol*] (SG) .... WAVO
Waycross, GA [*FM radio station call letters*] (BROA) .... WASW-FM
Waycross, GA [*FM radio station call letters*] (BROA) .... WWSN-FM
Waynesboro, TN [*FM radio station call letters*] (BROA) .... WMSR-FM
Weapon (MILB) .... wpn
Weather (WEAT) .... Wx
Weatherford, OK [*FM radio station call letters*] (BROA) .... KAYM-FM
Web of Science .... WoS
WEBS, Australia Index Series [*AMEX symbol*] (SG) .... EWA
WEBS, Austria Index Series [*AMEX symbol*] (SG) .... EWO
WEBS, Belgium Index Series [*AMEX symbol*] (SG) .... EWK
WEBS, Canada Index Series [*AMEX symbol*] (SG) .... EWC
WEBS, France Index Series [*AMEX symbol*] (SG) .... EWQ
WEBS, Germany Index Series [*AMEX symbol*] (SG) .... EWG
WEBS, Hong Kong Index Series [*AMEX symbol*] (SG) .... EWH
WEBS, Italy Index Series [*AMEX symbol*] (SG) .... EWI
WEBS, Japan Index Series [*AMEX symbol*] (SG) .... EWJ
WEBS, Malaysia(Free)Index Series [*AMEX symbol*] (SG) .... EWM
WEBS, Mexico(Free)Index Series [*AMEX symbol*] (SG) .... EWW
WEBS, Netherlands Index Series [*AMEX symbol*] (SG) .... EWN
WEBS, Singapore(Free)Index Series [*AMEX symbol*] (SG) .... EWS
WEBS, Spain Index Series [*AMEX symbol*] (SG) .... EWP

WEBS, Sweden Index Series [*AMEX symbol*] (SG) .... EWD
WEBS, Switzerland Index Series [*AMEX symbol*] (SG) .... EWL
WEBS, U.K. Index Series [*AMEX symbol*] (SG) .... EWU
Webster, MA [*FM radio station call letters*] (BROA) .... WORC-FM
Welcome Back [*Online dialog*] .... WB
Wellhead Protection Program [*Environmental Protection Agency*] (EPAT) .... WHP
Wellton, AZ [*FM radio station call letters*] (BROA) .... KBHV-FM
WESCO International [*NYSE symbol*] (SG) .... WCC
Wesley Jessen VisionCare [*NASDAQ symbol*] (SG) .... WJCO
West (GEAB) .... w
West Coast Lumber Inspection Bureau .... WCLB
West Fargo, ND [*AM radio station call letters*] (BROA) .... KQJD
West Germanic (BEE) .... WGmc
West Klamath, OR [*AM radio station call letters*] (BROA) .... KRAM
West Palm Beach, FL [*AM radio station call letters*] (BROA) .... WDJA
West Palm Beach, FL [*Television station call letters*] (BROA) .... WFLX-DT
West Pharmaceutical Services [*NYSE symbol*] (SG) .... WST
West Point Veterinary Medical Society (GVA) .... WPVMS
West Salem, WI [*FM radio station call letters*] (BROA) .... WKBH-FM
West Virginia Network .... WVNET
West Yarmouth, MA [*AM radio station call letters*] (BROA) .... WBUR
Western Atlantic (QUAC) .... WA
Western Lath/Plaster/Drywall Industries Association .... WLPDIA
Western Reserve Historical Society (GEAB) .... WRHS
Western Women Professional Bowlers (EA) .... WWPB
Westerville, OH [*FM radio station call letters*] (BROA) .... WEGE-FM
Westfield America [*NYSE symbol*] (SG) .... WEA
Westhampton, NY [*AM radio station call letters*] (BROA) .... WDRE-FM
Westinghouse Federation of Independent Salaried Unions .... FISU
Westower Corp. [*AMEX symbol*] (SG) .... WTW
Wetland Water Quality Model .... WWQM
Wetumpka, AL [*FM radio station call letters*] (BROA) .... WJWZ-FM
Wewoka, OK [*FM radio station call letters*] (BROA) .... KWSH-FM
Wheatland, WY [*FM radio station call letters*] (BROA) .... KZEW-FM
Wheaton, MD [*AM radio station call letters*] (BROA) .... WACA
Wheelchair Sports, USA [*An association*] (EA) .... WSUSA
Wheeling, MO [*FM radio station call letters*] (BROA) .... KULH-FM
White Gold [*Watch*] .... wg
White Gold Filled [*Watch*] .... wgf
White Gold Shell [*Watch*] .... wgs
White Hall, AR [*FM radio station call letters*] (BROA) .... KTRN-FM
White River Junction, VT [*FM radio station call letters*] (BROA) .... WWSH-FM
White Star, MI [*FM radio station call letters*] (BROA) .... WEJC-FM
Whitehall Jewellers [*NASDAQ symbol*] (SG) .... WHJI
Wichita Falls, TX [*AM radio station call letters*] (BROA) .... KWFS
Wichita, KS [*AM radio station call letters*] (BROA) .... KMYR
Wichita, KS [*FM radio station call letters*] (BROA) .... KZZD-FM
Wickenburg, AZ [*AM radio station call letters*] (BROA) .... KBSZ
Wide Field and Planetary Camera 2 .... WFPC2
Wide-Angle Free-Air Chamber .... WAFAC
Wide-Band Data Collection System (EOSA) .... WBDCS
Widely Integrated Distributed Environment .... WIDE
Widow (GEAB) .... wd
Wilber, NE [*FM radio station call letters*] (BROA) .... KFLV-FM
Wildlife Land Trust .... WLT
Wildlife Rescue Veterinarian Association of Japan (GVA) .... WRVJ
Willamette Indus. [*NYSE symbol*] (SG) .... WLL
Willard, OH [*FM radio station call letters*] (BROA) .... WHHA-FM
Willbros Group [*NYSE symbol*] (SG) .... WG
William McNamara Fan Club (EA) .... WNFC
Williams, AZ [*FM radio station call letters*] (BROA) .... KWMX-FM
Williamsburg, VA [*FM radio station call letters*] (BROA) .... WKLR-FM
Williamsport, PA [*FM radio station call letters*] (BROA) .... WPTC-FM
Willis Lease Finance [*NASDAQ symbol*] (SG) .... WLFC
Williston, FL [*FM radio station call letters*] (BROA) .... WTMG-FM
Williston, VT [*FM radio station call letters*] (BROA) .... WTBC-FM
Wilmington, NC [*FM radio station call letters*] (BROA) .... WBID-FM
Winamac, IN [*FM radio station call letters*] (BROA) .... WFRI-FM
Winchester, KY [*AM radio station call letters*] (BROA) .... WMJR
Winchester, OR [*FM radio station call letters*] (BROA) .... KLOV-FM
Winfield, KS [*FM radio station call letters*] (BROA) .... KBDD-FM
Wing (MILB) .... wg
Winmill & Co,'A' [*NASDAQ symbol*] (SG) .... WNMLA
Winnebago-Itasca Travelers (EA) .... WIT
Winneconne, WI [*FM radio station call letters*] (BROA) .... WVBO-FM
Winnipeg, AB [*FM radio station call letters*] (BROA) .... CKUW-FM

Winnipeg, MB [*FM radio station call letters*] (BROA) .... CJUM-FM
Winton Financial [*AMEX symbol*] (3G) .... WFI
Wireless Markup Language .... WML
Wisconsin Educational Media Association .... WEMA
Wisconsin Regional Primate Research Center (GVA) .... WRPRC
Wise, VA [*FM radio station call letters*] (BROA) .... WCVC-FM
Wit Capital Group [*Stock market symbol*] .... WITC
Witholding Tax .... W/tax
Without .... W/o
Witness (GEAB) .... wit
Witness (GEAB) .... wtn
Wittenberg, WI [*Television station call letters*] (BROA) .... WFXS
Wolfforth, TX [*Television station call letters*] (BROA) .... KBFA
Women in the Wind [*An association*] (EA) .... WITW
Women's Outdoor Challenges [*An association*] (EA) .... WOC
Women's Participation Ratio .... WR
Woodruff, SC [*AM radio station call letters*] (BROA) .... WDRF
Woodwork Institute of California .... WIC
Work Status (EPAT) .... WS

Worker Investment Act .... WIA
Working Class Hero Beatles Club (EA) .... WCH
Working Families Tax Credit .... WFTC
Workplace Violence .... WV
World Amateur Golf Council (EA) .... WAGC
World Association of Veterinary Educators (GVA) .... WAVE
World Association of Wildlife Veterinarians (GVA) .... WAWV
World Bocce Association (EA) .... WBA
World Encyclopedia of Contemporary Theatre [*A publication*] .... WECT
World Equine Veterinary Association (GVA) .... WEVA
World Federation of the Animal Health Industry (GVA) .... COMISA
World Islam Study Enterprise [*Tampa, Florida*] .... WISE
World Links for Development [*Program*] .... WorLD
World Standard Printed English .... WSPE
World Standard Spoken English .... WSSE
World Veterinary Association (GVA) .... WVA
World Wrestling Federation .... WWF
Worldloppet/American Birkebeiner [*An association*] (EA) .... WL
WTA Tour Players Association (EA) .... WTA
Wyman-Gordon [*NYSE symbol*] (SG) .... WYG

X-Y-Z
By Meaning

XL Capital Ltd'A' [*NYSE symbol*] (SG) XL
XOOM.com,Inc. [*NYSE symbol*] (SG) .... XMCM
X-Ray Imaging Experiment (EOSA) .... XIE
X-Ray Telescope .... XRT
Yankee Candle, Inc. [*NYSE symbol*] (SG) .... YCC
Yankeetown, FL [*FM radio station call letters*] (BROA) .... WBKX-FM
Yankton, SD [*FM radio station call letters*] (BROA) .... KCLH-FM
Yanzhou Coal Mining ADS [*NYSE symbol*] (SG) .... YZC
Yazoo City, MS [*FM radio station call letters*] (BROA) .... WMGO-FM
Yazoo City, MS [*Television station call letters*] (BROA) .... WMYC
Yeast Open Reading Frame .... yORF
Yellow Collared Macaw [*Bird*] .... YCM
Yellow Gold [*Watch*] .... yg
Yellow Gold Filled [*Watch*] .... ygf
Yellow Gold Shell [*Watch*] .... ygs
Yellow Naped Amazon [*Bird*] .... YNA
Yemen, Republic of (MILB) .... Ye
Yield .... yld
YOCREAM Intl. [*NASDAQ symbol*] (SG) .... YOCM

Young & Rubicam [*NYSE symbol*] (SG) .... YNR
Young Men's Hebrew Association (PROS) .... YMHA
Young Women's Christian Association (PROS) .... YWCA
Young Women's Hebrew Association (PROS) .... YWHA
Youngsville, PA [*FM radio station call letters*] (BROA) .... WTMV-FM
Your Own World [*Internet service*] .... YOW
Youth Attitude Tracking Study .... YATS
Yucca Valley, CA [*FM radio station call letters*] (BROA) .... KYOR-FM
Yugoslav Academic and Research Network .... YUNAC
Yuma, AZ [*FM radio station call letters*] (BROA) .... KLJZ-FM
Yuma, CO [*FM radio station call letters*] (BROA) .... KNEC-FM
Zale Corp. [*NYSE symbol*] (SG) .... ZLC
Zambia (MILB) .... Z
Zanesville, OH [*FM radio station call letters*] (BROA) .... WJIC-FM
Zero-Inflated Poisson Regression [*Statistics*] .... ZIP
Ziff-Davis ZDNet [*NYSE symbol*] (SG) .... ZDZ
Zimbabwe (MILB) .... Zw
Zoological Society of San Diego .... ZSSD
Zoological Survey of India [*Calcutta, West Bengal*] .... ZSI
ZZ Top International Fan Club (EA) .... ZZTIFC